The Dictionary of Contemporary Slang

Also by Jonathon Green
in Pan Books

Famous Last Words
A Dictionary of Contemporary Quotations

The Dictionary of Contemporary Slang

compiled by Jonathon Green
illustrations by Chris Burke

Pan Books London and Sydney

For Nick Cole
– whose researches have transcended all bounds of dedication

First published 1984 by Pan Books Ltd,
Cavaye Place, London SW10 9PG
9 8 7 6 5 4 3 2 1

ISBN 0 330 28412 6
Photoset by Parker Typesetting Service, Leicester
Printed and bound in Great Britain by
Cox & Wyman Ltd, Reading

Acknowledgements

No compilation of slang, ancient or modern, would be possible without the pioneering efforts of the late Eric Partridge. It would have been simple, but foolish, merely to pillage his work, and I have not done so; but in many areas, especially that of possible and likely etymologies I owe a great deal to his earlier studies. Thus I would take this opportunity of making due acknowledgement here.

On a more immediate level, I must thank many people, all of whom have made a contribution of some degree to the collection of words in this dictionary or to the progress and publication of the work as a whole. I cannot name every one, but particular thanks go to:

Don Atyeo, Rosie Boycott, Linda Brown, Colin Clarke, Katherine Clarke, Nick Cole, Peter Davies, Karen Durbin, Leslie Gardner, Arthur Green, Johann (Aka) Hashim, Kyle Cathie, David Leitch, Alan Marcuson, Andrew Payne, David Rattray, Susan Ready, Harriet Thistlethwaite, Pola Wickham.

SLANG IS A LANGUAGE
THAT ROLLS UP IT'S SLEEVES,
SPITS ON IT'S HANDS
AND GOES TO WORK.

Introduction

‘Slang is a language that rolls up its sleeves, spits on its hands, and goes to work.’
Carl Sandburg

Alongside Standard English, the ostensibly ‘pure’ language of formal speech and writing, of *Times* leaders and BBC erudition, stand several sub-species of language, less beloved of Eng. Lit. teachers, but none the less popular and possibly even more vigorous and entertaining for that very exclusion. These include *cant*: the language of the underworld; *jargon*: the special or occupational language and the ‘professional slang’ of a variety of interest groups; *colloquialism*: informal, conversational speech, used, as it were, through the dinner but not for the after-dinner speechifying; *solecisms*: the variety of linguistic irregularities; *dialects*: regional usages, ever more besieged by television’s bland mid-atlanticisms; and finally *slang*.

Definitions of slang abound. Aside from Carl Sandburg’s description above, one can choose from all of these. The Oxford English Dictionary (1933) talks of ‘either . . . new words, or current words employed in some special state’. Fowler (1926) has ‘the playing with words and renaming things or actions’. H. L. Mencken (1936) offers ‘the exuberance of mental activity and the natural delight of language making’. More recently the Reader’s Digest *Success with Words* (1983) claims, ‘slang seems to stand between the general words – the standard and informal ones available to everyone – and the in-group words . . . available to specific segments of the population’. Finally, the doyen of every slang lexicographer, Eric Partridge, who opined in *Slang: Yesterday & Today* (1933) ‘Slang, being the quintessence of colloquial speech, is determined by convenience and fancy rather than by scientific laws, philosophical ideals and absolutes, and grammatical rules . . . in short, it is catholic, tolerant, human and, though often tartly, humane. Inherent in human nature as a psychological tendency and potentiality, slang is indicative not only of man’s earthiness but of his indomitable spirit; it sets him in his proper place: relates a man to his fellows, to his world and the world, and to the universe.’ Or, in the words of Dr J. Y. P. Grieg, writing in the Edinburgh *Despatch* in 1938, ‘the commonest stimuli of slang are sex, money and intoxicating liquor’.

When, in 1937, Eric Partridge published the first volume of his monumental *Dictionary of Slang and Unconventional English*, synthesizing such previous collections as those of Grose (1785 and various editions to 1823), Hotten (1859), Farmer & Henley (1890–1904) and adding a wealth of new material, it was still possible to restrict a dictionary even of contemporary slang (although his was not) to the vocabulary of the United Kingdom. Fifty years later, such particularism has no justification. This is a dictionary of contemporary slang, and as such, while its sources may stretch back several hundred years, is attempting to delineate the slang of today's English-speaking world. To ignore the massive American presence in that world, as inescapable in language as in any other of its aspects, would be impossible. Thus these entries, some 11,500 in all, contain both British and American English, as well as all the other tongues, notably Yiddish and Romany, that have been absorbed into slang. Culled from novels, magazines, word studies, television, radio, film and popular music, they are intended to give a substantial cross-section of such slang as is spoken in England, America and Australia, and which appears in so many of the films, TV shows and pop songs that continue to transcend the boundaries of these major English-speaking nations.

For many years the single word 'slang' was used to include all those other sub-species of language mentioned above. That they have been latterly separated has not, of course, completely ruled out the many areas where particularly cant, jargon and dialect blend into more everyday slang usages. Indeed there is a good deal of slang that began in a far more specific context than it is now used. Such etymologies have been pointed out when possible. Nonetheless, it has been my intention to concentrate as much as possible on current, general slang. The one specialist area that does gain a large representation is cant, criminal jargon, and it seems only fair to include such material, given the massive output of such vocabulary in both film and television, neither of which medium would claim an audience composed exclusively of villains.

Slang evolves without respite. I would prefer to think that all these entries will remain in use, but there is little doubt that more and more will be coined. How many of the 'new boys' will stay the course is debatable, yet some must, just as a number of those included here have lasted centuries already, still excluded from 'respectable' speech, but locked forever into a less formal vocabulary. Often vivid, usually pertinent, albeit sometimes gross, slang is a vital part of everyone's daily speech. The 'fifth generation' of 'artificially intelligent' computers will doubtless take their toll on all sorts of language, but so long as man still talks to man, and not merely to machine, there will be a place in his heart, and his mouth, for slang.

Sources and selections

Slang is primarily a spoken, rather than a written language. Dictionaries, on the contrary, are printed codifications, of greater or lesser complexity. Inevitably the marriage of the two forms leads to certain difficulties. In the first place, one can hardly hope to establish a specific 'first use' of a slang word, and I have not attempted to do so. Instead I have attempted to find some form of source for the words that I have included. As the dictionary is intended to cover only modern, contemporary vocabulary, the books, magazines, films, radio and television programmes that I have cited are essentially post-1945 creations; indeed I have looked as far as possible only to the last decade or so. A glance through the bibliography should bear this out. Nonetheless, much of our slang, however popular in contemporary usage, dates back to the 19th century and well beyond. Thus I have included John Camden Hotten's *Modern Slang, Cant and Vulgar Words* (1859, 1860, etc.) as well as a number of older source-books, if only to underline the antiquity of many current terms. In the main, however, the accent is on the more up-to-date, and whether or not the terms so indexed come from an earlier era, the sources from which I have taken them prove irrefutably that they are still going strong. Unfortunately, as a solo compiler, I have not been able, nor have I tried, to read every available slang-laden work. Where I have been helped has been in the very wide spread of slang words in all manner of writing, both for print and for the large and small screen. I have done my best to assimilate as much as possible in the time available. There are, as will be obvious, a number of words for which I have been unable to provide a source, although I know, from my own or overheard use, that these words are popular and prevalent. I have included them on those grounds, even bereft of a suitable source.

Bearing in mind the various lyrical definitions of slang cited above, I have attempted on a more practical level to exclude as much 'fringe material' as possible. Thus I have minimized the appearance of jargon, or 'professional slang', other than in those instances where the slang of an 'in-group' has moved in more mainstream use. There is some cant, the criminal vocabulary, but once again, I have tried to cut down on the more arcane areas of safe-cracking equipment, pickpocketing methodology and other professional references. On the whole I have concentrated on the general slang in popular use among English, American and Australian speakers, with certain forays into social, rather than professional interest groups, notably 'Sloane Rangers', 'preppies', 'Valley Girls', drug users and homosexuals. I have also included some of the specific vocabulary of US urban blacks.

There is also a selection of *backslang*, a vocabulary in which words are simply turned on their heads for extra obscurity. Most essentially a spoken slang, these inclusions are spelt phonetically, rather than aiming at any absolute rules.

Jonathon Green — October 1983

Abbreviations

a.	adjective
abbrev.	abbreviation
acro.	acronym
aka	also known as
Aus.	Australian
backsl.	backslang
C.	century
Can.	Canadian
cf	compare
cp	catch phrase
derog.	derogatory
dial.	dialect
eg	example
esp.	especially
ex	from
excl.	exclamation
expl.	expletive
euph.	euphemism
Fr.	French
fr.	from
Ger.	German
ie	that is
Ital.	Italian
j.	jargon
journ.	journalistic
Lat.	Latin
lit.	literally
milit.	military
n.	noun
naut.	nautical
nb	note well
obs.	obsolete
orig.	original(ly)
p.ppl.	past participle
phr.	phrase
polit.	political
poss.	possible
prob.	probable
pron.	pronunciation
qv	which see
RAF	Royal Air Force
Rus.	Russian
S. Afr.	South African
SE	Standard English
Sp.	Spanish
sp.	spelling
spec.	specifically
UK	United Kingdom
US	United States
USMC	United States Marine Corps
USN	United States Navy
usu.	usually
v.	verb
v.i.	verb intransitive
v.t.	verb transitive
Yid.	Yiddish

a n. (drug use) (abbrev.) amphetamine; thus a-head (qv.): amphetamine user (cf: head) *Saunders.*

a (interj.) (Black use) yes, absolutely, certainly! (cf: fucking A) *Major.*

A1 a. excellent, perfect, first class; fr. the top rating of a ship at Lloyds of London *Hotten.*

ab n. (drug use) (abbrev.) abcess; the result of injecting with a dirty needle, and/or using adulterated narcotics *De Lannoy & Masterson.*

abc n. (abbrev.) *a*ce *b*oon *c*oon (qv.) *Folb.*

abdicated (homosexual use) ordered out of the public lavatory where one is looking for sex *Legman.*

Abe (derog.) a Jew; fr. abbrev. Abraham (cf: Abie Kabibble) *BvdB.*

abergavenny n. (rhyming sl.) a penny *Jones:J.*

Abie Kabibble n. (derog.) a Jew (cf: Abe) *Farrell.*

about right a. drunk *Dickson.*

Abyssinia! goodbye; corruption of 'I'll be seeing you!' *Whitcomb.*

ACAB (acro.) *A*ll *C*oppers *A*re *B*astards; popular tattoo in UK, esp. among Hells Angels, etc.

accidentally on purpose deliberately; of a supposed accident that deliberately discomforts a disliked target.

accommodation collar n. (US police use) an arrest made for no reason but to raise the officer's arrest record and thus improve his standing in the hierarchy *Green:2.*

AC/DC a. **1.** bisexual; **2.** (homosexual use) ambivalent as to taking an active or passive role in a relationship; both derive fr. opposite varieties of electrical current *Stanley.*

ace n. **1.** (US Black use) one single pill, either amphetamine, barbiturate or tranquilliser *Folb*; **2.** a detective *Algren*; **3.** one dollar *Caron.*

ace v. **1.** to do well; **2.** to defeat an opponent *Underwood*; **3.** (Aus. use) to stop, to cease; thus *ace it up*: stop it! *Baker.*

ace! term of endearment between any two males; the implication is of fondness and respect *Bukowski:6.*

ace boom boom n. see: ace boon coon *Folb.*

ace boon coon n. (US Black use) one's best and most trustworthy friend *Folb.*

ace coon poon n. see: ace boon coon *Folb.*

ace-deuce n. (gambling use) the number 3 in cards or in craps dice; fr. addition of ace (1) plus deuce (2) *Chandler: Notebk.*

ace in the hole n. a hidden asset; fr. poker use *Price:2.*

ace of spades n. (US Black use) the pudendum; fr. supposed resemblance of the shape of pubic hair *Neaman & Silver.*

ace out v. to defeat, to take something away; fr. poker use when ace is the highest card *Fiction Illus.3.*

aces a. wonderful, marvellous, excellent, etc.; both of objects and persons, thus 'you're aces!' *'Hill Street Blues', Thames TV, 1983.*

aces high n. (US prison use) an inmate popular amongst his peers (cf: aces) *Neaman & Silver.*

acid n. **1.** (drug use) d-lycergic acid diethylamide-25; a powerful synthetic hallucinogen based on ergot; discovered in 1943 by Dr Albert Hofmann of Sandoz Labs, Basel, and massively popularized in 1960s by Dr Timothy Leary, Ken Kesey (and his Merry Pranksters), rock groups and the 'alternative society' *Green:1*; **2.** cheek *Powis.*

acidhead n. a regular user of LSD (cf: acid) *Green:1.*

acid rapper n. one who takes extra-large doses of LSD *Wolfe:2.*

acid rock n. a musical style allegedly influenced by and purporting to recreate the sensations of LSD and similar psychedelics; orig. in 1960s but undergoing a minor revival in 1980s.

ackamaracka n. (UK prison use) deceit, tall stories, lies *LL.*

ackers n. (Br. Army use) money; fr. Egyptian *akka*: one piastre.

across the pavement (UK criminal use) any crime committed in the street *Powis.*

action n. **1.** any form of monetary deal or the profits from that deal; **2.** (gambling) the play in a gambling casino, in one of the games within that casino, or in any form of betting – track, cards, dice, etc.; **3.** pleasure, enjoyment, activity; usu. sexual.

action piece n. (US Black use) **1.** a pistol, a revolver, a shotgun; **2.** a woman *Klein.*

active a. (UK police use) an enthusiastic and efficient officer *Laurie.*

Acton Hilton n. (BBC-TV use) the BBC TV rehearsal rooms in Acton, London; the block that contains them resembles only facetiously a chain hotel.

actor n. (US Black use) anyone out to deceive, to project a phoney image *Major.*

act the nigger v. (US Black use) to draw unnecessary attention to oneself by foolish behaviour *Folb.*

AD n. (drug use) *d*rug *a*ddict (reversed to avoid confusion with the law's DA, district attorney) *Major.*

Ada from Decatur n. (gambling use) aka: *eighter from Decatur*, the point of eight in craps dice *Chandler: Notebk.*

Adam and Eve v. (rhyming sl.) to believe *Powis.*

addict n. (US cant) one who seemingly cannot resist the blandishments of confidence tricksters and falls for every variety of trick *Neaman & Silver.*

addled a. drunk; fr. SE *addle-pated*: stupid *Dickson.*

ad hocer n. (skiing use) a skier who arrives at a chalet without a previous booking; fr. Lat. *ad hoc*: for this purpose/for this occasion *Barr.*

advice n. (UK police use) a severe disciplinary reprimand *Laurie.*

afflicted a. drunk; the implication is of mental instability *Dickson.*

African golf ball n. (US Black use) aka: *African grape*; deprecating reference to the watermelon, a cliché Black foodstuff *Folb.*

Afro n. a Black hairstyle, esp. popular in 1960s, in which usually short crinkly black hair was allowed to grow out.

Afro set n. (US Black use) anywhere that Blacks use for talking or acting in furtherance of their own social and political betterment *Klein.*

Afs n. (S. Afr. use) derog. term for Africans, white use only *Marcuson.*

aggravation n. (UK police/criminal use) the difficulties that both sides of the professional law make for each other *Laurie.*

aggro n. (abbrev. aggravation); **1.** spec. violence enjoyed by skinheads, esp. at football matches, beating up Asians, etc.; **2.** any form of problems, difficulties, harassment *Newman:1*.

agony aunt n. the problem-solving (usu. female) columnists of papers and magazines to whom the lovelorn and generally wretched can write, their letters will be answered in print and/or privately.

a-head n. (drug use) one who specializes in consuming quantities of amphetamines *Green:1*.

aid n. (UK police use) temporary detective constable; fr. 'aid to CID' *Laurie*.

ain't holding no air (US Black use) to be unimpressive, to lack credibility; to lack the basic knowledge of taking care of oneself within the ghetto *Folb*.

ain't long enough insufficient money *Folb*.

air head n. (Valley Girls (qv) use) an idiot, a fool, someone who has nothing but air, and no brains, in his head (cf: bubblehead) *Harpers/Queen 1/83*.

air hose n. (US preppie (qv) use) loafers worn, as is preppie style, without socks *Bernbach*.

airmail n. (US use) throwing garbage out of windows instead of taking it to dustbins, loading it into disposal chutes, etc. *Selby:1*.

air out v. to go for a walk; orig. Black but now general use *Major*.

airs and graces n. (rhyming sl.) **1.** faces; **2.** braces; **3.** horse races *Jones:J*.

airy-fairy a. insubstantial, trivial, of minimal importance.

aka n. (cant) an alias, a false name; fr. abbrev. *a*lso *k*nown *a*s *Neaman & Silver*.

Aladdin's cave n. (UK police use) the home of a successful thief, or the place where he keeps his loot (cf: slaughter) *Laurie*.

Alan Whickers n. (rhyming sl.) knickers; fr. TV personality *Wright*.

Al Capone ride n. (US Black use) any old car, both the original Capone era models and more recent ones that lack the most up-to-date gimmicks and accessories *Folb*.

alderman's nail n. (rhyming sl.) tail *Jones:J*.

aled up a. drunk *Keyes*.

alf n. (Aus. use) unsophisticated, nationalistic, basic Aus. male; recently overtaken by ocker (qv) *Baker*.

alias a. (West Indian use) dangerous, violent *Thelwell*.

alias man n. (UK criminal, esp. West Indian use) a cheat, a hypocrite, anyone unethical *Powis*.

alive and kicking absolutely alert and lively; often as a response to a speaker who assumes the opposite of an (absent) person: 'No, he's still alive . . .'

alkied a. drunk *Dickson*.

alky n. (abbrev.) alcoholic *Underwood*.

all at sea a. **1.** confused; fr. losing one's bearings *Goulart*; **2.** drunk; fr. bobbing up and down and possibly vomiting *Dickson*.

all behind like a fat woman (cp) refers to tardiness or being slow.

all bets are off all deals are cancelled, all agreements are forgotten; in gambling use, no money can be won or lost *Higgins:2*.

all chiefs and no indians (cp, orig. milit. use) all officers and no 'other ranks'; also, for a situation where no one in a group of people wants to be anything but the boss.

all done by mirrors (cp) any event which seems remarkable but which obviously hides tricks beneath the surface.

all dressed up and nowhere to go (cp) both a literal description and one implying anticlimax or disappointment.

alley cat n. see: alley rat *Shulman*.

alley rat n. (US Black use) a particularly unpleasant, villainous and impoverished person *Major*.

alley-whipped a. unpaid despite one's having done the work required; fr. the hapless worker being taken out into the alley and beaten when money is requested *Safire*.

all fine and dandy excellent, perfect;

often in ironic use.

all-fired a. extremely, very much so; euph. for *hell-fired Chandler:LG.*

all get out very much, to a great extent; usu. prefixed by *as . . .*

all hot and bothered flustered, manically nervous; sometimes through the suppression of lust.

alligator n. (US Black use) any sexually aggressive male *Folb.*

alligator (rhyming sl. later; orig. 1950s cp.) 'see ya later, alligator . . . in a while, crocodile', popularized by Bill Haley and the Comets 1956 pop hit of the same name, and by the widely publicized use of the phrase by Princess Margaret *Cole.*

all in a. **1.** exhausted, utterly tired *Wilkinson*; **2.** drunk *Dickson.*

all in one n. an orgy; 'person' or 'orifice' is unstated *Klein.*

all mops and brooms a. drunk *Dickson.*

all mouth and trousers all talk and no action; a braggart, a fake (cf: all piss and wind) *'Minder', Thames TV, 1983.*

all my eye and Betty Martin utter, absolute nonsense *Hotten.*

all of a doodah in a fluster, in a state, very agitated.

all of a tiswas utterly confused, very excited; Central TV, 'Tiswas' children's light entertainment programme 1970s.

all of a tizzy see: all of a tiswas.

all one's born days ever, at any time at all.

all-originals a. (US Black use) Black people only; thus *all-originals scene*: a Blacks only party, etc. *Major.*

all over bar the shouting (cp) a foregone conclusion.

all over the board eccentric, unstable *McFadden.*

all over the place in a great mess, utterly disorganized.

all piss and wind all talk and no action (cf: all mouth and trousers).

all points bulletin n. (US campus use) a plea for help, with work, emotions, etc.; fr. police use; cf. APB *Underwood.*

all right! excl. yes indeed! I agree! etc. *Underwood.*

all that jazz all that sort of thing, usu. following a list of proper nouns '. . . and all that jazz'; *Capital Radio programme title 1983.*

all the beans (bingo use) 57; fr. Heinz 57 Varieties.

all the steps (bingo use) 39; fr. *The Thirty Nine Steps* by John Buchan.

all the twos (bingo use) 22; thus *all the threes*: 33; *all the fours*: 44 etc., up to *all the nines*: 99.

all the way general term of agreement, of encouragement and support.

all tits and teeth a female who capitalizes on her physical charms – esp. her smile and (presumably) large breasts – to make up for the lack of more subtle attractions.

all to cock unsatisfactory, mixed up, useless (cf: cock).

all wet a. drunk *Dickson.*

all wind and piss a loudmouth, a braggart, all talk and no action (cf: all mouth and trousers) *Powis.*

all wool and a yard wide (US cp) excellent, dependable person; fr. clothing trade self-promotions *Burroughs:Jr.*

almonds n. (rhyming sl.) almond rocks = socks *Powis.*

alphonse n. (UK criminal use) a ponce (cf: Charlie Ronce, Joe Ronce, etc.) *Powis.*

also-ran n. a useless person, a failure; fr. racing use.

ambidextrous a. (euph.) bisexual; fr. SE: capable of using both hands equally well (cf: AC/DC) *Neaman & Silver.*

ambulance-chaser n. a lawyer who specializes in representing the victims of street and other accidents and to whom he offers his services, which are accepted while the victim is still too shocked to make proper and rational arrangements *Green:2.*

amigo n. affectionate term of address; fr. Sp. 'friend' *'Hill Street Blues',*

Thames TV, 1983.

amp n. **1.** (drug use) (abbrev.) ampoule; **2.** (music business) (abbrev.) amplifier.

amster n. (Aus. use; fr. rhyming sl.) amsterdam = ram (fr. ramp, qv) = one who works outside a carnival, sideshow, strip club, etc., touting the pleasures inside and pulling in the punters (qv) *Baker.*

Amy-John n. a lesbian, often derog.; fr. Amazon *Maledicta.*

anchors n. brakes.

and how! general excl. of agreement or approval *Southern & Hoffenberg.*

Andrew n. the Royal Navy; fr. Lieut Andrew Millar (or -er); orig. sl. for man o'war *Powis.*

and then some! rejoinder to the last speaker: that's not all of it, either!

Andy Cain n. (rhyming sl.) rain *Jones:J.*

and you! (jocular cp) general admonition to anyone listening after one has made a given pronouncement to a given individual *Capital Radio 1983.*

angel n. aka: *angelina*: a passive homosexual *Legman.*

angel dust n. (drug use) PCP, phencyclidine – a dangerous hallucinogenic based on animal (pig) tranquillizer *Green:1.*

angel kisses n. freckles *Grogan.*

angel with a dirty face n. a covert, closeted (qv) homosexual *Legman.*

angle n. any plan which should benefit its maker; a gimmick *Fiction Illus.3.*

ankle-biters n. children; fr. their height and alleged propensities *Humphries:2.*

anna maria n. (rhyming sl.) a fire (domestic) *Jones:J.*

annihilated adv. (Valley Girls (qv) use) extremely drunk or intoxicated by some drug *Harpers/Queen 1/83.*

animal house n. aka: *animal zoo* that fraternity house on the campus of a US college that is generally rated the least efficient, the most degenerate and overall the one to avoid.

anno domini old age and its deleterious effects, esp. of physical prowess *Sharpe:2.*

answer is a lemon, the (derog. cp) a generally negative reply to a fellow speaker; fr. *lemon* anything useless, disappointing, etc.; also the fact that the fruit, like this cp, is sour.

ante up v. to pay out money; fr. poker use *Wodehouse:PGM.*

antsy a. twitchy, nervous, fr. 'ants in one's pants' *R. Stone, 'A Flag for Sunrise', 1981.*

any how disorganized, messy.

any old anything, whatever; a general term of vagueness; 'any old way', 'any old job', etc.

anywhere (drug use) possessing drugs, as in *are you anywhere* (cf: holding) *Burroughs:1.*

AOK intensified form of OK (qv): absolutely perfect, completely excellent, etc. (cf: A1).

APB (US police use) (abbrev.) *a*ll *p*oints *b*ulletin; general alert broadcast to all officers/vehicles; thus used generally by civilians to denote a search for a given person *McFadden.*

ape n. a thug, a hoodlum *rr.*

apehangers n. high, extra-long motorcycle handlebars, favoured by outlaw riders such as the Hells Angels; riding with such equipment one's arms dangle forward like those of an ape *Thompson.*

apeshit a. berserk, mad, crazy, extremely upset *Higgins:1.*

Apple n. (abbrev.) Big Apple (qv) *Price:3.*

apple n. (US Black use) **1.** the vagina; **2.** any pill/capsule coloured red (cf: reds); **3.** large-brimmed, oversized hat, in 1930s/40s style *Folb.*

apple fritter n. (rhyming sl.) bitter beer *Jones:J.*

apple-knocker n. **1.** spec. itinerant fruit worker; **2.** rural, unsophisticated person *Grogan.*

apple-polisher n. a toady, a sycophant; the apple being polished is that presented to the teacher by the class goody-goody (cf: wax up).

apples n. **1.** breasts *Folb*; **2.** (rhyming

sl.) apples and pears = stairs *Powis*.
apples adv. (Aus.) satisfactory; fr. 'apple-pie order' or rhyming sl. apples and spice = niçe *Humphries*.
apples and rice n. (rhyming sl.) nice, usu. used ironically, unlike 'apples' in Aus. use (qv) which is approving *Cole*.
april fools n. (rhyming sl.) **1.** stools; **2.** tools; **3.** football pools *Jones:J*.
april showers n. (rhyming sl.) flowers *Jones:J*.
apron n. **1.** a woman; **2.** a bartender; both uses stem fr. the representative garment *Major*.
area n. (US campus use) genitals; fr. abbrev. pubic area *Underwood*.
are you prepared? (homosexual use) excl. implying amazement or shock, both approving and disapproving *Stanley*.
are you ready? see: are you prepared? *Stanley*.
are you saving it for the worms? (Can. cp) addressed to a supposed virgin, this phrase is intended to shame her into intercourse *Neaman & Silver*.
argy-bargy n. argument, confusion, confrontation; fr. argument *Keyes*.
Aristotle n. (rhyming sl.) bottle; usu. abbrev. as *Arry Franklyn*.
arm n. penis *Milner*.
armed for bear very heavily armed; fr. hunting use *Himes:1*.
armpit n. the least appetizing, poorest, most rundown, and possibly dangerous, area of a given city or town; often as 'armpit of the universe' *Klein*.
army and navy n. (rhyming sl.) gravy *Cole*.
aroma n. (drug use) amyl nitrate (cf: poppers).
around the bend crazy, insane.
around the world licking and sucking the partner's body, incl. the genitals and sometimes the anus; usu. used by prostitutes as part of possible paid services *Legman*.
arrow n. a dart, used in the *arrows game*: darts *BBC-TV passim*.
arse n. **1.** spec. buttocks; **2.** fool, idiot; **3.** (Aus. use) cheek, effrontery; **4.** (Aus. use) sexual conquests, thus a woman/women *Wilkes*.
NB: for the purposes of this dictionary, the spelling *ass* (preferred in the US) has been used for many words and phrases otherwise found under *arse*.
arseholed a. very drunk *H. Page*.
arseholes! rubbish! nonsense! *BBC-2 TV 1983*.
arse over tit head over heels (cf: ass over appetite).
arsy-versy back to front (cf: arse over tit); corruption of vice-versa.
artful dodger n. (rhyming sl.) lodger; with the implication of the lodger's traditional interest in his landlady *Cole*.
Arthur n. (rhyming sl.) bank = Arthur Rank (cf: J. Arthur) *Powis*.
article nine (US criminal/drug use) Federal legal provision that states that anyone considered under the influence of drugs, esp. an addict, is thus not responsible for a given crime and will be sent to the Federal Narcotics Farm at Lexington, Ky. for supposed curing *Burroughs:Jr*.
artist n. an expert/devotee of a given activity; ie: piss artist, punchout artist (qqv), etc. *Powis*.
artsy-craftsy a. pretentious, humourless, self-opinionated; often garbed, metaphorically, in open-toed sandals, home-woven garments and resident in a converted mill *Whitcomb*.
arty n. (US milit. use) (abbrev.) artillery *Del Vecchio*.
arty-farty a. pretentious, overly intellectual/artistic, exhibiting superficial form and little positive content, etc. *L. K. Johnson*.
arvo n. (Aus. use) afternoon *Humphries:2*.
as a bean (Aus. use) general intensifier; ie: 'keen as a bean' *Ready*.
as easy as cake and ice cream see: piece of cake.
ask for the ring v. to practise anal intercourse (cf: bit of ring) *Folb*.
ass spec. buttocks, usu. with sexual connotation *Price:2*. *(See note under*

arse.)

ass fucking n. anal intercourse *Price:2.*

ass hammer n. (US campus use) motorcycle; fr. the battering one receives from its seat on one's own *Underwood.*

asshole n. spec. anus; thus derog. description of a given subject *Price:2.*

asshole buddy n. extremely close friend *Higgins:3.*

ass-kicker n. an aggressive, domineering person, a bully *Wolfe:2.*

ass-kisser n. sycophant (cf: ass licker, brown-noser) *Price:2.*

ass-licker n. a sycophant (cf: ass-kisser).

ass man n. a man who finds a woman's buttocks her most alluring feature (cf: leg man, tit man).

ass on backwards a. drunk (cf: can't find one's ass with both hands) *Dickson.*

ass over appetite head over heels (cf: arse over tit) *Algren:2.*

ass peddler n. anyone who sells their body as a prostitute, male or female *Major.*

asswipe n. **1.** spec. lavatory paper; **2.** derog. term of abuse *Price:1.*

as the actress said to the bishop (cp) turning what may have been a perfectly innocent phrase into a sexual innuendo; thus: 'Pull it out and we'll see how long it is.' 'As the actress said . . .'

at a pinch in an emergency; if really necessary.

at a rate of knots very fast; fr. naut. use.

at it involved in some form of criminality *Newman:1.*

atlas n. (US prison use) **1.** a very strong prisoner; **2.** a prisoner who attempts to carry out everything unaided; both fr. the mythical Atlas who held up the earth in his hands *Klein.*

at sparrow's-fart at dawn, early in the morning; usu. *up at . . .*

at the death in the end; in conclusion.

at the mark-up (UK criminal use) taking an unfairly large proportion of the loot or proceeds from a given swindle, robbery or whatever *Powis.*

at the micks causing trouble; fr. the mix, ie. mixing it *Powis.*

at the push-up (UK criminal/police use) stealing by pickpocketing amongst a large crowd *Powis.*

at the switch (UK criminal/police use) to steal property from a shop and then take it back and demand a cash refund *Powis.*

at the wash (UK police/criminal use) stealing from coats and jackets left hanging up in a washroom or public lavatory *Powis.*

attitude n. one's whole posture towards society, its rules and one's own place amongst them *'Hill Street Blues', Thames TV, 1983.*

Auntie n. **1.** (UK) the British Broadcasting Corporation; orig. use by independent TV companies, but now general; **2.** (Aus. use) (fr. UK origins) Australian Broadcasting Commission (ABC).

auntie n. ageing male homosexual *Jay & Young.*

Auntie Ella n. (rhyming sl.) umbrella *Jones:J.*

Auntie Nelly n. (rhyming sl.) belly *Wright.*

Aunt Jane n. see: Aunt Jemima *Major.*

Aunt Jemima n. (US Black use) a subservient, obsequious Black woman, the female version of Uncle Tom (qv); an early fast-food chain, 'Aunt Jemima's Kitchen', featuring pictures of a stereotype 'Black Mammy' existed in the 1960s *Folb.*

autograph n. (con-man use) a blank piece of paper which the victim is induced to sign and which may be used for some criminal purpose *Neaman & Silver.*

awash a. drunk *Dickson.*

away a. **1.** in prison; London use: any prison outside London *Cole*; **2.** (UK prison/police use) escaped, fr. gaol or police cells *Cole.*

awesome a. (Valley Girls (qv) use)

indicates tremendous approval *Harpers/Queen 1/83*.

AWOL (milit. use) (acro.) *a*bsent *w*ithout*o*ut *l*eave *Del Vecchio*.

awright! that's good, I feel great, etc. (phonetic trans. of US pron. of 'all right' as a greeting/excl.) *McFadden*.

axe n. any musical instrument, esp. guitar; fr. Black jazz use, when instrument more likely saxophone or trumpet *Green, 'Book of Rock Quotes' vol 1, 1977*.

axe v. to close down, to terminate, esp. of businesses, jobs *Capital Radio 1983*.

axle grease n. **1.** a thick application used for one's hair *Major*; **2.** semen *Klein*.

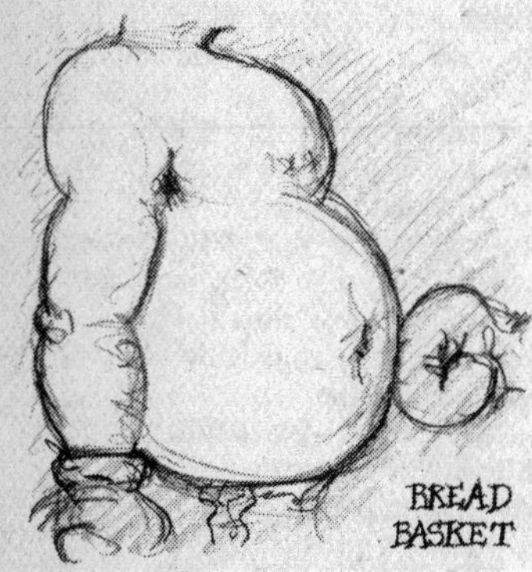

B n. (drug use) (abbrev.) benzedrine *Major.*

baa-lamb n. anyone mild, pleasing, amicable; often used by women of malleable men *Wodehouse:passim.*

babbler n. (Aus. use; rhyming sl.) babbling brook = cook, esp. in an institution, mining camp, farm, etc. *Wilkes.*

babbling brook n. (rhyming sl.) **1.** cook (cf: babbler); **2.** crook *Jones:J.*

babe n. **1.** a woman *Jones*; **2.** (Valley Girls (qv) use) a person of either sex *Pond.*

babes term of affection or simply address between either sex *Wolfe:1.*

baby n. **1.** (US Black use) term of affection/general address between men and women or men and men *Himes:1*; **2.** pet project, obsession, personal concern; 'it's my baby'.

babyblues n. human eyes, irrespective of actual colour.

babycakes term of affection between friends *Price:3.*

baby life n. (US prison use) the maximum sentence that a prisoner must serve – 6 yrs, 4 mths – before a parole board is bound to consider his case for the first time; baby = miniature.

Babylon n. (West Indian/Rastafarian use) **1.** spec. the police; **2.** Western society; **3.** any oppression or the forces that oppress the Black (Rasta) man. Babylon is opposed to Zion – the promised land of Africa, and esp. Ethiopia *Thelwell.*

baby-pro n. (US pimp use) a prostitute under the age of legal consent *Shulman.*

babysit v. (drug use) to take care of someone either under the influence of a drug (esp. LSD) or, more often, recovering from an unpleasant, drug-induced experience *Underwood.*

baby-sitting (journalistic use) looking after the source of a major story, often by staying with them in a hotel, expenses paid by the newspaper, so as to stop any rival paper obtaining the subject's interview *World In Action, Granada TV, 1983.*

baby-snatching marrying or having an affair with someone much younger than oneself; applies to either sex.

bachelor's baby n. (US Black use) an illegitimate child (cf: trick baby) *Klein.*

back alley deal n. (US Black use) any deal between one unsuspecting victim and the person who intends and succeeds in cheating him *Klein.*

back-ah-yard n. (West Indian use) the Caribbean, home *Powis.*

back door man n. **1.** an adulterous lover who comes in at the back door as the husband leaves by the front; **2.** one who practises anal intercourse *J. Morrison, song title 1968.*

back door parole n. (US prison use) dying in prison before one's sentence is over *Chandler: Notebk.*

back eye n. the anus; thus anal intercourse *Klein.*

backfire v. (euph.) to fart *Neaman & Silver.*

back-hander n. **1.** a bribe (cf: kickback); **2.** a slap in the face.

back jump n. (US Black use) anal intercourse, either hetero- or homosexual *Klein.*

backmark (US Black use) **1.** undersirable characteristic; **2.** spec. an informer, esp. in prison *Klein.*

back number n. an irrelevant person, a 'has been', esp. of a former lover, now discarded; fr. the previous and thus 'dead' editions of newspapers.

back of beyond n. anywhere considered by the speaker as inaccessible, outside the purlieus of civilization.

back of Bourke (Aus. use) the wilds, the back of beyond, the edge of 'civilization' *Ready.*

back off (excl.) go away! stop bothering a person *Major.*

back of the net (excl.) wonderful, perfect, fr. football commentator use to applaud a goal *Payne.*

back room boys n. unsung, anonymous but vital experts, inventors, scientists, theorists, etc. who provide much of the muscle behind a business, factory or other organization.

back seat driver n. anyone who offers unwanted advice to the person who is actually in charge or at least performing the task for which the advice is given.

back slice n. the anus, of a man or woman *Klein.*

back slit see: back slice *Klein.*

back to square one start again at the beginning; fr. early BBC radio soccer broadcasts when commentators directed their audience around a squared grid (printed in *Radio Times*), dividing the area of a soccer pitch, as they followed the progress of the ball.

back to the drawing board (cp) let's start again with new plans; used when one plan or idea has come to nothing *Manser.*

backward thinking (US Black use) confused,muddled thinking *Klein.*

bacon and eggs n. (rhyming sl.) legs *Jones:J.*

bad good; the inference being that the individual/object so defined is bad in Establishment eyes and thus good in those of any outlaw – criminal, drug, minority – culture, esp. in Black use (cf: vicious, mean, etc.) *Seale.*

bad-ass a. tough, aggressive, frightening *Price:2.*

bad-ass nigger n. (US Black use) an aggressive, tough black man who rejects the constraints and humiliation of the role the white authorities have selected for him.

bad boy n. (US Black use) clever, attractive black male *Folb.*

bad egg n. rogue, villain *Wodehouse:passim.*

baddest a. (US Black use) the very best, supreme *Folb.*

bad hat n. rogue, untrustworthy person *Wodehouse:passim.*

bad in the head a. (US Black use) eccentric, out of control; unhappy *Folb.*

bad lot n. see: bad egg, bad hat *Wodehouse:passim.*

bad-mouth v. to attack verbally, to slander *Big Ass Comics 1.*

bad news n. an unattractive, unpleasant person; an unpleasant situation *Underwood.*

bad nigger n. (US Black use) any Black who rejects the second-class role offered by the dominant white society (cf: bad-ass nigger) *Major.*

bad rap n. **1.** a serious criminal charge; **2.** an unfair criminal charge *PT.*

bad-rap v. see: bum-rap.

bad shape troubled or depressed state *Underwood.*

bad shit n. **1.** better than average marijuana (cf: bad); **2.** worse than average problems *Price:2.*

bad talk n. (US Black use) conversation or writing that considers and/or urges revolutionary attitudes and actions; such talk is 'bad' both in white eyes and as the prerogative of 'bad niggers' *Major*.

bag n. **1.** a measure of narcotics, sold as *nickel bag*: $5 worth, *dime bag*: $10, etc.; **2.** a contraceptive sheath *Price:2*; **3.** taste, occupation, preference: 'that's my bag'; fr. jazz use 1950s; **4.** old unattractive woman; fr. 19th cent. hag-bag *Wright*.

bag v. **1.** (drug use) to divide bulk purchases of drugs into smaller quantities for dealing *Larner*; **2.** (US Black use) to swallow semen or vaginal fluid during oral intercourse *Folb*; **3.** (Aus. use) to denigrate, to criticize *Wilkes*; **4.** v.t. (Valley Girls (qv) use) to hide something unpleasant from the speaker's sight (cf: bag your face!) *Harpers/Queen 1/83*.

bagel bender n. (derog.) a Jew; fr. bagel, a style of doughnut-shaped roll popular among Jews *Dunne*.

bagels n. (US use) bulges of fat that accumulate around the hips and thighs, usu. used of women despite their universality amongst the overweight; fr. the shape of the popular Jewish roll (cf: love handles) *Neaman & Silver*.

baggage smasher n. (film use) a clumsy person *Chandler: Notebk*.

bagged a. drunk; thus *to tie a bag on*, *to have a bag on Dickson*.

bagged v.i. arrested, caught *Higgins:1*.

bagged a. easy, simple, no problem (cf: in the bag) *Heller*

bagged out a. style-less, shappy, run-down; fr. resemblance to a bag lady (qv) *Pond*.

baggies n. **1.** (drug use) plastic food bags used popularly for holding small amounts of marijuana *Green:1*; **2.** (surfing use) loose-fitting 'boxer short' style of swimming trunks *Whitcomb*.

bag lady n. (abbrev.) shopping bag lady; a female derelict, usu. sleeping rough or in shelters, often an alcoholic or meths drinker, whose most cherished possessions are the numbers of (to an outsider) junk-filled shopping bags which festoon her as she walks and which never leave her side *Shulman*.

bag man n. go between, one who conveys a bribe from the one who offers it to the one who accepts *San Francisco Comics no.2*.

bag of bones n. **1.** (US Black use) marijuana cigarettes *Klein*; **2.** a noticeably thin person *Algren*.

bagpipe it v. (Valley Girls (qv) use) forget it *Pond*.

bagpiping n. intercourse under the armpit, generally a homosexual practise *Rodgers*.

bags I! (UK school use) that's mine, I want to do that!; an allied formula, mainly in prep schools, is *quis*? (Lat: who) to offer an object, to which the responses are *ego*! (Lat: I) if one wishes to make a claim, or *baggy* (bags I) *no par* (no part) if one wishes to be excluded.

bag your face! (Valley Girls (qv) use) general term of abuse, basically requesting a person to put their face into a rubbish bag and throw it away; general Aus. use: *go bag your head* predates this.

bag Zs v. (US preppie (qv) use) to nap, to sleep (cf: cop some Zs) *Bernbach*.

Bahama Mama n. (US Black use) a fat, unattractive 'Black Mammy', supposedly typical of West Indies *Folb*.

bail v. (US teen use) to leave, to play truant; fr. 'bail out' *Pond*.

bail up v. (Aus. use) to trap, to corner; orig. use to describe the 'stand and deliver' tactics of late 19th C. bushrangers *Ready*.

bait n. an attractive man or woman to lure a victim into a con-game or a mugging *Klein*.

bake v. (US prison use) to execute in the electric chair *Klein*.

bald-tyre bandits n. (UK criminal use) traffic police *Powis*.

bale of straw n. (US Black use) a white woman, esp. a blonde *Major.*
ball n. **1.** sexual intercourse *Price:2*; **2.** a good time *Price:2*; **3.** (rhyming sl.) ball of chalk = a walk *Powis.*
ball v. to have sexual intercourse *Price:2.*
ball and chain n. the wife *Major.*
ball and chalk n. aka: *ball of chalk* (rhyming sl.) walk *Cole.*
ball buster n. **1.** spec. a nagging woman (cf: break one's balls); **2.** any overbearingly unpleasant person or circumstances *Price:1.*
ballgame n. (US milit. use) any operation, esp. one involving contact with an enemy *Del Vecchio.*
balling the jack driving a truck very fast; working very hard; any speedy activity; fr. lumberjack use *N. Cassady, 'The First Third', 1971.*
ballocks n. **1.** excl. balls (qv)! rubbish!; **2.** testicles *Norman:1.*
balloon n. saloon bar of a public house; fr. rhyming sl. balloon car = bar *Powis.*
balloon v. to try out a new idea or concept; on the same lines as 'let's run it up the flagpole and see if anyone salutes *Higgins:5.*
balloon goes up (milit. use) the start of hostilities or of a given operation; either the onset of war or of events during that war *Pynchon.*
balloons n. conspicuously large female breasts *Klein.*
ball park figure a round figure for general estimation, assessment; fr. the rough estimate of fans watching a sporting event *Green:2.*
balls n. **1.** spec. testicles; **2.** by ext. fr. **1**: courage, bravery; supposedly quintessential male qualities; **3.** (excl.) rubbish, nonsense *Austin.*
balls-aching nagging. complaining (cf: bellyache, ball buster).
balls-up n. a blunder, an error *Price:3.*
ballsy tough, masculine, courageous (cf: balls) *White.*
balltearer (Aus. use) an aggressive woman (cf: ball buster) *Humphries:2.*
ball up n. (US use) a mess, a confusion; thus *to ball up*: to err, to blunder.
bally a. (euph.) bloody *Wodehouse:passim.*
ballyhoo v. to publicize to excess, often when the product cannot live up to the manufactured image; fr. carnival and fairground use.
baloney n. aka: boloney; nonsense, rubbish *Yellow Dog 22.*
bam n. (drug use) amphetamine; fr. Mex. *bambita Major.*
bamboozle v. to deceive, to fool, to hoax deliberately *Hotten.*
Bambi effect n. the turning in spring of a young (otherwise homosexual) man's fancy to (heterosexual) love; fr. the parting of the youthful Bambi and his erstwhile pal Thumper *Jay & Young.*
banana n. **1.** (US Black use) a light-skinned Black, esp. an attractive woman *Major*; **2.** (Black use) the penis *Klein.*
banana bender n. (Aus. use) Queenslander (cf: Bananaland) *Ready.*
Bananaland n. (Aus. use) Queensland; fr. the banana crop produced there *Wilkes.*
banana oil n. (US use) nonsense, insincere or hypocritical talk *Neaman & Silver.*
bananas a. crazy, eccentric *Woody Allen, film title, 1971.*
bananas n. (US criminal use) a homosexual *Legman.*
band n. (US Black use) a woman *Major.*
band-aid n. (US milit. use) a medic or corpsman; fr. US name for UK 'Elastoplast' *Del Vecchio.*
B & D n. (acro.) bondage and discipline, a sexual 'speciality' *Jay & Young.*
B & E (police use/cant) (acro.) breaking and entering *Higgins:2.*
band in the box n. (rhyming sl.) pox, venereal disease *Jones:J.*
bandit n. (UK police use) a villain, a criminal, usu. with a specific speciality: *knickers bandit*: steals

underwear from washing lines; *gas meter bandit*: steals from gas meters, or similarly paltry sums; *piss-hole bandit*: homosexual who solicits in public lavatories, etc. *Powis*.

band of hope n. (rhyming sl.) soap *Jones:J*.

band rat n. a woman who associates herself with musicians, usu. offering sex in return for proxy celebrity (cf: groupie) *Bruce:2*.

bang n. **1.** spec. an injection of narcotics; **2.** a blow; **3.** a thrill *Price:2*; **4.** sexual intercourse *G. Macdonald Fraser, 'Flashman & the Indians', 1983*.

bang v. to copulate; like many sl. terms involving sex, this implies an aggression irrespective of any affection (cf: poke, do, screw, etc.).

bang a. extremely, very; ie: 'bang in trouble' *Performance*.

bang around to make one's presence felt, with little practical result *Goulart*.

banged shot down *rr*.

banger n. **1.** a dilapidated motor car; fr. the noisy engine, parts dropping off, etc. *Powis*; **2.** a sausage; orig. naval use.

bang the bishop to masturbate *Barr*.

bang like a shithouse door (in a gale) v. to rate as an enthusiastic sexual performer; usu. said by men of women *Humphries*.

bang on v. to talk repetitiously and tediously *Whitcomb*.

bang on a. absolutely right, exactly so, etc. *Manser*.

bangtail n. (US Black use) a prostitute (cf: bang, tail) *Klein*.

bang to rights caught in the act *Norman:1*.

bang up v. **1.** to inject a narcotic drug; **2.** (UK prison use) to lock a prisoner in his/her cell *Norman:1*

bang-up a. first-rate, excellent *Hotten*.

bang up (against) aka: *bung up (against)*: very close.

banjaxed broken, ruined, smashed up; usu. Irish use *Terry Wogan, bk. title, 1980*.

banjo n. (Aus. use) a shovel; fr. shape *Wilkes*.

banjo v. (UK milit. use) to hit, to beat up *Green:2*.

bank n. (US prison use) a shot of a narcotic *Chandler:Notebk*.

banker n. (UK taxi-driver use) one of a series of routes that are most often requested by passengers, ie. Heathrow to the Hilton, etc.; fr. gambling use.

bank on v. to take for granted; to assume as a certainty; fr. gambling use *Runyon:1*.

bankroll v. to provide financial backing for a project, legal or otherwise *Fiction Illus.3*.

bar n. one pound sterling *LL*.

barbecue v. (US Black use) an attractive woman, esp. one who enjoys/offers oral sex *Major*.

barber v. to gossip, to chatter; fr. supposed predeliction of barbers to chatter on at their captive customers *Farrell*.

Barbie Doll n. a super-conformist, conventionally attractive, WASP (qv) American woman; fr. the name of a blue-eyed, blonde-haired designer labelled plastic doll *H. Thompson, 'The Great Shark Hunt', 1980*.

barbs n. (drug use) (abbrev.) barbiturates *Green:1*.

Barcoo salute n. (Aus. use) a characteristics gesture in Aus. of brushing away flies from one's face; fr. river and district of Queensland *Wilkes*.

bare-ass a. naked *Higgins:1*.

bareback a. making love without using a contraceptive sheath *Price:2*.

barf v. (usu. US campus use) to vomit *Underwood*.

barf! (interj.) general expression of disgust (cf: barf, v.) *Underwood*.

barf city n. (US teen. use) anything particularly unpleasant (cf: barf) *Pond*.

barfly n. the habitual occupier of a given bar, day in, day out *Schulberg*.

barf me out! excl. (Valley Girls (qv) use) exclamation indicating absolute disapproval *Harpers/Queen 1/83*.

barge n. a particularly large vagina

Klein.

barge in v. to interrupt rudely, to push one's way in *Seale.*

barker n. (UK criminal use) a small pistol; fr. late 18th C. 'barking iron' *Powis.*

barmy a. insane, eccentric; fr. dial. *barm*: yeast, thus frothing like fermenting yeast *Performance.*

Barnaby Rudge n. (rhyming sl.) judge; fr. C. Dickens character *Cole.*

barnet n. (rhyming sl.) Barnet fair = hair *Norman:2.*

barney n. a fight *Tidy.*

baron n. an influential convict within the prison; esp. one who trades in the prison currency, tobacco, thus verb: to baron (cf: daddy) *Norman:1.*

baroning selling contraband luxuries within the prison, carried out by prisoners (cf: baron) *LL.*

barrack v. (Aus. use) to support a given team or individual in a sporting context; unlike SE use, no antagonism implied, other than usual partisanship *Wilkes.*

barrack room lawyer n. any amateur, esp. in the services or in prison, who considers himself more expert in the law, esp. Queen's Regulations or prison rules, than any professional and who will offer services, often to their detriment, to his peers *LL.*

barrel v. (Aus. use) to knock down, to hit, esp. as a result of a tackle in football *Wilkes.*

barrelass v. to rush headlong, to charge at *Higgins:4.*

barrelhouse **1.** a brothel or cheap saloon; thus **2.** (jazz use) rough and tough unpretentious music that started off in the repertoire of the musicians who played for such saloons *Major.*

base! (Valley Girls (qv) use) excl. of approval at another person's cruel but accurate attack on a third (absent) party *Pond.*

base v. **1.** (drug use) (abbrev.) free-base (qv); **2.** to disparage, criticize, humiliate another person *Pond.*

bash n. a party *Klein.*

bash v. to hit, to batter *Performance.*

bash the bumps v. (skiing use) skiing through a crowded field of rich skiers *Barr.*

basic a. unexciting, unexceptional, uneventful *Underwood.*

basket n. **1.** (homosexual use) the male genitals *White*; **2.** (euph.) bastard *Humphries:2.*

basket case n. cripple, either mentally or physically *Price:2.*

basketeer v. (homosexual use) to wander the streets gazing at male genitals; this can provide some men with adequate satisfaction, others may be simply sizing up the available talent for later developments *Legman.*

basket picnic n. see: basketeer *Legman.*

bastard n. general term for a man, people; not esp. derog. *Humphries.*

basted a. drunk *Dickson.*

bat n. **1.** an unattractive woman, often old; **2.** a drunken binge, a spree, thus *go to bat Grogan.*

bat a. (US campus use) good, attractive, fr. play on *bad* (qv) *Underwood.*

bat and wicket n. (rhyming sl.) ticket *Jones:J.*

batchy a. silly, stupid *Sillitoe.*

bate n. .(UK society use) temper; orig. prep school/public school use, thus inevitably carried into adult life *Barr.*

bath bun n. (rhyming sl) **1.** sun; **2.** son *Jones:J.*

bato n. (US Black use) any Mexican, Puerto Rican or other Latin person *Folb.*

bat phone n. (UK police use) the officer's personal radio set; fr. 'Batman' comic-TV show superhero *Powis.*

bats a. crazy, insane, eccentric; abbrev. bats in the belfry (qv) *Dickson.*

batshit a. insane, crazy, fr. batty plus apeshit (qqv) *Price:3.*

bats in the belfry a. eccentric, crazy; often as verb: *to have bats . . .*

bat the breeze v. to chatter, to gossip; orig. milit. use.

batti n. (Jamaican use) the buttocks *Thelwell.*

batting average n. (US police use) an officer's current record of arrests, upon which his promotion may depend (cf: accommodation collar) *Neaman & Silver.*

battle v. (Aus. use) to struggle for a livelihood, to work in a low-paid job; both senses imply some self-congratulation *Lawson.*

battle (and) cruiser n. (rhyming sl.) boozer = public house *Cole.*

battle-axe n. a formidable (older) woman.

batty insane, crazy, eccentric; fr. Fitzherbert Batty, a 19th C. barrister whose certification as mad in 1839 caused much interest *Higgins:1.*

battyman n. (West Indian sl.) a homosexual, prob. fr. batti (qv) *Powis.*

bawl out v. to scold, to reprimand, to criticize; all such attacks are delivered at the top of the voice.

Bay City n. (US trucker use) San Francisco, Calif.; however, the fictitious (and massively corrupt) 'Bay City' created by Raymond Chandler is generally seen to be Oakland, Calif. *CB.*

bazoo n. mouth *Farrell.*

bazoom n. humorous pron. of bosom.

B.B. head n. (US Black use) an unattractive female; esp. one with short nappy hair *Folb.*

be a devil! take a risk!; I dare you!; usu. used facetiously to someone for whom the tiniest breach of 'normality' is a major event *Manser.*

beak n. **1.** judge, magistrate *Chandler Notebk.*; **2.** the nose *Wodehouse: RHJ.*

bean n. the head *Farrell.*

bean v. to hit on the head *Price:2.*

beanbag v. to have sexual intercourse *'Hill Street Blues', Thames TV, 1983.*

bean eater n. aka: *bean choker*; (derog.) Mexican *BvdB.*

beaner n. (Valley Girls (qv) use, although general derog.): Mexican (cf: bean eater) *Harpers/Queen 1/83.*

bean-feast n. a party, a celebration, usu. with food and drink; fr. early 19th C. tradition of employers giving their workers an annual banquet.

beano n. a party, a celebration; fr. bean-feast (qv) *Wolfe:2.*

beans n. **1.** (US Black use) any drug available in a pill form and swallowed as such *Klein*; **2.** dollars *Price:3.*

Bean Town n. (US trucker use) Boston, Mass. *CB.*

bear n. **1.** (US Black use) a particularly ugly wo man *Folb*; **2.** (US campus use) any difficult course (cf: gut) *Underwood*; **3.** (CB use) a policeman; fr. US Forest Service's mascot 'Smokey the Bear' (cf: smokies) *CB.*

beard n. (lesbian use) a male used as an ostensible lover or even husband, as a disguise for one's real preference *Maledicta.*

bear in the air n. (CB use) a police helicopter *CB.*

bear-leader n. an expert who teaches his pupils by example; fr. nickname for the tutors of the 18th C. who ferried their aristocratic pupils around the 'Grand Tour' of Europe *J. le Carré, 'Smiley's People', 1980.*

bear's paw n. (rhyming sl.) saw *Jones:J.*

beast n. (US Black use) **1.** white person; **2.** heroin *Klein.*

beastie n. (Valley Girls (qv) use) anyone considered outside the group talking, esp. if unattractive, empty-headed, etc. *Pond.*

beat n. (pimp use) a client who likes to be beaten, often bringing his own equipment with him *OUI 8/75.*

beat a. **1.** exhausted, tired out *Selby*; **2.** out of funds *Higgins:3.*

beat about the bush v. to avoid a given topic, to fail deliberately to come to the point *Humphries:2.*

beat a rap v. to be found not guilty in a court *Hoffman:a.*

beat around the bush v. see: beat about the bush.

beat feet v. (US campus use) to leave, to depart *Underwood.*

beat for v. to take a person's money, whether it is offered or not *Burroughs:1.*
beat it v. to go away, usu. as excl: *beat it! Manser.*
beat off v. masturbate (cf: beat one's meat) *Higgins:1.*
beat-off n. see: jerk-off (n.) *Underwood.*
beat one out of v. to cheat, to steal from, to defraud *Larner.*
beat one's chops v. see: beat one's gums.
beat one's dummy v. to masturbate *Folb.*
beat one's gums v. to talk incessantly.
beat one's hog v. to masturbate *Higgins:2.*
beat one's meat v. to masturbate *Junker.*
beat one to the punch v. **1.** (US Black use) to arrive at destination sooner than another person; **2.** to appreciate or understand something faster than another person; both fr. boxing use *Klein.*
beat out v. to overcome, to beat a rival *Algren.*
beats me! general excl. of incomprehension; I just can't understand it *PT.*
beat the rap v. to be found innocent of a charge in court *Dunne.*
beat-up a. dilapidated, run down, ageing *Price:2.*
beat up v. **1.** assault, attack (cf: stomp); **2.** to nag, harass *Higgins:1.*
beaut! (Aus. use) all-purpose Aus. term of approbation, can equally well be used as adj.; also as beauty! (pron. bewdy) *Humphries:2.*
beaver n. vagina, esp. in commercial pornography use *Higgins:2.*
beaver shot n. a close-up photograph or camera-angle on the female genitals; used in commercial pornography.
bebopper n. (US Black use) an inexperienced, naïve and on those grounds unpopular person; fr. the bebop jazz craze, new and sophisticated in 1940s, but archaic by 1980s *Folb.*
be brought out v. to be initiated into the homosexual life (cf: come out) *Legman.*
bed and breakfast (bingo use) 26; fr. 2/6d, at one stage the going rate for a B&B establishment *LL.*
be down (Black pimp use) to be prepared, aware *Milner.*
Bedpan line n. (British Rail use) the electrified commuter line between Bedford and St Pancras; post 1983, though the line, on diesel power, pre-existed without this name.
bedroom eyes n. a look in the eyes that invites its subject towards seduction *Algren.*
Beeb n. the British Broadcasting Corporation (BBC).
Beecham's pill n. (rhyming sl.) **1.** bill; **2.** still (photograph) *Jones:J.*
beef n. **1.** a complaint, a problem *Higgins*; **2.** a court case, usu. as defendant; **3.** (US Black use) penis *Folb.*
beef v. **1.** to complain; **2.** to engage in sexual intercourse *Underwood.*
beefcake n. a male pinup (cf: cheesecake).
beef bayonet n. the penis (cf: pork sword).
beef up v. to strengthen, to improve *Caserta.*
beefy a. well-built, muscled, stolid *Wodehouse:AAG.*
beemal n. (butchers' back-sl.) lamb *Cole.*
been and gone and done it (cp) mocking response to a confession of some minor error or peccadillo; usu.: 'now you've . . .' *Manser.*
been there to have seduced someone *Dury, 'Laughter', 1979.*
beer belly n. a fat stomach, the result of an excess of beer-drinking *Powis.*
beer bottle beat n. (pimp use) a client who likes to be beaten by a prostitute who is wielding a beer bottle *OUI 8/75.*
beer bust n. a drinking party that concentrates on beer *Whitcomb.*

beer gut n. see: beer belly *Cole.*
beer-up n. (Aus. use) a riotous, drunken party (cf: piss-up) *Wilkes.*
bees and honey n. (rhyming sl.) money *Franklyn.*
bee's knees a. wonderful, the best, perfect (cf: cat's pyjamas).
beetle-crushers n. large, heavy boots, often as worn by policemen, labourers or the army *P. MacDonald, 'X v. Rex', 1933.*
beetle off v. to leave, to wander off *Barr.*
beevos n. (US college use) beer; corruption of 'beverage' (cf: bevvy) *Bernbach.*
beezer n. the nose *Wodehouse:JO.*
beggar my neighbour (rhyming sl.) on the Labour = visiting the Labour Exchange/Unemployment Office to draw one's dole/unemployment benefit *Cole.*
beggar's lagging n. see: tramp's lagging *LL.*
begging for it a male comment on a woman who, supposedly if not actually, is inflamed with lust.
begorra! (euph.) by God! the cliché expletive of each and every stage Irishman yet created (cf bejabers!).
behind 1. involved with, concerned about, believing in *Michaels & Ricks*; **2.** (Black use) the cause of something *Milner.*
behind one's door (UK prison use) locked up in solitary confinement *Newman:3.*
beige a. (Valley Girls (qv) use) deeply tedious person *Pond.*
be-in n. (hippie use) fr. the original Human Be-in, Golden Gate Park, San Francisco 1967, a gathering of hippies for mutual admiration, smoking of cannabis and listening to music. The *-in* suffix extended around the hippie vocabulary, incl. *fuck-in*, *smoke-in*, *love-in*, etc. *Hoffman:a.*
be in the hot seat v. to be in a difficult, poss. embarrassing, certainly demanding position.
bejabers! (euph.) by Jesus! those stage Irishmen who do not say begorra (qv) will certainly say bejabers! many manage both.
bejazus (euph.) by Jesus; often in knock the bejazus out of (qv).
bell n. (US Black use) personal notoriety *Major.*
bell v. to call on the telephone *Payne.*
belle n. (homosexual use) a good-looking, young homosexual *Legman.*
bell ringers n. (rhyming sl.) fingers *Wright.*
bells n. (US Black use) (abbrev.) wedding bells; an expression of approval *Major.*
bellyache v. to complain, to moan *Higgins:2.*
bellyful n. enough, if not too much, satiety; esp. in have a bellyful (qv).
belly gun n. a small gun that is most effective when fired at short range, esp. when aimed at a victim's abdomen.
belly habit n. (drug use) pains in the stomach that may accompany withdrawal from continued heroin use *Major.*
belly up a. drunk *Dickson.*
belly up to v. to move straight at, to approach directly; fr. the pushing forward of one's stomach.
below the belt underhand, unfair, illegal, cheating; fr. boxing use which declares such blows as foul.
below the mahogany a. drunk; the mahogany is the bar, beneath which the drinker has slipped *Dickson.*
belt n. a measure of spirits.
belt v. to hit *Price:2.*
belt along v. to run fast, to hurry *Tidy.*
belted a. drunk *Dickson.*
belter n. an admirable, exciting, thrilling, etc. event or circumstance.
belt it v. to drive exceptionally fast *Humphries:2.*
belt it out v. to sing loudly and enthusiastically *Hoffman:a.*
belt one's hog v. to masturbate *Dunne.*
belt out v. to knock down; to destroy *Breslin.*
belt up! (excl.) be quiet, shut up!

Manser.
BEM n. (acro.) Bug-Eyed Monster(s); a popular category of science fiction writing and described as such by fans *'Twilight Zone' magazine: passim.*
be missing! (excl.) go away! a phrase first used by Chicago mobster Spike O'Donnell in rejecting the overtures/threats of Al Capone (*see 'Raymond Chandler Speaking', 1962*) *Chandler: LG.*
be my guest! (cp) help yourself, make yourself at home, etc.
bended knees n. (rhyming sl.) cheese *Wright.*
bender n. **1.** a bout of riotous drinking, often lasting several days and including random acts of excess, violence, etc. *Higgins:3*; **2.** a homosexual (cf: bent).
bend one's ear v. to chatter on interminably and probably tediously *Powis.*
bend one's elbow v. to have a drink *Powis.*
benies n. (US campus) (abbrev.) benefits, spec. those of the GI Bill that puts US service veterans through college for free *Underwood.*
bennies n. (abbrev.) benzedrine (cf: B) *Tuff Shit Comics.*
benny n. an overcoat *Folb.*
benny house n. a brothel which essentially caters for heterosexuals, but will obtain male prostitutes on request *Legman.*
beno fr. 'there'll be no fun': the period of menstruation and thus, traditionally, no sex *Rawson.*
bent n. a homosexual.
bent a. **1.** corrupt, esp. 'bent copper': corrupt policeman *Payne*; **2.** sexually eccentric, esp. homosexual.
bent as a nine bob note dishonest (of a person); stolen (of an object) *Cole.*
bent out of shape intoxicated by a drug, esp. cannabis or LSD, or extremely drunk *Goldman.*
benz n. (abbrev.) benzedrine (cf: bennies, B) *Norman:2.*
be one of the knights v. (homosexual use) to have syphilis *Legman.*
Berdoo n. San Bernardino, Calif. *Thompson.*
berk n. (rhyming sl.) Berkeley Hunt or Berkshire Hunt = cunt (qv) = fool, incompetent *Humphries.*
Berkeley Hunt n. see: berk *Cole.*
Berkshire Hunt n. see: berk *Cole.*
berries n. (US Black use) wine *Folb.*
best bib and tucker in one's best clothes.
best-built a. women with voluptuous figures *Higgins:1.*
betcha! fr. bet you! see: you bet!
Bethlehem steel (US Black use) a boastful description of the rigidity of one's erect penis; fr. the US steel producer *Klein.*
bet one's boots v. to be certain, to wager everything in total confidence *Dury, 'Do It Yourself', 1979.*
bet one's bottom dollar v. bet one's boots *Wodehouse: PGM.*
bet one's kettle v. to be drunk *Dickson.*
Betsy n. a revolver, a pistol *Runyon:1.*
better half n. the wife, usu. joking use *Manser.*
better than a poke in the eye with a blunt stick see: better than a slap in the belly with a wet fish.
better than a slap in the belly with a wet fish (cp) a situation that certainly might be worse.
between hell and high water caught between two extremes, neither of which is particularly palatable.
between the devil and the deep blue sea caught between two equally unappealing extremes.
between the rock and the hard place (mainly US use) see: between the devil and the deep blue sea; between hell and high water.
betwixt and between undecided, uncertain, 'neither one thing nor the other'.
bet your ass v. **1.** to bet heavily on an apparent 'sure thing'; **2.** excl.: .'you must be joking!' *Higgins:1.*
bet your life see: bet your ass; bet one's bottom dollar, etc.
bevvied a. drunk; fr. beverage

Wilkinson.

bevvy n. alcohol, esp. beer (cf: beevos) *Wright.*

beyond the rabbit-proof fence (Aus. use) very far away, beyond 'civilization' (cf: back of Bourke) *Bickerton.*

be your age! excl. of contempt, based in the condemnation of one who the speaker considers is acting childishly *Baker.*

bf (abbrev.) *b*loody *f*ool.

B-52 n. (US milit. use) a can opener; fr. the heavy bomber of the same name *Del Vecchio.*

B-girl (abbrev.) bar-girl: amateur prostitutes who solicit from bars *Goldman.*

bhani ghani (US Black use) a form of greeting (cf: what's happening?), poss. fr. Swahili: *abari gani* what's news? *Folb.*

bi a. (abbrev.) bisexual (cf: ambidextrous).

Bible-banger n. (US campus use) aka: *Bible beater*: a religious fanatic *Underwood.*

bible-puncher n. a religious person, usu. one who wishes to thrust their beliefs on any who will listen and many who would rather not.

biddy n. old lady, spec. Irish servant girl, fr. common Irish name *Bruce:1.*

biff v. **1.** to hit; thus; **2.** to kill, to murder *Goulart.*

big a. (gambling use) multiples of ten thousand; high stakes used in poker games where (as in drug use) the convention talks of *nickels* ($500) and *dimes* ($1000), thus *big nickel* $5000 and *big dime* $10000 *Al Alvarez, Sunday Times, 5/6/83.*

Big A n. (US trucker use) **1.** Amarillo, Texas; **2.** Atlanta, Georgia *CB.*

Big Apple n. New York City *Capital Radio, 30/9/83.*

big ass a. large, powerful, self-opinionated; fr. the supposed crushing power of such massive buttocks *Big Ass Comics, title 1969, Rip Off Press.*

big hit n. (US prison use) a long term of imprisonment, usu. 3 years or more (cf: big time) *Klein.*

big boat n. large, traditional American car, esp. station wagon *Price:3.*

big bucks n. large sums of money, esp. those earned by performers or stolen by criminals *Capital Radio, 29/6/83.*

big C n. (euph.) cancer; *the* horror disease (*pace* AIDS) of the 20th century which, as the supreme threat to life, cannot even be named in full without a shudder *Rawson.*

big cheese n. important person, influential figure, boss in a given situation/job *'Hill Street Blues', Thames TV, 1983.*

big deal! *excl.* what's important about that?, why bother me? *McFadden.*

big deal a. important, vital, urgent, impressive, etc. *McFadden.*

big Dick (from Boston) (gambling use) the point of ten in craps dice *Algren.*

Big Ditch n. the Atlantic Ocean.

big Deuce n. (US teen. use) Second World War *Sculatti.*

big E n. a brush-off, a rejection; *E* is abbrev. for elbow (qv) *Barr.*

big enchilada n. a phrase much the same as big shot, big cheese (qqv), momentarily very popular during the Watergate Scandal (1973/4) when the White House tapes used it variously to describe corrupt personnel *PT.*

big fish n. an important, powerful person *PT.*

biggie n. anything or anyone large, important, successful, esp. used in entertainment industries (cf: gorilla) *Dickson.*

Big Green (US college use) nickname for Dartmouth College *Bernbach.*

big H (drug use) heroin *Underwood.*

big hit n. (Aus. use, rhyming sl.) shit = excrement *Franklyn.*

big house n. (US criminal use) prison *Wodehouse passim.*

big jobs n. (US child use) excreta *Dury, 'Laughter', 1979.*

Big John n. (US Black use) the police *Folb.*

Big Kahoona n. (surfing use) a legendary monstrous 'perfect' wave – never encountered, but continually sought out *Whitcomb*.

big league a. important, substantial, powerful; fr. sporting use *Schulberg:2*.

big noise n. an important, powerful person.

big-note artist n. (Aus. use) braggart, esp. concerning alleged sums of money he possesses *Baker*.

big O n. orgasm *Jay & Young*.

big one n. £100, $100 *Higgins:3*; but $1000 *Higgins:4*.

big razzoo n. a gesture of extreme contempt or scorn (cf: razz, raspberry) *Chandler:LG*.

Big Red n. (US college use) Cornell University *Bernbach*.

big shot n. superior person, or one who claims to be (cf: big noise) *Price:2*.

big sleep n. death; coined by Raymond Chandler as title of his book, 1939.

Big Smoke n. (Aus. use) Sydney; fr. UK use for London (cf: smoke) *Humphries:2*.

big split n. (Aus. use) the act of vomiting *Humphries:2*.

Big T n. (US trucker use) Tucson, Arizona *CB*.

big time n., a. success, fame, power; fr. theatrical use: vaudeville theatres with top-line acts and thus only two shows per day, the opposite of small time (qv) *Whitcomb*.

big time n. (US prison use) a lengthy sentence, 3 years plus (cf: big bit) *Seale*.

big wheel n. an important, influential person, esp. in business (cf: big noise, etc.) *Chandler:LG*.

big wig n. a powerful, important person, often a politician or bureaucrat.

bike n. a promiscuous woman (cf: town bicycle) *Powis*.

biker n. a motorcycle rider, usu. a member of an outlaw motorcycle gang *San Francisco Comics 3*.

bilge n. nonsense, rubbish, piffle; fr. nautical use: bilgewater.

bilge artist n. aka: *bull artist*; a braggart, one given to boasting.

bill n. (taxi-driver use) the taxi-driver's licence *Powis*.

Bill n. **1.** (abbrev.) Old Bill (qv) *Newman:1*; **2.** (abbrev.) dollar bill (cf: billies) *Price:1*; **3.** $100 *Schulberg*.

billies n. (Valley Girls (qv) use) money, diminutive of bill (qv).

bill of goods false promises, a hoax, theories that are not followed up by practice *Uris*.

bill shop n. police station (cf: cop shop) *Powis*.

billy n. (US police use) the policeman's wooden club (cf: Mr Wood).

billy-jack a. (US Black use) unsophisticated, from the back woods *Klein*.

bim n. (abbrev.) bimbo (qv) *Chandler:LG*.

bimbo n. a young man or woman *Jay & Young*.

Bimi n. West Indian *Price:2*.

bimps n. (US campus use, spec. U. of Arkansas) french fried potatoes *Underwood*.

bin n. **1.** pocket *Griffith*; **2.** (abbrev.) loony bin (qv).

bind n. a problem, which 'ties one up' *Higgins:3*.

bindle n. (drug use) a small measure of narcotics, wrapped in a folded square of paper; fr. hobo use, a bindle was a bedroll which was carried folded up *De Lannoy & Masterson*.

bindle stiff n. a tramp, spec. one carrying a bedroll 'bindle'; formerly a migrant worker *Grogan*.

bingo n. (Can. prison use) a riot *Caron*.

bins n. **1.** binoculars, eyes *Wright*; **2.** glasses, spectacles *Payne:2*; **3.** pair of trousers, fr. bin: pocket *Norman:2*.

bint n. a young girl, fr. Arabic *Powis*.

bip bam thank you ma'am see: wham bam thank you ma'am *Major*.

Bird n. Thunderbird, a motor car *Higgins:2*.

bird n. **1.** (US Black use) an

experienced, tough female prostitute *Klein*; **2.** a girl; a girl-friend *Norman:1*; **3.** (rhyming sl.) bird lime = time = a prison sentence *Performance*; **4.** penis *Price:2*; **5.** (US milit. use) a helicopter *Del Vecchio*; **6.** (US campus use) an obscene gesture of dismissal, mockery; fr. flip the bird (qv) *Underwood.*

bird dog n. **1.** (US milit. use) a forward air controller, usu. in a single-engined propellor plane, directing military movements, bombing, etc.; fr. hunting use *Del Vecchio*; **2.** (US criminal use) a contact man for stock and bond thieves; fr. hunting use *AS 41 (1966).*

bird dog v. (US teen. use) to steal another person's girl-friend; to break up a school or college romance *The Everley Brothers, 'Bird Dog', 1958.*

birdie n. an effeminate male; fr. bird (qv) *Legman.*

birdseye n. (drug use) a small amount of narcotics *De Lannoy & Masterson.*

birdsnesting n. (skiing use) skiing through trees *Barr.*

Birmingham screwdriver n. a hammer; fr. supposed oafishness of the Birmingham worker who would rather hammer in a screw than use the correct tool; despite normal racial stereotypes (and their supposed jobs) a US usage *yiddish screwdriver* has been noted *c.*1939.

birthday suit n. the naked body; fr. the state in which one emerges from the maternal womb *Humphries.*

biscuits and cheese n. (rhyming sl.) knees *Jones:J.*

bit n. **1.** situation, circumstance, usu. with a descriptive noun: 'the whole punk bit', etc. *McFadden*; **2.** a prison sentence – any length (cf: big bit) *Selby:1.*

bitch n. **1.** (homosexual use) an effeminate male, supposedly the 'passive' partner in a homosexual couple *Folb*; **2.** (derog.) a woman; esp. Black pimp use *Milner*; **3.** (Can. prison use) an habitual criminal *Caron.*

bitch v. to complain *Price:2.*

bitch box n. (US army use) Tannoy, public address system; its announcements usually mean inconvenience or trouble for the troops (cf: bitch, v.) *Seale.*

bitchen a. see: bitchin.

bitchin a. (*excl.*) wonderful, great, esp. in surfer use: subseq. adopted by Valley Girls of 1980s Calif. *Wolfe:1.*

bitchin twitchin superlative form of bitchin (qv) *Pond.*

bitch off v. (US campus use) to annoy, irritate *Underwood.*

bitch's bastard n. (UK prison use) a severe, possibly violent warder *AS 41 (1966).*

bitch up v. to make a mess of things, to make a mistake *Sanchez.*

bite n. an attempt to obtain a loan *Runyon:1.*

bite v. to worry, to annoy; usu. in 'what's biting you/him/etc.?' *Howard.*

bite one's crank v. to fellate; fr. 'crank-handle'.

bite the bullet v. to suffer in silence; fr. the placing of a bullet between the teeth of wounded soldiers/sailors when undergoing surgery in pre-anaesthesia days *Dickson.*

bite the ice (Valley Girls (qv) use) excl. of dismissal, 'go to hell!' *Pond.*

bit of a lad n. a cheeky, self-possessed youth who 'fancied himself' (cf: Jack the Lad).

bit of all right n. an attractive female, usu. young.

bit of crackling n. an attractive girl.

bit of fluff n. **1.** any thing or person considered insignificant, ineffectual *Capital Radio, 1983*; **2.** an attractive, but otherwise unexceptional female *Chandler:LG.*

bit of how's yer father n. sexual intercourse; occasional use as general euph. 'swear like how's yer father' ('Cool for Cats', Squeeze) *Capital Radio 1983.*

bit of mess n. (UK criminal use) a prostitute's male lover, who is neither ponce nor client *Powis.*

bit of ring n. anal intercourse

Legman.

bit of slap and tickle n. sexual by-play, necking.

bit of spare n. an unattached female, usu. at a party or club *Powis.*

bit of stuff n. a girl, usually attractive; stuff = material and descends fr. mid-19th C. *bit of muslin*: a young girl, prob. a prostitute.

bit of the other n. sexual intercourse *May.*

bit on the side n. an affair; a lover other than one's regular partner (married or otherwise) *Farren.*

bit previous in poor taste, uncalled for (cf: out of order).

bit swift (UK criminal/police use) the taking of unfair advantage, usu. the complaint is made by the villain against the man who arrests him *Powis.*

bit thick a. unpleasant, insufferable, distasteful *Wodehouse:MOJ.*

blab v. **1.** spec. to confess; **2.** to talk; **3.** to inform *Higgins:1.*

blabbermouth n. a gossip, an indiscreet talker *Dunne.*

blabs in labs (US campus use) course in linguistics, the 'labs' are language laboratories *Bernbach.*

black n. (abbrev.) blackmail *LL.*

black a. depressed, sullen, irritable *Sillitoe.*

black and white n. US police car painted this *R. Newman, 'Jolly Coppers', 1979.*

black beauties n. (drug use) strong amphetamine capsules *Green:1.*

black bird n. (US Black use) particularly dark-skinned Black person *Folb.*

black bomber n. (drug use) strong capsules of amphetamine, coloured black *Green:1.*

black dust n. (US Black use) an extremely black-skinned person *Klein.*

black gang n. (RN use) stokers and engine room crew; fr. days of coal-powered ships.

black gungeon n. (drug use) especially potent form of marijuana *Green:1.*

Black justice n. (US Black use) Black self-determination; as opposed to white justice which Black radicals experience only as a prejudiced farce *Major.*

black-leg n. a strike-breaker (cf: scab) *BBC-1 TV, 1984.*

black moat n. (drug use) particularly potent variety of marijuana, with notably dark colouring *Green:1.*

blackmun n. the anus; in his novel *Myron* (1974) Gore Vidal, responded to a Supreme Court decision whereby any local authority can censor any book, play, film, etc., by replacing the 'bad' or 'dirty' words by the surnames of the current Supreme Justices: thus Blackmun, 'Whizzer' White: cunt; Powell: balls; Rehnquist: cock; Father Hill (a 'warrior against smut'): tits; Burger: to fuck.

black on black n. (US Black use) a car with black paintwork and all-black interior upholstery and fittings *Folb.*

black pope n. (relig. use) the head of the Jesuit order; fr. the colour of their clothes *BBC-1 TV, 1983.*

Black Power dance n. (US Black use) looting; fr. 1960s riots when militant US Blacks looted in the big city ghettoes *Major.*

black taxi n. (Aus. use) an official limousine that ferries government members, etc. to and from houses, appointments and the like *Wilkes.*

Black 360° a. (US Black use) intensely and specifically Black in personality and consciousness; 360° describes a complete circle *Major.*

black widow n. (drug use) black capsule containing amphetamine (cf: black bomber) *Underwood.*

black wings (Hells Angel use) performing cunnilingus on a menstruating black woman *Thompson.*

bladder n. newspaper; fr. Ger. *blatt*: newspaper *Runyon:1.*

bladder of lard n. (rhyming sl.) playing card *Jones:J.*

blade n. **1.** any knife *Higgins:1*; **2.** (US Black use) a Cadillac, because it is so 'sharp' (qv) *Folb.*

blag v. (UK criminal use) to steal *Capital Radio 1983.*

blagger n. a thief *Newman:1.*

blah n. pompous, banal, verbosity *Whitcomb.*

blah v. to speak in a blah (qv) manner *Whitcomb.*

blanco n. (US Black use) white person; fr. Sp. *Jones.*

blank n. **1.** (UK prison use) a rejection, esp. of a parole application (cf: knockback) *Obs. 1981*; **2.** (drug use) any powder sold as a narcotic but which is in fact absolutely without effect *Major.*

blank v. to ignore, wipe out, reject *Price:2.*

blanket man n. (US criminal use) an arsonist's accomplice who holds a blanket ready to douse the flames that may have started to burn the person actually setting the fire *Breslin.*

blanket party n. (US prison use) an initiation rite whereby a new prisoner is forcibly smothered in a blanket, then beaten up by his fellows *Folb.*

blarney n. nonsense, charming but empty chatter; fr. Irish use for traditional 'gift of the gab', a facility which is ensured by kissing the Blarney Stone at Blarney Castle, Eire *Dunne.*

blast n. an uproarious party *Underwood.*

blast v. to smoke marijuana or hashish cigarettes *Selby:1.*

blasted a. **1.** (euph.) damned *Rawson*; **2.** very drunk or heavily influenced by a given drug *Bernbach.*

blatherskite n. aka: *bletherskate* a voluble, boastful speaker *Dickens.*

blaze on v. (US Black use) to attack or knock down without warning *Folb.*

blazing a. general intensifier, esp. in 'a blazing row': a vicious argument (cf: flaming).

bleat n. (UK prison use) a petition to the Home Secretary for reduction or repeal of one's sentence; the weak chance this has of success is underlined by the allusion to the sound of a sheep *LL.*

bleed n. (US Black use) a Black person (cf: blood) *Folb.*

bleeder n. a person, with usu. but not invariable derog. implications *Performance.*

bleeding a. exclamatory adjective, intensifier: 'bleeding hell', etc. *Performance.*

bleeding dirt (homosexual use) aka: *the mouse* extorting money from homosexuals *Legman.*

bleed white v. to submit to excessive extortion; thus draining every drop of money/blood.

bless one's little cotton socks (cp) general expression of affection.

blew in v. to waste, usu. money.

blighter n. a person, usu. unfortunate or unpleasant; one who 'blights' a situation *Wodehouse:CW.*

Blighty n. England, orig. in Indian Army fr. Hindustani: *bilyati*: foreign; currently used ironically or in military/patriotic context (Falklands war reporting, etc.).

blimey! (excl.) denoting surprise or disbelief fr. 'God blind me!' (cf: gor blimey, Gordon Bennett).

blind n. (homosexual use) an uncircumcised penis (cf: near-sighted) *Legman.*

blind a. **1.** extremely drunk, often as phr. *blind drunk Farrell*; **2.** utterly, complete, ie: *steal them blind Eagles, 'Desperado', 1975*; **3.** negative intensifier: *not a blind bit of use*; *a blind word*, etc.

blinder n. a hard and exciting sporting encounter; esp. as *to play a blinder.*

blind Freddy n. (Aus. use) a person of absolute and unassailable incompetence; fr. a blind beggar in the streets of Sydney in the 1920s *Baker.*

blinding a. wonderful, terrific, perfect, etc. *Cole.*

blind pig n. an unlicensed drinking house; a speakeasy *Salisbury.*

blindside v. to take by surprise; fr. football use *Higgins:5.*

blind staggers n. extreme drunkenness *Dickson.*

blinker n. **1.** a camera *Chandler: Notebk.*; **2.** (US criminal use) a police surveillance helicopter *Folb.*

blind twenty n. (bingo use) 20; thus *blind thirty*; *blind forty*, etc. up to *blind ninety.*

blinking a. mild perjorative *Wright.*

blister n. an offensive person, usu. 'old blister' *Wodehouse:PGM.*

blitzed a. drunk; fr. Ger. *blitzkrieg*: saturation bombing tactics (cf: bombed) *Pond.*

blob n. the score of 0 in a cricket match *S. Sassoon, 'Diaries', 1983.*

block n. **1.** (UK prison use) the punishment cells *Cole*; **2.** a ban, a rejection (cf: blank) *Norman:2*; **3.** the head; but nearly always in 'knock one's block off' (qv) *Hotten.*

blockbuster n. anything enormous, gigantic; often used of a best-selling novel, film, TV series, etc.

block-buster n. **1.** orig.: the first Black family to move into a formerly all-white inner city area; **2.** current: the first white family to move back into an inner city area, driving out the poor minority tenants and starting the process of gentrification.

blocker n. (US criminal use) in a shoplifting team (cf: booster) the member who deliberately acts in a suspicious manner in order to divert attention from the real thief *Breslin.*

blocked a. intoxicated on a given drug, usu. cannabis or barbiturates *Keyes.*

bloke n. a person, a man *Performance.*

blood n. (Black use) (abbrev.) blood brother: term of address to fellow Black; by extn. general term of address (cf: bleed) *Price:2.*

bloodbath n. (boxing use) the (often dubious) division of a fighter's earnings; his manager is paid the actual cash and the boxer may well feel he has gained too small a share for his efforts *Heller.*

blood claat n. (West Indian use) lit. blood cloth, used to wipe away menstrual blood, thus highly derog. description of another person; also used as adj.

blood oath! (Aus. use) expression of agreement *Ready.*

blood wagon n. (skiing use) a stretcher *Barr.*

bloody n. (US preppie (qv) use) (abbrev.) bloody Mary; a drink of which the chief constituents are vodka and tomato juice *Bernbach.*

bloody a. a general negative intensifier, esp. in UK and Aus, where it is so widespread as to be termed 'the great Australian adjective'; bloody, like fucking (qv), is often inserted betw. the syllables of other words or phrases, eg: abso-bloody-lutely, not bloody likely, etc.

bloody-minded a. stubborn, unrelenting, deliberately inconsiderate in pursuing one's own opinions, ideas, etc.

bloomer n. an error, a slip (cf: blooper).

blooming a. (euph.) bloody *Humphries:2.*

blooper n. an embarrassing verbal error, often delivered by a public or authority figure to his own detriment (cf: bloomer) *Rawson.*

blort n. cocaine; fr. 'blow' + 'snort' (qqv) *Safire.*

blot n. (Aus. use) the anus (cf: freckle) *Wilkes.*

blotch n. (mainly school use) blotting paper *G. Willans & R. Searle, 'The Compleet Molesworth', 1959.*

blot one's copybook v. to make an error, both practical and behavioural.

blotto a. drunk *Wright.*

blow n. **1.** cocaine; **2.** a snort or sniff of cocaine *Milner.*

blow v. **1.** to fellate (cf: eat, go down on) *P. Roth, 'Portnoy's Complaint', 1969*; **2.** to depart, to walk away *rr*; **3.** to ruin, to upset, to destroy, to lose *Higgins:1*; **4.** of money: to squander, to waste *Breslin*; **5.** (musician use) to play music; orig. Black use, fr. blowing of various wind instruments; **6.** (US Black use) to talk enthusiastically and fluently; fr. jazz use: the lyrical playing of an

instrument *Seale*; **7.** (Aus. use) to boast, to brag *Wilkes*.
blow! (excl.) go away! *Jones*.
blow a fuse v. to explode with rage; fr. the fault that occurs when a wire is overloaded with electrical current.
blow a raspberry v. to make an obscene noise with one's lips, usu. intended to imply derision; fr. rhyming sl. raspberry tart = fart (qv).
blow ass v. to walk fast, to run off *Folb*.
blow away v. **1.** to shoot dead *Himes:1*; **2.** to impress, to bowl over *Bernbach*.
blow Black v. (US Black use) to talk about and/or initiate Black activism, social change, revolution and any similar form of racial advancement (cf: blow great guns) *Folb*.
blow down one's ear v. aka: *blow in one's ear*: to whisper *Powis*.
blowed (euph.) damned; usu. as in I'll be blowed! (qv) *Rawson*.
blower n. **1.** telephone; fr. earlier 'speaking tubes' down which one had to blow to alert the other person *Caron*; **2.** (bookmaker use) the betting shop public address system that broadcasts races, odds and results.
blow fire v. (US Black use) to do anything well and keenly, esp. dancing, musicianship *Folb*.
blow great guns v. **1.** to blow a violent storm; **2.** (by extension) to make a great fuss about something.
blowhard n. a boaster; a loud and egocentric talker *White*.
blow heavy v. (US Black use) to talk seriously of contextually vital matter (cf: blow Black) *Folb*.
blow in v. to arrive unexpectedly and casually; fr. image of being wafted by a chance breeze.
blow it! excl. of annoyance; euph. for a variety of 'stronger' synonyms, *fuck it*, *bugger it*, etc. *Manser*.
blow it out your ass! general excl. of derision, contempt or dimissal of the previous speaker's statement *Dunne*.
blow-job n. fellatio (cf: head) *Price:2*.
blow me down! excl. of surprise; fr. you could have blown/knocked me down with a feather (qv) *Manser*.
blown out a. shocked, exhausted, overcome *Price:2*.
blow off n. (US teen. use) anything considered exceptionally easy *Pond*.
blow off steam v. aka: *let off steam* to release one's (pent-up) emotions, thus, to become angry or noisy and excited; fr. railway use (cf: blow one's stack).
blow one away v. (teen. use) to astound, to amaze, etc. *Pond*.
blow one out v. **1.** to exhaust; **2.** to shock; **3.** for one of a couple to abandon the relationship *'Tucker's Luck', BBC-2 TV, 1983*.
blow one's cookies v. **1.** to vomit; 'cookies' = food consumed *Junker*; **2.** to fellate; 'cookies' = male genitals.
blow one's cool v. to lose control, to freak out (qv) *Hoffman:a*.
blow one's doughnuts v. (US campus use) to vomit *Bernbach*.
blow one's gasket v. see: blow one's top; fr. automobile imagery *Neaman & Silver*.
blow one's glass v. to perform fellatio on a man *Dunne*.
blow one's groceries v. (US campus use) to vomit *Bernbach*.
blow one's lunch v. to vomit *Junker*.
blow one's mind v. **1.** spec. to become intoxicated with a given drug or drugs; **2.** to surprise, to amaze *Uneeda Comix*.
blow one's nose v. to inform *Schulberg*.
blow one's own trumpet v. to boast unashamedly.
blow one's stack v. to lose control, to lose one's temper; fr. railroad use (cf: blow one's top) *Schulberg*.
blow one's top v. to lose one's temper; to lose one's sanity *Runyon:1*.
blowout n. a binge of eating, drinking and debauchery *Uris*.
blow out v. **1.** to reject, to break a promise, neglect a rendezvous, etc.; **2.** (UK police use) for a case, a theory, an accusation to fall through *Laurie*.
blow out of v. to leave, to depart

Gruber.

blow past v. to deceive, to fool, to confuse *Higgins:5.*

blow smoke up one's ass v. to confuse, to tell lies *Higgins:1.*

blow some tunes v. (US Black use) to perform cunnilingus *Folb.*

blow stick n. penis *Jay & Young.*

blow the gaff v. to reveal a secret, esp. a hoax or deception *Humphries.*

blow the skin flute v. to fellate *Legman.*

blow the whistle on v. to inform against someone; the whistle summons the police *Powis.*

blow through v. (UK police use) to phone through information, fr. blower *Laurie.*

blow-up n. a quarrel, an argument.

blow up v. **1.** to break down, both of people (usu. athletes) animals (racehorses, greyhounds) and machinery *Wodehouse:AAG*; **2.** to lose control, to lose patience, to become enraged *rr.*

blow your copper v. (US prison use) to lose good conduct credits *Chandler: Notebk.*

blub v. to cry, to burst into tears; usu. juv. use *BBC Radio 3, 1983.*

bludge v. (Aus. use) to impose on, to scrounge *Humphries.*

bludger n. (Aus. use) orig. a pimp; latterly a scrounger, a beggar, one who leeches on others for his subsistence *Ready.*

blue n. **1.** (US Black use) a dark-complexioned Black person (cf: blueskin: a half-caste, 18/19th C.) *Klein*; **2.** (Aus. use) a brawl, a quarrel; **3.** (Aus. use) a blunder, a mistake *Wilkes.*

blue a. **1.** pornographic; thus *blue movie*, etc. *Higgins:5*; **2.** depressed, unhappy, dissatisfied.

blue and white n. US police car, painted in those colours (as in New York) (cf: black and white).

blue angel n. (drug use) amytal barbiturate, which is packaged in blue capsules *Green:1.*

blue around the gills a. feeling and looking sick, esp. from an excess of alcohol *Dickson.*

blue balls a feeling of intense sexual frustration *Higgins:1.*

blue chips n. cast-iron, undeniable facts; fr. Stock Exchange use: ultimately dependable securities *PT.*

blue dangers n. (US criminal use) marked police cars (when painted blue, as in New York), blue uniformed police *Shulman.*

blue-eyed soul n. (musical use) a style of popular music in which white performers performed soul songs, usually the province of Black performers; most popular in 1960s *Capital Radio 1983.*

blue-eyed soul brother/sister n. (US Black use) any white who is accepted as genuinely friendly towards Blacks *Folb.*

blue feature n. (US milit. use) any indication of water, coloured blue, on a map *Del Vecchio.*

blue funk n. abject terror, utter cowardice.

blue meanies n. (hippie use) the establishment in general and the police (who wear blue) in particular; a short-lived perjorative, stemming fr. *Yellow Submarine*, an animated film featuring The Beatles (1968) in which the 'baddies' were so named.

blue noses n. a puritan, a killjoy; orig. an aristocrat (who had 'blue blood'), blue noses passed the repressive 'blue laws' that restricted the morals of many states.

blue papers n. (UK prison use) the papers that signify the imminent release of a prisoner serving a life sentence *LL.*

blue pencil v. to censor, to edit by cutting; fr. trad. colour of the editor's pencil.

blues n. **1.** (Aus. use) the police; fr. their uniforms *Humphries*; **2.** amphetamines; fr. 'Purple Hearts', a popular variety *c*1965; **3.** (orig. Black but now general use) misery, depression, unhappiness, etc.; **4.** (West Indians use) a shebeen, an illegal drinking club or a party where drink is sold without a licence *Powis.*

blue vein n. an erection; fr. that vein that runs up the penis *Newman:3.*

bluey n. **1.** (UK criminal use) lead; **2.** (orig. Aus.) a red-headed person *Powis.*

bluff n. (lesbian use) a female homosexual who can alternate between active/passive roles; fr. butch and fluff (qqv) *Stanley.*

blunt n. (drug use) any drug available in a blunt-ended capsule.

BMOC (acro.) Big Man On Campus *Junker.*

boasie a. (Jamaican) proud, boastful, showy; comb. of English 'boastful' and Yoruba *bosi* 'proud and ostentatious' *Thelwell.*

boat n. (rhyming sl.) boat-race = face *Norman:3.*

boat n. (US Black use) the vagina *Klein.*

bob and weave v. to avoid direct action, either confrontation, explanation, aggression, etc.; fr. boxing use *PT.*

bob a nob n. one shilling each; used when estimating the cost of meals, outings, tickets, etc.

bobbish a. healthy, in good spirits, well set up, cheery *Wodehouse:AAG.*

bobbles n. (US Black use) gaudy, flashy, ostentatious jewellery; fr. 'baubles' *Klein.*

bobby n. a British policeman; fr. Sir Robert Peel who established the force in 19th C. *Mandelkau.*

bobby dazzler n. anything or person seen as exceptional, wonderful.

bobby soxer n. teenage US girl, wearing (short) bobby-socks; orig. describing the fans of Frank Sinatra in 1940s and thus girls of late 1940s, 1950s who enjoyed pop music and its ancillary pleasures.

bobkhes n. fr. Yiddish: 'goat droppings'; an absurd idea, an insulting sum, price or proposition, esp. in show business use *Rosten.*

Bob's your uncle (cp) everything will be absolutely fine; there'll be no worries; fr. the apparently nepotistic choice by Tory leader Robert Cecil of his nephew Arthur Balfour as Chief Secretary for Ireland in 1900, a decision that was both surprising and unpopular *A. J. Langguth, 'Saki', 1981.*

bob up v. to appear (unexpectedly) *Wodehouse:GB.*

Boche n. (derog.) German *BvdB.*

bod n. (abbrev.) body *McBain:1.*

bod a. (US campus use) outstanding, exceptional *Underwood.*

bodger a. aka: *bodgie*: second-rate, worthless; fr. SE *bodge*: to mend badly, to patch up *Baker.*

bodgie n. (Aus. use) male equivalent to UK *teddy boy*; fr. bodger (qv) *Ready.*

body n. (UK police use) a person, esp. a suspect or wanted criminal *Newman:2.*

body and soul lashing n. (nautical use) a piece of rope tied around a sailor's oil-skins to provide a grip for rescuers if he fell overboard; also, on sailing ships, extra binding to keep the wind out of one's clothes *Channel 4 TV 1983.*

body lover n. a homosexual who prefers rubbing and fondling a body than anal penetration or fellatio *Legman.*

body queen n. (homosexual use) one who primarily looks for partners who specialize in body-building *Stanley* .

body-snatching (journalistic use) getting hold of a major source for an important story and holding on to them, usually in a luxury flat or five-star hotel, in order to get the story from them and ensure that no other paper can track them down (cf: baby-sitting) *'World In Action', Granada TV, 1983.*

boff n. a laugh, a joke; usu. show business use *Variety: passim.*

boff v. **1.** to copulate *'Hill Street Blues', Thames TV, 1983*; **2.** to hit, to assault *Runyon:1.*

boffin n. **1.** any form of scientific expert; **2.** spec. Scotland Yard fingerprint expert *Neaman & Silver.*

boffo superb, magnificent, excellent; usu. show business use *Goldman.*

boffola n. a laugh, esp. a loud 'belly laugh'; usu. show business use (cf: boff) *Variety: passim.*

bog n. lavatory (cf: dike) *Sharpe:1.*

bog v. to wet the end of a cigarette while smoking it.

bogart v. to hold on to a marijuana joint (qv) for longer than one's companions feel is fair; allegedly from the greediness in this area ascribed to the film star Humphrey Bogart *'Easy Rider', directed P. Fonda, D. Hopper, 1969.*

bogey n. aka: *bogie* policeman, detective *Norman:2.*

bog in v. (Aus. use) **1.** to start a task enthusiastically; **2.** to eat heartily; **3.** not to stand on any ceremony *Wilkes.*

bogtrotter n. (derog.) Irish person *BvdB.*

bogue n. (drug use) the sickness that follows an addict's withdrawal from regular narcotic use *Algren.*

bogue a. (US teen. use) (abbrev.) bogus; fake, uncool (qv) *Sculatti.*

boho n. (abbrev.) bohemian. eccentric *Wolfe:2.*

bohunk n. (derog.) a Slav; thus an oafish, dull, if muscular person (cf: honkie) *BvdB.*

boiled a. drunk *Dickson.*

boiler n. an old woman, often 'old boiler', without any remaining sexual appeal; fr. the old tough birds used for boiling chickens (cf: chick) *Powis.*

boilerplate n. standard practice; used by lawyers – the regular clauses in any contract – or media – the basic syndicated wire service stories used throughout the US newspaper system *Vidal.*

boilover n. (Aus. use) in sport, spec. horse-racing, an upset – the failure of a favourite to win *Wilkes.*

boing-boing n. tourist; implying the twanging of a rubberneck (qv) *Price:3.*

BO juice (US campus use) deodorant; fr. Body Odour *Underwood.*

boko n. the nose *Topper (comic) passim.*

boldacious a. (US Black use) excessive behaviour – over-aggressive, arrogant, unrestrained, etc. – that is inappropriate for a given situation; fr. SE *bodacious Klein.*

bold as brass a. arrogant, impudent, outspoken, shameless.

bollixed up ruined, messed up, performed very badly; US sp. of UK *bollocksed up Rawson.*

bollock n. (UK 'society' use) ball (hunt, charity, etc.); fr. pun on the mild obscenity *Barr.*

bollocking n. a severe telling off *Powis.*

bollock naked aka: *stark bollock naked*: totally naked, and thus revealing one's genitals.

bollocko a. naked, fr. bollock naked (qv) *Powis.*

bollocks! excl: rubbish, nonsense.

bollocksed up UK version of US bollixed up (qv).

bolshie a. uncooperative, subversive, Left-wing; fr. Russian Bolsheviks.

bomb n. drug use: see bomber *Larner.*

bomb n. (theatrical use) **1.** (UK) a major success; **2.** (US) a disaster, a flop *Goldman;* **3.** (Aus. use) a dilapidated, run-down old car *Wilkes.*

bombed a. **1.** drunk *Higgins:1*; **2.** intoxicated by a given drug *Powis.*

bomber n. (drug use) a very large and potent cannabis joint (qv) *Major.*

bomber n. (abbrev.) black bomber, a variety of amphetamine in a black capsule *Green:1.*

bomb off v.i. to fail to work, esp. of a computer program *Underwood.*

bombshell n. a shock, a surprise, usu. unpleasant; thus *drop a bombshell*: to deliver such a shock.

bonaroo (US prison use) fr. Fr. 'bon' = good *Chandler: Notebk.*

bonce n. head; created by 19th C. schoolboy who took word fr. *bonce*: a large marble *Performance.*

bonds n. (pimp use) the clothes with which a pimp bedecks his working girls; and, since his money has paid for them, 'binds' the girls to him *Neaman*

& Silver.

bone n. **1.** $1.00 *Himes:1*; **2.** the erect penis.

boned hit hard on the head; from the hard skull that is battered *Powis.*

bonehead n. fool, dullard, idiot *Farrell.*

boner n. **1.** an erection (cf: hard-on) *Price:2*; **2.** (school use) a mistake.

bones n. **1.** dice; esp. in 'roll them bones!'; fr. material originally used in making dice *Hotten*; **2.** (US college use) *1.* marijuana cigarettes (cf: joint); *2.* nickname for Yale U. ultra-secret, ultra-Establishment society 'Skull & Bones' (cf: spook) *Bernbach.*

bone-shaker n. a decrepit vehicle with, *inter alia*, inadequate springs, thus jolting its passengers.

bone up (on) v. to learn, to revise.

boneyard n. a cemetery *Chandler:LG.*

bonified (US Black use) competent, qualified, the right man for job; fr. Fr. *bon* = good *Klein.*

bonkers stupid, insane, eccentric *Capital Radio 1983.*

bonzer a. good, thus extremely, very *Humphries.*

boo n. marijuana (cf: bu) *Price:2.*

boob n. **1.** a fool, an idiot; fr. *booby 'Yellow Submarine', film 1968*; **2.** (UK criminal use) a prison *Obs. 1981.*

boob v. to make a mistake, to blunder.

boo-boo n. poss. fr. Yiddish *bulba* 'potato': a blunder, usu. embarrassing *Rosten.*

boob play n. a foolish action, an error, a blunder (cf: boob) *rr.*

boobs n. breasts; fr. obsolete *bubbies Higgins:1.*

boob-tube n. television; fr. the alleged mental state of regular watchers *Hoffman:a.*

booby-hatch n. aka: *booby hutch*: mental hospital; the first poss. fr. Coney Hatch, the second poss. fr. mad March hares.

boodle n. money *L. Charteris 'The Saint' books: passim.*

booferbox n. large radio/tape recorder/stereo particularly popular among ghetto youths (cf: Third World briefcase, ghetto blaster) *C. Clarke.*

boofhead n. fool, idiot, simpleton *Baker.*

boog a. (derog.) Black, Negro (cf: boogie) *Algren.*

boogaloo v. to dance; orig. Black use *Hoffman:a.*

boogie n. (derog.) Black *Price:1.*

boogie v. **1.** spec. to dance (cf: boogaloo); **2.** to enjoy oneself, have a party, a good time *Price:1.*

boogie-woogie v. (US Black use) to leave, to depart *Klein.*

boojie n. (US Black use) (derog.) a bourgeois Black; fr. bourgeois *Price:3.*

book n. **1.** a magazine, a periodical; mainly illiterate use; the bound variety are presumably an unknown quantity *Ian Dury, 'Razzle'*; **2.** (Black pimp use) a supply of names and addresses of clients (cf: working from a book) *Milner.*

Book n. the oral tradition that forms the basis of Black pimping; a good deal has been encapsulated in 'Pimp: The Story of My Life' by Iceberg Slim, 1967 *Milner.*

book v. **1.** to arrest, thus write down in a police charge book *Capital Radio 1983*; **2.** to note *Newman:1*; **3.** (abbrev.) bookmaking *Higgins:3.*

bookie n. (abbrev.) bookmaker *Performance.*

book it v. (US campus use) to study assiduously *Underwood.*

book the joint v. (US teen. use) to look over a place, to check it out (qv) *Pond.*

book up v. (US campus use) to study hard (cf: book it) *Underwood.*

boola-boola (US use) a. college chauvinism; fr. college sports cheer 'boola-boola' *Price:3.*

boolhipper n. (US Black use) a leather coat *Major.*

boom-boom n. (US juv. use) excrement *Neaman & Silver.*

boomer n. **1.** (Aus. use) anything considered exceptionally large or strong; fr. orig. use: a large kangaroo

Wilkes; **2.** (US use) a transient worker, a migrant; thus *boomer reporter*: a journalist who works on papers all over the country, never keeping one job for too long *Gruber*.

boondoggle n. a waste, of time, of money, of energy; esp. used by US govt. for a project that is considered to waste tax dollars *Green:2*.

boong n. (derog. Aus. use) Aborigine *Humphries:2*.

boonie n. a peasant, a country person; fr. *boondocks*: USMC use for hard rural areas *Price:2*.

boonie hat n. (US milit. use) soft hat worn by troops *Del Vecchio*.

boonie rat n. (US milit. use) an infantryman, a foot soldier, who fights and patrols through the jungles, swamps, etc. *Del Vecchio*.

boonies n. (abbrev. boondocks) **1.** (US milit. use) the field, the bush, the jungle; anywhere the troops operate that is not designated a firebase, a basecamp or occupied by civilians; fr. Tagalog *bundok*: mountain *Del Vecchio*; **2.** (US campus use) rural areas, the countryside – not necessarily rough or unpleasant *Underwood*.

boost v. to steal from large stores; fr. boost = raising up, which the booster (qv) does with the goods *Breslin*.

booster n. a shoplifter on a large and professional scale *Grogan*.

boot n. **1.** (US milit. use) any new recruit in the US armed forces; thus *boot camp*: basic training camp; *boot second lieutenant*: newly commissioned 2nd Lieut., etc.; fr. leggings worn by recruits to USN during training *Del Vecchio*; **2.** (US Black use) a fellow Black (USU. derog.); poss. fr. black boots? *Jones*; **3.** dismissal from a job; usu. as 'get the boot'.

boot v. (US campus use) to vomit *Bernbach*.

boot around v. to kick, usu. in a fight *Runyon*.

booted (US campus use) **1.** expelled; **2.** vomited *Bernbach*.

bootlicker n. a cowardly, obsequious person; one who curries favour, who sucks up (qv) **Seale.**

boot out v. to throw out, eject *Price:2*.

booty n. (US Black use) **1.** the female; **2.** spec. the vagina *Folb*.

booze n.v. drink; to drink.

booze artist n. a drunkard.

boozed a. drunk *Dickson*.

boozed up a. drunk *Dickson*.

boozer n. a public house *Powis*.

booze-up n. a drinking session *Tidy*.

bop n. **1.** a dance; **2.** (US Black use) foolish talk, prattle (cf: bebopper) *Folb*.

bop v. **1.** to fight *Salisbury;* **2.** hit; **3.** to walk in a carefree. bouncy way *Price:2*.

bo-peep n. (rhyming sl.) sleep; fr. the nursery rhyme character who lost her sheep while sleeping *Wright*.

bopper n. (abbrev.) teenybopper (qv) *Farren*.

boppers n. (US campus use) shoes *Underwood*.

bopping club a street gang who have regular fights with opponents *Salisbury*.

bopping gang n. street gang who are active fighters (cf: bopping club) *Jones*.

boracic a. (rhyming sl.) boracic lint = skint = out of funds *Payne*.

borax n. (US use) rubbish, lies, exaggeration; fr. cheap and shoddy material peddled by immigrant Jews.

borders n. (drug use) non-proprietory capsules of barbiturate powder sold on the black market and with inference of having been made up on the US/ Mexico border *Folb*.

bore stiff v. to bore completely; stiff = corpse-like.

bore the pants off v. to bore completely and totally.

borrow v. (UK police use) to arrest; a suspect is 'borrowed' from his family and friends (cf: claim) *Laurie*.

Borscht Belt n. (show business use) a circuit of predominantly Jewish hotels in the Catskill Mts, New York State; the musicians and comedians who perform there have named them for the favourite Jewish/Russian beetroot soup *Goldman.*

bosh n. nonsense, rubbish; Turkish wd. = worthless *Hotten.*

boss a. excellent, wonderful *Gothic Blimp Works no.4.*

Boss Charley n. (US Black use) the white, esp. those in authority *Bruce:2* (cf Mr Charlie).

boss-eyed a. squinting.

boss player n. (Black pimp use) a thoroughly experienced, professional, worldly-wise pimp who may even transcend pimping for superior occupations; can be applied to any admirable figure outside the pimp milieu *Milner.*

bot v. (Aus. use) to scrounge; thus *on the bot*: scrounging *Wilkes.*

bother n. trouble, difficulties; thus *in bother Laurie.*

botheration! mild exclamation of annoyance that precludes anything more lurid and thus taboo *Rawson.*

bottie n. (nursery use) the bottom, the buttocks.

bottle n. courage, bravery *Griffiths.*

bottle v. to collect money from a busker's audience.

bottle and glass n. (rhyming sl.) = arse, the buttocks *Cole.*

bottle baby n. an alcoholic tramp whose life has destroyed his sanity and reduced his mental age to that of an infant *Schulberg.*

bottle blonde n. one whose blonde hair is only dyed and comes not from nature but from a bottle *London Weekend Television 1983.*

bottle it v. see: bottle out *Robins.*

bottle out v. to be a coward, to run away, to back down from a challenge; to lose one's bottle (qv) *Griffiths.*

bottler n. **1.** (UK use) a coward, someone who bottles out (qv); **2.** (Aus. use) anyone outstanding, either in a positive or negative manner, tho' usu. congratulatory.

bottom drawer n. wherever an engaged girl starts collecting the necessities of her trousseau.

bottom line n. the end result, the final assessment; fr. Yid. *di untershte sture* to denote the final profit/loss figure on an account *Vidal.*

bottom man n. the submissive partner in a homosexual sado-masochist couple *Jay & Young.*

bottoms n. (US Black use) the least pleasant, the poorest part of a given ghetto or inner-city area *Klein.*

bottoms up! a popular toast before drinking; the bottoms are those of the glasses as the drinks are emptied into the drinkers' mouths.

bottom woman n. (Black pimp use) the most reliable and experienced of a pimp's stable of prostitutes *Shulman.*

bought it killed, esp. in battle *Sharpe:1.*

bougie a. (abbrev.) bourgeois: taking on the attitudes and lifestyle of the middle classes (cf: boojie) *Price:2.*

bounce n. **1.** (US criminal use) arrest and subsequent trial *Dunne*; **2.** (UK criminal use) fiddling and dishonest practice – adjusting invoices, stealing stock, etc. – by retail shop employees *Powis.*

bounce v. **1.** to pay a cheque, knowing that one has insufficient funds in one's bank account; for the bank to refuse to honour that cheque, marking it 'return to drawer'; **2.** to throw out; of a party, a place of entertainment, etc.; **3.** to dismiss from a job *Thompson:J.*

bouncer n. a large, tough man employed to keep order in given premises – often a pub, club, concert hall, etc. (cf: bounce **2**) *Powis.*

Bouncing Betty (US milit. use) a mine that springs a metre in the air prior to exploding; also known as *old step and a half* from the distance a soldier can cover between triggering the mine and being killed by it *O'Brien.*

bourbon a. (US teen. use) hazy, spaced out (qv), unable to focus mentally *Sculatti.*

bovver n. fr. Cockney pron. bother; fighting, disturbance, esp. that caused by skinhead youths (cf: aggro) *Robins.*

bovver boots n. high-laced boots preferred as footwear by skinhead youths; usu. merchandised under the brandname 'Dr Martins'.
bow and arrow n. (rhyming sl.) sparrow *Jones:J.*
bowl n. (drug use) a pipe used for smoking marijuana *Del Vecchio.*
bowler-hatted a. retired from active service and given a desk job in Whitehall *Green:2.*
bowsered a. drunk *Dickson.*
bow-wow n. juv. or facetious use: a dog.
box n. **1.** the vagina *Keyes*; **2.** the penis *Stanley*; **3.** (US prison use) a safe *Chandler: Notebk.*; **4.** a guitar *Powis*; **5.** television, fr. goggle box (qv) *Powis*; **6.** (US campus use) tape deck; fr. box = guitar (qv) *Underwood.*
box cars (gambling use) the point of twelve in craps dice *Chandler:Notebk.*
box clever v. to carry out any enterprise smartly and efficiently; fr. boxing use.
boxed a. drunk *Dickson.*
box lunch n. cunnilingus (cf: box **1**) *Keyes.*
boy n. (homosexual use) a male prostitute *Legman.*
boy n. **1.** champagne; allegedly fr. Edward VII's habit of merely saying 'Boy!' to an attendant page who automatically brought him a glass of that wine *A. Binstead, 'Pitcher in Paradise', 1903*; **2.** (drug use) heroin (cf: girl) *Green:1.*
boy-ass n. a boy who exists simply as a sex object for his homosexual partners *Legman.*
boy in the boat n. (lesbian use) the clitoris *Maledicta.*
boyo term of address, usu. Irish or (cliché) Welsh.
boysie n. general term of address to a male; S. London use *BBC-1 TV series 'Only Fools & Horses' passim.*
Boystown n. (homosexual use) the predominantly gay neighbourhood in West Hollywood (cf: Swish Alps) *White.*
boystown sound music popular in gay discos *K. Wilson.*
bozo n. **1.** fool, idiot *San Francisco Comic Book no.2*; **2.** tough, a thug *Farrell.*
brace and bits n. (US rhyming sl.) female breasts, plus pun on brace = pair *Neaman & Silver.*
bracelets n. (UK criminal use) handcuffs *LL.*
brace of shakes at once, immediately, usu. *in a . . .*
bracer n. a quick drink, intended to brace up the drinker prior to what may be a difficult undertaking *Southern & Hoffenberg.*
brahma a. anything good, enjoyable, attractive; fr. Hindu deity and Indian Army use *Dury.*
Brahms and Liszt n. (rhyming sl.) = pissed = drunk *name of wine bar in Covent Garden, London.*
brainchild n. an idea, an inspiration.
brains n. (UK police use) the CID; usu. ironic *Powis.*
brand X n. (US Black use) marijuana *Folb.*
brass n. **1.** money; esp. Northern UK use: 'where there's muck there's brass' and similar homilies *Thames TV series 1983*; **2.** audacity, gall, cheek; **3.** a prostitute; fr. rhyming sl. *brass nail* = tail (qv) *Performance*; **4.** (abbrev.) brasshat (qv).
brass balls n. anything severely challenging, esp. in a 'masculine' context *Powis.*
brassed off a. irritated, fed up, annoyed *LL.*
brasshats n. senior officers – both police and milit. use *Newman:1.*
brass monkey weather extremely cold temperature; fr. cp 'cold enough to freeze the balls off a brass monkey' *Whitcomb.*
brass tacks n. (rhyming sl.) facts; usu. in 'let's get down to brass tacks' and as such almost SE.
brass up v. to hand over money (cf: brass).
brassy a. of a woman: showy, flashy, ostentatious; implies a superficial bright, hardness, but also possible

prostitution (cf: brass **3**).

bread n. fr. Yiddish *broyt* money *Price:2.*

bread and butter n. **1.** (rhyming sl.) gutter *Jones:J*; **2.** one's basic income and the work that provides it *Bruce:2.*

bread and butter column (journalistic use) a column fuelled in the main by press agent handouts and similar varieties of free publicity for those who send it to the writer; such a column harms no one, puffs a great many and keeps the writer off the breadline *Bruce:2.*

bread and butter letter n. a letter of thanks sent to one's hostess shortly after having enjoyed her hospitality.

bread and cheese v. (rhyming sl.) sneeze *Jones:J.*

bread and lard a. (rhyming sl.) hard *Franklyn.*

breadbasket n. the stomach, fr. boxing use *Wright.*

breadhead n. an individual who is interested primarily in acquiring money; coined during the anti-money Sixties; fr. bread + head (qqv).

break n. an escape from prison *Waits.*

break a leg! (theatrical use) trad. term of encouragement to a fellow actor prior to their going on stage; the direct 'good luck' is paradoxically considered very bad luck *Green:2.*

break v. (journalist use) to happen; a story 'breaks'.

break an ankle v. (euph.) to become pregnant out of wedlock; orig. 18/19th C. UK, now survives mainly in US *rawson.*

break down v. (US Black use) to explain; to put the listener right *Folb.*

breaker n. **1.** Citizen's Band radio enthusiast *CB*; **2.** UK police use: shop-/housebreaker *Laurie.*

break-in n. (Valley Girls (qv) use) someone who is leaving *Pond.*

breaking n. **1.** (abbrev.) break dancing: dance style perfected in New York's South Bronx slums; dancers spin, whirl and twist, pivoting on heads, elbows, knees, etc.; performed to rap DJs (qv) *ES 21/9/83*; **2.** (abbrev.) breaking and entering (cf: B&E) *Newman:1.*

break it down v. (Aus. use) to give in, to desist *Wilkes.*

break it up! general admonition to move on, break up a meeting – of several people or a couple.

break one's ass v. **1.** to beat up someone; **2.** to hurt oneself; **3.** to work very hard *Price:2.*

break one's balls v. to attack, to complain, to nag; thus *ball-breaker*: the 'castrating female' who nags constantly and undermines the male concerned *Bruce:2.*

break one's chops v. **1.** to talk incessantly; **2.** to make a great fuss about something *Price:2.*

break one's ear v. to interrupt, to chatter continually *McBain:1.*

break one's luck (prostitute use) to encounter the first customer of the day *Milner.*

breaks n. luck, chance, opportunities; either *good breaks* or *bad breaks* *'Requiem for a Heavyweight', Channel 4, 1983.*

break squelch v. (milit. use) to break radio silence and start transmitting *Del Vecchio.*

break up v.t., v.i. **1.** to collapse in laughter; **2.** to cause someone else to laugh heartily.

breathe down one's neck v. **1.** to be physically close; **2.** to be in hot pursuit, or in competition.

breed n. (abbrev.) half-breed, derog. term for American Indian *BvdB.*

breeders n. (homosexual use) married homosexuals who produce children *Jay & Young.*

breeze n. simplicity, easy, no problems *Humphries:2.*

breeze along v. to visit, with inference of casual, unplanned dropping in *Humphries:2.*

breezer n. (Aus. use) a fart *Neaman & Silver.*

breezy a. bright and cheery *Wodehouse:AAG.*

brekker n. breakfast; fr. Oxford '-er' endings of 1920s *Wodehouse:PB.*

brew n. a pot of tea *Bleasdale.*
brew n. beer, ale; spec. in UK: Carlsberg Special brew, poss. the strongest canned beer on sale in UK *Greaser Comics.*
brew v. (drug use) to prepare heroin for injection by heating with water in a spoon or bottle cap (cf: cook) *Klein.*
brewer's droop n. temporary impotence due to the effects of alcohol on the erectile tissue *Humphries.*
brewski n. (US campus use) beer *Bernbach.*
brew up v. to make tea.
brick n. **1.** a reliable, kind, selfless person; fr. the solidity of the object *Vidal*; **2.** (drug use) one kilo (2.2 lbs approx) of marijuana (cf: key) *Green:1.*
brickie n. (abbrev.) bricklayer *Wilkinson.*
Bridewell v. (spec. Liverpool police use) a police station, esp. the cells it contains; fr. St. Bride's Well, 19th C. prison in London *Bleasdale.*
brief n. **1.** a barrister; whose legal commissions are his/her briefs *Newman:1*; **2.** (UK police use) a warrant to arrest or search *Powis.*
brig n. prison; esp. US milit. use *Wodehouse passim.*
bright n. (US Black use) a light-skinned Black person *Klein.*
brill! (abbrev.) brilliant! *Lucien Green passim 1983.*
brilliant n. (homosexual use) an obviously, exaggeratedly homosexual man *Legman.*
bring down n. anything depressing, either person or circumstance *Burroughs:1.*
bring down v. **1.** to attract; to make move in one's direction *Bruce:2*; **2.** to depress; fr. drug use.
bring home the bacon v. to deliver whatever was requested and required *Wodehouse:AAG.*
bring it in v. (poker use) for the player with the lowest exposed card to commence betting at the start of a round *Alvarez.*
bring oneself off v. to masturbate *Neaman & Silver.*
bring one up v. (US Black use) to criticize, to tell off *Folb.*
bring the house down v. to delight, to gain overall approval; fr. theatrical use.
briny n. the sea; fr. the salt water.
Bristol City (rhyming sl.) = titty = female breasts (cf: Bristols) *Cole.*
Bristols n. (fr. rhyming sl.) Bristol bits = tits = breasts *Norman:3.*
bro n. (US Black use) (abbrev.) brother; a fellow Black *Del Vecchio.*
broad n. **1.** a male homosexual prostitute; fr. broad = woman *Legman*; **2.** a woman *Big Ass Comics 1.*
broad in the beam a. fat, overweight, esp. around the buttocks; fr. naut. description of a ship.
broads n. playing cards *Powis.*
broadsman n. a card sharp *Powis.*
broke a. out of funds, impoverished, poor *Performance.*
broker n. someone who is usually broke (qv), a poor person *Runyon.*
broke to the wide a. aka: *broke to the world*: absolutely penniless.
brolly n. umbrella *Capital Radio 1983.*
bronco n. a young man, a novice in the gay world and thus somewhat rough; fr. Western use *Legman.*
Bronx cheer n. a loud, derisive noise, imitative of a fart (cf: raspberry) *Neaman & Silver.*
broom v. to disappear quickly; fr. the image of sweeping away *Chandler: Notebk.*
brooming off (taxi-driver use) illegal practice by cabbies whereby they refuse any fares other than those they consider maximally profitable, despite the regulation that they must take whatever fare presents itself; the rejected fare is 'swept' along to the next cab *Powis.*
brothel creepers n. suede shoes, often in lurid colours, with extra thick rubber soles, esp. popular among rock 'n' roll fans of 1950s (and in 1980s revival).
brothel stompers n. (US campus use)

see brothel creepers, although these 'respectable' versions have no great thickness of sole *Bernbach.*

brother n. (US Black use) form of address to fellow Black male (cf: bro) *Himes:1.*

brothers n. Black people; orig. in 1960s Black radical use, now used by both Black and white speakers with only residual polit. overtones *Higgins:2.*

brougham n. (US Black use) an elegant, expensive and prized motor car; fr. the smart carriages of 19th C. named for Lord Henry Brougham (1778–1868) *Klein.*

brown v. (homosexual use) to perform anal intercourse *Legman.*

brownbag v. to drink liquor from a bottle 'hidden' in the bag in which one purchases it from the liquor store; necessary in US states where drinking in the street is illegal *R. Stone, 'A Flag for Sunrise', 1981.*

brown bomber n. **1.** (Aus. use) a parking policeman *Ready*; **2.** a laxative pill *Pearce.*

browncoat n. (taxi/police use) the junior examiner at the Police Public Carriage Office in London (cf: whitecoat) *Powis.*

browned off irritated, annoyed; fr. accumulation of brown rust on fatigued or worn out metal *Norman:2.*

brown eye n. **1.** the anus; **2.** anal intercourse (cf: ring, brown).

Brown Family n. generic term for homosexuals; mainly obs.; referring to the predeliction for anal intercourse (cf: brown, brown eye, etc.).

brown hatter n. a homosexual *Cole.*

brownie n. a shot of whisky *Private Eye passim.*

Brownie point n. a commendation awarded to the Girl Guides' junior branch and thus usu. a sarcastic and backhanded form of compliment when handed out by adults *Underwood.*

browning n. anal intercourse; mainly obs. (cf: brown, brown eye, etc.) *Jay & Young.*

Browning Family n. the world of homosexuals (cf: Brown family) *Legman.*

Browning Sisters n. homosexuals in general (cf: Brown Family) *Legman.*

brown noser n. anyone who pays excessive court to authority – at school, in work, etc. (cf: ass-kisser, -licker) *Junker.*

brown stuff n. (drug use) opium *Burroughs:1.*

brown wings (Hells Angels use) anilingus or anal intercourse *Mandelkau.*

bruiser n. thug, spec. a boxer *Schulberg.*

brummy a. (Aus. use) second-rate, tawdry; fr. SE *brumagem* *Humphries:2.*

Bruno n. (US college use) Brown University *Bernbach.*

brush n. (Aus. use) a female; fr. pubic hair thereof *Wilkes.*

brush-off v. to ignore, to treat contemptuously, to dismiss *Hotten.*

brush one's teeth v. (US Black use) to perform cunnilingus *Folb.*

Brussels sprouts n. (rhyming sl.) Scouts *Jones:J.*

b.s. (abbrev.) *b*ull*s*hit *Del Vecchio.*

BSHs (acro.) *B*ritish *S*tandard *H*andfuls, cod-officialese to denote the female breast *Powis.*

btm n. coy abbrev. for bottom = posterior.

bu n. (drug use) marijuana (cf:boo) *Sanders:2.*

bub n. boy; used as derog. form of address, implying youth, insignificance, etc. *Motor City Comics.*

bubble n. (ski use) aka *egg*: telecabin *Barr.*

bubble n. (UK prison use: rhyming sl.) bubble and squeak = speak = information *Obs. 1981.*

bubble and squeak n. (rhyming sl.) a Greek *Cole.*

bubbled betrayed, informed against; fr. rhyming sl: bubble and squeak: to speak *Newman:1.*

bubble-gum (music business use) catchy, simplistic pop music aimed specifically at the pre-pubescent and early teenage female market, all, allegedly, prime consumers of bubble gum.

bubble-gummer n. a young girl, aged 10–14 *Jenkins*.

bubblehead n. foolish, careless person, with a brain full of air. (cf: airhead) *Esq 1983*.

bubbly n. champagne *Vidal*.

bubby term of address, mix of buddy + baby (qqv) *Price:3*.

buck n. (Liverpool police use) a tearaway, a young, aggressive criminal *James MClure, 'Spike Island', 1980*.

buck n. **1.** (abbrev.) buckshot, used to load shotgun shells *Higgin:1*; **2.** (US prison use) a priest *Chandler: Notebk*; **3.** a dollar; $100 *Laugh In The Dark*.

buck v. **1.** to desire, to work towards, aim for *Price:1*; **2.** to avoid, to resist.

buck and a half n. $150 *Higgins:2*.

bucket n. **1.** (homosexual use) the anus *Legman*; **2.** (Can. prison use) county prison; fr. rhyming sl. bucket and pail *Caron*.

bucket v. (Aus. use) to disdain, to denigrate, to despise *Wilkes*.

bucket (down) v. to rain very heavily.

bucket job n. (UK criminal use) aka: *bucket gaff*; a fraudulent company *Powis*.

bucko a. aggressive, overbearing, domineering *Wodehouse: JM*.

buck private n. (US milit. use) a private soldier who is 'bucking for' promotion; thus occas. other ranks in a similar position, eg: *buck colonel*, who wishes to be a general.

buckshee a. free, gratis; fr. *baksheesh*: a tip (Persian for a gift, a present); picked up by Middle East and Indian imperial troops and thus brought West *Wright*.

buck's night n. (Aus. use) a stag party, the party thrown for a bridegroom on the eve of his wedding *Bickerton*.

buckwheat n. (US Black use) a light complexioned Black person *Folb*.

buck up v. **1.** to encourage, to cheer up; **2.** as excl: cheer up! *Norman:2*.

bud n. **1.** a young, pubescent girl *Wolfe:2*; **2.** (Valley Girls (qv) use) marijuana; emphasizing its herbal origins *Harpers/Queen 1983*.

buddy n. friend, acquaintance *Laugh In The Dark*.

buddy-buddy a. exceptionally and overtly friendly, prob. insincerely so *Bruce:2*.

buddyseat n. pillion seat on a motorcycle *Selby:1*.

budgie n. (UK criminal use) a talkative person, esp, in police use, a minor informer; fr. the budgerigar, a popular UK cage bird, which can be taught to speak *Powis*.

bud sesh n. (US teen. use) getting together to smoke marijuana; fr. buddy session *Pond*.

buf n. (Valley Girls (qv) use) an attractive male; fr. 'beautiful' or 'beautiful fellow' *Pond*.

buffer n. genial old fool, a description more affectionate than critical *Hotten*.

bufu a. (Valley Girls (qv) use) homosexual, fr. buttfucker *Harpers/ Queen 1/83*.

bug n. **1.** an enthusiast, a fan, a devotee, who has a 'bug' in his/her head *Runyon*; **2.** (Can. prison use) homemade water heater for making coffee *Caron*; **3.** (espionage use) any form of electronic surveillance gadget *Higgins:5*; **4.** an insane, unstable person; fr. 'bugs in the head' and thus the unstable mobster Benjamin Siegel (1906–47) earned the nickname 'Bugsy' *Stone*.

bug v. **1.** to tap a telephone *Greenlee*; **2.** to annoy, irritate *Price:2*.

bug-eyed a. drunk; one's eyes are popping like those of some insects *Dickson*.

bugger n. fr. SE synonym for sodomite: a person, esp. *silly bugger*, *daft bugger*, etc; not necessarily perjorative.

bugger! syn. for damn! (qv) (cf: buggeration, botheration, etc.).

buggeration! general excl. of annoyance (cf: botheration).

buggerlugs n. general term of (affectionate) address, usu. among men *Waterhouse.*

bugger (it) up v. to make a mess of , to blunder *Higgins:2.*

bugger's grips n. the brushed back 'wings' of hair that adorn the temples of many upper class Englishmen; coarse rumour imputes these as the handholds for those who are positioning such partners ready for anal penetration *K. Payne.*

Buggins turn a sinecure that comes to all members of a given committee, board of directors, etc. so long as they remain members of that group and, in due course, inevitably take their turn at a given task.

bughouse a. insane, crazy *Schulberg:2.*

bughutch n. tatty, rundown, dirty cinema (cf: fleapit) *Waterhouse.*

bug out v. to leave, to run away *'Banty Raid', cartoon, Thames TV-1983.*

bug pass n. (Can. prison use) a prisoner so deranged that he is no longer responsible for his actions *Caron.*

bug juice n. (Can. prison use) depressant drug used for controlling violent or non-cooperative prisoners *Caron.*

bugle n. the nose; through which one blows.

bugle duster n. handkerchief *Humphries.*

buick v. to vomit; fr. the noise of the vomiting (cf: hughie, ralph) *Bernbach.*

built n. an attractive woman with a noticeably good figure *Breslin.*

built a. a well muscled man, poss. referring spec. to his penis. (cf: hung) *Price:1.*

built like a brick shithouse a very strong, muscled man, who resembles a squat, four-square, solid edifice.

bull n. **1.** (abbrev.) bull-dyke = lesbian *Dunne*; **2.** policeman, fr. Ger: *bulle*: (sl.) policeman or poss. Sp. sl. *bul*: policeman *Fiction Illus. 3*; **3.** (US criminal use) a veteran, long-term convict *Dunne.*

bull and cow n. (rhyming sl.) row *Powis.*

bullcrap n. see: bullshit *Southern.*

bull dagger n. a masculine lesbian (cf: bull-dyke) *Jones.*

bulldog n. (US newspaper use) the first edition (c.12 midnight) of a morning paper; the first (late morning) edition of an evening paper *Fiction Illus. 3.*

bull-dyke n. a masculine lesbian; usu. an unpleasant, excessively man-hating one (cf: bumper) *Big Ass Comics 1.*

bullet n. (poker use) an ace *Uris.*

bullet-proof a. immune, irrefutable.

bull-fiddle n. the double-bass *'Some Like It Hot', directed Billy Wilder, 1959.*

bullpen n. **1.** sport: the bench on which the batting team in baseball sit when not performing; **2.** police use: the holding cage in a precinct house *Himes:1*; **3.** any enclosure – college dormitory, factory changing room, etc. – where a group of men associate, gossip, etc.

bull session n. (US use) sitting around gossipping, often of men rather than woman (cf: bull) *King.*

bullsh n. (abbrev.) bullshit (qv) *Humphries.*

bullshit n. rubbish, nonsense, lies *Price:2.*

bullshit v. to tell lies, to tease, to confuse with false information.

bullshit artist n. anyone with a good line of persuasive, if insincere patter *Underwood.*

bully! (excl.) wonderful, excellent, fine! *PT.*

bully beef n. (UK prison use; rhyming sl.) chief (officer) (cf: corned beef) *Norman:1.*

bully for you! (excl.) well done! congratulations; usu. ironic/sarcastic use.

bullyrag v. to bully, to pressurize, to taunt *PT.*

bum n. **1.** the buttocks *Payne*; **2.** spec. a tramp, a vagrant *Powis*; **3.** (derog.) term of abuse for anyone unpleasant *Laugh In The Dark*; **4.** (boxing use) a poor, incompetent fighter *Heller*; **5.** a promiscuous girl, fr. bum: tramp (vagrant) used as tramp (promiscuous woman) *Bruce:2.*

bum a. useless, second rate, poor, inferior, etc; fr. bum = vagrant, tramp, etc. *Algren.*

bum v. **1.** to wander around; **2.** to beg *Price:3.*

bum-boy n. (derog.) homosexual male; fr. bum = buttocks.

bumchat v. to make statements to a woman with the sole interest in her seduction *S. Ford.*

bum deal n. a poor bargain, a mistaken agreement; fr. bum, a.

bumf n. paperwork, fr. abbrev. bumfodder, orig. Second World War milit. sl. *Dickson.*

bum-fluff n. very light growth of hair on the face of a boy who is on the verge of shaving.

bum-freezer n. a short jacket that stops short of covering the buttocks; orig. describing an Eton jacket, latterly the 'Italian' styles of 1950s and thence any short (men's) jacket *Whitcomb.*

bum map n. (US banking use) a cheque that is returned to drawer *Breslin* (cf: bounce **1**).

bummed out a. **1.** suffering from a bummer (qv) *McFadden*; **2.** drunk *Dickson.*

bummer n. **1.** (drug use) an unpleasant drug experience, esp. while using LSD *Green:1*; **2.** any unpleasant experience *Hoffman:a.*

bump n. spontaneous, cursory sexual intercourse *Klein.*

bump v. **1.** to dismiss an employee; **2.** to increase wages or, in gambling use, a bet.

bumper n. **1.** (cant) a pickpocket's assistant who bumps into the victim *Neaman & Silver*; **2.** a masculine lesbian *Legman*; **3.** (Aus. use) cigarette butt (cf: not worth a bumper) *Wilkes.*

bumpers n. breasts *Neaman & Silver.*

bump off v. to murder *Sharpe:1.*

bump into v. to meet by accident.

bum-rap v. to slander, to attack verbally, to catcall *Bruce:2.*

bum's rush n. forcible ejection, esp. from a bar or club *Goldman.*

bum steer n. **1.** spec. a false clue, thus; **2.** a mistake, the wrong direction *Humphries.*

bum trip n. see: bummer **1**.

bum-sucker n. sycophant, crawler (cf: ass-kisser, -licker, brown-noser).

bunch of fives n. the fist *Hotten.*

bunch punch n. (US campus use) group sex in which a number of males have sex with one female (cf: gang-bang) *Underwood.*

bunco n. (criminal use, esp. US) fraud; fr. *banco*, first used in US c.1870 *Powis.*

bunco artist n. a confidence trickster *Wodehouse:PGM.*

bunco squad n. (US police use) a special squad devoted to combating confidence tricksters (cf: bunco, pussy posse).

bunco-steerer n. (US criminal use) a member of a confidence trickster gang who persuades a victim to take part in the current swindle they are using to make money.

bundle n. a large amount of money *Grogan.*

bunfight n. a tea party, esp. with image of children struggling for sticky buns.

bung n. aka: *bunghole*; the anus *Legman.*

bung v. pass, throw *Payne.*

bung n., v. a bribe, to offer or give a bribe; usu. of police (UK) (cf: sling) *Powis.*

bungalow v. (US milit. use in Vietnam) to live with; fr. shack up (qv) *Neaman & Silver.*

bunged up a. stuffy, blocked, esp. of one's nose during 'flu or a cold.

bung ho! a toast when drinking; also synonym for 'goodbye' *Pynchon.*

bunghole n. see: asshole *Price:3.*

bunghole v. to sodomize *Bukowski:1.*

bungo n. (West Indian use) (derog.) crude, boorish, ignorant black person *Thelwell.*

bungy n. an eraser, a rubber; usu.

school use.
bun in the oven pregnant *Humphries.*
bunk n. nonsense, rubbish; fr. bunkum *Sanders:2.*
bunk down v. to sleep *Humphries:2.*
bunker n. a sodomite; fr. bugger (qv) *Legman.*
bunk off v. to play truant, usu. UK schoolchildren (cf: hop the wag).
bunkum n. nonsense, rubbish *Neaman & Silver.*
bunk up n. sexual intercourse *Norman:1.*
bunny n. **1.** (fr. rhyming sl.) rabbit (and pork) = talk *Newman:2*; **2.** (US Black use) a promiscuous woman, whose habits emulate the preoccupations of rabbits *Klein.*
buns n. the buttocks *Vidal.*
bunty n. a small, middle-aged woman, implying one's affection for a woman so-titled *Powis.*
buoyant a. drunk; 'my teeth are floating' *Dickson.*
burbed-out (US middle-class) conventional, poss. fr. Burberry coat *Price:3.*
burg n. a town, a city; fr. German *Big Ass Comics 1.*
burglar n. corruption of *bugger* (cf: bunker) *Legman.*
burgle v. to sodomize; fr. SE *bugger* *Neaman & Silver.*
burgoo n. fr. Hindustani: porridge or soup *P. MacDonald, 'X v. Rex', 1933.*
buried (US prison use) held incommunicado *Chandler: Notebk.*
burn n. (UK prison use) a smoke, a cigarette *LL.*
burn v. **1.** to cheat, defraud, fail to pay a debt *Bruce:2*; **2** (spec. drug use) to sell cut or second-rate drugs *Caserta*; **3.** to betray sexually *Two Lane Blacktop, 1971*; **4.** (US campus use) to grade harshly *Underwood*; **5.** to annoy, to infuriate, to embarrass *Pond*; **6.** to recognize *Higgins:1*; **7.** (UK criminal use) to open a safe using oxyacetylene cutting equipment *LL.*
burn down v. **1.** to shoot, to kill; **2.** to overdo, to use to excess *Burroughs:1.*
burned at annoyed with *McFadden.*
burnie n. (drug use) a half-smoked marijuana cigarette *De Lannoy & Masterson.*
burning down habit an extremely heavy addiction to narcotics (cf: oil burner habit) *Burroughs:1.*
burn one's shoulder v. to be drunk; with a cigarette? by falling on the stove? *Dickson.*
burnout n. one who has exhausted their capabilities; one who can no longer function efficiently within their own job or discipline *Price:3.*
burn rubber v. to drive a car very fast; fr. the smoking tyres *Tuff Shit Comics.*
burnt n. (fr. rhyming sl) burnt cinder = window (pron. winder) *Norman:2.*
burnt a. (US campus use) disppointed, esp. sexually *Underwood.*
burnt offering n. joking description of any food which has been burnt on the stove.
burnt out the victim of excess, too much drink and/or drugs, all of which has taken its toll both physically and, esp. mentally.
burn up v.t. to annoy, to irritate (cf: burnt at) *Runyon:1.*
burn-up n. fast riding of a motorcycle, esp. used by outlaw bike riders, Rockers, etc. *Mandelkau.*
burn with a low blue flame v. to be extremely drunk; fr. image of lighting the alcohol fumes pouring from one's mouth *Neaman & Silver.*
buroo n. unemployment office, Labour exchange; fr. bureau.
burst n. a spree, a party with much eating and drinking *Tidy.*
burst v. to beat up; usu. as a threat 'I'll burst him!'.
burst one's bubble v. (US campus use) to humiliate; to deflate someone's ego *Underwood.*
burton n. (rhyming sl.) Burton-on-Trent = rent *Powis.*
bush n. **1.** the female pubis *Dunne*; **2.** (drug use) marijuana, esp. as in Congo bush, African bush, etc. *Green:1*; **3.** (abbrev.) bush league (qv)

Higgins:1.

bushed exhausted, tired out; as if one had been wandering, lost, through the woods *Higgins:5.*

bushel and peck n. (rhyming sl.) the neck (cf: Gregory Peck) *Cole.*

busher n. an amateur, an unsophisticated person (cf: bush league).

Bushey park n. (rhyming sl.) a lark, thus a joke *Jones:J.*

bush league **1.** (baseball use) second rate teams, leagues, players; **2.** amateur, unprofessional, unsophisticated.

bush patrol n. **1.** sexual by-play, and thus; **2.** sexual intercourse *Neaman & Silver* (cf: bush **1**).

bush telegraph n. a network of gossip, rumours which brings news (often inaccurate) before the official sources.

bushwa aka: *bushwah*, *booshwa*, *booshwah*, *boushwa(h)*; euph. bullshit *Rawson.*

business end n. that part (practical or metaphorical) that really matters.

business girl n. prostitute (cf: working girl) *Powis.*

bust n. **1.** (US Black use) the police; fr. **2.** an arrest *Folb*; **3.** a failure *Runyon.*

bust v. **1.** to smash, to break up *Mandelkau*; **2.** to hit (with the fist) *Goulart*; **3.** to arrest; spec. to catch in possession of drugs *Price:1.*

bust a grape v. (US Black use) to engage in any form of hard, productive work *Klein.*

bust a gut v. to exert oneself strenuously.

bust caps v. **1.** (US milit. use) to fire a weapon; **2.** (drug use) to inject a narcotic (cf: cap).

busted a. **1.** see: bust v **3**; **2.** without money *Heller.*

Buster general US mode of address to any male.

buster n. a person, often an old and cantankerous one *Wodehouse:AAG.*

busting desperate; fr. bursting *Humphries:2.*

bustle-punching (UK police use) the action of the *frotteur*: using the anonymity of a dense crowd to rub one's penis against the nearby buttocks of defenceless women *Powis.*

bust one's ass v. work exceptionally hard *Higgins:3.*

bust one's chops v. see: break one's chops.

bust one's hump v. to work very hard *Higgins:1.*

bust one's nuts v. see: bust a gut.

bust-out n. an enormous feast (cf: blow-out) *Goldman.*

bust-out a. an intensifying adjective: extreme, tremendous, great, etc. *Bruce:2.*

bust some booty v. (US Black use) to perform sexual intercourse (cf: booty) *Folb.*

bust (someone) up v. to beat up, to hurt in a fight *Jones.*

bust up v. to end a love-affair.

busy n. a CID officer, a detective, as opposed to *flattie* (flatfoot, qv), the regular policeman *Powis.*

busy as a one-armed paper-hanger (cp) denotes extreme activity.

butch n. a masculine lesbian: or masculine male homosexual, opp. of femme (qv) *Jay & Young.*

butcher n. an inefficient surgeon, esp. one who practises cosmetic work *P. Roth, 'Goodbye Columbus', 1959.*

butchers n. **1.** (fr. rhyming sl.) butcher's hook = a look *Norman:2*; **2.** (Aus. use; fr. rhyming sl.) butcher's hook = crook (qv) = ill, sick. *Humphries:2.*

butt n. **1.** cigarette end *Price:1*; **2.** (abbrev.) buttocks *Bukowski:2.*

butter n. (US Black use) **1.** a woman; **2.** spec. buttocks *Folb.*

butter-and-egg man n. (US use) a small-town success, often a farmer who produces such commodities, who attempts to pass for a sophisticate in the big city *C. Connolly, Journals, ed. D. Pryce-Jones, 1983.*

butter baby n. (US Black use) a sexy, well-built female *Folb.*

butterball n. an overweight young

person *Whitcomb.*

butterbox n. **1.** (derog.) a Dutchman; fr. his country's product *BvdB*; **2.** a fop (fr. 1703); thus effeminate male *Humphries.*

butterboy n. a novice, in whose mouth butter would not melt; esp. a young policeman or a newly qualified taxi-driver *Powis.*

buttercup n. an effeminate male homosexual *Legman.*

buttered a. (US Black use) well turned out, elegant *Klein.*

buttered bun n. a girl who has had intercourse with one man and is about to repeat this immediately with a new partner. (cf: crumpet) *S. Hutt.*

buttered scone (bingo rhyming sl.) 1 (cf: Kelly's eye) *Wright.*

butterfinger n. one who cannot grasp anything properly when thrown to him/her.

butterflies in one's stomach nerves, apprehensions, tension.

butterfly n. (US Black use) an over-dressed, flashy person *Klein.*

butterhead n. (US Black use) a Black who, for whatever reason, is considered an embarrassment to his race *Major.*

butter up v. to flatter, to ingratiate oneself *Neaman & Silver.*

butt-fuck v. to subject to anal intercourse *Jay & Young.*

buttfucker n. one who indulges in anal intercourse.

butt in v. to interfere, to make a nuisance of oneself; fr. pushing forward like a charging bull.

buttinski n. one who intrudes, interferes; fr. butt in + suffix-ski *Schulberg.*

button n. **1.** policeman; fr. those upon his uniform *Chandler:LG*; **2.** the clitoris *Neaman & Silver*; **3.** the chin, esp. in *on the button*: a blow square on the chin and thus: exactly, perfectly, quite correctly *Farrell.*

button-down a. conforming, straight (qv); fr. the button-down collared shirts from Brooks Brothers (New York) that are the uniform of the US business establishment *McFadden.*

buttoner n. (UK criminal use) the member of a gang running a game of three-card monte (qv) who persuades passers by to bet on the inevitably fraudulent game; fr. buttonhole *Powis.*

button man n. (US Mafia use) a lower echelon member of a Mafia family (cf: soldier).

button mob n. a large group of uniformed police, esp. at a demonstration, a royal appearance, etc. *Powis.*

button one's lip v. to be quiet, to stop talking.

button up v. **1.** (abbrev.) button one's lip (qv); **2.** to close, to shut down, (govt. use) to withold information *PT.*

butt out! (excl.) go away, leave me alone, etc. (cf: butt).

butt-plunger n. (pimp use) a man who inserts a dildo into his own anus then walks around naked while the prostitute looks on *OUI 8/75.*

butty n. **1.** a friend, a 'mate'; usu. Northern UK use; **2.** a sandwich; fr. 'buttered bread'; thus *jam butty*, *chip butty*, etc.

buy n. (drug use) the purchase of a given drug.

buy v. to accept, to believe *The Roches, 'Nurds'.*

buy a ticket v. (US Black use) aka: *buy a wolf ticket*: to call one's bluff, to take on a challenge *Folb.*

buyer n. (UK criminal/police use) a receiver of stolen goods (cf: fence) *Powis.*

buy the farm v. **1.** to accept whatever is offered without query; to be conned or hoaxed; fr. image of a simple country person ensnared into a bad purchase by a smooth salesman *'Hill Street Blues', Thames TV, 1983*; **2.** to die *Rawson.*

buy the ring v. to perform anal intercourse (cf: bit of ring) *Folb.*

buzz n. a telephone call (cf: bell) *Wodehouse:AAG.*

buzz n. **1.** a rumour *Norman:2*; **2.** a pleasant sensation from taking a given drug, esp. barbiturates or cannabis *Grogan*.

buzz v. (US teen. use) to drive around town in one's car, looking for amusement (cf: cruise) *Pond*.

buzzard n. an old and unattractive person (cf: buffer) *Folb*.

buzz around like a blue-arsed fly v. to be excessively busy; often to the detriment of others.

buzzer n. police badge.

buzz off! (excl.) go away! *McBain:1*.

buzz the nab v. (Valley Girls (qv) use) to leave, to escape a situation; fr. buzz (drive around) and nab (abbrev. nabes: the neighbourhood) *Pond*.

BVDs n. underwear, from the popular brand name.

by George! mild excl.

by jingo! euph: by Jesus! *Rawson*.

by Jove! (euph.) by God! *Rawson*.

BYO (Aus. use) (abbrev.) Bring Your Own; refers to bringing drinks to a party or an unlicensed restaurant; sometimes BYOG: Bring Your Own Grog *Bickerton*.

C n. **1.** $100; fr. century. thus *C-note*:$100 dollar bill (cf: G) *Chandler: LG*;**2.** (drug use) cocaine (cf: H) *Burroughs: 1*.

cabbage n. cash, banknotes (cf: lettuce) *Klein*.

caboose n. the buttocks; fr. the cow-hide container stretched across the rear of the chuck wagon, when full it hangs down behind the wagon *Rawson*.

cad n. (US Black use) (abbrev.) Cadillac *Klein*.

caddy n. (abbrev.) Cadillac.

caff n. corruption of *café*, usu. cheap and cheerful *Payne*.

Cain and Abel n. (rhyming sl.) table *Wright*.

cake n. (US Black use) money *Shulman*.

cakehole n. the mouth, usu. abbrev. hole (qv).

cakes n. female breasts *Higgins: 5*.

calaboose n. fr. Sp *calabozo*: gaol; mainly US South/Western use *Runyon*.

calf n. **1.** 50p.; fr. rhyming sl: cow and calf = half = half a pound, orig. 10/–, now 50p *LL*; **2.** (US Black use) a Cadillac *Folb*.

California bankroll n. (Black and gambling use) a show bankroll in which the one large-denomination note is exhibited on the outside, concealing a quantity of small bills; a general slur to which all states, i.e. *Michigan bankroll*, are variously subject, depending on a speaker's prejudice *Folb*.

call-boy n. a male prostitute who can be hired on the phone. fr. call-girl (qv) *Jay & Young*.

call for hughie v. (UK 'society' use) to vomit (cf: cry hughie) *Barr*.

call-girl n. a female prostitute who can be hired by telephone (cf: call-boy).

call-house n. a brothel – homo- or heterosexual – that takes 'orders' for sex on the phone; previously the 'call' referred to the fact that girls could be 'called' for their services by the attendant customers *Legman*.

call it a day v. to stop, to go no further, to express satisfaction with progress.

call one out v. to challenge to a fight *Folb*.

call the punches v. see: call the shots *dl*.

call the shots v. to dictate a course of action, to say what should happen; fr. dice gambling use *McFadden*.

camp v. to act ostentatiously and outrageously in a homosexual manner; though by no means restricted – verbally or physically – to the gay world *Jay & Young*.

camp as a row of tents a. extremely, ostentatiously camp (qv).

can n. **1.** buttocks *Legman*; **2.** (drug use) quantity of marijuana (approx. 1oz) (cf: lid) *Folb*; **3.** (US cant) a safe

Caron; **4.** prison *Higgins: 1*; **5.** lavatory.

can v. **1.** to stop (a noise, an action, etc.) *Underwood*; **2.** to dismiss from a job, to throw out, to ignore; fr. can=buttocks *Farrell*.

canal boat n. (rhyming sl) the Tote *Jones: J*.

Canaries n. Norwich City Football Club.

canary n. **1.** (UK cant) an informer; thus *sing like a canary*: to inform without restraint *Cole*; **2.** (show business use) a female singer, usu. fronting a band.

cancel one's ticket v. to murder, to assassinate *Rawson*.

candy n. (US Black use) **1.** heroin, but see nose-candy; **2.** sexually desirable person of either sex; **3.** (drug use) any drug in capsule form *Folb*.

candy-ass n. weakling *Price: 2*.

candy-butt n. young, inexperienced male (cf: candy-ass) *Folb*.

candyman n. (US Black use) a man who sells drugs, women and any other desired commodity for a pleasant life. (cf: candy, nose-candy) *Klein*.

candy-striper n. US hospital voluntary auxiliary workers; fr. striped dresses they wear *Price: 2*.

can I speak to you? (UK criminal use) acknowledged code between a newly arrested criminal and his arresting officer; the topic of their conversation would be the possibility and quantity of a bribe which would secure the villain's freedom or at least a reduction in the charges (cf: do you drink?) *Powis*.

canned a. drunk; fr. canned up, and thus turned to liquid (?) *Dickson*.

cannibal n. one who indulges in oral sex *Major*.

cannon n. **1.** a large gun *rr*; **2.** the penis *Klein*; **3.** (US) a pickpocket; because he 'shoots at' a victim (?) *Chandler: Notebk*.

can of worms n. an unpleasant, complex and unappetizing situation *Variety 1983*.

canoodle v. to cuddle, to neck (qv) *Rawson*.

can opener n. (US cant) any tool used for the breaking open of a safe and invaluable when explosives would lead to discovery *Runyon*.

can't find one's ass with two hands (cp) to be very drunk *Dickson*.

can't hit a lick (US Black use) the inability to succeed in a given aim, esp. that of making money either legally or otherwise; fr. musical use *Klein*.

can't hit the ground with his hat a. (cp) extremely drunk *Dickson*.

can't see through a ladder a. (cp) extremely drunk *Dickson*.

can't win 'em all (cp) denoting commiseration over a disaster or disappointment, sometimes, but not necessarily, involving actual competition *Wodehouse: GB*.

Canuck n. (derog.) Canadian *BvdB*.

canyon n. the vagina (cf: yodel in the canyon) *Folb*.

can you see green in my eyes? (S. Afr. use) do you think I'm lying? *Marcuson*.

cap n. **1.** (abbrev.) capsule: containing a narcotic, usu. heroin. *Payne*; **2.** (US Black use) cunnilingus; a strained parallel to head (qv) *Klein*.

cap v. to transfer bulk drugs (in powder form) into capsules for sale *Green:1*.

cape of good hope n. (rhyming sl.) soap *Jones: J*.

caper n. a large scale crime, usu. involving a great deal of elaborate planning and aimed at very large sums of money, expensive pieces of jewellery, etc. the supposed lack of violence in such enterprises lent them this somewhat jovial, jokey air *Powis*.

cap on v. to attack someone verbally, to discredit someone *Folb*.

capper n. an anecdote that steals the limelight from a previous anecdote; a punchline *Bruce: 1*.

Captain Cook n. (rhyming sl.) **1.** a look *Humphries*; **2.** a book *Jones: J*.

capture n. an arrest and conviction for a crime *Norman: 1*.

caput finished, over, ruined, etc; fr. Ger. *kaputt*; done for.

caravan v. (US teen. use) to drive cars in groups and to perform a variety of elaborate manoeuvres on the street *Folb*.

card n. a character, a noticeable person, a likeable eccentric *Jones*.

card v. (US campus use) to request proof of age (in a bar) by producing one's identification card *Underwood*.

Carl Comedian n. (US campus use) derog. dismissal of a raconteur whose jokes and stories fail to make the desired impact *Bernbach*.

Carl Rosa n. (rhyming sl.) a poser, anyone pretending to be something that he/she is not; thus *the old Carl Rosa*: fraud *Powis*.

carney n. a carnival worker *Waits*.

carnies n. (Aus. use) (abbrev.) carnations *Humphries: 2*.

car park n. (rhyming sl.) a nark = an informer *Powis*.

carpenter's dream n. an available girl; 'flat as a board and easy to screw' *Price: 1*.

carpet n. (UK prison use) a three months' sentence; fr. the earlier assumption that prison workshops took just 90 days to produce a particular type of regulation size carpet *Norman: 1*.

carpet v. to reprimand, to criticize, to tell off, esp. in milit. use; the miscreant stands on the carpet in front of the superior's desk *Hotten*.

carpet biter n. one who becomes so enraged as to start chewing at the carpet.

carpy (UK prison use) fr. *carpe diem* ('make the most of the day' Lat.): to be locked away in one's cell at night *LL*.

carriage trade n. the upper classes; usu. ironically; fr. earlier divisions of transport *Chandler: LG*.

carrot crunchers n. visitors to London from the provinces and the countryside (cf: swedes) *Powis*.

carry v. to carry arms *Higgins: 1*.

carry a case v. (US criminal use) to be out on bail *Klein*.

carry a torch v. to mourn a dead love affair; to feel love without it being returned *Vidal*.

carrying see: holding *Major*.

carry on v. to have an adulterous relationship *Major*.

carry-on n. a commotion, an exciting event, a disturbance; often in phr. a *right/real carry-on Hotten*.

carry-out n. a cafe which specializes in food that can be packed and taken away for eating elsewhere *Jan Harold Brunvand, 'The Vanishing Hitchhiker', 1983*.

carry the can (for) v. to take the blame that should be another's.

cart v. to carry, to drag; thus *cart away*, *cart out*, etc.*Higgins: 1*.

cartnapping (retail industry use) the stealing of supermarket and self-service store trolleys *Dickson*.

carve a slice v. take a portion of the profits *Waits*.

carve-up n. **1.** any situation in which one feels oneself unfairly deprived of a desired aim or object; **2.** (UK prison/criminal use) a share-out of loot, profits, etc. (cf: carve a slice) *LL*.

carvie n. (UK prison use) one who helps carve-up, share, a ration of tobacco; a prisoner may take on a regular 'carvie' for periods of his sentence *LL*.

carving knife n. (rhyming sl.) wife *Jones: J*.

cas a. (Valley Girls (qv.) use) term of general approval for favoured clothing; abbrev. of casual *Pond*.

case n. (UK criminal use) a brothel *Powis*.

case v. **1.** to look over, to appraise, esp. prior to a robbery as in *case the joint Runyon*; **2.** (UK prison use) to discipline, to put on report *LL*.

case card n. the last card of the four available of each denomination to appear in the deal; thus *case ace*, *case deuce*, etc. *Algren*.

case dough n. (US prison use). limited money *Chandler: Notebk*.

case it around v. (Valley Girls (qv.)

use) **1.** to check out (qv.) a place or situation (cf: case); **2.** to move on to a new activity *Pond*.

case out v. **1.** to join forces for any undertaking; **2.** (excl.) go away! *Algren*.

case over v. to assess; to judge the quality; to look at *Price: 3*.

caser n. **1.** five shillings, fr. Yiddish *kesef*: silver *Norman: 4*; **2.** (UK prison use) a prison officer notorious for excessive discipline (cf: case **2**) *LL*.

case the joint v. to survey a house, shop, etc. with a view to subsequently robbing it *Caron*.

cash and carried (rhyming sl.) married (cf: cut and carried) *Jones: J*.

cashed up (Aus. use) wealthy, well-off, albeit temporarily *Wilkes*.

cash in one's chips v. to die; fr. gambling use, the action one takes on leaving a game *Humphries: 2*.

Caspar Milquetoast n. aka: *Casper Milktoast*: a cowardly, weak person. fr. the central character in the cartoon 'The Timid Soul' created by H. T. Webster, first pub. in New York *World*, 1924 *Waits*.

casper n. (US Black use) a particularly light-skinned black person *Folb*.

cast v.t. (UK police use) to be discharged fr. the police force *Laurie*.

cast nasturtiums v. joking corruption of cast aspersions.

cast the net v. (US pimp use) for a pimp to employ an experienced prostitute to lure a new girl into joining his stable (qv.) *Klein*.

Casuals n. working class UK youth who dress in the designer-labelled clothing of their society peers but whose accents and lifestyles remain resolutely proletarian *Harpers/Queen 8/83*.

cat n. a person, usu. male; from jazz use c.1950s poss. fr. 'alligator', early black use for worldly, smart, sophisticated male, abbrev. to gator, gate, cat (?) *Price: 2*.

cat v. to vomit *R. Kipling, 'Stalky & Co', 1908*.

cat and mouse n. (rhyming sl.) house *Jones: J*.

cat around v. **1.** (US campus use) to wander purposelessly about *Underwood*; **2.** to search for a sexual partner (abbrev.) tom-cat (qv.) *McFadden*.

catch n. the number of clients a prostitute has serviced within a given time *Klein*.

catch v. **1.** to attend, esp. a performance; **2.** to notice, to appreciate.

catch a buzz v. (lesbian use) to masturbate with an electric vibrator *Maledicta*.

catch a cold v. **1.** to get into trouble, poss. through impetuousness; **2.** to lose out financially, poss. after purchasing a supposed 'bargain' which proves to be otherwise.

catch one's death v. to catch a bad cold or 'flu.

catch one's tit in a wringer v. to find oneself in trouble, in an unpleasant situation. The most famous use was during the Watergate Affair when a leading figure suggested that were Katherine Graham, prop. of the Washington *Post*, to permit revelations on White House involvement, she would 'catch her big fat tit in a wringer' *Higgins: 2*.

catch some rays v. **1.** to sunbathe *Junker*; **2.** Valley Girls (qv.) use: goodbye; a feasible alternative farewell in sun-drenched California *Pond*.

cathouse n. brothel *Price: 1*.

catnip n. (drug use) inferior or fake marijuana *Folb*.

cats and kitties n. (rhyming sl.) = titties = breasts *Neaman & Silver*.

cat's pyjamas n. anything exceptional, superlative. (cf: the bee's knees).

cat's whiskers n. see: cat's pyjamas.

catting (US Black use) (abbrev.) tom-catting: looking for female company and/or conquests *Jones*.

cattle car n. (US Navy use) equivalent of Black Maria or paddy wagon (qqv.)

used by the USN's Shore Patrol *Pynchon*.

catty-cat n. (US Black use) the vagina (cf: pussy) *Folb*.

caught in a snowstorm under the influence of cocaine (cf: snow) *Chandler: Notebk*.

caught short desperate to visit a lavatory as soon as possible.

caught with one's trousers down surprised in an embarrassing position, or, on a metaphorical level, caught without adequate defences or preparation.

cauliflower n. (abbrev.) cauliflower ear, the sign of a boxer whose ears have taken too many punches to retain their original shape.

caution sign n. (US Black use) anyone who dresses in an excessively gaudy and vulgar manner, with many clashing bright colours *Folb*.

cavalier n. an uncircumcised penis, or the boy who has one (usu, school use) (cf: roundhead).

CCW (US police use) (acro.) Carrying a Concealed Weapon *Klein*.

cecil n. (US prison use) cocaine (US pron. *see*sul thus cf: C) *Chandler: Notebk*.

celebrity fucker n. anyone who courts the famous with the hope of enjoying some proxy fame (cf: groupie) *Wolfe: 2*.

cell task n. (UK prison use) ironic reference to the official cell tasks set prisoners; in fact a pin-up picture whose real life incarnation would obviously make a preferable 'task' to that set by the authorities *LL*.

cement-head n. (US teen. use) a gullible, conventional person *Sculatti*.

cement kimono n. (US gangster use) a method of disposing of a corpse by placing inside a barrel filled with wet cement and tossing the resultant lump into a river. (cf: wooden overcoat) *rr*.

cement overcoat n. see: cement kimono *Alvarez*.

central cut n. the vagina *Klein*.

centre man n. (US prison use) a sycophantic prisoner, who hangs around the centre of the goal where the staff tend to be found *Neaman & Silver*.

century n. $100 or £100 (cf: C) *Major/LL*.

cereb n. (US campus use) (abbrev.) cerebral: one who works exceptionally hard *Bernbach*.

certain age n. (euph.) middle-aged or older; usu. of women.

cha-cha v. (US Black use) to have sexual intercourse; fr. the dance *Folb*.

chair n. (abbrev.) the electric chair *Higgins: 1*.

chalice n. aka. *chillum*: a pipe used for smoking marijuana; when used by Rastafarians it takes on a sacred and ritualistic role, thus the 'religious' name *Thelwell*.

chalk n. **1.** (US Black use) a white person *Folb*; **2.** (rhyming sl.) Chalk Farm = arm *Powis*.

chalk eater n. (gambling use) a horse race better who always plays the short priced favourites; fr. the chalk used to write up the odds on the bookmaker's slate *Runyon*.

chalkie n. (Aus. use) school-teacher, who wields it *Wilkes*.

champagne trick n. a particularly wealthy/generous client for a prostitute (cf: trick) *Neaman & Silver*.

chance one's arm v. to take risks; fr. boxing use.

chancer n. anyone who risks their luck, usu. foolishly *Payne*.

chapper n. (UK criminal use) a policeman, fr. Yiddish *Powis*.

charge n. **1.** drugs in general, spec. marijuana *Norman: 2*; **2.** the effect of a given drug (cf: high) *De Lannoy & Masterson*.

changes n. any alteration in one's mental/emotional state; thus *go through changes*, *put through changes* (qqv.) *Major*.

charge n. (drug use) marijuana *Green: 1*.

charged (up) intoxicated by cannabis (cf: charge) *Powis*.

charity girl n. (US use) a promiscuous girl who 'gives it away for free'

Neaman & Silver.

charity moll n. (Aus. use) an amateur prostitute, or a professional who undercuts her peers *Wilkes.*

Charlie n. **1.** (drug use) cocaine *Burroughs: 1*; **2.** see: Mr Charlie.

charlie n. (Aus. use) **1.** a prostitute; **2.** a lesbian *Baker.*

charlie a. **1.** wary, fr. charley: a watchman (1812) *Norman: 2*; **2.** (UK 'society' use) flashy, ostentatious, not socially acceptable *Barr.*

Charlie Ronce n. (rhyming sl.) a ponce (cf: Joe Ronce) *Dury.*

charlies n. breasts; fr. Aus. rhyming sl. Charlie Wheeler = Sheila = a girl and thus her distinguishing characteristic *Dunne.*

Charlie's dead (school use) your slip is showing.

charming wife n. (rhyming sl.) a knife *Powis.*

charver v. to make love; fr. Parlyaree (theatrical slang.) chauvering: sexual intercourse; poss. fr. Fr. *chauffer*: to heat up *Norman: 2.*

chase the dragon v. to smoke heroin, sucking up the smoke of the drug which is burned on a piece of kitchen foil; the heated heroin liquifies and flows across the paper, gradually giving off smoke which is sucked into the smoker's lungs by a tube, also usually made of kitchen foil; the 'dragon' underlines the Oriental origin of much of the heroin found in the UK *Green: 2.*

chassis n. the female figure; thus *classy chassis*: an attractive figure, and thus an attractive woman; fr. motoring use *Neaman & Silver.*

chat n. verbal skills, fluency, articulacy, the ability to charm a victim with words alone *Norman: 2.*

chateaued a. (UK 'society' use) very drunk (on wine); puns on shattered and chateau *Barr.*

chatter box n. (US Black use) **1.** record player; **2.** telephone*Klein.*

chat up v. to attempt the first, verbal stages of seduction.

chazerai n. fr. Yiddish *chazer* a pig: a pigsty, a mess; cheap, worthless, rubbish *McBain: 1.*

cheap a. mean, miserly, grasping *Higgins: 5.*

cheap Charlie n. (US milit. use) any soldier who is less than generous when drinking in a bar, etc. *Del Vecchio.*

cheapie n. a mean person *Higgins: 3.*

cheapskate n. a mean, ungenerous person *Runyon.*

cheaters n. glasses, spectacles *Runyon: 1.*

cheat the starter v. to have a child out of wedlock; to become pregnant prior to the wedding *Neaman & Silver.*

check out v.t. to kill; fr. check out: leave a hotel, depart *Price: 2.*

check out v. **1.** to look over, sum up *Price: 2*; **2.** to die *Dunne.*

cheder n. a prison cell, fr. Yiddish *cheder* a small room, or a study *Powis.*

cheerio **1.** goodbye; **2.** a toast (cf: cheers).

cheers **1.** one of the most common toasts before drinking; **2.** thank-you; **3.** goodbye (cf: cheerio).

cheese n. **1.** aka: *head-cheese*: smegma that accumulates around the uncircumcised penis *Legman*; **2.** (US teen use) the best of a given type or style (cf: big cheese) *Sculatti.*

cheese v. **1.** to ejaculate *Klein*; **2.** to break wind (cf: fart) *Dunne.*

cheesecake n. **1.** a pin-up girl (cf: beefcake) *San Francisco Comic Bk no. 2*; **2.** easy, simple, no problems *Higgins: 1.*

cheesed off miserable, annoyed, fed up *Humphries.*

cheese-eater n. an informer; fr. euph. for rat: an informer *Grogan.*

cheese it! stop it! formerly Aus. cant but latterly general use, esp. by schoolchildren *Baker.*

cheesy a. **1.** (street gang use) disloyal *Salisbury*; **2.** false, hypocritical; fr. the 'say cheese' ritual for the summoning up of instant false smiles for the camera *Norman: 2.*

cherries n. (rhyming sl.) cherry hogs = dogs = greyhound racing tracks *Powis.*

cherry n. **1.** a female virgin; thus *bust a cherry*: to deflower; **2.** (homosexual use) anally virgin *Legman*; **3.** virgin; thus *harvest the cherries*: to take a youth and have his virginity taken *Price: 1*; **4.** (US milit. use) a fresh troop, one who has yet to be 'blooded' in combat *Del Vecchio*.

cherry-picking (business use) the reviewing of a number of competing ideas prior to selecting those most useful/profitable for one's own ends.

cherrypop v. to seduce and deflower virgins, usu. females.

chevy n. (rhyming sl.) chevy chase = face *Powis*.

chew face v. (US college use) to kiss *Bernbach*.

chew one's balls off v.t. to reprimand severely.

chew out v. to tell off, to harangue *Higgins: 1*.

chew the fat v. to converse, to talk over; fr. rhyming sl. = have a chat *Runyon*.

chew the rag v. see: chew the fat *Runyon*.

Chicago bankroll see: California bankroll *Folb*.

Chicago lightning gunfire *Chandler: Notebk*.

Chicago piano n. a Thompson sub-machinegun, which achieved notoriety as the preferred weapon of Chicago gangsters in 1920s and later *Fiction Illus. 3*.

Chicago typewriter n. a Thompson sub-machinegun,

chichi n. the female breast, fr. Mexican *Maledicta*.

chichi a. **1.** aka *shishi*: homosexual *Stanley*; **2.** affected, pretentious, 'pretty-pretty'.

chick n. a girl: fr. chicken, lively, perky and 'good enough to eat'; the opposite of cat (qv.) *Powis*.

chicken n. **1.** a coward; fr. that bird's alleged characteristic *Salisbury*; **2.** (US Black use) *1.* unattractive old woman; *2.* an aggressive woman (NB: both uses are direct reverse of usual white equivalents; cf: bad) *Folb*; **3.** underage boys (cf: mystery) *Jay & Young*.

chicken feed n. derisorily small amounts; of money or anything else *Himes: 1*.

chicken hawk n. an older male homosexual with a preference for young boys (cf: chicken queen) *McFadden*.

chicken out v. to be scared, to be too frightened to act *Farren*.

chicken queen n. older homosexual male who prefers sex with teenage boys (cf: chicken hawk) *Jay & Young*.

chicken ranch n. a brothel, fr. a house in Gilbert, Texas where poor farmers once paid for their pleasures with chickens *Neaman & Silver*.

chicken run n. teenage virility ritual involving the driving of two cars at high speed towards each other, or towards a dangerous obstacle: the first one to turn aside or brake is 'chicken' *'Rebel without a Cause', directed N. Ray, 1955*.

chickenshit cowardly, fearful *Higgins: 1*.

chi-ike v. to tease, to fool, to deceive *Sillitoe*.

chili n. (derog.) a Mexican; thus *chili-* as prefix to anything supposedly Mexican; fr. popular Mex. food.

chili chump n. aka: *chili pimp* (US Black use) a pimp who has only one girl working for him; an inexperienced pimp *Klein*.

chill n. death, assassination; fr. the cold corpse *Fiction Illus. 3*.

chill v. to murder, to assassinate.

chill out v. (US teen. use) to calm down, to control one's emotions *Pond*.

chimney n. (US Black use) a hat, fr. the chimney's position on top of the house *Major*.

china n. (rhyming sl.) china plate = mate = best friend *Powis*.

chinch n. a bedbug *Major*.

Chinee n. complementary ticket *Runyon*.

Chinese a. one of the racial stereotypes used in many contexts: the Chinese eye-shape, plus the supposed cunning of the wily Orientals always has 'Chinese' implying something slightly out of true, either physically, ethically, or otherwise (cf: French).

Chinese chance (US use) no chance whatsoever, no luck; fr. gold rush use, when Chinese worked otherwise abandoned claims *New York restaurant name, c.1982*.

Chinese cut n. a stroke that sends the ball in quite another direction from that in which the batsman aimed; 'Chinese' implying 'slanted' as in the racial clichés of oriental eyes *BBC Radio 3 1983*.

Chinese duckets n. complimentary tickets to a theatrical or sporting event (cf: Chinee) *Runyon*.

Chinese fire drill bedlam, chaos *Stone*.

Chinese No. 3 a variety of heroin, processed in Hong Kong and imported by Chinese smugglers. (cf: chase the dragon).

chingazo n. fr. taboo Sp. 'a fuck': sexual intercourse *Folb*.

Chink n., a. Chinese *Price: 2*.

Chink chow n. Chinese food *Underwood*.

chinky a. (US campus use) stingy, mean; fr. the tightness of one's wallet and pockets *Underwood*.

CHINS (US prison use) (acro.) *C*hildren *I*n *N*eed of *S*upervision (cf: MINS, PINS) *Neaman & Silver*.

chinwag n. a chat, a conversation *Humphries*.

chip v. (US criminal use) to carry out a small crime with only minimal profits *Klein*.

chip in v. to join in, to contribute; fr. poker use *Price: 2*.

chipper a. cheerful, lively, perhaps slightly drunk *Neaman & Silver*.

chippie n. **1.** carpenter, esp. theatrical, movie use *Wilkinson*; **2.** a promiscuous woman; a prostitute *Waits*; **3.** (abbrev.) fish and chip shop.

chippie v. to fool sexually; to betray *Waits*.

chippy n. a prostitute who does not really work at it full-time, a promiscuous young girl. *Price: 1*.

chippy v. to use narcotics, esp. heroin, only on an irregular basis rather than to be a habitual addict.

chippy on v. to cheat on one's wife or husband with a new sexual partner *Bruce: 2*.

chips n. buttocks *Selby: 1*.

chisel v. to cheat, thus *chisel out of*: to defraud *Greaser Comics*.

chiseller n. a cheat, a thief *Greaser Comics*.

chiv n. a knife; fr. Romany *Powis*.

chizz v. (school use) to cheat, to swindle; fr. chiseller (qv).

chocolate n. a black person.

Chocolate City n. the Black ghetto; any concentration of Blacks *Price: 2*.

choff n. food; fr. chow (qv.) + scoff (qv.) *Sanders: 2*.

choice a. excellent, first-rate *Pond*.

choirboys n. (US police use) innocent, novice policemen who work strictly by the rulebook *'Hill Street Blues', Thames TV, 1983*.

choke a darkie v. (Aus. use) to excrete *Humphries*.

choked a. upset, annoyed, depressed, having 'a lump in one's throat' *Performance*.

choked down (US Black use) well dressed, poss. fr. choker: a tie, thus one who wears a tie must look smart *Folb*.

choke off v. **1.** to upbraid, to reprimand; **2.** to silence (in mid-flow) *Wodehose: AAG*.

choker n. a disappointment, an annoyance (cf: sickener) *Norman: 3*.

chokes and croaks (US campus use) course in first aid and safety education *Dickson*.

chokey n. **1.** (UK prison use) punishment cells *Norman: 1*; **2.** prison *Dury*.

chokka aka: *chokker*: full to the brim; fr. choc full, choc a bloc *Capital Radio 1983*.

Cholo aka *Chico*: see *bato Folb*.

choof v. to leave, to go away; fr. UK early 20th C *teuf-teuf*: goodbye (?) *Baker*.

chook n. (Aus. use) a chicken *Humphries*.

choose off v. (US Black use) to challenge to a fight *Folb*.

choose up v. (US prison use) for an experienced inmate to select a newcomer as a homosexual partner, whether or not the latter agrees to act as one *Klein*.

choosing money n. (US pimp use) the voluntary donation of her earnings by a ho (qv.) to a pimp whom she wishes to start acting as her own pimp *Shulman*.

chop n. **1.** (Aus. use) share, portion *Wilkes*; **2.** food.

chop chop quickly, fast; fr. Chinese pidgin *Dunne*.

chopper n. a Thompson sub-machinegun, usu, gangster use (cf: Chicago piano, typewriter) *rr*.

chopper n.**1.** a helicopter *M. Herr, 'Dispatches' 1978*; **2.** a cut down, 'chopped' motorbike, spec. a Harley-Davidson, preferred for speed and style by outlaw motorcycle gangs, i.e. Hells Angels *San Francisco Comic 3*.

choppers n. teeth.

chopping sticks (bingo rhyming sl.) 6 *Wright*.

chops n. lips. mouth; fr. animal use and thus usu. derog *Sillitoe*.

chop the clock v. (car sales use) to tune back the mileometer in order to fool a customer into thinking a vehicle is less old than it actually is *J. Updike, 'Rabbit is Rich', 1982*.

chopstick n. slightly derog. Asian person *Folb*.

chosen a. (US prison use) selected, like it or not, as the homosexual lover (cf: punk) of an older, tougher inmate (cf: choose up) *Klein*.

chow n. food, esp. in an institutional setting, ie army messhall, prison, etc.; fr. Chinese *O'Brien*.

chowder-head n. (US teen use) see: cement-head *Sculatti*.

chow-hound n. (US milit. use) any serviceman who is especially keen on his food, runs to head the messhall queue, etc. *AS 41 (1966)*.

christen v. to mark or otherwise damage, esp. of a dog that reveals its lack of house-training.

Christmas! (euph.) Christ! *Rawson*.

Christmas hold n. (Aus. use) a squeeze of one's opponent's testicles; fr. pun on 'hand full of nuts (testicles)', a popular Yuletide pleasure *Wilkes*.

Christmas tree n. (drug use) **1.** stimulant (deximal spansules) **2.** depressant (butabarbital (Tuinal)) *Klein*.

Christopher Columbus! (euph.) Christ! *Rawson*.

chromo n.**2.** an ugly, distasteful person *Runyon: 1*; **2.** (Aus. use) a prostitute.

chubb v. (UK prison use) to lock up; fr. trade name of the locksmith *LL*.

chubby-chaser n. a man who prefers (unfashionably) plump or even fat women *M. Innes 1983*.

chuc n. (abbrev.) Pachuco = Mexican-American *Farina*.

chuck n. a verdict of not guilty: chucked out of court *Newman: 3*.

chuck v.**1.** to vomit; **2.** to throw *Performance*; **3.** to end an affair, to reject a lover.

chuck a dummy v. to vomit.

chucker-out n. a staff member at pubs, dance-halls, concert-halls and similar places of public entertainment to eject, by force if necessary, rowdy and undesirable people (cf: bouncer) *Dickson*.

chuck horrors n. see: chucks *Algren*.

chuck it in v. to give up, esp. of a job. or as excl. *chuck it in!* stop it! *Griffith*.

chucklehead n. dolt, simpleton, fool.

chucks n. **1.** Converse All-Star baseball boots; signed by designer Chuck Taylor *Jay & Young*; **2.** the craving for food that hits a heroin addict once he has withdrawn from using the drug – which on the whole destroys the appetite during its regular use. *Burroughs: 1*.

chuck up the sponge v. to give in, to surrender; fr. boxing use *Neaman & Silver*.

chuck you Farley! joking expletive, fr. 'fuck you, Charley!'
chuff n. (homosexual use) pubic hair *Maledicta*.
chuffed a. very pleased, delighted, happy *Barr*.
chug v. (abbrev.) chug-a-lug: to drink, esp. to down in one gulp or without putting down the glass *Price: 2*.
chummy n. (UK police use) address of anyone to whom the policeman is talking; a suspect *Laurie*.
chummy a. friendly; fr. chum *Higgins:2*.
chump n. anyone gullible, easily taken in *Milner*.
chump v. to trick, to deceive, to make someone a chump (qv) *Thompson:J*.
chump-change a. second rate, inferior, good only for fools *Price:2*.
chump job n. respectable, low-paying regular work (cf: nine to five) *Milner*.
chump off v. (US Black use) to look down on, to disdain *Klein*.
chunder v. (Aus. use) to vomit; according to Barry Humphries, the great popularizer of the word in his 'Barry Mackenzie' strip in *Private Eye* and on film, fr. nautical shout of warning 'watch under!'; Wilkes (op cit) also offers rhyming sl. fr. Chunder Loo of Akin Foo = spew = vomit; Chunder Loo featured in long-running series of ads for Cobra boot polish c.1910 *Humphries*.
chungo bunny n. (derog.) Black person; mispron. of jungle bunny (qv) *Higgins:1*.
chunk n. (Can. prison use) a handgun *Caron*.
chunk v. (US Black use) to discard, to throw away; fr. chuck (qv) *Klein*.
church key n. a can opener *Greaser Comics*.
church mouse n. (homosexual use) a homosexual who frequents crowded churches in order to fondle any potential sex partners *Legman*.
chutzpah n. fr. Yiddish: gall, cheek, outrageousness, audacity *Rosten*.
cinch n. a simple, easily attained thing; fr. *cinch*: grip tightly, thus something one can grasp easily *Grogan*.
circle jerk n. joint masturbation, often in competition, by a group of boys, poss. sitting in a circle.
circus n. a sex-show *Legman*
— city a fantasy place that acts as an intensifier for a given adjective or phrase; thus *nowhere city*, *forget-it-city*, *fun city*, etc. *Bruce:2*.
civvie n. a civilian, thus termed by members of the forces, the prison service, police, etc.
civvy street n. the world of civilian life, usu. service use.
claim v. (UK police use) to arrest (cf: borrow) *Laurie*.
clam n. **1.** (UK use) a tight-lipped person; **2.** (US use) a mean person.
clams n. dollars *Dunne*.
clam up v. to stop talking, to become deliberately secretive *Goulart*.
clap n. venereal disease *Price:1*.
clapped out a. worn out, useless; esp. of machinery, cars, etc. fr. clap (qv) and its deleterious effects, even on such things as could not possibly contract it *Capital Radio 1983*.
clapping for credit (US campus use) music appreciation course *Bernbach*.
claret n. blood *Performance*.
classic a. (US campus use) anyone or anything that is regarded as out of the ordinary, eccentric; inference is one of ironic appraisal *Bernbach*.
clean a. **1.** (Black pimp use) dressed in the height of current male fashion, perfectly groomed *Milner*; **2.** beyond any possible suspicion, guiltless *Higgins:1*; **3.** not using any form of drug; not currently addicted *Higgins:1*; **4.** (criminal use) without any form of incriminating identification; not carrying a gun *Grogan*.
clean out v. (gambling use) to take all of an opponent's money. (cf: take to the cleaners) *Powis*.
clean shot n. good luck, favourable opportunity *Higgins:1*.
clean to the bone a. (US Black use)

aka: *fonky to the bone, mod. . ., ragged. . ., silked. . ., tabbed. . .* exceptionally well dressed *Folb.*

clean up v. **1.** (Black use) to make excuses; to form an alibi *Milner*; **2.** to do very well out of a project; esp. in gambling use. (cf: take to the cleaners) *Pearce.*

clean up on to deal with successfully *Schulberg.*

clean up the kitchen (homosexual use) to practise cunnilingus *Legman.*

clean up the walls v. (US Black use) to chatter, to gossip, to talk nonsense *Seale.*

clear cut (US Black use) **1.** stylish clothes; **2.** pure drugs *Klein.*

clearly a. (Valley Girls (qv) use) totally, maximally, perfectly, etc. *Pond.*

clear off v. to leave, to depart, esp. as excl. *clear off*! *Manser.*

clear-up n. (UK police use) the identification and capture (ideally) of a known villain *Laurie.*

clever a. (Aus. use) in good health, in order, working well, etc., thus *not too clever*: generally negative response to 'how are you', 'how is it', etc. *Ready.*

click v. to work out exactly as planned; like a perfectly designed machine *rr.*

clickety-click (bingo rhyming sl.) 66.

click with v. to get on well, usu. with someone of the opposite sex *Wodehouse:AAG.*

cliff-hanger n. any suspenseful, threatening situation, although usu. one from which one is eventually delivered; fr. movie description of such silent-era serials as 'The Perils of Pauline' (starring Pearl White) in which the heroine, at an episode's end, was often literally hanging from a cliff *McFadden.*

climb all over v. **1.** to attack verbally; to reprimand; **2.** to maul sexually, usu. spoken by a female of a male.

climbing trees to get away from it aka: *got to swim underwater to get away from it; so busy I've had to put a man on to help*: (Aus. male cp) in answer to query 'getting any?' (qv) *Neaman & Silver.*

climb the rigging v. to lose one's temper, fr. RN use *Green:2.*

climb the walls v. to approach insanity through nerves, irritation, tension, etc.

clincher n. the ultimate solution, the culmination *Schulberg.*

clink n. prison; fr. the name of the Southwark gaol, demolished in the 18th C. *Sillitoe.*

clip v. **1.** to hit, to tap sharply *Runyon:1*; **2.** to defraud, to steal from (cf: welch, rip off) *Higgins:1.*

clip-joint n. a club or similar place of entertainment where the customers are deliberately and systematically defrauded under the guise of charging them for their pleasure *Norman:2.*

clipped a. circumcised (cf: roundhead).

clippie n. a bus conductress, who once clipped tickets.

clipping (UK criminal/police use) posing as a prostitute, obtaining the money, but absconding before intercourse takes place (cf: murphy game) *Powis.*

clit n. (abbrev.) clitoris *Southern & Hoffenberg.*

clithopper n. (lesbian use) a promiscuous lesbian *Maledicta.*

clitty n. the clitoris *Fiesta Magazine XIII:6.*

clobber n. fr. Yiddish (?); clothes *Norman:2.*

clobber v. to hit *Newman:1.*

clobbered a. drunk *Dickson.*

clobber one with v. to force an unpleasant/unwanted task or duty on someone.

clock n. the face *Sillitoe.*

clock v. **1.** to see, to recognize, to notice *Payne*; **2.** to hit *Price:2.*

clock a daffy v. (S. Afr. use) shoot a line (qv), tell a deceitful story with the intention of tricking the hearer *A. Marcuson.*

clock and a half? (taxi-driver use) the attempt by a crooked cabbie to get an innocent, usu. foreign, fare to pay an extra 50% of what is registered on the clock; some pretext may be put forward, but often just the phrase, delivered with confidence, is sufficient *Powis.*

clock in v. to arrive; fr. industrial time-keeping practice *Wodehouse:GB.*

clodpoll n. fool, incompetent *Dickson.*

close, but no cigar (cp.) commiserating with a 'near-miss' or a good try; fr. fairground use: the pitchman rewarded successful punters (qv) with cigars *C. Colegrave.*

closer n. (horse-racing use) a horse on whom the odds shortened drastically in the minutes prior to the race, but which still failed to win *Bukowski:1.*

closet a. secretive, clandestine, hidden; fr. homosexual use.

closet case n. (homosexual use) a homosexual who finds it difficult or impossible to admit his sexuality in public *Jay & Young.*

closet queen n. see: closet case *Stanley.*

cloth-ears n. general term of abuse, esp. to someone who at first seems to not have heard one's comment *Capital Radio*1983.

clothes n. (NY police use) (abbrev.) plain clothes; a detective *'Serpico', directed Sidney Lumet, 1973.*

clotheshorse n. an exquisitely well-dressed, fashionable person, although the implication is that beyond such perfection lies little else.

Cloud 9 paradise; anywhere exceptionally pleasant *Major.*

clout n. influence, esp. in politics; one who 'packs a punch' in government *PT.*

clout v. to steal *Higgins:3.*

clown n. fool, idiot; generally derog. application *Price:2.*

clown around v. to play the fool *Heller.*

cluck n. a dull, stupid person; with the brains of a chicken *Junker.*

clucky a. (Aus. use) pregnant; ref. is to a broody hen *Neaman & Silver.*

clueless a. stupid, ignorant, incompetent.

clue one in v. to explain, to offer information *Greenlee.*

clunk n. a fool, an idiot.

clunk v. to hit, to strike.

clunker n. worn-out, useless car *The Collected Trashman 1969.*

clutch n. (UK 'society' use) a dance (the activity, not the event) *Barr.*

C-note n. $100 bill (cf:C) *Fiction Illus.3.*

CNR strawberries n. (Can. prison use) prunes *Caron.*

coal burner n. a white man or woman who enjoys sexual relations with a black man or woman *Maledicta.*

coat and badge v. (rhyming sl.) to cadge; usu. in 'on the C. and B.'; fr. Doggett's Coat and Badge, awarded to Thames watermen who, with this prize, had the right to charge higher fares in their mid-19th C. heyday *Cole.*

Coat-hanger n. (Aus. use) the Sydney Harbour Bridge; fr. its shape *Wilkes.*

cobber n. (Aus. use) friend, mate; fr. UK dialect *cob*: to take a liking to someone; like the other great clichéd Aus. word bonzer (qv) (cf:ripper) cobber is now nearly defunct *Ready.*

cobbler n. (US cant) a forger, esp. of passports, currency and stocks and bonds *Neaman & Silver.*

cobblers! (rhyming sl.) cobblers awls = balls (qv) = rubbish! *Powis.*

cobitis n. (UK prison use) loss of appetite, poss. fr. eating too many prison loaves ('cobs') *LL.*

cobs n. testicles; fr. cobblers (qv).

cock n. **1.** general term of address, esp. Cockney use; in itself an abbrev. of Cockney *Wright*; **2.** the penis.; UK and northern states of US; **3.** the vagina: southern states of US (cf: nuts 2) *Grogan*; **4.** US southern campus use: a woman, viewed solely as a sexual object *Underwood*; **5.** a man who is easy to sponge on; spec. one who buys more than his necessary share in a pub *Powis*; **6.** nonsense, rubbish; also *load of old cock.*

cock a deaf 'un v. to pretend to be deaf, or at least to ignore by 'not hearing' the speaker *Norman:2.*

cockamamy a. confused, ludicrous, fake, fraudulent, absurd *Rosten.*

cock and hen (bingo rhyming sl.) 10 (cf: Downing Street) *LL.*

cock and hen n. £10 *EN 1957.*

cock a snoot at v. to disdain, to ignore, to turn up one's nose.

cock block v. (US Black use) to ruin another man's sexual activities by stealing his girl, interrupting his seduction etc. *Folb.*

cock doctor n. venerealogist *Higgins:1.*

cock-eyed a. **1.** very drunk, fr. the inability to coordinate physically that accompanies such a state *Farrell*; **2.** eccentric, odd; out of true, at an angle *Wodehouse:JO.*

cock-hound n. (Black use) a man devoted to sex before all things; fr. the Southern use of cock as vagina rather than penis *Milner.*

cock it up v. **1.** (UK use) to blunder, to make a mistake; **2.** (Aus. use) for a woman to offer herself sexually in an obvious manner *Wilkes.*

cockle and hen (rhyming sl.) ten, usu. £10 (cf: cock and hen) *Cole.*

cock linnet n. (rhyming sl.) minute *Jones:J.*

cock movie n. pornographic film *Simmons.*

cock off v. to fail, to blunder *Higgins:1.*

cock pluck v. (US Black use) see finger-fuck *Folb.*

cocksman n. **1.** an exceptionally virile man *Price:1*; **2.** (US Black use) a male prostitute *Major.*

cock sparrow n. (rhyming sl.) barrow *Jones:J.*

cocksucker n. **1.** spec. fellatrix; **2.** generally abusive term. (cf: motherfucker) *Price:2.*

cocktease v. to lead on in a sexual manner but never to permit actual intercourse. Thus one who does this is a *cockteaser* (cf: pricktease, -teaser) *Price:2.*

cock up v. to make a mess of; to blunder.

cocky general term of address to a man *Wodehouse: MOJ.*

coco n. (abbrev.) coconut: head *Runyon:1.*

coconuts n. (drug use) cocaine *De Lannoy & Masterson.*

codger n. a fellow, a man; usu. in 'old codger' with the implication of crotchety old age *Hotten.*

codology n. the practice of teasing; fr. cod: to tease, to hoax *Sex Pistols, 'Dead Horse', 1979.*

cods n. testicles; orig. Middle Eng. usage *Humphries.*

cod's roe n. (rhyming sl.) = dough (qv) = money *Wright.*

cods wallop n. nonsense, rubbish, drivel.

coffeeand n. (abbrev.) coffee and cakes: the cheapest meal available in a cafe or diner; thus, in context, referring to cheap, minimal, second-rate: *coffeeand role* in the theatre is a small part that will pay for little more than snacks *Selby:1.*

coffee and cocoa (rhyming sl.) say so; thus cp: I should cocoa (esp. in 'Billy Cotton Band Show' BBC Light Prog. 1950s) *Cole.*

coffeeand pimp n. a smalltime pimp, whose girls barely make him a living, let alone provide the high style to which he should aspire *Green:2.*

coffee grinder n. old and unstable propellor-driven aeroplane *Higgins:3.*

coffeehouse v. (poker use) to bluff a rival verbally rather than by betting *Alvarez.*

coffin nail n. a cigarette, presumably from nicotine's cancerous potential *Uris.*

cognoscenti n. (homosexual use) the world of homosexuals, its style, language, ethos, etc. *Legman.*

coin n. money *Variety 1983.*

coin v. to make a great deal of money.

cojones n. (Sp.) testicles; used both to mean the physical organ and the metaphorical courage, and in both cases a synonym for balls (qv); popularized first by the works of Ernest Hemingway and latterly by

Puerto Rican immigrants to US *Rawson.*

coke n. cocaine (cf: C, Charlie, girl, etc.) *Milner.*

coke stare n. (US Black use) the evil eye; a deliberately aggressive and unpleasant look *Folb.*

cold a. **1.** (sporting use) out of form, below par *Sanchez*; **2.** (US teen. use) unpleasant, difficult, unnecessary; and by bad = good thus: excellent, first rate, superb *E. Beyer.*

cold n. (butchers' sl.) frozen, thus imported meat *Cole.*

cold case n. (US Black use) a very bad situation *Folb.*

cold-cock v. to knock out unconscious. (cf: cold-deck) *Grogan.*

cold-cunt v. (lesbian use) to ignore, to brush off; fr. cold shoulder (qv) *Maledicta.*

cold-deck v. to knock unconscious; fr. knock cold (qv) and deck (qv).

cold in hand a. (US Black use) without money, broke (qv) *Major.*

cold meat n. a corpse; thus *cold meat box*: a coffin; *cold meat cart*: hearse.

cold shot n. (US Black use) unnecessary and aggressive behaviour *Folb.*

cold shoulder v. to ignore, to snub.

cold turkey n. withdrawal from heroin addiction without any assistance from medication *Grogan.*

collar n. (drug use) the strip of paper wrapped around a dropper to ensure a tight fit with the needle *Burroughs:1*; **2.** an arrest *Goldman.*

collar and tie n. a masculine lesbian; fr. the use of men's clothing *Legman.*

collect v. (Aus. use) to be hit by, to collide with, usu. of a car *Wilkes.*

college n. gaol *Runyon.*

collegiate fucking (homosexual use) body to body rubbing (cf: Princeton rub) *Jay & Young.*

collie n. (Jamaican use) marijuana, ganga; thus *collie-man*: ganga seller *Thelwell.*

colly v. (US Black use) to understand, to comprehend *Major.*

colly-wobbles n. feelings of tension, fear or sickness, usu. seen as stemming from the stomach *Hotten.*

colours n. (Hells Angel use) the emblems of the Hells Angels, ie an embroidered patch of a winged skull wearing a motorcycle helmet, the name Hells Angels, the name of the chapter (town, etc.), the letters MC: motorcycle club *Thompson.*

combo n. **1.** a group of musicians; abbrev. combination; **2.** (criminal use) combination lock (on a safe) *Bukowski:1.*

comboozelated a. (US campus use) drunk *Underwood.*

come n., v. an orgasm; to achieve orgasm; thus *come a river*: for a woman to have multiple orgasms *Price: 2.*

come a cropper v. to suffer an accident, usu. a fall *Wodehouse:CW.*

come across v. **1.** to pay-up, esp. reluctantly *Wodehouse:AAG*; **2.** to deliver, to surrender, esp. sexually *Humphries.*

come-along n. (police use) a chain manacle *Stone.*

come and get it! (ex milit. use) general cry indicating that a meal is ready.

come a purler v. to fall down, to trip over an obstacle, usu. sustaining some form of injury *Wodehouse:AAG.*

come clean v. to confess, to make an admission (cf: make a clean breast of) *Gruber.*

come down v. to occur; to turn out.

come down v. for the effect – good or bad – of a given drug to end.

come down on aka: *come down fonky, come down hard*: to talk to severely, to criticize heavily; to assault *McFadden.*

come-freak n. anyone who is obsessed with physical sex and the delights thereof (cf: come, v) *Shulman.*

come it v. to act aggressively, often with no grounds for so doing *Hotten.*

come off it! stop it! don't keep trying that line, etc. *Manser.*

come on n. patter, sales or seduction talk, a line (qv) *M. Jagger, K.*

Richard, 'I'll Take You To The Top', 1982.

come-on v. to appear; esp. 'come on tough, come on nasty' etc. *Safire.*

come-on boy n. a male prostitute who entices a client and then, instead of sex, has him beaten and robbed by a confederate (cf: murphy game) *Legman.*

come one's cocoa **1.** to ejaculate, and thus; **2.** (UK police/criminal use) to inform or to confess one's crimes *Powis.*

come one's fat v. see: come one's cocoa *Powis.*

come one's guts v. (Aus. use) to give information to the police (cf: come one's cocoa, fat).

come one's lot v. see: come one's cocoa *Powis.*

come on like gangbusters v. to come on strong (qv); fr. US radio serial of 1940s which featured hard-hitting, intrepid crimefighters *Bruce:2.*

come on strong v. to make one's presence and opinions felt *Thompson.*

come on to v. to approach reasonably aggressively; to solicit *Jay & Young.*

come out v. to declare oneself as a homosexual; fr. coming out of the closet (qv) *Jay & Young.*

comer n. an ambitious, go-ahead person, 'the coming man' *Dunne.*

come the big note v. (Aus. use) to boast, to set oneself as a richer/more important person than is true (cf: big-note artist) *Wilkes.*

come the old acid v. to act contrarily, aggressively, to argue *Austin.*

come the old soldier v. to deceive another for one's own benefit, esp. to avoid an unpleasant task; a veteran, supposedly, knows every trick when it comes to avoiding onerous duties *Wright.*

come the raw prawn v. to act resentfully or unpleasantly; to be rude *Humphries.*

come the tin soldier v. see: come the old soldier *Powis.*

come through v. take over in an emergency; carry out requirements *Higgins:1.*

come to a sticky end v. to meet great misfortune, esp. a violent death or a gaol sentence; usu. said of a person already condemned as 'a bad lot'.

come undone v. to find oneself in difficulties *Safire.*

come unglued v. to become mentally and emotionally unstable *Neaman & Silver.*

come unstuck v. see: come undone.

comics n. (US milit, use) topographical maps *Del Vecchio.*

Commie n. (abbrev.) Communist (cf: reds) *Vidal.*

commo n. (US milit. use) (abbrev.) communication *Del Vecchio.*

Commo n. (Aus. use) Communist; commie refers to those who live in rural communes *Ready.*

commode-hugging drunk (US campus use) extremely drunk, to the point of hugging the lavatory bowl and vomiting within (cf: drive the porcelain bus, etc.) *Underwood.*

completely a. (Valley Girls (qv) use) all purpose term of approval (cf: clearly) *Pond.*

compo n. (Aus. use) workers' compensation, payment for time lost after an injury at work *Ready.*

con n. **1.** (abbrev.) confidence man, confidence trick/game *Powis*; **2.** (abbrev.) convict; thus *ex-con*: former prisoner *Price:2.*

con v. to fool a victim in one or another form of confidence trick *Powis.*

con and coal n. (rhyming sl.) the dole *Wright.*

Conan Doyle n.,v. (rhyming sl.) **1.** boil (on the neck); **2.** to boil (a kettle) *Jones:J.*

con artist n. confidence trickster, fraud (cf: artist) *Bleasdale.*

conch n. (US campus use) (abbrev.) conscientious: a devotedly hard worker (cf: cereb, grub, etc.) *Bernbach.*

condo n. (abbrev.) condominium *McFadden.*

confusion n. (West Indian use) a

street fight, a riot *Powis*.

conk n. **1.** nose *Humphries*; **2.** head *Waits*; **3.** fr. congolene, a fiery liquid used in the artificial straightening of naturally kinky black (Negro) hair: hair that has been thus treated *Goldman*.

conk v. to hit, to knock out *Selby:1*.

conk out v. to collapse, to break down, to malfunction *Wolfe:2*.

connect v. to obtain drugs, usu. by keeping a specific appointment with the connection (qv) *Burroughs:1*.

connection n. a supplier of drugs *Grogan*.

Connie n. (abbrev.) Lincoln Continental *Higgins:2*.

cono n. (New York Sp. use) cunt; thus, girls in the context of potential seduction *Pynchon*.

cons n. **1.** (prison use) (abbrev.) convicts *Cole*; **2.** (UK police use) (abbrev.) previous convictions *Laurie*.

Cons basketball shoes; fr. trade name 'Converse All-Stars' (cf: chucks) *Price:3*.

contract n. a paid assignment to murder a given victim, thus, *take out a contract on Higgins:1*.

convictitis n. (UK prison use) the illusion, fostered by too long a career in the prison service, that every prisoner is about to attack one for no other reason than that one is a warder *LL*.

cook v. to tamper with, to falsify; thus 'cook the books', 'cook the accounts' *Hotten*.

cook v. for a musician or group of musicians to be playing in harmony and particularly creatively.

cook v. (drug use) to prepare a narcotic (esp. heroin) for injection by heating a solution of powder and water for use in a syringe *Tuff Shit Comics*.

cook a mark v. (cant) to calm down one's victim when he has been stripped of his money, possessions, etc. *Neaman & Silver*.

cooker n. (drug use) a container, usu. a bottle cap, in which the mixture of heroin and water can be heated prior to drawing it into a syringe and thence injecting it into one's arm *Larner*.

cookie n. an attractive woman. fr. cookie=biscuit, a common example of the equation of sex and food in sl.

cookie pusher n. a young man who errs to the 'feminine side of life' – tea parties, conversation, the niceties of dress and of gossip, art rather than sport, etc; fr. the cakes that such men are continually passing around such tea parties *Green:2*.

cookies n. any form of desired object: sex or money *Milner*.

cooking a. responsive, appreciative, esp. of an audience *Bruce:1*.

cook one's goose v. to give someone their due deserts *Farrell*.

cool n. **1.** (street gang use) a temporary armistice between opposing gangs *Salisbury*; **2.** temper, poise, attitude to life and ability to deal with it *Price:2*.

cool v. to calm down, to deal with a problem *Goldman*.

cool a. calm, self-possessed, aware, sophisticated *Price:2*.

cool cat n. a sophisticated, competent, unruffled, able person (cf: cat) *Squeeze, 'Cool for Cats', 1980*.

cooler n. **1.** (US Black use) a funeral home (cf: chill, cold meat) *Klein*. **2.** punishment/solitary confinement cells *Caron*.

cool head n. (US campus use) a calm, unflappable person *Underwood*.

coolie n. (street gang use) any youth unaffiliated to a gang *Salisbury*.

cool it v. calm down; often as excl. 'cool it!' *Underwood*.

cool off v. **1.** to become bored *Burroughs:1*; **2.** to calm down.

cool out v. to calm down *Price:2*.

cool the rock v. (Valley Girls (qv) use) to calm down, to restrain one's excessive behaviour *Pond*.

coon n. (derog.) (abbrev.) racoon; a Black person *Price:2*.

coon-lover n. see: nigger-lover *Breslin*.

coop n. prison *Wodehouse:MS*.

coop v. (US police use) to sleep while on duty – in a motel room or similar hideaway *'Hill Street Blues', Thames TV, 1983.*

coot n. **1.** (US campus use) the vagina; **2.** (US campus use) females considered solely as sexual objects *Underwood*; **3.** a fool, a simpleton; usu. as old coot, silly old coot, etc.

cootie n. (US Black use) an inexperienced, naïve young person, keen to improve his/her status *Klein*.

cooze n. **1.** vagina, thus derog. euph. for cunt (qv) *Stone*; **2.** by extension, female (usu. promiscuous) *Schulberg*.

cop n. (abbrev.) copper (qv).

cop v. **1.** spec. to buy drugs. cf: score **2.** obtain, purchase *Price:2*; **3.** (UK criminal use) to receive bribes, esp. of a policeman *Powis*; **4.** (US pimp use) to seduce a girl, spec. with the intention of making her into a ho (qv) *Shulman*.

cop a bird v. to fellate (cf: bird) *Legman*.

copacetic a. aka *copasetic*: excellent, OK, first rate. fr. Yiddish *Waits*.

cop a cherry v. to take a girl's virginity (cf: cherrypop).

cop a dose v. to catch venereal disease *Humphries*.

cop a drop v. (UK police use) to accept a bribe. (cf: bung) *Laurie*.

cop a feel v. to indulge in some form of petting, but not intercourse *Higgins:1*.

cop a heel v. **1.** (US cant) aka: *cop and heel* to run off, to escape *Klein*: **2.** (US prison use) to attack fr. behind *Chandler: Notebk*.

cop a moke v. (US prison use) to escape, to go on the run *Neaman & Silver*.

cop an attitude v. (US Black use) to take a negative stance on a given topic; to make one's own position adamant despite prevailing opinions and pressures *Klein*

cop and blow v. **1.** (Black pimp use) to exploit an unsatisfactory prostitute for as much money as possible before discarding her *Shulman*; **2.** (US teen use) to make a purchase and then leave; of fast food, drugs, prostitutes, etc. *Sculatti*.

cop a packet v. to gain a great deal, poss. more than one bargained for this can either be good – more money than expected – or bad – a longer gaol sentence than feared *LL*.

cop a plea v. (US criminal use) to plead guilty to a lesser charge in return for the dropping of a major one (cf: cop out 2) *Dunne*.

cop a squat (US Black use) sit down, make yourself at home *Klein*.

cop a tube v. (surf use) to catch a perfect wave *Pond*.

cop it v. usu. abbrev: cop it hot: to get into trouble, to suffer in a given way, spec. *cop a packet*: to be severely wounded or hurt.

cop one's joint v. to perform fellatio *Goldman*.

copout n. a coward, a runner away from problems, a weakling *Underwood*.

cop out v. **1.** to avoid a problem or a difficult situation; to run away; to give up trying; **2.** (US criminal use) to use legal plea bargaining to plead guilty to a lesser charge in return for having a major one dropped *Klein*.

cop out on v. to inform against *Bruce:2*.

copper n. **1.** a policeman; from the copper badges carried by New York City's first policemen, c. 1850 *Grogan*; **2.** (US prison use) good conduct marks; a prisoner who gains such marks is considered to resemble a policeman.

copper-hearted a. (US prison use) an informer by nature *Chandler: Notebk*.

copper v. to inform.

copper jitters n. (drug/criminal use) excessive fear of the police, verging on obsession *Burroughs:1*.

copper nob n. a red-headed person.

copping n. (UK criminal/police use) the practice by bent (qv) policemen, of taking bribes from criminals, either to turn a blind eye when necessary, to drop charges, lose evidence, etc. *Powis*.

copping clothes n. (US pimp use) particularly smart, legitimate suit of clothes, worn specifically to entice and seduce potential hos (qv) *Shulman.*

cop shop n. police station (cf: bill shop).

cop some z's v. to sleep *Milner.*

cop the lot v. to gain everything *Performance.*

cor! aka: *gor*: euph. for God, as in *cor blimey*: God blind me! *Wright.*

corked a drunk *Dickson.*

corker n. anything excellent, superlative, first rate *Mortimer.*

corksacking (euph.) cocksucking (qv); coined by Anthony Burgess in *NYT* 1972.

cornball a. naïve, unsophisticated (cf: corny) *Grogan.*

corned drunk; fr. corn whiskey *Runyon.*

corner v. aka *lawing* (UK criminal use) **1.** a confidence trick whereby shoddy goods are sold by pretending they are in fact high-grade stolen property and playing on the 'thrill' some people derive from such a purchase; **2.** arranging to sell stolen goods and then having fake 'policemen' break in, confiscate the goods and threaten the victim with charges of receiving; these charges can, naturally, be dropped in return for a bribe which is arranged by a fake 'solicitor' who makes sure there is no real police involvement by assuring the victim that he has no rights in law and that paying and shutting up is the best thing to do *Powis.*

corner cowboys n. idlers who while away their days standing and gossiping on street corners *Schulberg.*

cornhole v. to have anal intercourse *Jay & Young.*

corn on the cob n. (US Black use) sexual intercourse in which the partners are partially clad *Klein.*

cornpone n. a person obviously from the South of the US; fr. the food of the same name *Major.*

corny a. sentimental, naïve, unsophisticated; all such characteristics are attributed to country folk, surrounded by cornfields.

corporation cocktail n. coal gas bubbled through milk, a down-and-out alcoholic's tipple, although in an age of North Sea gas this drink is redundant.

corpse v. (theatrical use) to cause (intentionally or not) a fellow performer to forget their lines and/or laugh on stage *Green:2.*

corrode v.i. (US campus use) to be overcome with disgust or repulsion *Underwood.*

corroded a. (US Black use) unappealing, unattractive *Folb.*

COs n. (taxi driver use) police officers who specialize in checking on laws that affect cabs and their drivers *Powis.*

cossie n. (Aus. use) swimming costume *Humphries:2.*

cost ya! (abbrev.) it will cost you something: ie don't ask for favours, but most things can be done – for a price *LL.*

cot-case n. (Aus. use) an invalid *Humphries:2.*

cottage n. (UK homosexual use) anywhere male homosexuals gather for sex; often a public lavatory (cf: glory hole).

cotton n. **1.** (drug use) small piece of material through which heroin has been sucked up into a syringe and which can be boiled, when no better supplies exist, to extract one final emergency fix (qv) *Burroughs:1*; **2.** (US Black use) female pubis *Folb.*

cotton-picking a. derog. term of abuse implying second rate, vulgarity, etc. *Selby:1.*

cough v. to confess, to inform.

cough drop n. a 'character', a 'card' (qv) *Wodehouse: MOJ.*

cough up v. to reveal, to hand over (objects or information).

couldn't fight one's way out of a paper bag (cp) implying physical weakness on the part of the subject.

couldn't knock the skin off a rice-pudding (cp) contemptuous dismissal of a weakling, or supposed weakling.

couldn't organize a fuck in a brothel (cp) utterly incompetent.

couldn't run a piss-up in a brewery (cp) an individual of such minimal competence that even provided with everything necessary to achieve a given aim, that aim remains beyond him/her.

council houses n. (rhyming sl.) trousers *Powis.*

country cousin n. (rhyming sl.) a dozen *Jones:J*

cousin n. (homosexual use) the lover of another homosexual *Legman.*

cove n. a person, a man; fr. Romany *Wodehouse VGJ.*

cover one's ass v. to look after oneself *Higgins:1.*

cover the sheet v. (US police use) to make one's arrest quota *Neaman & Silver.*

cover-up n. an alibi, concealment, usu. illegal or at least unethical.

cow n. an obese, unattractive female.

cowabunga! (surf use) excl. of pleasure, victory (over the waves), etc. *Green:2.*

cowboy n. **1.** (US Black use) see *bad-ass nigger Folb*; **2.** a tradesman who ignores the basic ethics and business standards of his peers but aims only for money; thus *cowboy builder*, *cowboy plumber* etc *Bleasdale.*

Cowboy City n. (US trucker use) Cheyenne, Wyoming *CB.*

cowlick n. a hairstyle, smoothed down over the forehead, that looks as if a cow had licked it into place (cf: duck's arse, DA).

cowpoke n. cowboy *Chandler:LG.*

cow's n. (rhyming sl.) cow's calf = half = ten shillings *Norman:2.*

cowyard confetti n. (Aus. use) euph. for bullshit (qv) *Wilkes.*

cozzer n. policeman; fr. Heb. *chazer*: pig, thus harking back to *Lexicon Balatronicum* (1815) at least *Newman:1.*

crab v. to spoil, to upset, to ruin *rr.*

crabby a. nagging, cantankerous *Higgins:2.*

crack n. **1.** a joke; **2.** a try, a chance *Price:2*; **3.** a remark *Runyon:1*; **4.** vagina.

crack v. **1.** to work something out, to find a solution; **2.** to hit *Price:2.*

crack a bottle v. to have a drink *Hotten.*

crack a cherry v. to take a girl's virginity (cf: cop a cherry, etc.) *Grogan.*

crack a fat v. (Aus. use) to achieve erection *Humphries.*

crack a tube v. (Aus. use) to open a can of beer *Humphries:2.*

cracked a. insane, crazy, eccentric *Bleasdale.*

cracker n. **1.** poor Southern US white farmer *Bruce:1*; **2.** an attractive (young) female; usu. as in 'a little cracker'.

crackerbarrel a. homespun philosophies; fr. the cracker (biscuit) barrel that could once be found in every US small town general store, surrounded by ageing sages offering the wisdom of their lifetimes (cf: scuttlebutt).

crackerjack a. excellent, first class, superlative *Vidal.*

crackers a. mad, crazy *Humphries.*

crack it v. to achieve a successful (from the male point of view) seduction *Ready.*

crackle n. (UK criminal use) banknotes, usu. £5 and up *LL.*

cracko n. a madman, a lunatic (cf: crackpot) *Shulman.*

crack on v. to tell tales, to boast *Waterhouse.*

crack one's face v. aka: *crack a smile*: to laugh, to smile.

crack one up v. to make someone laugh *Price: 3.*

crackpot n. an eccentric *Dury, 'Laughter', 1981.*

crack something up v. to promote an event, object, idea, etc.

crack the books v. to open books, thus to read *Vidal.*

crack up n. a nervous breakdown, a mental collapse *F. S. Fitzgerald, bk* *title, 1936.*

crack up v. **1.** to laugh uproariously *Goldman*; **2.** to crash – a car, an airplane, etc. *Heller.*

crack wise v. to make a 'clever' comment that impresses no one (cf: wiseguy) *McFadden.*

cracky (euph) Christ (cf: crikey) *Rawson.*

cradle-snatcher n. an older person, usu. a woman, who prefers affairs with people substantially younger than they are.

crag n. (US campus use) irritable, nagging woman *Underwood.*

crank n. any form of amphetamine drug; such drugs 'crank up' one's bodily motor *Thompson.*

crank v. (Valley Girls (qv) use) all-purpose word; 'like you crank yourself together or you crank to school, or you crank up the radio . . .' *Pond.*

crank it out v. to write (usu. rubbish) more from duty than pleasure or interest; to be a hack writer *Higgins:5.*

crank up v. to inject narcotics with a hypodermic syringe *Caron.*

crap n. **1.** spec. excrement; **2.** rubbish, nonsense, anything useless *Bruce:1.*

crap v. **1.** to go to the lavatory, defecate; **2.** *crap around*: fool about, tell deliberate lies *Dunne.*

crapbrain n. general term of abuse, based on alleged stupidity of the recipient *'Hill Street Blues', Thames TV, 1983.*

craphouse n. **1.** lavatory; **2.** any unpleasant, dirty place; **3** (show business use) a small, unfashionable venue *Bruce:2.*

crap out v. **1.** to fail, to go wrong, to blunder; fr. the losing throws in dice *Laugh in the Dark*; **2.** to collapse, to become exhausted, to fall asleep *Goldman.*

crapper n. **1.** lavatory (cf: crap) *May*; **2.** the anus, the buttocks *Rawson.*

crappo a. disgusting, appalling (cf: crappy) *Price:3.*

crappy a. unpleasant, disgusting, vile, revolting; fr. crap (qv).

crap-shoot n. any situation in which luck, not judgement, is of paramount importance; fr. gambling game of craps.

crash n. (Aus. use) an excretion *Ready.*

crash v. **1.** to sleep, collapse exhausted, spec. after a bout of heavy drug (esp. amphetamine) use *Lou Reed, 'Take a Walk on the Wild Side', 1972*; **2.** (abbrev.) gate-crash: to appear uninvited at a given party or other function *Wodehouse:AAG*; **3.** (UK police use) to drop enquiries into a given case *Powis.*

crasher n. **1.** an uninvited guest at a party; **2.** someone who collapses from fatigue *Thompson*; **3.** a bore *Obs. 1983.*

crash-pad n. a flat or house in which any passing friends or strangers can find a bed at short notice (cf: crash) *Uneeda Comix.*

crawfish n. (US campus use) a stingy, mean person *Underwood.*

crawfish v. **1.** to grovel, to abase oneself before another *N. Mailer, 'The Naked and the Dead', 1947*; **2.** to back down, to renege on a previous statement, committment; fr. the movements of the fish *Chandler:LG.*

crawling a. infested with insects or vermin.

crazy **1.** keen on, enthusiastic. esp. as *crazy for Price:2*; **2.** (excl.) wonderful, amazing, etc.; mainly used in beatnik/bop jazz era of 1940s/50s.

crazy alley n. (US prison use) a special part of a prison used for insane prisoners *Chandler: Notebk.*

crazy-ass a. insane, utterly eccentric *Burroughs:Jr.*

crazy for extremely enthusiastic.

crazy house n. lunatic asylum, mental hospital *Dunne.*

cream n. semen.

cream v. **1.** to destroy, to beat up comprehensively, to overcome easily *Price:2*; **2.** to win a sporting competition decisively *Higgins:5*; **3.** to achieve orgasm.

creaming n. (UK criminal use) stealing from one's employer, usu. on a small, but protracted scale *Powis*.

cream one's jeans v. to ejaculate spontaneously (while dressed) on seeing a supremely erotic sight; often used only figuratively and meaning over-excited, even if not erotically *Humphries*.

cream puff n. (derog.) a homosexual or a generally weak man *Schulberg:2*.

cream puff freak n. (pimp use) a client who likes to throw gooey cakes at a girl and thus achieve sexual arousal *OUI 8/75*.

creamstick n. (US Black use) the penis (cf: cream, n.) *Klein*.

creamie n. an attractive and sexually malleable female *Bleasdale*.

crease v. to beat severely *Austin*.

creased a. exhausted, tired out.

crease up v. to collapse with laughter.

cred n. (abbrev.) credibility *Capital Radio 1983*.

creep n. an unpleasant person, poss. inference of some physical peculiarity, criminality *Price:2*.

creep v. **1.** to forego one's pride and beg unashamedly; to curry favour, to suck up to (qv) (cf: bootlick); **2.** (US pimp use) for a prostitute to distract her trick (qv) while an accomplice slips into the room and rifles his wallet; since he always has to pay in advance, he won't check his money till they have parted *Shulman*; **3.** to perform a theft, esp. the activities of a sneak thief *Norman*; **4.** (US campus use) to go out on the town *Underwood*.

creeper n. (UK cant/police use) a sneak thief *Cole*.

creeping and tilling (US Black use) diverting a store cashier's attention while a confederate opens and robs the till *Klein*.

creeping Jesus n. a whining, sneaking person.

creepsville n. any unappealling place *Underwood*.

creepy a. unpleasant, suspicious, menacing *Higgins:5*.

creepy-crawly n. an insect; usu. juv. use.

crew n. **1.** a gang, usu. football supporters, who engage in fights with rivals *Robins*; **2.** (US use) a gang of graffitti artists, rap singers or break dancers (qqv) *Wild Style, film 1983*.

crib n. **1.** a small, cheap brothel; fr. early 19th C. use: a room, a lodging *Salisbury*; **2.** a safe *Chandler: Notebk*; **3.** house, apartment, anywhere one lives *Price:2*; **4.** (student use) examination or other aids which help with answers to homework, or actual cheating in exams.

crib v. (student use) to cheat.

crib man n. (US cant) one who specializes in breaking into houses and apartments *Neaman & Silver*.

cribsheet n. see: *crib*.

crikey! (excl.) euph. for Christ! *Humphries*.

Crimea n. (rhyming sl.) beer *Wright*.

criminey! (euph.) Christ! *Rawson*.

Crimson n. (US college use) Harvard University *Bernbach*.

crinched a. (US campus use) bent, dented; fr. crimped + pinched *Underwood*.

crinkle top n. (US Black use) a female with an Afro (qv) or natural (qv) haircut *Folb*.

cripes! (euph.) Christ! *Rawson*.

crispy n. (Valley Girls (qv) use) anyone whose faculties seem impaired by an excess – of drugs, drink, etc – and is thus 'burnt out' *Pond*.

criss cross v. (US Black use) to deceive or cheat; development of double-cross *Klein*.

croak v. **1.** to die *Humphries*; **2.** to kill *Rawson*.

croaker n. doctor *Chandler: Notebk*.

crock n. (abbrev.) crock of shit: useless, unpleasant event or experience *Price:2*.

crocked a. drunk *Klein*.

crocko a. drunk *Dickson*.

crock of shit n. see: crock.

crombie n. overcoat, fr. trade name of a particular coat, particularly beloved by skinheads (qv) of late 1960s.

cronky a. (Aus. use) corrupt, dishonest, lying; fr. racing use *Humphries*.

crook **1.** defective, useless, unpleasant (of people) *Humphries*; **2.** ill *Humphries:2.*

crooked on (Aus. use) averse to, hostile to (cf: crook) *Wilkes.*

crop n. (US campus (spec. U. of Arkansas) use) fifth of a gall. of wine *Underwood.*

cross v. (abbrev.) double-cross: to betray, to let down *Schulberg.*

cross bar hotel n. (US use) prison *Neaman & Silver.*

cross-eyed a. drunk *Dickson.*

cross man n. (US Black use) anyone who manipulates others for his own advantage; fr. double-cross *Klein.*

cross up v. to betray, to double-cross *Chandler:LG.*

crotch n. a woman; a concentration on her physical sexuality *Higgins:3.*

crotch cheese n. unwashed vaginal secretion found in less than ideally clean females (cf: headcheese) *Klein.*

crow n. **1.** an unattractive woman *Runyon:1*; **2.** (UK criminal use) a lookout man in a street game of three-card monte (qv) *Powis.*

crowd pleaser n. (US police use) the officer's gun; an ironic use *Neaman & Silver.*

crow eaters n. (Aus. use) South Australians *Bickerton.*

Crow Jimism the reverse of anti-Black discriminatory Jim Crow laws (qv); thus guilt-induced affection for and fascination with Blacks by white liberals *Bruce:2.*

Crow MacGee a. (US prison use) no good, unreal, false *Chandler: Notebk.*

crown v. to hit over the head *Goulart.*

crown jewels n. male genitals *Stanley.*

crud n. **1.** spec. dried semen, on the body, clothes or bedlinen; **2.** any disease; **3.** dirt, in general *Selby:1*; **4.** an unappealing person *Underwood.*

cruddy a. useless, no good, lousy, second rate *Price:3.*

crude n. (US police use) a tip-off from an informer; as opposed to a communication, a complaint from a member of the public *Neaman & Silver.*

crude a. (US Black use) worthless, excess and as such useless *Klein.*

cruise v.t. to approach someone obviously with sexual intent; both for commercial or non-commercial purposes *A. Hanson.*

cruise v. **1.** spec. to search for sexual contacts by walking specific streets, areas, etc. **2.** to drive around, often along a town's main street, surveying the situation, looking for friends, girls to pick up, etc. *Tuff Shit Comics.*

cruise a. (Valley Girls (qv) use) easy, simple, useful; describing anything suitable for cruising (cf: cruise) *Pond.*

cruisemobile (Valley Girls (qv) use) any favoured car *Pond.*

cruiser n. **1.** prostitute *Higgins:1*; **2.** a marked police car that patrols given streets.

crumb crusher n. (US Black use) a baby who is just learning to eat solids *Klein.*

crumbly n. (UK 'society' use) an older person, c.50–70 (cf: wrinkly, dusty) *Barr.*

crumbs! (euph.) Christ! usu. child use only, prob. the mildest of such euphemisms.

crumb-snatcher n. see: crumb crusher *Folb.*

crumbum a. useless, awful, second rate, inferior *Price:3.*

crumby a. see: crummy *a. Sillitoe.*

crummy a. second-rate, inferior, unpleasant *Burroughs:1.*

crummy n. (logger use) pickup trucks that transport loggers to and from camps *Wolfe:2.*

crumpet n. a girl or woman; example of sex/food equation (cf: bit of crackling, cookie) *Humphries.*

crunch n. the ultimate aspect of a given situation, a more aggressive and crisis laden bottom line (qv); often in 'when it comes to the crunch . . .' *Dickson.*

cruncher n. (Aus. prison use) a small-time criminal *Neaman & Silver.*

crush n. **1.** a sexual interest in someone *The Roches, 'Nurds'*;

2. (lesbian use) the vagina *Maledicta.*

crush out n. (US cant) a means of obliterating the body and the evidence of a murder by putting the corpse into a car and the car through a junkyard crushing machine *Neaman & Silver.*

crust n. cheek, audacity, nerve *Wodehouse passim.*

crust of bread n. (rhyming sl.) the head (cf: loaf of bread) *Franklyn.*

crutch n. see: roach clip *Folb.*

cry hughie v. to vomit; fr. alleged noise the vomiting makes: herwaaagghh!! (cf: cry ralph, cry ruth) *Billy Connolly passim.*

crying a. general intensifier; esp. in crying shame (n) *Algren.*

cry ralph v. to vomit; fr. alleged sound of being sick (cf: cry huey, cry ruth) *Billy Connolly passim.*

cry ruth v. to vomit *Humphries.*

crystal n. powdered Methedrine *Goldman.*

cry Uncle! v. to beg someone to stop an action, to surrender *Jay & Young.*

cs (abbrev.) chickenshit (qv) (cf: bs) *Rawson.*

cube n. (drug use) morphine; fr. the shape of bulk supplies *Green:1.*

cuckoo a. crazy, eccentric, insane *Heller.*

cuddle and kiss n. (rhyming sl.) miss, thus a girl *Jones:J.*

cuff v. **1.** to hide a cigarette or marijuana joint (qv) inside the cupped fingers *Larner*; **2.** (US Black use) to hit, to fight *Folb*; **3.** to place on credit (cf: on the cuff) *Bukowski:6.*

cuffs n. (UK police/criminal use) (abbrev.) handcuffs *LL.*

cuffs and collars pubic hair that matches the colour of the visible hair; thus ostensibly proving that a woman is not dyeing her hair *Price:2.*

cull n. (US campus use) **1.** a socially unacceptable person; **2.** spec. fraternity use: anyone rejected for membership in fraternity/sorority; fr. hunting/countryside use *Underwood.*

cull bird n. (US campus use) any female considered socially/physically unacceptable *Underwood.*

culture fruit n. see: African golf ball.

culture-vulture n. anyone who battens on to the prevailing cultural trends in order to debase and exploit them for economic gain, irrespective of the aesthetic loss involved *Hoffman:a.*

cum v. to achieve orgasm; often found as alternative to come (qv) to enhance the sexual aspect of the otherwise common word *Bukowski:2.*

cum freak a man obsessed with sexual gratification (cf: cock hound) *Folb.*

cunt n. **1.** the vagina; fr. Middle Eng. orig., but taboo since 15th C.; among many (obs.) euphemisms is 'the divine monosyllable'; **2.** a fool, a dolt, an unpleasant person – of either sex (cf: prick).

cuntlapper n. **1.** general term of abuse *Higgins:3*; **2.** spec. cunnilinctor *Legman.*

cunt positive (lesbian use) the concept of appreciating the vagina despite its secondary image in a phallocentric world *Jay & Young.*

cupcake n. **1.** spec. the female breast *Higgins:4*; **2.** an attractive (young) female.

cuppa n. aka: *cupper*: a cup of tea *Performance.*

cup of tea n. personal preference; ie: 'she's my cup of tea . . .' etc.

curly (one) n. a tricky problem, a challenge.

curly wolf n. a tough, tricky character; fr. qualities of the animal.

currant bun n. (rhyming sl.) the sun *Cole.*

curse n. (euph.) menstrual period *'Serpico', directed S. Lumet, 1973.*

cushy a. soft, comfortable, easy, etc. *LL.*

cuss out v. to curse; to attack verbally, to criticize *Seale.*

custard and jelly n. (rhyming sl.) telly = television *Jones:J.*

custards n. (Aus. use) pimples, acne; fr. pus such eructations contain *Ready.*

cut n. **1.** (US sporting use) a pre-arranged point at which a group of competitors or recruits to a team are reduced by those who fail to achieve a given standard; thus *make the cut*: to continue on the team, in the competition, etc.; **2.** a share, of profits, of loot, of the proceeds of a robbery, etc.

cut a. drunk; fr. *cut one's leg*, a facetious ref. to a staggering drunk.

cut v. **1.** for a manager or agent to take a percentage of a client's money, esp. in boxing use *Heller*; **2.** to dilute a drug with some adulterant *Larner*; **3** (US campus use) to have sexual intercourse *Underwood.*

cut and carried a. (rhyming sl.) married (cf: cash and carried) *Jones:J.*

cut a side v. **1.** (US Black use) to have sexual intercourse; **2.** (musician use) to record a song, one side of a 45 rpm or a number of songs, one side of a 33 rpm record.

cut a slice (off the joint) v. to have sexual intercourse (male point of view).

cutchie n. (Jamaican use) a pipe used for smoking ganja, marijuana *Thelwell.*

cut down to size v. to reduce a person's (high) opinion of him/herself to a realistic estimate.

cutesie a. excessively sweet, cloying.

cutesie-pie **1.** see: cutesie; **2.** an attractive female, usu. young, poss. a given male's girlfriend.

cutie n. pretty young girl *Capital Radio 1983.*

cut it v. to manage, to deal with (difficult) situations *Price:2.*

cut it out! just stop that! *Manser.*

cut it up v. to have an uproarious good time; 'cutting the rug' *Thompson:J.*

cut loose v. **1.** to terminate, to let go, to get rid of *Milner*; **2.** to abandon restraints, either in one's action or, in an argument, in one's language and abuse.

cut no ice v. make no impression, fail to impress *Austin.*

cut off at the pass v. to intercept, to ambush: metaphorically as well as physically; fr. the cliché of many Westerns 'I'll cut them off . . .' *PT.*

cut (out) v. to leave *Selby:1.*

cuts and scratches n. (rhyming sl.) matches *Jones:J.*

cut that out! (excl.) stop doing that! *rr.*

cut the cake v. (US black use) to deflower a virgin *Klein.*

cut the crap! (excl.) don't try to fool me! stop talking rubbish! etc. *Southern & Hoffenberg.*

cut the mustard v. to come up to a given standard *Dury, 'Laughter'.*

cut the rug v. to dance.

cutthroat n. see: badass nigger *Folb.*

cutty n. (US Black use) a friend, a close intimate *Folb.*

cut up v. to divide, esp. money, loot *Higgins:1.*

cut up rough v. to react unpleasantly, to become annoyed *Wodehouse:VGJ.*

cut up rusty v. see: cut up rough.

cut up touches v. (US cant) **1.** to reminisce over old successes, major villanies, etc. **2.** to share out the spoils of criminal acts.

cuz (US Black use) fr. abbrev. cousin: form of address between black males *Folb.*

CYA (US civil service use) (abbrev.) Cover Your Ass (qv): the basic admonition to anyone, at any level, working in government.

D n. (Aus. use) (abbrev.) detective *Wilkes*.
da n. **1.** (abbrev.) *d*uck's *a*ss: a style of haircut popular in 1950s but still found *White*; **2.** (US campus use) (abbrev.) *d*umb *a*ss = fool, idiot *Underwood*.
dabs n. fingerprints *Powis*.
dachsie n. (abbrev.) dachshund *Barr*.
dad- (euph.) God; thus *dad-blamed*, *dad-blasted*, etc.: all reasonably mild exclamations.
dad and dave v. (Aus. use) **1.** (rhyming sl.) to shave *Bickerton*; **2.** fr. popular 1930s radio serial concerning various aspects of rural Aus. life: hayseed, peasant, unsophisticated person *Wilkes*.
daddy n. **1.** (UK prison use) a leader – through intimidation and other influence – of the inmates in a Borstal (cf: baron) *R. Minton, 'Scum', 1981*; **2.** a masculine lesbian (cf: papa) *Legman*; **3.** (US Black use) form of address to a black male; *daddy-o* (qv) beloved of 1950s white beatniks is now obs. *Himes:1*; **4.** the supreme example, the most important/powerful/well-known, etc.; often as *the daddy of them/us all*; **5.** 'Masculine' lesbian *Maledicta*.
daddy-o term of address; orig. black use, then permeated white beatnik and latterly hippie culture, generally obs. now *Bukowski:1*.
daddy one n. (US Black use) a lover or any man who provides for a given woman *Folb*.
daffadown dilly (rhyming sl.) silly (cf: daffy) *Jones:J*.
daffy a. eccentric, foolish; esp. in *daffy about*: madly in love with *Runyon*.
daft a. foolish, silly *Dury, 'Do It Yourself', 1979*.
dag n. (Aus. use) **1.** unenterprising person, a coward; **2.** a card (qv), a character *Humphries*.
dagger n. see: bull-dagger.
dago n. (derog) Italian (US), South American (UK).
Dago n. (US trucker use) San Diego, California *CB*.
dago red n. cheap, rotgut red wine, usu. drunk by alcoholics; orig. the cheap home-produced red wine made by Italian families and merchandized, during Prohibition, by Italian gangsters.
daily n. **1.** (abbrev.) daily help, charwoman; **2.** (fr. rhyming sl.) *Daily Mail* = tail = rear end; thus *up one's daily*: following close behind *Newman:1*.
daily-daily n. (US milit. use) anti-malaria pills that must be taken every day; pun on berri-berri (?) *Del Vecchio*.
Daily Getsmuchworse n. the *Daily Express Private Eye passim*.
Daily Mail n. **1.** (rhyming sl.) tail = buttocks *Powis*; **2.** (rhyming sl.) tale, thus a lie *Jones:J*.
dairies n. (US Black use) the female

breasts; fr. lactation *Folb.*

daisy n. **1.** anything particularly appealing, excellent; **2.** a male homosexual; **3.** (US Black use) a housewife *Klein.*

daisy chain n. a circle of people, hetero- or homosexual, all linked physically in mutual sex acts *Legman.*

daisy roots n. (rhyming sl.) boots *L. Donegan, 'My Old Man's a Dustman', 1960.*

daks n. (Aus. use) trousers; fr. trade name Daks, popular trouser tailors *Ready.*

damage n. the cost; usu. in 'what's the damage?' *Humphries:2.*

damager n. (boxing and theatrical use) joke corruption of word manager, implying his alleged effect on those whose livelihoods are in his hands *Powis.*

dame n. woman; often with the implication of promiscuity *McBain:1.*

damn all nothing, absolutely zero, etc.; euph. fuck all (qv) *Manser.*

damned clever, these Chinese (cp) remarking on some particularly ingenious invention; the attribution is less to the skill of the Chinese than to their supposed wiliness.

damn tootin' absolutely, completely accurate, no doubt at all *Farrell.*

damp n. the vagina *Southern & Hoffenberg.*

damper n. **1.** a small safe, a cashbox *Runyon:1*; **2.** (Can. prison use) solitary confinement, punishment cells *Caron*; **3.** anything which diminishes pleasure, which 'dampens' the warmth of one's emotions.

dance v. to steal from first or higher floors; dance implies Fred Astaire, thus stairs, up which the villain must climb *Powis.*

dance on one's lips v. to hit in the face; to kick *Folb.*

dance on the mattress v. to make love; to have sexual intercourse *Klein.*

D&D a. **1.** (police use) *d*runk and *d*isorderly; **2.** deaf and dumb.

dandy a. attractive, first-rate, excellent; a general term of approbation *Jenkins.*

dang a. (euph.) damn *Rawson.*

dap n. (US milit. use) a ritualistic handshake, differing as to unit, involving much slapping of palms, snapping of fingers, etc. (cf: give some skin, etc.) *Del Vecchio.*

dap a. (US Black use) (abbrev.) dapper, well-dressed; *dap to a tee*: very well dressed *Folb.*

daps n. gym shoes, tennis shoes *K. Clarke.*

darbies n. (UK police/criminal use) handcuffs; fr. a moneylender's bond of particular severity known as 'Father Darby's bands' *LL.*

Darby Kelly (rhyming sl.) belly, often as 'Darby Kel' *Powis.*

darkie n. (derog.) Black person *P. Tinniswood, 'The Home Front', 1983.*

dark meat n. Blacks, esp. as sex objects (cf: white meat) *White.*

darkness at noon (US campus use) the slide shows that form the basis of lectures in Art History *Bernbach.*

darn (euph.) damn; thus varieties incl. *goldarn*, *gosh darn* (both using euphs. for 'God') *Rawson.*

darry n. (UK prison use) a look; fr. 19th C. *derrey*: an eyeglass *LL.*

dash n. (Nigerian use) bribery; the money paid as a bribe *ST 6/2/83.*

dash! general euph, both for fuck (qv) damn (qv) etc.; fr. the — that a less candid age would use for the printed obscenity; thus *dash it*, *dashed*, etc. *Manser.*

dash in the bloomers n. sexual intercourse, usu. quick and adulterous *Higgins:5.*

date n. (Aus. use) the anus, the backside as a whole; fr. dot *Wilkes.*

date v. **1.** (Aus. use) to goose (qv) someone; fr. date, *n* (qv) *Wilkes*; **2.** to have an affair with someone, to be 'going out with' on a number of pre-arranged days *Price:2.*

daughter n. a male homosexual brought into the gay world by a homosexual friend *Stanley.*

Davy Jones' locker n. a watery grave;

fr. at least 1774.

daylight v. (US Black use) to enlighten, to explain *Klein.*

dead a. **1.** of glasses or bottles: empty *Biff Comix, 1981*; **2.** finished, lost, spec. arrested, captured *Higgins:3*; **3.** absolutely, extremely, very *Performance.*

dead as a dodo a. absolutely dead, utterly irrelevant (of information, news); fr. the bird last seen alive in Mauritius in the 1680s.

deadbeat n. a failure, a down-and-out *Fiction Illus:3.*

dead cert n. absolute certainty, esp. in race course betting *Sillitoe.*

dead duck n. a complete, irredeemable failure *Vidal.*

Dead End Street n. the vagina *Maledicta.*

deadhead v. to ride for free; to drive a cab, airplane, etc. without its usual load, passengers, etc. *Higgins:4.*

deadhead a. useless, spec. non-participant *Higgins:3.*

deadeye n. the anus *Klein.*

dead-eye dick n. (homosexual use) one who performs anal intercourse fr. nickname for a superlative marksman *Legman.*

dead from the neck up a. anyone considered particularly stupid.

dead man's shoes (US Black use) anything that one would rather not have to experience but which probably cannot be avoided *Klein.*

dead marine n. (Aus. use) an empty bottle (cf: dead soldier) *Wilkes.*

dead meat n. **1.** a corpse; **2.** a stupid, dull person *Klein.*

deadpan a. expressionless, fr. dead+pan (face) *Howard.*

deadpan v. to speak without expression, esp. in a situation that would normally demand some emotion *Price:3.*

dead pigeon n. a guaranteed and absolute failure, often in context of a forthcoming election *Vidal.*

dead set a. (Aus. use) absolute, perfect, exact, ideal, etc. *Humphries:2.*

dead set on a. fascinated by, obsessed with, in love with.

dead shot n. (US Black use) the insertion of the penis into either the vagina or anus *Klein.*

dead soldier an empty bottle.

dead time n. (US prison use) any time spent in prison which does not actually diminish one's sentence *Klein.*

dead to rights a. **1.** certain, sure; **2.** caught in the act (cf: bang to rights) *Algren.*

dead to the wide aka: *dead to the world*; utterly and completely exhausted *Sillitoe.*

dead 'un n. (Aus. use) in horse-racing, a mount that seems not to have been raced to its full capacity *Wilkes.*

deal v. to sell drugs, esp. marijuana (cf: connect) *Green:1.*

death on a. dealing very strictly and severely with employees, business partners, etc. *Klein.*

Dear John n. a letter concluding a relationship, usu. sent by the woman and received by the man, often in prison or serving in the forces *Pearce.*

death! (US school use) excl. of approval or admiration *E. Beyer.*

de-bag v. to remove someone's trousers, usu. as a somewhat heavyweight joke; fr. *bags*: trousers 19 C.-mid 20 C.; now obs. except in some (public) school use *Dickson.*

debs n. (street gang use) the girl-friends or girl members of a street gang *Salisbury.*

debut n. first homosexual experience *Jay & Young.*

debutante n. someone new to the gay life *Jay & Young.*

deck n. **1.** floor, the ground; fr. USN/USMC use *Norman:2*; **2.** (US contruction work) the roof of a building, or its highest floor at a given stage of building *Price:2*; **3.** (drug use) a measure of heroin (cf: bag) *Larner.*

deck v. to knock on to the ground *Bukowski:7.*

deck ape n. (US navy use) deck hand *Pynchon.*

deck up v. (drug use) to portion out

large measures of heroin into small portions (cf: deck, bag) *Larner*.

decoke v. (motorist use) to clean the spark plugs of accumulated carbon.

deeache n. (backsl.) head *Cole*.

deelo n. (backsl.) old *Cole*.

deelo nam n. (backsl.) old man *Cole*.

deenach n. (backsl.) hand *Cole*.

deep six v. **1.** (naut. use) to throw overboard *S. Llewellyn, 'The Worst Journey in the Midlands', 1983*; **2.** to get rid of, to abandon *Waits*.

defug v. (UK 'society' use) to open the doors/windows in order to get some fresh air into a musty/smoke-filled room *Barr*.

dekko n. a look, a view; fr. Hindustani *dekho*, a look *Humphries*.

Delhi belly n. food poisoning, epitomized in diarrhoea, suffered by tourists in India. Other localized versions of this problem include Cairo crud, Gyppie tummy, Rangoon runs, Hong Kong dog (cf: Montezuma's revenge) *Rawson*.

delok n. (butchers' backsl.) cold, ie. frozen/imported meat *Cole*.

delonammon n. (backsl.) old woman *Powis*.

demo n. (abbrev.) demonstration (of a political or pressure-group nature).

dep n. **1.** (police/criminal use) (abbrev.) deposition *Mortimer*; **2.** (UK prison use) (abbrev.) deputy governor *LL*.

dep n., v. (abbrev.) deputy; to act as deputy *Capital Radio 1983*.

depresso a. (US teen. use) depressing *Price:2*.

deputy do-right (US Black use) the police *Folb*.

Derby Kelly n. (rhyming sl.) belly (cf: Darby Kelly) *Franklyn*.

deri n. derelict house or other dwelling *Robins*.

dero n. (Aus. use) a derelict person, a down-and-out *Wilkes*.

derry n. see: deri.

destroyed (drug use) extremely high (qv) (cf: wasted) *Folb*.

dethroned a. (homosexual use) a queen (qv) who has been ejected from the public lavatory where he is looking for sex. (cf: abdicated). *Legman*.

detox n. (abbrev.) detoxification after a period of drug addiction *Jay & Young*.

deuce n. **1.** two dollars *Fiction Illus.3*; **2.** (drug use) two pills *Folb*.

deuce 25 aka *deuce and a quarter*: a Buick 225; any car with 225 hp engine *Folb*.

devil n. (US Black, esp. Black Muslim, use) white person *Folb*.

dew n. (US milt. use) marijuana *Del Vecchio*.

dewdrop n. a drop of mucus lodged at the opening of a nostril and hanging there prior to removal.

dex n. (abbrev.) dexedrine, a form of ampehtamine drug *Green:1*.

dexy n. see: dex *Green:1*.

DFFL (acro.) Dope Forever, Forever Loaded: a popular patch worn by Hells Angels, hippies, etc. *Thompson*.

dialogue n. (Valley Girls (qv) use) a conversation; esp. one person's monologue *Harpers/Queen 1/83*.

diaper n. (US Black use) a sanitary towel; fr. usual use: nappy *Folb*.

dibs n. money *Runyon*.

dibs on trad. expression claiming a share of, or the next turn with a given article *Uris*.

dick n. **1.** a detective *Fiction Illus.3*; **2.** the penis *Price:2*; **3.** (US teen. use) an unattractive male, esp. one who has an overly high self-image *Pond*.

dicked a. assured of success; fr. *dick* = penis, thus image of potency *Underwood*.

dickery n. (rhyming sl.) dickery dock = clock *Powis*.

dick gun n. (milit. use) gun for firing rubber bullets; which look extremely phallic *A.F.N. Clarke, 'Contact', 1983*.

dickhead n. a fool, an incompetent; a general term of abuse (cf: dick) *Bleasdale*.

dickless tracy n. (US cant) woman police officer; fr. puns on dick = detective (qv) and cartoon strip 'Dick Tracy' *Neaman & Silver*.

dickory dock n. (rhyming sl.) cock =

penis *Cole.*

dick peddler n. aka: *prick peddler*: a male prostitute who will only take active roles with his clients *Legman.*

dick teaser n. see: prick teaser.

dickty a. (US Black use) snobbish, haughty *Major.*

dicky a. out of order, sub-standard, not working as it should *Humphries:2.*

dicky-bird n. (rhyming sl.) a word *Norman:1.*

dicky dirt n. (rhyming sl.) shirt 'Dickie Dirts': chain of cut-price shirt and jeans shops in late 1970s London.

dicky-licker n. (derog.) a homosexual *Legman.*

diddicoi n. a gypsy; fr. Romany *Powis.*

diddies n. breasts; mispron./dial. use of titties (qv).

diddle v. **1.** to molest sexually; **2.** to have sexual intercourse; **3.** to cheat, to defraud *Hotten.*

diddler n. (Can. prison use) child molester *Caron.*

diddley-hop n. (street gang use) a top gang fighter *Larner.*

diddley-poo n. excreta; usu. children's use *Rawson.*

diddley-shit a. minimal, small, insignificant *Uneeda Comix.*

diddley-squat n. nothing, zero; thus *it don't mean diddley squat*: it is totally irrelevant, unimportant.

diddums (nursery use) term of soothing affection use by parent to child

diddy-bag n. aka: *ditty-bag* a small bag for various trifles, mainly US milit. use.

diddy-bop **1.** (Black use) pretentious Black person, pretending/trying to identify with whites; **2.** naïve, immature Black; **3.** Black bourgeois *Greenlee.*

diddy-bopping (milit. use) walking carelessly (cf: diddy-bop) *Baker.*

didies n. underpants *King.*

did I ever! general expression of intensification, ie: I certainly did! usu. in answer to a question.

did I fuck! excl. of negation, eg: 'Did I steal that car, did I fuck!'; similarly *will I fuck!* = no I certainly won't.

didn't ought n. (rhyming sl.) port (wine) *Powis.*

dido n. (US police use) a minor complaint by one officer against another *Runyon.*

die v. (show business use) for a performance to fail, to fall flat; esp. of a comedian who does not amuse *T 12/9/83*

diesel n. **1.** an overtly masculine lesbian *Goldman*; **2.** (UK prison use) prison tea; it tastes like derv *Obs. 1981.*

diesel-dyke n. see: diesel **1.** *Bruce:2.*

dig n. a sex show, fr. Black sl. *dig*: to look, to notice *Legman.*

dig v. appreciate, enjoy; from jazz fan use referring to music c. 1950s *Price:2.*

digger n. **1.** an Australian; fr. form of address used by miners in Aus. Goldfields of 19th C., spread after Aus. participation in First World War *Baker*; **2.** (Can. prison use) solitary confinement, punishment block *Caron.*

dig in v. to eat heartily; often as exhortation: 'dig in!'

dig in the grave n. (rhyming sl.) a shave *Cole.*

digits dealer n. (US cant) numbers racketeer *Neaman & Silver.*

dike n. **1.** see: dyke *Bruce:2*; **2.** (Aus. use) a lavatory, esp. a communal urinal use by schoolboys, soldiers, etc. (cf: bog) *Wilkes.*

dildo n. a fool, an incompetent, from the lack of autonomous competence of the sexual aid so named *Harpers/Queen 8/83.*

dill n. (Aus. use) a fool *Humphries.*

dillo n. (backsl.) old *Powis.*

dilly n. anything outstanding or remarkable; often used ironically *Thompson:J.*

dime n. **1.** (in general US use) the number ten (cf: nickel); **2.** (gambling use) $1000 *Alvarez*; **3.** (US prison use) 10-year prison sentence.

dime-a-dozen a. common, undistinguished; fr. the cheapness of such items *Vizinczey*.

dime bag n. (drug use) $10 worth of a given drug (cf: nickel bag) *Green:1*.

dinah n. nitroglycerine; fr. dynamite *Chandler:Notebk*.

din-din n. (juv. use) dinner.

dinero n. money; fr. Sp. *Goulart*.

ding n. **1.** (Aus. use) derog. term for foreigners, esp. Italians and Greeks *Wilkes*; **2.** (Aus. use) (abbrev.) wing-ding (qv.) *Wilkes*.

ding v. to break *Wolfe:7*.

dingaling n. **1.** (US Black use) the penis *Chuck Berry, song title 'My Dingaling', 1978*; **2.** idiot, fool *Underwood*.

dingbat n. a fool, an idiot *Higgins:4*.

ding-dong n. **1.** (rhyming sl.) a fight *Jones:J*; **2.** penis *Lou Reed, 'Sister Ray', 1968*.

dinge n. a Black; fr. dingey: shabby, grimy *Chandler:1*.

dinge queen n. a homosexual who prefers black partners *Stanley*.

dinger n. (Aus. use) anus, buttocks *Wilkes*.

dingleberries n. pieces of excreta clinging to the hairs around an inadequately cleansed anus *Green:2*.

dingo v. (Aus. use) to act in a particularly cowardly and treacherous manner, to exhibit the mannerisms of the dingo, the native Aus. dog, a despised creature *Wilkes*.

dingus n. **1.** penis *Neaman & Silver*; **2.** thingummijig, whatchamacallit, etc. *TZ*.

dingy a. (US campus use) silly, foolish (cf: dingbat) *Underwood*.

dining at the Y v. perform cunnilingus; fr. the conjunction of the thighs, plus a pun on the YMCA/YWCA *Humphries*.

dink n. an Oriental, esp. Vietnamese (cf: gook) *Higgins:1*.

dinki-di a. (Aus. use) real, genuine, fr. dinkum (qv.) *Humphries*.

dink-do (bingo rhyming sl.) 22 *Wright*.

dinkum a. (Aus. use) honest, genuine; esp. as *fair dinkum*: fair play, on the level; fr. UK dial. dinkum: fair share of work *Humphries*.

dinky n. (UK 'society' use) a large car; deliberate understatement and ref. to defunct brand of toy cars *Barr*.

dino n. tramp, hobo, layabout *Algren*.

dinosaur n. (US Black use) the penis *Folb*.

dip n. **1.** (abbrev.) dipshit (av.) *Underwood*; **2.** a pickpocket *Powis*.

diphead n. see: dipshit *Underwood*.

dip it v. see: dip one's wick *Dunne*.

dip one's wick v. to have sexual intercourse (of a male) *Humphries*.

dipping in business (US Black use) interfering in affairs that are none of one's concern *Klein*.

dipping in the bush v. to engage in cunnilingus *Klein*.

dippy a. crazy, eccentric, insane.

dipshit a. (derog.) second rate, inferior *Price:2*.

dipso n. (abbrev.) dipsomaniac; alcoholic *Fiction Illus.3*.

dipstick n. (euph.) dipshit (qv.) *Stone*.

dip the bill v. to take a drink *Chandler:Notebk*.

dip the fly v. (US Black use) to have sexual intercourse *Flob*.

dirt n. information, not necessarily, but often scurrilous; often as 'what's the dirt on. . .?' (cf: dish the dirt).

dirt farm n. (US Black use) any centre for (malicious) gossip (cf: dish the dirt) *Folb*.

dirt road n. the anus *Sanders:2*.

dirt tamper n. one who practises anal intercourse *Legman*.

dirty dishes n. (UK cant) planted incriminating evidence *Neaman & Silver*.

dirty dozens see: dozens *Folb*.

dirty dowager n. (homosexual use) an unkempt, ill-preserved older queen (qv.) *Legman*.

dirty great a. to imply great size in a given context; the most common use of *dirty* as an intensifier.

dirty leg n. a promiscuous girl *Jenkins*.

dirty look n. a disapproving glance or stare.

dirty money n. money that is considered not to have been earned honourably or respectably.

dirty old Jew (bingo use) 2 (cf: me and you).
dirty pool n. unfair, duplicitous *Jay & Young.*
dirty weekend n. a weekend spent either with one's lover (in the absence of one's spouse) or with one's spouse but mercifully relieved of one's children.
dirty whore (bingo rhyming sl.) 34.
discombobulate v. to discomfit, to perplex ('jocular use' *OED*) *Higgins:5.*
discover one's gender v. to come out (qv.); to accept one's homosexuality *Legman.*
dish n. **1.** an embarrassing story about a given subject's life *White*; **2.** an attractive female. (cf: crumpet, cookie, etc.).
dish v. to hurt, to stop another's plans, to frustrate.
dish it out v. to hand out, usu. punishment, blows, abuse, etc. *rr.*
dish out gravy v. (UK criminal/prison use) to hand out particularly severe sentences *LL.*
dish queen n. a homosexual who enjoys slandering his peers (cf: dish the dirt) *Stanley.*
dish the dirt v. to gossip maliciously, to slander *Selby:1.*
dishy a. attractive, pretty.
ditch v. to throw away, to dispense with, to abandon – both persons and things *Price:2.*
ditso a. useless, second rate, no good *Price:2.*
ditty-bop see: diddy-bop *Price:3.*
div n. a weakling *Dury.*
dive v. to perform cunnilingus *Legman.*
dive into the dark v. (US Black use) to have sexual intercourse *Klein.*
dive into the sky v. to penetrate the anus with one's penis *Klein.*
divine right n. (US Black use) the police *Folb.*
divvy n. (abbrev.) dividend; the annual financial share-out by a co-operative society.
divvy up v. (abbrev.) to divide up, usu. illicit profits *Wodehouse:PGM.*
dj (abbrev.) *d*inner *j*acket.
DJ (abbrev.) *d*isc *j*ockey *Capital Radio passim.*
do n. **1.** a party, a celebration, dinner, etc; often reasonably formal *Pynchon*; **2.** (US Black use) (abbrev.) hair-do *Folb.*
do v. **1.** to consume a given drug: ie *do coke* (qv.), etc. *Jay & Young*; **2.** to copulate with a girl or woman; **3.** to sue, to take to court, to charge with a crime; thus 'X was done for taking and driving away', etc. *Bleasdale*; **4.** to assault.
DOA a. (police use) (abbrev.) *D*ead *O*n *A*rrival *Dunne.*
do a Bertie v. (UK police/criminal use) to turn Queen's evidence against one's accomplices; fr. a criminal turned confessor: Bertie Smalls *Powis.*
do a bit v. **1.** (US prison use) to serve a prison sentence; **2.** show business: to perform a routine on stage *Goldman.*
do a bunk v. run off, escape, go into hiding *Sillitoe.*
do a crib v. (US criminal use) to break and enter premises for the purpose of robbery (cf: crib) *Klein.*
do a dry waltz with oneself v. to masturbate *Algren.*
do a fair lick v. to run fast *Sillitoe.*
do a foreigner v. for men contracted to one job to take time off illegally to tackle another, more lucrative one *Bleasdale.*
do a job v. (criminal use) to commit a crime, esp. a robbery.
do a job on v. **1.** to beat up; **2.** to make someone the victim of a confidence trick or allied hoax or deception.
do a Melba v. (Aus. use) to announce, with great fanfare, one's imminent retirement, only to return, time and time again, for another 'farewell' – a practice of the late Dame Nellie Melba (1861–1931) and many other 'showbiz greats' *Wilkes.*
do a mischief to v. (UK criminal use) to harm, to beat up.

do a number v. **1.** (drug use) to make and smoke a marijuana or hashish cigarette; **2.** make a fuss, become emotional, subject to emotional blackmail or at least some form of moral/friendship/ethical pressure; often *do a number on Dickson.*

do a powder v. see: take a powder *LL.*

do a runner v. (UK criminal/police use) to abscond from the police or to be on the run, prior to possible capture by the police *Powis.*

do a solid v. perform a great favour *Price:2.*

do as you like n. (rhyming sl.) a bike = bicycle *Powis.*

do a thing v. (drug use) to inject oneself with heroin *Klein.*

do a ton v. to drive a motorcycle or car at one hundred mph.

dob in v. (Aus. use) **1.** to betray, to inform against; **2.** to contribute (financially); **3.** dob oneself in: to let oneself in for problems *Humphries:2.*

do brown v. to deceive, to take in, to surprise; fr. cooking use *Hotten.*

dock v. to cut; use. in *dock one's pay*: retain a portion of one's wages; fr. SE *dock*: slicing off a dog's tail *Seale.*

dock asthma n. (UK police use) ironic reference to the gasps of alleged 'surprise' from the accused when the police produce their evidence in court *Powis.*

Dr Feelgood n. a doctor who obliges patients – often showbusiness or entertainment celebrities – with amphetamines or narcotics which, despite their user having no real medical need for them, guarantee 'good feelings'.

doctor's orders (bingo use) 9; fr. the Army's No. 9 pills, or the nine months of pregnancy *Wright.*

Dr Thomas n. (US Black use) a middle class Black aspiring to white status; as Uncle Tom but with professional qualifications *Folb.*

do-dad n. any object or gadget without a specific name *TZ.*

doddle n. anything absolutely simple or easy to achieve *Norman:2.*

dodge n. a trick, a gimmick, a means of avoiding problems, esp. those encountered in work *Thompson:J.*

dodgy a. dubious, unreliable: temporarily the cp (with its antonym 'swinging') of comedian Norman Vaughan, compere of TV's 'Sunday Night at the London Palladium'.

dodo n. an idiot, a dullard; fr. 'dead as a dodo' *Klein.*

do down v. to take advantage of someone, esp. financially or by talking behind their back in a derogatory way.

doesn't have a pot to pee in (cp) very poor.

doesn't know enough to come in out of the rain (cp) someone who is exceptionally stupid *Heller.*

does your mother know you're out? (cp) sarcastic comment to a person whom the speaker feels should be elsewhere, due to immaturity, foolishness, inexperience, etc.

dog n. **1.** (rhyming sl.) dog and bone = phone *Capital Radio 1983*; **2.** (derog.) an untrustworthy, vicious, traitorous, completely venal man *Milner*; **3.** weakness, cowardice *Higgins:3*; **4.** unattractive woman *Price:1*; **5.** (commercial use) anything that remains hard to sell, used by antique trade, auto business (esp. second hand cars), etc. *AS 41 (1966)*; **6.** (Aus. use) an informer *Wilkes*; **7.** euph. for dog excrement, thus 'there's dog all over the pavement'.

dog and bone n. (rhyming sl.) telephone *Jones:J.*

dog around v. **1.** to live a promiscuous life (cf: cat, v.) *Price:3*; **2.** (US campus use) to neglect one's academic work *Underwood.*

dog-ass a. inferior, second-rate, unpleasant *Jenkins.*

dog-end n. the last fraction of a cigarette. (cf. butt) *Norman:2.*

dog-face n. infantry soldier *Grogan.*

dog-food (drug use) heroin *Folb.*

dog fuck n. sexual intercourse in which entry is made from the rear.

dogger out n. (UK criminal use) a

lookout man *AS 41 (1966)*.

doggie n. (abbrev.) dog-face (qv.) *Selby:1*.

doggie bag n. a bag provided by some retaurants for customers to take home left-overs, ostensibly for later consumption by their pet dog *AS 41 (1966)*.

doggie (doggy) -do n. (euph.) canine excrement.

doggie-fashion n. see: dog fuck.

doggone general US intensifier (cf: ruddy, bleeding, etc.) *Rawson*.

doggy a. (US Black use) hard, mean, thoughtless *Folb*.

dog it v. **1.** to dress up; fr. put on the dog (qv); **2.** to malinger, to act lazily (cf: dog around 2) *Higgins:4*; **3.** (gambling use) to act weakly, to be a loser, to lack winning spirit; fr. abbrev. underdog (cf: pooch) *Alvarez*.

dog juice n. (US Black use) cheap liquor *Folb*.

dog-knotted for two lovers to be locked together during intercourse because of a vaginal muscle-spasm brought on by a sudden shock *Sharpe:1*.

dogs n. **1.** (fashion use) badly designed garments *AS 41 (1966)*; **2.** shoes; coined by US sportwriter Tad Dorgan (d.1929) in NY *Evening Journal AS 41 (1966)*; **3.** the feet *Runyon*.

dog's ballocks n. (journalistic use) the printed symbol **:-** (cf: dog's cock) *AS 41 (1966)*.

dogsbody n. any member of an organization who takes on all the menial and tedious tasks, often working for any senior person who gives out instructions *Dickson*.

dog's cock n. (journalistic use) a printed exclamation mark, thus **!** (cf: dog's ballocks) *Green:2*.

dog's dinner n. a distasteful mess (but cf: dressed up like a dog's dinner) *Legman*.

dog's nose n. (US criminal use) a paid informer *AS 41 (1966)*.

dogs of war n. mercenary troops; fr. F. Forsyth bk title, in turn fr. W. Shakespeare *Julius Caesar*.

dog tag n. a legitimate prescription for otherwise illegal narcotics; for a dog to be 'legal' (not a stray) it must have a labelled collar *AS 41 (1966)*.

dog watch n. (broadcasting use) programmes that are broadcast after midnight; orig. nautical use *AS 41 (1966)*.

dogswatch n. (journalistic use) a shift on a newspaper running fr. 9–12 midnight; fr. nautical use *AS 41 (1966)*.

do-hickey n. any nameless small object (cf: do-dad).

do in v. **1.** to inject a narcotic drug *Burroughs:Jr*; **2.** to kill, thus *do oneself in*: commit suicide *McBain:1*; **3.** to wear out.

doing a hundred (US Black use) to be in good shape, to be doing well; fr. one hundred per cent (qv) *Major*.

doings n. whatever objects are required to perform a given job.

doing the dutch v. (Can. prison use) to commit suicide *Caron*.

doing-up n. the wilful destruction of property as part of a gang war *Performance*.

do in the eye v. to cheat.

do it for myself v. (taxi-driver use) to take a (usually bargain) fare without putting it on the clock and thus having to pay it to the cab company *Price:2*.

do it like Mommy v. to act in a domesticated manner – doing the housework, shopping, etc. *Sculatti*.

do it on one's head v. aka: *do it on one's dick/prick*: to endure any challenging situation esp. a prison sentence with no difficulty *Grogan*.

do (it) up right v. to carry out fully and correctly, to achieve a set objective *Southern*.

do-jigger n. (US use) the penis *Neaman & Silver*.

dole-bludger n. (Aus. use) one who claims unemployment benefit either when work is available or while actually employed in 'the Black Economy'; the Aus. equivalent to UK 'dole scrounger' (cf: bludger) *Wilkes*.

doley n. (Aus. use) aka: dolie: anyone drawing unemployment benefit *Wilkes*.

doll n. **1.** an attractive (young) woman *Runyon*; **2.** (US campus use) a conceited young woman *Underwood*.

dollar n. five shillings, and thus obsolete outside films, books, etc. of a pre-metric era; fr. a time when exchange rate was four US $ to a £ sterling.

Doll City n. (US teen. use) a conventionally pretty girl (cf: doll) *Sculatti*.

dollface n. an attractive girl, or boy; often used as form of address 'Hey, dollface!'

doll up v. to dress up a person or an object *Uneeda Comix*.

dolly n. **1.** (abbrev.) dolly-bird; a pretty young girl, but particularly popular in 1960s 'Swinging London' *Keyes*; **2** (drug use) (abbrev.) Dolophine, a synthetic morphine *Goldman*.

Dolly Varden n. (rhyming sl.) the garden; fr. Charles Dickens character *Powis*.

DOM n. (acro.) *D*irty *O*ld *M*an; poss. an actual or alleged child molester but usu. any older man who makes obvious his preference for girls younger than he might be expected to pursue *Barr*.

donah n. **1.** attractive woman; fr. parlyaree (a form of theatrical/circus sl. deriving fr. Italian *donna*: a woman); **2.** (criminal use) the 'lady', the queen in a game of three card monte *Powis*.

done a. **1.** cheated (cf: ripped off) *Wilkinson*; **2** beaten up, assaulted *LL*.

done for a. without a chance, hopeless, defeated, lost, abandoned.

done like a dinner (Aus. use) see: done to a turn *Wilkes*.

done over worsted, put at a disadvantage, forced to lose out in a disagreement or struggle.

done thing n. whatever is currently accepted by a given group of people – professional, social, economic, etc.

done to a turn worsted, beaten, at a disadvantage; with image of being spit-roasted and defenceless.

done up see: done over.

done up like a kipper **1.** beaten up; **2.** caught red-handed by the police; ambushed during a crime *Cole*.

dong n. the penis *Price:2*.

donkey drop n. (cricket use) a full toss *M. Meyer (ed.), 'Summer Days', 1983*.

donkey-lick v. (Aus. use) to trounce, to beat comprehensively *Wilkes*.

donkey's years a very long time; fr. the length of a donkey's ears and the addition of an extra 'y'.

donnybrook n. a fight, a riot, a noisy brawl; fr. notorious Donnybrook Fair in Eire at which such events were a regular feature.

Dons n. Wimbledon Football Club *BBC-1 TV passim*.

don't argue n. (Aus. use) in rugby football, a straight-arm hand-off; fr. illus. in the trademark of Aus. company J. C. Hutton pty. Ltd *Wilkes*.

don't ask me statement of ignorance or lack of interest in a previous query.

don't call us, we'll call you (cp) semi-joking phr. of dismissal; fr. trad. theatrical use by producers/directors to auditioning actors whom, of course, they never do call *Manser*.

don't be funny (cp) don't be stupid (cf: don't make me laugh).

don't do anything I wouldn't do! (cp) exhortation to anyone who is leaving, esp. on holiday or in search of similar supposed pleasures; the inference is usu. sexual *Del Vecchio*.

don't fancy yours! joking reflex comment when two young men see two girls, irrespective of real charms *L. Deighton, 'Close-Up', 1974*.

don't get your bowels in an uproar (cp) don't make so much (unnecessary) fuss.

don't give a monkey's couldn't care less *Austin*.

don't give a rap (for) couldn't care less; fr. *rap*: halfpenny (orig. a form of small counterfeit coins in Ireland

18th C.) *Hotten*.

don't give me that (cp) you can't fool me (cf: tell it to the Marines) *Manser*.

don't have a clue has absolutely not the slightest idea *Wodehouse:AAG*.

don't hold no air (US Black use) to have little impact or effect on either people or event *Folb*.

don't just stand there – do something! (cp) urging a quantity, if not a quality of action.

don't know one's ass from a hole in the ground to be particularly stupid *R. Newman, 'Rednecks'*.

don't know shit from Shinola haven't the first idea about a given topic, to be particularly wrong in an opinion; Shinola is a black shoe-polish *Price:2*.

don't know (someone) from a bar of soap (Aus. use cp) implying absolute lack of acquaintance with a person mentioned or seen *Wilkes*.

don't give a tuppenny fuck couldn't care less.

don't know whether you're coming or going utterly confused, lost, disorientated.

don't make a production out of it (cp) 'don't make a mountain out of a molehill'.

don't make it a federal case don't make a minor problem into a major one *McBain:1*.

don't make me laugh (cp) don't be stupid, ridiculous (cf: don't be funny).

don't mind me (I only live/work/etc. here) (cp) a resentful cri-de-coeur from a speaker who feels his/her territory is being taken over by strangers.

don't shoot the pianist he's doing his best (cp) self-explanatory *Capital Radio 1983*.

don't spend it all at once (cp) usu. on handing over a small amount of money, in payment of a debt, etc.

don't strain yourself! (derisory cp) addressed to anyone deemed to be failing conspicuously at pulling their weight.

don't take any wooden nickels (cp) look out for yourself.

don't worry – it may never happen (cp) usu. offered as advice to someone looking especially miserable or worried.

doo-dads n. morsels, pieces, odds and ends *White*.

doodah n. **1.** anything for which one cannot remember the name; **2.** an emotional crisis, a nervous, tense state *Wodehouse:AAG*.

doodle the penis *Rawson*.

doodley-shit n. worthless rubbish, trash (cf: diddley-squat, etc.) *Farina*.

doofus (US campus use) odd, strange, eccentric *Underwood*.

doog a. (backsl.) good *Cole*.

doog eno (butchers' backsl) good one *Cole*.

doog gels (butchers' backsl.) good legs (of a passing woman) *Cole*.

doo-hickey n. anything to which one cannot immediately put a name, a thingammijig.

dooky n. excrement *Sanders:2*.

doolally a. mad, eccentric; fr. Indian Army Deolali sanatorium in Bombay *Waterhouse*.

do one's block v. to lose one's temper *Humphries*.

do one's dough v. to lose one's money, to spend up.

do oneself in v. to commit suicide; to put oneself in a deliberately unpleasant situation/position *Neaman & Silver*.

do one's head v. (US campus use) to take a given, preferred drug *Underwood*.

do one's nut v. see: do one's block *Powis*.

do one's stuff v. to perform as one is expected; to do one's duty; to exhibit a given speciality *Fleetwood Mac, 'Rumours', 1976*.

do one's (own) thing v. to behave as dictated by one's personal beliefs, wishes, idiosyncrasies, etc. *Wolfe:2*.

doonups n. (butchers' backsl.) pounds *Cole*.

doorstepping (journalistic use) hanging around on the doorstep, or some similar venue, of the possible and much sought after source of a major story *'World in Action', Granada TV, 1983.*

doover n. (Aus. use) penis *Humphries.*

do over v. **1.** to beat up *Austin*; **2.** to cheat, to defraud.

dope n. **1.** drugs *Price:1*; **2.** a fool, a dunce *Breslin*; **3.** information *Major.*

dope v. **1.** to drug; **2.** spec: to work out the potential of a racehorse prior to making one's bet *Runyon:1.*

dope out v. to work out; esp. in working out possible winners in a horserace *Gruber.*

doper n. a drug user, no specific choice required.

dope the ponies v. to work out possible winners amongst competing racehorses *Gruber.*

dopey a. dull, stupid, vapid *Bruce:2.*

do-rag n. (US Black use) the scarf or similar cloth that is used to bind up one's newly-straightened process (qv.) hairstyle *Klein.*

do-re-mi n. money *Thompson.*

dorf n. (US campus use) a fool, an eccentric *Underwood.*

do-right man n. a conformist, esp, one who follows rules within an institution *Klein.*

dork n. the penis; thus *dork-brain*: derog. description.

dorky a. (US campus use) odd, weird, bizarre (cf: dork) *Underwood.*

dorm n. (school use) (abbrev.) dormitory.

Dorothy's friends n. homosexuals; fr. 'Dorothy', the character played by Judy Garland (1922–69), still a deity to large parts of the gay world, in *The Wizard of Oz* (1939) *H. Page.*

dos a reno n. (butchers' backsl.) a sod *Cole.*

dose n. venereal disease *Norman:2.*

dosed up a. suffering from venereal disease.

do skippers v. to sleep around on floors, sofas; to have no permanent home *Norman:2.*

doss n. a place to sleep, a bed *R. Graves, 'Goodbye to All That'; 1929.*

doss down v. to fall asleep, usu. on floor or similar temporary accommodation *Norman:3.*

dosser n. tramp, vagrant, a homeless person *Wilkinson.*

dosshouse n. lodging house, night shelter or similar refuge for tramps, vagrants, etc. *LL.*

dot n. (lesbian use) the clitoris *Maledicta.*

do the dirty on v. to treat badly, to betray a trust, to cheat.

do the do v. (US Black use) to have sexual intercourse *Folb.*

do the full sesh v. (Valley Girls (qv) use) to indulge completely, to take to the limit; sesh = (abbrev.) session *Pond.*

do the lolly v. (Aus. use) lose one's temper, lose control of one's emotions, senses *Wilkes.*

do the nasty v. to have sexual intercourse *F. Zappa, 'Brown Shoes Don't Make It', 1966.*

do the natural thing v. (US Black use) to have sexual intercourse *Folb.*

do the party v. (UK criminal use) a stage in a game of three-card monte (qv.) whereby one of the gang apparently bets and wins (posing as just another bettor), thus encouraging the real victims to put down their cash *Powis.*

do the pussy v. (US Black use) to have sexual intercourse (cf: pussy) *Folb.*

do time v. serve a prison sentence *Higgins:1.*

dotty a. eccentric, odd; fr. *dotty on one's pins*: unsteady on one's legs, and thence in one's brain *Wodehouse:MS.*

double a. qualifying adj. that intensifies another adj: double-good, double-quick (qv), etc.

double v. (abbrev.) double-date: two couples going out together *Price:1.*

double-bagger n. (Valley Girls (qv.) use) an intensely unappealing person (cf: bag your face, bag lady) *Pond.*

double carpet n. (UK prison use) six

months imprisonment (cf: carpet) *Powis.*

double-clutch v. (drug use) to take more than one's share of a communally smoked marijuana cigarette; US grass (qv.) smokers ritually take only one puff before passing on their cigarette (cf: bogart) *Folb.*

double-dooring (US criminal use) a method of defrauding hotels whereby one arrives like any normal guest at the front door, but leaves by the back door – any form of illegal departure, leaving one's cases (filled with stones or telephone directories, etc.) *Breslin.*

double-doored a. (Can. prison use) from both ends *Caron.*

double-life man n. a bisexual *Legman.*

double-nickel n. (US trucker use) the freeway where there is a speed limit of 55 mph *Higgins:4.*

double-o v. to stare at, to look over, to check; the 'o' in question is an eye *Schulberg.*

double quick extremely fast *Dury.*

double sawbuck n. $20 *Chandler: passim.*

double shot n. two ejaculations of semen *Klein.*

double-whammy n. intensifier of whammy (qv.).

douchebag n. derog. term of general abuse; from the apparatus used for douching *Price:2.*

dough n. money *Price:1.*

dough-boy n. (US milit. use) a US soldier, orig. in Mexican War c.1847 in the flour and rice-based concoction that was a staple; subsequently replaced by GI, grunt, boonierat, etc. (qqv.).

dough-pop v. to defeat completely *Jenkins.*

do up v. **1.** to inject a narcotic; **2.** to deal with; esp. to beat up *Norman:2.*

douse the Edisons v. (US teen. use) to turn off the lights; fr. Thomas Alva Edison (1847–1931) *Sculatti.*

dowager n. (homosexual use) an elegant older queen (qv.) *Legman.*

down **1.** depressed; **2.** knowledgeable, aware, prepared *Folb.*

downer n. **1.** barbiturate, tranquilizer. *Green:1*; **2.** depressing, worrying situation. *Underwood.*

down-home a. pertaining to the customs, attitudes and general lifestyle of the US South; thus, unsophisticated, rural *Wolfe:6.*

Downing Street n. (bingo use) 10 (cf: cock and hen); fr. the residence of UK Prime Ministers at 10 Downing Street, London SW1.

down in the dumps miserable, unhappy, gloomy (cf: in the pits) *rr.*

down the drain lost, wasted, useless.

down the hatch! popular toast prior to taking a drink *Chandler:LG.*

down the pan wasted, lost, abandoned; the pan is that of the lavatory.

down the plug see: down the drain.

down there n. coy reference to the vagina *Waterhouse.*

down to responsibility *Powis.*

down to Larkin free; esp. of a round of drinks that are on the house (qv.) *Powis.*

down under n. Australia; supposedly sited 'underneath' the UK on the globe *Capital Radio 1983.*

do you need a boy? (drug use) surreptitious request for heroin (cf: boy) *De Lannoy & Masterson.*

do you think I'm made of money? aka: *I'm not made of money!* cp: admonishing someone – usu. a wife or child – who is spending the breadwinner's hard-earned cash with excessive abandon.

the Dozens aka: *Dirty Dozens*: a ritual game of testing a rival's emotional strength by insulting his various relatives, especially his mother, and taking similar insults in return (cf: signify) *Himes:1.*

drack n. (Aus. use) **1.** rubbishy, worthless goods; fr. Yiddish *dreck Baker*; **2.** an unattractive woman *Wilkes.*

draftnik n. (US campus use) one who has avoided the military service conscription; one of the -nik suffix words that developed post 1957 with the launch of the Russian Sputnik, the first of which was beatnik (qv.) *Underwood.*

drag n. **1.** dressing in the clothes of the opposite sex. orig. theatrical use and stressing the drag of a long dress along the floor, as opposed to tight-fitting trousers *Jay & Young*; **2.** a puff of a cigarette *Price:1*; **3.** a disappointment, a pity, a nuisance, a bore *Price:1*; **4.** a motor car; orig. a four-horse coach *Norman:3*; **5.** a street, thus *main drag*: the main street *Wright*; **6.** influence, pull *rr*; **7** (US milit. use) the final man in a platoon, bringing up the rear of a moving column (cf: point, slackman) *Del Vecchio.*

drag v. (UK police use) to steal from cars *Laurie.*

drag-ass a. tedious (of a thing); lazy (of a person) *Price:2.*

drag-dyke n. 'masculine' lesbian who chooses to dress in male clothing; the reverse of the usual drag (qv) *Jay & Young.*

drag one's tail v. to mope around, to look miserable; fr. a dog with its tail down.

drag-queen n. a feminine homosexual who prefers to dress as a woman *Stanley.*

drag the chain (Aus. use) orig. for a shearer who lagged behind the others; latterly a drinker who fails to keep up with the rest of his companions *Wilkes.*

Drain n. (London Transport use) the Waterloo and City Line *ES 1983.*

drapes n. clothes *Folb.*

drat (euph.) damn *Rawson.*

dratsab n. (backsl.) bastard *Cole.*

draw a blank v. to have no luck, to receive no reply to a request; fr. card playing use.

draw the crabs v. (Aus. use) to attract unwelcome attention, to draw enemy fire (actual or metaphorical) *Wilkes.*

draw the crow v. (Aus. use) to come off worst, usu. in a share-out or division of spoils. labour, prizes, etc.; fr. story in which a number of game birds and one crow were on offer and one hapless person 'drew the crow' *Wilkes.*

dreamboat n. a particularly attractive man or woman; the fuel of one's fantasies *Chandler:LG.*

Dream Street n. 47th Street, New York City, betw. 6th & 7th Aves.; home of the stage door to the Palace Theatre, HQ of American vaudeville. Coined by Damon Runyon *Fiction Illus.3.*

dreck n. fr. Ger. 'dung' **1.** spec. excrement; **2.** anything worthless, second-rate, rubbishy *Schulberg:2.*

dredge-heads n. habitual drinkers, who drink up the dregs in every glass *Price:3.*

dress down v. to tell off, to reprimand, to criticize.

dressed (US Black use) a car filled with every conceivable decoration, gimmick, and similar flashy adornment *Klein.*

dressed to the nines a. dressed up to the height of fashion.

dressed up like a dog's dinner a. dressed in the height of chic and fashion (but cf: dog's dinner) *AS 41 (1966).*

dressed up like a pox doctor's clerk a. (Aus. use) flashily dressed, over-dressed *Humphries.*

dress-up n. (pimp use) client who enjoys dressing up in the prostitute's clothes and makeup; may provide his own wardrobe *OUI 8/75.*

dreykop n. a trickster, a fraudsman, fr. Yiddish, lit. 'twisted head' *Powis.*

drill v. to shoot (dead); fr. drilling a hole.

drink n. **1.** the ocean, the sea; fr. Second World War RAF use *Dickson*; **2.** a bribe, a sum of money that would supposedly purchase 'a drink', but usu. much larger. *Newman:1*; **3.** a tip, a commission, a bonus *Performance.*

drink v. (UK police/criminal use) to be susceptible to bribery; thus code between newly arrested criminal and policeman 'Do you drink, officer?' (cf: can I speak to you?) *Powis.*

drink at the fuzzy cup v. (US Black use) to engage in cunnilingus *Folb.*

drinker n. an after-hours drinking club *Newman:1.*

drip n. **1.** venereal disease, spec. gonorrhoea; **2.** a weakling, a spineless person.

drip it up v. to purchase on extended credit, to use hire purchase (cf: on the drip) *BBC Radio 4, 1983.*

dripping a. (UK 'society' use) gutless, cowardly, weak (cf: drip) *Barr.*

dripping for it sexually eager *Maledicta.*

drive on (US Black use) to hit hard and without warning *Folb.*

drive one's hos v. (US Black use) to keep one's stable (qv) of prostitutes hard at work, observing one's rules and earning plenty of money *Klein.*

drive one up the wall v. to infuriate, to annoy intensely, fig. to the point of insanity (cf: climbing the walls).

drivers n. (US campus use) legs *Underwood.*

drive the porcelain bus v. (US campus use) to vomit; spec. when hugging the circular lavatory (steering wheel-shaped) bowl and vomiting therein *Bernbach.*

drongo n. (Aus. use) a fool, fr. 1920s racehorse that consistently finished last or thereabouts in 37 races, and was used as a name for a slow-witted figure in polit. cartoons in the Melbourne *Herald Humphries.*

droob n. (Aus. use) a useless, foolish, depressing person *Wilkes.*

drop n. **1.** (US Black use) an orphan *Major*; **2.** delivery, usu. of stolen goods, contraband, etc. *Payne.*

drop v. **1.** to knock down *Humphries*; **2.** to lose money *Higgins:3*; **3.** (drug use) to consume pills or any drug that can be taken orally *Green:1.*

drop a beast v. (UK 'society' use) to fart *Barr.*

drop a brick v. to make an error, a mistake, esp. verbally.

drop a clanger v. to make a social error, the awfulness of which reverberates around the assembled gathering.

drop a lug v. (Black pimp use) to confront someone either as to his character or his actions *Milner.*

drop a thumper v. to break wind (cf: fart) *May.*

drop dead! excl. of dismissal (cf: go to hell!).

drop game n. (US criminal use) a confidence trick whereby the victim is persuaded to pay money for a wallet, supposedly found and filled with money, but actually planted by the con-man *Klein.*

drop hairpins v. (homosexual use) to reveal one's sexual preferences by dropping broad hints. (cf: drop one's beads) *Stanley.*

drop it! (excl.) change the subject, stop talking that way, etc. *Himes:2.*

drop off the twig v. to die; as if one were a bird *Humphries:2.*

drop one in it v. to put someone deliberately into difficulties; 'it' is trouble, but the inference is also of excrement.

drop one out v. (police use) to dismiss from a list of possible suspects; to let off *Newman:2.*

drop one's beads v. (homosexual use) accidentally to reveal one's homosexuality by a slip of the tongue or other blunder (cf: drop hairpins) *Stanley.*

drop one's bundle v. (Aus. use) to panic, to lose (emotional) control *Wilkes.*

drop one's gear v. (Aus. use) to undress (of a female) *Ready.*

drop one's load v. (US Black use) to reduce tension by having sexual intercourse (cf: empty one's trash) *Klein.*

dropped (US campus use) unofficially but dedicatedly engaged to be married; fr. traditional gift by the man of a pendant or drop, bearing his initials *Underwood.*

dropper n. **1.** a paid killer *Chandler: Notebk*; **2.** an eye-dropper used by narcotics addicts as a makeshift syringe when custom-built hypodermics are unavailable *Lou Reed, 'Heroin', 1967*; **3.** (UK criminal/police use) a passer of dud cheques *Powis.*

drops n. **1.** money left in pre-arranged (secret) places for bribes, pay-offs, shares of a robbery, etc.; **2.** the weekly housekeeping money for one's wife *Powis.*

drop sticks v. (UK cant (West Indian use)) pickpocketing *Cole.*

drop the cue v. to die; fr. billiards (cf: take the last count, strike out, etc.) *Rawson.*

drop the hook on v. to make an arrest *Chandler:LG.*

drop trou v. (US campus use) (abbrev.) drop one's trousers; a classier version (supposedly) of mooning (qv) *Bernbach.*

drug p.ppl. of drag (qv): exhausted, disinclined, bored; thus 'I'm too drug to go out tonight . . .' *Sculatti.*

druggie n. **1.** (abbrev.) drugstore owner, druggist *Goldman*; **2.** (derog.) (and rarely used by anyone involved with drugs) a drug user.

drugstore (catering use) the trolley which holds the restaurant's cutlery *Breslin.*

drugstore cowboy n. a man, usu. a youth, who frequents drugstores for no other reason than meeting his friends, gossiping and wasting time *Farrell.*

drum n. **1.** house, home *Griffiths*; **2.** (Can. prison use) cell *Caron.*

drummed up artificially inflated, made to appear more important than reality allows *PT.*

drummer n. (US use) a salesman; fr. 'drumming up trade' + drum = house (which he visits) *Algren.*

drumming (UK criminal use) posing as a door-to-door salesman to tour houses and thus check out which ones are empty and thus ripe for robbery *Powis.*

drumstick case n. (US Black use) rape *Klein.*

drumsticks n. (US Black use) well-rounded thighs of an attractive woman *Klein.*

drunk as a . . . bastard, bat, beggar, besom, big owl, boiled owl, brewer's fart, a cook, a coon, a coot, a cooter, a dog, a fiddler, a fiddler's bitch, a fish, a fly, a fowl, a Gosport fiddler, a hog, a king, a little red wagon, a log, a lord, a monkey, a Perraner, a pig, a piper, a poet, a rolling fart, a sailor, a skunk in a trunk, a sow, a swine, a tapster, a tick, a top, a wheelbarrow.

drunk tank n. (US use) short-term lockup for a night's drunk arrests prior to sending them to court.

drunk to the pulp (US Black use) drunk to the point of passing out *Klein.*

drunky a. drunken; esp. with given name, 'Drunky John', etc. *Dickson.*

druthers n. an alternative choice, a preference; fr. 'I'd rather . . .' *Algren.*

dry-fuck v. to simulate intercourse by rubbing one's clothed body against that of one's partner *Bukowski:7.*

dry-hump v. see: dry-fuck.

dry land n. (US Black use) all clear; safety *Klein.*

dry-snap v. to fire a gun that is either empty, or does not have a round ready in the barrel *Higgins:2.*

dry up v. to stop talking, to refuse to give information (to the police) *Klein.*

d.t.s (acro.) delirium tremens; see: the shakes *Himes:1.*

dub n. (US campus use) **1.** cigarette *Underwood*; **2.** a failure, an incompetent, a novice.

dubber n. (US campus use) cigarette (cf: dub) *Underwood.*

dubbies n. female breasts *Farina.*

dubee n. aka: doobie (drug use): a marijuana cigarette *Folb.*

Dublin University graduate n. a particularly stupid person; an unexceptional example of the clichéd condemnation of the Irish as fools *Powis.*

dub up v. to lock up in a cell *Norman:2*

ducat n. a ticket, for theatre, sporting

event, etc. (cf: ducket) *Schulberg:2.*
Duchess of Fife n. (rhyming sl.) wife (cf: dutch) *Cole.*
duchess n. a girl who is making money in films *Chandler: Notebk.*
duck v. **1.** usu. in *to fuck, suck and duck*: to bend over preparatory to anal intercourse *Legman*; **2.** to avoid *Higgins:5.*
ducket n. a ticket (cf: ducat) *Runyon:1.*
ducket v. (Can. prison use) to be placed on report for punishment by the governor; fr. docket *Caron.*
duckies n. (US Black use) money *Klein.*
duck out v. **1.** to avoid *Salisbury*; **2.** to leave *'The Blue Parrot' (film), 1953.*
ducks n. term of address, generally affectionate or friendly *Sillitoe.*
duck's ass see: d.a.
duck's butt n. (US Black use) female with unkempt hair *Folb.*
duck shoot n. (milit. use) a simple operation, 'like shooting ducks on a pond' *Wolfe:5.*
duck-shoving n. (Aus. use) fighting for status, rank, position, esp. in polit. terms *Wilkes.*
duck soup n. anything simple, easy; any person easily persuaded or victimized *Runyon.*
ducky **1.** term of address (cf: ducks); **2.** a. sweet, delightful, charming; an example of the apparent charm (cf: chick) of farmyard animals.
dud n. a failure *Jay & Young.*
dude n. **1.** a man *Grogan*; **2.** (US campus use) a thing *Underwood.*
dudes n. men, people *Price:2.*
dudley n. (US teen. use) a failure, a loser; fr. dud (qv) *Pond.*
duds n. clothing *Vidal.*
due (police use) due to be arrested – as part of the everyday problems of a regular, known criminal – irrespective of whether the person in question had actually committed the crime of which he was suspected *Newman:1.*
duff n. buttocks *Rawson.*
duff a. useless, broken down *Austin.*
duff v. to blunder, to make a mess of *Underwood.*
duff around v. to sit about, to act lazily; fr. duff (qv) *Higgins:5.*
duffer n. **1.** (US prison use) bread; fr. UK prison: food, esp. pudding *Chandler: Notebk*; **2.** an incompetent, foolish person *Price:3.*
duff over v. see: duff up.
duff up v. to beat up *Sharpe:2.*
dugs n. female breasts *Wolfe:2.*
duji n. (drug use) heroin *Rattray.*
duke v. to fight with the fists *Bruce:2.*
Duke of Kent n. (rhyming sl.) rent *Powis.*
dukes n. fists *Runyon.*
duke it out v. to fight with fists *Price:2.*
Duke of York n. (rhyming sl.) fork *Wright.*
dukie n. (US Black use) excretion; thus *dukie hole*: the anus *Klein.*
dumb a. stupid *Price:2.*
dumb-ass a. stupid, unintelligent *Jenkins.*
dumb-bell n. idiot, fool *Wodehouse:AAG.*
dumbo n. a fool, a dullard (cf: dum-dum, lamebrain, etc.).
dum-dum n. fool, idiot (cf: dumbo, dummy) *Bruce:2.*
dummy n. **1.** a wallet *Norman:2*; **2.** (Can. prison use) bread *Caron*; **3.** a deaf mute *Powis*; **4.** a fool, an idiot *Dunne.*
dummy up v. to stop talking; to keep quiet *Pearce.*
dump n. an unpleasant, disgusting and unappealing place *Wilkinson.*
dump v. **1.** to knock down; fr. dump on the floor *Selby:1*; **2.** (US campus use) to defecate *Underwood.*
dump on v. to impose oneself on another person *McFadden.*
dump one's load v. to vomit.
dump truck n. (derog. male use) a car full of lesbians *Stanley.*
dunderhead n. fool, idiot, incompetent.
dunnee n. (Aus. use) lavatory *Humphries.*
dunnigan worker n. a thief who hangs around public lavatories, hoping

to steal from discarded coats, or take parcels, etc. that have been put down *Chandler: Notebk.*

dustbin lids n. (rhyming sl.) kids = children *Jones:J.*

dust-off n. (US milit. use) medical evacuation of casualties by helicopter *Del Vecchio.*

dust one v. (US Black use) to knock down, to beat up *Folb.*

dust-up n. a fight *J. Mortimer, 'Rumpole & the Golden Thread', 1983.*

dusty n. (UK 'society' use) very old person, 70 yrs and onwards (cf: wrinkly, crumbly) *Barr.*

dusty a. (US Black use) unclear, unable to predict the future *Klein.*

dusty bread n. (US Black use) a conventional, conservative girl *Klein.*

dutch n. wife; fr. rhyming sl: Duchess of Fife (qv).

Dutch n. (rhyming sl.) dutch plate = mate *Powis.*

Dutch courage cowardice that, fortified by generous quantities of alcohol, becomes (temporary) bravery; coined during various UK-Holland wars of 18th C. *Safire.*

Dutch treat n. an outing, visit to a restaurant, etc. in which costs are shared equally – ie there is no 'treat' at all in the sense of one party being entertained at the other's expense *Safire.*

Dutch uncle n. one who talks severely and critically, who lays down the law; usu. as *talk like a Dutch uncle.*

DV (US Black use) (abbrev.) Cadillac Coupe *De V*ille *Folb.*

DX (US milit. use) (abbrev.) direct exchange; also, to discard or dispose of, ultimately to kill *Del Vecchio.*

dyke n. lesbian *Jay & Young.*

dyke down v. (US Black use) to dress smartly *Klein.*

dynamite a. **1.** excellent, wonderful, first-rate; often as excl.' **2.** undiluted drugs *White.*

eager beaver n. an excessively earnest, keen person whose efforts are sometimes more notable for their sound and fury than their actual usefulness.

ear-basher n. a bore, a loudmouth who refuses to stop talking *'Minder', Thames TV, 1980*.

earhole v. to listen: to overhear *Norman: 2*.

ear-jerker n. (film use) a film in which the main attraction is the volume and predominance of the music; on the model of tear-jerker (qv.) *T 25/3/83*.

early a. (US Black use) up to date *Klein*.

early riser n. (US prison use) an inmate who is granted an early parole *Klein*.

earn v. (UK criminal use) to make a dishonest profit from a given crime *Powis*.

earner n. **1.** (UK cant) any job or plan that pays well, almost invariably criminal *Payne*; **2.** (UK police use) a bribe, often paid as regularly as more legitimate wages *Newman: 1*.

early-bird a. first of the day, ie:*early bird matinee Waits*.

early out n. (US milit. use) any serviceman who has 150 days or less remaining of his active service duty *Del Vecchio*.

earth (backsl.) three *Cole*.

earwig n. a lookout, one who listens for approaching steps, then checks their owner before admitting him/her *Performance*.

earwig v. (rhyming sl.) to twig = to understand *Jones: J*.

ease it v. (UK prison use) to relax, to let up on some form of crime or rule-breaking *LL*.

east and west n. (rhyming sl.) vest *Wright*.

easy a. **1.** sexually available, esp. in *easy lay*; **2.** equivocal, not caring one way or another when faced with a given choice.

easy as kiss my arse very simple indeed.

easy as pie very simple.

easy as taking candy from a baby aka: . . . *money from a child* cp: very simple, almost criminally so *'1-2-3', Len Barry, 1965*.

easy as winking see: easy as pie.

easy game n. see: easy ride *Klein*.

easy-peasy very simple; usu. juvenile use *S. Lewellyn, 'The Worst Journey in the Midlands', 1983*.

easy ride n. sexually available female.

easy rider n. any 'outlaw' motorcyclist; fr. film title 1969 *Underwood*.

easy street n. a secure, comfortable life; a situation free of problems, esp. material ones (cf: sitting pretty).

easy stuff n. see: easy ride *Klein*.

eat v. aka: *eat pussy, eat out*: cunnilingus *Price: 2*.

eat crow v. to suffer humiliations and

insults without responding in kind *Goldman*.

eat dirt v. to retract a previous statement, usu. incurring humiliation and embarrasssment by so doing *Underwood*.

eat hair pie v. to perform cunnilingus *Legman*.

eating bothering, usu, as in *what's eating you/him/etc.*; consumed by an obsession *Runyon*.

eating tackle n. teeth.

eat it v. (euph.) eat shit (qv.) *Higgins: 5*.

eat jam v. to lick the anus *Legman*.

eat my shorts! (US campus use) derogatory, dismissive phrase drop dead, go to hell, etc. (shorts, in US, are underpants) *Bernbach*.

eat one's ass off v. to criticize severely, to punish heavily *Chandler: LG*.

eat one's heart out v. to be consumed by jealously *Neaman & Silver*.

eat one's meat v. to fellate *Goldman*.

eat out v. to perform cunnilingus.

eat pound-cake v. (homosexual use) to suck a partner's anus *Legman*.

eat pussy v. to perform cunnilingus (cf: eat, pussy).

eats n. food *Price: 2*.

eat shit v. to suffer and accept humiliation; to humble oneself, usu. to attain a desired goal *Vizinczey*.

eat up v. to enjoy immensely.

ebony n. (US Black use) the quintessence of black sensibility *Klein*.

Edgar Britt n. (Aus. use) rhyming sl. see Jimmy Britt (qv.) *Wilkes*.

edge n. tension, usu. creative; concentration *Higgins: 3*.

edge city n. the extremes of experience, whether spiritual, physical, drug induced or whatever; usu. with overtones of fear and challenge (cf: — city) *Wolfe: 2*.

Edie n. a prostitute (working Piccadilly, Bayswater Rd and other cheap streets) (cf: Tom n.).

Edmundo n. (rhyming sl.) Edmundo Ros (Latin American band leader) = boss *Payne*.

Edna! (UK criminal use) rhyming sl. Edna May = on your way! *Powis*.

eel juice n. liquor *Chandler: Notebk*.

eemosh n. (backsl.) home *Cole*.

eenin (backsl.) nine *Cole*.

eeson n. (backsl.) to have a look *Cole*.

eevach a kool v. (backsl.) to have a look *Cole*.

eevige v. (backsl.) to give *Cole*.

effing (euph.) *f*ucking *Dury*.

effing and blinding using obscenities, 'bad language'.

eff off! (euph.) fuck off! *Rawson*.

egg n. **1.** a person, usu. qualified as *good egg, bad egg*, etc. *Farrell*; **2.** (US campus use) a conspicuously studious and intellectual student; abbrev. egghead (qv.) *Underwood*.

egghead n. intellectual, anyone considered to work with brain rather than brawn *Motor City Comics*.

egg in the nest (US Black use) to be pregnant *Klein*.

eggs in the basket n. (homosexual use) testicles *Legman*.

ego trip n. self-aggrandisement, boastfulness, egocentricity; fr. Freudian ego + drug culture trip (qv.) *Underwood*.

eightball n. **1.** (derog.) Negro, Black; fr. colour of the 8 ball in pool *Farrell*; **2.** a conventional, law-abiding person *Farrell*.

eight-pager n. small, illustrated eight-page pornographic booklet in which popular characters – Popeye, Mickey Mouse, Blondie, etc. – were crudely pastiched in erotic scenarios far removed from their everyday antics, (cf: Tijuana bible).

80-90 n. euph. amongst New York Hasidim: *putz* = prick; fr. numerical values '80' + '90' that are ascribed to Hebrew letters 'pay' and 'tzadik' that are in themselves a euph. for 'putz' *Safire*.

eighty-six v. to throw out, fr. rhyming sl.: eighty-six = nix = nothing *Price: 2*

elbow v. to get rid of, to dismiss (cf: big E) *Farren*.

elbow grease n. physical effort, fr. the movement of an elbow when its arm is rubbing or polishing hard.
elbow shaker n. (US Black use) one who reminds others of a forgotten or overlooked fact or event by digging them in the ribs *Klein*.
electric a. weird and wonderful, marvellous *Powis*.
elephant n. (rhyming sl.)Elephant and Castle = asshole (pron. arssle) = anus *Powis*.
elephant's trunk a. (rhyming sl.) drunk *Dury*.
elevated a. drunk; 'high' *Dickson*.
eleven-bravo (US milit. use) an infantryman; fr. 11-B, the number of his MOS (military occupational speciality), his army job description *Del Vecchio*.
Eli n. (US college use) Yale Universities, thus *Elis* members of Yale *Bernbach*.
elly-bay n. (Pig Latin) the belly *Runyon*.
elrig n. (backsl.) girl *Cole*.
elwoff n. (butchers' backsl.) fowl *Cole*.
emag n. (backsl.) game, usu. as a term of disgust or disappointment: 'what's your game?' etc. *Powis*.
embalmed a. very drunk *Neaman & Silver*.
emok nye (backsl.) come in *Cole*.
empty one's trash v. (US Black use) to have sexual intercourse; spec. to ejaculate (cf: drop one's load) *Neaman & Silver*.
encore (UK 'society' use) fr. Fr. 'more', used to mean wonderful, very good.
end n. that area of a football stadium, behind the respective goals, traditionally reserved for the hard-core supporters of home and away teams and the scene of most fighting *Robins*.
end-around n. the result, the final assessment, the bottom line (qv.) *Higgins: 1*.
end of the ball-game n. death; one of a number of games-playing/sporting metaphors for life's termination. (cf: cash in one's chips; struck out; throw in the sponge; etc., etc.) *Rawson*.
English culture sex advertisements: bondage and discipline (cf: French, Greek culture, etc.) *Neaman & Silver*.
English guidance (commercial sex use) bondage and discipline; fr. the popular assumption that all Englishmen enjoy such activities *Rawson*.
eno (backsl.) one *Cole*.
enob n. **1.** (butcher's backsl.) bone *Cole*; **2.** the penis, using 'bone' as synonym *Rawson*.
enthroned (homosexual use) a homosexual who looks for sex in public lavatories; fr. queen (qv.) (cf: abdicated) *Legman*.
equalizer n. a gun; reduces all before it to the same abject level *Runyon*.
erase v. to murder, to kill (cf: rub out) *Rawson*.
-erino suffix applicable to various words, generally implying intensification, further excellence, appeal, etc.
Errol Flynn (rhyming sl.) chin *Cole*.
esaff n. (backsl.) face *Cole*.
esclop n. (backsl.) the police *Powis*.
eskimo (US derog.) a Jew (cf: Ikey-Mo) *Rosten*.
esky n. (Aus. use) a portable drinks cooler, popularly filled with beer for cricket watching, etc; fr. eskimo, and thus chilliness *Ready*.
ethno n. (Aus. use) immigrants to Australia, of various ethnic persuasions *Wilkes*.
-ette all-purpose diminutive, often applied to otherwise unsuitable words.
euchred (Aus. use) exhausted, destitute; fr. card-game 'euchre' (orig. US) in which, if a player chooses to play a given round and fails to take 3 tricks, he/she is 'euchred' (*OED*) *Wilkes*.
even Steven fair shares.
ever so very much; usu. in 'thanks ever so!' and certainly not 'U' speech *Manser*.
everything but the kitchen sink an

undertaking that requires whatever is available, no matter what it is, relevant or not.

evif (backsl.) five *Cole*.

ex! (juv. excl.) (abbrev.) excellent; used in UK prep schools (cf: brill) *Lucien Green*.

ex n. (abbrev) ex-husband, ex-wife, ex-lover: the other half of a lapsed relationship *McFadden*.

excuse my French! genteel euphemism automatically offered after the speaker has sworn in public; as ever, Anglo-Saxons blame the French for anything remotely 'dirty' *Dunne*.

exercise the ferret v. to copulate *Humphries*.

extract the Michael v. consciously 'genteel' version of take the micky (qv.)

exxes (backsl.) six *Cole*.

expat n. (abbrev.) expatriate; applied to UK citizens living abroad.

eye n. (US prison use) **1.** detective; fr. logo of Pinkerton's detective agency; **2.** a warder *Chandler: Notebk*.

eyeball v. to stare at *White*.

eye doctor n. (homosexual use) one who practises anal intercourse *Legman*.

eye-eye! look at that!, what's all this! take a look around, etc. *LL*.

eyeful n. an attractive female.

eyes n. nipples or female breasts *Neaman & Silver*.

eye-opener n. **1.** the first drink of the day. (cf: phlegn-cutter); **2.** a surprise, a shock, not necessarily unpleasant *Bukowski: 1*.

eyes like pissholes in the snow deeply sunken eyes, often bloodshot to boot; poss. the result of an excess of alcohol.

Eyetie n. (derog.) Italian, fr. exaggerated 'Italian' pronounciation *Humphries: 2*.

eyewash n. rubbish, nonsense.

faastie a. (Jamaican use) rude, impertinent, impudent; fr. Surinam Creole *fiesti – nasty Thelwell.*

fab a. (abbrev.) fabulous; excl. of approbation, first popularized by the Beatles c.1963 but still used, often with an ironic intonation *Vidal*.

face n.**1.** a person; esp. in police use, a known criminal *Griffith*; **2.** a person, spec. a fellow mod (qv) c.1962; now the name of a magazine which, twenty years later, promotes much the same sartorial and ethical attitudes as did the mods in their day.

face-ache n. joc. form address, despite apparent rudeness of the phrase; the ache presumably comes fr. laughter.

face artist n. (US criminal sl.) a fellator *Legman*.

faced (US teen. use) extremely drunk; euph. fr. shit;faced (qv) *Bernbach*.

face-fucking n. fellatio in which one partner lies on his back with opened mouth *Jay & Young*.

face fungus n. beard and/or moustache *Humphries*.

facer n. a problem, an obstacle – both unexpected; anything that one must face up to *Laurie*.

face the nation v. (US Black use) to engage in cunnilingus *Klein*.

facial n. (pimp use) a client who likes the prostitute to sit on his face, sometimes after she has inserted a suppository or even when she is having intercourse with another man *OUI 8/75*.

factory n. (UK police use) a large, forbidding Victorian police station in the London Metropolitan area *Powis*.

fade n. (US Black use) a Black who immerses him/herself into the white world, and thus 'fades away' *Major*.

fade v. **1.** to put at a disadvantage; fr. dice use, implying that the shooter can match any throw that comes up *Breslin*; **2.** to leave; to vanish *Goldman*; **3.** (US Black use) to drop a topic of conversation; to change an unpalatable subject *Klein*.

faded boogie n. (US Black use) a Black informer; a Black who apes whites and loses his own ethnicity *Major*.

fading game n. (gambling use) a dice game in which players bet against each other rather than against the bank or house as in a casino (cf: head and head game) *Runyon: 1*.

fag n.**1.** (abbrev.) faggot (qv) *Jones*; **2.** cigarette; **3.** a bore, a chore; one is 'fagged out' (qv).

fag-end n. **1.** the butt of a cigarette; **2.** a fragmentary part of a speech or conversation which one might overhear, just as it tails off (cf: pick up fag-ends).

fagged out exhausted; fr. corruption of SE *fatigued* (?) *Wright*.

faggot n. a homosexual; prob. orig. 17th C. *faggot*: a promiscuous woman, thus playing on effeminacy and the multiple couplings of some homosexuals *Price: 2*.

faggotter n. (US Black use) a pimp who specializes in selling the services of male homosexual prostitutes *Klein*.

fag hag n. **1.** a woman, prob. heterosexual, poss. ageing, who courts and indulges the company of male homosexuals *Jay & Young*; **2.** a heterosexual male, irrespective of age, who prefers the company of homosexuals to that of his preferential peers *Price: 3*.

fag hots n. (homosexual use) cheap pornography aimed at the male homosexual readership *Maledicta*.

fagola n. homosexual (cf: faggot) *Vidal*.

fag tag n. (US campus use) see fruit loop (qv) *Bernbach*.

fag your face! (Valley Girls (qv) use) general term of dislike, euph: go fuck yourself! (cf: fug, bag your face) *Pond*.

fair crack of the whip! (Aus. excl.) be fair! *Humphries*.

fair dinkum! (Aus. excl.) homest! really! *Humphries*.

fair dos (Aus. use) general statement of agreement, acceptance.

fair enough! statement of acceptance, agreement *Baker*.

fair go n. (Aus. use) any situation which meets basic requirement of fairness to all without fear, favour or prejudice; fr. a call in a game of 'two-up' that indicated all relevant rules were satisfied and that the coins could be spun *Wilkes*.

fair-haired boy n. see: white-haired boy *Heller*.

fair one n. a street gang fight conducted under some sort of mutually recognized rules *Salisbury*.

fair pop n. a good opportunity, a fair chance.

fair shake n. (abbrev.) fair shake of the dice (qv) *Bruce: 2*.

fair shake of the dice! (Aus. excl.) be fair!

fairy n. homosexual male *Jay & Young*.

fairy snuff! corruption of 'fair enough' *Wright*.

fake it v. to pretend *McFadden*.

fake on one v. (US Black use) to ignore *Folb*.

fall v. (US criminal use) to be caught in illegal activities and subsequently arrested, tried and convicted *Klein*.

fall apart n. to collapse emotionally; to lose control of one's feelings *'Total Eclipse of the Heart', Bonnie Tyler, 1983*.

fall by v. to visit without prior warning; to drop in *Folb*.

fallen off the wagon a. drunk (cf: on the wagon) *Dickson*.

fall guy n. a patsy (qv); a victim who is chosen or forced to suffer punishments or difficulties that are in fact due to another person *Chandler: LG*.

fall money n. (US prison use) bail and legal fees; just in case one 'takes a fall' (qv) *Chandler: Notebk*.

fall off the wagon v. to resume drinking after a period of abstinence *Neaman & Silver*.

fall out v.**1.** to be overcome with laughter; **2.** to lose control of a situation; **3.** to fall asleep.

false face n. (US campus use) a hypocrite, an insincere person *Underwood*.

falsies n. a padded brassiere that accentuates the shape and dimensions of otherwise diminutive female breasts *Howard*.

family n. an intimate, either related in fact or emotionally *Powis*.

family jewels n.**1.** the male genitalia (cf: crown jewels); **2.** (CIA use) any secrets the revelation of which would embarrass and thus 'hurt' the agency and thus the USA *Green: 2*.

famous last words! (cp) don't you be so sure; offered to a speaker who has just made an absolute promise as to some future event.

fan v.**1.** to flaunt oneself deliberately to gain sexual interest *Major*; **2.** to conduct a search of a suspect's clothes *Runyon*; **3.** to pick pockets *Powis*.

fancy crib n. (US Black use) a fashionable, chic, well designed home (cf: crib) *Klein*.

fancy man n. a male lover, not always adulterous, but usu. referring to a married or older woman rather than a girl *Sillitoe*.

fancy pants n. an overdressed male, erring towards the effeminate in this preoccupation.

fancy pants v. to act suspiciously or uncharacteristically nervously, coyly *Chandler: Notebk*.

fang v. (Aus. use) to demand money; (cf: put the bite on) *Wilkes*.

fanny n. **1.** lies, a cover story *Newman: 1*; **2.** (US) the buttocks *Jay & Young*; **3.** (UK) the vagina *Keyes*.

fan one's ass v. (US Black use) to move one's buttocks in an exaggerated manner with the deliberate intention of attracting one's audience sexually; usu. of homosexuals (cf: fan one's pussy) *Klein*.

fan one's pussy v. (US Black use) a female version of the male fan one's ass (qv) *Klein*.

fantabulous a. incredibly wonderful; fr. comb. of fantastic + fabulous *Underwood*.

fantail a. (US prison use) a highly promiscuous prison homosexual (cf: fan one's ass) *Klein*.

far and near n. (rhyming sl.) beer *Wight*.

fare n. a prostitute's client; someone who 'pays for a ride' *Norman: 2*.

far gone a. drunk *Dickson*.

farm n. mental hospital *Dunne*.

farm v. (US campus (spec. University of Arkansas) use) to drink alcohol (cf: crop) *Underwood*.

farmer n. (US Black use) recently arrived Southern farm workers who persist in their country ways despite the pressing sophistication of the Northern cities *Klein*.

Farmington n. (US campus/prep school use) Miss Porter's School (for girls), Farmington, Conn. *Bernbach*.

far out! (excl.) amazing! remarkable! wonderful! fr. the mental 'space' entered under the influence of hallucinogenics *SF Comics*.

fart n. fool, unpleasant person, often older than the speaker; fr. the bodily function (cf: cunt, prick, etc.) *Underwood*.

fart v. to break wind *Higgins: 1*.

fart around v. waste time *Higgins: 1*.

fartarse around v. see: fart around.

fart off v. see; fart around.

fast **1.** amoral, illegal, corrupt; **2.** of a woman: promiscuous *Klein*.

fast black n. (UK 'society' use) a black London taxi *F. Fogarty*.

fast-fuck n. **1.** sexual intercourse that, through various circumstances, has to be hurried and brief; **2.** of a man: one who is unable to delay his own orgasm until his partner is satisfied too; a premature ejaculator *Klein*.

fast lane n. the active, competitive and ruthless world fought over by those of ambition and intent *Vidal*.

fast mover n. (US milit. use) the 1400 mph F-4 fighter bomber *Del Vecchio*.

fast talking Charlie n. (US Black use) a Jew (derog.) (cf: Mr Charlie) *Folb*.

fast track n. (US pimp use) those streets or blocks in a city where prostitutes work; spec. the East Coast cities as opposed to the slower California West *Shulman*.

fat a. (US Black use) pregnant *Klein*.

fat cat n. any successful, wealthy, influential person *Hoffman: a*.

fat chance! not a hope! no chance at all! *PT*.

fat city n. (US campus use) the process of gaining weight or the state of being fat *Underwood*.

Fat City n. success, wealth; often fr. criminal activities *Higgins: 3*.

fathead n. fool, idiot, often used affectionately as well as derog. *Wodehouse: PGM*.

father and mother of . . . general intensifier; usu. 'of a thrashing' or 'of a row'.

father and mother stuff n. (street gang use) attacking 'civilians' – non-gang members, women, children, the old *Salisbury*.

fat knot n. (US Black use) a substantial roll of dollar bills *Klein*.

fat lip n. unpleasant talk *Major*.

fatmouth a. braggart, noisy, loud-mouthed (qv) *Higgins: 1*.

fatmouth v. to argue, to answer back, to be cheeky *Folb*.

fats or fems n. (homosexual use) (abbrev.) fat or effeminate homosexuals, as described in gay ads *Jay & Young*.

fatso n. general derog. term addressed to a fat person *Chandler: LG*.

fave a. (abbrev.) favourite.

fave rave n. (teen. use) most favoured person, most enjoyable experience, preferred food, etc., etc.

fay n. (US Black use) (abbrev.) ofay (qv).

featherbedding n. (industrial use) the practice of making things easy for union members, of handing out easy 'jobs for the boys' *Green: 2*.

feathermerchant n. a physical weakling *Uris*.

feature with v. (Aus. use) to seduce a compliant female; coined by Barry Humphries for his strip character 'Barry Mackenzie' *Humphries*.

fed up a. irritated, annoyed, bored; intensified as *fed up to the back teeth*.

feeb n.**1.** (abbrev.) feeble, thus, a feeble, useless person; **2.** (butchers' backsl.) beef *Cole*.

feedback n. response, usu. negative or problematic *Higgins: 2*.

feed one a line v. to deceive through a cunning story, excessive charm, any verbal facility *Junker*.

feed one's face v. **1.** to stuff oneself with food; **2.** to indulge in oral intercourse *Klein*.

feed one stuff v. (US Black use) to deceive; to pass on false (and self-serving) information *Klein*.

feed the bears v. (CB use) to pay a parking fine, to get a parking ticket (cf: bear) *CB*.

feed the kippers v. to vomit over the side of a ship.

feel a draught v. (US Black use) to sense racial antagonism in one's conversation or dealings with whites *Major*.

feel froggy v. (US Black use) to feel like fighting (cf: froggy) *Folb*.

feeling no pain a. drunk *D. Leitch*.

feeling right royal a. drunk *Dickson*.

feel like death warmed up v. to feel absolutely appalling; often used by those suffering fr. hangovers.

feel one's collar v. (UK criminal/police use) to arrest, to place under suspicion; fr. the physical act of grabbing a villain *Newman: 1*.

feel one's oats v. to feel like sex.

feel up v. manual stimulation of a girl *Higgins: 1*.

felch queen n. homosexual who is stimulated by fecal matter *Stanley*.

fall off the back of a lorry ironic reference to goods that are obviously stolen; they didn't fall, 'they were pushed'.

fem n. see: femme *Klein*.

femme n. **1.** effeminate homosexual male *Jay & Young*; **2.** a feminine lesbian.

fence n. **1.** (Aus. use) a procurer of the sexually complaisant for such customers who prefer something out of the ordinary *Baker*; **2.** a receiver and seller of stolen property; thus *to fence* (cf: placer) *Caron*.

fey n. aka: *fay*: abbrev. of ofay (qv) *Burroughs: 1*.

F-40s (drug use) seconal; fr. pharmaceutical identification stamped on the capsule *Folb*.

fhb (cp) (abbrev.)*f*amily *h*old *b*ack; often used by mother when there is only enough food to feed the guests properly.

fib v. to lie, usu. children's use *Dunne*.

ficky-fick n. sexual intercourse, usu. in pidgin sl.

fiddle-fart around v. (US campus use) to waste time, to shirk duties *Underwood*.

fiddlesticks! (excl.) nonsense! rubbish!; earlier use meaning 'the penis', makes it a euph.

field nigger n. (US Black use)

working class, street Blacks, as opposed to Black bourgeoisie; fr. slavery era distinction betw. field and 'house' slaves *Seale*.

field of wheat n. (rhyming sl.) street *Jones: J*.

fiend on v. (US Black use) to show off, to outdo a rival *Folb*.

fifty cent bag n. (drug use) $50 worth of marijuana (cf: dime bag. nickel bag) *Folb*.

fifty: fifty usu. *50:50* alternating fellatio and sodomy between the same partners *Legman*.

figure v.i. to consider, to feel, to estimate; fr. totting up numbers *Runyon*.

figure v.t. to consider, to think of a person or object as; usu. *figure/ for . . . Runyon*.

figure out v. to work out, to understand *Price: 2*.

file v. (Black pimp use) an instruction to a prostitute to take note of present mistakes so as to avoid them in future; a parody of business use in the 'oldest profession' *Klein*.

filling station n. (US Black use) a liquor store *Folb*.

fill one in v. to explain, to give details *Wodehouse: PGM*.

fill one up v. (US Black use) to gratify and satisfy completely; with obvious sexual overtones, although sex need not enter the pleasure *Klein*.

filth n. the police, esp. the CID *Performance*.

fin n. **1.** (US Black use) a female hip that resembles in its opulent curve the fins on a 1950s model automobile *Klein*; **2.** a five dollar bill, abbrev. of finnif (qv) *Chandler: Notebk*.

financial a. (Aus. use) in credit, in the black, solvent *Bickerton*.

find the lady n. (criminal/gambling use) the three-card trick, three-card monte (qv), usu. played on the street; the 'lady' being a solitary queen alongside two nondescript cards.

fine and dandy n. (rhyming sl.) brandy *Jones: J*.

fine as wine (US Black use) any particularly attractive male or female *Folb*.

finger n. **1.** (UK police use) an unpopular person; fr. finger = informer (qv) *Laurie*; **2.** an informer *Runyon*.

finger v. to inform, to point out, to tip off *Runyon*.

finger artist n. (US Black use) a lesbian *Major*.

finger-fuck v.**1.** manual stimulation of the female genitals *Higgins: 1*; **2.** manual stimulation of a male's anus *Jay & Young*.

finger pie n. manually stimulating the female genitals (cf: hair pie) *The Beatles, 'Penny Lane', 1967*.

finger-pointing n. the making of (false) accusations *PT*.

finicky a. the manner of an obsessive, petty person, concerned with minutiae and as such often irritating to others.

fink n. **1.** company policeman, spy; **2.** police informer *Higgins: 2*; both terms, **1.** chronologically preceding **2.** come from *Pink*, an abbrev. for *Pinkerton*, the detective agency recruited to help break strikes.

finnif $5.00; fr. Yiddish: 'five' *Runyon: 1*.

finsburies n. (film/TV use) arc light; fr. rhyming sl. Finsbury Park = arc *Franklyn*.

fin up (US prison use) a sentence of five years to life *Chandler: Notebk*.

fire v. **1.** in sport, to work/play at maximum capacity; fr. an engine which is 'firing on all cylinders'; **2.** (US Black use) to strike a blow *Seale*.

fire away to start, usu. as excl. start what you're doing, say your piece, etc. *Manser*.

firebug n. arsonist *Higgins: 4*.

fire-eater n. a noticeably courageous person; with the supposed daring of the performer.

fire on v. (US Black use) disparage, ridicule (cf: blaze on) *Folb*.

fire power n. (US Black use) physical strength and ability *Folb*.

fire up v. (drug use) **1.** To pump the blood and heroin mixture out of the hypodermic into the vein or muscle *Klein*; **2.** to light a marijuana cigarette *Folb*; **3.** (US Black use) to excite sexually; to anger, to arouse emotionally *Klein*; **4.** (US campus use) to have sexual intercourse *Bernbach*.

firkin a. (euph.) fucking *Fiesta magazine passim*.

firm n. a criminal gang, large or small *Performance*.

first base n. (teen. use) initial advances on a girl; usu. implying the caressing of some part of the body or even the removal of some clothing; sucha base is always above the waist. Thus *second base*: similar explorations below the waist; such progress derives fr. baseball *Waterhouse*.

first bird n. (UK prison use) one's first experience of a prison sentence (cf: bird) *LL*.

first cab off the rank (Aus. use) the speediest one to react, the first one off the mark *Wilkes*.

first crack out of the box at once, immediately *Wodehouse: MOJ*.

first-nighter n. (US Black use) a one-time sexual encounter, unlikely to be repeated *Klein*.

firsts n. (US Black use) any Blacks who are the first to take on a specific job in a formerly all-white world *Major*.

first skirt n. (US milit. use) senior officer in Women's Army Corps (cf: top brass) *Neaman& Silver*.

fish n. **1.** (derog.) woman, fr. alleged smell of the vagina; **2.** (Can./US prison use) a new inmate; **3.** a prison homosexual *Caron*.

fish a. fresh, uninitiated, new, etc. *'The Mean Machine' dir. Albert S. Ruddy*.

fisherman's daughter n. (rhyming sl.) water, that which one drinks, rather than lakes, rivers, seas, etc. *Wright*.

fishing fleet n. (UK 'society' use) those girls who visit Hong Kong, and once many more centres of the British Empire, esp. India, in the hope of catching a rich husband *Barr*.

fish 'n' chip mob n. (Sandhurst use) unfashionable regiments and thus anyone considered socially unacceptable *Barr*.

fish or cut bait (cp) either carry out what you're doing or let someone else more competent get on with it while you take a secondary role (cf: shit or get off the pot) *PT*.

fish queen n. any man, homo- or heterosexual, who enjoys cunnilingus (cf: fish **1**) *Legman*.

fishy n. suspect, dubious; fr. the smell of rotting fish *SF Comics*.

fist v. see: fist-fuck *White*.

fist-fuck v. **1.** (homosexual use) to insert one's hand and forearm into the partner's anus or vagina *Jay & Young*; **2.** to masturbate.

fist junction n. (US Black use) that point of confrontation at which a physical fight takes over from mere words *Folb*.

fit n. see: works *Klein*.

fit a. tired out, exhausted *Underwood*.

fit as a Mallee bull (Aus. use) extremely healthy, in perfect physical condition *Wilks*.

fit to be tied furious, enraged, in need, therefore, of restraint *Vidal*.

fit to bust emotionally moved, either to rage or ecstasy, depending on context *Prices: 3*.

fit up n. any temporary structure, esp. a stage, boxing ring, etc. which can be assembled, then knocked down for assembly at another venue *Newman: 1*.

fit up v. to incriminate by using false evidence, both physical and verbal. (cf: stitch up, frame) *Newman: 1*.

five and dime a. insignificant, paltry; fr. small shops of the same name *Folb*.

five-day wonder n. (UK police use) a graduate of the special course at Bramshill Police College (cf: Shake 'n' Bake, etc.) *Laurie*.

five-finger discount n. (US Black campus use) the act and proceeds of shoplifting *Klein*.

Five-finger Mary n. one's hand, as used for masturbation (cf: Mrs

Hand . . .' shake hands with the wife's . . ., etc.) *Dunne*.

five in the South (gambling use) the point of five in craps dice *Chandler: Notebk*.

five to two n. (rhyming sl.) a Jew (cf: four by two) *Cole*.

fix n, v **1.** an injection of narcotics; to inject narcotics *Price: 1*; **2.** any corrupt deal, a bribe, a favour, etc.; thus *to put the fix in*: to ensure a plan or event favours whoever has paid the bribe, arranged the deal, etc.

fixing to v. to be about to do something, to intend to do something *Country Joe MacDonald, 'Feel Like I'm Fixin' to Die Rag', 1967*.

fix up v. see: fit up *Laurie*.

fizgig n. (Aus. use) a police informer *Baker*.

fizzing a. (euph.) fucking, mainly teen. use *Waterhouse*.

flach (backsl.) half *Cole*.

flack n. (show business use) publicity man; press agent; fr. the barrage of anti-aircraft fire – that assailed Second World War bombers; also poss. fr, the 'flags' that such people wave for their product *Goldman*.

fladge n. (abbrev.) flagellation, only when used in a sexual context (cf: B&D, English culture).

flag v. (homosexual use) to attract a stranger with the eyes or with a slight gesture of the head *Legman*.

flak n. interference; annoyance, problems *The Roches, 'Nurds'*.

flak catcher n. a civil servant, or similar figure in private industry, whose task is to intercept complaints, queries and similar problems coming from the public, before such problems reach his superiors *Wolfe: 4*.

flake n.**1.** a boring, unappealing, incompetent, undesirable person *Price: 3*; **2.** (US police use) see accommodation collar *Neaman & Silver*.

flake v. (US police use) to plant evidence *Neaman & Silver*.

flaked out a. exhausted *Humphries*.

flake off v. (US campus use) to depart, to go away *Underwood*.

flako a. drunk; fr. flaked out (qv) *Dickson*.

flaky a. second rate, unreliable, distasteful, possibly eccentric person. (cf: flake).

flaky ho n. (pimp use) an unstable, unreliable prostitute whose desire for clients and money is undermined by her inability to maintain a good front and economic and social discipline*OUI 8/75*.

flame v. (homosexual use) **1.** to look exaggeratedly 'feminine' in dress and style *Jay & Young*; **2.** spec. to wear makeup *White*; both meaning fr. 19th C. *flamer*: a conspicuous person who 'burns brightly'.

flamer n. (US prep school use) anyone who commits a major social error; thus the error itself; such blunders mean that one 'goes down in flames' *Bernbach*.

flaming a. mild perjorative, euph. fucking *Wright*.

flannel n. rubbish, nonsense; albeit plausible rubbish *Neaman & Silver*.

flannel v. to talk nonsense in a soothing, plausible manner, esp. for the purposes of charming a woman one wishes to seduce.

flap n. panic, excitement, commotion, ex milit. use since First World War *Powis*.

flapdoodle n. nonsense, rubbish (cf: baloney) *Wolfe: 2*.

flapping at the jibs (US Black use) to talk wildly, out of control, in a panicky, unrestrained manner; fr. flapping at the jaw/jowls/lip etc. *Seale*.

flapper n. (US Black use) **1.** the mouth; **2.** the penis *Klein*.

flapping track n. a small, unlicensed race track for horses or dogs *T. 13/3/84*.

flaps n. ears, usu. large ones *Powis*.

flap shot n. in pornographic still or moving pictures: close-up shot of the labia and open vagina *Green: 2*.

flaptabs n. ears *Sillitoe*.

flash n. **1.** (UK criminal use) a large bundle of notes; esp. when used in a three card monte (qv) game to entice poss. victims *Powis*; **2.** the initial physical effects of an injection of narcotics *Southern*; **3.** brief glimpse, esp. when offered to a man by a woman inadvertently revealing her thighs, breasts or genitals. *rr.*

flash a. ostentatious, showy *Norman: 2.*

flash v. **1.** to show off, usu. one's material possessions and gross self-esteem; **2.** (US campus use) to vomit *AS 50 (1965)*; **3.** to expose one's genitals *Bruce: 2.*

flash as a Chinky's horse (Aus. use) see *flash as as rat with a gold tooth.*

flash as a rat with a gold tooth (Aus. cp) extremely ostentatious *D. Leitch.*

flash case n. (US Black use) a satchel or bag that contains illegal drugs or any other contraband; fr. 18th C. (and later) use of *flash*; pertaining to criminality *Klein.*

flasher n. an exhibitionist *Powis.*

flash of light n. (rhyming sl.) a sight *Cole.*

flash on v. to have a sudden inspiration, memory, moment of absolute comprehension, etc. *McFadden.*

flash roll n. a sum of money that is revealed as proof that a given person, esp, a narcotics dealer or other criminal, is willing to do business; the money is 'flashed' (qv) before the client (cf: flash case).

flash-tail (US Black use) a female prostitute *Klein.*

flash the ash v. to hand around one's pack of cigarettes *Cole.*

flash the range v. (US prison use) the scanning of the area outside one's cell by using a small hand mirror to catch any reflections of approaching warders, etc. *Klein.*

flat a. (Aus. use) (abbrev.) flat out: exhausted, worn out *Humphries: 2.*

flatbacker n. (Black pimp use) a prostitute who specializes in quantity rather than quality in her clients *Milner.*

flatfoot n. policeman, detective *Fiction Illus. 3.*

flat fuck n. (lesbian use) sexual relations between two women, rubbing bodies together (cf: dry fuck) *Maledicta.*

flat joint n. a crooked gambling game or casino; orig. fair/carnival use, when a *flat* was a crooked or doctored 'wheel of fortune'.

flats n. **1.** playing cards; **2.** plastic credit cards *Powis.*

flatten v. to knock down *Humphries.*

flattie n. see: flatfoot; (cf: busy) *Powis.*

flat top n. (naut. use) an aircraft carrier.

fleabag n.**1.** a cheap, sordid hotel *Runyon: 1*; **2.** (pimp use) an old, worn out prostitute who is forced to seek equally run down clients, often on Skid Row or in cheap hotels, etc. *OUI 8/75*; **3.** (US Black use) troublesome, difficult person who tends, like fleas, to follow around and keep irritating the individual who has been made subject of his/her woes *Klein.*

fleapit n. cheap, tawdry, rundown cinema *Waterhouse.*

fleas and ants n. (rhyming sl.) pants *Wright.*

fleece v. to rob; esp. in a crooked sideshow or gambling game fr. the shearing of sheep (both actual and figurative).

fleshpot n. (US Black use) a woman, viewed strictly as a sex object *Klein.*

flesh-presser n. a politician who attempts to curry favour with the voters by shaking as many hands, kissing as many babies and patting as many backs as he can reach in a campaign (cf: glad hand).

flick v. (US Black use) to fail deliberately to turn up for work or school (cf: bunk off) *Klein.*

flick n.**1.** a knife with a spring-loaded blade; **2.** a razor blade with one side taped for holding as a weapon *Folb.*

flick my bic v. (US Black use) suggestion to a woman that she should stimulate one'e genitals with her hand; *bic* = a popular pen. *Klein.*

flicks n. the movies, the cinema; orig. *flickers*, denoting the slight jerkiness of early pictures *Humphries.*

flim-flam n., v. a confidence trick, a criminal hoax, to perpetrate such a trick or hoax.

flint n. (US Black use) a cigarette lighter *Klein.*

Flip n. (derog.) Filipino *Bukowski: 2.*

flip a. nonchalant, unconcerned, in control; abbrev. flippant *Price: 2.*

flip v. to lose control (cf: freak) *Price: 2.*

flip-flop n. (US prison use) an individual who first gains parole and then returns to the same jail after breaking the terms of that parole or committing a new crime *Klein.*

flip-flop v. to change direction; fr. computer use.

flip for v. to become fascinated, obsessed by.

flip oneself off v. (Aus. use) to masturbate *Wilkes.*

flip one's lid v. see: flip one's wig *Neaman & Silver.*

flip one's wig v. to lose one's temper; to lose one's sanity *Schulberg.*

flip-out n. an eccentric, a madman *Thompson.*

flip out v. see: flip.

flipping a. (euph.) fucking; esp. in *flipping heck*: fucking hell!

flip the bird v. (US campus use) to make an obscene gesture (cf: give the finger) *Underwood.*

flipwreck n. (Aus. use) a person who has (supposedly) masturbated themselves into physical and mental decline; pun on shipwreck *Wilkes.*

flit n. a homosexual *P. Wickham.*

flivver n. an automobile, spec. a Model T Ford *Runyon:1.*

floater n. **1.** (homosexual use) a gay prostitute who works only in towns where he is unknown and does not live *Legman*; **2.** a (social) error, a *faux pas* *Wodehouse:MOJ.*

flock n. see: stable *Klein.*

flog v. to sell; currently non-specific, but orig. with criminal overtones *Performance.*

flog one's mutton v. to masturbate (cf: flog the log, bang the bishop, etc.).

flog the log v. to masturbate *Junker.*

flood v. (US Black use) to have an erection, the penis 'floods' with blood *Folb.*

floor v. **1.** to accelerate the car – by pressing the relevant pedal down, thus *four on the floor*: a gearshift on the floor of the car, instead of on the steering wheel *Price:3*; **2.** to defeat utterly; fr. boxing or wrestling imagery.

floosie n. see: floozie *Southern & Hoffenberg.*

floozie n. a promiscuous young girl *McBain:1.*

flop n. **1.** a cheap room or bed; **2.** a drunk passed out and as such a possible victim for a robber (cf: lush-roller) *Burroughs:1*; **3.** (UK criminal/police use) anywhere a thief or gang can leave the loot so as to avoid detection during the immediate aftermath of a crime *Powis*; **4.** (US prison use) the rejection of one's application for parole (cf: knockback) *Klein.*

flophouse n. a lodging house or night shelter for tramps, down-and-outs, alcoholics, etc. *LL.*

flopover v. to assume a position with the buttocks in the air or with the body bent at 45° and the hands thus supported by the knees, either of which will permit the easy introduction of the penis into the anus or vagina *Klein.*

flopsweat n. (show business use) the nervousness and tension (and sweat) that overcome a performer at the thought of failure (a flop) on stage *Green:2.*

Florida n. (US prison use) the solitary confinement/punishment block, fr. the siting of such cells in the warmest areas of the prison, often underground *Klein.*

flossed up a. of a woman, made up

(cf: tarted up) *Powis.*

flounder n. (rhyming sl.) flounder and dab = cab = taxi *Laurie.*

flour mixer n. (rhyming sl.) *shikse* (Yiddish) = Gentile girl *Powis.*

flowery n. (rhyming sl.) flowery dell = cell (though usu. peter, qv) *Powis.*

flue n. (UK prison use rhyming sl.) screw = prison officer *LL.*

fluence n. (abbrev.) influence: delicate, subtle influence, either in business/polit./etc. manipulation or in actual physical acts, ie. the spinning of a cricket ball; also implication of *fluency D. Leitch.*

fluff n. **1.** (US Black use) the vagina *Folb*; **2.** young, attractive, but empty-headed girl *Chandler: Notebk*; **3.** the passive partner in a lesbian couple (cf: femme) *Stanley.*

fluff v. to make a mistake, esp. in theatrical use.

flummox v. to fool, to confuse, to overcome (by trickery), to avoid, to disappoint.

flunk (out) v. to fail an examination *Greenlee.*

flush n. the lavatory *Higgins:3.*

fluter n. a fellator (cf: skin flute) *Legman.*

fly a. smart, sharp, perspicacious; thus *fly boy*; not usu. very complimentary *Powis.*

fly a kite v. **1.** usu. with *go. . .*: a suggestion that an unwanted person should go away; **2.** to present a false front, a deceitful line of talk in order to persuade one's victim that one's intentions are other than that which they really are; **3.** to pass a dud cheque *Norman:2.*

flyboy n. a pilot, civil or military; usu. with slight implication of disdain or dislike *Bukowski:1.*

fly-by-night n.a. dubious, crooked, criminal; esp. of a businessman who takes one's money but fails to provide any or at least adequate recompense *Humphries:2.*

fly by the seat of one's pants v. to fly an aircraft using natural ability and daring rather than instruments and technology *BBC-1 TV 1984.*

flying a. exhilarated by using a drug (cf: high) *Higgins:1.*

flying blind a. drunk *Dickson.*

flying saucer n. a diaphragm *Junker.*

fly off the handle v. to lose control, to become extremely angry *Farrell.*

fly-over people inhabitants of those states of the USA over which one passes in an airplane flying from Coast to Coast; formerly 'middle America' *Wolfe:8.*

fly the coop v. to leave, poss. suddenly; fr. avian habits *Price:2.*

FNG (milit. use) (abbrev.) Fucking New Guy, used of new arrivals in a squad, platoon, etc. *O'Brien.*

fodder n. (UK 'society' use) well-cooked food; referring back to the stables that so many such speakers know and love *Barr.*

fog v. to shoot *Chander: Notebk.*

Foggy Bottom n. the US State Department; derived both fr. the name of an area of Washington, DC and from the 'foggy' obfuscations produced by its bureaucrats.

fold v. **1.** (journalist use) for a magazine or newspaper to cease from publication *J. G. Dunne, 'Quintana and Friends', 1981;* **2.** (poker use) to throw in one's hand; both uses imply the folding up and putting away of clothing *Alvarez.*

folding stuff n. cash money *Humphries.*

fold one's ears v. to lecture or advise someone at great and serious length *Major.*

fold up v. to collapse, to surrender; both defeats are under unbearable pressure; fr. poker use (cf: fold).

Follies n. (UK prison use) the Quarter Sessions *LL.*

follow one's nose v. (US Black use) to lead a law-abiding life, whatever temptations may exist to the contrary *Klein.*

fonfen n. the line (qv) created by con-men to further a given fraud or trick; fr. Yiddish *Powis.*

fonk (Black pimp use) the negative

aspects of funk (qv) *Milner.*

fonked out heavy (US Black use) very well dressed *Folb.*

fonky positive or negative intensifier depending on context; thus exceptionally good or bad; smelling sweet or vile, etc. *Folb.*

foodie n. (euph.) gourmet, one of a self-elected circle of London eaters, devoted to the best and newest in eating and drinking; coined by *Observer* food writer Paul Levy, 1981.

fool n. **1.** anyone excessively enthusiastic about a given activity or topic; thus *dancing fool, singing fool*; *writing fool* (drug use): a doctor who will write as many prescriptions for narcotics as there are people requesting them *Burroughs:1.*

fool around v. to conduct a promiscuous sex life; thus *let's fool around*: a suggestion by one of a couple that they should abandon speech for (sexual) action *Higgins:5.*

fool's gold n. (US criminal use) fake jewellery *Klein.*

foop v. (US campus use) to engage in homosexual acts fr. reverse of *poof* (?) (qv) *Underwood.*

fooper n. (US campus use) a homosexual *Underwood.*

football n. (drug use) a measure of one half grain of a narcotic *Goldman.*

foot-in-mouth disease n. aka: *dontopedology*: the continual problem of making grossly tactless or embarrassing statement *Neaman & Silver.*

footling a. incompetent, inadequate, mediocre *Wodehouse:AAG.*

footslogging hard, exhausting and protracted walking, orig. First World War milit. sl. *Wodehouse:AAG.*

for a motherfucker (US Black use) an intensifying expletive: 'he has guns for a motherfucker': he had a great many guns; 'I'm throwing bricks for a motherfucker'; I'm throwing bricks continually and passionately, etc. *Seale.*

for crying out loud! (euph.) for Christ's sake! *Manser.*

for days! (homosexual excl.) implies shock or amazement; fr. concept of having sex on and on for days *Stanley.*

forget it! (excl.) implies absolute dismissal of a suggestion, a concept.

forget you! (US teen. use) impossible, out of the question, no way (qv) *Pond.*

fork! (excl.) give!; thus *fork out, fork over*: to pay, to hand over money *Powis.*

fork n. (US cant) pickpocket *Neaman & Silver.*

for keeps for the duration, for a long time, for ever *Price:2.*

fork out v. to pay, to donate *Hotten.*

fork over v. to hand over, to give out *Sanders:2.*

forks fingers *Powis.*

form n. previous convictions. fr. horse-racing use (cf: previous) *Dury.*

for real honest, sincere, to be taken at face value *Junker.*

for sure (Valley Girls (qv) use) certainly, definitely, absolutely *Harpers/Queen 1/83.*

Fort Bushy (homosexual) the pubic hair *Maledicta.*

Forty-Deuce (US con-man use) 42nd Street fr. 8th Avenue to Times Square; the centre of New York's tourism/nightlife/underworld *Shulman.*

forty-eight (milit. use) forty-eight hour leave pass *Waterhouse.*

for yonks for ages, for a very long time; poss. fr. eons *Barr.*

foul up v. to ruin, to destroy, to blunder *Higgins:3.*

four by two n. (rhyming sl.) (derog.) Jew *Humphries.*

four-eleven-forty-four (4-11-44) n. (UK Black use) the penis *Neaman & Silver.*

four-eyes (derog.) anyone who wears glasses; overtones also of distrust of anyone 'intellectual' *Sillitoe.*

4-F useless, inferior, weak; fr. milit. specification for anyone unfit to serve *Uris.*

4-F Club Find 'em, Feel 'em, Fuck 'em and Forget 'em: the axiom for macho

US youth; Mae West in *I'm No Angel* (1933) tells her maid to 'find 'em, fool 'em and forget 'em' when it comes to men *Junker.*

four-flusher n. a cheat, a scrounger, one who fails to pay due debts; fr. poker use: a real flush requires five cards of the same suit, four is merely a bluff *Higgins:4.*

four-letter man n. **1.** (UK 'society' use) an unpleasant person; the four letters are perhaps s-h-i-t or c-u-n-t *Barr*; **2.** (US use) both as **1.** and as h-o-m-o (cf: three-letter man) *Neaman & Silver.*

four-letter words n. (euph.) obscenities, notably cunt, fuck, shit, etc.; thus six-letter. . .: bugger; and ten-letter: cocksucker, etc. (qqv).

four sisters on thumb street (US Black use) masturbation (cf: Mrs Hand and Her Five Daughters) *Folb.*

fourth of July n (rhyming sl.) tie *Wright.*

fox n. (Black use) a girl, a woman *Milner.*

foxed a. drunk *Dickson.*

foxy a. sexy, usu. Black use, but whites also *Price:2.*

FP (UK criminal use) False Pretences, fraud *LL.*

frag n. (US milit. use) (abbrev.) a fragmentation grenade *Del Vecchio.*

frag v. (US milit. use) the practice, as the US morale in Vietnam declined, of soldiers assassinating unpopular or incompetent officers and NCOs by tossing a fragmentation grenade at them during the heat of battle *Del Vecchio.*

frail n. girl, woman *Sharpe:1.*

frame n. (UK police use) the general situation, esp. that surrounding the suspects in a given crime (cf: in the frame) *Laurie.*

frame v. to trap a suspect (poss. innocent) by creating false evidence, witnesses etc. (cf: frame-up) *Fiction Illus.3.*

frame-up n. the concoction of criminal guilt or charges *Performance.*

frank and fearless n. (UK 'society' use) a discussion; fr. diplomatic/journalistic hyperbole/hypocrisy *Barr.*

fratting essentially abbrev. of fraternize, but used as euph. for fucking (qv) *Rawson.*

freak n. **1.** any person considered odd by the speaker; **2.** an obvious user of drugs, esp. cannabis and hallucinogens; **3.** (US milit. use) aka: *freq* radio frequency *Del Vecchio*; **4.** (Black pimp use) anyone with eccentric sexual tastes, habits; esp. one who enjoys sex for its own sake and does not ask for cash, a perversion in pimp ethos *Shulman.*

freak v. (abbrev.) freak out: to worry, to disturb, to cause severe anxiety (the extent of the disturbance varies totally as to context): orig. 1960s drug/hippie use.

freak fuck n. any variation on 'straight' heterosexual intercourse *Folb.*

freaking (euph.) fucking (qv) *Wolfe:8.*

freak off v. **1.** to offer sex for free, no cash required; **2.** to furnish a room or apartment; 'freak' here implies one's own tastes, but in interior decoration and not sex *Milner.*

freak out n. **1.** spec. any unpleasant experience caused by drug use, esp. with LSD; **2.** anxiety, ranging from twinges of fear to a full nervous breakdown, varying as to context.

freak trick n. (US prostitute use) any customer who requires out of the way sex or who attacks the girl physically *Neaman & Silver.*

freaky a. odd, bizarre, unnerving *Grogan.*

freckle n. (Aus. use) anus *Humphries.*

Fred n. (Aus. use) the average Australian (cf: Alf, ocker) *Wilkes.*

Fred's n. (UK 'society' use) nickname for Fortnum & Mason, the country's leading caterers, of Piccadilly, London *Barr.*

free-base v. a method of intensifying the effect of cocaine by heating it in combination with ether or other chemicals prior to inhaling it.

freebie n. **1.** (prostitute use) giving

one's sexual services without making a charge; **2.** any free sample, free trip, esp. press tours, promotions, etc.

free for all n. (US campus use) a sexually available female *Underwood.*

freeload v. **1.** to enjoy for free the pleasures that are made available to a celebrity or at an important event but become equally available to anyone who cares to struggle hard enough to grab them; **2.** in general use to define the taking of any benefits for which one has not made due efforts to deserve *O'Brien.*

freeloader n. a parasite, esp. those who form a celebrity's entourage and enjoy the crumbs from his various tables *Jenkins.*

free ride n. an easy time *PT.*

free shot n. the unpaid for services of a prostitute *Klein.*

free show n. the inadvertent revelation by a woman of her body – in all or part – glimpsed by a passing male (cf: flash).

Freeway Freddie n. (US Black use) any police in a patrol car *Folb.*

freeze v. to become silent, to quieten down, to refuse to answer questions or make conversation *Greenlee.*

freeze on v. to ignore, to snub, to reject *'Hill Street Blues', Thames TV, 1983.*

French a. a racial stereotype used in various contexts: the English (and thus US) belief in 'gay Paree' and its supposedly sex-obsessed denizens has long equated 'French' with sexy or, pejoratively, pornographic and 'dirty' (cf: Chinese).

french v. to fellate.

French active n. the passive (sucked) partner in fellatio *Jay & Young.*

French culture fellatio, obs. except in homosexual contact advertisements (cf: English culture, Greek culture) *Jay & Young.*

Frenchie n. a contraceptive sheath; fr. French letter (qv) *Sharpe:2.*

French kiss n. a deep kiss, using the tongue as well as lips (cf: soul kiss) *Jay & Young.*

French leave n. absenting oneself from a job or duty without prior permission *Higgins:4.*

French letter n. contraceptive sheath *Sharpe:1.*

Frenchman n. one who offers fellation to others for cash *Bukowski:1.*

French passive n. the fellator *Jay & Young.*

French tickler n. a contraceptive sheath with extra protrusions for added stimulation *Sharpe:1.*

frenchy n. a contraceptive sheath, fr. French letter (qv).

fresh a. familiar, cheeky, over-intimate *Higgins:1.*

fresher n. (student use) a student in his/her first term at a university; one of the last survivors of the Oxford '-er' suffix of the 1920s, which once offered 'Pragger Wagger': the Prince of Wales, 'wagger pagger bagger': waste paper basket, etc.

fresh hide n. (US Black use) a new lover or sexual partner; fr. hide: skin (usu. of an animal) *Folb.*

fress v. fr. Yiddish 'eat': to perform either form of oral intercourse, usu. cunnlingus *Goldman.*

frick and frack n. (US Black use) the testicles *Folb.*

fricking a. (euph.) fucking (qv) *Heller.*

fried a. (drug use) extremely high (qv) *Folb.*

fried, dyed, swooped to the side (US Black use) straightened Black hair which is attempting to emulate the texture and even colour of a white person's hair *Folb.*

friend form n. (US prison use) official papers that must be completed to facilitate outside visitors to the inmates *Klein.*

friend in need n. (US Black use) sarcastic reference to anyone who is continually looking for loans, free handouts, etc. *Klein.*

friendlies n. (milit. use) one's allies or those troops in one's own forces. Thus *friendly fire*: artillery or small-arms fire coming from one's own, misdirected side *Del Vecchio.*

frig v. (euph.) to fuck (av); orig. euph. for masturbate *Powis*.

frigging a. (euph.) fucking (qv) *Price:2*.

frighteners n. threats, violence, anything that will terrify a given person into doing what is required; thus *to put the frighteners on*: to intimidate, to harass *Performance*.

frip n. (US campus use) a weak, ineffectual person *Underwood*.

'Frisco speedball n. drug cocktail containing LSD, cocaine and heroin *Green:1*.

frisk v. **1.** (police use) to search, for weapons, illicit drugs, stolen goods, etc. *Selby:1*; **2.** (police use) to search a suspect, usu. briefly *LL*.

'Fro n. (US Black and campus use) (abbrev.) Afro: Black (and white) hairstyle where normally short, curly black hair is allowed to grow out in a bush around the head, supposedly in the style of one's African forbears.

Frog n. (derog.) French person *BvdB*.

frog n. **1.** (banking use) a cheque that is returned to drawer (cf: leaper, bum map) *Breslin*; **2.** (rhyming sl.) frog and toad = road *Powis*; **3.** (Aus. use) a contraceptive sheath; fr. French letter (qv) *Wilkes*.

frog and toad n. (rhyming sl.) road *London Transport poster 1983*.

froggy a. (US Black use) aggressive, belligerent, keen to fight; keen to start 'jumping' *Folb*.

front n. **1.** a respectable appearance; a mask for illegal activities *rr*; **2.** (criminal use, esp. pimps, con-men) anything one needs – fancy clothes, a clever line of patter, a personal style, a mental attitude – for the successful promotion of one's game (qv) (cf: more front than Brighton Beach) *Milner*.

front v. **1.** (Aus. use) to appear in front of *Wilkes*; **2.** to advance either money or any other commodity (esp. drugs) as a loan or a sample of goods on offer; when buying drugs the seller may ask for the money to be 'fronted' so he in turn, can make a bulk purchase from his superior in the sales chain.

front door n. (US Black use) the female genitals; as opposed to back door (qv) *Klein*.

front line n. (UK Black use) that area of a city where the Black community is most likely to clash with the forces of white law and order; All Saints Road, Notting Hill, Railton Road, Brixton, etc.

front one off v. (US Black use) **1.** to reveal information about another person that puts that person in an embarrassing or otherwise difficult position *Klein*; **2.** to be attracted to the company of another person not so much for their personality as for the outward show and physical beauty in the reflected glory of which one can bask *Shulman*.

fronts n. (US Black use) clothes, esp. suit or jacket *Folb*.

front street n. (US Black use) the main street of a town; that street on which most of the (illegal) action takes place (cf. fast track) *Klein*.

front-wheel skid n. (rhyming sl.) (derog.) Yid = Jew *Powis*.

frosty n. a chilled glass or can of beer *Humphries*.

fruit n. a male homosexual *Selby:1*.

fruitcake n. an eccentric, a peculiar person; fr. 'nutty as a fruitcake' (cf: nuts) *Dunne*.

fruit fly n. a woman who enjoys the company of homosexual rather than heterosexual males (cf: fag hag) *Stanley*.

fruit loop n. (US campus use) the small loop (ostensibly for hanging the shirt when no hanger is available) on the upper back of many shirts; such a loop, supposedly, can be used to hold a victim ready for buggery (cf: bugger's grips) *Bernbach*.

fruity a. sexually aroused; the fruit is 'ripe' for enjoyment.

fry v. (criminal use) to be electrocuted in the electric chair *Himes:1*.

fry one's hair v. (US Black use) to straighten one's hair (cf: conk).

F-60s (drug use) histadyl fr.

pharmaceutical identification stamped on the capsule.

F-66s n. (drug use) tuinal, fr. pharamaceutical identification stamped on the capsule.

fubar (milit. use) (acro.) *f*ucked *u*p *b*eyond *a*ll *r*ecognition *Uris.*

fubis (US milit. use) (acro) *f*uck you *b*uddy, *I*'m *s*hipping out (cf: I'm all right, Jack).

fuck n. **1.** sexual intercourse; **2.** a person, ie dumb fuck, crazy fuck, etc.

fuck v. **1.** to have sexual intercourse; **2.** an expletive, ie: fuck off, get fucked, etc.

fuck a duck! general expletive *Newman:1.*

fuck book n. pornography (cf: stroke book, eight-pager, etc.) *Pearce.*

fucked a. **1.** ruined, spoilt; **2.** unhappy, wretched.

fucked up a. 1. (drug use) extremely stoned (qv); **2.** (US milit. use) wounded or killed *Del Vecchio.*

fucked up and far from home in an utterly awful situation, miserable and lonely.

fuckfaced a. blear-eyed, half-awake *Price:2.*

fuckhead n. idiot, moron, fool, etc. *Bruce:2.*

fucking a. adj. form of fuck (qv).

fucking A/fuckin' A excellent, first rate *Price:3.*

fucking ada! exclamation, usu. implying disbelief, displeasure *Dury, 'Laughter'.*

fucking off wasting time, idling, lazing about *Seale.*

fuck off n. an idler, a lazy person.

fuck off! (excl.) go away!

fuck off v. to leave, to run away, to depart.

fuck over v. to hurt emotionally; to act cruelly, to interfere, to mess around with, to adulterate (ideas/objects) *Caserta.*

fuck that for a lark! (cp) don't expect me to get mixed up; that's a stupid idea, etc.

fuckup n. a failure, a loser.

fuck (it) up v. to make a mistake, to err, to blunder *Higgins:1.*

fuck you, Jack, I'm all right! (cp.) unalloyed selfishness; thus film title *I'm All Right, Jack*, 1958 (cf: fubis).

fuddy-duddy n. fussy, pernickety, narrow-minded person, often with assumption of their being old *Southern & Hoffenberg.*

fudge! usu. 'oh fudge!': euph. for fuck (qv) (cf: sugar) *Rawson.*

fug v. (euph.) fuck (qv); coined by N. Mailer in *The Naked and the Dead*, 1949.

full a. drunk *Wilkes.*

full as a... boot, bull, fiddler, goat, googy egg, goose, lord, tick.

full as a fairy's phone book a. (Aus. use) (poss. one-off for 'Sir Les Patterson'): extremely drunk; thus also *full as a state school hat rack, full as two race trains, full as a seaside shithouse on Boxing Day* *Humphries:2.*

full as an egg a. very drunk *Franklyn.*

full as the family po a. (Aus. use) extremely drunk *Wilkes.*

full bird n. (US milit. use) a full Colonel *Higgins:5.*

full buf n. (Valley Girls (qv) use) dressed up in one's finery, 'dressed to kill' *Pond.*

full house both syphillis and gonorrhoea *Powis.*

full of beans enthusiastic, excited, cheerful *Wodehouse:AAG.*

full of it (euph) full of shit (qv) *Gruber.*

full of piss and vinegar healthy in mind and body, full of energy and elan.

full of shit lying, spinning a line, telling tales, a generally unpleasant person or experience.

full scream (US Black use) total commitment; no holds barred *Klein.*

full sheet n. (UK prison use) a report against an officer for a serious offence against a prisoner *LL.*

full to the gills a. drunk *Dickson.*

full tour n. (US teen. use) a tedious experience (cf: three-hour tour) *Sculatti.*

full two bob n. (Aus. use) worthwhile, as good as advertised *Humphries.*

funch n. sexual liasons at lunchtime, fr. fuck (qv) + lunch; the trad. genteel term is *matinee* (cf: nooner) *Rawson.*

fungus n. see: face-fungus *Norman:2.*

funk n. cowardice, terror; thus *to funk it*: to avoid an issue or an act through fear *McFadden.*

funker n. a weakling, a coward *Barr.*

funky (Black use) **1.** sweat generated during sex; **2.** the odour of the female genitals; **3.** anything basic, elemental, earthy (cf: fonky) *Milner.*

funnies n. (abbrev.) funny papers = comic strips in daily/weekly newspapers *Dunne.*

funny farm n. a mental hospital *Napoleon XIV, 'They're Coming To Take Me Away, Ha! Ha!', 1966.*

funny man n. (US Black use) a homosexual male *Klein.*

funny money n. (criminal use) counterfeit money.

funny pages n. those pages which newspapers reserve for comic strips *PT.*

funny papers n. (US milit. use) topographical maps (cf: comics) *Del Vecchio.*

funny peculiar or funny ha-ha? (cp) asking the speaker whether 'funny' means odd or amusing *Manser.*

funt n. fr. Yiddish: one pound sterling.

fur n. the vagina (cf: beaver, pussy) *Underwood.*

furburger n. the vagina, esp. during the act of cunnilingus since then it is 'eaten' (qv) *Humphries.*

furphy n. (Aus. use) a groundless rumour; fr. one Furphy, the proprietor of sanitary carts used by the Australian forces in the First World War; the gossip and chat around these carts developed into the general word (cf: scuttlebutt) *Humphries:2.*

furry hoop n. vagina *Humphries.*

futy n. the vagina *Maledicta.*

futz n. **1.** spec: the vagina; **2.** euph: fuck (qv) *Rosten.*

fuzz n. policeman; poss. fr. fuss, since a detective makes a 'fuss' over criminality *Grogan.*

fuzzburger n. see: furburger *Simmons.*

fuzzy cup n. (US Black use) the vagina *Klein.*

G n. **1.** (abbrev.) grand = thousand (usu. dollars or pounds) (cf: K, C) *Runyon*; **2.** (drug use) one grain, usu. of morphine *Burroughs:1.*

g n. (US Black use) (abbrev.) goodies: the female genitals; the vagina *Folb.*

g a. (US teen. use) (abbrev.) gross (qv) *Pond.*

gab v. to talk; fr. 18th C. Scottish *gab* = mouth *Caserta.*

gabby a. talkative *Runyon:1.*

Gabriel n. (UK prison use) the chapel organist; fr. his angelic namesake *LL.*

gabriel n. (music use) a trumpet player; fr. the archangel who announces the 'last trump' *Major.*

gaff n. **1.** a gimmick, a hidden trick; fr. Fr. *gaffe*: a social error *Bruce:2*; **2.** house, home. orig. a fair, then a cheap music-hall or theatre *Performance.*

gaff a. excellent, simple; fr. gaffer **1** *Higgins:3.*

gaffer n. **1.** the boss; **2.** spec. the manager of a circus; thus **3.** the 'straight' front man for any form of fraud or marginal business. *Higgins:3.*

gag v. **1.** to make a joke; fr. 'choking' with laughter **2.** to choke *Price:2.*

ga-ga n. **1.** inexperienced, immature homosexual; **2.** homosexual foreplay *Legman.*

gaga a. crazy, eccentric *Higgins: 5.*

gage n. see: gauge *Southern.*

gag me with a spoon! (Valley Girls (qv) use) an expression of disgust *Harpers/Queen 1/83.*

galah n. (Aus. use) a fool, fr. the rose-breasted grey backed Aus. cockatoo 'much given to chatter' *Humphries.*

galah session n. (Aus. use) an interval set aside regularly on the Flying Doctor radio network for anyone who wishes to exchange news and gossip rather than make emergency calls; fr. the 'chattering' galah (qv) *Wilkes.*

gallon head n. (US Black use) **1.** a person with a large head; thus, traditionally **2.** an intelligent person *Klein.*

gam v. **1.** to fellate, fr. *gamahuche* (mainly 19th C.) *Keyes*; **2.** (US Black use) to boast, to show off; fr. 18/19th C. *gammon*: to tell tall tales, to hoax, to flatter insincerely *Major.*

gam n. leg, usu. female; fr. Fr. *jambe*: leg *Runyon:1.*

Game n. (abbrev.) pussy game: prostitution *Milner.*

game n. (US Black use) any means whereby one attempts to gain economic, psychological or other advantages over a rival or victim *Shulman.*

game v. any attempt to manipulate humanity for one's own ends, usually financial ones; to trick, to deceive *Milner.*

gammy a. lame, crippled; as in 'gammy leg', etc.

gander n. a look, a survey; fr. the

bird's long neck *Runyon.*

gang-bang n. **1.** multiple rape of a woman *Price:2*; **2.** (US Black use) a fight *Folb.*

gang-shag n. **1.** (white use) see: gang-bang; **2.** (US Black use) a riotous, noisy party *Major.*

gangster n. (US Black use) **1.** marijuana; **2.** a troublemaker; **3.** an aggressive, abusive person *Folb.*

gangster doors n. (US Black use) a four-door saloon *Folb.*

gangster ride n. (US Black use) an old-fashioned, large, poss. black car *Folb.*

gangster walls n. (US Black use) white-walled tyres *Folb.*

ganja n. aka: *ganga*, *gunja*: marijuana, spec. that grown in Jamaica *Green:1.*

gannet n. a glutton, a heavy eater; fr. the bird, orig. nautical use *LL.*

gaolbait n. a girl under the age of consent, with whom intercourse, even when mutually desired could legally lead to imprisonment for statutory rape *Norman:2.*

gaolbird n. a convict, or a former prison inmate *Price:3.*

gaol break n. (film use) time off from shooting for a meal break *Chandler: Notebk.*

gaolhouse lawyer n. (US/UK prison use) any inmate who has used his incarceration to study law, both for his own use and to advise other prisoners. Can also be used in derog. sense to imply amateurishness and interference.

gape n. (US Black use) anyone who is not part of the hip subculture and who thus 'gapes' in wonder/horror at its antics *Klein.*

garbage n. nonsense *Jay & Young.*

garbage mouth n. a regular, even obsessive user of obscenity/profanity *Underwood.*

garbage wagon n. a motorcycle that still retains its basic style and specifications, prior to being adapted to outlaw motorcycle gang use (cf: chopper) *Thompson.*

garbo n. **1.** (film use) a snobbish, standoffish person; fr. the actress Greta Garbo (1905–) whose most famous (if mythical) line declared 'I want to be alone' *Chandler: Notebk*; **2.** (Aus. use) garbage man, dustbin man *Humphries:2.*

garden n. (homosexual use) pubic hair (cf: grass, lawn) *Maledicta.*

garden gate n. **1.** (rhyming sl.) magistrate *Jones:J*; **2.** (bingo rhyming sl.) 8 (cf: Harry Tate).

gardening (cricket use) for the batsman to pat down supposed imperfections in the grass around his crease so as to ensure that the ball cannot take an awkward bounce *BBC Radio 3 1983.*

garden of Eden n. (US Black use) the vagina *Klein.*

gargle n. a drink.

gas n. **1.** (US campus use) idle or boastful talk *AS 50 (1965)*; **2.** a good time, plenty of fun; usu. Irish use, esp. in 'a great gas'.

gas v. **1.** to enjoy, to have a good time *Folb*; **2.** to chatter, to talk inconsequentially and continually; to offer only 'hot air' *May.*

gas and run v. to have one's car filled by a garage attendant, then drive off before he can obtain your money in payment *Whitcomb.*

gas-guzzler n. the traditionally enormous US automobile, profligate of petrol and dwarfing its European rivals; symbolic of the 1950s, out of favour in the energy-conscious '70s, but currently staging a renaissance (cf: boat).

gash n. **1.** spec. vagina; **2.** any girl or woman *Higgins:1.*

gash a. spare *LL.*

gash-eater v. one who performs cunnilingus *Legman.*

gassed a. drunk *Schulberg.*

gassy a. talkative.

gat n. a pistol or revolver; poss. fr. Gatling gun (?) *Sharpe:1.*

Gate n. (abbrev.) Notting Hill Gate, London W11.

gate fever n. (UK prison use) the nervous feeling that overtakes many prisoners as their sentence draws to its close *Cole.*

gatemouth n. (US Black use) a gossip, a loudmouth *Major.*

gauge n. (drug use) marijuana *Green:1.*

gawd n. (mispron./euph.) God.

gawdelpus n. an irritating or helpless person; often used of a child: 'you 'orrible little gawdelpus!'; fr. 'God help us'; unstated is 'what shall we do about you?'

gawp v. to stare *Algren.*

gay a. homosexual; (with the decline of derog. terms, such as queer, gay is nearly SE) *Stanley.*

gay and frisky n. (rhyming sl.) whisky *Cole.*

gayola n. (US cant) payoffs and bribes made to police to permit running of gay clubs fr. payola (qv) *Neaman & Silver.*

gazlon n. (UK criminal use) a small time, poss. timid thief, fr. Yiddish *gozlin*: a swindler, an unethical person *Powis.*

gazooney n. see: gonsi! *Legman.*

gazoopie n. aka: *gazupie*: a sex show *Legman.*

gazump v. (usu. estate agent use) to accept a stated price for one's property and then to raise that price, using as a threat, a supposed, but usu. non-existent 'offer' from elsewhere; alternatively the seller accepts one price and then, tempted by a genuinely greater offer, dumps the first buyer without sorrow or ceremony (cf: gessump).

gazungas n. breasts *Neaman & Silver.*

GB (abbrev.) goofball (qv) *Major.*

GBH (UK police/criminal use) (abbrev.) *G*rievous *B*odily *H*arm *LL.*

gd (abbrev./euph.) *g*od *d*amned *Bukowski:1.*

gear n. **1.** spec. drugs; **2.** a given object or objects, things *Performance.*

gear a. excellent, wonderful, just right; fr. 'that's the gear': that's the stuff, and at peak popularity one of the Beatles' supposed favourite words; currently used somewhat ironically (cf: fab).

geared a. (US criminal use) sexually aberrant *Legman.*

gear up v. to prepare oneself mentally and physically for dealing with the day; fr. motor car use *White.*

gee v. (US Black use) to have sexual intercourse; poss. fr. gee up, thus ride taken in a sexual sense *Klein.*

geechie a. (US Black use) unintellibible; fr. *geechie* the creole spoken by the inhabitants of the South Sea Is. off Georgia: gullah *Folb.*

gee-gees n. horses, esp. those on racecourses; thus *play the gee-gees*: to gamble on horseraces.

geek n. **1.** a carnival freak who specialized in biting the heads off live chickens *SF Comics*; **2.** (Valley Girls (qv) use) a vulgar lower class youth, fr. carnival use (qv) *Harpers/Queen 1983.*

geek v. (Aus. use) to stare at, to look at (cf: gig) *Ready.*

gee man n. (Aus. use) one who 'gees up' the potential customers into a sideshow, strip club, etc. (cf: amster) *Baker.*

geepie n. (pron. with hard 'g') a youthful hipster (cf: teenybopper) *Sculatti.*

geese n. (derog.) Jews *Runyon.*

geetoh n. GTO, a motor car *Higgins:1.*

gee up v. to provoke trouble deliberately, to tease maliciously *LL.*

gee willikins! mild, euphemistic excl.; usu. US juv. use.

geeze v. to inject narcotics; thus *geezed*: under the influence of narcotics; *geezer*: an injection of narcotics, the equipment with which one injects *Grogan.*

geezer n. a man. fr. 19th C. dialect *Performance.*

gelt n. fr. Yiddish: money; fr. Ger: gold *Norman:2.*

gen n. information, facts; fr. RAF 'general information' *Humphries.*

gendarmes n. fr. Fr: policemen *Runyon:1.*

George n. (air crew use) the automatic pilot in milit. and civil aircraft. Fr.

Second World War cp: 'let George do it I can't be bothered' *Green:2.*

georgia v. see: georgy *Major.*

georgy v. (US Black use) **1.** to trick or take advantage of a victim by using a variety of sexual lures; **2.** to hire a prostitute and then leave without paying *Himes:2.*

geri n. (abbrev.) geriatric, a derog. term for the old (and middle-aged) (cf: wrinklies).

german bands n. (rhyming sl.) hands *Jones:J.*

gertcha! fr. get along with you (cf) *Capital Radio 1983.*

gessump v. (UK prison use) to acquire anything by fraud or a confidence trick; (cf: gazump) *LL.*

gestaps n. (US Black use) the police; fr. *ge*heime *sta*ats*po*lizei, the Gestapo, the internal police force used by the German Nazi regime 1933–45 *Folb.*

get n. idiot, fool, poss. fr. *get*: child (one of his begetting) *Bleasdale.*

get! (excl.) go away! *Goulart.*

get v. as in *get yours*, *get theirs*, etc., to die, usu. by accident or through violence *Wolfe:5.*

get a bang out of v. to enjoy, to derive pleasure from, to get a thrill.

get a bee in one's bonnet v. to become obsessed by a given topic; also *have a bee . . .*

get a capture v. (UK cant) to be arrested *Norman:1.*

get across v. **1.** to irritate, to annoy; (US Black use) **2.** to succeed; **3.** to seduce; **4.** to acquire status; *Folb.*

get a fourpenny one v. to suffer physical harm, to be beaten up, spec. hit in the face.

get a glow on v. to get drunk; fr. the reddening of some drinkers' faces *Dickson.*

get a guernsey v. (Aus. use) to gain approval, to do well; fr. the award of one's team 'guernsey' (like the UK 'get one's colours', 'get one's cap') that marks one's selection to a given team *Wilkes.*

get a haircut v. (US Black use) to be cheated, robbed or in some way made to suffer by a woman *Major.*

get a hair up one's ass v. to be in a bad temper *Price:3.*

get a jag on v. to get drunk *Dickson.*

get a kick out of v. to enjoy, to appreciate (cf: kick) *Bruce:2.*

get a line on v. to understand (cf: line) *PT.*

get a load of v. to notice, to look at deliberately; usu. in a sexual context, 'get a load of that!', and used betw. males *Manser.*

get a load on v. to become drunk *Schulberg.*

get along with you! (excl.) implying general disbelief of the previous speaker *Manser.*

get an earful v. listen to *Capital Radio 1983.*

get an edge on v. to drink steadily, not to outright drunkenness, but to preserve a feeling of general inebriation *Higgins:5.*

get a snootful v. to be drunk (cf: snoot) *Dickson.*

get a shot of leg v. (US Black use) to have sexual intercourse *Folb.*

get away with murder v. to flout all proprieties with absolute success; to achieve the otherwise unacceptable *Higgins:4.*

get away (with you)! (excl.) don't try to fool me; don't tell lies, don't make me laugh, etc.; fr. SE meaning of physical movement *Breslin.*

get behind v. **1.** to make a commitment to an idea, a job, a person, etc. *Milner*; **2.** to understand; fr. hippie/drug use of 1960s *McFadden.*

get Chinese v. (US campus use) to succumb heavily to a given drug, usu. marijuana; the inference is the deviousness of the Chinese stereotype, rather than the presence of opium. *Bernbach.*

get clear v. to work out a given situation to its logical conclusion; fr. Scientology *clear*: the ultimate state of those who subject themselves to a scientology course *McFadden.*

get cold feet v. to become scared, to

back down on a previous promise or statement; the cold comes when one 'tests the water' of a situation and finds it chilly *Higgins:1*.

get cracking v. to start work, to get on with anything speedily and efficiently; fr. cracking a whip over one's team of horses *Humphries*.

get down v. (US Black use) **1.** to concentrate; **2.** to commit oneself; **3.** to do something especially well; **4.** as an excl.; this is popular when shouted between the lines of a disco record *Folb*.

get down dirty v. (US Black use) to become abusive, to cause trouble *Folb*.

get down fonky v. see: get down dirty *Folb*.

get down from the Y v. (US Black use) to fight *Folb*.

get down shitty v. see: get down dirty *Folb*.

get down with v. (US Black use) to become involved with; to enjoy *Folb*.

get gay with v. to tease, to provoke, to be flippant *Chandler:LG*.

get her! excl. of derision, mockery (both affectionate and otherwise); orig. homosexual use, 'her' being someone acting exceptionally affectedly, but now general use *Thames TV 1984*.

get this v. to die, usu. violently; poss. abbrev. 'get his deserts'.

get home with the milk v. to stay out all night and return only at dawn.

get hot under the collar v. to become increasingly ill-tempered *Neaman & Silver*.

get in bad (with) v. to earn disfavour, to get into trouble.

get in deep v. to become heavily involved; usu. in either crime or love *'The Stone Killer', film, 1973*.

get in line v. to conform.

get in one's eye v. (US Black use) to beat up *Folb*.

get in one's hair v. to annoy, to irritate; the image is of lice.

get into v. to penetrate either the vagina or anus *Legman*.

get into v.t. to become involved in something.

get into one's pants v. to seduce *Bukowski:1*.

get into one's ribs v. to borrow money; one's wallet is carried in a pocket near the ribs *Wodehouse:PGM*.

get it? do you understand? esp. referring to the point of a joke *T 1983*.

get it in the neck v. **1.** to be killed; **2.** to be punished severely; to suffer badly.

get it off one's chest v. to confess, to unburden oneself *Wodehouse:AAG*.

get it on v. to take positive action *Greenlee*.

get it on (with) v. to have sexual intercourse *McFadden*.

get it together v. **1.** to start a sexual relationship; **2.** to make a decision, to take action; **3.** to pull oneself together, to stop vacillating, etc.

get it up v. **1.** to achieve erection; thus, **2.** to maintain enthusiasm for a given idea, situation etc. (cf: hard-on for) *Higgins:5*.

get jack of v. (Aus. use) to resent, to be bored, with, fed up with *Humphries:2*.

get knotted! (excl.) go away, stop bothering (me); euph., get fucked *Manser*.

get lost! fr. Yiddish *ver farvalgert*: disappear, move on, go away *Rosten*.

get low v. (US campus use) to smoke marijuana; a reverse pun on usu. 'get high' (qv) *Bernbach*.

get more ass than a toilet seat to have an extensive and varied sex life *'The Deer Hunter', dir. M. Cimino, 1979*.

get next to (US Black use) to become lovers, to seduce *Capital Radio 1984*.

get off v. (drug use) to experience the effects of a given drug; fr. 'taking off' and getting 'high' (qqv) *Larner*.

get off on v. to enjoy *McFadden*.

get off one's back v. to stop annoying someone; to stop nagging or otherwise irritating *Big Ass Comics 1*.

get off one's case v. to desist from

harassing, to stop annoying *McFadden.*

get off with v. to seduce, to pick up and poss. go to bed with.

get one at it v. to tease, to drive into a fury *Norman:1.*

get one going v. **1.** to drive someone into a temper, to make one lose control through teasing; **2.** to drink heavily; 'one' = a drinking session *Dickson.*

get one's act together v. to calm down; to plan sensibly, to state a goal and aim for it *McFadden.*

get one's ashes hauled v. to have sexual intercourse; ashes a mispron. of ass (?) *Keyes.*

get one's ass in a sling v. to get into bad trouble, physical or otherwise *Higgins:4.*

get one's ass in gear v. to hurry up, to stop wasting time, to put some effort and commitment into one's activities, to start doing something useful and positive (cf: get one's act together) *Uris.*

get one's back up v. to annoy, irritate, infuriate; fr. the feline habit of bristling the fur when annoyed or frightened *Sillitoe.*

get one's bowels in an uproar v. to become excited, agitated *Schulberg:2.*

get one's cards v. to be dismissed from work; the cards in question are Insurance Cards, P45 forms, etc.; thus to *give one one's cards*: to dismiss *LL.*

get one's collar felt v. (UK criminal use) to be arrested *LL.*

get one's cookies v. to have sexual intercourse *Higgins:2.*

get one's dander up v. to lose one's temper; poss. fr. Romany *dander*: to bite *Neaman & Silver.*

get one's end away v. to have sexual intercourse *Humphries.*

get one's end in v. see: get one's end away *Wilkes.*

get one's feet muddy v. to have been in criminal trouble *Powis.*

get one's feet under the table v. to establish friendly relations; of a man, to start living with a woman.

get one's finger out v. to stop dawdling and lazing about and begin some constructive activity *Waterhouse.*

get one's goat v. to annoy someone; fr. the goat's propensity to butt when in a bad temper (?) *Neaman & Silver.*

get one's greens v. to have sexual intercourse; poss. fr. obs. *garden*: female genitals (cf: garden of Eden) *Rawson.*

get one's gun off v. to reach orgasm *Pearce.*

get one's head down v. to have some sleep *Newman:2.*

get one's head together v. to sort oneself out; to calm down *Wilkinson.*

get one's hooks on v. to grasp, to grab, to obtain; esp. when the object is most desired or currently held by a rival. (cf: hooks) *Wodehouse:GB.*

get one's jollies v. to enjoy oneself; to have sex *Goldman.*

get one's knickers in a twist v. to become excessively agitated over a problem or situation, to worry to extremes.

get one's leg over v. to seduce *May.*

get one's nose cold v. (drug use) to sniff cocaine, which has a numbing quality, esp. if, as more than likely, it has been adulterated with procaine or novocaine.

get one's nuts off v. to achieve orgasm, poss. through masturbation *Southern & Hoffenberg.*

get one's oats v. to gain sexual release.

get one's respect v. (US Black use) to ensure that one is treated in the manner to which one feels one should be accustomed, esp. in prison *Klein.*

get one's rocks off v. **1.** to enjoy oneself; **2.** to have sexual intercourse *Higgins:1.*

get one's shit together v. see: get one's act together *Jay & Young.*

get one's shoes full v. to become drunk *Dickson.*

get one's skates on v. to hurry up, to stop wasting time.

get one's thing off v. (US Black use)

to gain pleasure from any given act *Klein.*

get one's wings v. **1.** (drug use) to start using heroin *Grogan*; **2.** (Hells Angels use) to be initiated into an outlaw motor cycle club (cf: red wings, brown wings) *Thompson.*

get on v.t. (US Black use) to pursue a given goal, aim *Klein.*

get on one's tits v. to irritate, to annoy *Bleasdale.*

get on one's wick v. to irritate, to annoy; fr. rhyming sl., Hampton Wick = prick = penis (qv) *Neaman & Silver.*

get over v. (US Black use) to achieve a given goal *Klein.*

get rooted! (Aus. use) excl. of strong protest; euph. Fuck off! get fucked! *Baker.*

get shot of v. aka: *get shut of* to get rid of something/someone *Sillitoe.*

get it to the T v. succeed absolutely and perfectly *The Who, 'Quadrophenia', 1973.*

get some v. to have sexual intercourse; thus: *getting any? Higgins:1.*

get some big leg v. aka: *get some cock*, *get some pussy*, *get some tail*, *get some soft leg*: to have sexual intercourse *Folb.*

get some brown v. aka: *to get some brown sugar*; *get some duke*: have male homosexual intercourse *Folb.*

get some ink v. to receive newspaper/magazine coverage for one's actions, speech, etc. *Higgins:5.*

get straight v. (US campus use) to sober up, either from drink or drugs *Underwood.*

get stuck into v. **1.** to start a fight; **2.** to start any form of activity; the implication is one of enthusiasm and activity.

get stuffed! (excl.) euph. for get fucked! *Manser.*

get the ass v. (US campus use) to lose one's temper; to become annoyed (cf: get the red ass) *Underwood.*

get the bird v. to be jeered, mocked, etc.; esp. theatrical use and dating back to 16th C.; fr. the hissing noise that geese, and an unappreciative audience can make.

get the Book v. (UK prison use) **1.** to become religious while serving one's sentence; **2.** for a Prison Officer to be disciplined for internal offences, usu. suspended pending an inquiry *LL.*

get the boot v. to be thrown out; both of a place or of employment (cf: get the chop).

get the bullet v. see: get the boot, get the chop, etc.

get the bum's rush to be thrown out.

get the chop v. to be dismissed from one's job.

get the drop on v. to obtain an (unfair) advantage over someone fr. drop = knock down (qv).

get the fat off v. (Aus. use) to relieve someone of their money, usu. by some form of trick or con-game *Humphries:2.*

get the glory v. (UK prison use) to become suddenly and fervently religious while serving one's sentence *LL.*

get the hell out of Dodge v. (US campus cp) to leave, to depart; 'if you don't want to stay here, then get the hell . . .' *Underwood.*

get the lead out! hurry up, stop dawdling, get on with it! *'Minder', Thames TV, 1983.*

get the message v. to appreciate, to understand; orig. jazz use, but now general.

get them in v. to order a round of drinks; esp. as excl. get them in! *Waterhouse.*

get the needle v. to be extremely annoyed *Norman:2.*

get the order of the boot v. to be sacked from work; fr. Order of the Bath.

get the picture v. to understand, to appreciate.

get the red ass v. to bear a grievance *Jenkins.*

get the slingers v. to be thrown out, dismissed from a job *Norman:3.*

get the wind up v. to become

nervous; fr. 'get the wind up one's trousers' *Wodehouse:GB*.

get this! (excl.) now listen! this is amazing!, etc. *Capital Radio 1983*.

getting any? popular greeting between men; the 'any' in question is, of course, sex *BBC-1 TV 1983*.

getting off at Redfern (Aus. use) coitus interruptus; Redfern is the station immediately before Sydney Central (cf: getting out at Gateshead) *Wilkes*.

getting out at Gateshead coitus interruptus; spec. used by natives of Newcastle-upon-Tyne, Gateshead being the station previous to their own (cf: getting off at Redfern) *Wilkes*.

getting the mohawk (US teen. use) building up one's irritation into a genuine bad temper *Sculatti*.

get to v. **1.** corrupt, bribe, influence *Heller*; **2.** to effect, to influence emotionally *McFadden*.

get to first base v. make some preliminary headway in seduction (cf: first base).

get tore in v. (Scottish use) to fight vigorously *G. MacDonald Fraser, 'McAuslan in the Rough', 1974*.

get under one's skin v. **1.** to annoy, to irritate; **2.** to fascinate, esp. sexually; both meanings fr. insect infestation.

get up n. **1.** (US prison use) the date of one's release given by a parole board, and thus the day on which one 'gets up' in prison but goes to bed free (cf: wake-up, n.) *Klein*; **2.** lies, a ruse, a subterfuge; something 'got up' to allay suspicions/enquiries *Newman:1*.

get weaving v. to stop wasting time, to hurry up, etc. *Manser*.

get with v. to understand; to join in; to accept the majority line.

gfu (milit. use) (acro.) *g*eneral *f*uck-*u*p (cf: snafu) *Rawson*.

ghetto blaster n. large stereo tape recorder plus radio carried by ghetto youths (cf: Third World briefcase, wog box) *Capital Radio 1984*.

ghinny n. (derog.) Italian (cf: guinea) *Higgins:1*.

ghost v. (UK prison use) to move a prisoner from one gaol to another during the night, both departure and arrival taking place when the other prisoners are locked in their cells *Obs. 1981*.

ghosting (US milit. use) idling, avoiding duties (cf: Goldbrick) *Del Vecchio*.

gib teenuck n. (backsl.) (derog.) big cunt *Cole*.

gib teesurbs n. (backsl.) big breasts (of a passing female) *Cole*.

gift of the gab articulateness, charm, persuasiveness *Wright*.

gig n. **1.** spec. a musical performance at a given venue; **2.** a job. *Price:2*; **3.** (street gang use) an event, a party *Salisbury*; (Aus. use) **4.** a fool, an idiot *Ready*; **5.** a look, a glance *Wilkes*.

gig v. **1.** (Aus. use) to look at, to stare (as in obs. UK school sl: *giglamps*: spectacles) *Ready*; **2.** (music business use) to play at a given venue, to perform *May*.

giggle-house n. (Aus. use) mental hospital, lunatic asylum *Wilkes*.

gigo (acro.) *g*arbage *i*n, *g*arbage *o*ut: cp implying that one cannot expect poor input to produce, by some magic, excellent output; fr. computer jargon.

gigolo v. (US Black use) to steal a friend's lover; to cheat on one's lover or partner *Folb*.

gimp n. **1.** spec. a cripple; thus **2.** an incompetent, a useless person, a loser *Price:3*.

gimp v. (US campus use) to ruin, to spoil *Underwood*.

gimped in (US campus use) irregularly shaped, dented *Underwood*.

gimped up (US campus use) confused, at a loss, mixed up *Underwood*.

gimpy a. **1.** crippled; **2.** botched, second rate *Underwood*.

gin and fuck-it n. a girl, usu. foreign au pair or tourist, who can allegedly be seduced for the price of a drink in certain pubs where such pick-ups congregate.

gin and Jaguar belt n. (UK criminal/police use) the wealthy Home Counties areas around London, esp. ripe for robbery *Powis.*
ginch n. **1.** vagina *Junker*; thus **2.** an attractive female *Wolfe: 2.*
ginchy a. attractive, sexy (cf: ginch **2**).
ginger n. **1.** (rhyming sl.) ginger beer = queer = homosexual *Powis*; **2.** (Aus. use) a prostitute who robs her customer of his wallet (cf: murphy game) *Wilkes.*
gin-jockey n. (Aus. use) a white man who enjoys sexual relations with Aborigine women (cf: gin-shepherd) *Wilkes.*
ginnal n. (Jamaican use) trickster, confidence man *Thelwell.*
gink n. a useless, stupid person *Wodehouse: passim.*
ginney n. see: guinea *Dunne.*
ginormous a. incomparably huge; fr. RAF sl. great +*i*mmense + *e*normous.
gin-shepherd n. a white man who attempts to prevent miscegenation between his peers and Aborigine women (cf: gin-jockey) *Wilkes.*
ginzo n. (derog.) Italian (cf: guinea) *Higgins:1.*
girl n. (drug use) cocaine (cf: boy) *Green:1.*
GIs n. diarrhoea/dysentery suffered by US troops on foreign duties (cf: Delhi belly, Montezuma's revenge) *Rawson.*
gissa job! (cp) fr. dial., give me a job, used by character 'Yosser Hughes' in A. Bleasdale's 'Boys from the Blackstuff', 1982 *Bleasdale.*
gissum n. see: gizzum.
git n. see: get.
git-down time n. the start of a prostitute's working 'day', when she 'get's down to business' *Shulman.*
git-'em-up guy n. a hold-up man; a robber; fr. demand 'get your hands up!' *Runyon.*
git-go n. the beginning *Milner.*
gitty-gap n. (US campus use) a thing *Underwood.*
give! (excl.) explain! confess! *Rosten.*
give a blow v. to blow marijuana smoke directly from the cigarette into someone else's mouth, achieved by reversing the joint in one's own mouth and blowing (cf: shotgun) *Milner.*
give a body v. (UK police use) to inform, to betray the names of one's criminal associates; usu. as exhortation 'Go on, John, give us a body' (and we'll be kinder to you) *Cole.*
give a break v. to give a chance, to let off, to excuse, to give an opportunity.
give a damn v. to care.
give a flying fuck, couldn't v. couldn't care less *Price:2.*
give a leg-up v. to help someone over an obstacle, wall, etc.; both physical and figurative *Wodehouse:PGM.*
give a little leg v. to confuse, to tell tales *Higgins:2.*
give a shit v. to care, but also, not to care, ie: 'I could give a shit' (cf: give a damn) *Price:2.*
give a squeeze v. (UK cant) to give a chance (to) *Cole.*
give a stuff v. see: give a shit *Humphries.*
give a tumble v. to try out, to experiment *Powis.*
give cone v. (Valley Girls (qv) use) to fellate; fr. licking an ice-cream cone *Pond.*
give head v. to perform oral intercourse *Goldman.*
give (her) a length v. to make love to a woman.
give (her) one v. to have sexual intercourse.
give it a fly v. (Aus. use) see: give (something) a burl *Wilkes.*
give it a go v. make an attempt, give it a try *Capital Radio 1983.*
give it all that v. to boast, to show off *Powis.*
give it a whirl v. try something out.
give it to v. (US criminal use) to murder, to execute *Bruce:2.*
give it the gun v. to accelerate, to drive a car fast *rr.*
give it the herbs v. (Aus. use) to accelerate a car *Wilkes.*
give it up (homosexual use) an

aggressive demand from one male that another accept his advances, esp. in gaol *Klein*.

give jiggs v. to keep a lookout; (abbrev.) *jiggers*! look out! run for it! *Farrell*.

give one a bell v. to call on the telephone (cf: give one a buzz) *Humphries:2*.

give one a buzz v. to call someone on the telephone (cf: give a bell) *Wodehouse:AAG*.

give one a coating v. (UK police use) to give one a reprimand *Powis*.

give one a piece of one's mind v. to tell someone off severely *Neaman & Silver*.

give one a song and dance v. to tell fanciful tales for the purpose of confusing or tricking the listener *Chandler:LG*.

give one a tumble v. to go to bed with someone *Runyon:1*.

give one Larry Dooley v. (Aus. use) to beat someone, to punish *Wilkes*.

give one rocks v. to excite sexually, spec. to make a man have an erection *Bukowski:1*.

give one's best shot v. to make one's best efforts; often as 'give—one's best shot' *Whitcomb*.

give one's arse a chance v. derog. comment aimed at a talkative person; usu. prefaced by 'Why don't you shut up and. . .' *Powis*.

give one some curry v. (Aus. use) 'to make things hot' for someone, to attack (verbally or physically) *Wilkes*.

give one some stick v. to encourage action by making threats.

give one the bullet v. to dismiss from employment, to throw out *Norman:2*.

give one the brush v. to ignore, to snub; fr. *brush*: (abbrev.) brush off *Dunne*.

give one the business v. **1.** to have sexual intercourse *Neaman & Silver*; **2.** to tease, to taunt, to put at a disadvantage by one's own actions *Dunne*.

give one the creeps v. to worry, to perturb, to disgust *Price:2*.

give one the finger v. to make a manual gesture (the raised middle finger in the US, the 'V-sign' in the UK) to imply derision and disdain *McFadden*.

give one the glad eye v. to give someone of the opposite sex a glance that implies sexual attraction.

give one the old boracic v. to deceive, to tell tales; prob. fr. Aus. *poke borak*: to hoax, to confuse the credulous; itself fr. barrack: to jeer.

give (something) a burl v. (Aus. use) to give it a try *Humphries*.

give one the belt v. to get rid of, to throw out *Norman:2*.

give one the chop **1.** to kill or otherwise dispose of a person; **2.** to fire from a job.

give one the leather v. to kick a person *Runyon:1*.

give one the leg v. see: pull one's leg *Higgins:4*.

give one the office v. (UK prison use) to initiate a new prisoner into the rules and regulations, official and unofficial, of prison life *LL*.

give one the pink slip v. to hand over, to cede ownership of something to another person; fr. the pink slip which in the US proves ownership of a given car *Wodehouse:AAG*.

give one the pip v. to irritate intensely *Wodehouse:AAG*.

give one the runaround v. to deceive, to delay, to put off, to avoid – all such efforts usu. in order to give oneself some form of advantage, breathing space, etc. *Thompson*.

give one what for v. to give someone a hard time, to tell off severely, to beat, esp. of an errant child.

give over! stop it! almost always northern UK use.

give some body v. to accede to sexual advances *Klein*.

give some plank v. (US Black use) see: give some skin.

give some skin v. (US Black use) ritual palm slapping that forms greeting between Blacks or Black and knowledgeable white (cf: slap five).

give some spli v. (US Black use) see give some skin *Klein.*

give the business v. **1.** to kill *Rawson*; **2.** to deceive, to bamboozle.

give the chop v. to destroy, to abandon, to stop, to cut off *Dunne.*

give the dog a bone v. to have sexual intercourse *Squeeze, 'Cool for Cats', 1983.*

give the drummer some v. see: give some skin *Major.*

give the duke v. to slow hand-clap as a sign of disapproval of a given sporting event; fr. duke=hand *Heller.*

give the eye v. to appraise sexually *Selby:1.*

give the finger v. to make a derogatory gesture by raising the middle finger in the direction of the person targeted; the meaning is 'fuck off' (cf: flip the bird).

give the green light v. to give permission, to allow; fr. traffic lights/ railway signals *Wodehouse:AAG.*

give the gun v. to accelerate a motor car.

give the heat v. to murder, to kill (cf: heat) *Rawson.*

give the Man the play v. (US Black use) to inform (cf: Man) *Folb.*

give them away with a pound of tea ironic reply by criminal to questions referring to the origins of obviously stolen goods in his possession *Powis.*

give the once-over v. to look over, to assess *Price:3.*

give the rap v. to murder, to kill Rawson.

give the works to v. **1.** to harm; from actual murder to mere beating up *rr*; **2.** to make an effort in a given context, whether selling an item, shooting a line (qv), criticizing, etc. *Chandler:LG.*

give up one's face v. to permit oneself to indulge in oral intercourse at the insistence of a partner *Klein.*

give up rhythm v. (US Black use) for a woman, using body language, to indicate her sexual availability to a man with whom she is walking or dancing *Shulman.*

give up the store v. to surrender, to give in *PT.*

gizmo n. **1.** (drug use) the paraphanalia used for injecting narcotics; **2.** any (small) thing for which one has temporarily forgotten the correct name, a gadget, a thingumijig *TZ.*

gizzum aka: *gissum*: semen *Price:1.*

glad eye n. a glance of sexual interest; thus *give the glad eye*: to appraise sexually (cf: hard eyes).

glad hand v. to welcome enthusiastically, even excessively and very likely insincerely; often used of politicians and similar professional charmers. fr. the outstretched hand of greeting (cf: flesh-presser).

glad rags n. one's best and prob. gaudiest clothes.

glads n. (Aus. use) (abbrev.) gladioli *Humphries:2.*

glamour puss n. an ostentatiously well-dressed, lavishly made-up, etc. woman.

glass n. (US criminal use) a diamond; thus *genuine glass*: very high quality; *fake glass*: worthless *Klein.*

glassed (UK criminal use) cut in the face or body by a jab or slash from a broken bottle *Powis.*

glasshouse n. prison, (esp. UK milit. use) fr. glass-roofed North Camp military prison at Aldershot *Wodehouse passim.*

glass jaw n. (boxing use) a conspicuously weak jaw which breaks or fractures when hit and loses its possessor his fights *Dunne.*

gleep a cage v. (US cant, motorcycle gang use) to steal a car *Neaman & Silver.*

glim n. a lantern; esp. a dark lantern used by thieves *Norman:2.*

glimmer n. a beggar *Powis.*

glitterati n. those fashionable writers and academics and sundry critics, etc. who have transcended their usual obscurity into the dubious limelight of the New York and London gossip columns *Safire.*

glitzy a. fashionable, sophisticated,

chic; glamorous + ritzy (qv) *T 8/9/83.*

globetrotter n. (drug use) a narcotics addict who is continually on the move *Major.*

glom v. aka: *glaum*: to grab, to steal *Chandler: Notebk.*

glory hole n. **1.** the vagina *Stanley*; **2.** (homosexual use) a hole cut in the side of a public toilet cubicle; one man pushes his penis through while another, anonymous, man fellates him *Jay & Young.*

glossy n. (abbrev.) glossy magazine; usu. expensive women's fashion magazines – *Vogue*, *Harpers/Queen* (which has called itself 'the non-drip glossy, punning on both drip = weakling, dullard, and gloss paint), etc. a descendant of the earlier *slicks.*

glut n. (abbrev.) glutton (qv) *Legman.*

glutton n. (homosexual use) a man obsessed with sex to the exclusion of other considerations *Legman.*

glutton for punishment n. (homosexual use) a fellator who continues sucking the penis even when orgasm has been reached *Legman.*

G-man n. FBI agent, fr. Government-man *Runyon:1.*

GMBU (acro.) *G*rand *M*ilitary *B*alls-*U*p (cf: GMFU) *Motimer.*

GMFU n. (UK 'society' use) *G*rand *M*ilitary *F*uck-*U*p (cf: GMBU) *Barr.*

gnarly a. (Valley Girls (qv) use) general term of disapproval, disappointment, annoyance *Pond.*

gnat's piss n. derog. description of any liquid, but esp. alcohol, that is weak, thin, tasteless, etc.

gnaw the 'nana to perform fellatio *Humphries.*

go v. to say, to talk; 'I go "How are you" and he just goes "Lousy". . .' *Pond.*

go a bundle on v. to support wholeheartedly. fr. the betting of one's whole 'bundle' (bank-roll).

go all over town with v. see: around the world *Legman.*

go all the way v. a man who 'goes all the way' achieves satisfactory seduction; the woman who does so is willing to permit it *Rawson.*

go a million v. (Aus. use) to be utterly lost, in a totally hopeless position, at a total disadvantage *Wilkes.*

go (and) jump in a lake! (euph.) go to hell! (qv) *Manser.*

go and see a man about a dog v. (cp) an excuse to facilitate one's leaving; often when needing to visit the lavatory.

go and take a running jump (at yourself) aka: *go and take a flying fuck*: epithet of dismissal and distaste.

go ape v. to lose control, esp. of one's temper *Selby:1.*

go around the block v. to gain experience *'Hill Street Blues', Thames TV, 1983.*

gob n. mouth.

gob v. to spit *Wolfe:8.*

go bananas v. **1.** to lose emotional control, to become obsessed by; **2.** to delight in something absolutely, usu. ≃ over *Underwood.*

go bark at the moon (excl.) go away! get lost! fuck off! *Simmons.*

gobble v. to fellate *Legman.*

gobble box n. (US campus use) television set (cf: goggle box) *Underwood.*

gobble the goo v. to fellate *Legman.*

gobby a. see: gabby *BBC-1 TV 1983.*

go belly up v. (US use) to die; a dead fish floats belly up on the water *Neaman & Silver.*

go bent v. (UK police use) for a witness to retract a previous statement (that helps the prosecution) (cf: bent) *Laurie.*

go bent on v. to let down; to desert *Norman:2.*

gob job n. fellatio (cf: blow job, head).

go boil your head! (excel.) generally dismissive, euph. for go to hell! (qv).

go Borneo v. (US campus use) crazily drunk; fr. presumed antics of the 'Wild Man of Borneo' *Bernbach.*

gobshite n. a fool, a dupe.

go case v. to sleep with *Norman:1.*

go cold on v. to lose one's initial enthusiasm for a proposition, activity, etc.

go crackers v. to go mad, become insane, eccentric.

godawful a. especially appalling *Price: 2.*

goddam a. generally derog., to intensify one's dislike of a given person, object, etc. *McBain:1.*

goddie n. (backsl.) dog *Cole.*

God forbids n. (rhyming sl.) kids, children *Powis.*

god-help-us n. aka *gawdelpus* (qv): a difficult person, often a mischievous child *Wodehouse: MS.*

go down v. **1.** (US street gang use) to attack a rival gang *Salisbury*; **2.** to happen, to take place *McFadden.*

go down in flames v. to fail to complete a task, despite one's best efforts *Safire.*

go down like a lead balloon v. to find no favour whatsoever; usu. of an idea or suggestion.

go down (on) v. to practise oral intercourse, for either sex (cf. blow, eat) *Higgins:2.*

go down on v. to cause someone trouble, to harm someone *Stone.*

go down south v. see: go down (on) *Powis.*

go down the drain v. see: go down the plughole.

go down the plughole v. to be wasted, to be lost for ever; like bathwater.

go down the road v. to pursue a given policy or course of action, even if it proves unpleasant *PT.*

go down the tubes v. to fail badly; to collapse completely.

God's in heaven (bingo rhyming sl.) 7 *Wright.*

God slot (TV use) that period of early Sunday evening TV viewing set aside by law for mandatory, if marginal, religious broadcasting. *Green:2.*

God's own medicine n. (drug use) morphine (cf: mother nature's own tobacco) *Algren.*

goer n. a promiscuous, sexually available female *'Monty Python's Flying Circus', BBC-2 1969.*

gofer n. assistant, errand boy, anyone who is told to 'go fer . . .' some requirement *Price:2.*

go fish v. (homosexual use) an effeminate man, wishing to imply his approximation of a woman during sex, might claim 'I just go fish', ie: turn into a girl (cf: fish) *Legman.*

go for v. **1.** to accept, to believe *Higgins:1*; **2.** attack; **3** to find sexually or otherwise attractive or appealing *Howard.*

go for broke to commit oneself unreservedly; esp. in gambling or betting context (cf: shit or bust).

go for it! (US campus use) general exhortation to those present, urging them to act crazily, the intention being thus to have extreme fun *Bernbach.*

go for one's tea v. to die *Powis.*

go for the doctor v. (Aus. racing use) for one rider and his mount to move significantly ahead of the field *Obs. 3/7/83*; **2.** (Aus. use) in gambling, to bet all one's money *Wilkes.*

go for the whole shot v. make an absolute commitment; indulge oneself completely *McFadden.*

go for veg v. (US campus use) to become drunk *Underwood.*

go from the fists v. aka: *go from the shoulders*, *go from the Y*: to fight.

goggle (at) v. to stare (at) *Wodehouse: AAG.*

goggle box n. the television *May.*

go halves v. to share, to divide equally.

go hang v. **1.** to go wrong, to collapse (of a plan), to fail *PT*; **2.** (euph.) go to hell; thus 'tell him to go hang!'

go haywire v. to lose control, to go mad; poss. fr. the baling wire used by US farmers to mend implements that have gone wrong *Bukowski:2.*

go ahead up v. (US Black use) to take part in some form of activity with another person *Folb.*

go Hollywood v. to sodomize; fr. the cinematic capital, where it presumed such excesses are quotidian pleasures *Neaman & Silver.*

going down happening *Price:2.*

going for pinkslips racing cars with the winner gaining the other's vehicle; the pink (insurance) slip is proof of ownership.

go in the tank v. (boxing use) to lose a fight deliberately; fr. tank = swimming pool (cf: take a dive) *Dunne.*

go in the water v. (boxing use) to lose a fight deliberately; fr. take a dive (qv) *Dunne.*

go into a flat spin v. to lose perspective and orientation, to be come very confused; fr. flying use.

goitre n. (UK criminal use) a bulging wallet full of notes; fr. the physical ailment *Powis.*

gold n. money; fr. *gelt* (qv) *Burroughs:1.*

Goldberg n. (US Black use) any Jew, esp. the shopowners of Harlem and other ghettoes *Milner.*

goldbrick n. a shirker, a loafter, a lazy person; fr. trick of selling a supposed (in fact painted) gold brick to the gullible, thus getting money without working for it *Uris.*

gold dust n. (drug use) heroin, presumably the Chinese (brown) variety, but also fr. the high price *Underwood.*

golden doughnut n. (Aus. use) the vulva *Wilkes.*

golden duck n. (cricket use) to be given out at the first ball of one's innings.

golden girl n. (drug use) particularly high grade cocaine (cf: girl) *Folb.*

golden oldie n. anything vintage but still valued; spec. rock 'n' roll records of 1950s/early 1960s.

golden shower urolagnia *Shulman.*

golden shower queen homosexual who enjoys being urinated on *Stanley.*

gold watch n. (rhyming sl.) Scotch whisky; orig. the rare *waterbury watch* (19th C. use) *Powis.*

go like a bat out of hell v. to move exceptionally fast.

go like a bomb v. **1.** to go very fast; **2.** to work out very successfully (cf: bomb).

go like hot cakes v. of a product or commodity: to sell out quickly.

go like the clappers v. to run very fast; rhyming euph. for go like hell: clappers = bell, rhymes with hell.

golly! (euph.) God, extra-mild euph., usu. child use only *Wodehouse:AAG.*

go-long n. (US Black use) the police truck in which arrested people are taken to the local cells (cf: paddy wagon, hurry-up) *Major.*

GOM n. see: God's Own Medicine.

gome n. (US campus use) a devotedly hard worker *Bernbach.*

go nap on v. **1.** (UK use) to commit oneself fully; fr. gambling use: to bet all one's assets, **2.** (Aus. use) usu. in negative sense: 'don't/doesn't/etc. go nap. . .': to dislike, to avoid *Wilkes.*

gone a. **1.** insane, crazy, bizarre *Runyon*; this predates, and poss. outlives, **2.** (Jazz/beatnik use) weird and wonderful, lost in music, drugs, etc; esp. *gone cat.*

gonef aka *gonnif*: fr. Yiddish: a thief *Rosten.*

gone for a Burton gone away, esp. absent presumed dead; fr. Second World War RAF use; the 'Burton' is a particular beer *Powis.*

gone on obsessed by, esp. when in love *Goulart.*

goner n. a doomed person, anyone who cannot avoid an unpleasant fate *Big Ass Comics 1.*

gone to pot of a person: fallen in status, leading a degenerate life; of a thing: broken down, ceased from functioning properly or well *Hotten.*

gong n. (milit. use) a medal.

goniff n. aka: *gonef*, thief, fr. Yiddish *Schulberg.*

gonk n. (UK prostitute use) contemptuous description of a client; fr. large cuddly figures momentarily popular in 1960s *Powis.*

gonner n. see: goner *T 12/9/83.*

gonsil n. (US tramp sl.) a young, homosexual sidekick who accompanies a tramp *Legman.*

gonzo a. finished, defeated, useless; fr. gone + zo (cod-Italian suffix)

Higgins:5.

goob n. (US campus use) a small mole, spot or similar skin blemish, fr. goober = peanut *Underwood.*

goober n. **1.** (US campus use) a small child; fr. goober = peanut = a given small object or person *Underwood*; **2.** the penis *Rawson*; **3.** an idiot, a fool, an incompetent *Pond.*

good news n. an acceptable person, event, etc.; general term of approval *Barr.*

good ole boy n. **1.** a Southern man of any age who conforms to the prevalent cultural standards *White*; **2.** (US preppie (qv) use) a student who is considered of the right type by his peers *Bernbach.*

good on you! (Aus. use) general expression of approbation, thanks, etc. *Ready.*

good people n. **1.** spec. former criminals (US) who have retired from their various specialities; **2.** one's peers *Maurer.*

goods n. (US criminal use) stolen goods, contraband *Klein.*

good shot good try, even though one may have failed.

good stuff n. (US Black use) **1.** sexually sophisticated; **2.** effective, pleasant drugs; **3.** success in a confidence trick, in deception *Klein.*

good time n. **1.** (US prison use) the penis *Higgins:1*; **2.** (US Black use) an especially acceptable, likeable person *Klein.*

good-time n. (Can. prison use) time off for good behaviour *Caron.*

goof n. an eccentric, crazy person; fr. dial. *goof*: a fool *Thompson:J.*

goof v. to blunder, to make a mistake *Goldman.*

goofball n. a barbiturate; a tranquilizer *De Lannoy & Masterson.*

goof bender n. letting one's hair down, acting absurd just for fun *Price: 3.*

goofed a. inebriated with a given drug; esp. barbiturates (cf: goofball) *Selby: 1.*

goofer n. a homosexual prostitute who will take active roles in fellatio or anal intercourse.

go off v.t. to find a person or object unappealing, distasteful, tedious. usu. when one's feelings have been more positive before *Griffith.*

go off the boil v. **1.** to lose impetus, to lose enthusiasm; **2.** to calm down *Wodehouse: AAG.*

go off the deep end v. to lose control, to become extremely angry, depressed, to show any extreme of emotion *Jay & Young.*

go off the rails v. to err, to make a mistake *Wodehouse: PGM.*

goof off v. to act lazily, to mess around instead of working *SF Comics.*

goof on v. to laugh at, to find amusing *Goldman.*

goofy a. stupid, uncoordinated, inept *Wodehouse: YMS.*

goo-goo eyes n. an amorous glance directed at a loved, or hopefully soon to be loved one.

gook n. **1.** (US campus use) dull, stupid, foolish person; poss. fr. milit. use in Vietnam *Underwood*; **2.** (derog.) Oriental; originated by US troops in Korean War, perpetuated in Vietnam and thus spread into non-milit. use *Del Vecchio.*

goolies n. testicles; fr. *gullies*; marbles.

goombah n. a thug, a gangster; fr. Italian: godfather, one of the names (cf: M. Puzo, *The Godfather,* 1969) used for a leader of the Italian-American Mafia *Grogan.*

goon n. **1.** thug (cf: heavy); **2.** spec. non-union labour used for strike breaking, intimidation, etc. *Tuff Shit Comics.*

go on about v. to nag, to complain continually and habitually, to make a lengthy fuss.

go one-on-one v. to have a direct confrontation with another person.

goon squad n. a group of thugs, usu. organized for a specific purpose – strike-breaking, extortion, etc.

go on, twist my arm (cp) a joking pretence that the speaker has to be persuaded into doing something that is in fact very appealing and will require no second thoughts on doing it.

goop n. fool, idiot *Wodehouse: YMS.*

goose n. (US campus use) a socially unacceptable person; a fool *Underwood.*

goose v. to poke a finger into the anus or vagina to surprise or poss. titillate the recipent of such attentions *Selby: 1.*

goose's neck n. (rhyming sl.) cheque *Jones: J.*

go out poncing v. (UK police use) for vice squad officers actively to search the streets for working ponces *Laurie.*

go out with v. (UK police use) to share totally in a fellow officer's operations; the inference is that all the 'real' police work takes place out 'on the streets' *Laurie.*

go overboard v. to commit oneself completely, often as 'go overboard for . . .' *'Serpico', directed S. Lumet, 1973.*

go over the hill v. (prison use) to escape; orig. escaping fr. outdoors work gangs, using hills as cover from one's pursuers *Neaman & Silver.*

gopher n. see: gofer *Chandler: LG.*

go phut v. to collapse; fr. noise a bursting balloon makes *Wodehouse: AAG.*

gor blimey! (excl.) fr. God blind me *Wodehouse: AAG.*

Gordon & Gotch n. (rhyming sl.) a watch; fr. firm of book and periodical importers *Jones: J.*

Gordon Bennett! (excl.) euph. for gor blimey (qv) from US racing gambler of 19th C. *Payne.*

gorge out v. (US campus use) spec. description by students of Cornell University for those among them who leap to their deaths from a nearby bridge and into the gorge below *Neaman & Silver.*

gorilla n. **1.** (business use) a monster success, a smash hit *Safire*; **2.** (US prostitute use) a customer who likes to beat up his girl *Shulman*; **3.** a thug, a muscleman, a hoodlum *Fiction Illus. 3.*

gorilla v. (US Black use) to use violence; to rape *Folb.*

gorilla in the washing machine v. (US Black use) to perform cunnilingus *Folb.*

gorilla pimp n. (US Black use) a pimp who controls his girls by threats and actual violence (cf: sugar pimp) *Milner.*

go round with v. to fight with *Jones.*

gosh! (euph.) God! extra-nild euph., usually used only by children.

go spare v. to lose one's temper: to act crazily. *Norman: 2.*

go steady v. to maintain a regular relationship *The Beach Boys,* 'I Get Around', 1964.

go straight v. give up crime *Higgins: 2.*

go the big spit v. to vomit *Humphries.*

go the hang-out road v. to tell the complete truth; fr. 'let it all hang out' (qv) *PT.*

go the knuckle v. (Aus. use) to have a fist-fight *Wilkes.*

go the limit v.**1.** see: go for broke; **2.** to have sexual intercourse *Rawson.*

go the whole shot v. see: go for broke.

go through changes v. to undergo alterations in one's emotional or mental state or attitudes; development of hippie/drug use of 1960s (cf: put through changes) *Major.*

go through like a dose of salts to go very fast, to move very quickly.

go through the card v. to cover comprehensively and completely; fr. betting use, to bet on every horse in a given race *Powis.*

go to bat v. to take action, to involve oneself with a specific task or job, to take a stance; fr. baseball (or cricket in UK) use *Higgins: 4.*

go to blazes! excl. of dismissal, both of the person and his/her opinion or statement, fr. euph. of go to hell (qv) – where the fires of perdition burn.

go to buggery! general excl. of dismissal; syn. for go to hell (qv).

go to bye-byes v. (juvenile use) to go to sleep.

go to hell! general excl. (cf: go to blazes).

go to Mexico v. to become drunk; for US teenagers brief trips across the border usu. implied non-stop excess *Dickson*.

go to pieces v. to collapse emotionally.

go to sleep v. to die; perhaps the ultimate of such euphemisms, and equally popular when 'putting an animal to sleep' *Higgins: 1*.

go to the dogs v. to decline socially; to become rundown, dirty and turn into a tramp.

go to the pack v. (Aus. use) to decline – socially, economically, etc. (cf: go to the dogs) *Dennis*.

go to the races v. to die; fr. racing use (cf: throw up the cards, pegged out, etc.) *Rawson*.

go to town v. to make a great fuss, to concentrate on; fr. a rural sensibility that equates such efforts with urban life *Performance*.

got up a. dressed up particularly smartly for some occasion *White*.

got up like a pox-doctor's clerk (cp) describing someone who is very smartly (too smartly?) dressed.

got your eye full? (cp) addressed to someone who is staring, with undoubted suggestion that they should stop at once; this can be followed with 'want a picture?'

go under one's neck v. (Aus. use) to usurp another's privileges; to stop someone else's intended actions *Wilkes*.

go under the house v. (Black use) to perform cunnilingus *Legman*.

go up v. (abbrev.) go up the river (qv) *Himes: 1*.

go upside one's head v. (US Black use) hit in the face, beat up *Folb*.

go up the old dirt road v. to practise sodomy *Legman*.

go up the river v. to go to gaol; fr. the Hudson River which leads to Sing-Sing, New York State's major prison.

go up the wall v. to lose one's temper (cf: climb the walls) *Green: 2*.

gourd n. **1.** (esp. drug use) the head, (cf: out of one's gourd); **2.** (US campus use) a stupid, empty-headed person *Underwood*.

governor n. (UK police use) general address to a senior officer within the same squad *Laurie*.

go way down South in Dixie v. (homosexual use) to perform ani- or cunnilingus *Legman*.

go west v. to die; to end, to collapse; for one's 'sun to set' *Weight*.

go with v. **1.** to accept and act upon given plan or suggestion; **2.** to have an affair/relationship with someone *White*.

go with the flow v. to accept a situation and make no attempt to alter it; to act passively. a mass popularization of therapist Carl Rogers' dictum on 'floating with a complex streaming of experience' which was not so simplistic *Price: 2*.

goy n. (Yiddish) gentile; pl: *goyim* *Norman: 3*.

grab n. (UK prison use) pay *LL*.

grab v. **1.** to arrest *Higgins: 1*; **2.** to appeal to *People's Comics*.

grab-ass v. to play around, to mess about *Stone*.

grab-bag n. a random collection of items, ideas, people, etc. *Thompson*.

grabbers n. fingers *Sillitoe*.

graduate v. (US Black use) to increase, through knowledge and sophistication, one's status within the ranks of one's peers in the streets and the criminal milieu *Klein*.

graft n. **1.** corruption; **2.** the proceeds of corruption, political/criminal payments, etc.; both meanings stem fron SE graft: work, occupation; **3.** efforts, hard work; usu. physical, labouring work *Sillitoe*.

graft v. to work hard, to make an effort, to struggle *Powis*.

grafter n. a hard worker, one who perseveres fr. graft **3**.

grand n. thousand (usu. dollars or pounds) (cf: G, K).

grand bag n. (homosexual use) a large scrotum *Legman*.

grand duchess n. **1.** a female heterosexual who occupies a pride of place in a homosexual male coterie; **2.** an experienced, older, sophisticated male homosexual *Stanley*.

grandstand v. to make oneself conspicuous. *White*.

Grand Tour n. (US campus use) the traditional tour undertaken by recently graduated US college students in Europe; fr. the earlier practice of England's young aristocrats *Bernbach*.

granny n. (UK criminal use) a legitimate business that serves only as a front for criminal activities *LL*.

grape n. any form of liquor, wine and spirits *Chandler: Notebk*.

grapes n. **1.** (USAF use) the deck crew, wearing purple uniforms, who work on aircraft carriers *Wolfe:6*; **2.** (US Black use) the female breasts *Folb*.

grapevine n. a network of unofficial sources, rumours, half-truths, etc. which seems to spread the news around a given circle or group faster than any sanctioned announcement (cf: bush telegraph).

grass n. **1.** marijuana *Price: 2*; **2.** (homosexual use) pubic hair (cf: garden, lawn) *Maledicta*; **3.** (rhyming sl.) grasshopper = copper = informer *Performance*.

grass v. to inform, tell tales, betray *Norman: 1*.

grass-eater n. (US police use) a policeman who, while still corrupt, remains satisfied with what perks – materials and financial – his beat offers rather than canvassing for extras (cf: meat-eater) *Green: 2*.

grassfighter n. (Aus. use) anyone known for losing their temper and brawling in public, presumably in grassy areas *Neaman & Silver*.

graveyard shift n. (industrial use) the overnight shift, the late shift *Green: 2*.

gravy n. money *Higgins: 2*.

gravy a. wonderful, excellent, perfect *Underwood*.

gravy train n. a simple, heavily profitable situation from which one can benefit easily *Sharpe: 1*.

gray a. (Black use) any white person *Milner*.

grease n. **1.** (homosexual use) any form of lubricant – KY Jelly, etc. – that facilitates anal intercourse *Klein*; **2.** (abbrev.) greasers: motorbike riders, aka Rockers, as opposed to Mods *Mandelkau*; **3.** protection money *Chandler: Notebk*; **4.** (US campus use) a meal, food *Underwood*.

grease v. **1.** to corrupt, to bribe, to smoothe over problems, esp. fr. authorities *Fiction Illus. 3*; **2.** to kill, esp. military use (cf: grease-gun) *Del Vecchio*.

greaseball n. derog. description of any Latin race: Greeks, Puerto Ricans (cf: spic), various South Americans, etc. *Price: 2*.

grease-gun n. an automatic weapon *Higgins: 3*.

greaser n. (derog.) Mexican; and other Latin races *BvdB*.

greaser n. **1.** a 1950s Teddy Boy, his hair larded with Brylcreem or similar unguent; **2.** a motorcycle gang member (cf: rocker); **3.** (US campus use) an old-fashioned person, whose style harks back to 1950s youth cults.

greasy spoon n. a cheap cafe or restaurant; fr. the state of its cutlery and the texture of its product *Farren*.

Great Scott! euph. for Good God! *Rawson*.

great shakes a. very good, admirable *Price: 3*.

greefo n. aka: *griefo*, *greapha*: marijuana *De Lannoy & Masterson*.

Greek a. anal intercouse; often used on a prostitute's bill of sale *Price: 2*.

Greek culture n. anal intercourse, usu. in homosexual advertisement use; fr. the ethnic cliché that categorizes all (ancient) Greeks as sodomites (cf: English culture, etc.) *Jay & Young*.

green a. naïve, innocent, unsophisticated *Sillitoe*.

green n. aka: *long green*: dollar bills

Price: 1.
green-ass a. naïve, inexperienced (cf: green) *Algren.*
greenbacks n. dollar bills *Himes: 2.*
greener n. (abbrev.) greenhorn (qv) *Algren.*
greenhorn n. a novice, an unsophisticated person, esp. a new immigrant or a new arrival in the city from the country *Farrell.*
green hornet n. (Canadian cant) a Toronto motorcycle policeman; fr. cartoon superhero *Neaman & Silver.*
green house n. (drug use) a place known for selling drugs, esp. green-coloured marijuana *Klein.*
greenie n. (US campus use) beer, spec. Heineken lager which comes in predominantly green-labelled bottles or cans *Bernbach.*
greenies n. (UK 'society' use) money; like so many similar class usages, the -ie suffic underlines the lifelong addiction to nursery language (cf: greenbacks) *Barr.*
green niggers n. Irishmen; similar inferior status to black 'niggers' but 'green' (Irish) rather than black *Price: 2.*
greens n. (rhyming sl.) greengages = wages *Powis.*
green thumb n. (US Black use) someone who has the knack of making money; fr. the more usual gardeners' 'green fingers' *Klein.*
Gregory Peck n. (rhyming sl.) the neck *Cole.*
grey n. dull, boring, earnest, hard-working, esp. university use.
grey ghost n. (Aus. use) a parking policeman, who superseded the brown bomber (qv) *Wilkes.*
grief n. misery, problems, troubles.
grief v. (US campus use) to trouble, to bother, to annoy *Underwood.*
griff n. information, news; fr. *griffin*: orig. denoting a newcomer to the Indian Army or Civil Service and a greenhorn (qv) in general *LL.*
grifter n. swindler, confidence man *Fiction Illus. 3.*
grill v. to interrogate *X.*
grind n. **1.** hard, continuous, wearing work, esp. academic work *Price: 3*; **2.** a hard worker at school *Junker.*
grind v. **1.** to rub one's body, especially the genital area against one's partner while dancing; **2.** to have sexual intercouse *Price: 2.*
gringa n. (Sp.) white woman *Vidal.*
gringo n. (derog. Sp.) white man, usu. Mexican use, referring to white Americans *Vidal.*
gripples n. (US Black use) the anus *Klein.*
grisly a. (US teen. use) awful, disgusting, generally distasteful *Pond.*
gritch v. (US campus use) to nag, to complain; fr. gripe + bitch *Underwood.*
gritchy a. (US campus use) irritable, grouchy *Underwood.*
grizzle v. to whine, to cry slightly but continually; usu. of a child.
groaty a. (US teen/campus use) disgusting, unpleasant; fr. grotesque (cf: grotty, grody) *Underwood.*
groceries n. the vagina (one of many sl. sexual words with 'edible' connotations, cf: lollipop, jelly roll, hair pie, etc.) *Maledicta.*
grockle n. (UK 'society' use) an outsider, an unpleasant person, a yob (qv) *Barr.*
grody a. (Valley Girls (qv) use) disgusting, unpleasant; fr. grotty (qv), in its turn fr. grotesque *Harpers/ Queen 1/83.*
grody to the max a. (Valley Girls (qv) use) extremely, even more, disgusting (cf: grotty, max) *Harpers/ Queen 1/83.*
grog n. (Aus. use) alcohol, usu, beer; fr. 18th C. *grog = rum Humphries.*
groggy a. weak, unsteady, semi-conscious; fr. orig. meaning of drunken *Wright.*
groid n. (US southern campus use) (derog. abbrev.) Negroid: Black student *Underwood.*
groin n. (UK criminal use) aka: *groyne*: any ring containing a gemstone, esp. a diamond *Powis.*
grok v. to appreciate, to understand

and experience completely, usu. *grok the fullness*; popular hippie and mystic use *R. Heinlein, 'Strangers in a Strange Land'*.

groove n. **1.** a way of life, of thinking and dealing with people, events, etc. *Randy Newman, 'Trouble in Paradise', 1983*; **2.** a delight, a pleasure, anything enjoyable *Southern & Hoffenberg*.

groove behind v. to enjoy or appreciate a given situation or other stimulus *Farina*.

grooved very pleased, very happy *Bruce: 2*.

groove on v. see: groove behind *McFadden*.

groovy a. **1.** delightful, wonderful, pleasant, enjoyable, etc.; **2.** (Valley Girls (qv) use) passé, out of date, esp. when referring to the tastes and styles of the 1960s, during which time **1** was the only accepted meaning *Pond*.

grope v. (US homosexual use) to fondle a potential partner in order to assess response to one's advances *Stanley*.

gross a. disgusting; esp. in US teen and campus use *Underwood*.

gross out v. to disgust, to shock *Jay & Young*.

grotty a. disgusting, unattractive, fr. grotesque; especially popular during the Beatlemania era of the early 1960s (cf: groaty, grody) *Payne*.

ground n. (UK police use) a given police officer's area of operations (cf: manor, patch) *Laurie*.

grounded a. to be stopped from enjoying some normal right or pleasure; teenage use, fr. aerospace: aircraft that cannot fly *Price: 2*.

ground rations n. (US Black use) sexual intercourse *Major*.

Ground Zero n. the basic position; the start; the essentials; fr. military use *Higgins: 5*.

grouper n. see: groupie *Wolfe: 2*.

group grope n. an orgy *Stanley*.

groupie n. young girl who associates herself with rock bands, offering her body for their celebrity *J. Fabian & J. Byrne, book title, 1969*.

grouse a. (Aus. use) wonderful, attractive, excellent – all-purpose term of approval *Wilkes*.

grouse gear n. (Aus. use) teen expression for particularly attractive female *Ready*.

grove (p.ppl. to groove) to have taken great pleasure in something *Sculatti*.

grow horns v. (US campus use) to become angry; the horns of a bull rather than those of a cuckold *Underwood*.

growler n. (US campus use) lavatory *Underwood*.

grub n. (US campus use) a hard worker, one who works to the exclusion of other interests *Bernbach*.; **2.** (Aus. use) dirty, unkempt person; fr. grubby *Humphries: 2*; **3.** food; used since mid-17th C. *Price: 2*.

grub v. to beg, to scrounge *Selby: 1*.

grubber n. **1.** (US campus use) a disgusting, filthy person; fr. grubby *Underwood*; **2.** (Aus. use) a hospital, spec. a vagrants' casual night shelter; poss. link to US campus use *Wilkes*.

grubbies n. (US campus use) dirty, greasy old clothes *Underwood*.

grubble v. to rummage around, to search at random *Sanders: 2*.

grubstake n. enough money to buy one a meal (cf: grub).

grumble and grunt n. (rhyming sl.) cunt (qv) = female genitals *Franklyn*.

grunch! (US campus use) general excl. of annoyance or disgust; prob. fr. grunge (qv) *Underwood*.

grunge n. sticky, dirty, unpleasant substances *Underwood*.

grunge v. **1.** to whine, to complain; **2.** to assault, to attack, to terrify *Sanders: 2*.

grungy a. dirty, messy, unappetizing, unappealing *Junker*.

grunt n. a US Marine private soldier, supposedly fr. such a soldier's endless complaining; the Vietnam era successor to the doughboy (qv) *Webb*.

grunter n. (Aus. use) prostitute; fr. the (simulated) grunts of passion with which she embellishes her services (?)

Wilkes.

grunters n. old people out of sympathy with current youth enthusiasms (cf: wrinklies, crumblies, etc.) *ES 11/5/83*.

G-string n. (US Black use) any device – tampon, towel, etc. – used to staunch flow of menstrual blood *Klein*.

gub n. (Aus. Aborigine use) white man (cf: Mr Gub) *Wilkes*.

gubbins n. indefinite noun for any nameless object.

guck n. any form of sticky substance; ointment, cream *Performance*.

gucky a. (UK 'society' use) sickening, likely to make one vomit (of an event or person as much as of a food or drink) *Barr*.

Gucky n. (UK 'society' use) deliberate mispronunciation of Gucci, a favourite designer label for such speakers *Barr*.

guff n. **1.** (UK prep school use) a fart *Barr*; **2.**lies, nonsense, twaddle *Runyon*.

guinea a. Italian (derog.) (cf: ghinny, ginny) *Price: 2*.

guinea pig n. (US criminal use) an informer, a stool pigeon (qv) *Klein*.

guineas n. (US campus use) money; fr. obs. UK denomination of £1 1 shilling *Underwood*.

guinea stinker n. a cheap, malodorous cigar supposedly preferred by Italian-Americans (cf: guinea, ghinny, etc.) *Goldman*.

guinzo n. Italian (derog.) (cf: guinea) *Price: 2*.

gumdrop n. (drug use) barbiturate, spec. seconal; any kind of drug available in pill or capsule form *Folb*.

gum heel n. (US prison use) policeman (cf: gumshoe, rubber heels) *Chandler: Notebk*.

gumshoe n. A (private) detective; fr. supposedly rubber-soled shoes used for creeping around on investigations *Chandler: passim*.

gumshoe v. to creep around, esp. used of policemen or private detectives (cf: gumshoe, n.) *Schulberg*.

gumption n. intelligence, natural wit, shrewdness; fr. 18th C. dial: *gawm*: understanding, which also gives *gormless*: stupid, doltish *Wright*.

gum things up v. to make a mess (of pre-arranged plans); to ruin a satisfactory situation by one's interference *Wodehouse: PGM*.

gum up the works v. see: gum things up.

gun 1. (drug use) a hypodermic syringe; **2.** the penis *J. Hendrix, 'Hey Joe', 1966*.

gun v. to rev an engine hard *Griffith*.

gun for v. **1.** looking for someone with the intent of creating some form (violent or otherwise) of a confrontation; from the Western gunfighter usage of one man pursuing another; **2.** sexually interested in a person.

Gunga Din n. (rhyming sl.) chin (cf: Errol Flynn) *Wright*.

gunge n. a sticky mess, poss. when in the form of gravy or sauce, but equally often merely resembling such foods *Barr*.

gung-ho a. enthusiastic, usu, aggressively so; often describing soldiers or sportsmen; fr. Chinese *keng ho*: awe-inspiring, (lit. more fiery) *Whitcomb*.

gunner n. the shooter in a game of dice craps *Runyon: 1*.

Gunners n. Arsenal Football Club.

gunny n. **1.** (drug use) marijuana *Folb*; **2.** (US milit. use) gunnery sergeant.

gunsel n. see: gonsil.

guntz n. the whole lot; fr. German *ganz Norman, book title, 1962*.

gunzel v. (US Black use) to fight; fr. misreading of gonsil (qv) *Folb*.

gut n. **1.** an easy task; fr. college use (qv) *Price: 2*; **2.** (US campus use) an easy course *Farina*.

gut it v. (US campus use) to stay up all night working without any amphetamines for stimulation but purely through strength of will and character; fr. guts – bravery, rather than gut – simple *Underwood*.

gutless a. cowardly *Tidy*.

guts n. **1.** courage, bravery *Larner*; **2.** stomach *Price: 2*.

gutshoot v. to shoot in the stomach *Higgins: 3*.

gutso n. (derog.) a fat person.

gutstick n. (US Black use) the penis *Klein*.

gutsy a. brave (cf: guts).

gutted a. (UK prison use) sick and tired, sick to the back teeth *Obs. 1981*.

gutty a. (UK police use) tedious, irritating, hard to tolerate *Laurie*.

Guv n. (abbrev.) Guvner (qv) or governor (qv).

guvner n. (UK police use) address by any rank to their immediate superior from sergeants upwards *'The Sweeney', Euston Films, 1974, etc*.

Guy n. (rhyming sl.) Guy Fawkes = a walk *Powis*.

guyver n. (Aus. use) flattery, insincerity, pretence *Wilkes*.

Guz (Royal Navy use) abbrev. guzzle: Devonport, the naval home port where sailors can eat and drink without restrictions *BBC-1 TV 1984*.

guzzle v. **1.** to eat or drink messily or noisily; **2.** to choke *Runyon: 1*; **3.** to indulge in foreplay *Runyon: 1*.

gynae n. (abbrev.) gynaecologist *Barr*.

gyp n. a cheat, one who fails to pay his due debts; abbrev. of gypsy and as such an ethnic slur *Goulart*.

gyp v. to cheat, to swindle *rr*.

gyp joint n. anywhere, esp. a club, bar, etc., where the unwary will be swindled (cf: clip-joint, gyp).

Gyppy tummy n. stomach troubles, diahorrea; orig. that contracted in Egypt, but now extended to any such problems that UK tourists experience abroad or in ethnic restaurants at home (cf: Montezuma's revenge).

gypsy's n. (rhyming sl.) gypsy's kiss = piss = urination *Powis*.

gyrene n. (US milit. use) a Marine *Uris*.

H² (US preppie (qv) use) hot and heavy (of sexual or romantic partnerships) *Neaman & Silver*.

habe n. (abbrev.) habeas corpus: an order compelling its subject to attend court *Higgins:1*.

habit n. drug addiction *Grogan*.

hack n. **1.** (Oxford University use) undergraduates who attempt to maximize their chances of a job by creating for themselves the best possible sounding curriculum vitae while still at the university *Harpers/Queen 8/83*; **2.** (US use) a taxicab *Fiction Illus.3*; **3.** a reporter, a journalist; formerly derog., but recently popular, if tongue-in-cheek *P. Howard, The Times*; **4.** (US/Can. prison use) a prison guard *Caron*.

hack v. **1.** to irritate, to annoy *Underwood*; **2.** (US campus use) to vomit; fr. SE *hack*: to cough *Underwood*.

hack around v. **1.** to joke, to tease *Higgins:1*; **2.** to waste time *Higgins:3*.

hacked a. very angry *Goldman*.

hacker n. **1.** taxi-driver *Goulart*; **2.** run of the mill, average person; fr. hack-work *Higgins:3*.

hackie n. (US use) taxi-driver *Chandler:LG*.

hack it v. to manage, to bear a difficulty, to solve a problem; fr. physically hacking one's way through *Stone*.

had a. **1.** seduced, debauched; **2.** fooled, defrauded, conned (qv) *Algren: 2*.

had it up to here to be exasperated, to lose all one's patience.

had it with to be annoyed with, to lose patience with: 'I've had it with you', etc. *McFadden*.

hair n. (US campus use) courage, masculine prowess; thus, *to show hair*: for a sportsman to play aggressively and well *AS 50 (1965)*.

hairbag n. an unpleasant, disgusting and unappetizing person *'Hill Street Blues', Thames TV, 1983*.

haircut n. (UK prison use) a short term of imprisonment; in a local gaol from a few weeks up to 2 or 3 months; in a convict gaol fr. 3 to 5 yrs. *LL*.

hair of the dog n. a further drink of what one was drinking on the previous night in the hope of getting rid of the hangover that the initial drinking has caused; 'the hair of the dog that bit you' *Runyon:1*.

hair pie n. the vagina; fr. the pubic hair, plus pun on 'hare'; an example of sex = food (cf: finger pie).

hairy n. (Glasgow use) a poor female; the premise is that a better off woman would wear a hat and hide her hair *G. Macdonald Fraser, 'McAuslan in the Rough', 1976*.

hairy a. (US campus use + UK general) dangerous, exciting *AS 50 (1965)*.

hairy-assed a. **1.** madly, wildly,

extremely; **2.** overtly, aggressively masculine *Higgins:1.*

half elision of 'half-past. . .' in telling the time: 'half-ten', 'half-four', etc.

half a bar n. formerly 10 shillings, thus correntiy 50p *Powis.*

half a cock n. £5, fr. cock and hen (qv), rhyming sl: £10 *LL.*

half a crown (bingo use) 26, fr. old coinage 2/6 *Wright.*

half a mo wait a moment, hang on (qv); fr. half a moment.

half and half a. (US campus use) bisexual (cf: AC/DC) *Underwood.*

half a sheet n. see: half a bar.

half-assed a. incompetent, second rate *Higgins:1.*

half a stretch n. (UK criminal use) six months imprisonment *Norman:2.*

half a yard n. $50 *Caron.*

half-baked incompetent, inadequate, below a given standard *Obs. 6/2/83.*

half-brass n. a woman who associates with the prostitute milieu but is not a working girl herself *LL.*

half-cock at less than full speed, with less than total commitment, effort, etc; fr. mechanical use.

half-cocked a. second-rate, not fully capable, unfinished *Dury.*

half-cut a. more than mildly drunk but not yet incapable.

half-gone a. drunk.

half-inch v. (rhyming sl.) to pinch = to steal *Cole.*

half-iron n. a man who enjoys the company but not the specific predelictions of homosexuals; fr. iron hoof = poof (qv) *LL.*

half-lo (US drug use) (abbrev.) half-load: 15 bags (qv) of heroin, a typical purchase made by a small pusher (qv) *J. Breslin, 'Forsaking All Others', 1982.*

half-ounce v. (rhyming sl.) to bounce = to cheat, to shortchange *Cole.*

half-past two n. (rhyming sl.) a Jew *Franklyn.*

halfpenny dip n. (rhyming sl.) a ship *Jones:J.*

half pint n. see: half portion *Schulberg:2.*

half-portion n. a diminutive person *Wodehouse:AAG.*

half-saved n. an eccentric, a fool *Obs. 6/2/83.*

half seas over a. drunk; orig. nautical use; prob. fr. image of half-submerged in liquor.

half step v. (US Black use) to act in an inappropriate or ineffectual manner *Folb.*

half the bay over a. drunk *Dickson.*

half-way house (bingo use) 50; there are 100 numbers available to the caller.

half-wide a. reasonably intelligent, aware of what goes on and thus, in certain contexts, corruptible (cf: wide boy) *Newman:1.*

half your luck! (Aus. use) excl. signifying envy/jealousy of the person addressed *Ready.*

ham and egger n. an ordinary, run of the mill person *Higgins:1.*

hambone v. (Aus. use) for a man to strip off his clothes in public, prob. at a drunken party *Ready.*

ham hocks n. (US Black use) aka: *hocks*: female legs, ankles *Folb.*

hammer n. **1.** (US trucker use) the accelerator *Higgins:4*; **2.** (US Black use) very attractive black girl *Major.*

hammer v. **1.** (driving use) to drive at maximum speed; thus *put the hammer down*: to drive fast, to accelerate *Humphries:2*; **2.** to beat up, to hurt physically.

hammer ass v. to work very hard *Higgins:1.*

hammerhead n. (US campus use) anyone stupid and obstinate *Underwood.*

hammer man n. (US Black use) an authoritarian figure *Major.*

hammers n. (US Black use) female thighs *Folb.*

Hammers n. West Ham Football Club.

Hampsteads n. (rhyming sl.) Hampstead Heath = teeth *Cole.*

Hampton n. (rhyming sl.) Hampton Wick = prick = penis *Powis.*

Hampton rock n. (rhyming sl.) cock

= penis *Cole.*

-handed a. (police/criminal use) the size of a firm (qv) of criminals can be two-, three-, four, team- or mob-handed.

handful n. **1.** (prison use) five year sentence *LL*; **2.** £5 *EN 12/11/57.*

hand-gallop v. to masturbate *Higgins:2.*

hand gig n. (homosexual use) a homosexual prostitute who specializes in masturbating his clients or joining in mutual masturbation with them *Legman.*

hand in one's dinner pail v. **1.** to die; **2.** to resign from one's job *Wodehouse:PGM.*

hand job n. masturbation, often offered in a prostitute's price list *Price:2.*

handkerchief head n. (US Black use) a subservient, role-playing, white stereotypical Black woman, the female version of a Tom (qv) (cf: Aunt Jemima) *Folb.*

handle n. name, nickname, or title, now esp. fr. Citizen's Band Radio use, but in prison use at least c.1950 *Capital Radio 1983.*

handmedowns n. second-hand clothes, either given free or bought at a second-hand shop.

hand-reared a. possessed of a large penis *B. Aldiss, 'The Hand-Reared Boy', bk title.*

hands off (your) cocks, feet in (your) socks! (cp) jocular wake-up cry, orig. RAF, but general in services, institutions, and similar sites of dormitory accommodation *'Serpico', dir. S. Lumet, 1973.*

handsome a. excellent, wonderful; general term of approval (cf: sweet) *Cole.*

hang n. (US Black use) a job; which supports one's living *Major.*

hang v. turn, as in *hang a left*, etc. *Higgins:1.*

hang about v. see: hang around.

hang about! (excl.) wait a minute, don't go!

hang a Lilly v. to turn left (cf: hang a Louie) *Underwood.*

hang a Louie v. to turn left *Underwood.*

hang a Ralph v. aka hang a Ralphie: to turn right *Underwood.*

hang around v. to wait about, to linger in one place *Wilkinson.*

hand a U-ie n. make a U-turn *Humphries:2.*

hangers n. breasts *Price:2.*

hanging-up n. (taxi-driver use) the refusal of some drivers to take fares as they appear at a rank, and instead to hold back until something lucrative – a trunk-laden tourist, etc. – turns up *Powis.*

hang in there v. to maintain a position, usu. with implication of pressures to surrender *Manser.*

hang it up v. to give up trying, to accept defeat, to acknowledge that a target will never be achieved *Klein.*

hang loose v. **1.** relax, take things as they come; **2.** (excl.) relax! enjoy yourself! don't worry! (cf: hang tough) *McFadden.*

hang one on v. **1.** to hit someone, to have a fight *Farrell*; **2.** to be drunk *Dickson.*

hang one out to dry v. to treat particularly harshly; to make an example of an individual *Dunne.*

hang one to the all v. to punish severely *Underwood.*

hang out v. to meet, to collect together at a regular venue (cf: hang around).

hang out n. a place where a given group tend to meet *The Collected Trashman, 1969.*

hang tough v. to behave in an aggressive, tough manner; to persist in a course of action whatever the problems (cf: hang loose).

hang up v. to distress, to annoy *Keyes.*

hang up n. problem, delay, neurosis *Yellow Dog Comics 22, 1972.*

hang up one's harness v. (US western use) aka: *hang up one's tackle* to die *Adams.*

hang up one's hat v. (US western use) to die *Adams.*

hankypanky n. trickery, deceit; esp. of a sexual nature *Sanders:2.*
ha'penny n. the pudendum *Neaman & Silver.*
happening a. (Valley Girls (qv) use) fashionable, chic, up to the minute *Harpers/Queen 1/83.*
happy as a pig in shit (cp) utterly contented.
happy as Larry (Aus. use) perfectly happy, quite content *Lawson.*
happy bag n. (UK criminal use) the bag in which a shotgun is carried on an armed robbery; the gun makes the victim 'happy' to pass over his money *ST 3/4/83.*
happy hour n. orig. US, now general: a period, one or poss. two hours, when a pub or bar offers drinks at half price, usu. about 6 pm; the assumption is that those customers who arrive for the cheap drinks will become sufficiently tipsy to stay on for the more expensive ones.
harbour light (rhyming sl.) all right; usu. as 'all harbour' *Cole.*
hard n. **1.** an erection *Bukowski:1*; **2.** a thug, a hoodlum *Keyes.*
hard-ass a. tough, no-nonsense, uncompromising.
hard bit n. (US prison use) an unpleasant time in prison due to one's personality, one's crime (which may alienate other prisoners) inability to adapt, etc. *Klein.*
hard-boiled a. tough, mean, unpleasant; as in the lengthily cooked egg *R. Goulart, 'The Hard-Boiled Dicks', bk title, 1967.*
hard case n. a tough, ruthless person *Norman:2.*
hard-core n. serious, experienced, full-time *Grogan.*
hardeyes n. unpleasant look, disapproving stare (cf: glad eye) *Higgins:1.*
hardhead n. **1.** (Aus. use) a villain, a criminal *Ready*; **2.** see: bad-ass nigger (although such a name does reinforce one white cliche: that one can never knock out or hurt a black man by hitting him on his head, since it is too solid to damage) *Folb.*
hard-leg n. (US Black use) a man who devotes all his time and energies to pursuing the street life and the world of strictly male endeavour – pimping, hustling (qv), etc. *Klein.*
hard money n. cash, coins, change *Klein.*
hardmouth v. see: badmouth *Folb.*
hard-nose n. (gambling use) a bettor who will never let himself become excessively in debt to his bookmaker *Bukowski:1.*
hard-nose a. tough, uncompromising (cf: hard-ass) *Price:2.*
hard-on n. **1.** an erection: *to have a hard-on for*: to want something very much; to like or dislike a person particularly *Price:2*; **2.** term of address, usu. sarcastic and referring to someone's high self-esteem; fr. have a hard-on for (qv) *'Serpico', dir. S. Lumet, 1973.*
hard stuff n. **1.** spirits, as opposed to beer *Humphries*; **2.** (drug use) hard drugs, ie. narcotics, as opposed to soft, ie. tranquillizers, cannabis, etc. *Klein.*
hard-talk v. to employ pressure tactics in a sales pitch *Bruce:2.*
hard time v. a prison sentence that a prisoner finds difficult to undergo *Higgins:2.*
hard-up a. impoverished.
hardware n. (criminal/police use) guns, ammunition.
hard way n. (gambling use) the making of an even point in a dice game by throwing a pair rather than two separate numbers *Runyon.*
haricot n. (Aus. rhyming sl.) haricot bean = queen = homosexual *Humphries.*
harmola n. second rate boxer; the suffix -ola tends to imply some jocularity, in this case to the fighter's potential for causing harm *Schulberg:1.*
harmony hair spray n. the act of ejaculating into a woman's hair; fr. the popular hair spray of the same name *Cole.*

harness bull n. uniformed police officer; the 'harness' is the Sam Browne some forces in the US favour *Chandler.*

Harolds n. knickers, fr. rhyming sl.? *Humphries.*

harp n. Irish person *Higgins:3.*

Harrow drive (cricket use) a shot that while aimed in one direction goes in quite another one, often for a boundary *BBC Radio 3, 1983.*

Harry —ers verbal style orig. in services, affected in 1950s by 'society' and now widespread if obs.: various words prefixed by 'Harry' and suffixed by 'ers'; eg: Harry flakers (tired out, cf: flaked), Harry crashers (asleep, cf: crash out) etc. etc.

Harry Randall n. (rhyming sl.) candle; fr. UK music hall comedian, c.1900. *Wright.*

Harry Tate **1.** (bingo rhyming sl.) 8; **2.** late (Tate was a comedian popular 1900–1910) *Wright.*

Harry Wragg n. (rhyming sl.) fag (qv) = cigarette; fr. 1930s jockey and trainer *Franklyn.*

harvest moon n. (rhyming sl.) (derog.) coon = black person.

Harvey Nichol n. (rhyming sl.) a pickle = a problem, a difficult situation *Jones:J.*

Harvey Nichols n. (rhyming sl.) pickles; fr. the Knightsbridge store *Jones:J.*

has-beens n. (rhyming sl.) greens; usu. prison use *Cole.*

hash n. (abbrev.) hashish *Higgins:2.*

hash v. (US campus use) to wait on tables in college or local cafeteria/bar, usu. as part-time job to help pay for fees; abbrev. *sling hash*: to work as a waiter/waitress in a cafe *Underwood.*

hashover n. the after-effects of an evenings heavy indulgence in smoking hashish; fr. drinkers' hangover *Sanders:2.*

hassle n. a problem, a nuisance, anything requiring irritating effort *Price:2.*

hassle v. to annoy, to nag; to pressurize *Vidal.*

hatched, matched and dispatched the Births, Marriages & Deaths announcements in *The Times*; listings under Adoptions were proposed as *attached Barr.*

hatchet job n. **1.** (journalist use) a particularly vicious piece of writing, criticizing a person or artistic endeavour; **2.** (US campus use) a broken date *Underwood.*

hatchet man n. **1.** (criminal use) a man who is used to punish, or even murder selected victims on the orders of his boss; **2.** anyone who takes on, or is told to take on unpleasant tasks, such as, in a company, firing members of staff, broaching distasteful but necessary topics, etc.

hatchi n. (lesbian use) the vagina *Maledicta.*

hat up v. (US Black use) to leave, to exit *Klein.*

haul ass v. to leave, to escape, to run off *Wolfe:2.*

have v. (UK police use) to believe, to accept *Laurie.*

have a bash v. to make an attempt.

have a bellyfull (of) v. to lose patience, to become infuriated by irritating repetition; fr. mental, rather than physical satiety.

have a brass neck v. to be impudent, rude.

have a buzz on v. to be drinking, and mildly intoxicated but not drunk *Neaman & Silver.*

have a crack v. to attempt, to have a try *Higgins:3.*

have a cut off the joint v. to have sexual intercourse (fr. male point of view).

have a dash v. (abbrev.) have a dash of lavender: to be marginally homosexual *Legman.*

have a down on v. to feel hostile towards, to be prejudiced against.

have a field day v. for a task or problem to turn out infinitely simple; to have great and unopposed success; fr. hunting/shooting use *PT.*

have a few too many v. to be drunk *The Who, 'Tommy', 1969.*

have a hard-on for v. **1.** to care deeply about, to be extremely concerned about. **2.** to dislike intensely, of both persons and objects; fr. the sexual use, describing the erect penis (cf: hard, hard-on) *Higgins:1.*

have a heat on v. to be drunk *Runyon.*

have a hit on v. (business use) (of a project/person) to make an impact; to come into conflict *Safire.*

have a lash v. to take part in, to make a try at *Wilkes.*

have a line on v. to understand, to know what is happening; fr. racing use, the *line*: the daily details of the horses running and the odds on them *Higgins:2.*

have a little visitor v. to have a period; genteel euph.

have a mad on (with) v. to be annoyed (with) Goulart.

have a moustache v. to perform cunnilingus; fr. female pubic hair *Legman.*

have an in v. to have special contacts, in criminal use, to have such contacts within a place – ie, a bank – that is to be robbed *Powis.*

have a pop (at) v. to try, to make an attempt *Wodehouse:MOJ.*

have a ring through one's nose v. (US Black use) to be obsessed, to the point of foolishness, with one other person, usu. a lover, by whom one can be led *Folb.*

have a screw loose v. to be slightly eccentric, not altogether in control *Southern & Hoffenberg.*

have a shot at v. **1.** (UK use) to make an attempt, to have a try; **2.** (Aus. use) to make a sneering remark in someone's direction *Wilkes.*

have a shot in the locker v. to maintain one's potency or ability, sexual and otherwise.

have a skinful v. to be very drunk *Humphries.*

have a slash v. to urinate *Humphries.*

have a soft spot for v. to favour someone, even if such favouritism is neither sensible nor approved.

have a stick up one's ass v. to be totally and irredeemably boring; such a stick would render one physically, and thus mentally, rigid *Simmons.*

have big eyes v. to be particularly interested *Southern.*

have by the short and curlies v. to have at an extreme disadvantage, to control completely; fr. idea of grasping one's pubic hair *May.*

have by the short hairs v. see: have by the short and curlies.

have eyes for v. desire, wish for, usu. sexually *T 11/5/83.*

have had one's chips v. to have died; fr. poker use.

have it away v. **1.** to escape (from prison); **2.** to copulate.

have it away with v. **1.** to copulate with a given person; **2.** to steal a given object.

have it coming v. to deserve, to merit, usu. 'it' is unpleasant *Thompson:J.*

have it covered v. (US Black use) to have a situation well under control *Folb.*

have it in v. to have sexual intercourse *Mortimer.*

have it knocked v. to have a problem, and esp. life in general, absolutely under control.

have it off v. **1.** (UK criminal use) to carry out a successful crime *Powis*; **2.** (UK police use) to make a successful raid and arrest *Newman: 2*; **3.** to copulate *Norman:2.*

have it on one's dancers v. (UK criminal use) to run away, to escape (cf: have it away) *Powis.*

have it out v. to force a confrontation; to fight *Mandelkau.*

have it taped v. to have something worked out, assessed fully, etc; orig. milit. use: fr. tape measure.

have kidney trouble v. (homosexual use) to frequent public lavatories for sex *Legman.*

have kittens v. to worry to excess, to throw a fit, to succumb to one's emotions, often through worry or fear; fr. the nervousness of a pregnant cat.

have off v. (UK police use) to arrest; 'off the streets' *Laurie*.
have one cold v. to have at one's mercy, to have at a disadvantage.
have one mapped v. to have someone completely and accurately assessed; to work out another's movements and attitudes *Klein*.
have one on v. to deceive, to tease, to delude *Keyes*.
have one over v. to seduce, to deceive *Powis*.
have one's act together aka: *have one's act down, have one's game uptight, have one's shit together/down*, etc., to be in full control of a given situation, whether emotional, social, sexual, financial, whatever *Folb*.
have one's back teeth afloat v. to be very drunk.
have one's cock caught in a zipper v. to be in very bad trouble *Higgins:2*.
have one's greens v. to have sexual intercourse (cf: greens) *Mortimer*.
have one's guts for garters v. to punish comprehensively; to hurt.
have one's head up one's ass v. to be completely and deliberately stupid *Price:2*.
have one's nose in the air v. to act in a snobbish, superior manner (cf: high-hat) *Neaman & Silver*.
have one's nose open v.t. (Black pimp use) **1.** to produce sexual excitement in another person; **2.** to be infatuated with another person; both uses imply heavy breathing *Milner*.
have one's number v. to understand another person absolutely, for all their possible evasions and excuses (cf: peep one's hole card) *Stone*.
have (one) over v. to cheat, to defraud, to trick *Griffith*.
have one over a barrel v. to put at a great disadvantage; to inconvenience deliberately.
have one's heart in one's boots v. to be depressed, frightened.
have one's heart in one's mouth v. to be terrified, to be very apprehensive.
have one's pots on v. to be drunk *Runyon*.
have papers v. (US Black use) to be legally married *Folb*.
have smallpox v. (US cant) to be wanted on an arrest warrant *Neaman & Silver*.
have someone on v. to trick, to hoax, to lie *Humphries*.
have some rabbit in one v. (US Black/criminal use) **1.** to be an habitual absconder from institutions or situations *Pearce*; **2.** to be sexually active *Klein*; both meanings derive fr. the alleged obsessions of rabbits.
have something going v. to be involved in a close relationship, usu. sexual *Folb*.
have the drop on v. to place someone else at a disadvantage, in any confrontation, physical, mental, financial, etc.
have the flag out v. to have one's menstrual period.
have the hots for v. to desire sexually *Price:3*.
have the (dead) needle v. to be very angry.
have the painters in v. (US use) to have one's menstrual period *Neaman & Silver*.
have the rag on v. **1.** spec. to have a menstrual period *Bruce:2*; **2.** to act foolishly, eccentrically, to be annoyed *Higgins:1*.
have the slows v. (drug use) to be very high (qv); life outside one's head seems to crawl by *Folb*.
have too much on one's plate v. to be overburdened; esp. with work or commitments.
have two left shoes v. (US Black use) to be absolutely wrong *Klein*.
have whiskers v. to be old, to be out of date *Goulart*.
have you got a coat? (UK police use) have you settled on a suspect who can be realistically arrested? *Laurie*.
hawk v. (US Black use) to keep a suspicious and close watch on *Klein*.
hawk one's brown v. to work as a male prostitute (cf: brown).

hawk one's fork v. (Aus. use) to work as a prostitute; the 'fork' is the juncture of the legs and thus the vagina *Humphries:2.*

hawk one's mutton v. to work as a prostitute (either sex) *Norman:2.*

hawk one's pearly v. to act in a promiscuous manner, to offer one's body for sexual enjoyment *Sharpe:2.*

hawkshaw n. (esp. West Indian use) a detective; fr. 'Hawkshaw the Detective' created by Henry Cecil Bullivant in such books as *The Ticket-of-Leave Man* (1935), etc. *Powis.*

hay n. **1.** a small sum of money; usu. as 'that ain't hay', remarking on a substantial sum *Wodehouse:PGM*; **2.** marijuana *De Lannoy & Masterson.*

haybag n. a fat, poss. drunken old woman *Runyon:1.*

hay eater n. (US Black use) a white person *Major.*

haymaker n. a swinging punch which counts more on energy and ire than on skill and direction; once such a blow landed, the recipient would 'hit the hay (qv) *Farrell.*

hayseed n. a farmer, a simple peasant, poss. with hair still filled with hay.

HBI (UK police/criminal use) (abbrev.) *H*ouse *B*reaking *I*mplements *LL.*

head n. **1.** (US campus use) a person; fr. 1960s hippie use *Underwood*; **2.** the regular user of any kind of drug: *pot head*, *acid head*, etc. *Wolfe:2*; **3.** oral intercourse, usu. fellatio, but also cunnilingus; **4.** a hangover; thus 'I've got an awful head this morning' (cf: hair of the dog).

head and head game n. (gambling use) a dice game in which players bet against each other rather than against a bank (as in a casino game) *Runyon:1.*

head-banger n. **1.** a psychotic, a randomly, obsessively violent person; someone who lacks control of their temper *Wilkinson*; **2.** in music business, a fan of loud, monotonous, 'heavy metal music', usu. a denim-clad, patch-bestrewn youth who plays a make-believe (or even cardboard) guitar and shakes his head violently as he watches or listens to his heroes.

headcase n. an eccentric, a bizarre person.

head cook and bottle-washer n. a general factotum who may in fact carry out neither of these duties *A. Green.*

head hunt v. **1.** (US Black use) to look for trouble, to start a fight *Folb*; **2.** (business use) to recruit executives, often by poaching them, offering massive inducements, from rival companies *ST 6/3/83.*

heading n. using the top of the head to butt someone in a fight (cf: nutting) *LL.*

headlights n. the female breasts *Neaman & Silver.*

headshrinker a psychiatrist, psychoanalyst, etc. (cf: shrink) *Caron.*

heads up! excl. by lookouts for illegal street traders or street gamblers to warn of an approaching policeman *Powis.*

head up adv. in direct confrontation *Klein.*

heart n. (street gang use) courage, bravery, spirit *Salisbury.*

heart of oak (rhyming sl.) broke (qv) *Powis.*

heat n. **1.** weapons, arms *Greenlee*; **2.** pressure, esp. on criminals from the police *Fiction Illus.3*; **3.** (drug use) the heating of powdered heroin prior to smoking it (cf: chase the dragon) *'Hill Street Blues', Thames TV, 1983.*

Heat n. the police *Goldman.*

heater n. a pistol, revolver (cf: heat) *Wodehouse:PGM.*

heat's on the police are enforcing exceptional pressure on the community *C. Himes, bk title.*

heave v. to vomit; fr. the sensation in one's stomach *Bernbach.*

heave-ho n. rejection, ejection *Wodehouse:PGM.*

Heavens to Betsy! excl. of shock, horror, surprise *Higgins:4.*

Heavens to Murgatroyd! see:

Heavens to Betsy!.

heaver n. (US Black use) a self-styled great lover, esp. of the more earthy, animalistic type (cf: stud) *Klein.*

heavy n. a thug, a villain; esp. in cinema and theatre.

heavy a. **1.** (drug use) a hard drug – heroin, cocaine – rather than a soft one – cannabis, etc. *Burroughs:1*; **2.** intense *Price:2*; **3.** frightening, threatening; **4.** thuggish, violent; **5.** meaningful, important, emotionally strong; a general intensifier, esp. loved by late 1960s hippies and radicals, varying as to context *Hoffman:a.*

heavy v. to threaten, to menace.

heavy date n. a more than usually important meeting with one's boyfriend/girlfriend *R. Wild.*

heavy-duty a. tough, unpleasant *Price:2.*

heavy mob n. **1.** a gang of thugs *Norman:2*; **2.** (police use) physically tough officers used in violent situations; **3.** (UK police use) officers from the Flying Squad and, formerly, the Special Patrol Group *Powis.*

heavyweight n. an important person with power and influence *Jenkins.*

Hebe n. a Jew; fr. Hebrew *Price:1.*

heck (euph.) hell *Seale.*

hedge n. (UK criminal use) the crowd that gathers round an illicit street game of three-card monte (qv) *Powis.*

hedgehog n. (US campus use) male derog. term for unattractive female (cf: dog) *Underwood.*

heebie-jeebies n. unpleasant fantasies, nameless terrors, anything the mind can conjure up to produce nerves and fear *Hoffman:a.*

heel n. **1.** spec. a petty criminal; **2.** a dishonest, untrustworthy person *Humphries*; either fr. 'down-at-heel' or the image on an unwanted person, continually at one's heels.

heeled a. **1.** armed *Grogan*; **2.** rich; abbrev., well-heeled.

heel on v. (US Black use) to leave, to depart *Klein.*

heifer n. (US Black use) an unattractive, obese woman (cf: cow); **2.** (US campus use) any female *Underwood.*

heinie n. the buttocks; fr. euph. diminutive of hind end or hinder parts *Neaman & Silver.*

Heinie n. (derog.) German *Stone.*

Heinz n. (UK bookmaker use) any combination bet; fr. the '57 Varieties' *Wall St. Jour. 10/5/67.*

heist n. a robbery; fr. hoist *Grogan.*

hellacious a. (US campus use) wonderful, amazing, extraordinary *Underwood.*

heller n. (US campus use) exciting, dramatic party; fr. 'hell-of-a' good time *Underwood.*

Hello, John, got a new motor? cp of 'alternative' comedian Alexei Sayle, coined c.1980 and parodying the many 'Johns' and 'Jack the Lads' of London's East End and its Essex overspill *A. Sayle, 'The Train to Hell', 1984.*

hell's bells! mild. excl. *Wodehouse:AAG.*

hell's teeth! excl.; see hell's bells *Manser.*

Hell Week n. (US campus use) period of initiation for pledges to a college fraternity *Farina.*

hems n. (abbrev.) haemorrhoids *Klein.*

hen n. a woman; term of address in Central Scotland to a woman *J. Boyle, 'A Sense of Freedom', TV film, Channel-4 1983.*

hen party n. a women-only get-together; the opposite of a stag party (for men) but generally devoid of the drunken excess.

hen-pecked a. a man, usu. married, who is persecuted by the woman with whom he lives.

Henry n. (drug use) heroin *Green:1.*

hep a. aware, informed, sophisticated, in the know (cf: hip).

hep n. (abbrev.) hepatitis *Hoffman:a.*

herb n. (drug use) marijuana, esp. Jamaican term *Green:1.*

Herbert n. a simple person; thus *Herbert music*: music hall jokes mixed with rock music *G 28/3/83.*

herbs n. (Aus. use) speedy, powerful, responsive to the accelerator (of a car) *Humphries:2.*

herder n. (US prison use) a prison guard *Chandler: Notebk.*

here's how! popular toast when drinking *Manser.*

here's looking at you a toast before drinking, immortalized (and clichéd) after Humphrey Bogart's rendition in *Casablanca*, 1941.

here's mud in your eye! a toast when drinking *Schulberg.*

here we go (again) (cp) often stated with some resignation and implying distaste for some form of repetitious activity, speechifying, etc.

her indoors n. the wife; coined by Leon Griffiths in the *Minder* series on Thames TV, 1979 onwards *Payne.*

he-she n. homosexual male (cf: omee-palone) *Shulman.*

he who smelt it, dealt it (cp) often used as the answer to who cut the cheese (qv) disclaiming all responsibility for having farted.

Hey Rube! **1.** a call for help; **2.** a fight, orig. between circus/carnival people and local townspeople. 'Hey Rube' was the traditional rallying cry of circus or carnival employees when faced with any trouble from locals *Pynchon.*

hex n. a curse, s spell; fr. Yiddish *hexe*: witch.

hick n. any inhabitant of the countryside, a peasant, a farmer; fr. late 17th C. meaning: an easy victim to card-sharpers, and thus usu. a rustic *White.*

hickey n. a love bite, usu. on the neck *Junker.*

hickory-dock n. (rhyming sl.) clock *Cole.*

hide n. **1.** (music use) drums; fr. their skins *Major*; **2.** the human skin, thus one's life, esp. in 'save one's hide', etc. *PT.*

hi-de-hi. . .ho-de-ho popular style of greeting, and the requisite response; orig. 1940s, but real popularity arrived with BBC-TV's eponymous situation comedy, set in a 1950s holiday camp.

hide the salam v. (US preppie (qv) use) (abbrev.) hide the salami: to have sexual intercourse; usu. as in *to play hide. . .* also as *hide and salam* fr. W. Allen, *Annie Hall*, 1976 *Bernbach.*

high a. intoxicated with drugs or drink. or, poss, religious/spiritual enthusiasm *Underwood.*

high and goodbye n. (US Black use) unreliable person (poss. hi – hello – and goodbye?) *Folb.*

high diver n. cunnilinctor *Legman.*

Higher-Higher n. (US milit. use) the high command *Del Vecchio.*

high as a kite a. very drunk; fr. rhyming sl. tight = drunk *Cole.*

high-brow n. an intellectual or anyone the speaker considers to be one.

highfalutin a. snobbish, pompous.

high game v. (Black pimp and conman use) giving the mark (qv) less than he pays for but leaving him believing he actually had more than the basic price *Milner.*

high-hat v. to act in a superior manner towards others, to put on airs *Mandelkau.*

high monkey-monk see: high mucky-mucky *Dunne.*

high mucky-mucky n. a superior person, usu, derog.; prob. fr. Chinook jargon: *hiu muckamuck*: plenty food, denoting a powerful member of a tribe *Runyon.*

high on the hog living a comfortable, secure and well-off life; fr. the area of the choicest cuts of pork and its by-products (cf: life of Riley) *Price: 3.*

highpockets n. a tall man *Uris.*

high roller n. a heavy gambler *Fiction Illus. 3.*

high-siding (Black use) showing off, bragging, often in the ostentatious display of jewellery, flashy clothes and cars, etc. *Milner.*

high sign n. a warning, a recognition signal, a secret sign.

high-steppin' a. see: high-siding.

hightail (it) v. to leave quickly, to run off, to escape.

high-toned a. superior, stand-offish *Tennessee Ernie Ford, '16 Tons', 1956.*

high-up n. the boss, the leader; anyone senior, more powerful than the speaker.

high-wall job n. (UK criminal use) breaking and entering a factory or any similar building surrounded by a high wall (cf: second storey man) *Sillitoe.*

high, wide and handsome a. happy, pleasant, carefree, performing well and easily.

high yellow n. aka: *high yaller*: a Mulatto woman or girl *Himes: 1.*

hike v. raise *Variety 19/1/83.*

hincty a. **1.** suspicious *Chandler: Notebk*; **2.** snobbish; **3.** (US Black use) derog. ref, to any Black abandoning racial pride for attempts to ape white manners/styles.

hip a. sophisticated, *au fait*, aware, in tune with events, ideas and situations. as abbrev. for hipster (qv) the word had a more specific meaning to jazz/ beatnik buffs of 1950s, but now the general use is predominant *Price: 2.*

hip v. to initiate, to explain *Goldman.*

Hip City (US Black use) Cleveland, Ohio *Klein.*

hipidity n. (US campus use) hippie (qv) *Underwood.*

hippie n. 1960s teen cult member, preaching a philosophy of 'love and peace', backed by wide spectrum drug usage, esp. of cannabis and hallucinogens.

hipster n. the epitome of the 1950s Bohemian stance: the quintessence of cool (qv), in full retreat from emotional display, hymned by bop music and lulled by heroin into complete disaffiliation from humanity; currently merely historical.

hipsters n. the accumulations of fat around the thighs and stomachs of the overweight (cf: bagels) *Neaman & Silver.*

hired gun n. (business use) an executive who is hired for the performance of a particiularly tough task; fr. imagery of cinema Westerns; the task performed, he may well 'ride off into the sunset' (cf: headhunter) *Kidder.*

hist v. see: heist *Runyon.*

hit n. **1.** a murder, esp. a gangster killing; **2.** a puff on a marijuana cigarette. *SF Comics*; **3.** a portion of any drug: a tablet of amphetamine or barbiturate; a line of heroin or cocaine, etc.; **4.** (rhyming sl.) hit and miss = kiss *Powis.*

hit v. **1.** to pay *Higgins: 1*; **2.** to adulterate drugs prior to selling them (cf: cut) *Higgins: 1*; **3.** arrive at *Runyon*; **4.** to rob, to hold up *Higgins: 1*; **5.** to inject narcotics; spec. for the drug to register its immediate effect on the user *Goldman.*

hit-and-get n. (US conman use) the passing off of a con-trick in a town and then immediately 'getting out' of that town and starting over again *Thompson: J.*

hit and missed a. (rhyming sl.) (always in full) pissed (qv) = drunk *Powis.*

hitch n. (US milit. use) a term of enlistment in one of the US armed forces *Stone.*

hitched a. married.

hit for six v. to assert oneself decisively in an argument; to destroy any form of opposition; fr. cricket use.

hit it off v. to establish a relationship, to become friendly, to get on well *Sillitoe.*

hitman n. an assassin, usu. employed by some variety of organized crime. (cf: hit, v.).

hit me! (gambling use) invitation to the dealer to give one another card.

hit me and cut the rap! (US teen use) stop talking and just do what you came to do, give me what I want, etc. (cf: beat about the bush) *Sculatti.*

hit on v. **1.** to approach, usu, against the subject's wishes *Goldman*; **2.** to seduce; in pimp use, to attract a woman to one's team of prostitutes *Milner.*

hit some shit v. (US Black use) to encounter problems *Folb.*

hitter n. a success, a star, usu. with

overtones of violence, criminality *Price: 1.*

hit the books v. (US campus use) to study hard *Underwood.*

hit the bottle v. to drink heavily *Algren.*

hit the bricks v. **1.** exit, leave for the street, start walking; **2.** spec. to be discharged from a gaol sentence.

hit the deck v. **1.** to fall down; **2.** to throw oneself deliberately to the ground *Mortimer.*

hit the gas v. to accelerate in a motorcar *Selby: 1.*

hit the hay v. to go to sleep *Runyon.*

hit the high spots v. to go out for an evening's dining and dancing.

hit the jug v. to drink heavily *Dickson.*

hit the mainline v. to inject narcotics *Chandler: LG.*

hit the road v. to leave, to set out on a journey *Eagles, 'Desperado', 1975.*

hit the roof v. to explode with temper, to become extremely annoyed *Fiction Illus. 3.*

hit the sack v. to go to sleep (cf: sack out) *Bruce: 1.*

hit the sauce v. see: hit the bottle.

hit the trail v. to leave *Chandler: LG.*

hit the wind v. (US Black use) to leave quickly, to run away *Klein.*

hive off v. (Aus. use) to leave *Ready.*

ho n. Black pron. of *whore*: a prostitute *Milner.*

hock v. to pawn; thus *in hock* *Higgins: 3.*

hockshop n. the pawnbroker's shop.

hocky n. dog excrement *Neaman & Silver.*

hog n. **1.** penis *Higgins: 1*; **2.** (US campus use) male term for an unattractive female (cf: dog) *Underwood*; **3.** (drug use) pig tranquillizer, PCP, phencyclidine (cf: angel dust) *Green: 1*; **4.** (drug use) anyone who uses more narcotics than does the speaker *Burroughs: 1*; **5.** (Hells Angels use) a motorcycle (usu. Harley-Davidson) modified and cut down for outlaw gang use (cf: garbage wagon); **6.** (Black use) any automobile, esp. a Cadillac *Milner.*

Hogan's ghost! (Aus. use) general expression of amazement *Bickerton.*

hog-caller n. a loud and piercing scream, akin to those used by farmers calling their pigs *Bukowski: 1.*

hogwash! (excl.) nonsense! rubbish! *Jay & Young.*

ho-hum a. non-committal, inconclusive *Jay & Young.*

hoist v. (UK criminal use) to shoplift *Powis.*

hoister n. (UK criminal use) **1.** a pick-pocket; **2.** a shoplifter *Powis.*

hoity-toity a. aloof, snobbish; fr. haughty *Esq. 6/83.*

ho-jo n. (abbrev.) Howard Johnson's motel *Higgins: 2.*

hokey a. fake, false; fr *hokum* *McFadden.*

hold everything! see: hold it!

holding in possession of drugs *Burroughs: 1.*

hold it! (excl.) stop what you're doing; be quiet, etc. *Seale.*

hold one's horses v. to slow down, to show restraint.

hold one's noise v. to stop talking *Wilkinson.*

hold-out n. (pimp use) an unprofessional, undisciplined prostitute (cf: flaky ho) *OUI 8/75.*

hold paper on v. stand as a creditor to someone *Dunne.*

hold the baby v. **1.** spec. from stock market use: purchasing stocks which one then cannot sell; **2.** to be left to clear up a problem, to take an (unpleasant) responsibility *Performance.*

hold the bag v. (cant) for a villain to be left with full responsibility for a crime in which his associates have not been legally involved *'Serpico', directed S. Lumet, 1973.*

hold the can v. to take responsibility, usu. unwanted (cf: hold the baby **2**) *Humphries: 2.*

hold the phone v. wait, delay, 'hang on'; fr. telephone use *Capital Radio 1983.*

hold your water! (excl.) wait a

minute, don't get excited, etc. (cf: hold one's horses) *'The Mean Machine', directed Albert S. Ruddy.*

hole n. **1.** (abbrev.) cakehole = mouth; esp. on *shut one's hole Performance*; **2.** (US prison use) the punishment cells; **3.** see: ho *Milner*; **4.** the vagina *Folb.*

hole card n. a secret, which can be either a weakness which, once discovered, can be exploited or a hidden strength; fr. poker use; thus peep one's . . . (qv) *Runyon.*

hole in one! (excl.) absolutely correct! fr. golf use *Payne.*

hole in the wall a. second-class, inferior, small-time (qv) *Whitcomb.*

holes & poles n. (US campus use) sex education classes *Jay & Young.*

hole up v. to settle, to take up residence; poss. but not definite inference of hiding away, taking refuge *Wolfe: 2.*

holler v. to shout, to scream *Higgins: 1.*

holler copper v. to inform *Runyon.*

hollow tooth n. (UK police use) New Scotland Yard, fr. it's being 'rotten inside', ie, corrupt *Powis.*

Hollywood swoop n. (US Black use) an automobile manoeuvre whereby one cuts in front of another vehicle, stopping one's own car and thus forcing, the other vehicle to halt, à la TV police chase sequences. *Folb.*

hols n. (abbrev.) holidays *Capital Radio 1983.*

holy cats! excl. of surprise, dismay, alarm *Rawson.*

holy cow! excl. of surprise *Rawson.*

holy cripes! general excl. of surprise, alarm, etc. (cf: cripes) *Rawson.*

holy friar n. (rhyming sl.) a liar *Jones: J.*

Holy Joe n. **1.** anyone of a religious bent; **2.** spec. a clergyman, esp. in services or in goal. *LL.*

holy mackerel! mild excl; see holy smoke, Moses, etc. *Manser.*

holy Moses! see: holy smoke *rr.*

holy smoke! excl. of surprise, shock, wonder, etc. *rr.*

Home and Colonial n. (UK police use) London-based Regional Crime Squad which includes officers from the Metropolitan (home) and provincial (colonial) forces *Powis.*

home and dry safe and sound.

homeboy, homegirl n. (US Black use) **1.** someone who stays mainly at home; **2.** a neighbourhood person; **3.** a good friend (cf: Yiddish *landsman*) *X.*

home squeeze n. see: main squeeze *Folb.*

hominy gazette n. (Aus. prison use) internal prison rumours; fr. the main constituent of prison meals (cf: bush telegraph) *Neaman & Silver.*

homo n. (abbrev.) homosexual *Price: 2.*

hon (abbrev.) honey, general term of endearment, affection *rr.*

honcho n. leader, employer, boss, the head person of any job or other situation; orig. US forces use in Korea *Higgins: 1.*

honcho v. to lead, to direct others in a task or plan.

honest? do you really mean it?; are you joking? etc.

honey n. **1.** a girl, a woman *Higgins: 1*; **2.** a mistress *Higgins: 1*; **3.** (US campus use) female term for endearing, attractive male *Underwood.*

honey cart n. (airline use) disposal vehicles that flush out the lavatories of airliners (cf: honey wagon) *Green: 2.*

honey dipper n. (US milit. use) a latrine cleaner; fr. *honey*; excrement and urine *Neaman & Silver.*

honeyfuck v. **1.** to have sexual intercourse in innocent/idyllic circumstances; **2.** to have sex with a pre-pubescent girl.

honeyfuggle v. (euph.) honeyfuck (qv).

honeymoon n. (drug use) the early use of heroin, during which period the user can stop without any real physical or mental pain; prior to actual addiction *De Lannoy & Masterson.*

honeymoon cystitis n. a vaginal infection that supposedly stems from intensive intercourse, which in turn is supposedly the staple of honeymooning couples.

honeypot n. the vagina *Southern & Hoffenberg*.

honey wagon n. (US agricultural use) a manure cart used for cleaning out barns (cf: honey cart) *Neaman & Silver*.

honk n. (abbrev.) honkie (qv) *Burroughs: Jr.*

honk v.i. (US campus use) to be sexually aroused *Underwood*.

honker n. **1.** penis *Jay & Young*; **2.** (Valley Girls (qv) use) anyone considered odd, eccentric *Pond*.

Honkers n. Hong Kong, usu. amongst UK ex-patriates stationed or working in Far East *P. Theroux, 'Saint Jack', 1973*.

honkie n. a white person; fr. hunkie: orig. name for Poles who worked in Chicago stockyards *Price: 2*.

honk on v. (US campus use) to go away; to leave one alone *Underwood*.

honky-tonk n. **1.** a seedy bar which may also offer music, gambling, whores; fr. the honky-tonk piano that was often a feature of such establishments; **2.** the late Dick Emery used *hello honky-tonk(s)* as a cp but it may not survive his death.

honyok n. rustic, peasant *Gruber*.

hooch n. alcohol, liquor; fr. Alaskan Indian *hoocheno*: liquor *Chandler: LG*.

hood n. (abbrev.) hoodlum = gangster, thug *Fiction Illus. 3*.

hood n. **1.** (Aus. surfer use) the police *Humphries: 2*; **2.** an enemy agent; used passim by John le Carré in his fiction, but like other similar usages, either already espionage sl. or soon to become such (cf: babysit, mole).

hooey n. rubbish, nonsense.

hoof n. the human foot.

hoofer n. dancer *Bruce: 1*.

hoofing (show business use) dancing *T 15/3/83*.

hoof it v. to run *Farrell*.

hoof out v. to throw out, to expel.

hoo-ha n. nonsense, rubbish, twaddle *Humphries: 2*.

hook n. **1.** (US campus use) the telephone *Underwood*; **2.** (US milit. use) (abbrev.) hook-up: radio *Del Vecchio*; **3.** (US Black use) Jew (derog.) fr. popular stereotype of hooknosed Semites, see hooknose *Folb*; **4.** (abbrev.) hooker (qv); **5.** the pickpocket who actually steals the wallet, money etc. rather than his various accomplices (cf: wire) *Chandler: Notebk*. **6.** (US police use) anyone with sufficient power and clout (qv) to influence police management decisions, esp. in the giving to specific officers of choice assignments *Neaman & Silver*.

hook v. **1.** to addict to drugs; **2.** to engage in prostitution; **3.** to arrest, to catch in a crime *Higgins: 1*.

hook down v. to swallow *Wolfe: 2*.

hooker n. prostitute. fr. the redlight area of New York in 19th C: Corlear's Hook *Price: 2*.

hooking (UK police use) the practice of a dishonest informer who attempts to smear honest policemen and drag them into his own problems for his own ultimate benefit *Powis*.

hook, line and sinker n. absolutely, completely fr. fishing imagery.

hooknose n. (derog.) a Jew *Farrell*.

hooks n. human hands *Algren*.

hook shop n. a brothel; fr. hooker (qv) *Goulart*.

hoon n. (Aus. use) a procurer of prostitutes, but not a pimp to a specific girl or girls *Baker*.

hoop n. (US prison use) sodomy (cf: ring) *Legman*.

hoopdie swoop v. (US Black use) to move in on and pick up a man or woman with great speed and efficiency *Folb*.

hoopla n. fuss, commotion *Grogan*.

Hooray (abbrev.) hooray Henry (qv).

Hooray Henry n. aka: *Hoorah Henry*:rich young man given to much public exhibitionism, drunkenness and similar anti-social activities, all based on an excess of snobbish self-esteem *Runyon*.

hooroo! (Aus. use) goodbye *Ready*.
hoosegow n. prison; fr. Sp. *juzgado*: a tribunal or court of justice *Wodehouse passim*.
hoot n. **1.** (Aus. use) money, wealth *Wilkes*; **2.** a most amusing experience *White*.
hoot v. **1.** to laugh loudly; **2.** (Aus. use) to smell badly, to stink *Ready*.
hootch n. (US milit. use) in Vietnam, any form of shelter from a peasant hut, to a bunker, to an office building *Del Vecchio*.
hooter n. nose.
hoowah n. whore fr. New York pron. *Price: 2*.
hop n. heroin, opium *Chandler: 2*.
hope-to-die a. (US Black use) closest, most trusted, best; fr. affirmation 'Hope to die if . . .' *Folb*.
hophead n. (drug use) **1.** spec. heroin addict; **2.** user of any drug *Thompson*.
hop it! (excl.) go away, run along, etc. *Manser*.
hop joint n. a room or apartment where patrons gather to smoke opium or take heroin (cf: shooting gallery) *Runyon: 1*.
hop on a babe v. (US campus use) to have sexual intercourse; the inference is that the man, lacking greater finesse, has made a pounce (prob. when drunk) to initiate the activity *Bernbach*.
hopped up a. **1.** spec. of a car which has been improved beyond its basic specifications; **2.** excited *Price: 2*; **3.** under the affect of narcotics.
Hopping Sam (US milit. use) see Bouncing Betty *Rawson*.
hop the coop v. to escape, from any form of confinement, not necessarily prison *Chandler: LG*.
hop the wag v. to play truant from school (cf: bunk off) *Powis*.
horizontal rumble n. (US campus use) sexual intercourse (cf: rumble) *Bernbach*.
Horlicks n. (UK 'society' use) a mess *Barr*.
horn n. **1.** the nose; **2.** telephone *McFadden*; **3.** (US milit. use) a radio handset *Del Vecchio*; **4.** an erection *Higgins: 1*.
horn v. to inhale a narcotic *Goldman*.
horn in v. to interfere, to butt in, to intrude *Farrell*.
horn movie n. pornographic film *Simmons*.
horny a. sexually eager, aroused *Price: 1*.
horrors n. unpleasant experiences – usu. paranoid fantasies – brought about occasionally by the effects of smoking cannabis *Keyes*.
horry n. (Aus. use) (abbrev.) horizontal; copulation *C. Clarke*.
hors d'oeuvres n. (drug use) barbiturates or amphetamines; a prelude to harder (qv) pleasures *Folb*.
horse n. **1.** heroin *Grogan*; **2.** (Can. prison use) a smooth piece of wood with a string attached *Caron*; **3.** (rhyming sl.) horse and trap = clap = venereal disease, spec. gonorrhoea *Powis*.
horse around v. to joke, to mess about; fr. horse-play *Higgins: 3*.
horsefeathers (euph.) horseshit (qv) *Rawson*.
horse laugh n. a bad joke; hollow laughter *Chandler: LG*.
horseman n. (Can. prison use) a Mountie, a member of the Royal Canadian Mounted Police (RCMP) *Caron*.
horseplayer n. a gambler on horseraces *Bukowski: 1*.
horses n. (abbrev.) horsepower *Selby: 1*.
horse's ass fool, idiot *Farrell*.
horse's hangdown n. fool, idiot (cf: horse's ass) fr. the animal's penis, thus prick = fool *Higgins: 4*.
horseshit n. rubbish, nonsense (cf: bullshit) *Bruce: 2*.
horsewomen n. masculine lesbians *Legman*.
hose v. (homosexual use) to sodomize.
hose down v. (milit. use) to fire at, usu. with automatic weapons or aircraft weapons *Wolfe: 5*.
hostie n. (abbrev.) air hostess (cf:

stew) *Humphries: 2.*

ho stroll n. (US Black pimp use) the street or streets in a given town or city where prostitutes work regularly *Klein.*

hot a. **1.** urgent, fresh *SF Comics*; **2.** wanted by the police, suspect; **3.** stolen (goods); **4.** (sporting use) playing well, on top form *Sanchez*; **5.** (gambling use) enjoying a run of luck *Southern*; **6.** angry, annoyed *Jenkins*; **7.** sexy, sexually available; **8.** attractive, pleasurable; general term of approval.

hot chair n. the electric chair *Sillitoe.*

hot cross bun (rhyming sl.) on the run *Cole.*

hot dog n. successful gambler *Higgins: 3.*

hot-dogger n. (US teen/campus use) **1.** a show-off, a braggart; **2.** a successful, talented individual *Underwood.*

hot-fling n. (US Black use) an exciting sexual encounter with a new partner *Klein.*

hot foot n. see hot-foot v.

hot-foot v. to rush around; poss. fr. *hot foot* n., malicious trick played on an unsuspecting sleeper; matches are thrust end-first into the gap between upper and sole of the shoe (or between naked toes if vulnerable); these matches are lit and the shoe 'catches fire' or the flesh is painfully singed *Humphries: 2.*

hot for a. enthusiastic, keen on *Thompson.*

hothead n. anyone quickly inspired to rage, a short-tempered person *Safire.*

hot lot n. (UK police use) the flying Squad, or the defunct Special Patrol Group *Powis.*

hot on see: hot for *Seale.*

hot pants **1.** worried, anxious *Higgins: 2*; **2.** sexually eager *Chandler: LG.*

hot potato n. a problem, a difficult person, a trying situation; anything those concerned would prefer not to handle *Uris.*

hots n. **1.** sexual desire *Price: 2*; **2.** (US campus use) electric hair rollers *Underwood.*

hot seat n. **1.** the electric chair (cf: hot chair, hot squat); **2.** an unpleasant situation, esp. in a courtroom or public enquiry *PT.*

hot-shit a. see: big deal *Patti Smith, 'Piss Factory', 1976.*

hot shot n. the substitution of battery acid for white powdered heroin; when injected by the addict it causes instant death and leaves no trace *Grogan.*

hot-shot n. an important, influential person *Chandler: LG.*

hot squat n. the electric chair.

hot stuff form of address, often implying that the person in question has a higher opinion of him/herself than does his/her audience *Price: 3.*

Hottentot apron n. (lesbian use) elongated labia *Maledicta.*

hottie n. (abbrev.) hot water bottle *Humphries: 2.*

hot to trot n. enthusiastic for sex *McFadden.*

hot walker n. (horse race use) a groom who walks a horse in order to cool it down after a race *Higgins: 1.*

hot-wire v. to start a car without an ignition key by making the required connection between two wires *Higgins: 1.*

house n. (abbrev.) whore-house or house of ill-repute, a brothel *Heller.*

house v. (UK police use) to trace a person or any suspicious or wanted object to a given place *Powis.*

house nigger n. (US Black use) a Black employed, often as the 'token nigger', in a mainly white organization; fr. slavery difference between house and field niggers (qv) *Klein.*

how are they hanging? jocular male to male greeting; 'they' are testicles (cf: getting any?) *Schulberg: 2.*

how does that grab you? (cp) what do you think of that? (slightly aggressive inference, a challenge is assumed) *McFadden.*

how d'ye do n. (rhyming sl.) shoe *Cole.*

how high is a Chinaman? (cp) the answer to a statement or question which the speaker considers to be absurd or unanswerable; a pun on supposed Chinese name *How Hi*.

howl v.t. (US preppie (qv) use) to mock, to tease; fr. the 'howls of derision' that accompany this *Birnbach*.

how's about how about; adopted almost as his own property by disc jockey Jimmy Savile, who also talks not of boys and girls but of 'guys and gals' *BBC-1 TV, 'Top of the Pops', passim*.

how's it hanging? greeting: what are you up to, how are you, etc. (cf: how are they hanging) *Price: 1*.

how's tricks? greeting, (cf: what's happening) *Greaser Comics*.

hoy v. (Aus. use) to call; fr. the excl. *hoy! Ready*.

hubba! hubba! US teen term of approval, esp. when directed at a passing girl *Firesign Theatre, 'How Can You Be in Two Places at Once, When You're Not Anywhere At All', 1970*.

hubbie n. (abbrev./corruption) husband *May*.

Huey n. (US milit. use) UH-1 helicopter *Del Vecchio*.

hully n. (US Black use) especially fat person *Folb*.

humbug n. (Black pimp use) a false arrest on trumped up charges; fr. SE use as lies, deceit *Milner*.

humdinger n. a remarkable and excellent event *Wodehouse: JO*.

hummer n. (UK cant) an arrest on trumped up charges; fr. humbug *Neaman & Silver*.

hump v. **1.** to have sexual intercourse *Price: 2*; **2.** to carry (heavy) objects; esp. in milit. use: patrolling with a heavy pack, weapon, supplies, etc.; esp. popular in Aus. *O'Brien*.

hump 'em and dump 'em popular male cp suggesting seduction and then abandonment are best ways of relating to women (cf: 4-F Club) *Vidal*.

humper n. a carrier of heavy objects, esp. in rock music use for those who lift band's equipment.

humongous a. enormous, outsized, huge *'Mad Max 2', film, 1982*.

humpy n. (Aus. surfing use) an ideal surfing wave; its back is suitably 'humped' *Humphries: 2*.

Hun n. (derog.) German *BvdB*.

hun n. (abbrev.) hundred: $100 *Milner*.

hung a. having a large penis *Price: 1*.

hung for a. (US teen. use) in need of, lacking *Sculatti*.

hung for bread a. impoverished, out of money *Bruce: 2*.

hung like a horse a. a well-endowed male.

hungry a. **1.** ambitious, enthusiastic, driven; **2.** (UK police use) an officer who is extra-keen to make arrests *Laurie*.

hungry croaker n. (drug use) a doctor who for one reason or another is willing to prescribe drugs for any user who asks for them (cf: writing doctor) *Klein*.

hung up a. **1.** obsessed *Underwood*; **2.** delayed *Caserta*.

hung up on a. obsessed with; esp. in love with someone *Norman: 3*.

hunk n. an attractive, rugged, well-built male; possibly somewhat unintelligent (cf: beefcake) *Underwood*.

hunkie n. see: honkie.

hunko a. short, stocky physique *Price: 1*.

hunky a. strong, attractive, well-built man *Jay & Young*.

hunky-dory a. excellent, first rate, all as it should be *David Bowie, album title*.

hunt v. (Aus. use) to drive away, to chase off *Wilkes*.

hurl v. (Aus. use) to vomit *Humphries*.

hurricane lamp n. (rhyming sl.) tramp *Cole*.

hurry-up n. a police patrol car *Norman: 2*.

hurry-up wagon n. (UK criminal use) a Black Maria or police van *LL*.

hurt v. (street gang use) to wound

severely: to kill *Salisbury*.

hurt for v. to want something desperately, usu. to alleviate current unhappiness *Underwood*.

hurtin' for certain a. (US Black use) ugly *Folb*.

hurting a. **1.** generally miserable; **2.** (drug use) urgently needing narcotics to sustain one's regular dosage *Higgins: 1*; **3.** (Black pimp use) in financial difficulties *Milner*.

hurting dance n. sadness, frustration, jealousy, usu, in a relationship where A has B 'doing a hurting dance' *Price: 2*.

hurting for a. in great need of, desperate for *Higgins: 1*.

husband n. the supposedly 'aggressive' partner of a homosexual couple *Legman*.

hush-hush a. most secret, undercover *Vidal*.

hush money n. a bribe paid to ensure that embarrassing facts are suppressed *Higgins: 3*.

hush up v. to keep secret, to hide *Wodehouse: MOJ*.

husky n. a tough male, a thug *Howard*.

hustle n. any get-rich-quick scheme; a means of seduction *Higgins: 1*.

hustle v. to offer a sale of drugs to a person *Carson*.

hustler n. **1.** gambler or player of pool, bowling, etc. who uses skill and possibly cheating to make a living against lesser opponents *Price: 1*; **2.** a prostitute of either sex *Price: 2*; **3.** (US campus use) a male who succeeds in his conquests of females *Underwood* .

hydraulic n. (Aus. use) a light-fingered person, who'll 'lift anything that isn't nailed down' *Wilkes*.

hype n. **1.** (abbrev.) hypodermic syringe, thus; **2.** a heroin addict *Grogan*; **3.** (pimp use) a prostitute who works simply to support her narcotic addiction *OUI 8/75*.

Hype n. aka: *the Bill*: the short change swindle in which the criminal persuades a shopkeeper that he has paid with a larger denomination note than he actually has, thus gaining extra change *Burroughs: 1*.

hype v. **1.** to promote a person or commodity through an excess of overzealous, grandiose publicity, esp. in rock business use, fr. hyperbole; **2.** (US Black use) to outsmart, to make a fool of *X*.

hyper a. (abbrev.) hyperactive: tense, over-emotional, betraying one's feelings, esp. towards an attractive person *McFadden*.

hypo n. (drug use) (abbrev.) hypodermic syringe (cf: works) *Algren*.

I am sure (Valley Girls (qv) use) (abbrev.) I am sure that you are wrong/ that I don't want to do what you suggest / etc.; intensified as *I am so sure pond*.

I can't handle this (teen. use) general term of apprehension, disentanglement from a difficult situation; popular among drug users who are finding a given experience too intense *Pond*.

ice n. diamonds *Wodehouse, bk. title, 'Ice in the Bedroom', 1961*.

ice v. to murder, to kill (cf: chill) *Stone*.

iceberg n. **1.** an unemotional person *Folb*; **2.** (Aus. use) anyone who enjoys an early morning swim in the icy ocean waters *Wilkes*.

ice cream freezer n. (rhyming sl.) a geezer = a male person *Powis*.

iced a. (US prison use) in solitary confinement *Major*.

iced to the eyebrows a. extremely drunk *Chandler: LG*.

icing expert n. (homosexual use) a fellator *Legman*.

icky a. distasteful, nauseating, unpleasant, esp. in juv. use. *Rosten*.

icky-poo a. (children's use) disgusting, nasty, unpleasant, usu. with overtones of stickiness *Higgins: 5*.

I couldn't care less statement of absolute disinterest, although the opposite sentiment, albeit hidden, may be the true one.

I could do that a favour (cp) remarked by a man of a passing female; the 'favour' would of course be sexual.

ID v. (police use) to identify *Newman: 1*.

IDB (UK 'society' use) (acro.) *I*n *D*addy's *B*usiness; used by young men to describe their occupation *Harpers/ Queen 8/83*.

idiot board n. (TV use) the cue cards used as prompts for a TV performer; ths cards are held up by the *idiot girl Green: 2*.

idiot box n. the television, implying that TV watchers are less than normally intelligent *Underwood*.

I don't believe this! excl. of disbelief that extends beyond mere lack of simple credence into a denial that one could ever have landed in such a mess, that others could have created such horrors, that such stupidity could exist, etc. *Safire*.

I don't give a fuck intense version of I couldn't care less (qv).

I don't know (teen. use) all-purpose term that is used less as a definite statement than as an alternative to 'er' or 'Y'know' as a sentence-breaker; usu. pron: I dunno *Pond*.

iffy marginal, not wholly acceptable, unpalatable *Newman: 3*.

if it moves, salute it; if it don't paint it (milit. cp) supposedly the advice for a successful services career.

if you can't beat 'em, join 'em (cp) a statement of cynical resignation, not to mention the justification for a number of otherwise self-abasing acts.

if you can't do the time, don't do the crime (UK cant cp) self explanatory (cf: time) *Cole.*

ig man n. (US Black use) (abbrev.) ignorant man *Klein.*

ignant a. (US Black use) ignorant, stupid person; fr. pron.

I hear you a 'deeper' way of saying 'I understand', 'yes'; one supposedly 'hears' with every fibre of one's being *McFadden.*

ikey mo n. (derog.) a Jew; fr. Isaac Moses *Humphries.*

I'll be blowed! general excl. of surprise, shock, etc.

I'll eat my hat! statement of utter disbelief: if such and such is true/ happens, the . . .; the most famous instance of the phrase was uttered by a BBC commentator at the 1938 FA Cup Final who promised, 'If there's a goal now, I'll eat my hat'. There was, and to his credit, he did.

illegitimis non carborundum (cp) don't let the bastards grind you down; the 'Latin' translation is hardly accurate.

I'll freeze, Bill (US teen. use) cp: thank you, but no; a polite rejection of an offer or suggestion *Sculatti.*

ill piece n. (homosexual use) an unattractive and (therefore) unpopular homosexual *Stanley.*

illy-whacker n. (Aus. use) a professional confidence man, esp. the itinerants who follow fairs and country shows; fr. spieler (qv) *Wilkes.*

in a coon's age over a very long period; fr. the lifespan of a racoon *Runyon.*

in a jam in trouble, facing a problem *Higgins: 3.*

in a jiffy very quickly, in a moment *Performance.*

in a mucksweat frightened, flustered, under tension.

in and out like a fiddler's elbow (cp) rapid and enthusastic copulation.

in and out man n. (UK criminal use) a thief who burgles a house when an opportunity arises, rather than making elaborate plans, etc. *EN 12/11/57.*

in a pickle in a mess, in difficulties *Hotten.*

in a pig's ass (excl.) completely impossible, absolutely not! *Price: 2.*

in a pig's ear see: in a pig's ass *'Minder', Thames TV 1983.*

in a pig's eye see: in a pig's ass.

in a spot in trouble, in difficulties; (abbrev.) in a spot of bother.

in a twitter nervous, worried; fr. Second World War RAF sl. *twittering ringpiece*: a state of extreme nervousness *Wodehouse: AAG.*

in bondage (US Black use) indebted to, under the control of; with a biblical inference *Klein.*

incoming n. (milit. use) hostile fire, esp. shellfire, that is aimed at and bombarding the speaker *Del Vecchio.*

in dock out of work, out of circulation; fr. naut: dry dock where ships are laid up for repairs *Norman: 3.*

indoor money n. (UK criminal use) reserve cash for use in day to day life, rather than the proceeds of a given robbery *Newman: 1.*

industrial debutante n. a prostitute who specializes in attending US business conventions *Rawson.*

in dutch in trouble, out of favour *Farrell.*

info n. (abbrev.) information *rr.*

in front in advance, beforehand (cf: front, v.) *Bruce: 2.*

in hock indebted to, owing (both money and metaphorical debts) *Algren: 2.*

ink n. **1.** (US Black use) cheap wine *Major*; **2.** a mention in the newspapers; fr. the printers' ink used *Dunne.*

ink v. to sign a contract *Higgins: 5.*

inked a. (Aus. use) drunk *Neaman & Silver.*

inky-dinky n. (US Black use) a particularly dark American black *Major.*

in like Flynn a dead certainty, esp. in

areas of sexual conquest; fr. the alleged sexual prowess of the actor Erroll Flynn (1909–59).

in mourning (UK 'society' use) dirty fingernails, thus edging the hands, like mourning paper, in black *Barr*.

inner man n. the stomach, one's appetite (for food) *Neaman & Silver*.

in one's birthday suit (euph.) naked *Rawson*.

in one's corner on one's side; fr. boxing use.

in one's cups a. drunk *Neaman & Silver*.

in orbit a. drunk; extremely high (qv) *Dickson*.

in pig a. pregnant *N. Mitford, 'The Pursuit of Love', 1945*.

in queer Street in trouble, esp. financial *Powis*.

in Shit Street in difficulties, facing problems, etc.

in shtuck aka: *in shtook*: fr. Yiddish: in trouble *'Minder', Thames TV, 1980*.

inside in prison *Caron*.

inside man n. (UK criminal use) in a three-card monte (qv) team, one of the shills (qv) who pose as normal bettors but act only to encourage the real victims of the game *Powis*.

in spades to the greatest extent; very much, extremely – any form of intensifier; fr. card use *Runyon: 1*.

instant boot camp n. (US campus use) the act of vomiting; fr. boot (qv) and the military training 'boot camp', a notably vile environment *Bernbach*.

interior decorating n. (UK 'society' use) sexual intercourse during the day *Barr*.

international milk thief n. (UK police use) ironic term for any petty villain *Powis*.

interrupter n. (UK police use) a court interpreter *Powis*.

in the altogether a. naked *Rawson*.

in the bag a. drunk *Higgins: 4*.

in the bag certain, easy, no problem *Higgins: 3*.

in the barrel (US business use) actually fired already or likely to be fired from one's job.

in the box seat (Aus. use) in fill control, in a position of dominance, power; box seat = driving seat in a (horse-driven) coach (cf: in the driving seat) *Wilkes*.

in the buff a. naked; fr. the colour of 'white' flesh *Neaman & Silver*.

in the cellar (sports use) at the bottom of a league or similar points table; Wodehouse favours 'down among the wines and spirits' (generally obs. now): miserable, feeling low, down in the dumps *Bukowski: 2*.

in the chair buying a round of drinks; fr. chairing a meeting *'Only Fools and Horses', BBC-1 TV 1983*.

in the closet **1.** spec. for a homosexual to hide his sexual predelictions; **2.** to hide away *Higgins: 2*.

in the death in the end *Norman: 2*.

in the dog-house out of favour, in disgrace; supposedly consigned to the dog's kennel rather than one's hearth and home *AS 41 (1966)*.

in the driving seat in control, running things, on top of a situation; fr. the controlling position in a vehicle (cf: in the box seat).

in the frame (UK criminal/police use) under suspicion, usu. with some grounds, of having committed a given crime; fr. racetrack use, the frame holds the numbers of the winning horses in a race; and, from villain's point of view, implying a frame-up (qv) *Mortimer*.

in the hole (gambling use) in debt, owing *Seale*.

in the money rich, successful in a wager; fr. racing use: those horses that finish 1–2–3 'run in the money', thus paying out to those who bet on them *Wodehouse: MOJ*.

in the peek n. (UK prison use) in an observation cell, into which a man is placed if, for instance, he has smashed up his cell or shown similar signs of instability *LL*.

in the pink a. extremely fit, well and cheerful; fr. abbrev. in the pink of condition *Dunne*.

in the pits a. depressed, miserable (cf:

down in the dumps) *Neaman & Silver*.

in the pudding club pregnant (cf: bun in the oven).

in the rude a. (genteel euph.) naked *Joe Orton, 'Entertaining Mr Sloane', 1964.*

in the saddle performing sexual intercourse, usu. of a male who is 'riding' *Dunne*.

in the soup a. in trouble, in difficulties.

in the stretch almost complete; fr. racing use: the stretch: the last part of the course *Grogan*.

in the tank a. drunk *Dickson*.

in the wrapper a. very drunk *Higgins: 5*.

into **1.** interested in, involved with; **2.** owing money to *Higgins: 1*.

in your eye! (US campus use) term of general derision, dismissal, contempt *Bernbach*.

irey a. (Jamaican (Rasta) use) powerful and pleasing *Thelwell*.

Irish a. a general racial epithet; the Irish seem eternally condemned as slow-witted, bungling peasants; thus Irish — will invariably imply such negative qualities (cf: Chinese, French, etc.).

Irish jig n. (rhyming sl.) **1.** wig *T 26/9/83*;**2.** cig (arette) *Wright*.

iris out v. to leave unobtrusively; fr. film use: the contracting of the picture to the dimensions of a small dot and thence a blank screen *Wodehouse: PGM*.

iron n. **1.** (rhyming sl.) iron hoof = poof = homosexual *Scaffold, 'Thank You Very Much', 1967*; **2.** gun *Higgins: 2*; **3.** a motor car *'The Killers', directed Don Siegel, 1964*.

iron cross n. (US Black use) extremely unfavourable circumstances from which it is hard to extract oneself *Klein*.

iron tank n. (rhyming sl.) bank *Jones: J*.

irvine n. (US Black use) the police *Folb*.

Irving n. (US use) a dull, uninformed, obnoxious person (cf: Melvin) *Neaman & Silver*.

I should be so lucky! (cp) initimating envy on behalf of a speaker who has just been informed of another's luck; the word-pattern implies Yiddish origin.

I should cocoa! (cp) (esp. popular in BBC Radio 'Billy Cotton Bandshow' 1950s): you must be joking, don't make me laugh, etc. fr. rhyming sl: cocoa = say so. *Powis*

Island n. the Isle of Wight, thus HMP Parkhurst which is situated there.

island-hopping n. the practice amongst (rich) tourists of touring around the islands of the West Indies, the Aegean Sea or similar hot and inviting spots.

Isle of Wight (rhyming sl.) all right *Powis*.

issue n. (Aus. use) everything, the lot, all there is *Ready*.

I suppose n. (rhyming sl.) nose *Capital Radio, 1983*.

it derog. reference to a casual, picked up partner, as opposed to a lover *Legman*.

it n. (US Black use) the quintessence of black being, spirit, sensitivity, etc.

item n. a couple; fr. such fashionable couples being items for newspaper gossip columnists *Price: 3*.

it'll all come out in the wash (cp) problems, etc., will all be made clear in due course, no matter how daunting at present.

it looks like rain (cant cp) an arrest – poss. of the speaker – seems likely *Neaman & Silver*.

it's a breeze (rhyming sl.) it's easy *Cole*.

it's one o'clock at the water-works (coy cp) your fly is undone *Rawson*.

it's the beer talking (cp) the excuse, usu. in a public house, for breaking wind.

it's your baby (cp) that's your problem *Manser*.

it's your corner it's your turn to pay, usu. in a pub *Powis*.

it's your little hip pocket (US Black use) you're in very great trouble

Himes: 2.

it takes two to tango (cp) sexual intercourse, esp. adulterous, requires two people, not just a lustful male.

Ivan n. a generally stupid East European person; fr. popular Russian name *Powis*.

I wouldn't know statement of dismissal, uninterest (cf: don't ask me).

I wouldn't trust him/her as far as I could throw him/her (cp) implying absolute lack of faith in its object.

j n. (drug use) (abbrev.) joint (qv).

jack n. **1.** (rhyming sl.) jack and jill (usu. pl) = pills: the pills of heroin in which the drug is issued to registered addicts in the UK *Green*; **2.** (abbrev.) blackjack *Runyon*; **3.** a detective, orig. northern dial., now general *Powis*; **4.** (rhyming sl.) jack tar = bar *Powis*; **5.** general term of address to a man *'Hill Street Blues', Thames TV, 1983*; **6.** (Aus. use) venereal disease *Wilkes*.

Jack-a-dandy n. (rhyming sl.) brandy *Cole*.

jackanape n. (US Black (radical) use) an undisciplined albeit enthusiastic member of a radical movement; one who finds it hard to put the general good before his/her own pleasures; fr. SE use, orig. one who acts like an ape. *Seale*.

Jack and Jill n. (rhyming sl.) hill, bill, till, pill *Cole*.

jack around v. **1.** mess about, usu. with sexual, adulterous overtones *Jenkins*; **2.** (US campus use) to tease *Underwood*.

jackdaw n. (rhyming sl.) jaw *Jones: J.*

jacked (Aus. use) angry, annoyed, fed up *Bickerton*.

jacked out (US campus use) annoyed, irritated, angry *Bernbach*.

jacked up a. **1.** (US teen. use) upset, anxious, waiting anxiously for time to pass *Sculatti*; **2.** (Aus. use) infected (usu. with venereal disease) *Wilkes*.

jacket n. **1.** (drug use) (abbrev.) yellow jacket = nembutal, a tranquilizer *De Lannoy & Masterson*; **2.** (US police use) the file on a given criminal, recording previous convictions, etc. (cf: form) *Algren*.

jacking off (gambling use) **1.** racking up the pool balls; **2.** shaking dice with a movement that might be seen as resembling masturbation (cf: jack off, v.) *Klein*.

jack in the box v. (US criminal use) to break and enter a house, apartment *Klein*.

jack in the box (US Black use) the state of having one's penis inside one's partner's vagina *Klein*.

jack it in v. stop doing something; to give in *Dury, 'Do It Yourself'*.

jack job n. (US campus use) unfair treatment *Underwood*.

Jack Jones n. (rhyming sl.) alone *Cole*.

jack of (Aus. use) bored with, tired of, etc.

jack off v. **1.** (drug use) to pump backwards and forwards with the plunger of the hypodermic without finally injecting the blood and heroin mix into the arm; fr. both the up and down gesture of masturbation, and the figurative 'jacking off' instead of reaching a climax *Klein*; **2.**to masturbate (cf: jerk off) *SF Comics*.

jack-off n. derog. form of address; lit: masturbator *Bruce: 1*.

jack roller n. a thief who specializes in

attacking the vulnerable: drunks, vagrants, etc. *Shulman.*

jacks (rhyming sl.) jack's alive = five, thus £5.00 *Norman: 2.*

Jack's alive (rhyming sl.) five *Cole.*

jack shit absolutely nothing; always used with a qualifying negative vb., *you don't know jack shit about* . . . etc. *Underwood.*

jacksie n. anus, usu. in *up your jacksie*: derog. response to an unpalatable idea or opinion *May.*

Jack the Lad n. a show-off; anyone particularly pleased with himself and keen on ensuring everyone knows it *Dury.*

Jack the Ripper n. (rhyming sl.) a kipper; fr. the 19th C. mass-killer; also kippers are slit open *Wright.*

jack up v. **1.** (drug use) to inject narcotics (cf: jack off); (US Black use) **1.** to assault, to attack; **2.** to have sexual intercourse *Folb*; **4.** to interrogate (by the police); to stop and search *Seale.*

jag n. a breakdown, an emotional collapse; often as a crying jag: lengthy and profound sobbing *Jay & Young.*

Jag n. (abbrev.) Jaguar motor car.

jake all right, OK, satisfactory *Farrell.*

jake flake n. (US Black use) anyone interested in themselves above anything or anyone else *Klein.*

jakes n. lavatory; orig early 16th C., when SE *Wolfe: 2.*

jalopy n. a (decrepit) car *Waits.*

jam n. **1.** a problem, a difficult situation; usu. *in a jam Chandler: LG*; **2.** (Black use) cocaine; **3.** semen *Jagger & Richards, 'Some Girls', 1977*; **4.** (homosexual use) a heterosexual male; **5.** foreplay between two homosexual men *Legman*; (US Black use) **6.** the vagina; **7.** an attractive woman *Folb.*

jam v. **1.** for musicians to play together without set scores or arrangement for the pleasure and the spontaneous music thus created *Price: 2*; **2.** (Black pimp use) to sniff cocaine *Milner*; **3.** (US teen. use) to leave, to exit fast *Pond*; **4.** to arrest; to put in an unfavourable position *Klein*; **5.** to ruin, to make a mess of *Algren.*

Jamdung n. (Jamaican) Jamaica; fr. *jam*: press, *dung*: down; refers to oppression of the Jamaican proletariat *Thelwell.*

jam fag n. a homosexual with no other sexual interests *Legman.*

jam house (Black pimp use) a place where cocaine can be both purchased and then snorted in convivial surroundings *Milner.*

jam it v. to drive a car or bike fast *Thompson.*

jam it! threatening exclamation, abbrev. of *jam it up your ass Bukowski: 1.*

jam jar n. (rhyming sl.) motor car *Capital Radio 1983.*

jamoke n. fellow, person, man *Higgins: 4.*

jam one up v. (US Black use) **1.** to rape; **2.** to beat, to overpower; **3.** to talk forcefully *Folb.*

jam-pot n. the anus *Legman.*

jam-rag n. a tampon or protective towel.

jam roll n. (rhyming sl. UK prison use) parole *Obs. 1981.*

jam tart n. (rhyming sl.) sweetheart, thus girlfriend *Cole.*

jane n. a girl, a woman *Grogan.*

jap v. (street gang use) to ambush one's rivals; fr. Japanese attack on Pearl Harbor (?) *Salisbury.*

JAP n. (acro.) *J*ewish *A*merican *P*rincess: a rich, spoiled Jewish girl *Rosten.*

jar n. (drug use) a quantity of pills, usu. 500/1000 (cf: lid) *Folb.*

jarhead n. an alcoholic, a heavy drinker *'Hill Street Blues', Thames TV, 1983.*

jarred a. drunk *Dickson.*

J. Arthur n. (rhyming sl.) J. Arthur Rank (for the cinema magnate, 1888–1972) = wank = masturbate, thus, by extension, a fool *Powis.*

jasper n. (US Black use) a lesbian, fr. white *jasper*: man, guy *Folb.*

java n. (US/Can use) coffee. thus also obs. *jamoke*: strong black coffee, fr.

Java + Mocha (two brands) *Caron*.

jaw v. to talk.

jawbone v. to talk, to chatter *Grogan*.

jawbreaker n. a word that the speaker considers so long or complex that its pronunciation threatens to be harmful.

jazz n. idle chatter; slightly deceptive conversation *Greenlee*.

jazz v. (US Black use) to have sexual intercourse *Folb*.

jazz around v. lead a fast life, mainly in pursuit of sex *Pynchon*.

jazz up v. to brighten up, to improve, to make more gaudy *Jay & Young*.

jazzy a. bright, colourful.

JD (acro.) *J*uvenile *D*elinquent *Grogan*.

jeff v. (US Black use) to use a given line of talk to deceive or seduce another person; thus *tight jeff*: well-rehearsed patter, *slack jeff*: spontaneous ad libbed chatter *Klein*.

jel n. (Valley Girls (qv) use) an appalling, unacceptable person; fr. jello (jelly) -brain *Pond*.

jello squad n. (US campus) an imaginery gathering or club of all those students considered beyond the social pale of their peers on campus *Underwood*.

jelly n. (UK cant) (abbrev.) gelignite *Powis*.

jelly baby n. secretions from the anus or vagina during/after intercourse *Klein*.

jellybox n. the vagina *Southern & Hoffenberg*.

jellyfish n. a weak, ineffectual, cowardly person *Stone*.

jelly roll n. (US Black use) the female genitals *Folb*.

jelly sandwich n. (US Black use) sanitary napkin *Folb*.

Jem Mace n. (rhyming sl.) face; fr. prizefighter, 1831–1910 *Wright*.

jemmy n. (UK criminal use) a short housebreaker's crowbar.

jerk n. a fool, an idiot, a failure; orig. fr. jerk off (qv) but such onanistic inference is generally irrelevant *Price: 2*.

jerk around v. to waste one's time, to irritate; fr. jerk off, v. *Bruce: 2*.

jerking the gherkin masturbation *Humphries*.

jerk off v. **1.** spec. to masturbate; **2.** to mess around, to waste time, energies *Price: 2*.

jerk-off n. (derog.) useless person; lazy incompetent (cf: jack off).

jerk one's chain v. to annoy, to distract forcefully; as an owner drags on a dog's lead to control it *Higgins: 1*.

jerkwater a. small-time, second-rate, mediocre; fr, jerkwater town (qv) *Thompson: J*.

jerkwater town n. a small, insignificant town; known only for its water tower and trough from which a train could scoop water from between the tracks without actually stopping (cf: tank town) *Runyon*.

Jerry n. (derog.) German *Sillitoe*.

jerry n. a chamber pot; fr. jereboam, usu. a double-magnum of wine *Hotten*.

jerry a. aware, knowledgeable, informed; fr. 19th C. UK verb: to recognize, to discern, detect *Runyon*.

Jesus H. Christ! general excl., the H. is redundant other than for rhythm *'Hill Street Blues', Thames TV, 1983*.

Jew/Jewish the Jew as a racial stereotype requires greater space than available here, as do the arguments pro/con the inclusion of such vilifications; in short Jew = money to his gentile peers (unlike the Scot who equals money but inventive/brave/etc. with it) and the words below bear this out (cf: Chinese, French, Irish, etc.).

jew v. (derog.) to cheat financially *Goldman*.

Jew canoe n. **1.** (US use) a Cadillac *Dunne*; **2.** (UK 'society' use) a Jaguar *Barr*.

Jewish lightning n. (derog.) deliberate arson in order to gain the insurance on an otherwise unprofitable business.

Jewish piano n. (derog.) cash register *Powis*.

Jewish typewriter n. (derog.) a cash

register *Powis*.

Jewy Louis n. (UK 'society' use) (derog.) flashy, vulgar style of interior decoration, poss. featuring (fake) Louis XV, XVI furniture *Barr*.

Jew York n. (UK 'society' use) (derog.) New York; fr. large Jewish population therein (cf: Yidney).

jib v. (US Black use) to talk; poss. fr. 19th C jib: underlip; also fr. flapping jibsail on a ship (?) *Seale*.

jib-jibe n. (US Black use) talk that goes in one ear and out the other *Klein*.

jiblet n. (drug use) barbiturate *Folb*.

jibone n. aka: *jabone* **1.** a greenhorn (qv), an innocent, a newly-arrived immigrant; **2.** a heavy, a thug, a muscleman; as which **1** was often used *Price: 2*.

jick head n. (US Black use) a drunkard; fr *jiggins*: a fool (?) *Major*.

jiffy n. a very short time *Humphries*.

jig n. (abbrev.) jigaboo (qv) *Dunne*.

jigaboo n. aka: *zigaboo*; derog, term for a Black person; fr. alleged 'natural rhythm' which has Blacks jigging around.

jig-a-jig n. sexual intercourse; often found in pidgin slangs.

jiggered **1.** (euph.) damned; with some feeling of confusion also *Rawson*; **2.** exhausted, worn out *Keyes*; **3.** drunk *Dickson*.

jiggery-pokery n. tricks, deceit, lies, underhand activities in general; fr. Scots *jouk*: a trick.

jigglers n. (UK criminal use) skeleton keys for use on pin tumbler locks; fr. sleight-of-hand required to turn lock *Powis*.

jill off v. (lesbian use) to masturbate, the 'feminized' jack off (qv) and the other of the nursery rhyme characters *Maledicta*.

Jim n. (US Black use) title for a fellow Black man, usu. as shorthand for making gesture of friendship *Bruce: 2*.

jim n. (US Black use) jewellery, diamonds; fr. gem *Klein*.

Jim Crow a. white racist discrimination vs. Blacks and the Jim Crow laws that embody it; fr. early 19th C. Kentucky plantation song with chorus 'Jump Jim Crow' and a blackface entertainer Thomas Dartmouth Rice who performed it c.1829 *W. Safire, 'Safire's Political Dictionary', revised edn., 1978*.

Jiminy Cricket (euph.) Jesus Christ! *Rawson*.

jim-jams n. (abbrev.) pyjamas, usu, children's use *Humphries: 2*.

jimmies n. (Aus. use) a fit of nerves; see Jimmy Britts *Wilkes*.

jimmy n. **1.** (rhyming sl.) jimmy riddle (qv) *Payne*; **2.** US version of jemmy (qv).

Jimmy Britts n. (Aus. use; rhyming sl.) the shits = terrified, scared, fr. Britt, a boxer who toured Australia during the First World War *Bickerton*.

Jimmy Hix **1.** (UK criminal use; rhyming sl.) fix = injection of narcotics *LL*; **2.** (gambling use) the point of six in craps dice *Chandler: Notebk*.

jimmy o'goblins n. *money*.

Jimmy Riddle n. (rhyming sl.) piddle = urinate.

Jimmy Skinner n. (rhyming sl.) dinner *Wright*.

Jimmy Woodser n. (Aus. use) anyone who drinks alone; or a drink that is taken by oneself *Lawson*.

jims n. (UK prostitute use) men who like to watch prostitutes at work (or just 'dirty old men' in sex bookshops, etc.) but offer no actual sexual threat *Powis*.

jing-jang n. (lesbian use) the vagina *Maledicta*.

jinny n. a speakeasy or unlicensed drinking place; fr. gin available there *Chandler: Notebk*.

jive v. to lie, to confuse, to tease; thus *jive about with*; to play with, to mess around *Price: 2*.

jive a. fake, phoney, deceitful, unappealing *Greenlee*.

jive and juke v. (US campus use) to have a very good time *Underwood*.

jive-ass a. derog. term of abuse; (cf: jive) *Jones*.

jive hand n. (US Black use) an undesirable situation which puts one person at an unfair disadvantage; one is dealt 'a bad hand' *Klein*.

joanie a. (Valley Girls (qv) use) out of date, unfashionable *Pond*.

joanna n. (rhyming sl.) piano *Cole*.

job a. (UK police use) anything involved in police work, ie: 'a job dog', 'a job car', etc.; all police work is known as 'the job' and the magazine of the Metropolitan Police is 'The Job' *Laurie*.

job n. **1.** (US campus use) bowel movement *Underwood*; **2.** (criminal use) the committing of a given crime, often with a qualifying name, thus 'The Barclays Bank job', etc. *Mortimer*.

job v. (Aus. use) to hit, to beat up *Wilkes*.

jobbed a. (UK cant) framed up on false evidence (cf: flake, verbal) *Neaman & Silver*.

jobbers n. (taxi-driver use) freelance, journeymen cabbies who hire their vehicle and work on the clock (qv) *Powis*.

jobsworth n. minor factotum whose only status comes from enforcing otherwise petty regulations, fr. 'more than my job's worth to let . . .' *Farren*.

jock n.**1.** (US campus and sports use) a sportsman; fr. the athletic supporter 'jock strap' worn by such performers *Underwood*; **2.** (abbrev.) disc jockey *Harry Chapin, 'I Am The Morning DJ'*; **3.** (abbrev.) jockey *Higgins: 1*.

Jock n. a Scot *Payne*.

jocker n. one who practises anal intercourse *Legman*.

jockey n. **1.** a masculine lesbian *Legman*; **2.** any form of driver, esp, cabs, buses; **3.** a worker in a given job: *swab jockey*: washer-up; *pump jockey*: petrol pump attendant *Dunne* etc.

jockey v. to struggle for a place, esp. the lead in a race; fr. racecourse use *Selby: 1*.

jock major n. (US campus use) to major in physical education *Simmons*.

jocks n. **1.** sportsmen; **2.** the practitioners of various jobs, ie: *construction jocks*, etc. *Higgins: 1*.

Jody n. (US Black use) mythical seducer 'Joe de (the) grinder' who specializes in married women or those with boyfriends; also derided by US troops as the lover who takes the 'girl you've left behind' *Klein*.

joe n. **1.** coffee; fr. Java (qv) *Schulberg*; **2.** an ordinary person, as in *college joe*, etc. (cf: Joe Blow) *Teresa*.

Joe Blake n. (rhyming sl.) cake *Wright*.

Joe Blakes n. (Aus. use, rhyming sl.) snakes (which one sees) and thus = delirium tremens.

Joe Blow n. an average member of the public.

Joe Bonce n. (rhyming sl.) a ponce, a procurer of prostitutes (cf: Charlie Ronce) *Cole*.

Joe Gurr n. (rhyming sl.) stir = porridge = prison *Wright*.

Joe Public n. the general public (cf: Mr Average) *T 3/3/83*.

joes n. (Aus. use) a fit of depression *Dennis*.

joey n. (UK prison use) any form of contraband – letters, parcels, etc. – smuggled into a prison *LL*.

john n. **1.** (homosexual use) an older man who supports a younger one without actually sharing a long-term relationship with him *Stanley*; **2.** the lavatory *Price: 2*.

John n. **1.** (prostitute use) a client *Selby: 1*; **2.** any anonymous male; ex *John Doe*, police, legal jargon for anonymous male suspect, victim, etc. *Fiction Illus. 3*; **3.** general term of address, irrespective of actual name; ie 'Hello, John, got a new motor', etc. *Norman: 2*.

John Bull (Aus. use; rhyming sl.) full, thus drunk *Humphries*.

John Hancock n. signature; fr. the particularly large signature of J.H. on the US declaration of Independence 1776.

John Henry n. (US Black use) a hard-working Black man, tough and indomitable in the face of appalling challenges *Major*.

john hop n. (Aus. use; rhyming sl.) cop = policeman *Neaman & Silver*.

John Law n. policeman, esp. a senior one *Powis*.

Johnny— used as a prefix, as in Johnny-darkie, Johnny-gyppo, etc.; these days tends be used facetiously/ironically.

Johnny at the rat hole n. an exceptionally enthusiastic, greedy person *Runyon*.

Johnny-be-good n. (US Black use) the police *Folb*.

Johnny Bliss n. (Aus. use; rhyming sl.) piss = urination *Wilkes*.

Johnny-come-lately n. a novice, an unsophisticated person, a recent arrival or recruit *Bruce: 2*.

Johnny Horner n. (rhyming sl.) corner *Jones: J*.

John Q. Public n. the average, law-abiding citizen.

John Thomas n. the penis *Humphries*.

joint n. **1.** a marijuana or hashish cigarette *Price: 2*; **2.** (US use) prison *Milner*; **3.** any place, esp. a bar or club *Breslin*; **4.** the penis *Goldman*.

join the great majority v. to die; all the dead of thousands of years of humanity *Neaman & Silver*.

jointman n. (Can. prison use) any prisoner who behaves like a guard *Caron*.

jo-jos n. (Can. prison use) a bulky coat without pockets *Caron*.

joker n. a man, a person; usu. with implications of incompetence *Price: 2*.

jolt n. an injection of a narcotic *Goldman*.

jones n. a heroin habit (qv) *Grogan*.

Joe Ronce n. (rhyming sl.) ponce, procurer (cf: Joe Bonce, Charlie Ronce) *Cole*.

jolly d. (public school use) wonderful, excellent, fantastic.

J/O scene n. (homosexual use) (abbrev.) jerk off (qv); mutual masturbation *Jay & Young*.

josh v. to tease.

joskin n. old man, old gaffer *Runyon*.

journo n. (Aus. use) journalist *Ready*.

joxy n. (lesbian use) the vagina *Maledicta*.

joy n. (drug use) marijuana *Folb*.

joy bang n. (drug use) an occasional injection of a narcotic by anyone who is not addicted.

joy buzzer n. (lesbian use) the clitoris *Maledicta*.

joy juice n. (US campus use) beer *Underwood*.

joy pop n. see: joy bang *Algren*.

joy trail n. the vagina *Dunne*.

Judas Priest! general excl., euph. for Jesus Christ! *'Hill Street Blues', Thames TV, 1983*.

Judy n. girl, woman, mainly Liverpool dial. *Keyes*.

Judy with the big booty n. (US Black use) a fat female *Folb*.

jug n. **1.** prison; thus *jugged*: in prison *Wodehouse: AAG*; **2.** a drink, esp. a pint of beer *Norma, : 2*; **3.** a bank *Caron*.

jugged a. imprisoned *Chandler: LJ*.

jughead n. a drunkard.

jugs n. breasts; by the use of physical resemblance, large breasts *Price: 2*.

jug-up n. (Can. prison use) mealtime *Caron*.

juice n. **1.**interest on a debt or loan (cf: vigorish) *Higgins: 3*; **2.** influence: political, criminal, anything involving corruption, pay-offs, favours *Bruce: 2*; **3.** spec. electricity (theatre, TV, film use); **4.** enjoyment, satisfaction, stimulation *Price: 2*; **5.** alcohol *Powis*.

juice v. **1.** to bribe, esp. in context of organized crime paying off the authorities *Chandler: LG*; **2.** to add interest to a loan, debt *Higgins: 3*.

juiced a. drunk *Gothic Blimp Works no 4*.

juice-freak n. (US campus use) cf. juice-head *Underwood*.

juice-head n. a heavy drinker, an alcoholic.

juice house n. (US Black use) liquor store *Folb*.

juice man n. (US cant) the collector of loans for an illegal loan shark (qv) *Neaman & Silver*.

ju-ju n. (drug use) **1.** any drugs in capsule form; **2.** marijuana cigarettes *R. Chandler, 'Farewell My Lovely', 1940.*

juke v. (US campus use) **1.** to dance; **2.** to have a good time (at a party); both fr. juke box, but itself fr. juke: cheap, raucous music played at similarly inclined roadhouses, cafes and brothels (cf: jive and juke) *Underwood.*

jump n. the beginning, the outset *Goldman.*

jump v. **1.** to ambush, to make a surprise attack *Mandelkau*; **2.** to have sexual intercourse *Powis.*

jump bad v. to misbehave *Price: 2.*

jump bail v. (criminal/police use) to leave the country and thus avoid a possible prison sentence while remanded on bail prior to one's trial *Wodehouse: MOJ.*

jump down one's throat v. to become furious with someone, often for no apparent reason.

jumped up a. conceited, arrogant; the implication is of one who no longer 'knows their place'.

jumper n. (UK cant) a jump lead carried by criminals to start stolen cars without using an ignition key *Powis.*

jumping a. lively, energetic, exciting *McFadden.*

jumping cat n. (US Black use) **1.** a sophisticated, poised older person; **2.** anyone successful in their occupation, legitimate or criminal *Klein.*

jump salty v. to be annoyed, irritated; to take offence *Waits.*

jump steady n. (US Black use) alcohol, which ensures that one keeps 'jumping' *Folb.*

jump the gun v. to act prematurely; fr. sporting use: in a false start a competitor will set off before the starting pistol has been fired *Manser.*

jump the last hurdle v. to die; fr. racing/running use (cf: take the long count, etc.) *Rawson.*

jump the rails v. to lose control, to disappear; fr. horseracing use *Chandler: LG.*

jump up and down v. (US Black use) to have sexual intercourse *Folb.*

jump-up man n. see: jump-up merchant *Powis.*

jump-up merchant n. one who steals fr. lorries, trucks, etc. *Norman: 2.*

jumpy a. nervous, irritable *Higgins: 1.*

Junction n. the area of South London near Clapham Junction railway station *Nell Dunn, 'Up The Junction', (1965).*

jungle bunny n. (derog.) Black person; fr. alleged origins in the jungle *Price: 1.*

jungle juice n. any form of strong, home-distilled liquor, often made of jungle-grown fruits and plants, herbs, etc. by soldiers with no 'regular' drinks.

jungle mouth n. (US campus use) bad breath *Underwood.*

jungly a. (UK 'society' use) disorganized, chaotic, less than smart *Barr.*

junior jumper n. (US Black use) a juvenile (under 16) who commits rape and robbery (cf: R&R) *Neaman & Silver.*

junk n. **1.** any unspecified objects, poss. worthless; poss. merely dismissive *Goulart*; **2.** (drug use) heroin *Goldman.*

junk v. to reject, to throw away, to abandon *Bruce: 2.*

junker n. a near-derelict but just driveable second-hand car; one step from the junkyard *Burroughs: Jr.*

junk food n. the products of the burgeoning world of 'fast-food' restaurants such as McDonalds, Burger King, Spudulike, etc. etc.; the implication, and to many palates, the actuality, is that such food is indeed junk, ie: rubbish.

junk hawk n. a heroin user whose entire existence centres on the drug *Grogan.*

junkie n. heroin addict *Price: 2.*

just a tick wait a moment *K. Waterhouse, 'In The Mood', 1983.*

just like mother makes it (cp)

perfect, ideal; often, but not necessarily referring to food or drink *Wodehouse: MOJ*.

just quietly (Aus. use) strictly between you and me *Wilkes*.

just seven (gambling use) the point of seven in craps dice *Chandler: Notebk*.

just the job see: just the ticket.

just the ticket perfect, ideal, exactly as desired and required *ES 19/5/83*.

just what the doctor ordered anything perfect, ideal, excellent; with extra implication of acting as a cure for previous problems.

juvie n. (US criminal use) Juvenile Hall; reform school *Major*.

K **1.** (civil service use) (abbrev.) Knight; **2.** (abbrev.) kilo-: use of the prefix denoting 'one thousand' as one thousand dollars; of late K has replaced the former equivalent G (qv) *Higgins: 1.*

kab edis n. (butchers' backsl.) backside or rump, both human and as a cut of meat *Cole.*

kak v. to vomit *Sanders: 2.*

ka-ka n. (juv. use) excrement *Neaman & Silver.*

kaker n. fr. Yiddish 'excrement': **1.** anything unpleasant or distasteful; **2.** cannabis (cf: shit) *Cole.*

kale n. money; its 'green-ness' connotes the vegetable (cf: cabbage, lettuce) *Farrell.*

Kanaka n. Hawaiian *BvdB.*

kanga n. a pneumatic drill; orig. fr. *kangaroo shit*, because it jumps up and down *Cole.*

kangaroo n. (rhyming sl.) a Jew.

Kangaroo Valley Earls Court, London; base for many expatriate Australians *Humphries.*

Kansas City roll n. see: California roll *X.*

karsy n. aka: kazi: spec. lavatory; thus any messy unappealing place that resembles one *Performance.*

kate and sidney (rhyming sl) steak and kidney *Jones: J.*

kate karney n. (rhyming sl.) the army *Jones: J.*

kaycuff foe! (backsl) fuck off! *Cole.*

kaylack v. (backsl.) talk *Cole.*

kaynab n. (butchers' backsl.) bank *Cole.*

kayrop n. (butchers' backsl.) pork *Cole.*

kazoo n. anus, buttocks; often in *up the kazoo Rawson.*

KB (UK prison use) (abbrev.) knockback (qv).

kecks n. knickers *Keyes.*

keel n. the buttocks; fr. nautical use *Neaman & Silver.*

keel over v. to collapse, to fall over; fr. nautical use *Austin.*

keen a. competent, appealling (in clothing), sharply dressed, etc. *Klein.*

keep ahead of the game v. to have a given situation under control *Folb.*

keep a stiff lip v. (US Black use) to keep quiet, to maintain a secret *Klein.*

keep banker's hours v. to act lazily; fr. the relatively brief periods during which a bank remains open for public business *Neaman & Silver.*

keep cave v. (UK school use) to keep a lookout, fr. Lat. *cave* = beware.

keep chickie v. to maintain a lookout (during a crime) *Grogan.*

keep mum v. to keep quiet; thus 1940s exhortation to secrecy: 'be like Dad: keep Mum' *Powis.*

keep nit v. (Aus. use) to act as lookout *Wilkes.*

keep one's cool v. to remain calm, despite circumstances to the contrary *McFadden.*

keep one'e ear to the ground v. to be on the lookout, to take note of developments *Schulberg: 2.*

keep oneself to oneself v. to lead a solitary life; to resist interfering in the business of others.

keep one's end up v. to do one's duty, to carry out one's share; fr. cricket use.

keep one's hair on v. to keep calm, to keep one's temper.

keep one's nose clean v. to lead a law-abiding, upright life; to avoid dangerous temptation; to resist interfering in things that are not one's business *Chandler: LG.*

keep one's pants zipped v. to retain control over one's ambitions, desires, conversation, etc.; such temptations are not always sexual *Higgins: 5.*

keep one's pecker up v. to stay cheerful, despite possible adversity; 'never say die!' (cf: pecker) *Hotten.*

keep on the straight and narrow v. to maintain a regular, law-abiding life.

keep stum(m) v. to keep quiet, to say nothing (cf: stumm & crum).

keep tabs on v. to keep under surveillance, to take note of *Higgins: 1.*

keep taking the tablets (cp) carry on with one's prescribed medicine; used in response to a statement that implies madness or eccentricity on behalf of the speaker *Manser.*

keep the ball rolling v. to maintain the progress of a situation *A. Powell, title of 4 vols of autiobiography, 1976/82.*

keep the cap on the bottle v. to suppress the publication of facts/information deleterious to oneself *PT.*

keep the cork on v. to maintain control of one's emotions *Thompson: J.*

keep the lines open v. to maintain communication; fr. telephone lines *McBain: 1.*

keep-up n. (US Black use) anyone who looks after the home, spec. a maid *Klein.*

keester n. see:keister *Bruce: 2.*

keister n. **1.** the anus, buttocks *Legman*; (US cant) **2.** a safe; **3.** a burglar's bag of safe/house-breaking tools.

kelly's eye (bingo use) 1 (cf: buttered scone).

kelt n. (US Black use) a white person *Major.*

kerb-crawling v. to drive a car slowly along the pavements of areas where prostitutes are known to operate and thus to make a pick up; this practice all too often leads to punters (qv) approaching quite innocent women.

kerfuffle n. a fuss, a row, a flap (qv).

key n. (drug use) one kilo of marijuana or hashish *Green: 1.*

key in v. to focus on; fr. film use, the key light focusses directly on a single actor *Price: 3.*

K-factor n. (skiing use) (abbrev.) Kraut-factor; the number of Germans visible on the slopes *Barr.*

KG (US police use) (acro.) *K*nown *G*ambler *Neaman & Silver.*

khyber n. (rhyming sl.) khyber pass = ass = buttocks *Powis.*

ki n. (UK prison use) cocoa; fr. nautical use *LL.*

KIA v. (US milit. use) to shoot dead or otherwise kill in combat; fr. milit. j. abbrev. *K*illed *I*n *A*ction *Del Vecchio.*

kibitz v. to watch (a gambling game) and to comment/advise but not to participate; fr. German *Kiebitz* a lapwing, a noisy and inquisitive bird. In German *kiebitzen* means to look over a cardplayer's shoulders *Kosten.*

kibitzers n. spectators in a gambling club or casino who do not play but watch and/or advise those who do; thus any non-participating adviser/observer *Performance.*

kick v. to stop taking an addictive drug; fr. kick the habit (qv) *Bruce: 2.*

kick n. **1.** the sensation any place or situation produces *Burroughs: 1*; **2.** pocket esp. in trousers *Wodehouse: TJ.*

kick about v. to make a fuss, to complain; fr. kick up a fuss *Farrell.*

kick around v. to hang about, to

wander aimlessly.

kick (it) around v. to discuss, to debate a topic *PT*.

kick ass v. **1.** to beat up someone; to fight; **2.** (US campus use) to have a good, if boisterous time *Underwood*.

kickback n. commission on a payment made by the payee to the customer; usu. a genteel euph. for bribe *Price: 2*.

kicker n. the last, most problematical piece of information *Fiction Illus. 3*.

kick in the ass n. see: kick in the pants.

kick in the pants n. **1.** a setback, a grave disappointment; **2.** anything that urges one on to greater effort, commitment, etc.

kick-off n. the beginning, the start; fr. soccer use *Wodehouse: MOJ*.

kick off v. to die *Higgins: 3*.

kick (something) off v. to start, to set in motion *Greenlee*.

kicks n. thrills, pleasure *Higgins: 2*.

kicksies n. trousers *Hotten*.

kick the bucket v. to die *Sillitoe*.

kick the gong around v. to use drugs, esp. heroin/morphine *Chandler: Notebk*.

kick the habit v. to stop taking an addictive drug, usu. heroin *Bruce: 1*.

kick the stuffing out of v. to maltreat, to beat up severely *Farrell*.

kick the tin v. (Aus. use) to make a financial contribution *Wilkes*.

kick up daisies v. to die (cf: push up daisies).

kick upstairs v. to promote an official or executive who cannot actually be dismissed but whose value in his/her current role is no longer useful to the organization *Capital Radio 1983*.

kid v. to tease, to joke with, to pretend, to fool *Higgins: 1*.

kiddiwink n. a young child.

kiddo n. a child; esp, as a greeting: 'Hey, kiddo' *C. MacInnes, 'Absolute Beginners', 1959*.

kidney n. the female womb *Klein*.

kidney wiper n. the penis; obvious extension of kidney (qv).

kid-simple n. (homosexual use) an obsessive lover of young boys *Legman*.

kife n. a bed *Powis*.

kike n. (derog.) a Jew; poss. rhyming with Ike (cf: Ikey Mo); or fr. Yiddish *kikel*: a circle, the mark used by some illiterate Jewish immigrants – rather than a cross – when signing papers at Ellis Island, NYC, c.1900 *Higgins: 3*.

ki-ki n. **1.** bisexual; **2.** a homosexual who is equally happy in active or passive sex roles *Stanley*.

Kilburn n. (rhyming sl. UK police use) Kilburn Priory = diary, spec. that used by an officer for writing up evidence that will be given in court *Powis*.

kill v. **1.** to convulse with laughter, to bowl over, to surprise *Goldman*; **2.** (theatre/TV/film use) to turn off a given light or lights *Green: 2*.

killer a. (US teen. use) wonderful, amazing, etc. (cf: kill **1**) *Pond*.

killing a. (UK 'society' use) very funny; thus 'that really kills me' etc. *Barr*.

killing floor n. (US Black use) anywhere used for the purpose of sexual intercourse *Folb*.

kill one's dog v. to drink heavily *Dickson*.

killout n. (US Black use) a fascinating person, enthralling topic or thing *Major*.

kimible n. (US Black use) the exaggerated, identifiable pimp walk poss. fr. (arms) akimbo *Klein*.

kindness n. (US Black use) a sexual favour; thus, *to do a kindness*: to indulge sexually *Klein*.

king a. (Aus. surf use) excellent, wonderful, perfect *Humphries: 2*.

king n. (Aus. use) (abbrev.) kinghit: a knockout punch or blow *Wilkes*.

King Dick a. (rhyming sl.) thick (qv) = stupid, dull *Wright*.

kinky a. odd, bizarre, eccentric, spec. sexually perverse *Performance*.

kip n. **1.** a bed; **2.** the place where one sleeps, one's home; both uses fr. orig. 18th C. a brothel *Norman: 2*.

kip v. to sleep *Norman: 2*.

kipe v. (US campus (spec. University

of Arkansas) use) to steal *Underwood*.

kiphouse n. see: dosshouse *LL*.

kipper n. (Aus. use) (derog.) Englishman; fr. the herring which, after processing, has become 'two-faced with no guts' *Wilkes*.

kishke n. fr. Rus: intestine; the guts *Rosten*.

kiss v. **1.** (US teen. use) (abbrev.) kiss goodbye: reject, do without, etc. *Sculatti*; **2.** to fellate or perform cunnilingus *Legman*.

kiss ass v. to be subservient, sycophantic *Jones*.

kisser n. **1.** the mouth *Wright*; **2.** the whole face *Runyon*.

kiss goodbye v. to reject, to do without.

kiss my arse! general cp. of contempt or dismissal *J. Joyce, 'Ulysses', 1922*.

kiss my tuna! (Valley Girls (qv) use) all-purpose excl. of rejection; tuna = vagina and the implication is that the oral sex that is invited is *de facto* distasteful *Pond*.

kiss of death n. a person or object contact with whom or which invariably proves fatal – metaphorically if not practically.

kiss off n. conclusion, farewell, termination (usu. with sense of one party compelling it on the other) *Jay & Young*.

kiss off v. to reject, ignore, spurn, toss aside *Higgins: 5*.

kiss one's ass goodbye v. to give up completely; to abandon all hope.

kiss the dog v. (US cant) for a pickpocket to steal from the person with whom he/she is face-to-face *Neaman & Silver*.

kiss the porcelain god v. (US campus use) to vomit (cf: drive the porcelain bus) *Bernbach*.

kiss the worm v. to fellate *Legman*.

kissyface n. (US teen/campus use) the act of kissing *Underwood*.

kite n. **1.** (Can. prison use) a contraband letter or note smuggled in/out of gaol. *Caron*; **2.** (US prison use) any form of written document, memo, etc. used within a gaol *Folb*; **3.** a dud cheque; thus *kiting*: passing dud cheques for fraud; a bouncing (qv) cheque 'flies away' *Norman: 2*; **4.** (US campus use) an inveterate drug user, who stays 'high as a kite' *Underwood*.

kitted up a. dressed, clothed *Humphries*.

kitty-cat n. (US Black use) **1.** a Cadillac; **2.** a female (cf: pussy) *Folb*.

Kiwi n. New Zealander; fr. the national bird.

klick n. (US milit. use) a kilometre *Del Vecchio*.

kludge n. anything thrown together more by luck than judgement and with little style or sophistication, though sufficient workability for those who assembled it; fr. computer jargon *Kidder*.

klutz n. fr. Ger 'a log': a stupid, clumsy person *Grogan*.

knacker v. to harm, to ruin *Tidy*.

knackered a. worn out, exhausted; fr. SE: horse-butcher *Wilkinson*.

knackers n. testicles *T 13/7/83*.

knee v. (abbrev.) knee in the testicles.

kneecap v. an extra-legal 'punishment' esp. beloved of and poss. introduced by the IRA, whereby victims are shot through the kneecaps and, while painfully crippled, are not actually killed. *Humphries: 2*.

kneel at the altar v. (US prison sl.) to fellate *Legman*.

knees up n. a party, a celebration, fr. Cockney popular song 'Knees Up Mother Brown!'

knee trembler n. sexual intercourse when both partners are standing up; popular with cheap prostitutes or with couple who have nowhere to lie down *Norman: 2*.

knickers! excl. meaning rubbish! piss off! (qv), etc.; general negation of the preceding speaker's opinion, demand, etc. *Powis*.

knight of the golden grummet n. (US criminal sl.) one who enjoys anal intercourse; fr. naut, grummet = rope ring; gold = excrement *Legman*.

knobs n. **1.** the female breasts *Folb*;

2. (US Black use) stylish, up to date shoes with shined toecaps *Seale*.

knock n. (Aus. use) a promiscuous female *Wilkes*.

knock v. **1.** (UK criminal use) to cheat, to defraud, to con (qv) *LL*; **2.** to criticize *Higgins: 3*; **3.** to have sexual intercourse *Keyes*; **4.** (US Black use) to kill *Klein*.

knock about v. to travel around rather than settle down *Sapper, 'Jim Maitland', 1923*.

knockabout man n. (Aus. use) pickpocket *Baker*.

knock at the door (bingo rhyming sl.) 4 *Wright*.

knockback n. (UK prison use) the rejection of one's application for parole (cf: flop).

knock back n. a rejection *Humphries*.

knock cold v. to knock unconscious (cf: cold-cock).

knock down drag out n. a vicious fight in which one participant is knocked unconscious *White*.

knocked a. under control, at one's mercy: 'I've got it knocked'.

knocker n. **1.** a critic *Keyes*; **2.** a gambler who refuses to pay his debts (which cannot be enforced legally in the UK) *Performance*.

knockers n. breasts *Tidy*.

knock for a loop v. to surprise completely, to devastate *Heller*.

knocking-shop n. a brothel *Hotten*.

knock it off v. stop doing something *Dury, 'Do It Yourself'*.

knock it on the head v. to stop doing something; to finish a task; fr. the final blow of a hammer that drives in a nail (?).

knock it out v. **1.** (US Black use) to have sexual intercourse; **2.** (journalism use) to write something quickly, with neither style nor concentration.

knock off v. **1.** (criminal use) to steal; **2.** (police use) to arrest; **3.** to seduce *Powis*.

knock-off n. a fake, a copy; used in fashion trade – cheap copies of 'model' garments – in antiques – cheap reproductions – etc.

knock off a piece to seduce a girl, piece is abbrev: piece of ass (qv) *Schulberg*.

knock one's block off v. to injure physically, usu. in form of a threat: 'I'll knock . . .'

knock on together v. to have an affair *Sillitoe*.

knock-out! (excl.) wonderful! perfect! *Capital Radio 1983*.

knock-out n. a surprise *Wright*.

knock out v. **1.** to impress, to overwhelm, to delight *Keyes*; **2.** to earn a given sum of money; ie 'knocking out £200 per week' etc.

knock over v. to rob, usu. with violence; of person or places *Tuff Shit Comics*.

knock the bejazus out of v. see: knock the stuffing out of.

knock them cold v. aka: *knock them dead* for a performer or performance to devastate an audience with its excellence.

knock the stuffing out of v. to beat severely.

knock up v. to make pregnant *Price: 2*.

know how many beans make five v. to be alert, to be aware of given facts/information.

know one's number v. to understand another person, to assess a situation (cf: peep one's hole card) *Heller*.

know one's onions v. to be well informed, to be aware.

know the ropes to understand how to do a given task, fr. sailing use.

know the words and music v. (homosexual use) to understand and partake in the gay sub-culture *Legman*.

know what's what v. to be aware of the facts, abreast of a situation.

know where the bodies are buried v. to have special knowledge of a situation, esp. of its less appealing side, that gives one power over those who nominally control it; the threat, rather than the use of blackmail *Wodehouse: PGM*.

knuckle n. a fight, violence; fr. the fist used therein *Robins*.

knuckle down v. to succumb, to surrender (cf: knuckle under) *Hotten*.

knucklehead n. derog. term of abuse, description for any foolish, stupid, slow person; the knuckles pressed to the forehead imply the intensity of thought *Folb*.

knuckle sandwich n. a blow from a fist *Humphries*.

knuckle under v. to surrender, to accept something one dislikes but is not strong enough to fight; one falls beneath a rival's knuckle (qv) *Schulberg*.

knucks n. (abbrev.) brass knuckles, worn over the fist to ensure victory in a fistfight *Farrell*.

Kojak v. (US teen. use) to find a parking space in an area where such discoveries are at best rare; fr. US TV show 'Kojak' whose eponymous hero seems to possess this facility *ad nauseam Sculatti*.

Kojak with a Kodak n. (CB use) policeman manning a radar speed trap; fr. popular TV show and make of camera *CB*.

kong n. (US Black use) home-distilled whisky; fr. King Kong (film 1933) and thus denoted great strength *Major*.

konk v. (Black use) to straighten one's otherwise naturally curly hair (cf: process) *Selby: 1*.

kook n. an eccentric, albeit an acceptable one.

kooky a. odd, eccentric (with overtones of charm) *Goldman*.

kool toul! (backsl.) look out! *Cole*.

kosher a. honest, legitimate, above-board; fr. Yiddish: according to the Jewish dietary laws, thus kosher meat, etc. *Runyon*.

KP n. (Aus. use) common prostitute *Baker*.

Kraut n. (derog.) a German; fr *sauerkraut*: a form of pickled, shredded cabbage, beloved of the nation *Higgins: 2*.

krazin n. (US campus use) a load of utter rubbish; absolute nonsense *Simmons*.

Kremlin n. (UK police use) New Scotland Yard *Powis*.

Kreskin v. (US teen. use) to prophesy, to work out intuitively, to foresee; fr. US TV magician 'Kreskin' *Sculatti*.

kurve n. prostitute; fr. Yiddish kurveh *Powis*.

kvetch n. to complain, to delay, to nag, fuss; fr. Ger. squeeze, press *Rosten*.

labonza n. the buttocks; the pit of the stomach *Neaman & Silver.*

labour n. (abbrev.) labour exchange: the employment exchange, the job centre *Norman:2.*

lace curtain n. (homosexual use) a long foreskin *Legman.*

lace-curtain Irish n. genteel petit-bourgeois Irish-Americans; who adorn their windows with such items *Bruce:2.*

lace curtains n. the genitalia of an uncircumcised male *Stanley.*

laced a. drunk; one's blood is 'laced' with alcohol *Dickson.*

la-di-dah n. (rhyming sl.) a cigar *Powis.*

la-di-dah a. **1.** stuck up, arrogant, snobbish; **2.** effeminate, affected, a sissy *Humphries:2.*

ladies n. (Black pimp use) prostitutes *Milner.*

lady n. (pimp use) sophisticated, classy prostitute whose talents mean she can make her own rules as to those she sleeps with and what she charges for the pleasure *OUI 8/75.*

Lady Five Fingers n. masturbation (cf: Mrs Hand . . .).

lady killer n. a sexually successful man; sometimes, however, only in his own eyes *Thompson:J.*

lady lover n. a lesbian *Legman.*

Lady Snow n. (US Black use) a respected upper-class white woman *Klein.*

lag n. a convict, a prisoner (cf: lagging) *Norman:1.*

lagging n. (UK criminal use) **1.** any prison sentence; **2.** a sentence of more than two years imprisonment; both fr. orig. meaning: transportation to the penal colonies *Norman:2.*

lagging station n. (UK prison use) a long-term prison *Obs.1981.*

lahteeache (backsl.) all right *Cole.*

laid back n. soothing, peaceful, passive, calm; used both of people and music; fr. the physical position (cf: mellow) *White.*

laid out (US Black use) well-dressed *Klein.*

laid to the bone (US Black use) clothes cut so well that they seem pasted to the wearer's figure *Klein.*

laid to the natural bone (US Black use) naked *Folb.*

lair n. (Aus. use) a show-off, an extrovert *Ready.*

lairize v. (Aus. use) to brag, to boast, to show-off *Wilkes.*

lairy a. (Aus. use) flashy, ostentatious, vulgar, showy; fr. lair (qv) *Dennis.*

lakes n. (rhyming sl.) Lakes of Killarney = barmy = mad *Powis.*

Lakes of Killarney n. see: lakes *Cole.*

lamb n. a young homosexual boy (cf: chicken) *Legman.*

lamb-time n. (US teen. use) spring *Sculatti.*

lame n. (abbrev.) lame-brain (qv).

lame a. drunk *Dickson.*

lame-brain n. an incompetent, a fool *Price:2.*

lame duck n. (US polit. use) a President who has been defeated in November's election but will not actually leave his office – in which his decisions are *de facto* irrelevant – until January; this usage can extend to any similarly-placed officials *Green:2.*

lamp v. to look at, to assess visually; fr. 19th C. *lamp*: eye *Farrell.*

Lancashire lasses n. (rhyming sl.) glasses (spectacles) *Franklyn.*

landsman n. a fellow-countryman; fr. Yiddish, thus spec. a fellow Jew (cf: paisan).

lard-ass n. **1.** a lazy, good-for-nothing person *Bukowski:1*; **2.** an overweight person *Uris*; both miscreants sit on their posterior and do nothing but cultivate 'lard'.

lare n. (Aus. use) a ruffian, a tearaway (qv); fr. abbrev. of larrikin.

lark n. **1.** any form of activity, occupation *Norman:3*; **2.** a game *Performance.*

lash-up n. a home-made assembly, essentially amateur, but quite adequate for a limited period; refers to material objects, organizations, ideas, etc. *Higgins:5.*

latch on to v. **1.** to understand, to grasp *Sillitoe*; **2.** to take hold of, to attach oneself to *Thompson:J.*

later! (abbrev.) see you later; goodbye *McFadden.*

later for that phrase of dismissal; I can't be bothered (now) *Seale.*

launder v. to 'de-criminalize' corruptly or illegally gained money by 'washing' it through a casino till or a bank. The 'dirty' notes, etc. are deposited and 'clean' cash is issued, without the taint of scandal (cf: dirty money) *PT.*

laundromat n. any situation, often a game of chance, in which illicit money can be laundered (qv); pun on the do-it-yourself laundry shops *Alvarez.*

lavender a euph. for homosexuals and anything referring to them *Legman.*

law n. the police *Norman:2.*

lawing n. see: corner **2** *Powis.*

lawn n. (homosexual use) pubic hair; if the pubic hair is shaved, a *mowed lawn* (cf: garden, grass) *Maledicta.*

lay n. **1.** sexual intercourse; **2.** a person with whom one makes love, usu. as a *good lay* or a *bad lay*, etc. *Price:2.*

lay v. **1.** to make love to *Price:2*; **2.** (US Black use) to over-indulge in drugs or drink to such an extent that one is laid on one's back *Klein.*

layabout n. a voluntarily unemployed male, usu. involved in some minor criminality *Norman:2.*

lay an egg v. to fail completely, esp. show business use; *Variety* headlined the morning after the 1929 Crash: 'Wall Street Lays an Egg' *Goldman.*

lay back aka: *lay low, lay up* (US Black use) **1.** to relax; **2.** to do nothing specific; **3.** to have sexual intercourse *Folb.*

lay-by n. (Aus. use) a deposit on and the subsequent purchasing by instalments of a given article in a shop *Ready.*

lay dead v. (US Black use) to do nothing, to stop everything *Folb.*

lay down n. (UK police use) a remand in custody *Powis.*

lay down v. to give in to another, to accept *Folb.*

lay down merchant n. one who specializes in passing forged banknotes *Norman:2.*

lay down one's knife and fork v. to die (cf: hand in one's dinner pail) *Neaman & Silver.*

lay in v. (US prison use) to stay in one's cell at any time when one might usually be out of it *Klein.*

layin' and playin' (US Black use) to be idling around the house, usu. with one's woman *Klein.*

lay into v. to attack physically.

lay (it) on the line v. to be absolutely honest; to declare one's feelings, one's attitude *Junker.*

lay it out v. (lesbian use) to admit and poss. flaunt one's sexual preference (cf: lay (it) on the line) *Maledicta.*

lay on v. **1.** to give, esp. of drugs; **2.** to provide; **3.** to tell, to impose facts upon *Jay & Young*.

lay off! a warning: keep away! stop doing a given action.

lay out v.t. to knock someone out in a fight.

lay rubber v. to drive off at speed, spinning the wheels as one accelerates away.

lay some on me! (US Black use) invitation to swap ritual handslaps as form of black-to-black greeting *Klein*.

lay some pipe v. to have sexual intercourse.

lay the leg v. (US prison use) to sodomize *Legman*.

lay the lip v. (US prostitute use) to fellate *Legman*.

lay the scene on v. to explain, to outline a situation (cf: scene) *Bruce:2*.

lay tight v. (US Black use) to stay calm, to retain one's grip of a situation *Klein*.

lay up v. to hide; to rest *Grogan*.

LB n. (drug use) one pound weight, fr. 1 *lb*. (cf: OZ) *'Hill Street Blues', Thames TV, 1983*.

LD (US Black use) (abbrev.) Cadillac *El*dorado *Price:2*.

lead down v. (milit. use) to fire at; fr. lead bullets.

lead-foot v. to move slowly and clumsily *Fiction Illus.3*.

lead on, Macduff (cp) exhorting someone else to take the initiative; a corruption of 'lay on, Macduff' in Shakespeare's *Macbeth*.

lead-pipe cinch n. absolute certainty *Algren*.

lead up the garden path v. to trick, to deceive deliberately, to tease.

lean and linger n. (US rhyming sl.) finger *Runyon*.

lean green n. (US teen. use) money (cf: green, greenbacks) *Sculatti*.

leaning house n. (US Black use) a brothel or a place where illicit meetings, drug sales, etc. take place *Klein*.

lean on v. to pressurize, to persuade, poss. with violence or threats of violence *Vidal*.

lean over backwards v. to make every effort towards a given end; the inference may be altruistic or self-aggrandising.

leap and you will receive (US Black use) ritual challenge to a fight, ie: come and get it! *Folb*.

leaper n. **1.** (drug use) any form of stimulant, amphetamine, etc. *Green:1*; **2.** a dud cheque, drawn against inadequate funds (cf: bounce) *Breslin*.

leapfrog n. (pimp use) a client who hires a number of prostitutes to play leapfrog while he watches (and masturbates) *OUI 8/75*.

Leaping Lena (US milit. use) see Bouncing Betty *Rawson*.

learn a new way v. turn to homosexuality *Higgins:1*.

leary a. aka: *leery*: bright, alert, intelligent; thus suspicious of someone *Newman:1*.

leather n. **1.** (homosexual use) the anus *Legman*; **2.** a wallet *Runyon:1*.

leather v. **1.** to beat, to kick *Hotten*; **2.** (homosexual use) to perform anal intercourse *Legman*.

leather medal n. (US sports use) the booby prize, the wooden spoon (qv).

leatherneck n. a Marine, both UK and US use; early US marine uniforms had a leather neckband.

leather piece n. (US Black use) any garment, esp. coat, made of leather *Wolfe:4*.

leave before the gospel v. to practise coitus interruptus (cf: get out at Gateshead; get off at Redfern) *Neaman & Silver*.

leave for dead v. to defeat absolutely; to leave far behind in any form of competition.

leave it out! stop doing that! *Dury, 'Do It Yourself', 1979*.

leave off! (excl.) stop it! (esp. in sense of stop telling lies) *Newman:1*.

lech n. **1.** (abbrev.) lecher; **2.** sexual desire; fr. lechery *Stone*.

leech n. a parasite, a sponger; fr. the blood-sucking creature *Larner*.

leeky store n. (US Black use) liquor store *Folb*.

leery a. **1.** bad tempered, disagreeable, cheeky *Powis*; **2.** cunning, underhand (cf: leary) *Keyes*.

lefthanded a. undesirable, unpleasant, evil; the lit. translation of Lat. *sinister*.

left off! (US campus use) (excl.) jokey reversal of more generally popular right on! (qv) *Underwood*.

lefty n. **1.** a left-handed person; **2.** a political radical, of left-wing ideology.

leg n. (US campus use) (abbrev.) dirty leg (qv) *Underwood*.

legal eagle n. a lawyer, the implication is of an astute one; technically rhyming sl.

leg art (newspaper use) pictures of women revealing their legs (cf: cheesecake).

leggner n. (UK prison use) a twelve month sentence, pun on stretch (qv) a leg *LL*.

leggy a. a girl with particularly attractive legs; esp. loved by tabloid newspapers who offer 'leggy lovely' as a noun.

leg it v. to run away *Newman:1*.

legit a. (abbrev.) legitimate; and as such the description of anything that, in context, might be considered as otherwise; thus *on the legit*: conducting an honest life/business, etc. *Algren*.

legless a. drunk; to the extent of falling over.

leg man n. a man who prefers a woman's legs to any other part of her anatomy (cf: ass man, tit man).

leg opener n. a drink given to a girl in the hope of getting her drunk enough for seduction *Humphries*.

legs eleven (bingo use) 11.

leg-shake artist n. (Aus. use) a pickpocket *Baker*.

legs up to her arse (cp) male description of a woman with exceptionally long (and attractive) legs.

leg work n. **1.** (US tramp use) to have intercourse between the thighs or the buttocks (but without actual penetration of the anus) *Legman*; **2.** any job that requires a great deal of walking *Fiction Illus.3*.

lemon n. **1.** (US Black use) a light-skinned black person *Major*; **2.** anything undesirable, esp. females; fr. sourness of the fruit *Wodehouse:MOJ*.

leo-time n. (US teen. use) August, fr. astrological sign 'Leo' *Sculatti*.

les n. (abbrev.) lesbian *Norman:2*.

lesbo n. (abbrev.) lesbian *Legman*.

leso n. (Aus. use) lesbian, *Wilkes*.

letch n. (abbrev.) lecher *Bukowski:2*.

let it all hang out v. (hippie, currently new therapy use) to cast aside any restraints, to do what one wants, to act from the heart.

let it ride v. to ignore, to forget; fr. dice gambling where a winning bet is not picked up from the table but left to be gambled again *Howard*.

let me hold some change (US Black use) please give me some money *Seale*.

let one have it v. to kill, esp. with gunfire *rr*.

let one's game slip v. (US Black use (though, general use also)) to lose control of a situation, a plan, an objective, etc. *Folb*.

let one's hair down v. (homosexual use) to relax one's inhibitions; poss. in homosexual use prior to more widespread use *Legman*.

let's be having you! (cp) time to start work, get out of bed, etc. *Manser*.

let's boogie (US teen. use) let's go, let's be off *Pond*.

let the dog see the rabbit (cp) give someone a chance to get on with a given task.

lettuce n. money (cf: cabbage, kale) *Humphries*.

level v. to admit, confess; to be honest *Runyon:1*.

Levy v. (rhyming sl.) Levy and Frank = wank = masturbate *Powis*.

lezzie n. (abbrev.) lesbian.

LF see: long firm *Powis*.

LF gear n. the proceeds of a long firm (qv) fraud, sold off at greatly reduced prices; sometimes, to tempt those who find such sales romantic, perfectly legitimate, if shoddy, goods are advertised as 'LF gear' *Powis*.

libber n. a feminist, a member of the Women's Liberation Movement; usu. derog. (male) use *Shulman*.

liberate v. to steal; fr. 1960s radical use, on the Proudhon principle that 'property is theft' but likewise with a degree of irony/self-mockery given the 1960s obsession with 'freedom' and 'the revolution'; with further irony, the 'radical' use stems fr. Second World War 'liberating forces' who 'freed' commodities as well as people *Payne*.

lick n. **1.** a blow; **2.** (rock music use) a particular phrase of music, ie *guitar lick*.

lick v. to defeat, to beat *Wright*.

lickety-split anything fast; some onomatopoeic overtones.

licking n. a beating, a defeat *Tidy*.

lick my froth! (Valley Girls (qv) use) general term of abuse, dismissal (cf: kiss my tuna!) *Pond*.

lid n. (drug use) quantity of marijuana, approx 22 gms; fr. the quantity of the drug that fills a popular tobacco tin lid *Green:1*.

lie doggo v. to remain hidden and quiet; like a stalking dog *Powis*.

Life n. (US Black use) the subculture of crime, pimping, drug dealing, etc. that makes up the alternative world of the streets *Milner*.

lifeboat n. (US prison use) a pardon, the commutation of a sentence *Chandler: Notebk*.

life of Riley n. the good life; the materially satisfactory life, a comfortable existence *Price:3*.

lifer n. **1.** (prison use) anyone serving a life sentence *BBC-TV 1983*; **2.** (US milit. use) a career soldier; also used as derog. term for anyone who appears excessively keen on milit. discipline and its administration to his peers *Stone*.

lift v. **1.** to arrest, esp. N. Ireland use by both Army and police *Wilkinson*; **2.** (criminal use) to steal.

lift one's game v. (US pimp use) to improve one's situation – financially, emotionally, intellectually, etc. *Shulman*.

ligger n. a hanger on; spec. in entertainment industry: a freeloader (qv). fr. *l*east *i*mportant *g*uest (?) or linger: hang around *NME*.

light v. (US Black use) to enlighten someone with general or specific knowledge *Klein*.

lighten up v. (US Black use) to calm down, to cease from an action *Folb*.

light into v. to attack verbally, to criticize, to nag *rr*.

light off v. to have an orgasm *Higgins:2*.

light of love n. (UK prison use; rhyming sl.) Gov = prison governor *LL*.

light out v. to leave, to run away, to escape.

lightweight n. an insignificant person, a weakling. *McFadden*.

like all-purpose, absolutely meaningless interj. that breaks a sentence but has no effect on the meaning: 'it's, like, cold . . .', 'I feel, like, sick', etc.; orig. in beatnik/jazz worlds c.1950s *Pond*.

like a bat out of hell moving very quickly.

like a dose of salts very quickly; usu. *go through (you) like a . . .*

like a good 'un enthusiastically, keenly *Norman:2*.

like a rat up a drain very quickly; usu. in sexual context: *up that like a . . . Humphries*.

like a spare prick at a wedding (cp) absolutely useless; the assumption is that only the bridegroom is necessary *Barr*.

like billy-o most enthusiastically, strenuously, speedily: general expression of energy or effort.

like crazy intensely, excessively, obsessively, etc. *PT*.

like fuck! aka: *like hell!*: general excl. of negation and denial. (cf: did I fuck!).

like it or lump it v. to accept a situation, willingly or not; often as *well, you'll have to . . .*
like nobody's business very well, excellently, very quickly.
like taking candy from a baby (cp) extremely easy *Wodehouse:MOJ.*
like winking very quickly *Hotten.*
likkered a. drunk; fr. 'liquored' *Dickson.*
Lilley and Skinner n. (rhyming sl.) dinner *Powis.*
Lilly (drug use) seconal, fr. manufacturer's name on the pill.
lily n. **1.** anything remarkable or particularly outstanding (cf: lulu) *Runyon*; **2.** an effeminate male; **3.** a homosexual who fears to reveal his sex life; *Legman*; **4.** (US Black use) a white person *Folb.*
Limbo Room n. (Can. prison use) a place where corporal punishment is administered to prisoners *Caron.*
Limey n. English person; (abbrev.) lime-juicer (obs); fr. the former habit of serving UK sailors lime-juice as a preventative against scurvy *Price:2.*
limo n. (abbrev.) limousine; esp. in show business use.
line n. **1.** (drug use) a portion of heroin or cocaine scraped into a line across a mirror in order for it to be sniffed into the nostril *Green:1*; **2.** a smooth verbal style aimed at seduction or at persuading someone else to accept an idea or plan; esp. in sexual or business contexts.
linen n. (rhyming sl.) linen draper = newspaper *Norman:2.*
lines n. (US Black use) **1.** words in general; **2.** persuasive patter aimed at seduction *Folb.*
line-up n. **1.** a police identification parade *Price:2*; **2.** gang-rape *Salisbury.*
line up on v. (homosexual use) to gang-fellate or sodomize *Legman.*
lion's lair n. (rhyming sl.) chair *Wright.*
lip n. **1.** cheek, back-talking *Norman:1*; **2.** lawyer; fr. concept of his 'talking back' (as in cheekiness) in defence of his client *Chandler: Notebk.*
lip off v. to talk rudely, cheekily, provocatively *Dunne.*
lippy n. (abbrev.) lipstick *BBC-TV 1982.*
lippy a. cheeky, verbal, talkative, loudmouthed (cf: lip) *Jenkins.*
LIQ (US Black use) (abbrev.) *LIQ*uor store *Folb.*
liquid cosh n. (UK prison use) major tranquillizers used to restrain (for short- or long-term periods) rebellious or 'difficult' prisoners *Cole.*
liquid laugh n. vomit *Humphries.*
liquid lunch n. a meal that consists (almost) entirely of alcohol *Humphries:2.*
liquor's talking a situation in which indiscretions and/or garrulous speech are put down to drunkenness *Dickson.*
lit **1.** see: lit up; **2.** (US Black use) to be shot *Klein.*
little black book n. the volume in which every bachelor supposedly keeps lists of available and willing female company.
little boy blue n. (US Black use) the police; fr. uniform colour *Folb.*
Little Eva n. (US Black use) a loud-mouthed white girl *Major.*
little green men n. a popular description of the putative inhabitants of outer space.
little jobs n. (children's use) urination (cf: big jobs) *May.*
little Joe n. (gambling use) the point of four in craps dice *Algren.*
little Josie (gambling use) the point of four in craps dice *Chandler: Notebk.*
little madam n. a young girl who acts, and considers herself, both older than her years and superior to her peers *Humphries:2.*
little man n. see: little man in the boat *Klein.*
little man in the boat n. (US Black use) the clitoris *Klein.*
little Miss Roundheels n. a promiscuous girl *Thompson:J.*
little office n. (euph.) lavatory *Humphries:2.*

little people n. (US milit. use) in Vietnam, the enemy; fr. the stature of the Vietnamese *Del Vecchio*.

little pretty n. (US Black use) an attractive male *Folb*.

little sister n. aka: *little pal*: the vagina *Maledicta*.

little stranger n. an unborn foetus; often illegitimate or of unknown paternity *Vidal*.

lit to the gills a. drunk *Dickson*.

lit up a. drunk.

lit-up (US milit. use) under fire *Del Vecchio*.

lit up like a Christmas tree a. very drunk *Dickson*.

lit up like Broadway a. aka: *lit up like Times Square*: very drunk *Neaman & Silver*.

lit up like Main street a. very drunk *Dickson*.

Litvak n. a Jew whose family come fr. Lithuania and as such considered lower-class by Polacks (qv) *Goldman*.

live a. (US teen. use) excellent, wonderful; thus *a live one*: an admirable person or object *Pond*.

live high on the hog v. to live in general and to eat in particular with great self-indulgence *Neaman & Silver*.

live it up v. to have a good time, to enjoy oneself *Capital Radio 1983*.

live one n. **1.** (cant) the ideal victim for a proposed hoax, fraud, etc. *Selby:1*; **2.** (homosexual use) a generous rich client for a prostitute *Legman*.

living end n. the extreme, the absolute limit.

living off the tit living in luxury, over protected; 'breast-fed' *Higgins:2*.

Lloyd n. (rhyming sl.) Harold Lloyd = loid (qv); fr. the silent-film star, (1893–1971) *Powis*.

load n. (US Black use) **1.** the intense urge to have sex; **2.** a large amount of semen in the testes; **3.** heavy responsibility *Klein*.

loaded a. **1.** drunk; **2.** intoxicated with a given drug *Jay & Young*; **3.** rich, either in actual cash or simply, esp. in prison use, in possessions such as tobacco *Norman:3*.

loaded for bear fully prepared for all problems, esp. the hardest ones. fr. hunting use: bear-shooting requires heavy armament.

loaded to . . . sl. synonyms for drunk, incl: *. . . the barrel*, *. . . the earlobes*, *. . . the gills*, *. . . the guards*, *. . . the gunnels*, *. . . the hat*, *. . . the muzzle*, *. . . the Plimsoll Mark*, *. . . the tailgate*. *Dickson*.

load of reg load of rubbish, nonsense; fr. milit. reg: (abbrev.) regimental: stickler for discipline, esp. petty, nonsensical rules *Cole*.

loaf n. head, esp. brains, intelligence; thus *use one's loaf*: to act sensibly; fr. rhyming sl. *loaf of bread* = head *Performance*.

loan shark n. the supplier of private loans at maximum interest *Higgins:3*.

lob n. **1.** a dull, stupid person; fr. Yiddish *lobbas*: rascal *Runyon:1*; **2.** penis *Selby:1*; **3.** (UK prison use) pay *LL*.

lob in v. (Aus. use) to arrive, to turn up *Wilkes*.

lobster n. (US Black use) a rich person *Klein*.

lobster shift n. the evening shift after the day workers have gone off *Price:2*.

lock v. (US pimp use) to ensure a ho's (qv) fidelity (emotional and economic) to a given pimp (cf: bonds) *Shulman*.

lock assholes v. to fight *Price:2*.

lock into v. to become part of a plan, a group, etc; to join.

loco a. insane, crazy; fr. locoweed: a narcotic weed that affects cattle in South-West US *People's Comic*.

locoweed n. marijuana. fr. the plant that affects cattle (cf: loco) *Southern*.

Lofty nickname for both very tall and very short men; for the latter see BBC-TV series 'It Ain't 'Alf 'Ot, Mum' 1970s passim.

loid n. (abbrev.) celluloid (often actually plastic, as in a credit card): pieces of plastic used to slip open Yale-style locks when housebreaking (cf: Lloyd) *Powis*.

lollied informed against, grassed (qv); poss. fr. *lollypop* = shop (qv) *Powis.*

lollies n. female breasts; which can, like the sweet, be sucked.

lollipop n. (US Black use) a sucker (qv) who has been 'sucked', ie: taken advantage of *Klein.*

lollipop man/woman n. a man or woman who supervises children crossing the road near a school; fr. the sign on a pole which they carry, and their role in tending children.

lolly v. (prob. rhyming sl.) lollypop = shop = inform to police *Newman:1.*

lolly n. money *Performance.*

lollygag v. to waste time doing nothing but standing around chattering about little, and going nowhere *Greenlee.*

Lombard Street to a China orange (cp) the longest possible odds.

loner n. a solitary person, not necessarily lonely, who prefers to work and live alone *Grogan.*

lone wolf n. a solitary person, usu. male; he may enjoy many acquaintances and be by no means a recluse, but permits no one to penetrate his façade.

long bit n. (US prison use) a term of imprisonment over 38 months which must be completed prior to becoming eligible for parole *Klein.*

long con n. any trickery and cheating that is carefully planned for perfect execution (cf: short con).

long firm n. (UK criminal/police use) a fraudulent scheme whereby a firm is set up, small orders placed and paid for to establish good credit; then a massive order is made, its contents quickly sold off, often below par, and the firm vanishes, the warehouse is shut down and the debts, this time huge, are never paid. *J. Pearson, 'The Profession of Violence'.*

long green n. money, fr. colour of dollar bills.

long-hair n. a hippie (qv) among whose 'badges' was extra-lengthy hair *Stone.*

long-haired a. intellectual, aesthetic; always derog. use, fr. the apparent necessity for the cultured to abandon the 'short-back-and-sides' cut; thus *long-haired music*: the classics, etc.

long johns n. long woollen winter underwear, combinations.

longshot n. a slim chance; fr. gambling use, a bet laid at long odds on an unlikely contender *Shulman.*

long (thin) streak of piss n. an unflattering description of a tall, thin person.

long-tailed 'un n. large denomination sterling note, £10, £20, £50 *Powis.*

long time no see (cp) I haven't seen you for a long time.

long-winded a. (homosexual use) a man who takes a long time to reach orgasm *Legman.*

loo n. the lavatory.

looey n. (US milit. use) (abbrev.) lieutenant (pron. 'lootenant') *Uris.*

loogan n. idiot, fool, incompetent *Runyon.*

looie n. (US milit. use) lieutenant (pron. 'lootenant') *Jones.*

looker n. **1.** an attractive woman *Bukowski:7*; **2.** (pimp use) a client who wishes only to look at a prostitute, usually naked, and occasionally fondle her breasts; **3.** a voyeur *OUI 8/75.*

lookism n. (homosexual use) evaluating a stranger purely on the basis of their physical appeal or lack of it *Jay & Young.*

look sharp v. **1.** to hurry up, to get on with; **2.** to dress smartly, fashionably (cf: sharp) *J. Jackson, LP record title, 1979.*

looks like a wet weekend (Aus. cp) used by a girl announcing, or a boy registering the onset of a menstrual period *Neaman & Silver.*

looks like he/she lost a pound and found sixpence (cp) of anyone who looks notably downcast.

looks like he wouldn't piss if his pants were on fire (cp) describing someone monumentally stupid *Thompson:J.*

look what the wind's blown in (cp) facetious greeting to a new arrival, or remark to a companion concerning that arrival.

loon n. a fool, an idiot; such people are supposedly 'moonstruck', fr. Lat. *luna*: moon *Higgins:5.*

loon about v. to act crazily, irresponsibly *Mandelkau.*

loon pants n. trousers featuring exaggerately flared bottoms, esp. beloved of early 1970s hippies; ads in *Melody Maker* passim.

loony a. eccentric, insane (cf: loon) *Wodehouse: JO.*

loony bin n. mental hospital or similar institution *Price:2.*

loony doctor n. psychoanalyst, psychiatrist, etc. *Wodehouse: COJ.*

loony farm n. see: loony bin.

looped a. (US campus use) drunk, fr. obs. *loop-legged Underwood.*

loop-the-loop n. (rhyming sl.) soup *Powis.*

loopy a. eccentric, crazy *Price:3.*

loose ends n. (US Black use) spare money available for loans *Klein.*

loot n. money *Selby:1.*

Lord love a duck! mild. excl. of surprise, etc. *Wodehouse:MOJ.*

Lord Lovel n. (rhyming sl.) shovel: only US use now *Wright.*

Lord Mayor v. (rhyming sl.) to swear *Jones:J.*

Lord Muck n. a hypothetical aristocrat, snobbish and conspicuous in his contempt for lesser mortals, but (since he is Lord *Muck*) in fact no better than they are.

lose one's bottle v. to back down, to turn cowardly (cf: bottle).

lose one's cool v. to lose one's dignity or self-possession, to lose one's temper (cf: freak out) *SF Comics.*

lose one's doughnuts v. (US campus use) to vomit (cf: blow one's doughnuts) *Bernbach.*

lose one's gender v. (homosexual use) to abandon homosexuality for the safer world of heterosexuality *Legman.*

lose one's lunch v. (US campus use) to vomit (cf blow one's lunch) *Bernbach.*

lose one's marbles v. to go mad, lose control *Higgins:3.*

lose one's rag v. to lose one's temper *P. MacDonald, 'X v. Rex', 1933.*

lose one's rudder v. to be drunk; and thus lose one's sense of direction *Dickson.*

lose the ball v. to find oneself in an increasingly difficult situation; to lose control of one's life, work, relationships, etc. fr. sporting use *Safire.*

loudmouth n. **1.** a braggart, a boaster; **2.** spec: a lawyer *Higgins:4.*

lounge lizard n. a smooth and highly plausible fortune- or sex-hunter who works his charms in the lounges of hotels; an adventurer (cf: saloon bar cowboy).

louse up v. to make a mess of, to ruin; usu. deliberately.

louse one up v. to cause a person difficulties, to cause trouble *rr.*

lousy with full of (a given commodity, type of person, etc); fr. orig. milit. (First World War) ref. to infestations of lice *Wodehouse:PGM.*

love handles n. the spare tyre (qv) of flesh around a portly stomach that may be seen in a kinder light by those who appreciate the Rubensesque figure (cf: bagels) *Bernbach.*

love it to death v. to enjoy or to love to extremes; in ironic use, to deplore *Price:2.*

love juice n. (US Black use) semen *Klein.*

lovely n. a pretty young girl; fr. SE adj. use.; esp. popular with tabloid press, seaside entertainers, etc.

lovely grub! (cp) implies approval of whatever is being considered, whether actual food or not.

lowdown n. privileged information, intimate details *Gruber.*

lower the boom (on) v. to reprimand severely; to put an end to someone's misbehaviour; fr. USN use *Green:2.*

low in the saddle a. drunk, and thus slumped over *Dickson.*

lowlife n. a criminal, or someone who may well be.
lowlife a. (US Black use) unpleasant, aggressive *Folb.*
low neck and short sleeves n. (homosexual use) a circumcised penis *Legman.*
low rent a. cheap, unappealing, distateful, unfashionable *Wolfe:5.*
lox jock n. (derog.) a Jew; fr. *lox* = smoked salmon, supposedly a favourite Jewish dish *Dunne.*
LTR (abbrev.) *L*iving *T*ogether *R*elationship: marriage in all but the legalities *McFadden.*
lubricated a. drunk (cf: neck oil) *Dickson.*
luck into v. to come up with a stroke of luck *Breslin.*
luck out v. to strike lucky *Higgins:3.*
lucozade n. (rhyming sl.) spade (qv) = black person *'Minder', Thames TV 1983.*
Lucy Law n. (homosexual use) police *Stanley.*
lucy locket n. (rhyming sl.) a pocket *Jones:J.*
ludes n. (abbrev.) quaalude; methaqualone *White.*
lug n. **1.** ear; fr. Scots dial. *Powis*; **2.** large, stupid man; lug: to drag, to haul; such a heavyweight would need to be dragged along, mentally or physically *Tuff Shit Comics.*
luggage n. (US teen. use) bags under the eyes *Sculatti.*
lugger n. **1.** (US criminal use) in a shoplifting team (cf: booster) the accomplice (usually two) who helps the actual thief remove the stolen goods from the store *Breslin*; **2.** (Can. prison use) a smuggler of contraband in/out of the prison *Caron.*
lulu n. **1.** anything remarkable, exceptional, wonderful; **2.** an ironic use of **1**: a disaster, an abject failure *Tuff Shit Comics.*
lumber v.t. to persuade, to trick *Norman:2.*
lumbered burdened with, trapped *Keyes.*
lumme! excl. of surprise, wonder, shock, disbelief; fr. 'Lord love me!' *Wilkinson.*
lump v. to hit someone over the head with a lump of stone or a brick *Selby:1.*
lumpy chicken (US milit. use) fr. loud and clear *Del Vecchio.*
lunch n. oral intercourse (cf: eat, fress).
lunchbox n. (US campus use) a simpleton *Underwood.*
lunch hooks n. fingers *Algren.*
lunchy a. (US campus use) **1.** dull, stupid, absent-minded; fr, out to lunch (qv); **2.** carefree, light-hearted, jokey; **3.** unfashionable, out of style *Underwood.*
lunger n. a mouthful of spit and mucus *Wolfe:8.*
lungs n. female breasts *Jenkins.*
lunk n. oaf, curmudgeon; (abbrev.) lunkhead (qv) *Waterhouse.*
lunkhead n. absolute fool, idiot, incompetent.
lurk n. (Aus. use) dodge, racket or scheme; fr. 19th C. UK cant: to pretend some form of distress in order to raise money from the credulous *Humphries.*
lurkola n. (Aus. use) fr. lurk (qv) homegrown version of US/UK payola (qv) *Baker.*
lurky a. (US campus use) seedy, untrustworthy, weird *Underwood.*
lush n. **1.** a drunkard; fr. Lushington; **2.** alcohol *Selby:1.*
lush v. **1.** to become drunk; **2.** (abbrev.) lush-roll (qv) *Hotten.*
lush it around v. to become drunk *Farina.*
lush it up v. see: lush it around.
lush-roll v. to rob a drunk; fr. lush (qv) *Selby:1.*
lush-worker n. one who robs drunks, esp. in subways *ST 1983.*
lust dog n. (US campus use) male term for allegedly promiscuous female *Underwood.*

M n. (drug use) (abbrev.) morphine (cf: GOM) *Green:1*.

MA n. (US milit. use) (abbrev.) Mechanical Ambush: any US set booby trap *Del Vecchio*.

ma aka: *mother*: a derog. title put before a man's name to imply his homosexuality *Legman*.

Ma and Pa store n. small corner store selling necessities; traditionally owned and run by a family *Rosten*.

Mac general term of greeting in USA; no specific ref. to Scotsmen implied *Southern & Hoffenberg*.

McAlpine fusilier n. Irish labourer working for the construction firm McAlpines, or any similar firm *Powis*.

macaroni n. **1.** (rhyming sl.) pony = £25 *Jones:J*; **2.** (US Black use) the middle man, usu. a pimp, who stands between the john (qv) and the ho (qv) *Klein*.

macaroni with cheese n. a hustler (qv) who involves himself in a wide variety of activities – pimping, drug-selling, gambling games, etc. (cf: macaroni) *Klein*.

McCoy (abbrev.) the real McCoy (qv) *Chandler: Notebk*.

macer n. a thief, a villain, fr. early 19th C. *Powis*.

machine n. (US campus use) a motorcycle *Underwood*.

macing n. cheating, esp. at three-card monte (qv) *Powis*.

mack n. (US Black use) a seductive line (qv) used with the intention of charming a member of the opposite sex (cf: mack, a.) *Folb*.

mack a. (Black pimp use) anything pertaining to a pimp: pimp shoes, etc. *Milner*.

mackery n. pimping *Algren*.

macking making verbal advances to someone of the opposite/same sex with a view to seduction *Jones*.

Mack man n. a black pimp; fr. Fr. argot *maquereau*, lit. mackerel, pimp; thus *hard-mack*: a pimp who rules through threatened or actual violence; *sweet mack*: a gentle pimp who prefers to use charm, aka *sugar pimp*; *Milner*.

mack on v. aka: *mack to*: to attempt the seduction of a given person *Folb*.

mac out v. (US teen. use) to overeat, to gorge oneself, esp. on junk food (qv); fr. McDonald's hamburger chain, and their major seller: the Big Mac *Pond*.

mad a. (Aus. use) generally intensifying adj. of approval: 'you mad bastard', etc. *Ready*.

Madam n. the proprietor of a male or female brothel *Legman*.

madam n. nonsense, rubbish, esp. in *load of old. . .*

mad as a cut snake (Aus. use) completely deranged, utterly furious *D. Leitch*.

mad as a wet hen (cp) extremely angry.

made (US Black use) one who has had

their hair straightened, usu. of females *Major.*

made man n. (US criminal use) a formally initiated member of the US Mafia *Teresa.*

mad minute n. (US milit. use) a weapons free-fire test and practice session *Del Vecchio.*

mad money n. saving set aside for some spontaneous, unscheduled expenditure, usu. on pleasure *Austin.*

Maggie's Drawers n. (US milit. use) flag waved on a rifle range to signal 'target missed' *Uris.*

maggie's pie n. (US Black use) the female pudendum (cf: magpie's nest) *Klein.*

magpie's nest n. (US Black use) the female pudendum *Klein.*

magoozlum n. rubbish, trash; poss. fr. Hollywood use of *magoo*: the gooey ingredient of 'custard pies' *Chandler:LG.*

maharishee n. (drug use) marijuana; fr. Maharishi Mahesh Yogi, popular 1960s guru with Beatles and other hippies (qv) *Folb.*

mahogany flat n. (US Black use) an expensive, well-furnished and situated apartment or home *Klein.*

main n. (abbrev.) mainline (qv) *Burroughs:Jr.*

main bitch n. **1.** aka: *main ho*, main stuff: (Black pimp use) the favourite prostitute among those a pimp controls; **2.** (general use) a man's favourite girlfriend *Folb.*

main chance n. the principle opportunity one may have for making money, attaining a goal, taking advantage of one's rivals, etc; thus one who has *an eye for the main chance*: a smart operator (qv).

main drag n. the main street *Runyon.*

mainline n. the vein into which an addict injects narcotics *Lou Reed, 'Sister Ray', 1968.*

mainline v. to inject narcotics directly into a vein (cf: skinpop) *Southern.*

mainliner n. a drug addict who injects narcotics into the vein *Fiction Illus.3.*

main man n. best friend, most important person *Price:1.*

main squeeze n. most favoured person, usu. lover *Price:2.*

major a. (US teen. use) all-purpose term of great approval (cf: serious) *Pond.*

make v. **1.** to attain a given goal: *make the team*, *make a club*, etc.; **2.** to seduce; **3.** to recognise; **4.** to attend, to go to *Bruce:2.*

make n. (police use) an identification *McBain:1.*

make a beeline for v. to go directly towards; not really based on nature, however.

make a bomb v. to become very rich.

make a car v. to break into parked cars in order to steal any valuables left inside them *Burroughs:1.*

make a clean breast of v. to confess, to own up unreservedly; fr. 'getting it off one's chest' (cf: come clean).

make a dead set for v. to make it clear to someone that he/she is the object of one's affections.

make a dog's dinner out of v. to make an appalling mess.

make a Federal case (out) of v. to take very seriously, esp. when speaker feels the problem is really minor, 'to make a mountain out of a molehill'; in the US legal system, the Federal legislature often implies greater severity *Schulberg.*

make a killing v. to make a profit by gambling; whether at the races, on the stock-market, in a casino, etc.

make a pass v. **1.** attempt to harm, attack; **2.** see: make a play for *Higgins:3.*

make a play for v. to make sexual advances towards a member of the opposite (or the same) sex, to attempt seduction *rr.*

make a run v. to go out buying a given commodity, esp. drugs, but also groceries, liquor, etc. *Jones.*

make a sandwich v. a sexual position in which two men have simultaneous vaginal and anal sexual intercourse with the same woman. *Folb.*

make book v. to run a bookmaking

operation *Dunne.*

make change v. (US Black use) to work or otherwise obtain money for staying alive *Major.*

make for a stash v. stealing the drugs another addict has hidden and using them oneself *Burroughs:1.*

make ignorant v. (UK criminal use) to irritate, to annoy *Powis.*

make it v. **1.** to be successful *Grogan*; **2.** to have sexual intercourse *Higgins:1*; **3.** to move, to get on, to depart *Jones.*

make like v. to imitate; thus *make like a chicken*, etc. *Major.*

make one v. **1.** (prison use) to plan and effect an escape *Obs. 1981*; **2.** (general cant) to put together plans for a crime, esp. a robbery, then carry out that crime *Newman:1.*

make one out v. to plan an escape from prison *Newman:3.*

make one right v. (US Black use) to feel good, esp. as a result of drug use *Folb.*

make one's bones v. (US Mafia use) to arrange and carry out one's first contracted murder *M. Puzo, 'The Godfather', 1969.*

make one's rep v. (criminal use) to establish oneself as a successful, respected criminal *A. Karpis, 'The Alvin Karpis Story', 1971.*

make out v. **1.** to succeed; **2.** to seduce a woman; **3.** to indulge in a variety of sexual foreplay, petting but not necessarily intercourse *SF Comics.*

make out artist n. a man renowned for his sexual prowess *NYRB 17/3/83.*

make pee-pee v. to urinate, usu. children's use *Bukowski:1.*

make the fist v. (US radical, esp. Black radical use) to make the Black Power sign of the clenched fist *Folb.*

make the legal move v. (US teen. use) to get married *Sculatti.*

make the scene v. **1.** understand, appreciate a situation, experience *Lou Reed, 'Run, Run, Run', 1966*; **2.** to go somewhere (cf: scene) *Bruce:2.*

makings n. (drug use) the tobacco, cannabis and cigarette papers required for the production of a joint (qv).

malflor n. (US use) a lesbian; fr. Puerto Rican/Sp. *Maledicta.*

mallet n. (US Black use) the police; fr. their repressive role *Folb.*

mama n. **1.** (Hells Angel use) the girls who ride with the Hells Angels, available for communal sex and allied indignities, aside from the *old ladies*, the actual girl-friends of the riders *Thompson*; **2.** a feminine lesbian (cf: papa) *Legman.*

mammy-jammer n. (euph.) motherfucker (qv) *Major.*

mammy-rammer n. (euph.) motherfucker (qv) *Jones.*

mammy-tapper n. (euph.) motherfucker (qv) *Jones.*

mams n. (S. Afr. use) breasts; fr. mammaries *Neaman & Silver.*

man n. **1.** a drug dealer *Goldman*; **2.** the police *Larner;* **3.** a criminal boss; **4.** any superior figure; esp. used by prisoners of their warders or of whites by blacks *Seale.*

man a-hanging n. (US Black use) a person in trouble *Klein.*

M & Ms n. (drug use) barbiturates, amphetamines, drugs available as pills; fr. US sweet (like UK 'Smarties') name *Folb.*

M and S nickname for Marks & Spencer group of department stores; alternative, considered more vulgar: *Marks* or *Marks and Sparks* (the firm's house magazine is called *Sparks*).

manhole n. (US Black use) a hangout (qv), esp. for men only *Klein.*

man in the boat n. (US Black use) the clitoris *Klein.*

manky a. unpleasant, disgusting, poss. smelly, poss. fr. Fr. *manqué*: lost *Dury, 'Do It Yourself', 1979.*

manor n. area of operations; home base, usu. police use *Payne.*

mantee n. a masculine lesbian *Legman.*

man with a paper ass n. (US Black use) anyone who is all talk and little or no action; fr. the empty mouthings embodied in the Maoist 'paper tiger'

Folb.

man with fuzzy balls n. (US Black use) a white man; there is a theory that fuzz (qv) = police derives from this *Folb.*

map n. the human face *Wodehouse:CW.*

maps n. (musician use) sheet music *Major.*

maracas n. female breasts, fr. musical instrument *Maledicta.*

mare n. ill-tempered, unpleasant woman (cf: cow, bitch) *Powis.*

mariweegee n. (drug use) marijuana; fr. pron. *Folb.*

marj n. aka: *marge*: (abbrev.) margarine *'Fiesta' magazine 10/83.*

mark n. a sucker, the potential and actual victim of a conman *Caron.*

marker n. **1.** (US Black use) the bait that lures a victim into some form of swindle or other fraud *Klein*; **2.** an IOU for a gambling debt *Higgins:3.*

mark one's card v. to explain, to point out, to warn *Newman:1, Norman:2.*

marks n. (drug use) see tracks *Burroughs:1.*

mark up v. to bruise, to leave scars after a fight *Performance.*

marv n. (US teen. use) a highly intelligent person, a scholar; fr. marvellous *Pond.*

marvy a. (abbrev.) marvellous, usu. teen. use.

Mary! homosexual exclamation; orig. Elizabethan use, abbrev. Virgin Mary *Stanley.*

mary n. marijuana *Bukowski:1.*

Mary Ann n. (rhyming sl.) hand *Cole.*

maryanne n. (drug use) marijuana *Green:1.*

Mary Ellen n. (Liverpool use) market women; spec. women who work as cleaners on liners, etc. *Bleasdale.*

maryjane n. marijuana. cannabis *Jay & Young.*

mary poppins n. breasts *T. Wolfe, NY 'Herald Tribune Sunday Magazine', 1965.*

mary warner n. marijuana, cannabis; fr. pron. *Green:1.*

Masers n. (abbrev.) Maserati *Higgins:5.*

masher n. a man who forces his unwanted attentions on women; generally obs.; poss. fr. Romany *mash*: to lure, entice *Bruce:2.*

mash it on me v. (US Black use) **1.** to give one what one is due; **2.** to pass over stolen or contraband goods *Klein.*

mash the fat v. (US Black use) to have sexual intercourse *Folb.*

massive a. (Valley Girls (qv) use) term of great approval (cf: awesome) *Harpers/Queen 1/83.*

master-dog n. (US Black use) the supreme authoritarian figure (usu. a white man) within a institutional hierarchy *Klein.*

mat n. (US Black use) one's regular sweetheart, one's wife *Major.*

match n. (drug use) (abbrev.) matchbox, approx. half ounce of marijuana (cf: lid) *Folb.*

matchbox n. **1.** see: match; **2.** (criminal use) an easily robbed target; no stronger than matchwood *Klein.*

mate n. friend *Griffith.*

mauler n. brass knuckles (cf: maulers) *Chandler:LG.*

maulers n. hands *Wright.*

mauley n. signature, fr. maulers (qv) *Powis.*

maven n. expert, connoisseur; fr. Yiddish *Rosten.*

maw n. (US Black use) **1.** mouth; **2.** vagina *Klein.*

maxed out a. very drunk (cf: max out) *Dickson.*

maximum n. (US prison use) the longest time one must serve of an indeterminate sentence *Klein.*

max out v. to indulge to extremes *Channel-4 TV 1983.*

Mayfair Mercenary n. a girl whose indeterminate class is transcended by her beauty and her ambition to frequent the wealthy salons of Mayfair and similar smart environs; often the 'mistress', 'girl-friend' or 'companion' of the men in the same places; coined by P. York in *Harpers/Queen* c.1980.

mazel n. (Yiddish) luck (always good).

mazuma n. money; fr. Yiddish *Wodehouse passim.*

MCP (abbrev.) *M*ale *C*hauvinist *P*ig; much beloved by early 1960s/70s feminists but now obs. other than amongst tabloid journalists and late arrivals *McFadden.*

meal ticket n. anyone who provides money or a livelihood for someone else – who thus needs to make less effort for themself *Payne.*

mean a. aggressive, unpleasant; also used positively, on 'outlaw' premise of bad = good (cf: bad, vicious, etc.) *Price:2.*

me and you (bingo rhyming sl.) 2 (cf: dirty old Jew) *Wright.*

mean-hair a. (homosexual use) unpleasant, cruel *Thompson.*

meany n. a mean, tight-fisted person; usu. juv. use *Goulart.*

measure one's dick v. putting under suspicion, checking records on a suspect *Higgins:1.*

meat n. **1.** a man; usu. a powerful man; **2.** the penis; **3.** prey, as in 'he's my meat' referring to a potential victim; **4.** the vagina *Price:2.*

meat-eater n. (US police use) a policeman who, not content with such payoffs, bribes and perks that are freely offered, actively compels people to offer him such monies (cf: grass-eater) *Green:2.*

meathead n. general term of abuse; implying that mere flesh, rather than brains, occupies one's skull *'Hill Street Blues', Thames TV, 1983.*

meat market anywhere that people – homo- or heterosexual – gather for the primary purpose of finding sexual partners (often used in universities to describe first-year parties) *Stanley.*

meat rack n. (homosexual use) any place where homosexuals display their charms to potential tricks (qv) or trade (qv); one London 'rack' is in Piccadilly Circus, next to the County Fire Office *White.*

meat shot n. in pornographic still or moving pictures, a close-up of the genitalia, male or female.

meat wagon n. (UK prison use) a wagon for conveying prisoners to and from court, police stations, prisons, etc. *Norman:1.*

mechanic n. a card sharp *Breslin.*

meddle v. (US campus use) **1.** to have sexual intercourse; **2.** to be intimate, but not spec. on a sexual level *Underwood.*

medico n. doctor *Wodehouse:AAG.*

meet n. **1.** (abbrev.) meeting; appointment; **2.** spec. a meeting for the purchase of drugs *Payne.*

meg v. (film use) to direct a film; fr. *megaphone*, a vital part of the director's armoury in the days of silent films *Variety passim.*

mega a. (US teen. use) superlative, extra-special, etc. *Pond.*

megabucks n. enormous sums of money, usu. in context of film or book deals; on model of nuclear *megadeath*: 1m deaths *Vidal.*

megger n. (film use) film director, fr. use of megaphone by directors during silent film era (cf: meg) *Variety passim.*

megsmen n. petty criminals and cheats, orig. *magsman*: card sharp, fr. mid-19th C. *Powis.*

mellow n. (US Black use) a favourite boy/girlfriend; a good friend of either sex *Folb.*

mellow a. calm, peaceful, unconcerned with the material or painful; (cf: laid back) a state often induced by smoking cannabis *White.*

mellow out v. to calm down (oneself or others); to relax mentally *White.*

mellow yellow n. **1.** (US Black use) a Mulatto girl *Folb*; **2.** (drug use) a variety of LSD, poss. obs. *Green:1* fr. song title by Donovan 1967.

melted a. drunk *Dickson.*

melted butter n. (US Black use) an attractive female, esp. a Mulatto, and thus fr. skin tone *Folb.*

Melvin n. a dull, tedious, and otherwise distasteful person (cf:

Irving) *Neaman & Silver.*

member n. (US Black use) a fellow black person *Folb.*

Memphis Glide n. a style of dancing *Price:2.*

mensch n. fr. Yiddish: a 'real man'; implication is of character and integrity rather than sexual or physical prowess *Bruce:2.*

mental a. insane, crazy, out of one's mind *Sillitoe.*

mental job n. one who is, or potentially might be insane *Rawson.*

Merc n. (abbrev.) Mercedes Benz *Performance.*

Mercedes n. (US Black use) an elegant woman with good looks and an atrractive figure; fr. the automobile of the same name and status *Folb.*

merchant n. a person, esp. a specialist in some kind of trade or profession, often criminal; synonym for general use of artist (qv) *Norman:2.*

mercy! homosexual excl., overtones of (campy) 'Southern belle' *Stanley.*

mercy Mary! homosexual excl. of surprise *Stanley.*

merry-go-round n. (US Black use) anyone who is attempting to deceive or swindle another person *Klein.*

mesc n. (abbrev.) mescalin *McFadden.*

meshugge n. fr. Yiddish: crazy, obsessed, weird *Rosten.*

mess about v. **1.** to indulge in varying degress of sexual intimacy (cf: mess around); **2.** to waste time, wander off the subject, distract one's attention, etc.' epitomized in Kenneth Williams' cp 'Stop messing about!' used in various Kenneth Horne BBC-Radio comedy shows and in 'Carry On. . .' films since.

mess around v. (US campus use) to have sexual intercourse *Underwood.*

messed up (drug use) extremely intoxicated by a given drug (cf: wasted, wrecked, destroyed, etc.) *Folb.*

mess one's mind v. to disturb and harm emotionally *M. Jagger & K. Richard, '19th Nervous Breakdown', 1966.*

mess over v. to harm, to interfere with someone, to annoy *Seale.*

mess up v. to assault; to ridicule *Folb.*

mess with v. **1.** to use; **2.** to become involved with *Grogan.*

mess with nature v. (US Black use) to lose one's potency, esp. through excess use of narcotics or alcohol *Folb.*

Met. n. (UK criminal/police use) (abbrev.) Metropolitan Police (serving London) *Newman:1.*

meter thief n. (UK police use) term of contempt for petty villain who steals from gas/parking meters, etc. *Powis.*

meth n. (abbrev.) methedrine *Higgins:1.*

metho n. (Aus. use) metholated spirits, beloved by extreme alcoholics *Humphries:2.*

me-tooing following suit, climbing on a bandwagon *Higgins:5.*

Mexican breakfast n. (US (Texas) derog.) a cigarette and a glass of water, ie: nothing nourishing at all *Safire.*

Mexican green n. (drug use) a grade and type of marijuana *Green:1.*

Mexican stand-off n. any situation in which neither party is willing to back down from a stated position but simultaneously neither party has a superior edge; the result is that both parties give in and walk off *Green:2.*

mf (abbrev.) *m*other*f*ucker (qv).

mic n. (drug use) (abbrev.) microgram, the basic measurement of LSD; an average LSD trip (qv) requires approx 250 mics *Hoffman:a.*

Mick n. Irish person; fr. Michael, a common Irish name (cf: Paddy) *Higgins:3.*

mick n. (Aus. use) Roman Catholic; fr. use of Mick as an Irish and thus often RC person (qv) *Wilkes.*

mickey n. **1.** a small bottle of wine or spirits *Folb*; **2.** (abbrev.) Mickey Finn (qv).

Mickey Finn n. a knockout drug, poss. chloral hydrate, mixed into an unsuspecting victim's drink; fr. an eponymous saloon keeper of Chicago, c.1896–1906. *Wodehouse:MOJ.*

Mickey Mouse a. second rate, badly made, artificial *Price:2.*

Mickey Mouse n. (theatrical rhyming sl.) the house, the audience *Jones:J.*

middle-cut n. (US Black use) the vagina *Klein.*

middle finger n. a prostitute's trick that ensures each client arrives at a speedy orgasm and the girl can maximize her nightly earning potential *Klein.*

middle leg n. the penis *Neaman & Silver.*

midnight n. (US Black use) a particularly dark black person *Folb.*

miffed a. annoyed; fr. 17th C. *miff*: a petty quarrel.

mike-mike n. (US milit. use) one millimetre *Del Vecchio.*

mileage n. **1.** experience; **2.** a criminal record *Shulman.*

military medium (cricket use) gentle, medium paced bowling which goes straight up and down the wicket *BBC Radio 3 1983.*

milk v. to defraud, to extract money from *Higgins:1.*

milk and water a. weak, diluted, adulterated; 'milk and water socialism', etc.

milkers n. female breasts; (cf: norks) *Rawson.*

milko n. (Aus. use) a milkman *Humphries:2.*

milksop n. coward, weakling *Dickson.*

mill n. (abbrev.) million, usu. dollars *Higgins:3.*

million n. a sure bet, fr. 'a million to a bit of dirt' *Norman:2.*

million dollar wound n. (US milit. use) any wound that guarantees the victim a passage out of a war zone and back to the USA; equivalent to UK *Blighty wound* in First World War *O'Brien.*

miln up v. (UK prison use) to lock into a cell; fr. name of a popular locksmiths *LL.*

Milwaukee goitre (US use) a beer belly; fr., *inter alia*, 'Schlitz: the beer that made Milwaukee famous' as did the many beers brewed for the predominantly Ger. immigrant population *Neaman & Silver.*

minces n. (rhyming sl.) mince pies = eyes *Normal:1.*

mind v. **1.** to protect, to act as a bodyguard *Payne*; **2.** (UK police use) to bribe regularly *Laurie.*

mind-blowing a. astounding, amazing, remarkable; usu. stemming from hallucinogenic drug use *Wolfe:2.*

minder n. **1.** (journalistic use) a reporter, often large and aggressive, who doubles as the bodyguard of anyone a paper has persuaded to give them exclusive material and/or interviews on a major story *Thames TV 1983*; **2.** criminal's bodyguard; strong-arm man *Performance.*

mind one's p's and q's v. to be careful, prudent, polite, cautious; poss. fr. 'please and thank-you'; basic manners taught to infants *Hotten.*

mind tripper n. (US campus/teen. use) anyone seen as eccentric, odd, abnormal; fr. mind + tripper (qv) *Underwood.*

minge n. the vagina; fr. Romany.

minge bag n. derog. term for an unpleasant or disliked female; fr. minge (qv) *Bleasdale.*

mingy a. mean, tight-fisted, miserly *Sillitoe.*

mini n. (abbrev.) miniskirt; orig. created as *the* fashion (*pace* Courreges boots) of the 'swinging Sixties', more recently resurgent in the 1980s.

minimum n. (US prison use) the least amount of time one must serve of an indeterminate sentence (cf: maximum) *Klein.*

mink n. (Black use) pretty, sexy young woman (cf: fox) *Milner.*

minnow n. (US campus (spec. University of Arkansas) use) a 12 oz. bottle or can of beer *Underwood.*

MINS n. (US prison use) (acro.) *M*inors *I*n *N*eed of *S*upervision (cf: CHINS, PINS) *Neaman & Silver.*

misery n. a depressing person.

mishegaas n. (Yiddish) nonsense,

absurdity *Goldman*.

Miss (homosexual use) a title prefixed to a given name to imply that the subject's homosexuality is known or obvious *Legman*.

Miss Ann (US Black use) a white girl, usu. derog. *Major*.

Miss Amy n. (US Black use) a young white girl *Folb*.

Miss Lillian n. (US Black use) white female of any age *Folb*.

miss the bus v. aka: *miss the boat*: to lose an opportunity, forfeit a chance, etc.

Miss Thing (homosexual use) greeting to a fellow homosexual male *White*.

Mr Average n. the average member of the public (cf: Joe Public) *Wham, 'Wham Rap', 1983*.

Mr Charlie (Black use) any white man (cf: Boss Charlie) *Greenlee*.

Mr Cracker n. (US Black use) a white person (cf: cracker) *Folb*.

Mr Do-You-Wrong n. (US Black use) a man who mistreats women *Folb*.

Mister Ed n. (US teen. use) **1.** an unimpeachable inside source; **2.** a trusted sidekick; fr. Ed McMahon, regular on US TV's 'Johnny Carson Show' *Sculatti*.

Mr Firstnighter n. a sophisticated, upper-class person, or one who poses as such; fr. US radio show 'Mr Firstnighter' of 1930s featuring a white-tie-and-tails star *Price: 2*.

Mr Gub (Aus. Aborigine use) the white man; fr. gub: diminutive of garbage. (cf: Mr Charlie) *Wilkes*.

Mr Peanut n. (US Black use) white male *Folb*.

Mr Right n. the ideal lover/husband for anyone so searching, male or female; thus Miss Right *Jay & Young*.

Mr Ten Per Cent **1.** spec. an agent, usu. in show business, who takes 10% (at least) of his/her client's earnings; **2.** any form of middleman, esp. between interest groups and politicians, who arranges 'favours' and directs influence for some cut of the subsequent profits.

Mr Thomas n. (US Black use) see Uncle Tom *Folb*.

Mrs Palm and Her Five Daughters the hand, as used for masturbation *Humphries*.

mitt n. a hand *Humphries*.

mittens n. boxing gloves *Heller*.

mitt man n. (US Black use) a religious charlatan who use his flock's credulity to make himself a sumptuous income *Major*.

mixer n. a gossip, usu. deliberately malicious; one who 'stirs things up'.

mix it v. to fight *Keyes*.

mizzled a. drunk *Dickson*.

MO (criminal use) *modus operandi* = way of working = the distinguishing work methods of a given criminal or gang *Dunne*.

Mob n. the US Mafia *Price: 1*.

mob-handed accompanied by a large gang *Griffith*.

mob it v. (film use) for extras to break out of their specified places *Chandler: Notebk*.

Moch n. derog. Jew, abbrev. of mockie (qv) *Bruce: 2*.

mockie (derog.) a Jew *Rosten*.

mod n. **1.** (US use) fashionable, up to date, abbrev. of modern: **2.** (UK use) member of a teenage cult orig. c.1961 who wore specifically distinguishing clothes, rode motor scooters and fought their main rivals, the motorbike riding, leather-clad rockers (qv).

mod squad n. plain clothes police, usu. young and dressed in the prevailing teenage and early 20s fashions, who look for crime in colleges and local youth centres.

mogadored a. (rhyming sl.) floored, thus beaten, defeated *Cole*.

mojo n. **1.** any drug; **2.** morphine *De Lannoy & Masterson*.

moll n. a woman, esp. a gangster's girl-friend *Farrell*.

moll buzzer n. pickpocket who specilizes in women as victims *Chandler: Notebk*.

Molly n. (rhyming sl.) Molly Malone (qv) = 'phone *Powis*.

mollycoddle n.,v. weakling, mother's

darling, milksop (qv); to indulge such a person in such weaknesses *Dickson*.

mollydooker (Aus. use) left-handed; poss. fr. duke = fist and moll = woman, with derog, sense that a woman, like a left-handed person, would be clumsy (?) *Wilkes*.

mollyfock n. (euph.) motherfuck *Wolfe: 2*.

Molly Malone n. (rhyming sl.) telephone *Jones: J*.

Mom and Pop stores n. small, corner stores stocking just the bare essentials (cf: Ma and Pa store) *Price: 3*.

Mom-Dad-Buddy-and-Sis shorthand for the clichéd American nuclear family *Wolfe: 2*.

momma term of address to any female.

momma's game n. (US Black use) see the dirty dozens, a ritual that depends heavily on mutually abusing the participants' mothers *Folb*.

mo-mo n. aka: *momo*: a moron; fr. repetition of the abbrev. 'mo' *Price: 2*.

momser n. lit. bastard, fr. Yiddish, but catch-all term implying everything from great affection to deep dislike (cf: bastard) *Schulberg: 2*.

Monday morning quarterback n. an amateur critic of specialist activities; spec. a non-playing football fan who delivers his opinions on a Monday of the pro games the previous Sunday *P. Roth, 'Our Gang', 1971*.

Monday pills n. (US milit. use) anti-malaria pills taken once a week *Del Vecchio*.

mondo a. (Valley Girls (qv) use) completely, absolutely; fr. Ital. mondo: the world (cf: —city) *Pond*.

money for jam anything, incl. money, that is gained for a minimal amount, if any, of effort, and available for purely pleasurable expenditure *Wodehouse: MOJ*.

moneymaker n. female genitals or buttocks *Rechy: 1*.

money to burn n. spare cash, available for spontaneous excess (cf: money for jam).

monicker n. name; poss. fr. monogram *Burroughs: 1*.

monkey n. **1.** (drug use) (abbrev.) monkey on one's back = narcotics addiction *Algren*; **2.** (derog.) general insult *Higgins: 1*; **3.** (UK criminal use) a padlock *Norman: 2*; **4.** £500; $500 *LL*.

monkey v. to tamper, fiddle with, usu, in destructiove clumsy manner.

monkey on one's back to be addicted to narcotics, esp. heroin *Bruce: 2*.

monkey's cousin (bingo rhyming sl.) 12 (a dozen) *Wright*.

monkey's tails n. (rhyming sl.) nails *Jones: J*.

monotony n. (US campus use) one's single, steady girl-friend; pun on monogamy, and its tedium *Underwood*.

monster n. **1.** (UK prison use) sexual offenders, child molesters, etc. (cf: nonce, Rule 43) *Newman: 3*; **2.** (US milit. use) PRC-77 radio, used for secure transmissions; fr. the radio's weight and complexity *Del Vecchio*.

monte n. **1.** (criminal/gambling use) (abbrev.) three-card monte (qv), the three-card trick *Powis*; **2.** (Aus. use) an absolute certainty; fr. 'three-card monte' (qv) a card game played only by conmen *Wilkes*.

Montezuma's revenge n. diarrhoea or in worse cases, dysentery as suffered by tourists with tender stomachs; the specific monarch ruled Mexico c.1500 and the food-poisoning that some tourists suffer is laid at his posthumous feet (cf: Gyppy tummy) *Obs. 1983*.

monthlies n. the menstrual period *Bukowski: 1*.

moo n. a (foolish) woman; fr. 'moo-cow'; often as 'silly old moo' (cf: cow, mare, bitch) *BBC TV, 'Til Death Us Do Part', 1960s passim*.

moocah n. (drug use) marijuana (cf: mu) *Green: 1*.

mooch n. **1.** spec. beggar; **2.** general derog. term *Stone*.

moody n. **1.** complaints, ill-temper, depression *Keyes*; **2.** deceit, lies, verbal trickery; fr. rhyming sl.

Moody & Sankey = hanky-panky *Franklyn*.

moody a. illicit, stolen *Thames TV 1984*.

mook n. see: mooch *Price: 2*.

moolah n. money *Sanders: 2*.

moon n. a month *Powis*.

moon n. (abbrev.) moonshine = illicit liquor *Higgins: 2*.

moon v. to drop one's trousers and underpants to present one's bare buttocks to onlookers; often performed through a car window (cf: drop trou) *Greaser Comics*.

moon (around) v. to wander around wretchedly lost in thought, often a victim of unrequited passion.

moon-ass n. an infatuated person who moons around for an unattainable love-object *Price: 3*.

mooner n. (US police use) a pathological lawbreaker; presumably fr. the effect of the moon on his mind *Neaman & Silver*.

moonlight v. to work at two jobs on each day in order to boost one's income; the second may well be unknown to the employer of the first and is usu. night work *Illustrated Fiction vol. 1, 1976*.

moonlighter n. (US Black use) a prostitute *Klein*.

Moor n. (UK police/criminal use) HMP Dartmoor.

moosh n. term pf address; fr. Romany mush = a man *LL*.

mootah n. aka: *mooter, muta* : marijuana *Green: 1*.

moppet n. a pre-teen girl *Wodehouse: JO*.

mop up v. to carry out conclusively; esp. of a gangland or military shooting *rr*.

moral n. a certainty; usu. in 'it's a moral . . .' *Humphries: 2*.

more ass than a toilet seat (cp) conspicuous sexual prowess, usu. in 'he gets . . .' *'The Deer Hunter', directed M. Cimino, 1979*.

more front than Brighton beach (cp) exceptionally cheeky, daring; pun on 'sea-front' and front: cheek, gall *'Only Fools and Horses', BBC-1 TV, 1983*.

more hide than Jessie (Aus. use) immensely cheeky; fr. a favourite elephant Jessie (1872–1939) who could be visited at the Taronga Park Zoo *Wilkes*.

more kicks than ha'pence (cp) of any situation which yields more trouble than it is worth.

more power to your elbow (cp) generally encouraging; the augmented elbow would doubtless be used for bending (cf: bend the elbow) *Capital Radio 1983*.

more pricks than a second-hand dartboard a description of a promiscuous female, usu. *She's had . . .*

morning after the night before the state of being hungover after an excess of alcohol.

morph n. (drug use) (abbrev.) morphine *Green: 1*.

Moss Bross n. Moss Brothers of Covent Garden, the country's leading hirers of dress clothes.

Motel Hell n. (US teen. use) any situation or place that is considered appalling or unacceptable – a job, a bad place to stay, a relationship, etc. *Sculatti*.

mother n. **1.** (abbrev. motherfucker (qv) *Himes: 1*; **2.** (Black use) effeminate male; **3.** homosexual who introduces another into the gay world (cf: daughter) *Stanley*.

mother fist and her five daughters n. the human hand, as used for masturbation *Jay & Young*.

motherflunker n. (euph.) motherfucker (qv) *Rawson*.

motherfouler n. (euph.) motherfucker (qv) *Major*.

motherfucker n. **1.** (white use) supreme insult/expletive based on the incest taboo *Price: 2*; **2.** (black use) a wide variety of meanings, fr. good to bad, often as a black-to-black term of affection; also simply meaning 'thing'; frequently abbrev. to *mother Seale*.

mother ga-ga n. (homosexual use) a fussy, gossipy, interfering older queen

(qv) *Legman*.
mothergrabber n. (euph.) motherfucker (qv) *Rawson*.
motherhugger n. aka: *mammyhugger*: euph. motherfucker *Major*.
motherjiver n. (euph.) motherfucker (qv) *Major*.
motherjumper n. (euph.) motherfucker (qv) *Farina*.
motherless a. (Aus. use) general intensifier; thus a bastard *Wilkes*.
mother-love n. a homosexual male having sex with a heterosexual woman *Legman*.
motherlover n. (euph.) motherfucker (qv) *Major*.
mother nature n. (drug use) marijuana *Peter Townshend, 'Tommy', 1969*.
mother nature's own tobacco n. (drug use) marijuana (cf: God's own medicine).
mother-raper n. (euph.) motherfucker (qv) *Himes: 1*.
Mother's Day n. (US Black use) the day when welfare cheques arrive from the government *Klein*.
mother's ruin n. (rhyming sl.) gin (though the 'rhyme' is not immediately apparent) *Cole*.
Mother Superior n. (homosexual use) an older, experienced and open homosexual *Legman*.
motivate v. to force oneself to do something which one dislikes *Milner*.
motor n. (abbrev.) motor car *Capital Radio 1983*.
motorcycle n. (US Black use) a woman (who can supposedly be 'ridden') (cf: bike).
motor-mouth n. an indiscreet person who cannot stop talking *Higgins: 1*.
motorway n. (skiing use) a broad, easy piste *Barr*.
motsa n. (Aus. use) a big gambling win, a large sum of money; poss. fr. Hebrew *motsa* = unleavened bread, and which resembles an outsize round biscuit, and thus an enormous coin (?) *Wilkes*.
mount n. (US Black use) a promiscuous female; who is 'ridden' *Folb*.
mount v. to have sexual intercourse *Folb*.
mountains n. (US Black use) large, noticeable female breasts *Klein*.
mountain wop n. derog. term of abuse for an Italian *Selby: 1*.
mouser n. **1.** moustache *Runyon*; **2.** (US tramp sl.) a homosexual *Legman*.
moustache Pete n. original Italian immigrants to New York, typified by their heavy moustaches; also original members of the US Mafia *Price: 1*.
mouth like the inside of an Arab's underpants (cp) referring to such ghastly physical feelings as are concomitant with a hangover.
mouth music n. the practice of cunnilingus *Powis*.
mouth off v. to boast, to brag.
mouthpiece n. a lawyer *rr*.
mouth-worker n. (homosexual use) a fellator *Legman*.
mouthy a. boastful, cocky *Robins*.
move on v. see: fire on *Folb*.
move one's ass v. to hurry up, to get a move on *Pynchon*.
mover n. an ambitious person; who moves both himself and others physically and emotionally *Caron*.
moves n. ideas, plans, ability to deal with various situations *Higgins: 1*.
moxie n. courage, guts, nerve *Rosten*.
mozzle n. phonetic pron. of mazel (qv).
MTF (UK 'society' use) *M*ust *T*ouch *F*lesh; of an overly amorous young man *Mortimer*.
mu n. (drug use) marijuana; fr. moocah (qv) *Green: 1*.
muck about v. to pretend, to act half-heartedly, to give less than total commitment, to tease *Mandelkau*.
mucker n. **1.** a friend; **2.** (euph.) fucker (qv).
muck-hole n. a filthy, unappetizing place or room *Performance*.
muck in v. to join in. to lend a hand, esp. in a dirty or unpleasant task *Wright*.

mud n. opium; fr. colour and consistency *Burroughs:*1.
mudcrusher n. (US Black use) an extreme form of bully, whose aim is to crush everyone into the ground *Klein*.
muddy waters n. (US Black use) the loss of a man's erection prior to or during sex. *Folb*.
mud flaps n. (US Black use) noticeably large feet *Klein*.
mud-kicker n. (pimp use) an unreliable, unprofessional prostitute (cf: flaky ho) *OUI 1975*.
muff n. the vagina; fr. supposed resemblance.
muff-diver n. cunnilinguist *Goldman*.
muffin n. the vagina *Higgins: 3*.
mug n. **1.** the face *Wright*; **2.** a fool *Gothic Blimp Works no. 2*; **3.** derog. description of any given person *Norman: 2*; **4.** the potential victim of a confidence trick or form of deception.
mug v. **1.** (US campus use) to kiss *Underwood*; **2.** (police use) to take identification pictures for prison/court use *Higgins: 2*; **3.** to make funny faces; esp. show business/theatrical and film use; **4.** to rob, usu. in the street and often with violence; orig. to garotte; thus *mugger* one who carries out such assaults.
mug book n. reference book used for casting purposes in theatre, TV and films; contains pictures of actual and aspirant stars, etc. *Chandler: LG*.
muggle n. (drug use) a cigarette with marijuana or hashish substituted for some of the tobacco and packed back inside it *Major*.
muggles n. (drug use) marijuana *Green: 1*.
mug punter n. a sucker in any game of chance or at a racecourse (cf: punter).
mugs away! trad. excl. in darts matches when the winners of the previous game tell the losers to start the next contest.
mug's game n. a foolish endeavour, pointless effort *Sillitoe*.
mug-shot n. picture taken by police or in prison for identification of prisoner; fr. mug = face (qv).
mug's ticker n. (UK criminal use) a piece of worthless jewellery or a dud watch Powis.
mug up v. **1.** to learn, to memorize; orig. theatrical use: 'paint one's mug' = face *Hotten*; **2.** (US Black use) to put on one's hat; to leave *Klein*.
mule n. **1.** unattractive female *Price: 3*; **2.** (smuggling use) an otherwise innocent person used to bring contraband goods, drugs, etc. through customs for a fee; fr. use of mules as beasts of burden. *Payne*.
mule mouth n. (US Black use) anyone who works regularly as a police informer *Klein*.
mulla n. money (cf: moolah) *N. Cassady, 'The First Third', 1971*.
mullahed (sp. unknown) (UK prison use) beaten severely *Cole*.
mulled up a. drunk *Runyon*.
Mulligan stew n. (tramp use) a stew made of whatever meats and vegetables are available *Waits*.
mulligrubs n. the blues (qv) *Major*.
mullyfogging (euph.) motherfucking (qv) *Wolfe: 2*.
mum a. silent, quiet.
mum n. (UK criminal use) one's mistress of many years or one's wife, but *not* one's actual mother *Powis*.
mumbo-jumbo a. meaningless nonsense *Thompson*.
mummy v. (US Black use) to beat a person to death, thus to make him/her into an Egyptian-style mummified corpse *Klein*.
mump v. to beg *Powis*.
mumper v. (US Black use) to travel around, to partner on someone's travels; prob. fr. UK 17th C. 'genteel beggar' who lived by nomadic begging along English roads *Klein*.
mumping n. (UK police use) for a policeman to accept cheap or free goods and services from friendly tradespeople (cf: mump) *Laurie*.
munchies n. the craving for food, often sweet or in an otherwise unlikely combination of flavours, that afflicts smokers of hashish or marijuana (cf:

chucks) *Green: 1.*

munger n. aka: *munga*: food; fr. Fr./Ital. root for 'eat', poss. since First World War *C. Clarke.*

munt n. (S. Afr. use) (derog.) Black person; fr. *muntu*: a person *Marcuson.*

murphy n. a potato; fr. the common Irish surname and the assumption that potatoes are the supreme Irish staple.

murphy game n. (criminal use) for a prostitute to lure a client either to a room or a deserted alley, hallway, etc. and then, instead of having sex, the client is beaten and robbed by a male accomplice, who may just strike, but may also pose as an aggrieved father, lover, brother, etc. *Green, 'The Directory of Infamy', 1980.*

muscle n. strength; strong-arm thugs used by gangsters *Higgins: 1.*

musclehead n. a stupid, if brawny man *Price: 1.*

muscle in v. to force an entrance; to use violence to gain something one desires *rr.*

mush n. **1.** the face; **2.** greeting: similar to *mate*; orig. Romany *moosh*: a man *Powis.*

musher n. (UK taxi-driver use) an owner driver; fr. mushroomer, one who has to get up early to earn a day's wages (cf: mushie).

mush faker n. an umbrella repairer; fr. mush abbrev. mushroom: an umbrella *LL.*

mushie n. (taxi-driver use) a cabbie who owns his own cab *Powis.*

music n. talking, esp. complaints or nagging *Higgins: 2.*

muski n. muscatel, cheap wine *Bukowski:*1.

muso n. (abbrev.) musician, usu. in rock'n'roll bands *'The Boy Who Won The Pools', LWT, 1983.*

mustang n. **1.** (US Black use) an independant woman who is 'hard to ride' *Klein*; **2.** (US milit. use) an officer who has been commissioned from the ranks *Green: 2.*

must have swallowed the dictionary (cp) referring to a person who habitually prefers longer to shorter words.

mutt n. a dog *Runyon.*

Mutt and Jeff a. (rhyming sl.) deaf; fr. US cartoon characters, orig. by Bud Fischer in 1930s *Cole.*

Mutt and Jeff v. (police/criminal use) for police interrogators to take the parts of the 'good/sympathetic' and 'bad/potentially violent' officers when attempting to gain information from a suspect. Such 'roles' are assumed only for the situation in hand *Cole.*

mutton n. **1.** the penis (cf: mutton dagger) *Humphries*; **2.** the vagina *Norman: 2.*

mutton dagger n. the penis *Humphries.*

muzzle n. fr. Yiddish *mazel* (qv): luck *Norman: 1.*

muzzler n. a homosexual, spec. a fellator *Legman.*

muzzy a. **1.** vague, befuddled, confused; **2.** drunk *Dickson*; both meanings fr. SE bemused.

my ass! (excl.) don't try to fool me! you should be so lucky! I wasn't born yesterday!, etc. *Pynchon.*

my foot! (euph., excl.) see: my ass! (qv) *Chandler: LG.*

my man (US Black use) term of endearment and address between two Black men *'Hill Street Blues', Thames TV, passim.*

MYOB (acro.) *M*ind *Y*our *O*wn *B*usiness.

my old guv'ner n. my father *Powis.*

mystery n. an unknown young girl, often recently arrived in London from provinces *Norman: 2.*

mystery mad aka: *mystery punter*: any man who prefers his sex and/or relationships with mysteries (qv) *Neaman & Silver.*

nab n. (US Black use) a policeman, who nabs (qv) a villain *Major.*

nab v. to catch, esp. of a policeman's arrest *Wright.*

nabes n. (abbrev.) neighbourhoods, esp. local cinemas *Variety.*

naff a. in poor taste, unappealing, unfashionable; orig. prostitutes' use: nothing *'The Comic Strip Presents', Channel-4 TV, 1983.*

naff off! (excl.) go away! euph. fuck off (qv). *Waterhouse.*

nag n. (US pimp use) a woman who takes her time over making her daily money from her clients; fr. nag: lazy horse *Klein.*

nail v. **1.** to seduce, to pin down *Jenkins*; **2.** to charge with a debt *Higgins:3.*

nailed a. found out, thwarted, arrested *Higgins:1.*

nail 'em and jail 'em (US Black use) the police *Folb.*

nail-head n. (US Black use) an unattractive female, esp. one with short, nappy hair (cf: BB head) *Folb.*

nail one to the wall v. **1.** to punish severely; **2.** to beat up comprehensively.

naked a. **1.** (US Black use) without a gun, without possessions or money; generally at a disadvantage *Klein*; **2.** (US campus use) exactly, completely true, affirmative (often as a response to a previous statement) *Underwood.*

naked jazz n. basic, raunchy, lowdown (qv) jazz music *Major.*

nam n. (backsl.) man *Cole.*

name of the game n. the most important aspect of a given situation; whatever matters most.

nammo n. (backsl.) woman *Cole.*

nana n. fool, idiot, incompetent; esp in *a right nana*; fr. abbrev. for banana, soft (punning on soft = stupid) fruit.

nancy-boy n. aka: *nance*: derog. homosexual, effeminate male *Legman.*

nanny goat n. (rhyming sl.) coat, boat *Jones:J.*

nanny-goating (rhyming sl.) courting (imperfect rhyme) *Wright.*

napper n. head *Wright.*

nappy a. **1.** (US Black use) crinkly, short black hair; disliked by those Blacks who aspire to the straight hair of whites *Klein*; **2.** Black, as in *nappy music*; fr. Black hair style *Price:3.*

Nap Town n. (US trucker use) Indianapolis, Ind. (cf: Circle City) *Klein.*

narc n. **1.** spec. (abbrev.) narcotics agent; **2.** any informer *SF Comics.*

narco n. (abbrev.) narcotics officer *Goldman.*

narc one over v. to betray a drug dealer or user to the narcotics police *Stone.*

narco squad n. (abbrev.) narcotics squad *SF Comics.*

nark n. a police informer; fr. Romany

nak: nose (cf: grass) *Hotten.*

nark v. **1.** to annoy, to irritate; **2.** to inform to the police (cf: grass) *Hotten.*

narked a. annoyed *Performance.*

nark it! shut up!, stop it! *'Z Cars', BBC-TV, 1964.*

narrowback n. (derog.) Irish person *Higgins:5.*

narrow squeak n. a lucky and hairsbreadth escape *Wodehouse:MOJ.*

Nashville n. (US Black use) any unsophisticated, suburban, middle-American town or person *Klein.*

nasty n. sexual intercourse *F. Zappa, 'Brown Shoes Don't Make It,' 1966.*

nasty a. (US Black use) exciting, particularly enjoyable; sexy (cf: bad) *Randy Newman, 'Trouble in Paradise', 1983.*

natch (abbrev.) naturally *Hoffman:a.*

natter v. to chat, to gossip. poss. fr. nag + chatter (?) *Humphries.*

natural n. **1.** an idiot, a fool; fr. a state of nature, thus untutored, unsophisticated, etc. *Obs. 6/2/83*; **2.** the ideal person for a given situation, often the potential victim for a confidence trick *Higgins:3*; **3.** see: Afro; **4.** (gambling use) in craps dice, a throw of 7 or 11.

natural-born man n. (US Black use) a 'real' (heterosexual) man; a good lover, an honest, unpretentious person; the premise is that a 'natural' person is not hidebound by social conditioning, etc. *Folb.*

natural woman n. (US Black use) female version of natural-born man (qv) *Folb.*

naughties n. sexual liaisons, intercourse *Humphries.*

Naughton and Gold (rhyming sl.) cold; fr. music hall duo *Wright.*

naughty n. sexual intercourse.

naughty a. (police/criminal use) criminal, violent, corrupt *Payne.*

naughty bits n. the genitals; this quite deliberate euph. coined c.1969 by the Monty Python's Flying Circus comedy team *BBC-2 TV, 1969 passim.*

naus n. pron. as abbrev. of nauseating and commonly used with a derog. inference, but in fact fr. rhyming sl. Noah's = Noah's Ark = nark = police informer *L. Brown, 20/4/83.*

nay-nay n. female breast (cf: ninnies) *Bruce:1.*

NB (UK 'society' use) (acro.) no background; note appended to names of potential male escorts by debutantes or their mothers *T 18/7/83.*

NBG (acro.) *N*o *B*loody *G*ood.

near-sighted a. (homosexual use) an uncircumcised penis with its tip protruding slightly above the foreskin (cf: blind) *Legman.*

near the mark somewhat corrupt, not wholly honest *Newman:1.*

neat a. pleasant, satisfactory, attractive; term of general approval according to context *Jenkins.*

neatnik n. someone devoted to neatness and order *McFadden.*

nebbie n. (abbrev.) Nembutal, a barbiturate (cf: nembie) *Selby:1.*

nebbish n. fr. Yiddish *nebech*: a born loser *Norman:3.*

neck n. **1.** audacity, daring; (abbrev.) brass neck; thus *stick one's neck out*: to chance one's luck *Howard*; **2.** (US campus use) (abbrev.) redneck (qv) *Underwood.*

neck v. to pursue sexual pleasure that stops short of intercourse; usu. teen use and practice (cf: snog).

neckbreak v. (US Black use) to move swiftly *Major.*

necklaced (US Black use) extremely hip (qv): 'laced by the neck' *Klein.*

neck-oil n. alcohol *Tidy.*

necktie party n. a hanging, usu. an illicit, impromptu lynching.

Ned Kelly n. (Aus. rhyming sl.) belly *Humphries.*

need a foghorn v. (US preppie (qv) use) to be utterly confused, lost *Bernbach.*

needle n. resentment, bitterness, irritation *Powis.*

needle v. to annoy, to tease maliciously (cf: wind up) *Norman:2.*

needle and thread n. (rhyming sl.) thread *Wright.*

needle match n. (sporting use) any

contest in which more than merely sporting rivalry divides the opponents; such a match will quite probably be violent, or at least ill-tempered.

needle freak n. **1.** (pimp use) a sadistic client who derives pleasure from hiring a woman with large breasts and paying her for every needle she permits him to stick into the flesh *OUI 8/75*; **2.** (drug use) one who injects themself with narcotics and other drugs and who is often as stimulated by the act of injection as by the action of the drug *Underwood*.

Negro n. (US Black use) formerly the accepted name for the Black race, since 1960s radicalization, the preferred word is *black* and thus Negro implies the old-fashioned, subservient Uncle Tom (qv) style of Black person *Folb*.

nellie a. **1.** overtly homosexual, effeminate man *Jay & Young;* **2.** general term of disparagement *Capital Radio 1983*.

nelly n. (US campus use) a lesbian *Underwood*.

nembie n. (abbrev.) Nembutal, a barbiturate (cf: nebbie) *Burroughs:1*.

Nelson in cricket, the score of 111, spec. the English team (of any era) unlucky number; fr. the Admiral's attributes: one eye, one arm, one anus *BBC Radio 1983*.

nemmo n. (backsl.) woman *Powis*.

nerd n. an unpleasant person; anyone outside a given peer group and who thus fails to fit in with 'the gang' *SF Comics*.

nerd pack n. (factory use) a plastic, sectioned liner for the breast pocket that keeps pens from soiling the cloth (cf: nerd) *Kidder*.

nerf v. to bump another vehicle slightly with one's own car *Junker*.

nerk n. (UK public school use) fool, yob, generally unappetizing/ unacceptable person (cf: nerd) *Barr*.

Nervo n. **1.** (rhyming sl.) Nervo and Knox (former music hall comedy team) = pox = spec. syphilis *Powis*; **2.** the box = television *Wright*.

nervy a. **1.** nervous, scared, cowardly; **2.** daring, audacious, pushing one's luck *I. J. Singer, 'The Brothers Ashkenazi', tr. J. Singer 1980*.

nest **n. 1.** (US pimp use) the women who make up the pimp's stable (qv) of prostitutes *Klein*; **2.** the vagina *Klein*.

net (backsl.) ten *Cole*.

nettled a. annoyed, irritated *Sillitoe*.

never been kissed aka: *never had it* (bingo use) 17; fr. supposed sexual innocence of a 17-year-old girl.

never happen (cp) used to dismiss any idea that the speaker cannot support.

never-never n. the hire purchase system; one never finishes paying for one's purchase, also Peter Pan's 'Never-Never Land' (cf: on the drip).

neves n. **1.** (backsl.) seven; **2.** (UK prison use) a seven-year sentence *Norman:1*.

nevis (backsl.) seven *Cole*.

new fish n. (US prison use) a new inmate *Pearce*.

Newgate gaol (rhyming sl.) a tale, esp. of the 'hard-luck' variety *Cole*.

Newington Butts n. (rhyming sl.) guts = stomach *Dury*.

newsie n. newspaper seller, usu. US/Aus. use.

News of the Screws n. nickname for the *News of the World* (UK Sunday paper) punning on its propensity for sex stories.

newted a. drunk, fr. pissed as a newt (qv) *May*.

NG (acro.) *No Good* *Caron*.

Niagara Falls n. (rhyming sl.) balls = testicles *Cole*.

nice (US Black use) feeling well, happy, at one with the world *Major*.

nice bit n. (US prison use) see: long bit, big bit *Klein*.

nice one, Cyril! (cp) general term of approval; fr. Cyril Knowles, a Tottenham Hotspur footballer, 1960s.

nice work - if you can get it (cp) implying fairly open jealousy of the previous speaker.

nick v. **1.** to arrest; **2.** to steal; thus *on the nick*: going stealing *Dury*.

nick n. **1.** prison; **2.** police station, esp.

its cells *Laurie*.

nicked a. (UK prison use) **1.** put on report to the governor for an infringement of prison rules *Obs. 1981*; **2.** arrested *'The Sweeney', Thames TV, 1974.*

nickel n. (general US use) the number five *Del Vecchio*; **2.** (US prison use) a five-year prison sentence *Klein*.

nickel-and-dime a. smalltime, second rate, insignificant *Stone*.

nicker n. pound sterling *Performance*.

nick off v. to leave, to depart, to go from one place to another.

niff n.,v. **1.** *n.* an unpleasant smell, a stink; **2.** *v.* to smell unpleasantly, to stink *Wodehouse:AAG*.

nifty a. neat, smart *Fiction Illus.3*.

nifty n. an attractive girl.

Nigerian lager n. Guinness stout; fr. its colour *'Minder', Thames TV, 1982.*

nigger n. (derog.) Black person, by extension any non-white, but, in a reverse racism, taking pride in such epithets, used by radical Blacks of each other *Seale*.

nigger box (US Black use) television (cf. wogbox) *Klein*.

nigger-driving n. (US Black use (fr. orig. in South)) the working of Blacks to exhaustion by white bosses *Klein*.

nigger-flicker n. (US Black use) a weapon, usu. a small knife or a razor blade with one side heavily taped to preserve the user's fingers *Folb*.

nigger fronts n. (US Black use) extreme stylishness in dress *Folb*.

niggerish a. lazy, couldn't-care-less; fr, spurious stereotype of Blacks as lazy people *Heller*.

niggerlipping wetting the end of a cigarette while smoking it *Price:3*.

niggerlover n. (derog.) term of abuse, usu. aimed at a white lacking in the necessary loathing of Blacks *Selby:1*.

nigger-rich (Black use) deeply in debt but loaded down with glossy, flashy status symobls – car, jewellery, etc. *Milner*.

nigger's bankroll n. (US Black use) see California bankroll *Folb*.

niggly a. ill-tempered, obsessed with irrelevancies and petty problems.

night-cap n. (US Black use) a small skull-cap worn by many black men *Klein*.

night-cap n. a final drink before bed, or before the bars shut *Goulart*.

night clothes n. (US criminal use) dark close-fitting clothes used when committing a breaking and entry at night *Klein*.

night-club v. to go out at night for enjoyment at clubs, bars, parties, etc. *Grace Jones, LP title, 1980.*

night hawk n. (US criminal use) one who specializes in stealing at night *Klein*.

night stick n. (US Black use) anyone who lives their life in clubs and bars and generally indulges themself as a 'night person' *Klein*.

night watchman n. (cricket use) a poor batsman who is sent in in place of a superior player after a wicket has fallen near the end of a day's play and the team does not wish to chance that superior wicket *BBC Radio 3, 1983 Test Match commentaries passim.*

nignog n. (derog.) Black person; fr. nigger (qv) *Le Carre*.

NIGYYSOB (acro.) *N*ow *I*'ve *G*ot *Y*ou, *Y*ou *S*on *O*f a *B*itch: shorthand for a position reached between patient and therapist during an encounter session.

-nik general suffix; coined 1957 after launch of Russian Sputnik. First -nik word was *beatnik*, orig. by Herb Caen in *San Francisco Chronicle Joyce Johnson, 'Minor Characters', 1983.*

Nina with her hair down (gambling use) the point of nine in craps dice *Chandler: Notebk.*

nineteenth hole n. the bar at a golf club; spec. used by golfers but understood more widely *Neaman & Silver*.

nine to five n. a regular, routine, uninspiring job; fr. the hours most usually worked.

ning-nong n. (Aus. use) stupid, foolish person *Humphries*.

ninnies n. female breasts; fr. sense of

'child' (cf: nay-nays) *Rawson*.

Nip n. (abbrev.) Nipponese: derog. Japanese *Sanchez*.

nip v. to scratch, to give a superficial wound *Klein*.

nipper n. a small child, who nips around *Performance*.

nisht aka: *nicht* fr. Yiddish: nothing *Norman:2*.

nit n. fool, idiot; fr. nitwit (qv) *May*.

nit-nit! shut up! *LL*.

nitty gritty n. basics, essentials, the grass roots *Seale*.

nitwit n. idiot, fool scatterbrain *Jenkins*.

nix v. to forbid, to veto, to say 'no'.

nix no *E. Presley, 'Jailhouse Rock', 1958*.

no account a. useless *Pearce*.

noah's ark n. (rhyming sl.) **1.** park; **2.** nark (qv) = informer, when pron. naus (qv) *Jones:J*.

nob n. **1.** (abbrev.) nobility; the aristocracy, upper classes *Norman:3*; **2.** penis *Humphries*.

no better than he/she should be (cp) admitting that the person in question is simply human, warts and all; often used of a woman who is considered promiscuous.

no biggie (US teen. use) don't worry, it's all right, etc.; fr. no big deal (qv) *Pond*.

nobbing n. sexual intercourse *P. Marchbank*.

nobble v. **1.** (racing use) to interfere with a horse in order to spoil its chance of victory; **2.** *jury nobbling*: the interference with the impartiality of a jury – through threats or bribes – either by a defendant or his/her friends *Mortimer*; **3.** to ruin anything deliberately; esp. to impede a rival *Wodehouse:AAG*.

no-brand cigarette n. aka: *no-name cigarette*; a marijuana cigarette *Folb*.

no chance no hope whatsoever; general term of dismissal or negation.

nod v. to lapse into unconsciousness after an injection of heroin *Larner*.

noddy n. (UK police use) (abbrev.) noddy bike; so-called from the fact that riders in motion could not salute their seniors who therefore ordered 'When you see me, nod your head!' *Laurie*.

no dice impossible, out of the question, on no account *Runyon*.

nod out v. to fall asleep, esp. after an injection of heroin (cf: nod) *Burroughs:1*.

no fear! absolutely not, not a chance, etc. *Manser*.

noffka n. aka: *nafka*: fr. Yiddish: a prostitute *Bruce:1*.

no flies on (cp) as in 'no flies on me/her/etc.' implying the smartness and imperviousness to trickery of the speaker or subject.

no freak n. (pimp use) a client who wishes the prostitute to simulate the role of a rape victim, screaming 'No!' and 'struggling' before he overpowers her *OUI 8/75*.

noggin n. the head *Price:2*.

no go impossible, pointless (cf: no chance).

no hoper n. a good-for-nothing, a loser, a derelict *Bickerton*.

no joy excl. of despair, disappointment, bad luck, etc.

no kidding?/! are you serious?/I'm absolutely serious.

no-knock n. a clause in US drug laws that permits police to enter premises without knocking first, and thus ensure surprise and probable arrests *Hoffman:a*.

nola n. (US criminal sl.) a homosexual male; fr. the female name *Legman*.

nommus! (London market use; back sl.) warning cry on sighting a policeman, lit. 'someone' *Powis*.

no muss, no fuss (business use; cp) no problems, either practically or emotionally *Kidder*.

non n. (US Black use) a physically unco-ordinated person; a poor athlete; fr. non-performer (?) *Folb*.

nonce n. (abbrev.) nonsense: sexual offender, spec. of young children *Cole*.

non compos a. (abbrev.) *non compos mentis*: (Lat.) 'not of sound mind', thus **1.** eccentric, crazy; **2.** drunk.

nondescript n. an unmarked police car used for surveillance, etc. *Newman:1.*

nong n. (Aus. use) an idiot, a fool, a general derog. description; fr. non compos (qv) *Ready.*

no-no n. an impossibility *Jay & Young.*

noodle n. head *Runyon.*

noodle n. a fool, a dull person.

nookie n. sexual intercourse, by extn. anyone who seems likely to be simply seduced. poss fr. obs. *nug*: to fondle *Jay & Young.*

nooner n. (Aus. use) a lunchtime seduction, often of a secretary by a businessman. *C. Clarke.*

no rest for the wicked (cp) said of/by someone who, while in no way wicked, is kept very busy; said with pride rather than rancour.

no risk! (Aus. use) excl. of agreement, negating any other possibility than that just proposed *Ready.*

norks n. (Aus. use) breasts; fr. Norco Co-Operative Ltd, butter manufacturer of NSW *Humphries.*

north and south n. (rhyming sl.) mouth *Powis.*

North Pole n. (rhyming sl.) arsehole *Wright.*

NORWICH (acro.) (k)*N*ickers *O*ff *R*eady *W*hen *I* *C*ome *H*ome; used on the back of envelopes, orig. by British forces (cf: SWALK).

nose n. **1.** cocaine; which one inhales; **2.** (US prison use) a police spy. fr. orig meaning of nark (qv) *Chandler: Notebk.*

nose around v. to search, to look over, to survey *Fiction Illus.3.*

nose candy n. cocaine (cf: candy **1.**) *Schulberg.*

nosh n. food *The Nosh Bar, a long-lived delicatessen/cafe in Gt. Windmill Street, Soho.*

no shit! (excl.) you don't say! goodness me!; usu. ironic use *Higgins:5.*

nosh-up n. a feast.

no skin off my ass (cp) no problem, no worries *Thompson:J.*

no skin off my nose! (cp) I don't care; it doesn't bother me *Dunne.*

no soap nothing doing, not a chance, no hope of that; poss. ex. US rhyming sl. bar of soap = dope, hence = no deal *Farrell.*

nosper n. (backsl.) person *Powis.*

no stuff (US Black use) no fooling, no lies, absolutely honest and sincere *Major.*

no sweat (excl.) no problem; don't worry; it's all right *Higgins:1.*

not a bean nothing at all, esp. of money *Chandler:LG*

not a brass razoo (Aus. use) absolutely penniless *Wilkes.*

not a hope in hell no chance whatsoever.

not all there a. eccentric, insane, crazy *Hotten.*

not an earthly no chance at all, absolutely impossible *Manser.*

not a sausage absolutely nothing (cf: sausage and mash) *Laurie.*

not backward in coming forward brash, direct and to the point (cf: accidentally on purpose).

notch n. the vagina *Rawson.*

notes n. pounds sterling *Capital Radio 1983.*

not give a hoot v. not to care less about a given subject/person *Wodehouse:MOJ.*

not half! (excl.) certainly! really! absolutely! *Manser.*

nothing doing absolutely not, not a hope/chance (cf: no dice) *Manser.*

nothing to write home about insignificant, unexciting (despite rumours to the contrary).

not much chop (Aus. use) unimpressive, substandard, no good; fr. Hindi *Chhap*: a brand *Wilkes.*

not much you wouldn't (cp) rejecting the previous speaker's protestations: don't fool me, you certainly would.

not my cup of tea not to my taste *Green:2.*

not on your life! (cp) no way at all, totally impossible.

not on your Nellie! (cp) not a chance (qv), absolutely impossible; fr. not on your Nellie Duff, rhyming sl. = puff = breath (of life), thus not on your life (qv) *Norman:1.*

not playing with a full deck a. not completely sane or competent; fr. card use *Price:2.*

not ready for people a. (US Black use) one who acts stupidly, childishly, who calls attention to their own idiocies *Folb.*

not so dusty a. actually, rather good, not as bad as expected or advertised.

not the foggiest not the first idea, no clue whatsoever; usu. as 'I haven't the foggiest', in answer to a query *Manser.*

not the full quid a. (Aus. use) mentally deficient, not all there (qv) *Wilkes.*

not to have both oars in the water (US campus use) anyone considered slightly insane, eccentric, odd *Bernbach.*

not tonight, Josephine (cp) general term of refusal; spec. of sex; allegedly first pleaded by the Emperor Napoleon to his wife.

not worth a bumper (Aus. use; cp) worthless, useless; fr. bumper (qv) *Wilkes.*

not worth a fart in a noisemaker (US cp) utterly useless *King.*

not worth a hill of beans absolutely useless *'Casablanca', 1941.*

not worth a light pointless, useless, worthless *Dury, 'Laughter', 1979.*

not worth a pisshole in the snow absolutely useless *Higgins:5.*

no way! (excl.) absolutely not; you must be joking! you can't fool me! etc. *Powis.*

nowhere n. an undesirable, tedious person, place, event or idea *Major.*

nowhere city n. irrelevant, pointless, of no use at all *Price:2.*

NQOCD (US preppie (qv) use) *N*ot *Q*uite *O*ur *C*lass, *D*ear *Barr.*

NSIT (UK 'society' use) (acro.) *N*ot *S*uitable *I*n *T*axis; note attached to the name of a prospective male escort by a debutante or her mother *T 18/7/83.*

nubian n. (US campus (spec. University of Arkansas) use) a socially unacceptable person; used for whites and Blacks despite obvious racist base *Underwood.*

nuddy a. naked, undressed; usu. a coy euph. used by those who find any sexual reference embarrassing (cf: down there).

nudge, nudge, wink, wink, know what I mean, say no more (cp) popularized by Eric Idle in 'Monty Python's Flying Circus' BBC-2 TV c.1969; Idle was dressed as a spiv and was making heavily sexual innuendos.

nudger n. (cant) pickpocket's assistant who nudges victims in a pre-selected direction, often into a crowded lift *Neaman & Silver.*

Nueva York n. New York; some reference to the large Puerto Rican population, but on the whole, merely an affectation *Pynchon.*

nuggety a. (Aus. use) chunky, squat, thickset; fr. shape of a gold nugget *Lawson.*

number n. **1.** a marijuana or hashish cigarette *Green:1*; **2.** (homosexual use) a casual partner picked up from the street, bar or baths *Stanley*; **3.** a performance; a scene, a display of excessive emotion *Goldman.*

number-cruncher n. (computer use) a large, sometimes slow machine which is used to make its way through volumes of maths that would defeat, by quantity rather than complexity, mere human efforts. *Green:2.*

number-cruncher course n. (US campus use) any course that involves a large amount of maths *Underwood.*

number one **1.** (US criminal use) first degree (pre-meditated) murder *Folb*; **2.** (milit. use) the best, fr. Korean and Vietnam wars (cf: number ten) *Webb.*

number ones n. (children's use) urination *May.*

numbers n. (gambling use) popular form of street gambling that involves predicting a combination of the winning numbers at a given racetrack; esp. widespread in US Black community.

number ten (milit. use) the worst, fr. Korean and Vietnamese Wars (cf: number one) *Webb.*

number twos n. (children's use) excretion *May.*

numb-nuts n. an idiot, a fool *Price:3.*

numbskull n. a fool, an idiot, an incompetent.

numero uno a. fr. Sp: number one, thus the best – of objects or persons *Price:1.*

nut n. **1.** the head *Wright*; **2.** (entertainment use) the break-even sum in a theatre or cinema after which profit starts *Vidal*; **3.** an insane person; thus *nut doctor*: any form of mental health specialist; *nut house*: mental hospital *Price:2.*

nut v. to butt one's opponent in the face, usu. the bridge of his nose, using one's own forehead.

nutcake n. a fool, an idiot, an eccentric *Higgins:5.*

nutcase n. an eccentric, an odd person.

nut house n. asylum, mental hospital *Thompson:J.*

nuts n. **1.** testicles *Price:2*; **2.** (US Black use) the clitoris (cf: cock) *Neaman & Silver.*

nuts a. insane *Price:2.*

nuts about obsessed with, usu. in the context of love *Baker.*

nuts and bolts the basics of a situation, the fundamental issues (cf: brass tacks).

nuts and sluts (US campus use) course in abnormal psychology *Bernbach.*

nutter n. a lunatic, an eccentric *Norman:2.*

nutting using the top of one's head to butt an opponent during a fight; such a blow can often end the fight instantly (cf: heading) *LL.*

nutty foolish, pleasantly eccentric; esp. in *nutty as a fruitcake SF Comics.*

nut up v. (US campus use) to lose one's temper completely, to go berserk *Underwood.*

nymph n. see: nympho *Bukowski:2.*

nympho n. (abbrev.) nymphomaniac, an allegedly sexually insatiable woman *Time Out, 3/84.*

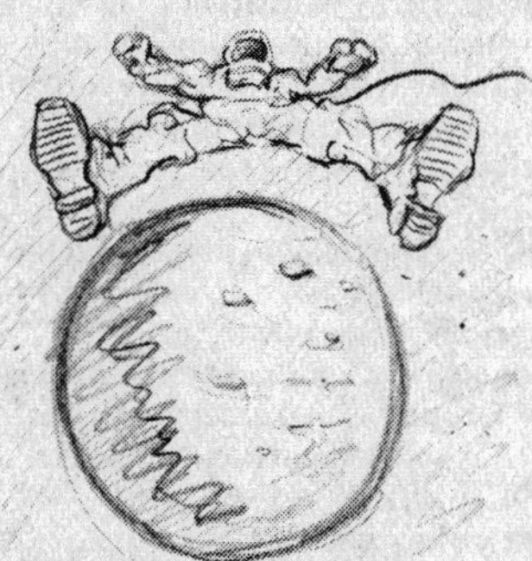

O n. (drug use) opium *Green: 1.*
oat (backsl.) two *Cole.*
oats n. sexual satisfaction.
obbo n. (UK police use) (abbrev.) observation (on a criminal, illicit club, etc.) *Laurie.*
OBC n. (US prison use) (acro.) *o*ld, *b*rutal *c*onvict; who uses experience and power to take advantage of younger, newer inmates *Neaman & Silver.*
obo n. (police use) observation, *on obo*: on surveillance of a criminal or place where a crime might occur *Newman.*
ocker n. (Aus. use) boorish, loutish, unsophisticated, ultra-nationalistic Australian; his rise, and celebration, coincided with the Labour govt. of Gough Whitlam c.1974; a corruption of Oscar, and popularized in a character named 'Ocker' portrayed by Aus. actor Ron Frazer in a TV series c.1975.
ock it! (excl.) (US campus (spec. University of Arkansas use) stop it *Underwood.*
OD v. (acro.) overdose (on drugs) *Jay & Young.*
oddball n. eccentric, odd, bizarre person *Uneeda Comix.*
odds v. to risk, to take a chance *Newman: 1.*
ofay a. white; fr. Yoruba *ofe* 'a charm that lets one jump so high as to disappear', thus trouble (the cause of such vanishing), thus a white man (the essence of trouble) *Southern.*
off n. (sporting use) the start of any race, esp. that of horses or dogs.
off v. **1.** to kill, esp. 1960s/70s radical use *Higgins: 2*; **2.** to have sexual intercourse (fr. male point of view) *Rawson.*
off-beat a. unconventional, out of the ordinary; fr. musical use *Bruce: 2.*
off-brand a. (US Black use) odd, eccentric, peculiar, bizarre *Folb.*
off-brand cigarette n. (drug use) a marijuana cigarette *Folb.*
off-colour a. (US criminal use) homosexual *Legman.*
office n. **1.** (US pimp use) wherever the pimp conducts his business, in this case, often the street or a neighbourhood bar; this borrowing of a trad. businessman's word, is common to such occupations as civil and military pilots: *office* = cockpit, and many others; **2.** (US prison use) a signal *Chandler: Notebk.*
off like a bride's nightie (Aus. use) extremely fast, very speedy *Wilkes.*
off one's bean a. **1.** insane, eccentric (cf: bean) **2.** drunk *Dickson.*
off one's cake a. crazy, insane (cf: off one's nut) *Bleasdale.*
off one's chump a. see; off one's rocker, off one's onion, etc.
off one's feed a. depressed, miserable, nervous.
off one's gourd a. insane, crazy

McFadden.

off one's nut a. mad. insane *Wright.*

off one's onion a. see: off one's rocker *Wodehouse: AAG.*

off one's rocker a. insane, crazy *Wodehouse: IJ.*

off-sider n. (Aus. use) assistant, helper *Bickerton.*

off the block n. local, a neighbour, a peer – always implying membership of the working class; someone who lives on the same street *Seale.*

off the cuff impromptu, spontaneous action or speech; fr. the practice of writing jokes or information on one's cuffs to aid a performer's memory.

off (the) beam wrong, mistaken, misdirected; often as *way off beam* fr. RAF use, refers to radio beams that guide aircraft.

off the hook out of trouble, freed of an difficult situation.

off the top the first and poss. most attractive portion of any share-out, legal or otherwise *Klein.*

off the top of one's head spontaneously, extempore, ad lib *Bruce: 2.*

off the track behaving badly, making mistakes, out of order (qv) *Howard.*

off the wall a. **1.** difficult, obstreperous, strange, peculiar; **2.** bizarre, peculiar *Greenlee*; **3.** spontaneously *McFadden.*

oggin n. (nautical use) the sea: fr. hog-wash *Green: 2.*

oh, my dear n. (rhyming sl.) beer *Wright.*

-oholic widely used suffix based on the obsessive nature of an *alcoholic*: thus *chocoholic*: one who cannot stop consuming chocolate, *bookoholic*: an obsessive reader, etc.

oik n. an unpleasant youth, a yob (qv) *May.*

oil n. **1.** (US Black use) alcohol, esp. wine *Folb*; **2.** graft, bribery, and the money for paying it (cf: juice, grease) *Major.*

oil burner habit n. an extremely heavy level of heroin addiction *Grogan.*

oiled a. aka: *oiled up*; drunk *Dickson.*

oil it v. (US campus use) to stay up late studying; fr. 'burning the midnight oil' *Underwood.*

oil out v. to escape one's responsibility, to escape from an onerous duty or similar situation; to slide away as if well-lubricated.

oily n. **1.**(rhyming sl.) oily rag = fag = cigarette; **2.** (prison use) a solitor's clerk, sometimes a solicitor, both of whom visit their imprisoned clients to 'clean up' their pre-trial problems *Cole.*

OK corruption of *orl korrect* and thus since at least 1839 a general term of agreement; despite the many conflicting claims as to the etymology of OK, this is that accepted by the *OED* Supplement (vol. III O–Scz, 1982 p.40).

oke-dokey see: OK *The People's Comic.*

okey-dokey (US Black use) **1.** white values and opinions; **2.** a swindle, a confidence trick *Major.*

old biddy n. old woman, fr. biddy = Bridget *Dunne.*

Old Bill n. the police *Newman: 1.*

old bill n. a police station *Robins.*

old boiler n. an old and unattractive woman (cf: boiler).

old cocker n. fr. Yiddish: *alte cacka*: old man, usu. disreputable *Price: 2.*

old coot n. foolish and/or cantankerous old person *Chandler: LG.*

old dog n. (US Black use) an expert in a given field *Klein.*

old Dutch n. the wife; fr. rhyming sl. Duchess of Fife (qv) *May.*

old Ear-ie see: on the Erie *Runyon.*

old enough to know better (cp) implying that someone who has just committed some blunder should not have done so.

old-fashioned look n. a disapproving glance.

old identity n. (Aus. use) anyone who has lived in the same place for a long time; a regular resident *Humphries: 2.*

oldie n. (usu. teen. or youth use) the old, esp. those over 40, or at least those who fail to share or appreciate the nuances and delights of the current version of the rebellious youth culture (cf: dusty, geri, wrinklies).

oldie but goodie n. something no longer fashionable or chic but still beloved by its owner/wearer/user (cf: golden oldie) *McFadden*.

old lady n. **1.** mother *Price: 2*; **2.** girl-friend; **3.** wife (actual or common law).

old man n. a woman's lover or husband.

old moody n. a cunning trick, a fraud; thus *to pull the old moody Norman: 1*.

Old Nassau n. (US college use) Princeton University *Bernbach*.

Old Nick Satan, the devil *Farrell*.

old one-two n. a knock out blow, either in an actual fight or as a metaphor; fr. boxing use *Heller*.

old sweat n. any veteran, orig. milit. use; fr. the sweating that resulted from one's labours *Wodehouse: MOJ*.

old timer n. (pimp use) an experienced, older but not necessarily run down prostitute; such women are often used to train up their younger recruits to a pimp's stable (qv) *OUI 8/75*.

oliver n. (abbrev.) Oliver Twist: a deliberately incorrect entry in a ledger; usu. bookmaker use: fr. rhyming sl. Oliver Twist = fist, thus to write *Powis*.

olly n. (rhyming sl.) fr. Oliver Reed (UK actor, 1938–) = speed = amphetamine drugs *Cole*.

OMCD (homosexual use) (acro.) *O*ut of *M*y *C*lass, *D*arling *Jay & Young*.

omee n. (theatrical use) a man; fr. 19th C. theatrical sl. *parlyaree* and one of the few survivors still in use (cf: polone).

omee-polone n. (theatrical use) a homosexual, fr. *parlyaree* wds for man and woman (cf: omee, polone).

on (backsl.) no *Cole*.

on, to be v. to be in agreement, to offer one's commitment, one's support; usu, as 'are you on?', 'I'm on!', etc.

on a bat a. drunk, on a drinking binge *Dickson*.

on a bender on a drinking spree *Dickson*.

on a brannigan a. very drunk *Dickson*.

on a bust drinking heavily *Dickson*.

on a good wicket in a secure, rewarding position; fr. cricket use. Thus *on a sticky wicket*: in difficulties, or about to face them *Humphries: 2*.

on a hiding to nothing with absolutely no chance; esp. in a sporting contest *ES 8/2/83*.

on a pension (UK police/criminal use) anyone receiving regular bribes *Powis*.

on appro (abbrev.) on approval *Wodehouse: PGM*.

on a promise (UK police/criminal use) awaiting a promised event, poss. money, a bribe, a tip-off, a material gift, etc. *Powis*.

on a rush (poker use) to be winning a succession of hands with unassailable ease *Alvarez*.

on a skate drinking heavily *Dickson*.

on at critical of, nagging, telling off.

on a tight leash **1.** deeply infatuated; **2.** kept under extreme control.

on a tipple a. very drunk *Dickson*.

on a toot on a spree, usu. involving drink, drugs and/or degeneracy *Wodehouse: PGM*.

once a week n. (rhyming sl.) cheek *Powis*.

once in a blue moon extremely rarely.

once in a month of Sundays (cp) exceptionally rarely.

oncer n. **1.** one pound note *J. le Carré, 'The Little Drummer Girl', 1983*; **2.** (homosexual use) a homosexual who never repeats a sexual encounter with any one partner but continues to seek new people *Legman*.

on contract (US police use) regularly accepting bribes *Neaman & Silver*.

on dab (UK police use) to be on a

disciplinary charge *Laurie*.

on doog (backsl.) no good *Cole*.

one n. (US Black use) (abbrev.) one big lie *Klein*.

— one nothing, not a single one: usu. with qualifying negative, eg 'He won't get dime one out of me', etc. *'Hill Street Blues', Thames TV, 1983*.

one away! (UK prison use) the cry of alarm from prison officers, signifying an escape.

one bill n. $100 (cf: bill) *Major*.

one brick short of a load not all there, slightly insane, eccentric *Humphries: 2*.

one-eyed brother n. the penis *Caserta*.

one-eyed scribe n. (US Black use) a monumental liar; an insignificant person, poss. because they cannot be trusted to tell the truth *Klein*.

one-eyed trouser snake n. the penis *Humphries*.

one for the road n. (cp) a final drink before parting; presumably coined prior to the invention of the internal combustion engine.

one good woman n. (US Black use) the ideal soulmate, helpful, considerate, sympathetic, prob, sexy too; hardly a feminist paradigm *Klein*.

one-hand magazine n. a pornographic magazine, used as an aid to masturbation (cf: stroke book) *Wolfe: 5*.

one hundred per cent feeling very well, cheerful, high-spirited, etc.

one-legged race n. masturbation *Dury, 'Laughter', 1979*.

one-lunger n.a single cylinder motorcycle *Selby: 1*.

one night stand n. **1.** an affair that lasts only a single night *Higgins: 1*; **2.** (rock business use) the giving of only one performance in a specific venue prior to moving on.

one off the wrist the act of masturbation.

one of these morning's you'll wake up and find yourself dead (cp) addressed to a very dozy, dull person.

one-on-one a. person-to-person, intimate *McFadden*.

one over the eight a. drunk; the eight being pints, a supposed 'safe' amount of beer.

one percenter n. (Hells Angel use) an outlaw bike rider; that 1 per cent of motorcycle users who refuse to abide by the rules and the law *Thompson*.

one-pot screamer n. (Aus. use) aka: *two-pot screamer* one who cannot hold their liquor without becoming obstreperously drunk; they only need one or two drinks before they lose all control *Bickerton*.

one-shot credit n. (drug dealer use) for the dealer to allow a client to default on a payment once only; any subsequent slip-ups will be met with violence *Thames TV, 1983*.

one's number to be up v. to die; to lose one's opportqnity or chance; to meet with one's unpleasant fate *rr*.

one to meet n. an appointment *Newman*.

one-two-three at once, immediately, speedily *Larner*.

on fire (US campus use) anyone who has just made a glaring social error (cf: flamer) *Bernbach*.

on flake (US Black use) passed out, unconscious (cf: flaked out) *Folb*.

on ice **1.** in reserve; **2.** out of the way *Price: 2*.

on it indulging (poss. to a noticeable excess) in a given drug, drugs or alcohol.

on jankers in prison; esp. in UK milit. use *Wodehouse passim*.

on my life! (excl.) an affirmation of absolute truth in the face of an audience's scepticism. one of those cliché phrases forced on every stage Jew *Payne*.

on offer liable to problems *Newman: 1*.

on one's ass, to be v.i. to pester, to harass, to annoy *Dunne*.

on one's case v. to harass, to persecute, to pursue *McFadden*.

on one's high horse arrogant, acting superior, etc. *Neaman & Silver*.

on one's Jack (rhyming sl.) Jack

Jones = alone *Norman: 4*.

on one's job (US Black use) well in control; successful at a given task *Folb*.

on one's last legs *in extremis*, 'at the end of one's tether', in great and seemingly irrefutable distress.

on one's Pat (Aus. use; rhyming sl.) Pat Malone = alone (cf: on one's Tod) *Wilkes*.

on one's say-so on one's word of honour, on trust.

on one's Tod (rhyming sl.) Tod Sloan = alone; fr. the jockey *Norman: 2*.

on one's uppers in great poverty, without any money, broke (qv); fr. the uppers of one's shoes, the soles having long since worn away, unmended through lack of cash *Powis*.

on speakers on speaking terms; usu. only found amongst devotees of Jessica Mitford's 'Hons & Rebels' 1960.

on spec at a risk, without making a firm decision; fr. speculation.

on the ball sophisticated, aware, up to date; fr. sporting use *Junker*.

on the bash **1.** working the streets as a prostitute (cf: bash) *Norman: 2*; **2.** (Aus./NZ use) to go out on a heavy bout of drinking.

on the bat **1.** out for a good, drunken, sexy, brawling time; **2.** working as a prostitute *LL*.

on the batter see: on the bat *LL*.

on the battle (Aus. use) working as a prostitute (cf: on the bat, batter, etc.) *Neaman & Silver*.

on the bottle (UK cant) stealing by picking pockets in a crowd *Cole*.

on the beam (US Black use) right on course, heading in the right direction *Klein*.

on the blink malfunctioning, working badly *Dunne*.

on the booze drinking heavily *Dickson*.

on the bottle **1.** drinking heavily; **2.** (UK use) working as a male prostitute; fr. rhyming sl. bottle and glass (qv); **3.** (US use) working in any form of prostitution; fr. rhyming sl. as **2** *Cole*.

on the bow see: on the elbow *Powis*.

on the bricks in the street, esp. of a prostitute's beat *Dunne*.

on the button **1.** right on target, usu. of a blow *Runyon*; **2.** up to the minute; fully aware *Higgins: 2*.

on the case (US pimp use) for a prostitute to be earning steadily and regularly from a given client *Klein*.

on the chopping block in a very disadvantageous position.

on the clock (taxi-driver use) the hiring of a cab by a freelance taxi-driver who then pays its owner a percentage of what is on the clock at the end of his working with the cab *Powis*.

on the coat (Aus. use) out of favour, 'getting the cold shoulder' *Wilkes*.

on the corn (Aus. prison use) to be serving time in goal; fr. hominy diet therein *Neaman & Silver*.

on the cuff on account; for free; fr. earlier practice of pencilling debts in shops or bars on a (celluloid) cuff *Higgins: 2*.

on the deck (milit. use) at ground level ; usu, air force term *Wolfe: 5*.

on the dot with perfect timing, absolutely promptly *Wodehouse: AAG*.

on the double fast, fr. milit. double-time *Capital Radio 1983*.

on the drip purchased on the hire purchase scheme; one's cash just drips away (cf: on the never-never).

on the earhole (UK criminal use) on the scrounge *Powis*.

on the earie (criminal use) cf: on the earhole *Schulberg*.

on the edge a. (US campus use) nervous, neurotic *Underwood*.

on the elbow on the scrounge *Powis*.

on the Erie! (US prison use) aka: *on the Ear-ie*: (excl.) be quiet, someone is listening! *Chandler: Notebk*.

on the fence (homosexual use) turning to heterosexuality (cf: lose one's gender) *Legman*.

on the flip side on the other side, on the reverse, 'on the other hand'; fr.

record industry use *McFadden*.

on the floor a. **1.** (rhyming sl.) poor *Cole*; **2.** drunk *Dickson*.

on the fritz a. **1.** drunk *Dickson*; **2.** of machinery: broken down, not working.

on the game involved in prostitution *Norman: 2*.

on the go active, lively.

on the grog a. aka: *on the sauce, on the juice*, etc.: very drunk.

on the hill a. pregnant *Selby: 1*.

on the hoof passing by; casual *White*.

on the hook playing truant *Pynchon*.

on the hop running away, escaping, on the run.

on the house free, a gift of the management, publican, etc. *'Minder', Thames TV, 1980 passim*.

on the hurry up at great speed, in a hurry *Powis*.

on the Jersey side on the wrong side, usu. jazz sl.; New York (esp. Manhattan) is the 'right side' *Goldman*.

on the job engaged in sexual activity *Capital Radio 1983*.

on the knocker **1.** (UK criminal use) touring houses, ostensibly to buy or sell goods, but specifically to trick or bully people into selling heirlooms, antiques, etc. for minimal prices *Powis*; **2.** (Aus. use) at once, on demand, esp. of cash payments *Wilkes*.

on the lam on the run from prison *A. Karpis, 'The AlvinKarpis Story', 1971*.

on the level honest; straightforward *Higgins: 2*.

on the line at stake; fr. gambling use *Grogan*.

on the make looking to benefit oneself, ambitious, keen to do whatever will be most useful for one's own advancement; esp. sexually *Waits*.

on the money excellent, perfect, just right; fr. betting use *W. Allen, 'Manhattan', 1979*.

on the Murray cod (Aus. use) in gambling, rhyming sl. on the nod = betting on credit *Wilkes*.

on the muscle **1.** (US prison use) quarrelsome, ready for trouble, picking fights *Chandler: Notebk*; **2.** working as protection for a top gangster *Schulberg*.

on the needle (drug use) addicted to narcotics.

on the nest (US use) pregnant *Neaman & Silver*.

on the never-never bought by the hire purchase credit system (cf: on the drip).

on the nod under the influence of heroin *Burroughs: 1*.

on the nose **1.** (UK use) in betting, a wager on the winning horse: '£5.00 on the nose' . . .; **2.** (Aus. use) unpleasant, lit. smelly, and thus offensive morally/aesthetically as well as in the nostrils *Wilkes*.

on the outer (Aus. use) to be unpopular, to be out of favour *Wilkes*.

on the outs to be out of luck, money, favour, popularity, etc. *D. McLintick, 'Indecent Exposure', 1983*.

on the pavement (UK police use) an arrest carried out in the street *ST 3/4/83*.

on the plastic (UK criminal/police use) using stolen credit cards for a variety of frauds and swindles *Powis*.

on the QT surreptitiously; on the quiet *Vidal*.

on the rag **1.** menstruating; thus, by derivation; **2.** irritated, testy, bad-tempered *Underwood*.

on the ran-dan on a spree *Howard*.

on the razzle indulging in a series of parties, binges, and general self-indulgent excesses.

on the rebound a relationship that is initiated less through attraction than to exorcise one that has recently collapsed.

on the rocks (drinkers' use) with ice-cubes or cracked ice.

on the Rory (rhyming sl.) Rory O'More = on the floor = penniless *Powis*.

on the sauce drinking heavily and consistently *Neaman & Silver*.

on the shelf **1.** put on one side for unspecified future use; **2.** of a girl: unmarried and, given the married state of most of her contemporaries, worried about it; feeling that as a person she is becoming **1** *Hotten*.

on the short end (gambling use) at the unfavourable end of the odds; thus in a 20-1 bet the 1 is the short end *Heller*.

on the skids on a social and economic decline; fr. mixture of a slide downwards and skid row (qv) *Humphries: 2*.

on the slate on credit; fr. practice of writing such debts on a slate *Payne*.

on the sleeve using narcotics; fr. the rolling up of a sleeve prior to the injection *Algren*.

on the spot (US police/criminal use) marked for death, the subject of a contract (qv) for assassination *Himes: 1*.

on the square living an honest, law-abiding (and tedious) life (cf: square) *Algren*.

on the stick efficient, aware, in control (cf: on the ball) *Price: 3*.

on the stones **1.** homeless; **2.** in the open air, usu. referring to a fight, often with sidebets and between local champions, arranged outside the normal boxing world *Robins*.

on the street out of gaol; in public life *Higgins: 1*.

on the take (criminal use) of a policeman – one who accepts bribes *Austin*.

on the tiles out all night having a riotous good time; fr. the nocturnal exploits of cats; usu. in a '*a night on . . .*' *Hotten*.

on the tin (US police use) free, gratis; fr. those gifts and favours – often free meals, drinks – obtained by showing one's official badge.

on the trot hiding away from the police to avoid an arrest; usu. by leaving one's home/town, etc. *Newman: 1*.

on the up and up in an increasingly favourable, lucky, pleasant situation.

on the whiz working as a pickpocket, one of the *whiz mob Powis*.

on the wagon voluntarily stopping drinking alcohol. orig, abbrev. for 'on the water-wagon' *Norman: 3*.

on the wire generally known, going the rounds of gossip and rumour (cf: bush telegraph) *X*.

on the wrist free, esp. in police (US) use for obtaining food, drink etc. on the strength of a badge *Greaser Comics*.

on tick on credit *Sillitoe*.

on top of having sexual intercourse with *Wilkinson*.

on velvet secure, cheerful, a life without problems *Schulberg*.

on your bike! (excel.) go away, be off with you.

oogie n. (Southern US campus use) derog. reference to Black students; fr. boogie (qv) *Underwood*.

OP (Can. prison use) (acro.) *O*ff *P*rivilege, restricted *Caron*.

op n. (abbrev.) a surgical operation *Humphries: 2*.

open game n. (US pimp use) a prostitute with no specific affiliation to one stable (qv) *Klein*.

open slather n. (Aus. use) a situation with no restrictions or limits to one's wishes *Wilkes*.

operator n. **1.** the controller of a gambling game; **2.** a major criminal *Higgins: 1*.

OPM (acro.) *O*ther *P*eople's *M*oney: the ideal commodity in the eyes of any entrepreneur; if one's deals fail, one loses nothing of one's own; if they work out one is profiting without investment *NYT 2/82*.

oppo n. (abbrev.) opposite number: best friend *Minder, Thames TV, 1980*.

orb v. (US teen. use) to stare at, to look over (cf: eyeball) *Sculatti*.

orchestra stalls n. (rhyming sl.) balls (qv) = testicles *Jones: J*.

ordinary n. (US Black use) one's regular female companion *Klein*.

oreo n. (US Black use) derog. description of a fellow Black whose colour may be Black, but whose opinions, attitudes, lifestyle and goals are all taken from white society and standards; fr. 'oreo cookie' a popular US biscuit which is black on the outside and white within.

original (Black use) a fellow Black person; thus *all-originals party*: a party for Blacks only *Milner*.

originals n. (Hells Angel use) the Levi jeans and jacket (with sleeves cut off) which are worn at an Angel initiation ceremony liberally soiled and 'worn in' and which the rider wears every day until they fall to pieces *Thompson*.

Oscar n. (Aus. rhyming sl.) Oscar Asche = cash *Humphries*.

ossifer n. joking, slightly derog. ref to a police officer.

ossified a. extremely high (qv) on a given drug; a pun on stoned (qv) *Folb*.

OT & E (UK 'society' use) (acro) *O*ver-*T*ired and *E*motional; usu. describing a fractious child *Barr*.

OTT see: over the top.

Otto n. (derog.) German, with implication of lumpenprole stolidity *Price: 3*.

out (abbrev.) out of pocket, poor, in debt *Higgins: 1*.

out and out n. (US Black use) a totally unacceptable person; fr. 'an out and out villain/nightmare', etc. *Klein*.

outasite a. excellent, wonderful, top quality (cf: out of sight) *The People's Comic*.

outers **1.** unacceptable, distasteful; fr. out of order (qv) *Cole*; **2.** (UK criminal use) a means of escape *Powis*.

outfit n. **1.** (UK prison use) whatever is needed for attempting a given escape *LL*; **2.** the equipment – needle, spoon, cotton, etc. – used for narcotic injection (cf: works) *Grogan*; **3.** (US campus use) anyone seen as odd or eccentric, who fails to fit in *Underwood*.

outfront open, honest, uninhibited (cf: upfront) *Wolfe: 2*.

outhouse n. (US prison use) a 'half-way house' or hostel, in which newly released prisoners or parolees can learn to re-acclimatize themselves to the 'real' world *Klein*.

outlaw n. (Black pimp use) a prostitute without a regular pimp; any independent prostitute; thus outside the pimp 'laws' *Milner*.

out like a light collapsing – through a blow, drink, drugs, exhaustion – instantly.

out of it **1.** unable to function adequately because of one's intoxication by drugs or alcohol; **2.** tired, exhausted *Underwood*.

out of left field a. peculiar, eccentric, in poor taste; fr. baseball use *Goldman*.

out of line breaking rules, unacceptable, out of the ordinary *J. Jackson, 'I'm the Man', 1980*.

out of one's brain a. intoxicated with drugs *The Who, 'Quadrophenia', 1973*.

out of one's gourd a. extremely affected by a given drug, usu. cannabis or a hallucinogen; fr. gourd = head *Wolfe: 2*.

out of one's mind a. **1.** intoxicated, either through drink or drugs; **2.** crazy, insane *Higgins: 3*.

out of one's nut a. see: out of one's mind *Bruce: 2*.

out of one's skull a. see: out of one's mind *Bruce: 2*.

out of order unacceptable, excessive, in bad taste: of events, behaviour, people *Dury*.

out of pocket (Black use) unacceptable, tasteless behaviour; fr. pool use when an 'out of pocket' shot causes a player to miss a turn (cf: out of order) *Milner*.

out of sight a. excellent, first rate, exceptional (cf: outasite, far out) *Seale*.

out of state a. (US campus use) pun on out of sight (qv) *Underwood*.

out of the blue surprising, quite unsuspected; a 'bolt from the blue' (sky).

out of the box a. (Aus. use) exceptional, well above average *Wilkes*.

out of the picture a. irrelevant,

unimportant; fr. cinema use.
out of this world a. fantastic, amazing, wonderful, etc.
out of whack off centre, out of true, out of order *Bruce: 1.*
out of your tree a. out of your mind, insane *Price :2.*
out on a limb in a difficult situation, in trouble; the limb is one found on a tree.
out on one's ear ejected unceremoniously, thrown out.
outside a. (Can. prison use) out of prison; the world of free people *Caron.*
out to lunch a. **1.** crazy, eccentric, weird; **2.** intoxicated by drink or drugs both imply a secretary announcing 'he's not here' of her boss (cf: not all there).
out with disenchanted with, opposed to *Seale.*
over a barrel in another's power, at a great disadvantage; thus *to have over a barrel*: to dominate, to control.
overboard a. over-enthusiastic, very keen; thus *to go overboard Higgins: 1.*
overs n. (UK criminal use) proceeds of a theft that can, if not carefully disposed of, become vulnerable themselves to further theft, poss. by one of the gang *Powis.*
over the fence (Aus. use) extreme, beyond the bounds of taste (cf: beyond the rabbit-proof fence, over the top) *Wilkes.*
over the hill n. a deserter from the armed forces *R. Stone, 'A Flag for Sunrise', 1981.*
over the hill a. worn out, finished, useless, too old *Dury, 'Laughter', 1979.*
over the hill ho n. see: fleabag *OUI 8/75.*
over the moon a. extremely cheerful, most delightful; cliché response attributed to sportsmen, esp. soccer players, when interviewed about a successful game or competition (cf: sick as a parrot).
over the side (UK police use) to be about one's private business, usu. sexual, when one should be on duty, fr. nautical use *Laurie.*
over the top beyond the usual bounds (of taste, of behaviour, etc.), esp. entertainment use where often cut to OTT (qv) *J. le Carré, 'The Little Drummer Girl', 1983.*
over the top a. very drunk *Wilkinson.*
Oxford scholar n. (rhyming sl.) a dollar (qv) = 5s. = 25p *Jones: J.*
oyster n. a girl (cf: spear the bearded clam) *Schulberg.*
OZ n. (drug use) one ounce of marijuana (cf: LB) *Green: 1.*

p.a. n. (acro.) *p*ublic *a*ddress system.

pace v. (US Black use) to live a fast, exciting and varied life *Klein.*

pachuco n. aka: *cholo*; a Mexican-American street gang youth *AS 50: 1–2 (1975).*

pack v. to live as a female tramp, travelling the country; fr. the backpack she carries *Klein.*

pack 'em v. (Aus. use) to be frightened; fr. image of holding back fear-induced diarrhoea *Lambert.*

packet n. **1.** a large sum of money, esp. in win a packet *Wodehouse:MOJ*; **2.** (UK gay use) the genitals, male or female (cf: box, basket) *Maledicta.*

pack in v. to stop.

pack it in v. to stop doing something; usu. as a command *Dury, 'Do It Yourself'.*

pack peanut butter v. to engage in anal intercourse *Folb.*

pad n. a place, house or apartment. orig. an opium den, thence to beatnik use: where one could smoke cannabis, currently general use (if dated) *Grogan.*

pad a bill v. the fraudulent addition of items to a bill or to expense account statements in order to obtain money that one is not actually owed *Heller.*

padding crib n. (US criminal use) a place to hide or to rest; fr. 19th C. UK cant *Klein.*

paddy n. (US Black use) **1.** white man, though not always Irish; **2.** spec. policeman; fr. large numbers of Irish on the force *Seale*; **3.** (UK prison use) (abbrev.) a padded cell for prisoners who have 'done their nut' (qv) in one way or another *LL.*

Paddy Irishman; fr. common Irish name: Patrick (cf: Mick) *Greenlee.*

paddy wagon n. (criminal/police use) the vehicle in which arrested people are transported to the local police station or gaol; either fr. paddy, abbrev. padlock, or Paddy, inference that most US police would be Irish *Seale.*

padre n. a (military) chaplain *Hotten.*

pads n. (UK prison use) (abbrev.) padded cell (cf: paddy) *LL.*

page three girl n. a pin-up; fr. the use by tabloid newspapers of under-dressed models in their pages as part of their ongoing rivalry; the *Sun* launched the battle and still has its girl on p.3; the *Daily Mirror* followed with p.5, but has recently excised such girls and the *Daily Star* offers p.7, but with colour to boot.

pain in the ass n. an annoying person *Higgins:1.*

pain in the neck n. an annoying person, a euph. for pain in the ass (qv) *Wodehouse:PGM.*

paint the town red v. to go on a spree.

paisan n. an Italian; usu. used by fellow-members of that race in an affectionate and congratulatory manner (cf: landsman) *Heller.*

Paki aka *Pakki* (derog. abbrev.) Pakistani.

Paki-bashing racially motivated attacks on the UK Pakistani community, esp. by white skinhead (qv) youths (cf: queer-bashing).

pal n. a friend, an accomplice; fr. Romany.

paleface n. a white person *J. Pilger, 'The Last Day', Thames TV 1983.*

paleface nigger n. (US Black use) a highly disliked white person; whose skin does not save him from opprobrium usu. heaped on Blacks *Klein.*

pally a. friendly, affectionate fr. pal (qv) (cf: chummy) *Wodehouse:AAG.*

palm v. to pass over money as a bribe *Higgins:5.*

palm-presser n. a politician who attemps to curry favour and win votes by shaking hands with anyone he/she meets (cf: flesh-presser).

palooka n. a boxer, usually one who is both large and stupid; coined by Jack Conway (d.1928) of *Variety* magazine, and given wide currency by Ham Fisher's comic strip 'Joe Palooka' (launched 1930) *Schulberg.*

palsy-walsy a. overly friendly fr. pal (qv) + reduplication *Wodehouse:AAG.*

pan n. face *Runyon.*

pan v. to survey, to look around; fr. film use *Price:3.*

pancake n. attractive young girl; an example of sex as food (cf: cookie, etc.) *Runyon.*

panhandler n. one who begs in the street; fr. a begging-bowl *Burroughs:1.*

panic stations n. a crisis, a drama; orig. naval use and punning on 'action stations'.

pan out v. to work out, to result in; fr. panning for gold *'Minder', Thames TV, 1983.*

pansy n. (derog.) effeminate homosexual male (cf: nola) *Legman.*

panther piss n. homebrewed liquor *Bukowski:2.*

panties n. (US prison use) the underwear worn by a prison homosexual *Klein.*

pants v. to remove someone's trousers whether they like it or not mainly juv. use (cf: debag) *Dickson.*

papa n. a masculine lesbian; fr. juv. use: father *Legman.*

paper n. **1.** a measure of heroin, contained in a folded square of paper (cf: bindle) *Grogan*; **2.** any form of money order, IOU, financial documents others than actual cash *Higgins:3.*

paper hanger n. (criminal use) one who habitually passes bad cheques; fr. pun on decorator *Breslin.*

paper pusher n. the lowliest rank of bureaucrat/clerk; the implication being that he never writes on, only pushes, paper *PT.*

papers n. cigarette papers, esp. when used for rolling marijuana joints (qv) *Folb.*

paracki n. paraldehyde *Higgins:1.*

paraffin lamp (rhyming sl.) a tramp *Dury.*

parallel parking n. (US preppie (qv) use) sexual intercourse *Bernbach.*

paralytic a. extremely drunk, to the point of passing out cold *Bernbach.*

paranoid a. frightened, worried, disturbed; all non-clinical uses orig. in 1960s hippie era, often occasioned by an excess of drug use; fr. 'Paranoia: functional psychosis characterized by delusions of grandeur and persecution, but without intellectual deterioration. . .' *C. Rycroft, 'A Critical Dictionary of Psychoanalysis', 1968.*

pardon my French 'genteel' euph.: excuse my swearing *Mortimer.*

par for the course (cp) as expected, predictable, nothing special.

park a custard v. (UK 'society' use) to vomit *Barr.*

parking n. (US teenage rite) couples use the boy's car parked in a discreet spot for petting and poss. intercourse *Higgins:1.*

parking place n. the buttocks

Neaman & Silver.

park your carcase an invitation to 'sit down'; US radio comedian Harry Einstein (1904–58) used the pseudonym 'Parkyakarkus'.

parlour pink n. a Socialist whose activism is limited by the confines of his dinner table and does not extend on to the streets, let alone the barricades.

part brass rags v. to part on bad terms; fr. naval custom of two sailors when on good terms sharing their cleaning rags *Wodehouse:AAG.*

particulars n. (US prison use) any member of the authorities with immediate effect on a prisoner's life: a warder, the sentencing judge, the parole board, etc. *Klein.*

party n. any form of sex act, usu. provided by a prostitute *Legman.*

party v. to enjoy oneself *Seale.*

party hop v. to move from one party to the next and so on during the course of a single evening and night (cf: island hop) *Underwood.*

party pooper n. a spoilsport; one who sabotages the pleasures and enjoyments of their companions, whether at a party or other amusement *Whitcomb.*

pash n. a crush (qv); usu. between junior and senior pupils of girls' schools; fr. passionate *R. Boycott, 'A Nice Girl Like Me', 1984.*

pass v. **1.** for a Jew to pretend to be a Christian *Bruce:2*; **2.** for a homosexual to appear straight (qv) to those he/she encounters *Jay & Young.*

pass in one's dinner pail v. to die.

passion-killers n. any female underwear deemed to reduce the chances of (male) exploration; orig. milit. use.

passion pit n. (lesbian use) the vagina *Maledicta.*

passion wagon any vehicle, often a van, in which teenage boys hope to seduce girls.

paste v. to hit *Wright.*

pasting n. a violent assault, a beating up *Runyon:1.*

past praying for utterly hopeless, usu. of a person, poss. of a broken down car.

patacca n. fr. Ital.: worthless rubbish, spec. fake jewellery such as counterfeit Cartier watches, etc. *Powis.*

patch n. (UK police use) a policeman's area of operations (cf: manor) *'Parkin's Patch', TV series title, c.1975.*

patch v. (Can. prison use) to arrange for bribes to be paid, corrupt deals to be made, etc. (cf: fix) *Caron.*

Pat Malone (rhyming sl.) alone (cf: Tod Sloan) *Humphries.*

pat one down v. to submit someone to a body search *Higgins:1.*

patootie n. attractive young girl *Esq. 1977.*

patsy n. a fool, a sucker (qv); fr. the popular Irish name, Patrick and thus an example of racial cliché, in this case Irish stupidity *Variety 1983.*

pattin' leather (US Black use) a reference to being out of work *Folb.*

pavement princess n. (Citizens' Band radio use) prostitute *CB.*

paws n. hands *Hotten.*

paybacks n. (US Black use) the retaliation by one person for insults or bad treatment from another; fr. financial use *Klein.*

payday stakes n. (gambling use) betting on credit, against the guarantee of one's forthcoming wages *Seale.*

pay-off n. **1.** a final payment for services rendered; **2.** the denouement of a book, film or play; **3.** one's deserts.

pay-off queen n. (homosexual use) anyone who regularly pays for his sex *Legman.*

payola n. the practice (ostensibly illegal and generally denied by its practitioners) of bribing (with cash or kind) those with access to the public to tout a given product; esp. common in the record business where disc jockeys are offered massive inducements to push a certain record or artist. Major scandals in the US c.1959 supposedly ended payola, but such optimism is quite illusory and cosmetic at best (cf: lurkola).

pay one's dues v. to undergo (usually) undesirable experiences before one attains a given desirable goal; the moral stance is unsaid *Bruce:1.*

PC (UK police/criminal use) (abbrev.) *P*revious *C*onviction *LL.*

pc (UK 'society' use) (abbrev.) *p*ost*c*ard *Barr*; **2.** (medical use) (abbrev.) Pinky Cheater = thin rubber gloves used during gynaecological examinations *Southern & Hoffenberg*; **3.** (abbrev.) *p*olitically *c*orrect, ideologically pure, etc. Esp. popular among US Women's Movt, New Left, etc. *Maledicta.*

P check n. (UK milit. use) (abbrev.) personality check: for establishing identification *A.F.N. Clarke, 'Contact', 1983.*

PDA (US preppie (qv) use) (acro.) *P*ublic *D*isplay of *A*ffection; kissing and cuddling in public *Neaman & Silver.*

pdq (abbrev.) *p*retty *d*amn *q*uick.

pea n. (Aus. use) the ideal, the perfect choice, the favourite; fr. 19th C. UK use *Wilkes.*

peacemaker n. (US Black use) **1.** the penis; **2.** a pistol or revolver (not only Black use) *Klein.*

peach n. a pretty young girl *Klein.*

peachy a. wonderful, excellent, delightful, etc. *Uris.*

peak v. **1.** to reach the limit of a particular experience; **2.** (drug use) the two hours or so in an LSD trip when the hallucinogen is at its most powerful.

peanut gallery n. **1.** spec. the top gallery, the 'gods' in a theatre; **2.** ignorant, vociferous spectators *Grogan*; both meanings assume a large consumption of peanuts by those so defined.

peanuts n. anything insignificant, petty; esp. money, wages *Schulberg:2.*

pearl diver n. a dish washer in a hotel or restaurant *Chandler: Notebk.*

peas in the pot a. (rhyming sl.) hot *Cole.*

peasouper n. a very dense fog; orig. the pollution-based London fogs, but since the Clean Air legislation of 1950s, any exceptionally impenetrable fog.

peck n. **1.** (US Black use) food *Klein*; **2.** see: peckerwood.

peck v. (US Black use) to eat *Klein.*

pecker n. penis *Selby:1.*

peckerwood n. (US Black use (mainly)) white person (derog.) fr. the red woodpecker, symbol of whites, rather than the black crow, symbol of blacks *Folb.*

pecking and necking n. (US Black use) sexual foreplay, kissing and cuddling *Klein.*

peckish a. hungry (cf: peck) *Hotten.*

pecks n. (drug and street gang use) food *Salisbury.*

pedal one's dogs v. to leave, to go away; esp. as an order 'pedal your dogs!'; fr. dogs = feet (qv) *Goulart.*

peddle pussy v. to work as a prostitute *Alvarez.*

pee v. to urinate; fr. abbrev./euph. for piss (qv) *Price:2.*

peek freak n. a homosexual voyeur who watches two other men during sex; fr. SE peek: to glance at, albeit briefly *Stanley.*

peel v. to strip off one's clothes *Klein.*

peel down v. see: peel.

peep n. a word; thus *not a peep*: saying nothing *Runyon:1.*

pee-pee lover n. (homosexual use) one who prefers the youngest boys for sex; fr. childish *pee-pee*: penis *Legman.*

peeper n. **1.** a private investigator; with implications of voyeurism *Chandler:LG.* **2.** (abbrev.) Peeping Tom: a voyeur *Laurie.*

peepers n. eyes *Humphries.*

peep one's hole card v. (US Black use) to work out a person's hidden motives, ideas, opnions, etc. *Klein.*

peer queer n. see: peek freak *Stanley.*

pee-wee n. nickname for any

noticeably small person.
peg v. to recognize *Jay & Young.*
pegged off under surveillance: fr. peg (qv) *rr.*
pegged out dead; fr. cribbage use (cf: cash in one's chips, etc.) *Rawson.*
peg-house n. a male brothel; fr. East Indian equivalents where the boys allegedly sat on wooden pegs to maintain a well-distended anus *Legman.*
peg out v. to die *Wright.*
pelter n. a horse; esp. a fast one *Runyon:1.*
pen (abbrev.) penitentiary *Farrell.*
pen and ink v. (rhyming sl.) stink *Norman:2.*
pencil geek n. (US campus use) (derog.) anyone who works more devotedly than his/her peers see fit *Bernbach.*
pencil-pusher n. **1.** a clerk; a white-collar worker *Selby:1*; **2.** a journalist *'Hill Street Blues', Thames TV, 1983.*
pencil-squeezer n. masturbator *Dury, 'Clever Bastards', 1978.*
penitentiary agent n. (US cant) a lawyer who seems to be working more for the courts and police than for the defence of his client *Neaman & Silver.*
penman n. (UK criminal use) a forger *LL.*
penny-ante a. small-time, second-rate, insignificant; fr. poker use *Vidal.*
penocha n. (US Black/Sp. use) vagina *Folb.*
people n. (US Black use) narcotics agents *Major.*
pep-em-ups n. (drug use) amphetamine; thus *pep pills Folb.*
pepper and salt (US Black use) black and white people running together in the street *Klein.*
pepper 'em up v. (US Black use) **1.** to prepare for something; **2.** to get drunk or high (qv) on drugs; **3.** to work out in a gym; **4.** to fight and possibly injure one's assailant; all imply some preparatory seasoning *Klein.*
pepper-kissing a. negative intensifier, thus no good, useless, etc. *Folb.*
peppy a. cheerful, enthusiastic.
perch n. (US campus (spec. University of Arkansas) use) a pint of liquor *Underwood.*
percher n. (UK criminal/police use) **1.** a gullible victim for a swindle or con-game; **2.** a simple arrest *Powis.*
percy n. the penis *Humphries.*
perfecto! (excl.) wonderful, excellent, perfect *'Hill Street Blues', Thames TV, 1983.*
perform v. (UK criminal use) to commit a given crime *LL.*
perishing a. general intensifier: *perishing cold*, *perishing hard*, etc. *Green:2.*
perk-up v. to improve, to cheer up.
perky a. jolly, cheerful.
perp n. (US police use) (abbrev.) perpetrator; the accused criminal *Neaman & Silver.*
persuader n. a weapon, usu. pistol or revolver, which persuades victims to its wielder's point of view *Klein.*
perv n. (abbrev.) pervert, spec. child-molester.
perv about v. to search for potential sexual conquests; the use of perv here is facetious rather than an actual reference to any sexual eccentricity.
pete-man n. (Can. prison use) safebreaker (Cf: peter **2**) *Caron.*
peter n. **1.** the penis *Jay & Young*; **2.** safe; **3.** cell *Cole.*
Peter-Jay n. (US Black use) the police *Folb.*
peter-man n. safecracker.
Petricelli n. (US Black use) a high fashion suit, fr. brand-name of tailors *Klein.*
petrified a. very drunk; fr. sense of being turned to stone rather than that of fear *Neaman & Silver.*
petrols n. (Aus. rhyming sl.) petrol bowsers = trousers *Humphries.*
pg (drug use) (abbrev.) *p*arago*r*ic; a cough medicine based on opium linctus which heroin addicts use when no stronger drugs are available *Burroughs:1.*
PH (drug use) (acro.) *P*urple *H*earts: amphetamine pills (cf: blues) *Keyes.*
pheasant plucker n. reverse of

'pleasant fucker', and always used ironically to attack the person so named *Dury*.

phiz n. face; fr. physiognomy *Algren*.

phlegm-cutter n. the first drink of the day, usu. that taken by an alcoholic soon after waking up (cf: eye-opener) *Higgins:5*.

Phoebe n. (gambling use) the point of five in craps dice *Algen*.

phone freak n. (pimp use) a client who arranges to phone up a prostitute and listen while she runs through a pornographic monologue and he masturbates *OUI 8/75*.

phoney n. (homosexual use) a mean or cheap client for a gay prostitute *Legman*.

phonus balonus a. rubbish, nonsense (cf: baloney) *Runyon:1*.

photo finish n. (rhyming sl.) (a pint of) Guinness (stout) *Cole*.

physics for poets (US campus use) course in basic physics for arts specialists *Birnbach*.

pi a. (abbrev.) pious, always in a derog. sense of self-righteous, unctuous, poss. hypocritical.

piano n. (US Black use) spare ribs; fr. resemblance to keys *Major*.

piccolo and flute n. (rhyming sl.) suit (cf: whistle and flute) *Jones:J*.

pick n. (cant) (abbrev.) pickpocket *Neaman & Silver*.

pick a bone with v. to argue with *Klein*.

pickaninny n.(derog.) Black, Negro; spec. a Black child *Dunne*.

picking up the vibrations (homosexual use) watching other men perform a sex show; all-male voyeurism; fr. hippie use, when pleasures were more cerebral *Legman*.

pickled a. drunk (cf: stewed) *Dickson*.

pick man n. (Can. prison use) one who picks locks *Caron*.

pick-me-up n. any form of drink that relieves the physical and mental state of the imbiber; esp. used for those concoctions advertised as curing hangovers *Wodehouse:MOJ*.

pick-up n. a casual sex partner, met and seduced without previous introduction.

pick up v. **1.** to accost for possible sex *Legman*; **2.** (drug use) to use narcotics *Burroughs:1*.

pick up fag-ends v. to listen in to other people's conversations and attempt to comment upon them or join in; often as in juv. admonition 'don't pick up fag-ends'.

pick up the soap for v. to permit oneself to be sodomized; from the posture necessarily adopted for both activities *Legman*.

pick up the tab v. **1.** to pay a bill, usu. in a restaurant; the implication is one of treating one's fellow eaters *Wodehouse: PGM*; thus **2.** to take responsibility, to accept the consequences.

picnic n. **1.** (UK use) any simple, pleasurable experience; **2.** (Aus. use) an unpleasant, tricky experience, fr. ironic use of **1**; **3.** thus (both UK/Aus.) *no picnic*: an understated description of an unpleasant experience.

piddle v. to urinate.

piddle around v. to mess about, to waste time (cf: piss around) *Thompson:J*.

piddling a. small, insignificant, irrelevant *Bukowski:2*.

pie a. easy, simple; usu. in *easy as pie* *Wodehouse:PGM*.

pie n. (US campus use) an attractive, sexually desirable female (cf: cookie, pancake, etc.) *Underwood*.

piece n. (drug use) **1.** a quantity of heroin, approx. 1 oz *Larner*; **2.** a quantity of cocaine, approx. 1 oz. *Milner*; **3.** (abbrev.) piece of ass (qv); **4.** a gun, thus; **5.** the penis.

piece of ass n. a woman, girl; not derog. but dismissive *Green, 'Book of Rock Quotes', 1977*.

piece of cake n. simple, easily achieved, no bother (cf: easy as pie) *McFadden*.

piece off v. to bribe, to pay off; to give out a 'piece' of cash *Goldman*.

piece of piss supremely easy.

piece of the action n. share of proceeds, esp. of a robbery *Higgins:1*.
pieces n. (US Black use) clothes (cf: leather piece) *Folb*.
pie-eater n. (Aus. prison use) small time criminal (cf: cruncher) *Neaman & Silver*.
pie-eyed a. drunk *Neaman & Silver*.
pie in the sky n. fantasies, fond hopes and illusions; fr. Joe Hill (hero of the 'Wobblies'; the Industrial Workers of the World, prototype US union) song 'The Preacher and the Slave' with its ironical line 'There'll be pie in the sky when you die'.
pig n. **1.** (US horse-racing use) a slow or otherwise useless horse, not to be betted on *Bukowski:1*; **2.** (US campus use) a female considered to be promiscuous and sexually available *Underwood*; **3.** the police; despite 1960s radical obsession with this use, it existed at least as early as 1815; **4.** any straight (qv) person, member of the Establishment or authorities *Tuff Shit Comics*.
pig brother n. (US Black use) (derog.) any Black who informs against his own people to the (white) police *Folb*.
pigeon n. **1.** (abbrev.) stool pigeon (qv) *Burroughs:1*; **2.** (criminal use) a sucker, a victim, a mark (qv) the opposite of rook (qv).
pigger n. (US Black use) a very fat female *Folb*.
pigging a. intensifier; euph. for fucking (qv) *Austin*.
pighead n. a stubborn, uncompromising person *Safire*.
pig heaven n. **1.** (US Black use) a police station *Folb*; **2.** a fantasy paradise that would delight the gross rather than the fastidious.
pig-ignorant a. extremely stupid.
pig it v. to live in squalor, albeit unworried by that squalor.
pig-mouth n. see: pigger *Folb*.
pig out v. to overeat massively (cf: mac out) *Price:3*.
pigs! general excl. of disgust, contempt, negation, etc.
pig's ear n. **1.** a mess, chaos, usu. *make a pig's ear of. . .*; **2.** (rhyming sl.) beer *Powis*.
pigshit n. nonsense, rubbish; synonym for bullshit (qv).
pig sty n. a police station (cf: pig heaven) *Cole*.
pig style (US Black use) living in filthy circumstances *Klein*.
piker n. a mean, grasping person; one who will not take the least risk, esp. to help others *Chandler:LG*.
pikey a. vagrant; fr. orig. piker: a tramp who walked the turnpikes *Dury*.
pile n. a large sum of money, a fortune; esp. in 'I've made my pile. . . etc. (cf: bundle, packet).
pile v. (US Black use) to have sexual intercourse *Folb*.
pile-up n. a car crash, esp. one involving a number of vehicles.
pile up some Zs v. (US teen. use) to get some sleep (cf: cop some Zs) *Sculatti*.
pill n. an unpleasant person, a weakling, a bore *rr*.
pilled up a. under the influence of amphetamines or barbiturates *Mandelkau*.
pillhead n. a regular user of amphetamine or barbiturate drugs.
pill out (hot rod use) to accelerate sharply from a standing start and thus leave traces of rubber tyres on the tarmac *'American Graffitti', directed by G. Lucas*.
pill popper n. a regular user of any drugs in pill form – barbiturates, amphetamines, etc. *Jay & Young*.
pills n. testicles; fr. pill = ball = testicle *Humphries*.
pimp a. (US Black use) stylish, expensive; fr. the enviable status of the pimp in Black street culture *Folb*.
pimp crazy a. (Black pimp use) a prostitute who goes from one sadistic, abusing pimp to another, apparently unable to break the habit *Milner*.
pimp dust n. (US Black use) cocaine; an expensive status symbol, to be used without regard to cost *Folb*.

pimped down a. (Black use) dressed in one's finest clothes, groomed to perfection *Milner*.
pimp fronts n. (US Black use) particular style of dress associated with pimps) *Folb*.
pimple n. the head *Runyon*.
pimple and blotch n. (rhyming sl.) Scotch (whisky) *Jones:J*.
pimpmobile n. a flashy, ostentatious car, potentially the choice of a pimp, but not restricted to such drivers (cf: spivmobile, pimp ride).
pimp post n. aka: *pimp rest*: the armrest between driver and passenger in a car *Folb*.
pimp ride n. (US Black use) an expensive car, thus suitable for a pimp *Folb*.
pimp's arrest n. when a pimp, who has to maintain a running bail bond for each prostitute he runs, has his girl arrested deliberately in order to retrieve that money; often occurs when the ho (qv) decides she wants a new pimp *Milner*.
pimp shades n. aka: *pimp tints*: style of dark glasses affected by pimps *Folb*.
pimp socks n. (US Black use) ultra-thin nylon socks, usu. with pattern of vertical stripes *Seale*.
pimp stick n. (Black pimp use) two wire coat hangers twisted together to make an improvised and vicious whip *Milner*.
pimp stride n. (US Black use) style of walking, associated with pimps, in which the subject rolls fr. side to side *Folb*.
pimpsy a. (UK 'society' use) far too easy, utterly simple *Barr*.
pin v. to mark down visually, to notice *Goldman*.
pinch n. **1.** an arrest *rr*; **2.** (drug use) a small amount of marijuana, enough for perhaps two cigarettes *Folb*.
pinch v. to arrest; a police use that took up the orig. meaning: to steal *Wodehouse: AAG*; **2.** to steal; since 18th C.
pinch-hit v. to act as substitute, esp. in an emergency; fr. baseball use *NYRB 29/9/83*.
pineapple n. a bomb; a grenade; fr. shape *Runyon*.
pinhead n. a stupid person *Safire*.
pin-jabber n. any drug user who injects his preferred drug *Chandler: Notebk*.
pink n. (US Black use) a white person; fr. real 'white' skin tone *Folb*.
pink elephants n. the supposed fantasy creatures that traditionally appear to those in the throes of delirium tremens.
pinkie n. a very light coloured Black person *BvdB*.
pink lady n. (drug use) Darvon (propoxyphene); fr. colour of drug *Folb*.
pinko n. a Communist sympathizer (cf: red) *Junker*.
pinktea n. (homosexual use) an upper-class homosexual who stands aloof from the pleasures and problems of less insulated peers *Selby: 1*.
pinktoes n. (US Black use) a Black man's white girl-friend *Major*.
pinky n. (lesbian use) a passive lesbian (cf: femme) *Maledicta*.
pin money n. small sums of money allotted to a woman for house-keeping; sometimes the money earnt by a woman at a part-time job.
pinned eyes in which the pupils are reduced, irrespective of the light available, to pinpricks; the basic sign of a heroin addict *Grogan*.
pin on v. to accuse, to lay the blame on someone; fr. SE: to attach *rr*.
pin one's ears back v. to defeat, to punish – verbally or physically.
pin position n. (taxi-driver use) the first cab in a rank *Powis*.
PINS (US prison use) (accro.) *P*ersons *I*n *N*eed of *S*upervision (cf: CHINS, MINS) *Neaman & Silver*.
pins n. legs (rarely in singular) *Wright*.
pipe n. the penis (cf: lay some pipe) *Folb*.
pipe down! (excl.) be quiet, shut up! fr. nautical use *Gothic Blimp Works no. 5*.
pipped a. beaten; (abbrev.) pipped to

the post *Wodehouse: Ukridge, 1924.*

-pipper n. (milit. use) *one-pipper*: second lieutenant; *two-pipper*: first lieut; fr. 'pips' that denote their rank on uniforms.

pippin n. a perfect example of whatever is under discussion; usu. *it's a pippin*; fr. the name of an apple *Wodehouse: PGM.*

pipsqueak n. an insignificant person *Wodehouse: JM.*

pirates n. (UK police use) motorized traffic police *Powis.*

piss v. to urinate; fr. Middle English usage.

piss and vinegar energy, enthusiasm, cheekiness *Uris.*

piss around v. to waste time, to mess about (cf: piddle around).

piss artist n. a regular drunk *Humphries.*

piss away v. to waste *Bukowski: 7.*

piss blood v. to worry excessively, to make a great fuss *Higgins: 1.*

piss broken glass v. to have venereal disease, esp. gonorrhoea; one of the first symptoms is pain during urination *Powis.*

piss-cutter n. generally obnoxious person *Uris.*

pissed a. **1.** (US use) annoyed; **2.** (UK use) drunk *Price: 2.*

pissed as a fart a. very drunk.

pissed as a newt a. very drunk.

pissed off a. furious, very annoyed *Seale.*

pissed to the ears a. extremely drunk *Bruce: 2.*

pissed up a. very drunk *Barr.*

piss elegant a. pretentious, ostentatious, self-obsessed male homosexual *Stanley.*

pisser n. **1.** (US pro football use) a particularly rough tackler *Jenkins*; **2.** (general use) a tough, purposeful person *Schulberg*; **3.** hilariously funny (cf: piss oneself) *Selby: 1.*

piss flaps n. the labia *Cole.*

pisshole n. **1.** spec. urinal, lavatory; **2.** any house, room or place that could be described as **1** *Performance.*

piss in one's pocket v. to curry favour, to be extremely close to someone, to ingratiate oneself *Humphries: 2.*

piss it v. to succeed with no difficulty whatsoever; to win very easily; often used of racehorses, greyhounds and similar sports *Barr.*

piss off v. **1.** to annoy; **2.** to leave *Newman: 1.*

piss oneself v. to laugh uproariously.

piss one's pants v. to be utterly terrified *Higgins: 1.*

piss on one's parade v. shatter illusions, ruin an otherwise satisfactory situation *Price: 2.*

piss or get off the pot see: shit or get off the pot *Uris.*

pisspoor very poor, both financially and qualitatively *Major.*

pisspot n. drunkard *Higgins: 4.*

piss-proud an early morning erection, more indicative of the need to urinate than of lust *'Minder', Thames TV, 1980.*

piss-take v. to tease.

piss-up n. a drunken party (cf: beer-up) *Keyes.*

pissy-ass n. insignificant, useless *Higgins: 3.*

pistol n. the penis (cf: gun, rod, piece, etc.).

pit n. **1.** a real mess, esp. a room that is so disordered *Underwood*; **2.** bed *Powis.*

PITA n. (acro.) *P*ain *I*in *T*he *A*rse (qv).

pitch n. **1.** (US campus use) an unattractive, unpleasant, if promiscuous female; fr. pig + bitch *Underwood*; **2.** see: angle *Himes: 2*; **3.** prostitute's territory; **4.** area used by a three-card monte team; **5.** the line (qv) used by a swindler or a legitimate salesman *Powis.*

pitch a bitch v. (US Black use) to complain, to fight, to cause a disturbance *Major.*

pitch and toss n. (rhyming sl.) the boss *Jones: J.*

pitcher n. (US Black use) the male partner in heterosexual intercourse, the dominant partner in male homosexual intercourse; fr. baseball use *Klein*.

pitch fly n. someone who takes over another's street-selling position without permission *Powis*.

pit city n. a wretched, depressing situation (cf: —city; pits).

pits n. **1.** the depths of despair; a situation, object or person who is totally undesirable *Jay & Young*; **2.** (US campus use) body odour; fr. armpits *Underwood*.

pit stop n. (skiing use) a break from skiing for drinks *Barr*.

Pitt Street farmer n. (Aus. use) aka *Collins Street farmer*: a businessman (Pitt Street, Sydney; Collins Street, Melbourne are the respective financial centres) who owns or shares a farm from which he takes annual profits but rarely visits *Wilkes*.

pitty a. (US campus use) messy, untidy, disgusting; fr. pit (qv) *Underwood*.

pixie n. a homosexual man; a synonym for fairy (qv) *Legman*.

pixillated a. drunk *Dickson*.

pizzazz n. style, glamour *Higgins: 5*.

pjs n. pyjamas.

placer n. middle-man who places stolen goods with safe purchaser (cf: fence) *Newman: 1*.

plain n. (Irish use) Guinness stout; the basic Irish drink *T 25/7/83*.

plain sailing simple, straightforward, easy *Wodehouse: GB*.

plank v. to have sexual intercourse; fr. 19th C.use: to lay down (cf: lay) *Wolfe: 3*.

plant n. (US police use) see: stakeout *McBain: 1*.

plant v. to bury a body *Dunne*.

plant v. **1.** to hide *Burroughs: 1*; **2.** (police/criminal use) for the police to hide evidence in the clothes, home or car of a suspected person in order to ensure they have something with which to charge their victim *PT*.

plaster v. **1.** to hit (cf: paste); (US Black use) **2.** to flatter; **3.** to shoot someone *Klein*.

plastered a. drunk *Mandelkau*.

plastic a. synthetic, false, phoney *F. Zappa, LP, 1966*.

plastic job n. plastic surgery *Chandler: LG*.

plate v. to fellate; fr. rhyming sl. plate of ham = gam (qv) *J. Fabian & J. Byrne, 'Groupie', 1969*.

plates n. (rhyming sl.) plates of meat = feet *May*.

play n. (US Black use) any form of action *Klein*.

play v. to bet on; thus *play the horses*, *play the dogs Higgins: 1*.

play around v. to have a number of affairs, lovers, entanglements.

play-away n. (UK 'society' use) a weekend staying in the country; poss. fr, sporting imagery *Barr*.

play ball v. to co-operate; fr. 'playing a game' with *Higgins: 2*.

play checkers v. (homosexual use) to move from seat to seat in a cinema in search of a receptive sex partner (US checkers = UK draughts) *Legman*.

play chicken v. **1.** aka:*play chick*: to keep a lookout *Selby: 1*; **2.** (US Black use) to intrude on another (man's) sexual advances *Folb*.

play chopsticks v. (homosexual use) mutual masturbation *Legman*.

played out a. exhausted, finished, worn out; fr. gambling use: all one's chips/cash have been lost.

player n. (Black use) **1.** a man who uses his wits and charm to obtain money and other favours from wealthy white women; **2.** a pimp *Shulman*; **3.** anyone who uses intelligence, wit, brains to gain objectives, incl. businessmen, politicians, etc. as well as criminals *Milner*.

play fathers and mothers v. to have sexual intercourse; the adult version of children's sex games, the main alternative one being *playing doctors and nurses*.

play footsie v. to nudge someone's foot with yours – out of sight of companions – as a possible prelude to further intimacy; thus to indulge in the cautious sounding out of any relationship – economic, political, etc. *Humphries*.

play funny buggers v. see: play silly buggers *Bleasdale*.

play gooseberry v. (teen. use) for an unwanted third party to hang around a couple who would prefer to be left alone; abbrev. of gooseberry fool *Waterhouse*.

play hardball v. to act ruthlessly and single-mindedly in pursuit of a goal; fr. baseball use *Vidal*.

play hard to get v. for a girl (usu.) to resist sexual advances, though not necessarily to reject them altogether.

play hookey n. to truant from school (cf: bunk off) *Larner*.

play hoop-snake with v. (homosexual use) mutual fellation; homosexual soixante-neuf *Legman*.

playing out of the pocket (US Black use) **1.** to be cheated or tricked ; **2.** to let something happen without noticing it *Klein*.

playing too close (US prison use) becoming over-familiar and invading the privacy of a fellow inmate *Klein*.

play it cool v. to act disinterestedly; to control every emotion.

play night baseball v. to have sexual intercourse *Neaman & Silver*.

play one's cards right v. to behave sensibly: to act in one's best interests *Higgins: 3*.

play one too close v. (US Black use) to involve oneself too intimately and without invitation, in another person's life *Klein*.

play past v. (US black use) to circumvent obstacles. mental as well as physical *Milner*.

play pocket billiards v. to play with one's genitals through a trouser pocket.

play possum v. to pretend to be dead; fr. the animal.

play ring a rosie v. (US use) to fool about, to make great effort with no result; fr. the children's game *'The Stone Killer', film, 1973*.

play second fiddle v. to take a secondary, subsidiary role; fr. orchestra use.

play silly buggers v. to act uncooperatively; to mess around, to cause a deliberate nuisance.

play stuff v. (US Black use) to deceive by a smart line of verbal patter *Klein*.

play the chill v. to ignore, to avoid, to act coldly towards *Runyon*.

play the con v. pretend, attempt to swindle or deceive *rr*.

play the dozens v. (US Black use) to compete in ritualized mutual insults (cf: dirty dozens) *Jones*.

play the duck v. to avoid; fr. duck out (qv) *Runyon*.

play the field v. to enjoy a variety of lovers; fr. horserace betting: spreading one's money around several horses instead of concentrating on one *Jay & Young*.

play the heel v. to act unpleasantly, to be mean, cruel *rr*.

play the hop v. to play truant from school (cf: hop the wag) *Cole*.

play the nut role v. to pose as a shambling incompetent in order to swindle or otherwise trick a possible victim *Klein*.

play the Tom v. see: Tom, Uncle Tom *Folb*.

play with oneself v. to masturbate *Joe Jackson, 'I'm the Man'*.

plead v. (police/criminal use) to plead guilty; never innocent *Laurie*.

plead the fifth v. to avoid committing oneself, to refuse to take an action or make a statement; fr. criminal habit of using the Fifth Amendment to the US Constitution (no one is obliged to give testimony that will incriminate themself) to avoid prosecution.

pleasure and pain n. (rhyming sl.) rain *Jones: J*.

plonk n. cheap or second rate wine. the brand-name 'Plonque' was merchandized in the early 1970s; it lived up to its name *Mortimer*.

plonk v. **1.** to copulate (cf: plank); **2.** to put down.

plot n. the place where three-card monte (qv) teams operate: the street, an alley or doorway, a deserted lot, etc. *Powis*.

plot up v. (UK police use) to study a

criminal's personality, habits, technique and associates prior to making an arrest *Laurie*.

plot up v. (UK cant) for a gang or group to seek out and establish territory in a given place– soccer stadium, club, crowded place, etc; fr. plot of land *Cole*.

plow v. (US use) to have sexual intercourse *Bruce: 2*.

plow the back forty v. (US use) to have sexual intercourse; fr. plow (qv) plus agricultural imagery *King*.

PLU (UK 'society' use) (acro.) *P*eople *L*ike *U*s (cf: NQOCD).

pluck n. (US Black use) **1.** wine; fr. grapes that are plucked or pluck = courage; **2.** an attractive female *Folb*.

pluck v. (US Black use) to choose one's woman *Klein*.

plucked (US Black use) sexually satiated; euph. for fucked (?) *Folb*.

plug v. **1.** (homosexual use) to perform anal intercourse *Legman*; **2.** to shoot *Laugh in the Dark*; **3.** to hit, usu. with the fist *Wodehouse: AAG*; **4.** to perform sexual intercourse, usu. male use *Underwood*.

plugged in abreast of the times, fashionable, *au courant Safire*.

plugugly n. a thug, a hoodlum *Wodehouse: EBC*.

plumb n. a very serious error *Major*.

plumber n. (US Black use) a man with a frequent and varied sex life *Folb*.

plunk v. **1.** to pluck the strings of guitar; **2.** to place, usu. *plunk down* (cf: plonk).

po n. the lavatory; fr. chamber-pot, and Fr. pron. pf *pot de chambre*.

pocket pool n. playing with one's genitals through a trouser pocket *Junker*.

pocket roll n. (US Black use) a roll of paper money kept in the pocket *Klein*.

POed (US teen. use) pissed off (qv) *Pond*.

poet's day n. Friday; fr. acro: *p*iss *o*ff *e*arly, *t*omorrow's *S*aturday *Cole*.

po-faced a. arrogant, stand-offish, humourless.

poggler see: pogue **1.** *Powis*.

pogue n. **1.** (UK criminal use) purse, wallet *Powis*; **2.**(homosexual use) a young boy; thus USMC use *poguey bait*: sweets *Legman*.

poindexter n. (Valley Girls (qv) us) an intellectual, bookish person; fr. pointy-head (qv) *Pond*.

point n. (drug use) a hypodermic syringe *Folb*.

point percy at the porcelain v. to urinate *Humphries*.

points n. single units of percentage *Higgins: 3*.

pointy-head a. (derog.) intellectual, cultured *Jones*.

poison n. an unpleasant person, best to be avoided *Klein*.

poisoned a. (US Black use) pregnant *Klein*.

poke n. a wallet; fr. Fr. *poche*: pocket *Burroughs: 1*.

poke v. to have sexual intercourse *R. Newman, 'Trouble in Paradise', 1983*.

poke along v. to walk slowly *Klein*.

poke one's mouth off v. (US Black use) to lose one's temper *Klein*.

poker n. (US criminal use) a single-barrelled shotgun *Klein*.

pokey n. gaol, usu. small, local; fr. pokey condition or fr. Fr. *poche*: pocket, and thus sense of 'putting away' (?) *Runyon*.

pol. n. **1.** (UK prison use) fr. Polly Parrot: a talkative person, a chatterer or gossip *LL*; **2.** (US use) (abbrev.) politician.

Polack n. **1.** (derog.) a Pole *Bruce: 2*; **2.** (Jewish use) a Jew whose family come from Poland (cf: Litvak).

pole n. the penis *Folb*.

pole v. to perform sexual intercourse; usu. male use *Underwood*.

polecat n. (US Black use) a dirty, untrustworthy woman *Klein*.

pole hole n. the vagina *Folb*.

policy n. (US criminal use) the numbers (qv) racket.

polish the apple v. (UK prison use) to curry favour, to act the sycophant; see apple-polisher *LL*.

politician n. **1.** a flatterer, a clever talker; **2.** (US prison use) anyone who gains good jobs and maximum privileges *Neaman & Silver*; both uses take a dim view of the SE use.

politico n anyone involved in politics, both conventional and 'alternative' activists *Hoffman: a.*

polluted a. extremely drunk; fr. the state of one's bloodstream (?) *Bernbach.*

polone n. (theatrical use) female; one of the few surviving examples of *parlyaree*, the 19th C. showmans', costers' and actors' slang, based mainly on corruption of Italian (cf: omee).

poly bag n. (abbrev.) polythene bag, usu. the carrier bags available in shops and supermarkets *Wilkinson.*

pom (abbrev.) pommy, pommie (qv) *Humphries.*

pommy n. (Aus. use) aka: *pommie*: English person; fr. abbrev. of pomegranate, punning on immigrant *Humphries.*

Pompey n. (RN use) Portsmouth; also general use, as in Pompey Royal, a Hampshire-brewed beer (cf: Guz).

Pompey whore (bingo rhyming sl.) 24 *Franklyn.*

pom-pom n. (US criminal use) a pump-action shotgun; fr. the naval armament *Klein.*

ponce n. **1.** spec. one who lives off the earnings of one or more prostitutes; **2.** derog. epithet for any given male; NB: many 'ponce' usages and combinations show the very different status of such a man in the UK compared with the US pimp (qv) *Norman: 2.*

ponce around v. to wander aimlessly, live as a good-for-nothing.

ponce off v. **1.** to live off immoral earnings; **2.** to scrounge (money) from someone *Norman: 2.*

ponce up v. to ornament (an object), to dress up (a person); both meanings implying some ostentation and flashiness.

poncy a. affected, ostentatiously 'artistic', poss. homosexual; there is no actual link in this use to a pimp or procurer *Barr.*

pong n. smell; usu. reserved for use in mass market children's comics or by 'society' speakers who retain much juvenile vocabulary from school (cf: bate, etc.) *Barr.*

pongo n. (New Zealand use) (derog.) British person: developed fr. 19th C. use: a monkey, thence a marine, a soldier.

pontoon n. (UK prison use) 21 month sentence; fr. card use *EN 12/11/57.*

pony n. **1.** £25 *Payne*; **2.** (rhyming sl.) pony and trap = crap = excretion *Newman: 3.*

pony in white n. (UK criminal use) £1.25 in silver coins *LL.*

pony up v. to pay one's debts, one's dues *Higgins: 4.*

poo n. **1.** (US preppie (qv) use) (abbrev.) shampoo = champagne *Bernbach*; **2.** exrement, usu. children's use only. fr. excl. announcing an unpleasant smell *Lucien Green.*

pooch n. **1.** dog *Capital Radio 1983*; **2.** (gambling use) a loser; fr. pooch = dog = abbrev. underdog *Alvarez.*

poodle n. (US Black use) a sexy or classy female (cf: fox) *Klein.*

poof n. homosexual (cf: poove) fr. 'camp' cries of 'pooh!' or 'poof!' *Performance.*

poof v. (US campus use) to kiss *Underwood.*

poof about v. to act in an ostentatiously homosexual manner.

poofta n. see: poofter *Robins.*

poofter n. homosexual male (cf: poof) *Le Carré.*

poon n. **1.** (Aus. use) simpleton, fool, useless person (cf: nong) *Wilkes*; **2.** (abbrev.) poontang (qv).

pooned up a. (Aus. use) flashily dressed, usu. of youths looking to pick up girls; poss. fr. US use of poon (qv) *Wilkes.*

poontang n. vagina, thus a nubile girl; fr. *putain* = whore (Fr.) *Junker.*

poop n. **1.** rubbish, tripe, nonsense *Uneeda Comix*; **2.** news, information, gossip, often as *hot poop*: fresh information, etc.; **3.** excrement; **4.** the buttocks; *Neaman & Silver*.

poop-butt n. (Black use) **1.** a lazy person (cf: drag-ass); **2.** a young, immature person *Milner*.

poop-chute n. the anus *Klein*.

pooped a. exhausted, tired out *Farrell*.

pooper n. penis *May*.

pooper-scooper n. a small scoop used by the cleanliness-minded for removing traces of their dog's excreta (poop, qv) from urban pavements *Capital Radio 1983*.

poophead n. (US campus use) a fool, a dullard *Underwood*.

poopie-plops n. (juv. use) excrement *Neaman & Silver*.

poor-mouth v. to belittle *Price: 2*.

pootbutt n. see: poopbutt *Folb*.

poove n. homosexual (cf: poof) *Private Eye: passim*.

poozle n. vagina *Big Ass Comics 1*.

pop n. **1.** (horseriding use) a horse's jumping ability *Barr*; **2.** aka: *pops*; father; fr. papa *LL*; **3.** (juv. use) a fizzy drink; **4.** champagne; fr. the uncorking process.

pop v. **1.** to feel elated, extremely pleased, enthusiastic *Price: 2*; **2.** spec. to inject a drug; thus *skin pop*: to inject under the skin rather than into a vein; **3.** to hit; **4.** to swallow pills *Selby: 1*; **5.** (US campus use) to take amphetamines specifically for staying up and working all night *Underwood*; **6.** to pawn; thus *popshop*: pawnbrokers.

pop corn n. anyone with a legitimate job, rather than a criminal or a hustler (qv) *Burroughs: 1*.

popcorn a. (Black use) lightweight, second string, unintelligent (cf: peanuts) *Milner*.

popcorn pimp n. (US Black use) a small-time, ineffectual pimp; a man who claims to be, but is not a pimp *Shulman*.

popeyed a. drunk *Dickson*.

pop off v. **1.** to exit, to vanish; **2.** to die *Runyon*.

pop one's cork v. **1.** to surrender sexually; to come to orgasm *Shirley Bassey, 'Big Spender', 1967*; **2.** to lose one's temper, to lose patience.

pop one's nuts v. to achieve male orgasm.

popped a. arrested *Larner*.

poppers n. (drug use) amyl nitrate (cf: poppers); fr. the necessity to break open the ampoule that contains the drug.

poppy n. money *Powis*.

poppycock n. nonsense, rubbish; orig. euph. for excreta *Rawson*.

popsy n. a female, usu. young and attractive *Wodehouse: MOJ*.

pork n. a fool *Price: 1*.

pork v. to have sexual intercourse, fr. male point of view (cf: pork sword) *Higgins: 4*.

pork sword n. the penis (cf: mutton dagger, beef bayonet).

porky n. (rhyming sl.) pork pie = a lie *D. Leitch*.

porridge n. imprisonment: fr. the staple morning diet of such establishments in the UK *Norman: 2*.

Porsche n. (US Black use) a female whose body, like the car, is small, rounded and compact *Folb*.

posh a. smart, pertaining to the upper classes; 'of obscure origin' (*OED Supp. O–Scz* 1982, which rejects traditional 'port out starboard home' derivation) *McBain: 1*.

possesh n. possession: a homosexual boy who is used for sex by the tramp he accompanies *Legman*.

pot n. **1.** (abbrev.) pot belly: an enlarged stomach, usu. developed through excessive drinking; fr. pots of ale (cf: beer gut) *Humphries: 2*; **2.** marijunana, hashish. fr. Sp: *potaguaya Higgins: 2*.

pot and pan n. (rhyming sl.) old man *Wright*.

potato n. (Aus. rhyming sl.) potato peeler = sheila = woman, girl-friend *Humphries*.

potatoes n. money *Runyon*.

potatoes in the mould (rhyming sl.) cold (cf: taters) *Cole*.

potato jack n. illicit liquor, distilled in US prisons *Higgins: 1*.
pot-boiler n. a literary or similar work created purely for the money; to keep the creator's 'pot boiling'.
potsy n. (US police use) badge, identification card; fr. the tin (used for pots) that allegedly makes badges *McBain: 1*.
potted a. drunk; fr. pot = flagon.
potty a. crazy, eccentric *Humphries*.
pound (US prison use) a five year sentence (cf: pound note) *J. Breslin, 'Forsaking All Others', 1982*.
poundcake n. an attractive woman (cf: pancake, cookie, etc.) *Neaman & Silver*.
pound note $5.00; fr. an exchange rate of five dollars = £1 *Runyon*.
pound note geezer n. rich man (orig. Aus.) *Norman: 2*.
pound one's ear v. to sleep; fr. tramps attempting to sleep in the boxcars of US railroads as they bumped over the rails *Gruber*.
pound salt up one's ass v. usu, as a rebuke: go . . .: go to hell, stick it up your ass (qv) etc.
powder one's nose v. to use a toilet, rather than a 'powder-room' *Rawson*.
powder puff n. (derog.) effeminate male homosexual (cf: poof) *Legman*.
pow-wow v. chat, converse with, talk to; fr. US Indian use *Burroughs: Jr*.
pox n. venereal disease; fr. 16th C.
poxy a. unpleasant, dirty, disgusting (cf: pox) *Performance*.
prang v. to crash one's car; fr. Second World War RAF use (cf: shunt) *Humphries: 2*.
prat n. an idiot, a fool; fr. orig. use: buttocks, posterior *Dury, 'Laughter', 1981*.
pratt for v. (homosexual use) to indulge – actively or passively – in anal intercourse; fr. prat(t): buttocks *Legman*.
prawnhead n. (Aus. use) fool, simpleton, general derog. term *Ready*.
preggers a. pregnant.
preppie n. (US college use) anyone who attends one of the major US 'prep schools' (St Paul's, Choate, Groton, Miss Porter's, Dana Hall, etc.), the equivalent of UK public (private) schools. The graduates of such schools – the children of the US establishment – share similar codes, styles, language and society *Bernbach*.
prescriptions n. (drug use) any drug that comes primarily in pill form: barbiturates, amphetamines, etc. *Folb*.
presents n. (US Black use) white spots on one's fingernails, supposedly auguring good luck *Klein*.
pressed a. (US Black use) very well dressed; fr. state of one's clothes *Folb*.
press flesh v. to shake hands, usu. of a politician on a campaign tour to meet the electors *Higgins:5*.
press ham v. (college use) to press a bare buttock against a window and hopefully shock passers by (cf: moon) *Junker*.
pressie n. aka *prezzie* (UK 'society' use) (abbrev.) present *Barr*.
press one's hair v. (US Black use) to straighten one's hair (cf: conk) *Folb*.
previous n. (abbrev.) previous convictions (cf: form).
prick n. **1.** the penis; **2.** an idiot, a fool, an incompetent *O'Brien*.
pricktease v. to lead on sexually but stopping short of intercourse. The woman or man (in homosexual context) who so acts is a *prickteaser*.
priest n. a celibate; fr. status of such clerics *Higgins:1*.
priggling a. pregnant; mix of in pig and preggers (qqv).
prime cut n. the vagina *film title, 1972*.
primed a. drunk; thus ready to 'explode into action' *Dickson*.
prime one's pump v. to excite sexually *Dunne*.
Princeton rub aka *Princeton-First-Year n.* (homosexual use) body to body rubbing (cf: collegiate fucking) *Jay & Young*.
prison wolf n. (Can. prison use) a prisoner who prefers women when free, but turns to men when imprisoned *Caron*.

privy-queen n. (homosexual use) a homosexual who seeks sex in or around public lavatories *Legman.*
pro n. **1.** (abbrev.) professional: an expert in a given field spec. *the pro*: the professional employed by a golf club; **2.** (abbrev.) prostitute *Price:1.*
process n. (US Black use) straightened hair *Folb.*
prod n. the penis *Underwood.*
prod v. to engage in sexual intercourse; usu. male use *Underwood.*
professional woman n. (euph.) prostitute (cf: working girl) *Milner.*
promo n. (abbrev.) promotion: publicity, PR, etc. *Higgins:3.*
promoted pimp n. (US Black use) **1.** a pimp who gives advice to other pimps or to their prostitutes; **2.** a method of getting money *Klein.*
prong n. **1.** penis; **2.** an erection *Higgins:1.*
prong v. to seduce.
pronto immediately, at once; fr. Sp. *Humphries.*
prop up v. **1.** (abbrev.) proposition, thus to make a proposition *Powis*; **2.** to arrange, to suggest, to fabricate a story *Powis.*
prospect n. **1.** (Hells Angels use) a recruit to an outlaw motorcycle gang prior to any initiation rites *Mandelkau*; **2.** (homosexual use) a potential client for a street prostitute *Legman.*
prossie n. prostitute *'Minder', Thames TV, 1980.*
prosso n. (Aus. use) prostitute *Ready.*
provider n. (poker use) one who habitually loses when playing and thus provides his fellow-players with regular wins *Alvarez.*
pseud n. (abbrev.) pseudo-intellectual; derog. description, often of quite genuine, if pretentious intellectuals, who offend their perhaps less academic critics *Private Eye: passim.*
pseudie tudie n. an architectural style popular in the Home Counties; it features fake beams and the other appurtenances of (Hollywood-style) Elizabethan & Tudor England.
psychedelic to the bone (US Black use) extremely intoxicated by a given drug, but not necessarily a hallucinogen *Folb.*
psyched to death a. (US teen. use) extremely excited (cf: psych up) *E. Beyer.*
psycho n. (abbrev.) psychopath *McBain:1.*
psych out v. **1.** to astonish, to amaze *Underwood*; **2.** to frighten or at least perturb someone else by playing on their inner fear; **3.** to lose emotional control.
psych up v. to put oneself into a confident, aggressive, etc. frame of mind as preparation for adequate dealing with a given situation *Jay & Young.*
PT (acro.) *P*rick *T*easer (qv).
pta (US Black use) (abbrev.) **1.** *p*ussy, *t*itties and *a*rmpits; **2.** a bad-smelling female *Folb.*
P-town n. Philadelphia *Jay & Young.*
public n. (abbrev.) public bar *Robins.*
puck n. (US campus use) anyone deemed socially unacceptable *Underwood.*
pud n. **1.** (US teen./campus use) the penis *Underwood*; **2.** fool, idiot *Price:3.*
pud a. (US campus use) soft, easy, esp. of course-work *Underwood.*
puddlejumper n. a small car *Higgins:3.*
puff n. see: poof.
pug n. a prizefighter, a boxer; esp. one who relies more on savagery than skill; fr. pugilist *Fiction Illus.3.*
puggy n. a tough, a hoodlum; fr. pug (qv) *Wolfe:1.*
puke n., v. vomit; to vomit *Price:2.*
pukka a. genuine, correct, honest; fr. Hindi *pakka*: substantial.
pull n. **1.** (horseracing use) a horse that is deliberately pulled up and stopped from winning so as to improve its odds in a subsequent, more important race *Bukowski:1*; **2.** an arrest (cf: tug) *Norman:2*; **3.** influence

(cf: clout) *Hotten*.

pull v. **1.** to arrest, to stop and search on the street *Capital Radio 1983*; **2.** to seduce *Keyes*.

pull a coat v. to draw attention, to point out, to nag *Price:2*.

pull a job v. carry out a robbery or other criminal act *Higgins:1*.

pull an act v. to put on a show with the intention of deceiving or defrauding someone *Neaman & Silver*.

pull a quick park v. (US Black use) to make a snappy pick-up of a sexual partner *Folb*.

pull a stroke v. to attempt and/or get away with anything outrageous or daring *Dury*.

pull a train v. to be the subject of gang rape, esp. amongst Hells Angels; the female is the engine, her assailants the rolling-stock *Thompson*.

pull down v. to earn money, usu. with a wage specified as object *Price:2*.

pull one's finger out v. to get on with something; to stop malingering and commit oneself to positive action *'Minder', Thames TV, 1983*.

pull one's joint 1. spec. masturbate; **2.** to whine, complain (cf: jerk off) *Higgins:3*.

pull one's leg v. to tease.

pull one's pisser see: pull one's leg (qv) *Bleasdale*.

pull one's pud(ding) v. to masturbate *Junker*.

pull one's punches v. to restrain oneself, esp. in conversation/speech; fr. boxing use *Dickson*.

pull one's socks up v. to make greater efforts, to improve one's performance.

pull one's wire v. to masturbate.

pull the plug on v. to terminate, to bring to an end, usu. abruptly; fr. electrical use.

pull time v. (US prison use) to be sentenced to a term of imprisonment *Klein*.

pull to a set v. (US Black use) to attend a party *Folb*.

pull your head in! excl. of annoyance: mind your own business, don't interfere; fr. the action of the tortoise *Ready*.

pump n. **1.** a gun, spec. a pump-action shotgun *Folb*; **2.** a promiscuous female *Underwood*; **3.** the heart *Dunne*.

pump v. to ask questions, esp. to interrogate (in a police station) *Sillitoe*.

pump iron v. to work out with weights, to practise bodybuilding.

pump jockey n. petrol pump attendant *Thompson*.

pumpkin head n. a person with an abnormally large head *Klein*.

punch n. (US campus use) a promiscuous female; one who is always getting 'banged' (qv) (?) *Underwood*.

punch v. (US campus use) to engage in sexual intercourse *Underwood*.

punch house n (US Black use) a party frequented by pimps and their women; usu. an orgy *Klein*.

punching bag n. (boxing use) a fighter who has no real abilities and is useful only as the recipient of a fortunate opponent's punches *Runyon:1*.

punch in the mouth n. cunnilingus *Simmons*.

punch-out artist n. anyone who enjoys and is expert in beating up his opponents with his fists *Thompson*.

punch-up n. a fight, in the street, a pub, etc. *Norman:4*.

punchy a. **1.** (boxing use) punch drunk, a boxer who has taken too many punches and is becoming eccentric; **2.** disorientated, eccentric, out of control *Higgins:1*.

punishment n. (homosexual use) taking an extra-large penis either in the mouth or the anus *Legman*.

punk n. **1.** nonsense, rubbish; **2.** (US campus use) second-rate, inferior *Dickson*; **3.** a youngster, a child *Runyon*; **4.** (US prison use) a young inmate used for sex by older, stronger peers. **5.** a young criminal or street gang member *Price:1*.

Punk n. mid-1970s youth cult, started in UK, spread to US by such apostles as the Sex Pistols, Malcolm McLaren, etc. Where the hippies (qv) had been bourgeois, punks were proletarian, complaining not against a consumer society but against their exclusion from its delights; they specialized in bizarre hair styles (mohican, multicoloured) ripped clothes, and safety pins, through flesh as well as fabric.

punk a. second-rate, inferior, distasteful *Humphries:2*.

punk v. to engage in anal intercourse *Folb*.

punk out v. to display cowardice *Price:3*.

punt v. to gamble, to wager.

punt v. i. (US campus use) to give up, esp. of one's work *Underwood*.

punt around v. **1.** to try one's luck, esp. when looking for a given person *Newman:1*; **2.** (UK police use) to go out on patrol, and gambling on an arrest *Laurie*.

punter n. **1.** spec: gambler (cards, dice, horses, dogs, etc.); **2.** member of the general public, esp. when in role of customer; **3.** the victim of a confidence trickster's schemes; **4.** (skiing use) a guest at a chalet.

punt off v. (US campus use) to forget, to put to the back of one's mind *Underwood*.

puppethead (US teen. use) any gullible, conventional person, esp. one who permits hearsay to 'pull their strings' in matters of current taste *Sculatti*.

puppies n. feet (cf: dogs) *Runyon*.

puppy n. (US Black use) **1.** a small penis; **2.** small bottle of wine; **3.** love-sick young man; **4.** sexually inexperienced male *Folb*.

puppy dog n. see: puppy (**3**, **4**) *Klein*.

purler n. a crash, an accidental fall *Wodehouse: CW*.

push n. (Aus. use) **1.** criminal gang (orig 1860s use); **2.** a crowd *Humphries*.

push v. (abbrev.) push off (qv) *ES 21/4/83*.

push v. **1.** to sell; **2.** spec. to sell drugs *Higgins:3*.

push along v. to leave (cf: push off).

pushed a. lacking, bereft; thus *pushed for cash*, *pushed for time Barr*.

pushed out of shape a. upset, angry *Underwood*.

pusher n. a seller of drugs *Burroughs:1*.

push iron v. see: pump iron *Klein*.

push off v. to leave *Humphries:2*.

push off! (excl.) go away.

pushover n. a person or situation that presents no difficulties or problems *Heller*.

push the boat out v. to spend heavily, usu. on pleasure, eating, drinking etc., often treating others also.

push up the daisies v. to die *Wright*.

puss n. **1.** see: pussy *Southern & Hoffenberg*; **2.** face; fr. Irish *pus*: mouth *Higgins:3*; **3.** the 'female' of a lesbian couple (cf: pussy) *Powis*.

puss gentleman n. (US Black use) a weak male; fr. pussy (qv) *Klein*.

pussy n. **1.** vagina; **2.** coward, implications of homosexuality *O'Brien*; **3.** women, poss. sexually available, in general; **4.** (UK criminal/police use) a fur coat *Powis*.

pussy a. scared.

pussycat n. **1.** (US Black use) the vagina *Folb*; **2.** a weak or at least amiable and passive person *Stone*.

pussyfoot v. to compromise, to act in a cowardly or weakly manner; fr. the animal's cautious movements *Dickson*.

pussy in a can n. (US prison use) sardines sold in a can at a prison commissary; fr. derog. ref. to the vagina (cf: fish) *Klein*.

pussy posse n. (US police use) the Vice Squad, esp. those members who deal with prostitutes (cf: bunco squad) *Higgins:2*.

pussy-whipped a. any man who is dominated by a woman, esp. wife or girl-friend.

puta n. (US Sp. use) a prostitute *Folb*.

put a dent in one's hip (US Black

use) to cost an appreciable amount of cash; one's wallet is carried on one's hip *Klein.*

put a hurting on v. (US Black use) to cause deliberate harm to someone *Klein.*

put a name up v. to inform against someone, often to save one's own skin (cf: body) *Newman:1.*

put a notice on v. (criminal use) arrange to have someone murdered (cf: contract) *Austin.*

put a sock in it v. to stop talking, to be quiet; the sock would gag a mouth *Wodehouse:MS.*

put away v. **1.** imprison; **2.** (show business use) for a comedian to score a big laugh from the audience *Goldman*; **2.** (UK police/criminal use) to inform against and thus be instrumental in having imprisoned *Powis.*

put-down n. verbal attack, criticism, condemnation *Vizinczey.*

put down v. to deride, to slander, to attack verbally, to tease.

put down a routine v. to hoax or otherwise persuade someone with a clever story *Burroughs:1.*

pu the elop (backsl.) up the pole = pregnant *Cole.*

put her on the block/corner v. (US Black use) to have a woman working for one as a prostitute *Folb.*

put in one's two cents v. to make a contribution, usu. gratuitous and/or malicious, to an argument or conversation *Algren:2.*

put in the acid v. (UK criminal use) to inform against *Powis.*

put in the poison v. to slander, to malign a person's character, esp. in court *Laurie.*

put it about v. to indulge in a wide-ranging sex life *Humphries.*

put it across v. to cheat or confuse someone.

put it all together v. to consolidate one's position, to work out one's life satisfactorily *McFadden.*

put it around v. to circulate information; esp. of police who attempt thus to use the criminal grapevine (qv) to glean specific facts *Powis.*

put it in the wind v. (US Black use) to leave *Folb.*

put it on the street v. to make available for general consumption; usu. of gossip, information, etc.

put it where the monkeys shove their nuts (euph.) shove it up your arse!

put lead in one's pencil v. to cheer up, to strengthen; esp. in sexual context *Humphries.*

put-on n. a joke, a hoax *Thompson.*

put on v. **1.** to tease, to joke with; to deceive for one's own gain *Goldman*; **2.** to eat; fr. put on the feedbag; often specifying the food: *putting on the chicken pie* etc. *Runyon.*

put on a crosstown bus v. (US Black use) to mislead deliberately *Major.*

put one away v. to knock out, to win a fight *Bukowski:2.*

put one in v. (Aus. use) to inform against; 'one' = a report or the person thus 'put in gaol' (?) *Wilkes.*

put one on v. to hit; 'one' = a blow.

put one's ass in a sling v. to cause someone extreme trouble, whether actually physically damaging or not *Dunne.*

put one's back up v. to annoy, to irritate; fr. the risen hairs on a cat's back that denote, *inter alia*, aggression.

put one's business on front street v. (US Black use) to make indiscreet disclosures about another person *Klein.*

put one's checks in the rack v. to die; fr. gambling use *Runyon:1.*

put oneself about v. to lead an active social life *Powis.*

put one's face on v. (female use) to put on make-up; however, gaining male currency among teenagers who enjoy make-up. *T 29/6/83.*

put one's flags out v. to have a menstrual period *Humphries.*

put one's foot down v. to insist, to be adamant; fr. a pettish stamp of the foot *Wodehouse:VGJ.*

put one's foot in it v. to make an error; it = 'the shit'.
put one's hand up v. to confess; fr. classroom practice *Newman:1.*
put one's head on the block v. to declare oneself openly; to take a risk or a stand that may be dangerous; fr. the chopping-block *Teresa.*
put one's nose out of joint v. to discomfit, to embarrass, to irritate *Vidal.*
put one's papers in v. (US and UK police use) to submit one's resignation *Neaman & Silver.*
put one's shirt on v. (gambling use) to bet heavily *Wodehouse: MJ.*
put one together v. to plan a crime *Newman:1.*
put on front street v. (US Black use) to reveal secrets about another person, esp. those they would prefer to be kept secret *Klein.*
put on hold v. to delay, to postpone, to defer; fr. telephone etiquette (cf: put on the back burner) *Price:3.*
put on ice v. **1.** to put aside a project or idea for later development, or use; **2.** (police use) to hide away a sensitive witness so as to stop their being killed by a wanted criminal; **3.** to maintain a distant, minimally emotional relationship (cf: play the chill).
put on jam v. (Aus. use) to put on airs *Neaman & Silver.*
put on the back burner v. to consider for a later date; to reserve one's judgement; to postpone *Dickson.*
put on (the) dog v. to assume airs and pretensions (but, cf: wear the dog) *Neaman & Silver.*
put on the feed bag v. to eat *Gruber.*
put on the guiver v. (UK criminal use) to affect an upper-class accent; fr. *guiver lad*: a working class dandy (19th C.); itself fr. *guiver*: flattery, humbug, show fr. Hebrew word meaning pride *Powis.*
put out to offer oneself for sex *Price:2.*
put out one's hand v. to go through a drunk's pockets looking for cash, valuables *Burroughs:1.*
put out one's lights to knock unconscious; fr. *daylights*: eyes *Hotten.*
putrid a. drunk (cf: stinking) *Dickson.*
put the arm on v. to pressurize with threats of violence; to extort 'protection' payments *Vidal.*
put the bag on v. to halt, to interfere with, to bring to a standstill *Humphries:2.*
put the bee on v. **1.** to air one's obsession, fr *a bee in one's bonnet*; **2.** see: put the bite on *Schulberg:2.*
put the bite one v. **1.** to extort, to blackmail *Wodehouse: CW*; **2.** to ask for a financial loan *Runyon:1.*
put the black on v. to blackmail *Dury.*
put the blast on v. **1.** to attack verbally, to criticize severely *Runyon*; **2.** to shoot dead *Chandler: LG.*
put the block on v. to interfere with, to stop.
put the blocks on v. (UK prison use) to tighten up regulations that have become temporarily lax *LL.*
put the boot in v. to kick someone as part of a fight *Humphries.*
put the bubble in v. (UK criminal use) to inform; fr. bubble (qv) *LL.*
put the bull on v. to pressurize, to act aggressively towards; fr. the animal *Breslin.*
put the cosh on v. to pressurize; to compel (cf: under the cosh) *Norman:2.*
put the cross on v. to mark for death *Chandler: Notebk.*
put the finger on v. to betray, to inform against *Algren.*
put the freeze on v.i., v.t. (US Black use) to stop *Folb.*
put the frighteners on v. (UK criminal use) to menace, blackmail, threaten with violence. *Performance.*
put the hammer down v. to drive fast, esp. used by truck drivers.
put the hammer on v. to attack verbally, to slander *Higgins:1.*
put the hard word on v. to make demands (esp. financial or sexual) of someone *Baker.*

put the kibosh on v. to spoil, to ruin; fr. kibosh: nonsense, rubbish *Hotten.*

put the leather in v. to kick someone during a fight *LL.*

put the lid on v. to cover up, to hide; esp. of a newspaper story that is offensive or embarrassing to a given Establishment *Chandler: LG.*

put the mockers on v. to wish the worst of luck; to curse; poss. fr. Hebrew *maches*: a plague *Norman:2.*

put the mozz on v. (Aus. use) to jinx, to cause another person trouble, to inconvenience (cf: put the mockers on) *Wilkes.*

put the scream out v. (criminal use) to put out an alert for a given person *Austin.*

put the screws on v. to pressurize; fr. thumbscrews *Gruber.*

put the shoe on the left foot v. (US Black use) to put blame where it does not belong *Klein.*

put the shoe on the right foot v. (US Black use) to place blame where it duly belongs.

put the shuck on v. to trick to deceive, to fool (verbally); fr. shuck (qv) *Underwood.*

put the skids under v. **1.** to sack someone from a job; **2.** to make someone else hurry up, usu. in doing their work.

put the sleeve on v. to arrest *Runyon:1.*

put the squeeze on v. to pressurize, esp. for money *Humphries:2.*

put the touch on v. to attempt to borrow money *Goldman.*

put the whisper on v. to inform against *Austin.*

put the wind up v. to worry, to frighten *Norman:2.*

put the wood in the hole v. shut the door; usu. as a command.

put through changes v. to alter another person's mental or emotional state, opinions or attitudes (cf: go through changes) *Major.*

put up a black v. to make a mistake; poss. fr. two black balls hauled to the mast of RN ships when a ship was out of control.

put up job n. a pre-arranged, and usu. criminal or at least deceptive, plan.

put up or shut up! (cp) 'put your money where your mouth is!'; fr. gambling use.

putz n. **1.** fr. Yiddish: the penis; thus, by extension; **2.** an idiot, a fool, a simpleton *Price:2.*

PV n. (US prison use) *P*arole *V*iolator *Klein.*

Q n. (US criminal/police use) (abbrev.) San Quentin Prison, California *Dunne.*

Q boat n. (UK police use) unmarked police radio car for surveillance and similar uses; fr. First World War naval vessels that masqueraded as merchant ships *Powis.*

QE v. (UK prison use) to turn Queen's Evidence, thus to inform *Obs. 1981.*

quack n. **1.** (US Black use) a homosexual; who 'ducks down' for sex (?) *Klein*; **2.** doctor, irrespective of abilities *Humphries.*

qualified a. (Black pimp use) experienced, of a prostitute *Milner.*

quandong n. (Aus. use) a girl who accepts any amount of gifts but still refuses to cede her sexual favours. fr. a fruit which is soft on the outside but hard inside *Wilkes.*

quarter to two n. (rhyming sl.) a Jew *Franklyn.*

quashie n. (Jamaican use) country bumpkin, peasant, stupid person *Thelwell.*

queeb n. (US teen. use) any small problem, esp. mechanical *Sculatti.*

queen n. effeminate (older) homosexual male *Performance.*

Queen's Park Ranger(s) n. (rhyming sl.) stranger(s); fr. the West London football club *Cole.*

Queen's Row (homosexual use) the Boston (Mass.) Public Gardens *Jay & Young.*

queer a. homosexual; (currently near-taboo in fashionable liberal circles, thus see gay).

queer as a nine bob note a. unusual, particularly suspicious; the phrase survives the demise of the currency *Powis.*

queerbait n. an effeminate young boy who attracts, or is supposed to attract older male homosexuals *Jay & Young.*

queer-bashing n. beating up (and robbing) male homosexuals; those who do this are unaffected by current rejection of queer as derog.

queer detail n. (US police use) branch of the Vice Squad specializing in homosexual crime (cf: pussy posse) *White.*

Queer Street n. any difficult situation *Hotten.*

quick n. (US Black use) instantly available money *Klein.*

quick and dirty see: quick fix *Kidder.*

quick fix n. any kind of instant remedy, poss. not the best one for long-term dependance *Safire.*

quickie n. spontaneous and brief sexual intercourse *Price:2.*

quick on the trigger a. bright, intelligent, alert *Dunne.*

quick starts n. (US campus use) rubber soled sneakers; popular for those who need to make a speedy exit *Underwood.*

quid n. pound sterling *Performance.*

quids in to be doing well; fr. image of

making a successful bet and the money thus gained *LWT 1984*.

quiff n. **1.** the vagina *Junker*; **2.** females, esp. sexually available ones *Dunne*.

quill n. (drug use) a folded over matchbook cover which hides a narcotic drug *Major*.

quim n. vagina; poss. fr. Celtic *cwm*: a valley *Big Ass Comics 1*.

quit v. to die *Major*.

quitter n. (horseracing use) a horse that is leading the field but unaccountably fails to win the race *Bukowski:1*.

quod n. prison; fr. the quadrangle in which felons exercised *Wodehouse: passim*.

quoit n. (Aus. use) anus, buttocks; 'round with a hole in it' *Wilkes*.

raas n. (Jamaican use) abusive term, fr. English 'your ass'.

raasclat n. (Jamaican use) extreme derog. term; fr. English 'ass cloth'.

rabbit n. **1.** a poor player, esp. in golf or tennis; **2.** (US Black use) a white person *Folb.*

rabbit v. (rhyming sl.) rabbit and pork = to talk *Norman:1.*

rabbit fever n. (US criminal use) **1.** the compelling desire to run off whenever things get difficult; **2.** the compulsion to attempt escapes from any form of imprisonment *Pearce.*

rabbit skin n. (US college use) one college diploma or degree; fr. the fur tippet worn by graduating students.

rabbit's paw n. (rhyming sl.) jaw *Cole.*

race off v. (Aus. use) to seduce *Wilkes.*

rack n. bosom, breasts *Greaser Comics.*

rack v. **1.** to sleep, fr. USMC rack: bed; **2.** to seduce a woman, to make love *Price:2;* **3.** (music business use) to categorize the varieties of rock music into their separate groups, and thus place them on separate racks within a store *Capital Radio 1983.*

rack attack n. (US campus use) a sudden onset of sleepiness *Underwood.*

racked a. tired out, exhausted; fr. rack = bed *Underwood.*

racket n. a noise *Dury, 'Laughter', 1979.*

rackets n. organized crime. fr. 19th C. UK cant racket: trick, plan *Tuff Shit Comics.*

rack monster n. (US campus use) sleepiness, exhaustion *Underwood.*

rack off! (Aus. use) go away! piss off! (qv) *Wilkes.*

rack out v. to fall asleep, to go to bed *Underwood.*

rack pick n. (US Black use) a comb designed specifically for use on a natural or Afro (qqv) hairstyle *Folb.*

rad a. (Valley Girls (qv) use) extreme, excessive, very much; a general intensifier that comes from SE use of radical as 'basic, essential, from the roots' and eschewing political overtones *Pond.*

Raddie n. an Italian living in London, orig. spec. in Clerkenwell *Powis.*

radishes! (US campus use) general excl. of disgust and annoyance *Underwood.*

rado n. (US Black use) (abbrev.) Cadillac El D*orado* (cf: LD) *Folb.*

Rafferty's Rules (Aus. use) no rules whatsoever, anything goes; not fr. an individual, but mispron. of 'refractory' *Bickerton.*

rag n. **1.** sanitary towel; abbrev. jam-rag (qv) *Price:1*; **2.** (derog.) newspaper *O'Brien*; **2.** (abbrev.) wet rag: a weak person *Price:1*; **3.** (Valley Girls (qv) use) an unpleasant person *Pond.*

rag baby n. (US Black use) a poor, ill-clothed girl who is nonetheless attractive *Klein.*

rag box n. (US Black use) the vagina *Klein.*

ragged down heavy (US Black use) exceptionally well-dressed (cf: rags) *Folb.*

ragged out a. (Valley Girls (qv) use) appalling, unattractive, etc. (cf: rag **3**) *Pond.*

raggedy-ass a. poor, badly dressed, impoverished *Bruce:2.*

rag head n. (US Black use) anyone who is not absolutely up to date with current information, gossip, style, etc. *Klein.*

ragmop n. (US Black use) an unkempt, messy person *Major.*

rags n. (US Black use) clothes *Folb.*

rags and bones n. (US Black use) the corpse of a poor person *Klein.*

rag top n. a soft-topped motor car; a convertible *Whitcomb.*

railbird n. (gambling use) a fan or spectator who crowds round the rails that surround a big game in a casino *Alvarez.*

railroad v. **1.** to arrest, try and convict without allowing the person concerned due process of law; to imprison on trumped up charges and faked evidence; to accelerate the legal process in order to ensure – through inadequate defence, legal knowledge, etc. – that a person will be found guilty and sentenced, even though their trial is ostensibly 'fair' *Seale*; **2.** (US campus use) to use influence in the pursuit of personal interests *Underwood.*

railroad whiskey n. (US Black use) cheap wine; fr. Santa Fe brand, the name of a US railroad *Folb.*

rainbows n. (drug use) any form of pill in a coloured jacket *Bukowski:1.*

rainmaker n. (sporting use) in Aus. Rules football, an exceptionally high kick that 'hits the clouds' *Channel-4 TV, 1983.*

rain on v. to kill, to make suffer *Waits.*

rainy-day money n. funds set aside to deal with unforseen difficulties *Performance.*

rainy days n. (US Black use) hard times *Major.*

raise Cain v. to cause as much trouble as one can; fr. Adam's wicked son, Cain *Neaman & Silver.*

raise hell v. to cause a good deal of trouble deliberately (cf: raise Cain) *PT.*

raise sand v. (US Black use) to cause a stir; to cause commotion; to fight; fr. image of kicking sand in someone's face *Klein.*

raise up v. (US Black use) **1.** to leave a place; **2.** spec. to be given leave or parole to leave a prison *Klein.*

rake it in v. to make a great deal of money; poss. fr. the croupier's rake in a casino.

rally v. (US campus use) to have a good time *Underwood.*

rally v. (US campus use) to act utterly madly, drunkenly, obstreperously *Birnbach.*

ralph n. vomit, fr. the noise made while vomiting (cf: buick, hughie) *Underwood.*

ram n. (Aus. use) a trickster's confederate who encourages the public to lose their money in a given con-game; fr. ramp (qv) and fr. the animal's horns, pushing at the victim *Baker.*

ramp n. any form of swindle or fraud *Newman:1.*

ramrod n. the penis *Klein.*

R and R **1.** (US milit. use) rest and recreation; temporary leave from active service *Del Vecchio*; **2.** (US police use) rape and robbery *Neaman & Silver.*

randy a. sexually aroused, eager *Higgins:5.*

range n. (Can. prison use) open area outside cells *Caron.*

rank a. second-rate, inferior, disgusting; fr. SE: rotten *Selby:1.*

rank v. (street gang use) to insult, often by ritual insults directed at the other person's mother (cf: dirty dozens) *Salisbury.*

rank one's style v. aka: *rank one's game/action/play*: deliberately to obstruct another's sexual advances (cf: cock block) *Folb*.

rannygazoo n. nonsense, irrelevant, irritating activity *Wodehouse:AAG*.

rap n. **1.** a blow, a hit *Higgins:1*; **2.** (Aus. use) congratulations, a word of praise, a boost *Wilkes*; **2.** (Aus. use) congratulations, a word of praise, a boost *Wilkes*; **3.** conversation; speech; **4.** a criminal charge, allegation.

rap v. **1.** to talk, to converse; thus rap session: an intense conversation; by extension, in new therapy use: an encounter group *Uneeda Comix*; **2.** to hit *Selby:1*.

rap on the real v. (US Black use) to speak sincerely, honestly *Klein*.

rap parlor n. current euph. for massage parlour, itself a cover for a store-front organization behind which, while legitimate massage may be available, men pay for a variety of sexual service from 'relief massage' (masturbation) to full intercourse *Rawson*.

rap sheet n. criminal record (cf: form, previous) *Higgins:1*.

rapt a. (Aus. use) overjoyed with, carried away, delighted: fr. irraptured + wrapped up in *Ready*.

rashing n. (US Black use) a mixture of thrashing and harassing *Klein*.

raspberry n. (rhyming sl.) raspberry ripple = cripple *Dury, interview, 1978*.

raspberry tart n. (rhyming sl.) **1.** heart; **2.** fart *Cole*.

raspy . **1.** (US Black use) unattractive, unkempt *Folb*; **2.** (Valley Girls (qv) use) excellent, wonderful (by bad = good syndrome) *Pond*.

Rastus n. (derog.) black man; fr. cliché Black name in slave era *Vidal*.

rat n. **1.** an unpleasant person; **2.** an informer.

rat ass n. term of abuse *Southern & Hoffenberg*.

ratbag n. derog. description or address *Humphries*.

rat bastard n. general term of abuse *Southern & Hoffenberg*.

ratchet-mouth v. talking nonsense, talking for the sake of hearing oneself talk *Higgins:4*.

rat fuck v. **1.** orig. campus use: a prank, a practical joke; **2.** devel. to electoral 'dirty tricks' à la Campaign to Re-elect the President (CREEP) in 1972, sabotaging the opponent's campaign by illicit means.

rat fucker n. a home-made tool which approximates a car's starting-handle *Simmons*.

rat-hole v. to hide away, to save up money, to hoard *Thompson:J*.

rat on v. to betray *Higgins:2*.

rat one out v. to betray, to inform against *Larner*.

rat one's hair v. to backcomb one's hair in order to create the once popular 'beehive' style, somewhat recreated by current teenage 'punk' fashions *Jan Harold Brunvand, 'The Vanishing Hitch-hiker', 1983*.

rat prick n. general term of abuse.

ratshit a. unpleasant, disgusting, annoying.

ratshit! general excl. of annoyance or distaste *Farina*.

ratted a. (UK 'society' use) drunk *T 18/7/83*.

rattle v. to unnerve, to frighten *Wodehouse:AAG*.

rattle one's beads v. to complain; usu. homosexual use *Stanley*.

rattle one's dags v. (Aus. use) to hurry up, to get a move on (cf: dags) *Bickerton*.

rattler n. **1.** (UK police use) the London underground railway *Powis*; **2.** a promiscuous girl *Cole*.

ratty a. **1.** rundown, ramshackle, unkempt *Price:3*; **2.** irritated, annoyed, obstreperous *Sillitoe*.

raunchy a. sordid, degenerate, excessive, seedy *Wolfe:2*.

rave n. **1.** a party; **2.** (theatre use) a highly congratulatory review *Norman:2*.

raver n. anyone devoted to having an energetically good time with variations of 'dope, sex and rock 'n' roll' as to individual taste and situation.

raw a. **1.** naked *Runyon*; **2.** inexperienced, a rookie, unsophisticated (cf: fish).

raw deal n. unfair, harsh treatment, particularly poor luck; usu. fr. point of view of victim.

raw sole n. (US Black use) a virgin Black girl (cf: fish, n., a.); pun on soul (qv) *Klein*.

rays n. sunshine.

razoo n. (Aus. use) a small amount of money; usu. in phrase 'not a brass razoo' (qv): absolutely penniless *Humphries:2*.

razor n. **1.** a notably 'sharp' person *Klein*; **2.** (rhyming sl.) razor blade = spade (qv) = Black person *Cole*.

razz v. to tease, to heckle, to barrack; fr. rhyming sl. raspberry tart = fart (qv) *Price: 2*.

razzle-dazzle v. (US Black use) **1.** to hang around; to loiter; **2.** to pretend something has happened/is happening when in fact nothing is *Klein*.

reach v. (US Black use) to help *Klein*.

reader n. **1.** (UK prison use) any form of reading matter, books, magazines, comics, etc. *LL*; **2.** (US police use/cant) warrant for arrest, 'wanted' poster; **3.** (cant) small-time thief who follows delivery men to their destination, having sneaked a look at the label, then claims to be the official recipient *Neaman & Silver*.

readers n. (gambling use) a crooked deck of cards which a cheat can read from the backs *Runyon:1*.

readies n. (abbrev.) ready money; cash, rather than cheques, etc. *Performance*.

read one's beads v. (homosexual use) chastise, berate, attack someone verbally *Stanley*.

read them and weep (cp) accept my superiority, like it or not; fr. poker use, a phr. used as the winner of a pot reveals his/her winning hand.

read the riot act v. to tell off severely and threateningly; fr. 19th C. and earlier practice of reading Riot Act to unruly crowds prior to attacking with police or troops if they refused to calm or disperse *Farrell*.

read the Rocks and Shoals v. (USMC use) to tell off, to upbraid (cf: read the riot act) *Uris*.

ready a. (US Black use) aware, sophisticated, prepared to deal with the real world *Folb*.

ready n. (abbrev.) ready money (cf: readies) *Austin*.

ready-eyed fully aware of a given situation in all its ramifications, both obvious and hidden *Powis*.

real babe n. (US teen. use) an admirable, attractive person of the opposite (or preferred) sex *Pond*.

real deal n. (US Black use) see bottom line *Klein*.

real grit n. (US Black use) the absolute truth, the essential facts (cf: nitty-gritty) *Klein*.

real McCoy n. the genuine article, fr. Norman Selby 'Kid McCoy' (1873–1940) a boxer in the US (cf: real McKay) *R. Boycott, 'Batty, Bloomers & Boycott', 1982*.

real McKay the genuine article, the real (and superior) thing; fr. the self-esteem of Scots in general and McKay's in particular (cf: real McCoy) *R. Boycott, 'Batty Bloomers & Boycott', 1982*.

real man n. (US prison use) a prisoner well-respected by his peers *Neaman & Silver*.

real woman (US Black use) a heterosexual woman (cf: natural woman) *Folb*.

reaming n. see: rimming *Jay & Young*.

ream job to lick and suck the anus, usu. homosexual use *Klein*.

rear-ender an automobile accident in which one vehicle hits the back of another *McFadden*.

recluse n. (US prison use) one who has been inside a prison for five years or more without hearing from anyone in the free world *Klein*.

recoup v. (US criminal/Black use) to start off fresh and determined on one's release from prison, undeterred by a few years' absence from the world; fr.

recouping one's losses *Klein.*

recce n. (abbrev.) reconnaissance; orig. milit. use, now a general term for making a preliminary exploration, assessment, etc.

red n. **1.** (UK criminal use) gold (cf: red stuff) *LL*; **2.** (US (Texas) use) chilli.

Red n. (abbrev.) Red Coat, a staff member of a Butlins Holiday Camp *Obs. 12/6/83.*

red a. **1.** communist (cf: pinko); **2.** (abbrev.) redneck (qv) *White.*

red ass n. bad temper, irritation *Underwood.*

redball n. (US milit. use) in Vietnam, an enemy trail or road *Del Vecchio.*

red band n. (US prison use) a trusty; fr. the red band around his arm that denotes his privileged status *Norman:1.*

red boys n. (Royal Agricultural Coll, Cirencester use) fire extingushers. *Barr.*

red Biddy n. the cheapest red wine, beloved of down-and-outs.

red dog on a white horse (US Black use) a woman having her menstrual period *Folb.*

redhot n. (US Black use) a highly aggressive, volatile person *Klein.*

red lane n. **1.** the throat *Hotten*; **2.** the vagina.

red-light v. to throw someone out of a car or other vehicle and force them to walk home, often over a great distance; they watch the rear-lights recede into the distance (cf: shellroad) *Runyon.*

redloch n. (butchers' backsl.) shoulder, both human and as a cut of meat *Cole.*

red Mary n. (US Black use) a menstrual period *Folb.*

redneck n. a peasant, esp. Southern US poor farmer who is stupid and racist *Jay & Young.*

red pants n. irritation, bad temper *Underwood.*

reds n. **1.** barbiturates, fr. colour of pills. (cf: whites, yellows, purple hearts) *Dury*; **2.** Communists, fr. predominant colour symbolizing world revolution.

Red Sea pedestrian n. (Aus. derog. use) a Jew, fr. the exploits of the Hebrews during their Exodus from Egypt *Humphries:2.*

red stuff n. gold; esp. jewellery *Powis.*

redtape n. bureaucratic interference and obfuscation, inevitably leading to problems and delay for those which it entangles.

red-tapers n. bureaucrats, civil servants *Sanders:2.*

red wings (Hells Angels use) cunnilingus with a menstruating woman *Mandelkau.*

reeb n. (London backsl.) beer *Powis.*

reefer n. **1.** marijuana; **2.** a marijuana cigarette; both meanings fr. greefo (qv) *SF Comic.*

reeking a. drunk (cf: stinking) *Dickson.*

reel in the biscuit v. (US campus use) to seduce a girl successfully *Bernbach.*

reet a. ideal, perfect, excellent, quintessential; fr. mispron. of right.

reffo n. (Aus. use) (abbrev.) refugee, derog. term for any European (esp. Italian, Greek, Yugoslav) immigrants to Australia; the late 1930s influx of Jews to the US created 'refujew' *Humphries:2.*

regular guy n. a thoroughly good person – in the speaker's opinion his/her peer, intellectually, in sense of humour, opinions, politics, etc. *Farrell.*

regular Joe n. a conventional (conservative) person (cf: Joe Public) *Price:3.*

rehash n.,v. a recreation, a post-mortem of an event; to discuss once more, to assess the past, either immediate or distant.

reimburse v. (US Black use) to lose one's life for the refusal or inability to pay off a debt or favour *Klein.*

reload v. (conman use) to let a victim win at a game of three-card monte (qv) prior to having him bet a larger sum, which he will inevitably then lose *Powis.*

REMF n. (US milit. use) (acro., pron. 'rimph'): *R*ear *E*chelon *M*other-*F*uckers; used by combat troops *Del Vecchio*.
Renee n. girl-friend; fr. the popular name *G 28/3/83*.
rep n. (abbrev.) reputation; spec. a member's standing and status in a street gang *rr*.
repap n. (backsl.) paper *Cole*.
repeat v. a genteel euph. for burping or farting; the food is 'repeating' itself.
repo man n. (abbrev.) repossession man: one who is employed by finance companies to repossess goods on which the owner is defaulting as to his payments.
reppock n. (backsl.) copper = policeman (cf: esclop) *Cole*.
reptiles n. (US Black use) shoes, fr. the skins used for many popular styles *Klein*.
rescue station n. (US Black use) liquor store; ironic corruption of rescue mission: a centre for alcoholics and other down-and-outs *Folb*.
resting a. (theatrical use) a euph. for unemployed; the US version is *at liberty Green:2*.
result n. a successful outcome to a given endeavour: a sporting victory; an arrest for policemen; a lucrative robbery for villains, etc. *Newman:1*.
retchtub n. (butchers' backsl.) a butcher *Cole*.
rettes n. (US preppie (qv) use) (abbrev.) cigarettes *Bernbach*.
re-up v. to reenlist, to join up again; fr. milit. use *Price:3*.
rev. v. (UK 'society' use) to improve, to gee up; fr. motor car use *K. Clarke*.
revo n. the Revolution; that unspecified explosion that stands as a grail for radicals everywhere.
RF (acro.) *R*at *F*uck (qv).
RFD queen n. a homosexual living in a rural area, outside the main gay world; fr. *R*ural *F*ree *D*elivery *Legman*.
rhino n. money *LL*.
rhubarb n. nonsense, rubbish, fr. actors' traditional muttering of 'Rhubarb' to provide background in crowd scenes *Austin*.
rib v. to tease, to make fun of *Goulart*.
ribby a. **1.** fr. on the ribs: short of money, broke (qv); **2.** second rate, poor quality *Powis*.
ricer n. (derog.) an Asian person; fr. the predominant Oriental staple *Folb*.
rich a. surprising, highly unlikely; usu. *that's rich*.
Richard n. (rhyming sl.) Richard the Third = bird = girl (friend) *LL*.
Richard the Third (rhyming sl.) **1.** bird = girl (friend) (cf: Richard); **2.** (theatrical use) the bird, ie booing from an audience *Franklyn*; **3.** a turd *Cole*.
rick n. an error, a mistake; poss. abbrev. ricket: a mistake or fr. bookies' sl. *rick*: a spurious bet *Austin*.
ricket n. a mistake, a blunder *Norman: 2*.
ride n. **1.** an automobile *Folb*; **2.** sexual intercourse *'Not The Nine O'Clock News', BBC-2 TV, 1980*.
ride a blind piece v. (homosexual use) to fellate an uncircumcized penis *Legman*.
ride punk v. (US Black use) aka: *ride pussy, ride the bitch's seat*: for a woman to sit between two men in a car *Folb*.
ride shotgun v. to sit in the seat next to the driver in a car; fr. stagecoach era use of a shotgun-wielding assistant who sat next to the coachman and protected him against marauding Indians, bandits, etc.
ride the deck v. (US prison use) to perform anal intercourse *Legman*.
ride the planks v. (Aus. surf use) to go surfing *Humphries: 2*.
ride the porcelain Honda v. (US campus use) to have diarrhoea (cf: drive the porcelain bus) *Bernbach*.
ride the rag v. (US Black use) to have a menstrual period *Folb*.
ride the wagon v. (US Black use) to enjoy a pleasant experience on a given drug *Klein*.
ride tough v. (US Black use) **1.** to be intoxicated by a drug; **2.** to be riding in a noteworthy car *Klein*.

ridgie-didgie a. (Aus. use) genuine, honest; fr. Uk cant *ridge* = gold in 17th C.*Baker*.

riff n. (US Black use) familiar or habitual words; fr. jazz use *Folb*.

rig n. **1.** (truck driver use) a truck; **2.** (drug use) the needed used to inject narcotics *Underwood*.

rig a jig v. (US Black/pimp use) to set up a potential trick (qv) or victim for deception or for his paying one of the pimp's girls for sex *Klein*.

right a. extremely, very; thus, a *right bastard*, a *right good 'un,* etc.

right arm! (US campus use) see: right on! *Underwood*.

righteous a. **1.** of people: honest, trustworthy, honourable; **2.** of things, esp. drugs: excellent, first-rate *SF Comics*; **3.** ideologically pure *Seale*.

righteous moss n. (US Black use) white people's hair *Major*.

right guy n. (US prison use) a popular prisoner, respected by his peers (cf: real man) *Neaman & Silver*.

righto! (excl.) certainly! *Performance*.

right on! (excl.) excellent, perfect, exactly right; orig. Black use but taken up by white hippies, radicals, etc; fr. 'right on time' *Seale*.

right sort n. a promiscuous girl *Cole*.

right up one's alley absolutely as one wishes, specifically to one's taste *W. Allen, 'Manhattan', 1979*.

rigid a. drunk, and passed out *Dickson*.

rim v. to stimulate the anus with the lips and tongue (cf: ream) *Jay & Young*.

rim-job n. see rim.

rim queen n. a homosexual who enjoys anilingus *Stanley*.

rim slide n. (US prison use) a silent but foul-smelling fart *Klein*.

ring n. the anus, the buttocks.

ring v. to alter a car for the purposes of using it as a getaway vehicle, hold-up van, etc. *Newman: 1*.

ring a bell v. to remind one of something, to jog one's memory.

ringburner n. (UK 'society' use) diarrhoea, the runs (qv) (cf: ring) *Barr*.

ring-ding n. fool, second-rate person, no-hoper; poss. fr. a punch-drunk boxer who has 'bells ringing' in his head *Farina*.

ringer n. **1.** a fake, someone posing as a person they are not; esp. a pool or bowling hustler (qv) who pretends not to be an expert; **2.** a horse or dog substituted either for a better or a worse animal for the purposes of those betting either for or against it; **3.** a second-hand car made up to look better than it is; **4.** one who specializes in stealing then improving second-hand cars for sale in UK or Europe *Powis*.

ring (her) bell v. to produce (female) orgasm during intercourse.

ring (his) bell v. to concuss, esp. in US football use when this may well follow a clash of helmets *Green: 2*.

ring it on v. to outwit, to fool *Powis*.

ring one's chimes v. to have or to give a partner an orgasm.

ringside n. (show business use) in a nightclub or similar establishment, those tables nearest to the stage; fr. boxing use *Bruce: 2*.

ring the changes v. (UK criminal use) to defraud, to deceive, esp. by passing counterfeit money *LL*.

rinky-dink a. cheap, second-rate *Underwood*.

rip and tear v. (rhyming sl.) to swear *Cole*.

ripe a. drunk *Dickson*.

rip her guts down v. (US Black use) to copulate aggressively, sadistically, but with implication that both partners achieve mutual satisfaction *Klein*.

rip into v. **1.** to start a fight; **2.** to criticize harshly (cf: tear into).

rip joint n. (US campus use) any store that charges exorbitant prices to students; fr. rip-off and joint (qqv) *Underwood*.

rip off n. a fraud, a cheat, a disappointment *Seale*.

rip off v. **1.** to steal, to cheat *Tuff Shit Comics*; **2.** to kill, to assassinate *Milner*.

rip off artist n. **1.** a thief; **2.** a prostitute who specializes in robbing her clients and as such is more thief than purveyor of commercial sex *OUI 8/75*; **3.** any form of cheat, emotional as well as material *Price: 3*.

ripped a. extremely intoxicated on drink, drugs or a mixture *Mandelkau*.

ripped to the tits a. an extreme version of ripped (qv).

ripper a. (Aus. use) excellent wonderful, perfect, etc.; has replaced the obs. *bonzer*; but cited in Hotten 1860 *Humphries: 2*.

rip-snorter n. anything exceptional or remarkable and of which the speaker approves.

rise and shine! jocular wake-up call; sometimes preceded by 'wakey-wakey!' (cf: hands off (your) cocks . . .).

ritzy a. smart, chic, fashionable; fr. the Ritz Hotel, once the epitome of such attainments.

roach n. the unsmoked portion of a marijuana/hashish cigarette; fr. cockroach *Performance*.

roach clip n. a small spring clip or pair of tweezers used to hold the last fragments of a marijuana cigarette, which is otherwise too hot to hold in one's fingers.

roach killers n. extremely pointed shoes for men, popular in New York c.1960s; fr. idea of their stabbing cockroaches (cf: winkle-pickers) *Price: 1*.

road brew n. (US campus use) aka: *roadies, road sauce*: beer *Bernbach*.

road dog n. (US Black use) an extremely initimate friend (CF: running partner) *Klein*.

roadie n. (music use) road crew, member of rock band's support unit who sets up and dismantles stage, equipment, etc. *May*.

roaf (bacsksl.) four *Cole*.

roak v. (US Black use) to beat savagely about the head *Klein*.

Robert E. n. (rhyming sl.) Robert E. Lee = pee = urination *May*.

rock n. **1.** diamond *Higgins: 1*; **2.** a man who is sturdy and solid both emotionally, physically and in his character.

rock 'n' roll (US milit. use) firing a weapon on full automatic; the weapon tends to move violently around *Del Vecchio*.

rockers n. UK youth cult who wore leather, rode powerful motorbikes and fought their ritual rivals, the mods (qv); latterly the hard-core rockers developed into a UK version of the US Hells Angels.

rocket n. a severe reprimand or telling off.

rockets n. (US Black use) bullets *Major*.

rock of ages n. (rhyming sl.) wages *Cole*.

rock out v. (US Black use) to collapse, to be exhausted *Folb*.

rocks n. **1.** the testicles; **2.** courage, bravery *Higgins: 5*.

rocks for jocks (US campus use) undergraduate course in 'introductory geology' *Birnbach*.

rock spider n. (S. Afr. use) an Afrikaaner *Marcuson*.

rod n. **1.** penis *Gothic Blimp Works No. 4, 1969*; **2.** a gun *Runyon*; **3.** an overcoat *Powis*.

rodded a. carrying a gun.

rodge n. a fact, anything that's true; fr. airforce roger = message received and understood *Underwood*.

Rods n. (UK 'society' use) Harrods (cf: Freds) *Barr*.

rod walloper n. masturbator; fr. rod **1.** (qv) *Humphries*.

rofe n. (UK prison use) fr. backsl. four-year sentence *LL*.

roger v. to have sexual intercourse, to seduce; fr. the name often given to bulls in 18th C. *Keyes*.

roll v. to rob. usu. *roll a drunk Burroughs:*1.

roll n. (abbrev.) bankroll *Higgins: 3*.

roll a number v. to prepare a marijuana cigarette (cf: number).

Roller n. a Rolls Royce car *Dury*.

roller n. **1.** a pickpocket who specializes in stealing from drunks (cf:

lushworker) *Chandler: Notebk*; **2.** (US criminal use) a policeman who specializes in stopping people on the street for an instant search in the hope of finding stolen goods or drugs *Klein*; **3.** (US Black use) one who keeps moving continuously; **4.** (drug use) a vein that rolls as one attempts to insert a needle *Klein*.

rollick v. (rhyming sl) (euph.) bollick = tell off, reprimand; thus 'a good rollicking' and 'rollicks!' *Cole*.

roll in v. aka: *roll up*: arrive, come home *Higgins: 3*.

rolling a. **1.** (abbrev.) rolling with money: very well off *Schulberg*; **2.** very drunk; fr. one's gait *Dickson*.

rolling in the aisles a. very much amused, reduced to near-hysterical laughter; fr. theatrical use referring to a comedian's success *Wodehouse: MOJ*.

roll in the hay sexual intercourse, with implication of spontaneity, adultery, *al fresco Higgins: 5*.

roll out v. (US campus use) to leave, to depart *Underwood*.

roll them bones! (gambling use) throw those dice! used with consciousness of slight archaism and only in the context of a crap game.

roll-up n. a handmade cigarette of papers and tobacco *Cole*.

roll with the punches v. to take events as they come and not to be unbalanced by problems; fr. boxing imagery *Higgins: 1*.

roll your own (US Black use) invitation to make yourself at home, do whatever you fancy; fr. rolling one's own cigarettes *Klein*.

roman candle n. (RAF use) the failure of a parachute to open and the resultant plunge to his death of the parachutist.

Roman culture n. orgies, group sex; fr. popular fantasties of the 'decline and fall' of Rome *Rawson*.

romp n. (horseracing use) an easy win, thus *to come home in a romp*: to saunter past the winning post, out-distancing all rivals.

romp it v. (US campus use) to accelerate in a car *Underwood*.

roof it v. to have sex on the roofs of New York apartment buildings *Sanders: 2*.

rook v. to cheat, to swindle, to steal; fr. allegedly larcenous character of the bird (cf: pigeon) *Hotten*.

rookie n. a novice, a beginner, a new recruit; esp. in milit., police, sports use; poss. fr. recruit *Runyon: 1*.

rooks n. see: rocks *Klein*.

room to rent n. (Valley Girls (qv) use) a stupid person, whose brain is 'vacant' *Harpers/Queen 1/83*.

rooster n. (US Black use) a sexually active male; fr. the farmyard bird *Folb*.

rooster time n. (US teen. use) the early morning, 'cock's crow' *Sculatti*.

root n. **1.** the penis; **2.** the person with whom one has intercourse; more usu. the female of the two.

root v. to have sexual intercourse.

rooted a. (Aus. use) exhausted, crippled, out of action *Humphries: 2*.

rooter n. a sports fan *P. Roth, 'The Great American Novel', 1973*.

root-faced a. humourless, sanctimonious, censorious; fr. a face carved into the hard twists of a tree root *Humphries: 2*.

root for v. to support, esp. a sports team *Grogan*.

rootiepoot n. (US Black use) see pootbutt *Folb*.

rope n. (drug use) a vein *Goldman*.

rope in v. to involve, to include *Higgins: 4*.

ropey a. second-rate, inadequate, mediocre, rundown, etc.; poss. fr. RAF use: an obsolete aircraft, overburdened with a variety of ropes.

rorty a. (Aus. use) rowdy, noisy, esp. of a party; fr. obs. SE (19th C.) *Humphries: 2*.

Rory n. **1.** (UK prison use; rhyming sl.) Rory O'Moore = door (of one's cell *LL*; **2.** (rhyming sl.) floor *Wright*.

Roscoe n. a handgun *Chandler: Notebk*.

rose among the thorns n. (US pimp

use) a good-looking prostitute in a stable (qv) of less attractive women *Klein*.

rosewood n. (US Black use) a policeman's nightstick; fr. wood from which it was made *Major*.

rosiner n. (Aus. use) any form of stiff drink, a pick-me-up *Wilkes*.

Rosy Lea (Lee) n. (rhyming sl.) tea.

rotgut n. cheap whisky; fr. its effects *X*.

rot n. rubbish, nonsense; esp. in talk rot *Wodehouse: MOJ*.

rotten a. (Aus. use) very drunk *Wilkes*.

rough end of the pineapple (Aus. use) hostile or unfair treatment *Wilkes*.

rough-house v. to fight, to beat up *Goulart*.

rough it v. to live deprived of life's material comforts; not simply to be poor, but to volunteer oneself – as in camping, the forces, etc. – for such hardy existence *Wodehouse: AAG*.

roughneck n. **1.** a thug, a hoodlum, a fighter *Heller*; **2.** a labourer on an oil rig *Green:2*.

rough trade n. (homosexual use) a violent sexual partner; often a man who is or poses as a construction worker, serviceman, truck driver, motorcyclist, etc., with appropriate costumes, often of leather.

roundball n. (US Black use) basketball (as opp. to football, played with an oval ball) *Folb*.

rounder n. (Can. prison use) anyone who knows their way around the underworld *Caron*.

roundeye n. **1.** the anus; **2.** a white person, as opposed to an oriental (cf: slant).

round file n. (US campus use) wastepaper basket *Underwood*.

roundhead n. **1.** (drug use) any drug contained in a capsule with curved ends *Folb*; **2.** a circumcised penis, the boy who has one (usu. school use) (cf: clipped).

round house v. (US pimp use) for a prostitute to go around the world (qv), licking, sucking and fucking (qv) every orifice and erogenous zone her client has to offer *Klein*.

round the houses n. (rhyming sl.) trousers *Cole*.

rouser n. (drug use) any type of amphetamine or stimulant drug which 'gets one up' *Klein*.

rout v. (US campus use) to engage in sexual intercourse *Underwood*.

rower n. (UK prison use) an argument; fr. row *Obs. 1981*.

row in v. **1.** (criminal use) to allow someone to join a scheme, a conspiracy *Norman: 2*; **2.** (UK police use) to implicate a given suspect in a given crime *Laurie*.

row out v. (UK police use) to exonerate a given suspect from a given crime *Laurie*.

Roy n. (Aus. use) a chic, sophisticated 'trendy' Australian; the opposite of Alf (qv) *Wilkes*.

royal a. (Jamaican use) any Black person from a race other than West Indian *Thelwell*.

Royal Mail n. (rhyming sl.) bail,usu. criminal/prison use *Cole*.

rozzer n. **1.** policeman; poss. fr. Romany *roozlo*: strong; or fr. *roast*, a villain *Humphries*; **2.** (US Black use) a rubber contraceptive with small protrusions for extra stimulation of the vagina *Klein*.

R/S (sex advertisements use) (acro.) rough stuff; incl. sadomasochism, urolagnia (cf: water sports, golden showers), infibulation (piercing of nipples), rubberwear, etc. *Neaman & Silver*.

rub v. (US Black use) to criticize *Klein*.

rubadub m. sexual intercourse; esp. quick and spontaneous *Southern & Hoffenberg*.

rub-a-dub n. (rhyming sl.) pub *Norman: 2*.

rubbed a. murdered, killed; fr. rubbed out = erased.

rubber n. a contraceptive sheath.

rubber v. to look around, to gaze at; fr. rubberneck *Howard*.

rubber boot n. contraceptive sheath *Higgins: 3.*

rubber cheque n. a bouncing cheque (qv) that is not honoured by the writer's bank.

Rubber City n. (CB use) Akron, Ohio *CB.*

rubber heels **1.** the Special Branch; **2.** the internal investigations department of Scotland Yard, policing the police *Austin.*

rubber johnny n. contraceptive sheath.

rubberneck v. **1.** (US Black use) masturbation, self-fellation (if one is acrobatically capable) *Klein*; **2.** to act as an obvious tourist; fr. visitors to New York City craning their necks to view the high buildings *Wolfe: 2.*

rubbidy n. see: rub-a-dub *Humphries.*

rubbin' one's nubbin female masturbation *Maledicta.*

rubbish n. (UK police use) everyday, mundane and undemanding police duties *Laurie.*

rubbish v. **1.** to attack verbally, to slander *Humphries*; **2.** to treat badly, with disrespect *BBC Radio 3 1983.*

rube n. a fool, an unsophisticated person; fr. carnival use and 'yokel' name: Reuben *Norman: 1.*

rub in v. to emphasise, often with malicious pleasure *Wodehouse: IJ.*

rub out v. murder, assassinate, kill *Fiction Illus. 3.*

rub up v. to stimulate the penis to erection using the hands *Higgins: 1.*

rub up the wrong way v. to annoy, to infuriate; fr. stroking a cat against the 'grain' of its fur.

rubyfruit n. the female genitals; fr. colour and supposed appearance; best known as title of Rita Mae Brown's 'Rubyfruit Jungle' *Maledicta.*

ruck n. a fight, an argument; abbrev. ruckus (qv) also fr. ruck: to disturb, orig. clothes and thence tempers *Norman: 2.*

rucker n. an arguer, a combative person *Norman: 2.*

rucking n. a severe reprimand *Norman: 1.*

ruckus n. a fight, a celebration, a noisy party or demonstration *Himes: 1.*

rude a. (euph.) sexual *Barr.*

rude parts n. (euph.) genitals, male or female (in the latter case extended to breasts also) *Barr.*

ruffle n. **1.** (homosexual use) the passive partner in a lesbian relationship; poss. fr. 19th C. *rufus*: the pudendum *Stanley*; **2.** (US Black use) a fight *Klein.*

rug n. toupee, hairpiece, usu. show business use; it lies on/covers one's bald patch *Price: 3.*

rug beat n. (US Black use) a noisy, festive party where the dancing 'beats the rug' *Klein.*

rugby team (bingo use) 15 *Wright.*

ruggsy a. aka: *warry* British milit. use (esp. paratroops), a consciously 'macho' image, featuring torn T-shirts, faded fatigues, large boots, and larger muscles *Green: 2.*

rug rat n. a small child who is still crawling on the carpet (cf: ankle-biter).

rugy n. (US Black use) unattractive; ill-tempered; elision of 'rude guy' (?) *Folb.*

ruin v. (homosexual use) deliberate exaggeration of one's effeminacy to shock fellow gays *Stanley.*

Rule 43 (UK prison use) voluntary solitary confinement for the sake of a prisoner's safety: child molesters, rapists, etc. choose this in preference to the natural justice of their peers *Newman: 3.*

rum a. odd, peculiar, strange *Wright.*

rumble n.v. **1.** (US use) a street gang fight *Price: 1*; **2.** (UK use) a fight *Payne.*

rumble v. **1.** to discover, to find out *Powis*; **2.** (drug use) to be searched by the police *Burroughs: 1.*

rum-dum n. a heavy drinker, a rummy (qv); fr. rum, the drink *Runyon.*

rummy a. odd, peculiar, bizarre; fr. rum (qv) *Wodehouse: YMS.*

rummy n. a drunkard.

rump v. (US Black use) to copulate *Klein.*

rumpot n. a drunkard *Runyon: 1.*
rumour n. (teen. use) anything considered dead, finished or currently irrelevant *Sculatti.*
run n. (Hells Angels use) full scale club outing involving all the Hells Angels in a given chapter and devoted to maximum excess in all possible areas of activity *Wolfe: 2.*
runabout n. (US Black use) facts on a given situation *Klein.*
run a double train v. (US Black use) for two men to penetrate a woman simultaneously – by the vagina and the anus (cf: make a sandwich) *Folb.*
run a line v. see: shoot a line *Klein.*
run a tight ship v. to keep full control of a given situation; to be an efficient organizer or leader; fr. nautical use *Vidal.*
rundown n. explanation, the facts.
run down game v. (Black pimp use) to explain the principles of the pimping business, both from experienced pimps to novices and from the pimp to his girls, telling them the tricks of their tricks (qv).
run down one's best game v. (US Black use) to make one's best, cleverest and most skilful efforts *Shulman.*
run down some lines v. (US Black use) **1.** to make conversation; **2.** to attempt seduction by smooth talking *Folb.*
rung a. cars supplied with false plates, documents, etc. for use in a robbery (cf: ringer) *Newman: 1.*
run-in n. an argument, a controversy, a fight *Wolfe: 2.*
run in v. to arrest; run in to gaol *Southern & Hoffenberg.*
run into the ground v. to persist in an action or in speech to the extent that all meaning and importance is lost; fr. driving a car or riding a horse until it collapses.
run it down v. to explain, to point out facts *Seale.*
runner n. (UK police/criminal use) one who is on the run from the police *Powis.*
runners (Aus. use) track shoes, training shoes.
running down assessing, going through *Price: 2.*
running partner n. (US Black use) a close friend with whom one pursues most of one's daily activities *Folb.*
running with allied to, in partnership with, on the same side as *Seale.*
run off at the mouth aka: *run off at the jaw/jibs*: to talk to excess and to the irritation of one's audience *Folb.*
run one on v. to arrest.
run one way and look another v. (US Black use) to act in a duplicitous manner; to cheat deliberately *Klein.*
run out of road v. for a motorcar (or its driver) to fail to negotiate a curve properly and to skid off the road rather than turn the corner.
run out on v. to abandon, to leave suddenly *Goulart.*
run over v. to victimize *Seale.*
run rings around v. to beat comprehensively; to make one to look foolish.
runs n. diahorrea (cf: trots) *Tidy.*
run sets on v. aka: *throw sets on, roll sets on:* to hit with combination left and right punches (cf: one-two) *Folb.*
run up side o' your head v. (Black use) to beat up *Milner.*
run with the ball v. to take on a problem and tackle it on one's own initiative, rather than passing the buck; fr. US football or UK rugby use *Dickson.*
ruptured duck n. (US milit. use) the lapel pin or pocket insignia worn by an honourably discharged US serviceman; thus the honourable discharge itself *Chandler: LG.*
rush n. the immediate and intense feeling that follows the injection of heroin into a vein *Tuff Shit Comics.*
rush v. **1.** to show intense interest in something or someone; **2.** (US campus use) to pay court to a student with the hope of having them join a given fraternity.
Russki n. (derog.) a Russian *BvdB.*
rust-bucket n. (Aus. use) a car that is

noticeably and dangerously rusty *Wilkes*.

rusty a. exhausted; out of practice.

rusty dusty n. the buttocks, esp. with the inference that someone has been sitting around doing nothing – thus they are 'rusty' and 'dusty' from lack of movement *Burroughs: 1*.

rusty-gun a. veteran policeman *Grogan*.

Ruth Buzzy n. (US Black use) a plain-looking woman; fr. the actress best known for her work on 'Rowan & Martin's Laugh-In', c.1967. *Folb*.

RWV (UK police/prison use) *R*obbery *W*ith *V*iolence *LL*.

ryache n. (backsl.) chair *Cole*.

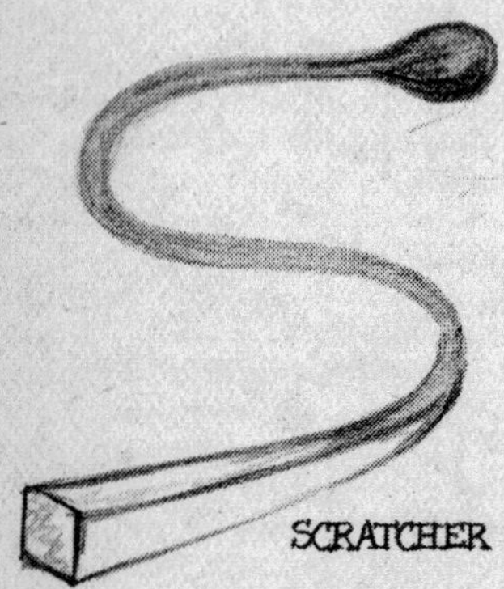

sack n. **1.** a bed *Austin*; (US Black use) **2.** an uncoordinated, unathletic person who just lies dumpily around *Folb*; **3.** one's home; fr. its being where one sleeps (cf: rack) *Klein.*

sack v. to dismiss from a job.

sacked out a. fast asleep *Bruce:2.*

sack it up v. (US Black use) to terminate, to bring to a conclusion *Klein.*

sack lunch n. see: box lunch *Folb.*

sack mouth n. (US Black use) one who talks too much; a gossip; thus a large, gaping mouth *Folb.*

sack o' nuts n. (US Black use) the scrotum; fr. nuts (qv) *Klein.*

sack out v. to fall asleep, to go to bed; fr. sack (qv) *Goldman.*

sad sack n. a miserable, depressed (and depressing) individual, usu. thus singled out in an institution – prison, army, etc. *E. Presley, 'Jailhouse Rock', 1958.*

sack time n. time spent asleep, in bed *Fiction Illus.3.*

safe n. (abbrev.) safety: a contraceptive sheath *Rawson.*

safe screw n. (UK prison use) aka: *safe twirl*: a prison officer who can be trusted to permit or even join in various illicit goings-on, transactions etc. *LL.*

sail close to the wind v. to take risks, esp. with a set of rules and regulations fr. naut. use.

sail into v. to attack, physically or verbally.

St Grotlesex n. (US preppie (qv) use) a portmanteau description of St Marks, St Paul's, Groton and Middlesex *Bernbach.*

saint n. (US police use) a highly scrupulous, incorruptible officer; such virtues, within the Force, are presumably near-saintly *Neaman & Silver.*

Sally Ann aka: Sally Army: (abbrev.) Salvation Army (cf: Salvo) *Powis.*

salmon n. (rhyming sl.) salmon and trout = snout = tobacco *Powis.*

salmon trout n. (rhyming sl.) snout = tobacco; esp. in prison use *Cole.*

saloon bar cowboy n. a man who specializes in picking up women who, like him, can be fround frequenting the saloon bars of public houses (cf: lounge lizard).

salt and pepper n. (US criminal use) black and white police car (cf: black and white) *Folb.*

salty a. irritated, annoyed; feeling sour *Selby:1.*

salty dog n. (US Black use) one who uses an excess of obscene language *Klein.*

Salvo n. (Aus. use) Salvation Army (cf: Sally Ann) *Baker.*

sam v. to cheat, to deceive; fr. 19th C. sammy: a fool, thus to treat as a fool (?) *Powis.*

Sam and Dave n. the police; fr. well-known soul duo *Folb.*

Sambo (derog.) Black man; first OED citation 1704, popular name in slavery era; also fr. children's bk 'Little Black Sambo' *BvdB*.

same difference n. exactly the same thing, thus no difference at all.

same ol' same ol' (US Black use) usual routine or situation *Major*.

samfie n. (Jamaican use) confidence trickster *Thelwell*.

samfu (UK milit. use) *s*elf-*a*djusting *m*ilitary *f*uck-*u*p (cf: snafu) *Rawson*.

Sam Hill n. (euph.) hell, usu. as in 'What in (the) Sam Hill. . .!' *Rawson*.

sand n. (Can. prison use) sugar; since 19th C.

sandbag v. **1.** to ambush, to take by surprise fr. the silent, deadly weapon employed *PT;* **2.** (motor racing use) to drive very fast; **3.** (poker use) to resist raising the bet when immediately possible in the hope of making a larger raise later on.

S&M (acro.) sado-masochism *Jay & Young*.

sandwich man n. (US Black use) a man having sex with two women *Klein*.

sango n. aka: (Aus. use) *sanger* a sandwich (cf: sarnie) *Ready*.

SAN man n. (US prison use) (acro) *S*top *A*t *N*othing man; dangerous and violent *Neaman & Silver*.

sanno n. (Aus. use) sanitary carter or inspector *Ready*.

sanpaku a. out of touch, out of balance – physically and spiritually; fr. Zen use: visibility of the white of the eye below the iris as well as (as usual) on either side; fr. Jap. *san*: three + *haku*: white *Burroughs:Jr*.

Santa Claus n. (US Black use) a vulgar, gaudy, flashy and tasteless dresser fr. the department store Santas (cf: caution sign) *Folb*.

sap n. **1.** a weighted blackjack made of leather and lead; **2.** a fool *Price:2*.

sapfu (milit. use) (acro.) *s*urpassing *a*ll *p*revious *f*uck-*u*ps (cf: snafu) *Rawson*.

Sappho n. a lesbian; thus *sapphic*: code word for female homosexuality *Legman*.

sappy a. foolish, stupid; fr. sap (qv) *Higgins:5*.

sarky a. (abbrev.) sarcastic; usu. juv. use.

sarnie n. a sandwich *Payne*.

sass v. to answer back, to check.

sassy a. cheeky, spirited, back-talking *Folb*.

sassy box n. (US Black use) [the vagina of] a saucy young girl *Klein*.

satchel n. anus; into which things may be put *Higgins:1*.

satellite v. to hang around; fr. satellites circling a planet *Price:3*.

saturated a. very drunk; a lit. description of the bloodstream *Dickson*.

Saturday Night Special n. a small handgun, often used in the many fracas that occur over Saturday night in a big US city *Price:2*.

sauce n. drink *Higgins:1*.

sauced a. drunk *Neaman & Silver*.

sauce hound n. drunkard, alcoholic *Schulberg*.

saucepan lid n. (rhyming sl.) Yid = Jew *Norman:3*.

sausage and mash n. (rhyming sl.) cash *Cole*.

sausage dog n. a dachshund; fr. its German origins (cf: dachsie).

save one's bacon v. to escape safely, from a place or situation; fr. 18th C. cant bacon = loot *Wright*.

savvy a. intelligent, aware; fr. Fr. *savoir*: to know *Higgins:1*.

saw n. (US Black use) the owner of a cheap rooming house *Major*.

sawbones n. a doctor, a surgeon *Klein*.

sawbuck a. $10; thus *double sawbuck*: $20 *Fiction Illus.3*.

sawed off a. see: sawn off.

sawn-off a. short; the presumption being that a short person was at one stage taller.

sawn off n. (abbrev.) a sawn off shotgun *Higgins:1*.

sawski n. see: sawbuck *Burroughs:1*.

say a mouthful v. **1.** (homosexual use) to reprove a fellow homosexual in detail and at great length *Legman;*

2. to say something important (and true).

say something v. (US Black use) to make an important statement, to say something profound *Major*.

says you! aka: *sez you*: general excl. of contempt, dismissing as beneath argument the previous speaker's words.

SBD (teen. use) (acro) *S*ilent *B*ut *D*eadly/silent but dangerous: said by anyone smelling a hitherto unannounced fart *Neaman & Silver*.

scab n. **1.** (US Black use) an exceptionally unattractive female *Folb*; **2.** (industrial use) a strikebreaker, a blackleg (qv) fr. 16th C. scab: a scurvy rascal, thence to current use by 18th C.

scads n. large quantities.

scag n. see: skag *Grogan*.

scag hag n. (homosexual use) see: fag hag *Stanley*.

scale v. (Aus. use) to practise any form of fraud, deception, confidence trick *Wilkes*.

scalp v. **1.** (theatre use) to tout tickets at above face value price; orig. Stock Exchange use: buy shares very cheap, then sell below the prevailing price; theatre scalpers (qv) look for greater profits *Variety: passim*; **2.** (US Black use) to perform cunnilingus *Klein*.

scalper n. a ticket tout *Runyon*.

scam n. **1.** a plan, a scheme *Goldman*; **2.** spec. a large scale plan to smuggle and distribute illegal drugs *Grogan*.

scammered a. (US prison use) homosexual *Legman*.

scampi belt n. the middle class commuter villages around London where, in the late 1950s/early 1960s, it was considered fashionable to eat scampi; of late scampi is reserved for the 'basket meal' trade and such areas should perhaps be renamed 'the fresh pasta belt'.

Scapa Flow v. (rhyming sl.) to go (cf: scarper) *Cole*.

scaredy-cat n. (juv. use) anyone who is, or appears frightened.

scare the pants off v. to terrify *Wodehouse:AAG*.

scare the shit out of v. to terrify (cf: scare the pants off).

scare up v. to obtain, usu. with some difficulty and poss. by threatening the supplier *Salisbury*.

scare the bejazus out of v. to terrify completely and utterly *Higgins:5*.

scarf v. **1.** to eat, esp. to gobble up, to eat aggressively; fr. scoff (qv) *Price:2*; **2.** (US campus use) to throw away, to abandon *Underwood*.

scarper v. to escape; to run off fr. Scapa Flow (qv) *Humphries*.

scat n. **1.** an itinerant, a tramp *Wilkinson*; **2.** (US Black use) the vagina *Folb*; **3.** (abbrev.) scatology: defecation for sexual purposes *Jay & Young*.

scat v. to leave, to go away, fr. scatter *Sillitoe*.

scatter n. a bar, anywhere one can purchase drinks *Runyon*.

scene n. **1.** choice, preference (cf: bag); **2.** a place, esp. a party; **3.** any situation *Greenlee*.

schitizi a. (abbrev.) schizophrenic, loosely used as crazy, insane *Bukowski:1*.

schizzed a. very drunk, supposedly producing schizophrenia in the sufferer *Bernbach*.

schizzout to lose control mentally, to exhibit the signs of insanity; fr. abbrev. schizophrenic *McFadden*.

schlemiel n. fr. Yiddish; fool, useless person *Pynchon*.

schlep v. fr. Ger *shleppen*: to drag: to carry an inconvenient weight for an equally inconvenient distance; or just to travel further than one might prefer *Norman:3*.

schlepper n. second-rater, loser *Goldman*.

schlock n. cheap, inferior merchandise; anything defective; fr. Yiddish *schlock*: a curse.

schlock shop n. flashy but cheap clothes store *Goldman*.

schlong n. penis *P. Roth, 'Portnoy's Complaint', 1969*.

schlub n. a fool, a moron; fr. Yiddish

Goldman.

schlubette n. a dumb, stupid, young girl, fr. schlub (qv) *Price:3.*

schmaltz n. fr. Yiddish 'fat': mawkish, over-emotional, esp. in show business use *Norman:3.*

schmeck n. heroin, fr. Yiddish 'to hit' (cf: smack) *Green:1.*

schmecker n. fr. Yiddish: heroin user *Grogan.*

schmeer n. fr. Yiddish: situation, circumstance, usu. 'the whole schmeer' *McFadden.*

schmo n. (euph.) schmuck (qv) *Rosten..*

schmooze v. to flatter, to butter up; fr. Yiddish *Stone.*

schmuck n. fr. Yiddish: 'penis'; a fool, an unpleasant person *Price:2.*

schmutter n. clothes; fr. Yiddish *shmatte*: rags *M. Jagger, K. Richard, 'Some Girls', 1981.*

schmutz n. filth, dirt; fr. Yiddish *Goldman.*

schnook n. fool, idiot; fr. Yiddish *McFadden.*

schnorrer n. fr. Yiddish: beggar *Gruce:2.*

schnozzle n. fr. Yiddish: the nose *Wright.*

schnozzola n. the nose *Vidal.*

school v. (US Black use) to explain a situation or a plan to someone else *Klein.*

schoolbook chump n. (US Black use) 1. an overly studious person; **2.** a naïve, innocent person, who has no knowledge beyond his/her books *Folb.*

schoolboy n. (US Black use) a neophyte in the street life; an apprentice criminal *Klein.*

schoolboy scotch n. (US Black use) wine *Folb.*

schoolie n. **1.** (abbrev.) schoolgirl *Newman:2*; **2.** (Aus. use) schoolteacher *Wilkes.*

school of hard knocks n. personal experience – as opposed, by those who attribute their education to this institution, to the soft option of actual academic life. (cf: university of life) *Whitcomb.*

school one v. to explain a situation *X.*

schpritz v. to attack, to slander; fr. Yiddish 'to spray' *Bruce:2.*

schtick n. aka: *shtik*, *shtick* (qv): affair, event, happening *Price:2.*

schtup v. fr. Yiddish: to have sexual intercourse *Bruce:1.*

schvug n. fr. Yiddish: black *Price:2.*

schwartze n. fr. Yiddish 'black': a Black person *Bruce:2.*

scoff n. food (cf: scarf) *Caron.*

scoff fishheads v. to have a difficult time, to encounter problems *Maledicta.*

scone n. (Aus. use) head *Ready.*

scone v. (Aus. use) to hit someone on the head *Ready.*

scoop n. (US teen./campus use) important, fresh information fr. journalist use (cf: poop) *Underwood.*

scoop v. to arrest (cf: lift) *Higgins:2.*

scoop the pool v. to make a major profit, fr. poker use *Sharpe:1.*

scoot off v. to run away.

scoots n. (US campus use) diarrhoea (cf: runs) *Underwood.*

scope n. the erect penis, fr. abbrev. telescope *Farina.*

scope v. (US campus use) to look for males, usu. female use; fr. telescope *Underwood.*

scope on v. (US Black use) to stare at intently, usu. with sexual interest *Folb.*

scope out v. to look over, to stare at, to investigate *Price:3.*

scorch n. (US Black use) best quality, top-rank goods; fr. *scorcher*: something exceptional *Klein.*

scorcher n. **1.** an attractive and sexually voracious female *May*; **2.** a very hot day; often found in tabloid press in cliché headline 'Phew! what a scorcher' *Sun passim.*

score n. the situation, the facts, what is going on; usu. as in *know the score*; **2.** £20; fr SE *Newman:1*; **3.** (criminal use) the profits from a robbery, fraud or similar criminal act *Teresa.*

score v. **1.** to buy drugs *M. Jagger, K. Richard, 'Sister Morphine', 1970*;

2. to seduce *Jay & Young.*

score between the posts v. (Aus. use) to have sexual intercourse, to seduce a female; fr. sporting use *Wilkes.*

score yoks v. to make people laugh *Price:3.*

scotch pegs n. (rhyming sl.) legs *Jones:J.*

scotia! (US Black use) OK (qv), okey-doke, etc. *Klein.*

Scotland Yard n. (US Black use) plain clothes police; fr. films featuring UK detectives (?) *Klein.*

Scouse n. Liverpudlian; fr. popular local stew: lobscouse *Payne.*

scrag v. to beat up, to harm, to kill; fr. orig use: to hang or garotte *Runyon.*

scram v. to escape, to run off; fr. scramble (?) *Wolfe:2.*

scramble n. **1.** (US Black use) money *Klein*; **2.** (US teen. use) any effort to stretch a thinning resource beyond realistic limits; fr. sl. for the effect achieved by a balding man who attempts to comb his hair to maximum effect *Sculatti.*

scrambling for the gills v. to have a bad time, to meet problems *Maledicta.*

scran n. food *Powis.*

scrap n. a fight; fr. 18th C.: a blow, a punch *Farrell.*

scrape n. an abortion; fr. the operation on the uterus *White.*

scrape v. (Aus. use) to have sexual intercourse *Wilkes.*

scrape the (bottom of) the barrel v. to make do with the most mediocre people, objects etc. simply because no others exist.

scratch n. money; a commodity for which most people must *scratch in the dirt Caron.*

scratcher n. (UK prison use) a match *LL.*

scratch for work v. (UK police use) to look desperately for an arrest; pun on usual meaning *Laurie.*

scratchman n. (US cant) a forger; fr. the drawing and etching he performs *Neaman & Silver.*

scratch sheet n. the daily racing form; fr. scratch: a zero handicap; first pub. 1917 in New York *Selby:1.*

scream n. **1.** a complaint, esp. against criminal activities, or to the police *Norman:2*; **2.** (US preppie (qv) use) ice cream *Bernbach.*

scream v. (US Black use) to inform to the police *Klein.*

screamer n. (US campus use) anything exceptionally challenging, difficult; esp. work *Underwood.*

screaming a. (US Black use) fantastic, amazing, extreme *Klein.*

screaming abdabs n. the horrors, utter disgust, abhorrence; usu. as in 'gives me the screaming. . .'; spec. delirium tremens.

screaming blue murder in a state of hysteria; utterly and completely overwrought or terrified *Sillitoe.*

scream sheet n. tabloid newspaper; fr. journ. use *screamer*: exclamation point, with which such papers' headlines are studded *Schulberg.*

scream some heavy lines v. (US Black use) **1.** to impress with one's smart talk; **2.** to debate or argue intensely and emotionally *Folb.*

screw n. prison officer; orig. a skeleton key, thus (?) to prison meaning (cf: twirl) *Cole.*

screw v. **1.** to cheat, swindle, take advantage of *Jay & Young*; **2.** to copulate; poss. the most common eg. of sex = violence; **3.** to break into, to rob; orig. with a skeleton key, see: screw, n. *Powis*; **4.** to stare intently at someone *Powis.*

screw around v. **1.** to indulge a promiscuous sex life; **2.** aka: *screw off*: to waste time, take time off *Price:2.*

screwball n. an eccentric, an out-of-the-ordinary person *S. Vizinczey, 'An Innocent Millionaire', 1983.*

screwdriver n. (UK prison use) Principal Officer who 'drives' his subordinate 'screws' (qv) *LL.*

screwed a. in trouble, in great difficulties; fr *screw*: to have intercourse (cf: fucked).

screwer n. burglary *Norman:1.*

screw it! (excl.) the hell with it! forget

it! etc.; euph. fuck it! (qv) *Underwood.*

screw it on v. to drive one's car or motorcycle very fast *Thompson.*

screwsman n. a skilled housebreaker *Powis.*

screw the arse off v. aggressive, vigorous copulation; a 'macho' man would always promise to make love in this way.

screw up v. to make a mess, to blunder badly; euph. fuck up (qv) *Underwood.*

screwy a. foolish, stupid, insane; fr. have a screw loose (qv) (?) *Laugh In The Dark.*

scribe n. newspaperman; fr. SE: a writer *Runyon.*

scrimshank v. to shirk one's work, to laze around; orig. milit. use; thus *scrimshanker*: one who acts thus.

scrub v. to cancel; to wipe out, to forget *Norman:1.*

scrubber n. promiscuous girl, usu. young *Norman:2.*

scrub it v. to forget something, to ignore, to let it pass *LL.*

Scrubs n. (UK police use/cant) HMP Wormwood Scrubs, London (cf: Ville) *Cole.*

scruff a. messy, unkempt; fr. scruffy *Pond.*

scrumptious a. delicious, extra-tasty; nearly always of food; usu. juv. use.

scrunge n. filth, mess, dirt *Underwood.*

scrungy a. filthy, messy, dirty, disgusting *Underwood.*

scuffer n. policeman, mainly Liverpool dial; fr. *scufter Keyes.*

scumbag n. **1.** spec. contraceptive sheath; **2.** derog. term of general abuse *Price:2.*

scummy a. unpleasant, disgusting *Keyes.*

scumsucker n. derog. term of general abuse (cf: cocksucker).

scuttlebutt n. gossip, rumour; fr. USN use, orig. scuttlebutt was the ship's water barrel, around which sailors gathered and gossipped (cf: furphy) *Bruce:1.*

scuzzy a. unkempt, down at heel, ragged *Price:2.*

sea food n. (homosexual use) sailors *Legman.*

seat n. the buttocks.

secko (Aus. use) a sexual pervert, usu. prison use *Wilkes.*

second closet n. (homosexual/lesbian use) the hiding of one's specific sexual preferences and practices even if the basic fact of homosexuality can be admitted *Jay & Young.*

second-storey job n. a break-in, spec. one that involves climbing above ground level.

second-storey man n. a thief who climbs into buildings above the ground floor *Fiction Illus.3* (cf: high-wall job).

section eight n. **1.** spec. section eight discharge: discharge from the US army on grounds of mental instability; thus: **2.** insanity, instability *Price:1.*

seddity (US Black use) Blacks attempting to ape whites; fr. absurdity (?) *Folb.*

seducer n. (US Black use) one who supplies the means of making fast, poss. illegal, money *Klein.*

see (backsl.) yes *Cole.*

see a dog about a man v. to urinate (cf: see a man. . .) *Neaman & Silver.*

see a man about a dog v. to visit the lavatory *Rawson.*

seedy (US Black use) common nickname for a dealer in pills *Klein.*

seeing-to n. **1.** of a woman: sexual intercourse; **2.** of a man: beating up, violence *A.F.N. Clarke, 'Contact', 1983.*

see off v. to deal with, to dismiss, to defeat.

see-saw n. (US Black use) an up and down, uncertain relationship *Klein.*

see the King v. to have sexual intercourse; orig. to be sophisticated, knowing *Mortimer.*

seeyabye! (Valley Girls (qv) use) goodbye! fr. see ya plus goodbye *Pond.*

see you in court general cp. used as synonym for 'goodbye'.

seg n. (US campus use) (acro) *s*hit-eating grin *Simmons.*

sell a boy v. (homosexual use) for one man to obtain the services of a boy at a given price and then to offer him to a second man for the actual sex *Legman.*

sell a pup v. to deceive, esp. in business or financial transactions fr. stock market j. pup, a worthless investment *AS 41 (1966).*

sell a wolf ticket v. (US Black use) **1.** boast, brag; **2.** talk nonsense, lie *Seale.*

sell one on v. to convince, to persuade, to convey enthusiasm.

semolia n. (US Black use) a fool *Major.*

send away with a flea in one's ear v. to dismiss sharply, to throw out after telling someone off severely *Wodehouse:MOJ.*

send down v. to imprison; fr. walking down the steps fr. the dock (at the Old Bailey) back to the cells.

send her down Hughie! (Aus. use) general appeal to the gods for rain; Hughie is also the mythical deity of surfing and as such invoked by surfers who want suitable waves *Baker.*

send on a humbug trip v. (US Black use) to send on a wild goose chase, a fool's errand *Folb.*

send to the cleaners v. aka: *take to the cleaners*: to defraud, outwit and, usu. thus deprive of one's every penny *Powis.*

send up v. **1.** (US criminal/police use) to imprison; poss. fr. 'send up the river; (qv).

send up v. to mock, to tease, esp. to paraody or imitate.

senior out v. (US teen. use) to give up the teen. lifestyle, to act like an adult (in the rejection of teen. excess) *Sculatti.*

septic n. (Aus. use; rhyming sl.) septic tank = Yank = American *Wilkes.*

serious a. (UK 'society; use) all-purpose intensifier, thus serious drinking, seriously rich, etc. *Barr.*

serve n. (Aus. use) negative criticism, a reprimand *Wilkes.*

serve v. (drug use) to sell narcotics *Burroughs:1.*

set n. **1.** (Black use) wherever the nightlife takes place; consciously using the movie meaning with everyone involved acting out their parts of the drama *Milner*; **2.** (poker use) three of a kind *Alvarez*; **3.** (US milit. use) a party; fr. **1** *Del Vecchio.*

set mouth v. (US Black use) to gossip, to malign *Folb.*

set one back v. cost a good deal, to be expensive *Humphries:2.*

settle one's hash v. to deal with someone who has wronged you; to take revenge.

set to rights v. to put straight, to set right.

set-up n. **1.** a situation planned to put a third party in a position of weakness, poss. to be murdered; **2.** any situation, experience *Burroughs:1.*

set up v. to place a potential victim in a position of weakness, esp. a target for murder.

set-up man n. (criminal use) someone who organizes and plans major robberies, recruits those who carry them out, disposes of the loot, etc. *Burroughs:1.*

seven digits n. (US Black use) telephone number (in the multiple exchanges of the major cities) *Klein.*

sew v. (US Black use) to masturbate; fr. the up-and-down motions of the hand *Major.*

sewermouth n. (US campus use) anyone who regularly use obscenities or profanities *Underwood.*

sew up v. to conclude, to possess completely, to finalize *Hoffman:a.*

sexpot n. very attractive man or woman *Jay & Young.*

Sexton Blake n. (rhyming sl.) **1.** cake; **2.** fake; fr. fictional detective created by 'Hal Meredith' (Harry Blyth) in *The Halfpenny Marvel* magazine, 1893 *Jones: J.*

sexy a. (media use) anything that pulls in audiences, readers, etc., thus usu. violence, disaster, scandal, etc.; orig. used by *Sunday Times* Insight team,

1960s *D. Leitch*.

shack v. (abbrev.) shack up (qv) *Bukowski: 6*.

shack job n. the person with whom one lives; a relationship *Bukowski: 5*.

shackle up v. (tramp use) to cook a midday meal*LL*.

shack up v. to live with; to have sex with *Goldman*.

shades n. dark glasses, sunglasses *Performance*.

shadow n. (US campus use) (derog.) Black (cf: shadow) *Underwood*.

shaft n. **1.** woman's body, considered simply as a sexual object *Algren*; **2.** unfair treatment *Underwood*.

shaft v. **1.** to have sexual intercourse with a woman; **2.** to defeat, defraud, harm *Wofe: 2*.

shafted a. **1.** treated unfairly; **2.** stood up by one's date; **3.** suffering a broken relationship.

shag a. (US prison use) worthless *Chandler: Notebk*.

shag v. to copulate; since 18th C. *Humphries*.

shag ass v. to work hard, to move fast, to expend effort and energy *Underwood*.

shagbag n. a very promiscuous woman, usu. with implication of the physical deterioration that such promiscuity has supposedly brought (cf: bag).

shagged out a. exhausted *Keyes*.

shagger's back n. (Aus. use) a particularly painful backache *Ready*.

shag like a rattlesnake v. to make love very enthusiastically; usu. a term of recommendation used by one male to another of a female they both find attractive *K. Waterhouse, 'Billy Liar', 1959*.

shake n. (US campus use) a party; fr. the dancing therein *Underwood*.

shake a leg! get on with it! wake up! (both lit. and figuratively).

shakedown n. blackmail, extortion; fr. shaking the clothes until money falls out *Jay & Young*.

shake-em-up n. (US Black use) white port and lemon juice *Folb*.

shake hands with an old friend v. to urinate *Rawson*.

shake hands with the wife's best friend v. **1.** to masturbate; **2.** to urinate *Humphries*.

Shake 'n' Bake n. (US milit. use) a sergeant who attended NCO school and gained rank after only a short time in uniform; fr. brand name of popular US instant food; thus similar synomyms: *Ready Whip, Nestle's Quick Del Vecchio*.

shakes n. delirium tremens, the shaking associated with an alcoholic who has been deprived of sufficient drink to achieve normality (cf: screaming abdabs) *Price: 2*.

shake the dew off the lily v. to urinate *Neaman & Silver*.

Shaky City n. (US trucker use) Los Angeles, Calif.; fr. frequency of earthquakes along the San Andreas Fault *CB*.

shall I put a bit of hair on it? (cp) directed at a workman who is failing to put something into something else; the hair in question would be female and pubic.

sham on v. (US Black use) to cheat, to deceive *Folb*.

shamus n. detective, esp. private operative; fr. Seamus, the common Irish name of many policemen *Fiction Illus. 3*.

shandy (rhyming sl.) chandelier = queer.

shanghai v. to kidnap, to abduct; fr. alleged practice of pressing men into service at the port of Shanghai *Price: 2*.

shank n. (US prison use) a knife *Caron*.

shape up v. (police use) to develop satisfactorily *Newman: 2*.

shape up v. to improve one's behaviour, activities, attitude, etc. *Newman: 1*.

shark n. **1.** a sharp operator, a crooked businessman; **2.** (abbrev.) loan shark (qv).

sharking n. the practice of a private credit company taking high interest on loans *Higgins: 3*.

sharp a. **1.** intelligent, perceptive; **2.** fashionable, ie *sharp dresser Higgins: 1*.

sharp end n. the challenging, demanding and sometimes unpleasant aspect of an experience; fr. the bow of a boat *T 18/7/83*.

sharpie n.**1.** a slick operator; one who lives and hopes to prosper by their wits *Goldman*; **2.** (Aus. use) member of a crop-haired teen cult, the equivalent of the British skinhead (qv) *Wilkes*.

sharpshooter n. (us Black use) a sexually adept and active person (cf: rod, gun, etc.) *Klein*.

shaver n. a person, often as *young shaver*; a child, or young person; fr. at least 1630 *Vidal*.

shazzam v. to flash dramatically, fr. comic strip excl. Shazam! *White*.

shebeen n. an unlicensed drinking place, an illegal late night drinking club *Powis*.

sheeny n. (derog.) a Jew; poss. fr. Ger, *schin*: a miser, a petty thief, a cheat; or fr. the 'sheen' of Brylcreemed hair affected by early immigrants *Bruce ; 2*.

sheep n. a mild, weak, acquiescent person; fr. the animal's characteristics.

sheepish a. (US campus use) long-haired (of males) *Underwood*.

sheepskin n. a college diploma; fr. the fur that graduates wear for the graduation ceremony.

sheet n. **1.** newspaper, magazine *Gruber*; **2.** (US criminal use) an official police record *Major*.

sheet! (euph.) shit (qv) *Hoffman: a*.

sheila n. (Aus. use) a female; fr. Gaelic *sheela*: girl, opp. of Paddy (qv) *Humphries*.

shekels n. fr. Hebrew: money *Wright*.

shellacking n. a severe beating or defeat *Runyon*.

shell-back n. ultra-conservative, slow-witted person; fr. image of a turtle *Humphries*.

shell out v. to hand over, usu. money; fr. the removal of a seed from a shell *Humphries: 2*.

shell-road v. to throw a person, often a woman who refuses to have sex. out of a vehicle and thus force them to walk home an inconvenient and possibly embarrassing distance (cf: redlight) *Runyon: 1*.

she-man (derog.) homosexual (cf: he-she, omee-polone).

shemozzle n. a fuss, a disturbance; fr. Yiddish.

Sherlock Holmes n. (US Black use) the police; fr. Conan Doyle's super-sleuth *Folb*.

schicer n. aka:*sheister*: a cheat, spec. one who refuses to pay a debt (cf: welsh) *Powis*.

shicker a. drunk, fr. Yiddish *Humphries*.

shicker n.v. alcohol, to drink (usu. to drunkenness) *Humphries*.

shift the weight v. to place the blame on someone else *Klein*.

shikse fr. Yiddish: **1.** a Gentile girl; **2.** a char-woman.

shill n. (gambling use) a house player (in a casino); a member of the three-card monte (qv) team who appears to be another innocent gambler and who thus lures the actual punters (qv) into losing more money: fr. abbrev. *Shillaber*: one who publicizes a circus, carnival, etc. *Jenkins*.

shim-sham n. (US campus use) feelings of unease, of nervousness *Underwood*.

shin n. (US prison use) any contraband gun or knife *Chandler: Notebk*.

shin battle (street gang use) a fake, practice battle *Salisbury*.

shine a. (derog.) Black, Negro *Dunne*.

shine on v. (US Black use) to ignore *Milner*.

shiner n. a black eye *Farrell*.

shingle short a. (Aus. use) 'not all there', eccentric *Wilkes*.

shirtlifter n. (Aus. use) male homosexual *Humphries: 2*.

shit n. **1.** spec. excrement; **2.** (drug use) cannabis; heroin *Green: 1*; **3.** trouble, problems, difficulties

Jenkins; **4.** an event, a thing, circumstance usu. as 'what is this shit?' etc. *Price: 2.*

shit v. (abbrev.) bullshit (qv).

shit a brick! (excl.) extreme surprise, annoyance *Humphries.*

shit a brick aka: shit bricks v. to tremble with extreme fear *Price: 2.*

shit and derision! general excl. of annoyance.

shit and wish v. (US Black use) cp fr. phrase 'shit in one hand and wish in the other; see which fills up first' *Klein.*

shit-bird n. (derog.) general term of abuse *Higgins: 1.*

shit detail n. any unpleasant/dirty task; fr. milit. use *Higgins: 3.*

shite n. derog. form of address; fr. shit (qv) *Bleasdale.*

shit-eating grin n. a smug, self-satisfied smile *Selby: 1.*

shit, eh (Aus. use) expression of moderate astonishment or irony *Ready.*

shitface n. **1.** an unpleasant, distasteful person *Underwood*; **2.** a drunken party *Price: 2.*

shitface a. (usually shitface drunk: extremely drunk.

shithead n. derog. term of general abuse *Price: 2.*

shitheap n. a dirty, unpleasant, disgusting place.

shitheel n. generally derog. term of abuse *Jenkins.*

shit hits the fan difficulties start to happen, usu. such problems have been expected to occur sooner or later *Higgins: 1.*

shithook n. **1.** (US campus use) a foolish, clumsy person *Underwood*; **2.** (US milit. use) CH-47 'Chinook' helicopter; (cf: campus use) *Del Vecchio.*

shit-hot a. extremely, superlatively, especially.

shithouse n. **1.** spec. lavatory; **2.** any dirty, messy, disgusting place *Performance.*

shit jacket n. (US Black use) outside lavatory *Klein.*

shitkicker n. **1.** spec. a farmer or other country person; **2.** a fool, a person of meagre intelligence. *NYRB 17/2/83.*

shitkicking music n. music that makes the hearer want to get up and dance, shout, sing, generally have a good, boisterous time *Pynchon.*

shit list n. a list pf people one considers distasteful, untrustworthy and otherwise unacceptable.

shit on a shingle n. (milit. use (mainly)) minced beef on toast.

shit on a stick n. (US Black use) a self-appointed tough guy, more words than action *Klein.*

shit oneself v. to be terrified, fr. physical effect of great fear *M. Mayer, 'Summer Days', 1983.*

shit on from a great height v. to be extremely unpleasant, to make a great deal of trouble for someone else.

shit or bust v. to make a last, absolute gamble (cf: go for broke).

shit, or get off the pot! (cp) either make a decision or let someone else do it; allegedly remarked by then Vice pres. Richard Nixon to Pres. Eisenhower when the latter was showing insufficient enthusiasm for his aide in 1952.

shit-scared a. terrified (cf: scare the shit . . .)

shit-stick (US prison use) **1.** a billy-club; **2.** the penis, esp. when used for anal intercourse *Klein.*

shit-stirrer n. a malicious gossip, causing trouble for its own sake.

shit stompers n. (US campus use) **1.** cowboy boots; **2.** cowboys *Underwood.*

shitter n. **1.** spec. a thief who likes to excrete inside the places he robs *Higgins: 3*; **2.** lavatory *Dury, 'Do It Yourself', 1979.*

shit through one's teeth v. to lie blatantly *Klein.*

shitty a. unpleasant, disgusting *Higgins: 1.*

shitwork n. unpleasant, unwanted, probably dirty occupations *Robins.*

shiv n. a knife (cf: chiv) *Price: 2.*

shlemiel n. fr. Yiddish: a fool, a

clumsy person, a misfit, a gullible person. etc. *Rosten*.

shlock n. fr. Yiddish: **1.** shoddy, cheap article; a phoney person; **2.** spec. drugs, fr. *shlock* = junk, thus lit. drugs *Rosten*.

shmeer v. fr. Ger: grease: to flatter, to bribe *Rosten*.

shmegegge n. a fool, a loser, a useless person *Price: 3*.

shmooser n. a flatterer, a sycophant; fr. Yiddish.

shocks for jocks (US campus use) course in introductory engineering *Bernbach*.

shoe n. (US Black use) **1.** a smartly dressed person; fr. Jazz use of 1950s *Major*. **2.** (US campus use) highly acceptable person; fr. Black use of shoe (qv) *Bernbach*.

shonk n. (derog.) a Jew; prob. fr. shonnicker (qv) *LL*.

shonnicker n. (derog.) a Jew; fr. Yiddish = a small trader or pedlar *Farrell*.

shoo-fly n. (US cant) **1.** a plain-clothes policeman on observation duty *Neaman & Silver*; **2.** an undercover policeman who spies on his colleagues *ST 23/10/82*; both fr. song lyric 'Shoo fly! Don't bother me'.

shoo-in n. a dead certainty; usu. in political use *Vidal*.

shook on (Aus. use) infatuated with, obsessed with *Wilkes*.

shoot! (excl.) surprise, indignation, etc., poss. euph. for shit (qv) *Seale*.

shoot a cat v. (UK 'society' use) vomit (cf: cat) *Barr*.

shoot a line v. to concoct a smooth patter with the specific aim of seduction (cf: line).

shoot blanks v. (US Black use) to engage in idle conversation; words that have no 'target' *Folb*.

shoot down v. **1.** to reject an invitation to dance, or go for a date (qv) *Price: 1*; **2.** (US campus use) to humiliate, to ridicule *Simmons*; **3.** to reject a line of argument; to overrule an opinion *Seale*.

shoot-'em-up n. (US Black use) a Hollywood Western movie; fr. the predominant activity *Major*.

shooter n. **1.** (gambling use) the player currently throwing the dice in a game of craps; **2.** (UK police/criminal use) a gun *Performance*.

shoot for the sky v. (gambling use) to bet one's entire funds against one's opponent's entire funds.

shoot from the hip v. (business use) to attack a problem head-on, to be a hard-nosed (qv) performer; fr. movie Westerns where gunfighters and cowboys 'shoot from the hip' *Kidder*.

shoot gravy v. (drug use) for a narcotics addict to reinject his own cooked (qv) blood *Major*.

shooting gallery n. a place, often an apartment or an abandoned building used by a number of heroin addicts to take the drug and nod out (qv) *Grogan*.

shoot off v. **1.** ejaculate *Jay & Young*; **2.** to leave quickly.

shoot off at the mouth v. to boast, to brag *May*.

shoot on v. aka: *shoot jokes on*: to mock, to tease, to discredit *Folb*.

shoot one's best mack v. (US Black use) to make an all-out effort at seduction by one's persuasive conversation (cf: mack, macking) *Folb*.

shoot one's bolt v. to have given everything one has, to be incapable of further effort *Heller*.

shoot one's load v. to ejaculate *Jay & Young*.

shoot one's mouth off v. to talk, esp. in loud or boastful way *Humphries*.

shoot one's star v. (US Black use) **1.** to arrest a homosexual; **2.** to perform anal intercourse *Klein*.

shoot one's wad v. to ejaculate.

shoot-out n. **1.** a gun battle; **2.** a decisive confrontation *Seale*.

shoot out one's marbles v. (US Black use) to go crazy (cf: lose one's marbles *Klein*.

shoot over v. to go quickly to a place *PT*.

shoot some hoop v. (US campus use)

to play basketball *Underwood*.

shoot the breeze v. to gossip, to talk idly (cf: bat the breeze).

shoot the bull v. see: shoot the shit *Pearce*.

shoot the dozens v. see: play the dozens *Folb*.

shoot the moon v. to abscond from a house or flat, taking one's furniture and possessions, but avoiding payment of any outstanding rent, utility bills, etc.

shoot the regular v. (US Black use) to chatter on in the usual, predictable manner; 'shit' is unspoken *Klein*.

shoot the shit v. to banter, chatter, gossip *Price: 2*.

shoot the squirrel v. (US campus use) to catch a glimpse of a girl's panties or pubic hair *Underwood*.

shoot the thrill v. (US Black use) to lead a promiscuous and varied sex life *Klein*.

shoot through v. (Aus. use) to leave, to exit *Humphries*.

shoot to kill v. to aim ruthlessly for a goal without reservation or compromise *Klein*.

shoot up v. to take narcotic drugs by injection *Price: 2*.

shop v. to inform; orig. 16th C. to imprison *Powis*.

short n. an automobile *Price: 2*.

short n. (US Black use) a cigarette butt *Klein*.

short a. **1.** (US prison use) of a prisoner with only a few weeks or days of a sentence to be served out *Burroughs: Jr*; **2.** (US milit. use) near the end of a given term of duty, spec. the twelve-month tours of Vietnam (cf: wake-up) *Del Vecchio*.

short arm n. the penis (cf: third leg). *Neaman & Silver*.

short-arm inspection n. (milit. use) medical inspection of the genitals; fr. short arm (qv).

short con n. (US criminal use) any variety of confidence trick that can be peformed spontaneously and on the spot, with no elabrorate props, preparation, etc. *Thompson: J*.

short dog n. (US Black use) a small bottle of cheap wine *Folb*.

short-end money n. (gambling use) money bet on the possibility of a given team or individual (esp. in boxing) losing a contest (cf: on the short end) *Schulberg*.

short end of the stick unfair treatment; deliberately engineered bad luck *Uris*.

shorts n. the last few puffs of a discarded cigarette (cf: short) *Grogan*.

short stuff n. (US criminal use) a quick and spontaneous con trick, thought up on the spur of the moment and workable only while the target is on hand (cf: short con) *Klein*.

short time n. **1.** (prison use) a short sentence; or a short part of one's sentence left to run; **2.** (milit. use) a short-service commission or a short period of enlistment; **3.** (prostitute use) the time spent with one client before taking on a new one; rather than spending a whole night with the same man *Norman: 2*.

short-time girl n. basic, cheap prostitute who satisfies her client's immediate need and then looks for her next customer *O'Brien*.

shot n. **1.** a measure of spirits; **2.** an opportunity, a chance *Dunne*; **3.** an injection of a narcotic drug *Price: 2*.

shot a. exhausted, completely used up *Higgins: 3*.

shotdown a. (US campus use) miserable, useless, distasteful *Underwood*.

shotgun n. (drug use) to blow cannabis smoke into someone else's mouth by reversing the cigarette inside one's own mouth and blowing; the other person places their open lips near the stream of smoke and inhales for as long as they can manage (cf: give a blow).

shotgun seat n. the seat nest to that of the driver in a car; fr. stagecoach use 'riding shotgun' (qv) *Price: 3*.

shot in the arm n. anything – verbal, physical, stimulant – that cheers one up, energizes one, etc.; fr. an injection.

shout n. **1.** turn to order a round of drinks; thus *your shout*, *my shout*, etc.; **2.** (UK police use) a call on the car/personal radio indicating an emergency, the scene of a crime, etc.; also used by London Fire Brigade for alarms coming over the teleprinter *Laurie*.

shove it! excl. of dismissal and rudeness; abbrev. of 'shove it up your ass!' *Vidal*.

Shovel City n. (US teen. use) anything one really digs, ie appreciates and enjoys; a pun on the tool *Sculatti*.

shovel and broom n. (US rhyming sk.) room *Runyon*.

shovel shit v. to talk nonsense, esp. in an attempt to defraud or deceive someone *Bukowski: 1*.

shovel shit against the tide v. (cp) to make great effort without any concomitant success *Higgins: 5*.

shove off v. to leave, to go away, usu, in form of an order to someone else.

shove one's oar in v. to interfere (where one is not wanted) *Wright*.

shovin' and pushin' (US Black use) trying as hard as possible to succeed *Klein*.

show a leg! wake-up call; orig. used to ensure that the leg (in an institution) was masculine and not, illicitly, female.

showboat v. to show off, esp. by parading oneself in front of an audience *Esq. 6/83*.

shower n. an unimpressive group of people; abbrev. of *shower of shit*.

showhouse n. (homosexual use) a brothel; a place where homosexuals can meet openly, sex is usually performed off the premises *Legman*.

show one's cards v. to reveal oneself, usu. to a greater extent than desired; fr. poker use (cf: peep one's hole card) *Farrell*.

show it v. to become obviously drunk *Dickson*.

show out n. (UK police use) a sign between a policeman and his informant who meet in a public place that means 'all clear' to speak *Laurie*.

show out v. to lead on, to deceive *Norman: 3*.

show the flag v. (UK 'society' use) to attend (apparently reluctantly) any official function; with the image of white administrators displaying Imperial might to the natives, the inference is that the function will have been organized for less socially acceptable people *Barr*.

shred the tube v. (Valley Girls (qv) use) to go surfing (cf: tube) *Pond*.

shrimp n. a small, weak, insignificant person; fr. the fish.

shrink n. **1.** fr. head-shrinker: a psychoanalyst, psychiatrist, etc. (cf: trick-cyclist) *Price: 2*; **2.** (US campus use) tight-fitting sweater (for girls) *Underwood*.

Shrinksville n. a state of mind in which it is advisable for the person so afflicted to consult a psychoanalyst (cf: shrink) *Safire*.

shtarka n. fr. Yiddish: **1.** a strong, brave man; a big shot (qv); used ironically *Rosten*; **2.** a thug, a hoodlum *Goldman*.

shtarker n. see: shtarka *Goldman*.

shtick n. (show business use) one's stage speciality, one's act, esp. of a comedian's monologue *Bruce: 2*.

shtum fr. Yiddish: quiet, silent, dumb *Performance*.

shuck n. a hoax, a lie, deceit; often in shuck and jive (qqv) *The People's Comic*.

shuck v. to defraud, to cheat, to fool *The People's Comic*.

shuck and jive see: shuck, jive *Seale*.

shuck down v. to strip off one's clothes, to undress; fr. shucking corn *Vidal*.

shucks mild excl. of surprise, regret, annoyance, etc. *Capital Radio 1983*.

shuffle n. (US Black use) a Black man deliberately playing dumb and acting out the white man's stereotyped view of his race; the shuffling walk, along with shiny smiles and natural rhythm are major parts of this image *Klein*.

shuffle v. (street gang use) to have a

fistfight *Salisbury*.

shuffled out of the deck a. dead, fr. card use (cf: go to the races, etc.) *Rawson*.

shufty n. a brief glance, a quick look; fr. Arabic orig. Second World War use.

shunt n. a car crash, esp. in professional drivers' use *'Minder', Thames TV, 1983*.

shuteye n. sleep, rest.

shut eyes n. (US police use) a sexual offender; fr. the pervert's suggestion to his youthful victim, 'Now just shut your eyes . . .' *Neaman & Silver*.

shut one's trap v. to be quiet; usu. as demand: *shut your trap! Farrell*.

shut someone down v. **1.** spec. to beat a rival in a drag race; **2.** to gain a victory.

shuttle butt n. (US campus use) a fat girl, esp. as to the buttocks *Underwood*.

shut your face! shut up, be quiet, etc. *Manser*.

shy n. (abbrev.) shylock (qv) *Higgins: 3*.

shylock n. one who supples private loans fr. the villain of Shakespeare's 'Merchant of Venice' (cf: loan shark) *Runyon*.

shyster n. a crooked lawyer; fr. shicer (qv).

Siberia n. (US prison use) solitary confinement cells *Chandler: Notebk*.

sick n. the illness that accompanies withdrawal from drug addiction *Grogan*.

sick a. **1.** annoyed; worried *Newman: 1*; **2.** suffering from withdrawal symptoms when addicted to narcotics, esp. heroin *Lou Reed, 'Run, Run, Run', 1966*.

sick as a parrot a. extremely depressed; sick usually means mentally rather than physically distressed; the cliché response attributed to many sportsmen, esp. soccer players and managers, after a loss or defeat (cf: over the moon).

sickener n. anything depressing, disappointing, frustrating (cf: choker) *Payne*.

sickie n. **1.** (Aus. use) a day's sick leave *Wilkes*; **2.** anyone considered to be 'sick in the head': insane, crazy *McFadden*.

sicko n. a mentally unstable person, with overtones of sexual perversion.

sic on v. to set on, to have someone attack; fr. sicking a dog on to a given victim *rr*.

sides n. records.

sidies n. sideburns; popular in Beatlemania era.

sidity aka: *saddity*: showing off, arrogant, egotistical fr. early 20th C. 'side'; affectations, airs *Selby: 1*.

sight for sore eyes n. a welcome appearance; often used as an affectionate greeting: 'you're a sight for sore eyes'.

sightseers n. (gambling use) see: hedge *Powis*.

signify v. (Black use) **1.** to cause trouble, to stir things up; often purely for fun, whatever the actual results; **2.** to pretend to a greater sophistication than one actually possesses *Milner*.

sil n. (abbrev.) silly about: a lesbian involved in an affair *Legman*.

Silicon Valley n. Santa Clara County, California: home of the USA's microchip technology industry; the 'chips' are made from silicon *Esq. 6/83*.

silent city n. (US Black use) a graveyard *Klein*.

silk n. **1.** a Queen's Counsel; fr. the material of their gowns, rather than the cotton of a junior barrister's *Newman: 1*; **2.** (US Black use) a white woman; fr. texture of her hair *Major*.

silk and satin n. (drug use) any combination of amphetamines and barbiturates or tranquilizers *Folb*.

silks n. (US Black use) expensive clothing, poss. actually silken *Klein*.

silk stocking n. (US Black use) a rich person; who might have worn them *Klein*.

silly as a two-bob watch (Aus. use cp) very silly indeed *Wilkes*.

silly-billy n. a fool, a simpleton; fr.

traditional clown's stooge in mid-19th C. fairs/circuses, Silly Billy *Vidal*.

silvertail n. (Aus. use) a wealthy person *Neaman & Silver*.

silvery spoon n. (rhyming sl.) coon (qv) = Black *Dury*.

simoleons n. money, usu, dollars *'Hart To Hart', LWT, 1983*.

simp n. (abbrev.) simpleton *Junker*.

simple pimp n. (Black use) one who barely manages as a pimp and has no hope of transcending that level of employment within the criminal hierarchy *Milner*.

Simple Simon n. (US rhyming sl.) diamond, usu. diamond ring *Runyon: 1*.

Sin City n. (US trucker use) Las Vegas, Nevada; fr. its lurid reputation *CB*.

sing v. to make a confession to the police *Laugh in the Dark*.

singer n. an informer *Runyon*.

sing like a canary v. (UK police/criminal use) to make a full confession to the police *Powis*.

sinker n. a doughnut; fr. habit of dunking one's doughnut into one's coffee *Schulberg*.

sip at the fuzzy cup v. (US Black use) to engage in cunnilingus *Folb*.

sissy n. (derog.) effeminate homosexual male *Jay & Young*.

sister n. (homosexual use) fellow (male) homosexual; also used by lesbians for their peers *White*.

sister-act n. **1.** a homosexual couple; **2.** a homosexual man having sex with a heterosexual woman *Legman*.

sisters n. Black womanhood; dating esp. fr. use by Black radicals in 1960s *Seale*.

sit a woman v. (US Black use) to entertain a woman *Klein*.

sit-com n. (media use) (abbrev.) situation comedy: 'Steptoe & Son', 'The Good Life', 'All in the Family', etc. (cf: soap opera).

sit down v. (US teen. use) to make a telling, lasting impression; to have a major effect *Sculatti*.

sit eggs v. (US Black use) to overstay one's welcome; fr. a hen awaiting its chicks *Klein*.

sit-me-down n. the buttocks *Rawson*.

sit on v. to suppress, to keep quiet *PT*.

sit on it and rotate! general term of abuse suggesting that a hard and painful object be thrust into the victim's anus *'Hill Street Blues,' Thames TV, 1983*.

sit on one's face v. for a woman to position her vagina directly above a man's mouth, either literally sitting or squatting above his face, in order to facilitate cunnilingus *Green, 'Book of Rock Quotes', 1977*.

sit on one's stuff v. (US Black use) to work as a prostitute *Folb*.

sitter n. **1.** (cricket use) a very easy catch *BBC Radio-3 passim*; **2.** an easy target, both in shooting and in metaphor.

sit tight v. to stay where one is, esp. to stand firm and unruffled in the face of adversity *rr*.

sit on the throne v. to use a lavatory *Rawson*.

sitting pretty a. secure, safe, enjoying an easy life, esp. as to material things *Wodehouse: AAG*.

sit-upon n. (genteel euph.) buttocks.

six and four n. (drug use) heroin that has been adulterated and weakened by mixing one portion of pure heroin to six or four of sugar *Larner*.

six-foot bungalow n. a coffin *Rawson*.

six man n. (Can. prison use) a look-out *Caron*.

sixteen-year-old after shave n. (US Black use) very cheap and nasty wine *Folb*.

sixty-eight fellatio: 'you suck me and I'll owe you one' (cf: 69) *Maledicta*.

sixty-nine fr. Fr. *soixante-neuf*: mutual oral-genital stimulation *Price: 1*.

size queen n. (homosexual use) one who is obsessed by the size of penis a potential partner can boast *Stanley*.

sizzle v. (US Black use) to be exceptionally prone to arrest, esp. when holding drugs and acting in an

outrageous manner nonetheless (cf: hot) *Major*.
skag n. aka: *scag*: heroin *Tuff Shit Comics*.
skank n. unattractive, easily available girl *Price: 1*.
skank v. (West Indian use) to steal.
skate a.v. (US campus use) easy, simple, esp. of work; a course one can skate through *Underwood*.
skedaddle v. to rush off, to scamper, to escape *Humphries*.
skeet v. (US Black use) to have sexual intercourse *Klein*.
sketch a. (US campus use) risky, dangerous; abbrev. sketchy *Underwood*.
skew-whiff a. crooked, cock-eyed (qv); thus drunk (cf: squiffy).
skezag n. (drug use) pig Latin -ez- insertion, fr. skag (qv) heroin; *Stone*.
skid artist n. (UK criminal use) an expert get-away car driver used on robberies; the speedily driven car skids around the corners *Powis*.
skidlid n. a crash helmet *T 8/6/83*.
skid marks n. stains on one's underwear *Humphries*.
skid row n. the centre, in any town or city, for down-and-outs, alcoholics, tramps, etc. *Bukowski:6*.
skied a. (US campus use) pun on psyched up (qv): ready for anything *Bernbach*.
skillet n. (US Black use) a Black person *Major*.
skimmish n. beer, alcohol; usu. vagrant use *Powis*.
skin n. a dollar *Motor City Comics*.
skin and blister n. (rhyming sl.) sister *Dury*.
skin-flicks n. pornographic films *Higgins:5*.
skinflint n. a mean person *BvdB*.
skinflute n. (US Black use) the penis *Klein*.
skin game n. (US Black use) a card game, spec. tonk or coon can *Klein*.
skinhead n. UK teenage youth cult whose main identifying features are bald heads, large 'bother' boots, turned up jeans and braces; they provide much of the 'heavy' element of the neo-Nazi National Front.
skin me! (US Black use) invitation to give me some skin (qv) *X*.
skinned a. deprived of one's money, esp. after gambling unsuccessfully.
skinner n. (Aus. use) in gambling, a betting coup *Wilkes*.
skinning see: skinpop *Larner*.
skinpop v. (drug use) to inject a narcotic beneath the skin rather than directly into a vein (cf: mainline) *Goldman*.
skins n. cigarette papers, esp. those used for rolling cannabis joints (qv).
skint a. without money, out of funds corruption of *skinned* (cf: broke) *Griffiths*.
skin the cat v. (US Black use) to have sexual intercourse *Folb*.
skin worker n. (US cant) a shoplifter *Neaman & Silver*.
skip v. to leave, to escape, to run off *Sharpe:1*.
skip it! forget it, don't bother, etc. *Howard*.
skipper n. (UK police use) a sergeant *Laurie*.
skippering sleeping in derelict, empty houses; orig. 16th C. *skipper*: a barn *Wilkinson*.
skippy n. (US Black use) an effeminate homosexual male *Major*.
skip tracer n. an investigator who tracks down those who default on hotel and other bills *Fiction Illus.3*.
skirt n. a woman, usu. an attractive woman *rr*.
skirt-chaser n. a Don Juan, a habitual and dedicated ladies man.
skite v. (Aus. use) to boast or brag; fr. Scot. blatherskite: a noisy person *Bickerton*.
skive (off) v. to neglect one's duties, one's work; orig. milit. use.
skiver n. a 'lazybones', a skirker; fr. skive (qv).
skivvies n. underwear *Pynchon*.
skoofer n. (drug use) aka: *skoofus, skroofus*: marijuana cigarette *Folb*.
skrungy a. unappealing, unappetizing, disgusting.

skulk v. (US campus use) to steal *Underwood.*
skull n. (US Black use) cunnilingus (cf: head) *Klein.*
skull and crossbones n. (US Black use) **1.** poison, thus; **2.** anyone who is 'poison', esp. one who disrupts one's plans *Klein.*
skulldrag n. (US Black use) any activity that taxes the mind or emotions *Major.*
skulled a. intoxicated by a given drug or by an excess of alcohol; fr. out of one's skull (qv).
skullneck v. to decapitate *Wilkinson.*
skunked a. very drunk; from *drunk as a shunk Neaman & Silver.*
sky n. **1.** (rhyming sl.) sky rocket = pocket *Norman:2*; **2.** (US Black use) a policeman; fr. colour of uniform *Neaman & Silver.*
sky v. (US milit. use) to leave (cf: sky off) *Del Vecchio.*
sky off v. (US Black use) to depart, to exit *Klein.*
sky pilot n. a priest *Caron.*
slab n. (US Black use) $1 *Klein.*
slabbed and slid a. (UK prison use) dead and gone, or certainly long since departed from the prison and thus the immediate knowledge or interest of those left behind *LL.*
slabs n. (backsl.) balls = testicles *Cole.*
slack n. freedom, relief of pressure; *give some slack*: to let someone relax, to stop pressurizing *Price:2.*
slackman n. (US milit. use) the second man in a platoon or patrol when marching, immediately behind point (qv) (cf: drag) *Del Vecchio.*
slag n. **1.** a promiscuous woman; **2.** any unpleasant person; **3.** general term for a group of unpleasant people: 'the slag' *Norman:2*; all derive fr. 18th C. *slag*: coward, fr. slack-mettled.
slag v. (abbrev.) slag off (qv) *T 11/2/83.*
slag off v. to critize, slander, attack verbally *Robins.*
slam v. **1.** to criticize particularly harshly *Klein*; **2.** to hit, to kill.
slambang a. rough, tough, aggressive *PT.*
slammer n. prison; fr. the slamming shut of cell doors *Higgins:1.*
slamming a. (US Black use) overwhelming, extraordinary, very big; fr. 19th C. UK use *Klein.*
slam off v. to die *Chandler: Notebk.*
slams n. (US prison use) cell doors, fr. the sound they make when shut (cf: slammer) *Klein.*
slant n. aka: *slant-eye*: derog. Oriental (cf: roundeye **2**) *BvdB.*
slap n. make-up, esp. in theatre use; one 'slaps it on' *Norman:3.*
slap-bang a. exactly, completely, perfectly; usu. as *slap-bang in the middle.*
slap-dab directly, straight at, immediately *Runyon.*
slap-dash a. careless, enthusiastic if less than puntilious, happy-go-lucky.
slap five v. mutual hand-slapping ritual used by Blacks (and some whites) for greeting, emphasis, congratulation, etc. (cf: give me five, give me some skin) *Price:2.*
slap-happy a. cheery, slightly eccentric; fr. boxing use: someone whose brain has suffered from an excess of fighting (cf: punchy) *Himes:2.*
slapping aka: *slip-slapping*: see slap five *Milner.*
slapping the plank see: slap five *Klein.*
slap the pavement (US Black use) to walk around *Klein.*
slash n. urination *LL.*
slash v. (US Black use) to demolish someone verbally; with a 'rapier-like' wit *Klein.*
slats n. the ribs; fr. resemblance *Runyon:1.*
slaughter n. (UK criminal use) an immediate dumping ground for recently stolen property, prior to sharing it out or hiding it more permanently and securely *'Minder', Thames TV, 1983.*
slaughterhouse n. (US Black use)

anywhere a couple can indulge in sexual intercourse (cf: killing floor) *Folb.*

slave n. (US Black use) work, any form of job *X.*

slay v. **1.** (homosexual use) to gossip maliciously behind a third party's back; **2.** to reduce to complete hysterical laughter; to amaze or shock.

sleaze n. an unappealing, seedy person; fr. sleazy (qv) *Higgins:4.*

sleazy a. of a person: unpleasant, poss. criminal, generally distasteful; of a thing: dirty, rundown, decayed.

sledge n. (criminal use) (abbrev.) sledgehammer, thus one who carries a sledgehammer for use in a bank-robbery, an assault or other violent crime *Mortimer.*

sledge v. (cricket use) the barracking and abusing of a batsman by fielders in order to disturb his concentration; fr. sledgehammer *ST 13/2/83.*

sleeper n. **1.** (US campus use) a lazy, useless person *Underwood*; **2.** (media use (publishing, films, records, etc.)) any product that gains acceptance and success only slowly; **3.** (drug use) any form of sleeping pill *Green:1.*

sleeping Jesus n. (US Black use) **1.** a dull, tedious person; **2.** a person who is nodding out (qv) under the influence of heroin; both senses punning on creeping Jesus (qv) *Klein.*

sleepy time girl n. a promiscuous female; a given man's mistress *Chandler:LG.*

slewed a. drunk; off-balance *Norman:3.*

slice n. **1.** the vagina (cf: prime cut, etc.); **2.** (record business use) a 45 rpm record – a slice of an album (if seen as a circular cake) *Whitcomb.*

slice of life n. aka: *spice of life*: the vagina *Klein.*

slicer n. (US Black use) a knife *Folb.*

slick a. fashionable, smart, stylish, clever *Underwood.*

slicker n. a dandy, a smart dresser *Farrell.*

slicks n. (US milit. use) see: Hueys *Del Vecchio.*

slickster n. (US Black use) a cheat, a smooth talker, a hustler (qv) *Folb.*

slick-'em-plenty n. (US Black use (derog.)) a Jew, implying the clichéd critique of Jews as sharp (dishonest) businessmen *Folb.*

slide n. **1.** an establishment where transvestites can solicit normally dressed males *Legman;* **2.** (US three-card monte (qv) use) the member of the con-team who keeps an eye out for police and warns the rest so that all can 'slide off' in time *Shulman.*

slide v. to be forgiven, pardoned, ignored *Underwood.*

slide by v. (US Black use) to drop in uninvited, without previous notice *Folb.*

slidewalk n. (US Black use) a specific style of walking: one foot takes normal paces, the other drags; one hand is tucked into the side, the other is positioned with the wrist pressed to the waist and the elbow sticking out (cf: diddy-bopping) *Klein.*

slim n. (US prison use) a police spy *Chandler: Notebk.*

sling v. (Aus. use) to pay a bribe or a commission, esp. on one's winnings at gambling (cf: bung) *Bickerton.*

slinger n. (UK criminal use) one who passes forged notes *LL.*

sling off v. (Aus. use) to mock, to tease *Wilkes.*

sling one's hook v. to leave; poss. nautical, poss. mining origins *Dury.*

sling out v. to eject, to throw out *Griffith.*

sling shot n. (US Black use) a sanitary napkin *Folb.*

slip (her) a length v. to make love to a woman.

slip it to v. to have sexual intercourse with *Humphries.*

slit n. **1.** the vagina, thus; **2.** a female *P. Roth, 'The Great American Novel', 1973*; **3.** (derog.) an Asian or Oriental person; fr. shape of eyes *Folb.*

Sloane Rangers n. close-knit (essentially female) coterie representing the late teen/early twenties members of the UK aristocracy and such peers as they admit. Coined in *Harpers/Queen* magazine in 1978 by Peter York in an article that defines and explains the type. The specific name stems from the status of Sloane Square, London, SW1 as the centre of all SR life, style, etc. *Bernbach.*

slob n. fr. Slavic *zhlub*: coarse fellow: lazy, dirty, unkempt good-for-nothing man *Selby:1.*

slop chute n. (USMC use) any bar or restaurant on a Marine base *Uris.*

slope n. (derog.) an Oriental, esp. Vietnamese, Korean; fr. shape of eyes *O'Brien.*

slopped a. drunk; fr. general sloppiness, of speech, mind, etc. *Dickson.*

sloppy seconds n. a girl who has just copulated with one man and about to take on a second *Carson.*

slosh v. to hit.

sloshed a. drunk; fr. 19th C. *slosh*: drink *Dury.*

slot n. (Aus. use) a prison cell, usu. criminal use; into which one is put *Wilkes.*

slouch n. (pimp use) an eccentric, lazy, unprofessional prostitute (cf: flaky ho) *OUI 8/75.*

slow burn n. the gradual development of an intense fury, slowly brought to a peak, rather than simply exploding with rage.

slow con n. a fraudulent scheme in which the victim is nurtured slowly and carefully towards his/her downfall (cf: short con) *Pearce.*

slow 'em ups n. (drug use) barbiturates, tranquillizers, which act as soporifics *Folb.*

slow one's row v. (US Black use) to lower one's profile; to keep off the streets, perhaps through fear of police or rival criminal interest *Klein.*

slow on the trigger n. stupid, dull *Thompson:J.*

slow walker n. (US criminal use) one who follows postmen on their rounds with the intention of stealing the mail they have just delivered *Breslin.*

slug n. **1.** a bullet; **2.** a measure of a drink *Selby:1.*

slug v. to hit.

slugger n. **1.** a fighter, professional or otherwise, who relies on brute force rather than skill for his conquests fr. slug = hit *Heller*; **2.** (US campus use) a sexual success, a seducer (cf: hitter) *Underwood.*

slum n. fake, paste jewellery; fr. 19th C. UK cant: trickery and skill; a false document or begging letter *Runyon.*

slummy n. an ill-dressed, unattractive female *Klein.*

slums and bums n. (US campus use) course in urban local government fr. decayed housing, tramps *Dickson.*

slush n. **1.** (criminal use) forged, counterfeit money *LL*; **2.** (publishing use) unsolicited, and thus almost inevitably unpublished and rejected manuscripts *Green:2.*

slush fund n. an emergency fund for unforeseen expenditure, esp. that which may be illegal or extra-legal; such funds came into prominence during the Watergate Affair of 1972–4 *Pynchon.*

slyboots n. cunning, deceptive person, usu. with overtones of affection rather than an expression of outright disapproval *Vidal.*

slygrog n. (Aus. use) liquor sold without benefit of a licence *Bickerton.*

sly, slick and wicked n. (US Black use) an individual who plans to be caught out in a small act of deceit and thus facilitate plans for a larger con trick *Klein.*

smack n. **1.** fr. Yiddish *schmeck* = hit; thus heroin (cf: hit) *Velvet Underground, 'Heroin', 1966*; **2.** (US conman use) the use of a specially doctored coin for heads-or-tails gambling; the name comes from the conman's smacking his hand on the coin as he catches it *Thompson:J.*

smacked out a. under the influence of heroin; fr. smack (qv).

smackers n. pounds sterling; orig. US $1 *Humphries.*

smackeroos n. pounds sterling *T 21/9/83.*

smack freak n. heroin addict (cf: smack) *Price:2.*

smack in the eye n. a rebuff, a rejection, a severe and surprising disappointment.

small change n. an insignificant, weak person; fr. monetary use *Waits.*

small potatoes a. insignificant; of little worth, irrelevant *Teresa.*

small time n.,a. mediocrity, failure, the second rate, unprofitable fr. theatre use: a vaudeville circuit for second-rate acts which offered three or even more programmes per day (cf: big time).

smart-ass n.,a. anyone who considers himself cleverer than his peers and than his own actual intelligence warrants *The People's Comic.*

smart cookie n. a bright, opportunistic person *rr.*

smart guy n. see: wise guy.

smartiepants n. general term of light-hearted abuse *May.*

smart money n. **1.** spec. the way in which experienced gamblers bet; **2.** good sense *Higgins:3.*

smart mouth n.,v. see: bad mouth *Folb.*

smarts n. wit, intelligence *Grogan.*

smash n. **1.** small change; orig. counterfeit money, then rhyming sl., cash *Burroughs:1*; **2.** (show business use) a great success, (abbrev.) smash hit *Performance*; **3.** (US Black use) wine; back-formation fr. smashed (qv) (?) *Folb.*

smashed a. **1.** very drunk *Junker*; **2.** intoxicated with a given drug, esp, cannabis or LSD *Wolfe:2.*

smashing a. wonderful, delightful, excellent; mainly juv. use.

smear and smudge n. (rhyming sl.) judge *Wright.*

smell a rat v. to be suspicious, of persons or situations *Sillitoe.*

smiling faces n. (US Black use) hypocrites, false friends *Klein.*

smoke n. **1.** (derog.) a Black person (cf: shadow) *Dunne*; **2.** any cheap, rotgut alcohol, spec. denatured alcohol shaken up with water and drunk by down and out alcoholic tramps *Himes:1*; **3.** (drug use) marijuana; **4.** (US campus use) one dollar; so small a sum 'goes up in smoke'.

Smoke, the n. London, as regarded from the provinces.

smoke v. to throw very fast, usu. of a ball *Underwood.*

smoked haddock n. (racing use, rhyming sl.) the Paddock *Franklyn.*

smoke out v. **1.** (US Black use) to impress; to outdo *Folb*; **2.** to entice into the open, to lure out; fr. hunting/rural use.

smoke stack n. (US Black use) a particularly Black person *Folb.*

Smokey n. traffic policeman, Highway Patrol; fr. US traditional country character 'Smokey the Bear' *Higgins:4.*

smoking a. (US Black use) very urgent, very excited; esp. in sexual context *Klein.*

smooching n. kissing and cuddling, standing up and dressed *Price:1.*

smoodge v. (Aus. use) to ingratiate oneself, to cuddle up, to suck up (qv); fr. Yiddish *schmooze* or SE *smudge*: to caress *Dennis.*

smoothie n. a sophisticated, smart person – both mentally and physically *Thompson:J.*

smother n. a coat, a wrap; fr. smother: to hide, to cover up *Norman:2.*

smush n. the mouth; fr. mush (qv) *Runyon:1.*

smut n. pornography, obscenity; since such items are 'dirty'.

smut-butt n. (US campus use) (derog.) Black student *Underwood.*

smut-hound n. one who is obsessed by the tiniest trace of obscenity, esp. in the arts or media; thus a censor;

coined by H. L. Mencken and one of the coinages of which he was 'vainest' *AS 41 (1966)*.

snafu (milit. use) (acro.) *s*ituation *n*ormal: *a*ll *f*ucked-*u*p coined c.1940 by anon. member of British Army *Byrne*.

snag v. **1.** to grab *Price:3*; **2.** (street gang use) to attack an individual without warning *Salisbury*; **3.** (US Black use) to have sexual intercourse *Folb*.

snags n. (Aus. use) sausages; rarely used in singular *Wilkes*.

snake n. (street gang use) a spy *Salisbury*.

snake v. (US campus use) to steal someone else's date *Underwood*.

snake-eyes (gambling use) the point of 2 (a pair of ones) in craps dice *Chandler: Notebk*.

snake in the grass n. (rhyming sl.) looking glass, mirror *Cole*.

snake's house n. (Aus. use) lavatory; fr. rhyming sl. snake's hiss: piss *Humphries*.

snaky a. devious, underhand, cunning; fr. the Eden myth.

snap n. anything easy, a simple task, achievement (cf: snip) *Selby:1*.

snap assholes v. see: lock assholes *Uris*.

snap it up v. to speed up, to hurry up; often as a command *Chandler:LG*.

snapper n. (homosexual use) the foreskin *Legman*.

snatch n. **1.** spec. the vagina; **2.** women, girls *Selby:1*.

snatch v. **1.** to kidnap *Runyon*; **2.** (US Black use) to threaten someone by grabbing their lapels and talking menacingly into their face *Klein*.

snazzy a. smart, fashionable, brightly coloured; fr. snappy + jazzy (?).

sneak job n. housebreaking *Runyon*.

sneaky a. underhand, crooked *Seale*.

sneaky Pete n. cheap, rotgut wine; its effects 'sneak up' on the drinker *Salisbury*.

sneaky-Pete v. to creep quietly, to move stealthily *Pynchon*.

sneeze v. to kidnap *Chandler: Notebk*.

sneeze in the cabbage v. to perform cunnilingus *Legman*.

sneeze it out v. to confess (cf: cough up) *Klein*.

sneezer n. prison *Runyon:1*.

snide a. **1.** spec. counterfeit (money), thus; **2.** fake, unpleasant, mean *Norman:2*.

sniff n. **1.** narcotics; fr. the method of consuming them *Black Uhuru, 'Chill Out', 1982*; **2.** rumour *Robins*.

sniffer n. **1.** (pimp use) a client who enjoys sniffing a prostitute's dirty panties *OUI 8/75*; **2.** (derog.) investigator from the DHSS who checks on the validity of unemployment benefit claims *Bleasdale*.

sniffy a. disdainful, arrogant; fr. sniffs of contempt.

snifter n. an alcoholic drink; fr. the brandy glass, shaped to be warmed by the hands and for the fumes, so intensified, to be sniffed *Wodehouse:GB*.

snip n. **1.** a bargain; **2.** anything simple, an easy task (cf: snap) *Capital Radio 1983*.

snipe n. **1.** cigarette end (cf: fag-end, butt-end) *Algren*; **2.** (USN use) a fireman or other member of a ship's engine-room gang *Pynchon*.

snipe v. (US Black use) to kill; fr. milit. use *Folb*.

snipe on v. (US Black use) to malign, to criticize, to gossip about someone; fr. milit. marksman *Folb*.

snippy a. hypercritical, complaining over petty problems; cutting down other people *Vidal*.

snitch n. **1.** an informer *Goldman*; **2.** the nose *Wright*.

snitch v. **1.** to inform; **2.** to steal *Wodehouse:AAG*.

snitcher n. an informant, a tell-tale *Sanders:2*.

snockered a. drunk *Price:3*.

snog v. to enjoy sexual preliminaries, stopping short of intercourse, usu. of teenage experimentation (cf: necking) *May*.

snoop v. to pry, to interfere, to listen

in.

snoot n. the nose *Runyon.*

snooter n. (drug use) anyone who inhales heroin or cocaine rather than injects it; fr. snoot (qv).

snootful n. an alcoholic drink; hence to *have a snootful*: to be drunk *Wodehouse:MOJ.*

snooty a. snobbish, stand-offish; one who looks down their nose (cf: snoot) *May.*

snooze job n. anything especially boring *Gene Hackman LWT, 1982.*

snorker n. (Aus. use) **1.** sausage, thus; **2.** penis *Humphries.*

snort v. to inhale narcotics, usu. cocaine or heroin, through the nostrils *Larner.*

snort n. a gulp of alcohol *Runyon.*

snot n. **1.** mucus; fr. 15th C. *Price:2*; **2.** (abbrev.) snotnose **2** (qv) *Thompson:J.*

snotnose n. **1.** a small child with a running nose; a grubby child; **2.** an arrogant, snobbish person (cf: snotty).

snotrag n. handkerchief; fr. snot **1** (qv) *Humphries.*

snotty a. superior, snobbish, stuck-up *Price:2.*

snout n. **1.** tobacco *Norman:1*; **2.** the nose *Higgins:2*; **3.** an informer (cf: snitch) *Newman:2.*

snow n. **1.** (Aus. school use) a blond-haired weakling, the butt of bullies who will call him 'snow!' *Humphries:2*; **2.** (Aus. use) derog. description of Italian or other Latin race; fr. snow: a white-coloured haircream à la Brylcreem and supposedly favoured by such men *Humphries:2*; **3.** cocaine; fr. colour and consistency *Vidal*; **4.** bluff, bluster, lies; abbrev. snow job (qv) *Higgins:2*; **5.** (US Black use) a white girl *Klein.*

snow v. to fool, usu. by overwhelming with slick patter (cf: snow job).

snow bird n. (drug use) a cocaine user; fr. snow (qv).

snow bunny n. a girl who frequents the ski slopes as much for the sex as for the sport *Humphries:2.*

snow-dropping n. (UK criminal use) stealing washing from unguarded clotheslines *LL.*

snowed over a. (US campus use) obsessively in love, infatuated *Underwood.*

snowed under a. over-burdened with work, commitments, responsibilities, etc.

snowfall n. see: snow job *'Taxi', Thames TV, 1983.*

snow in one's game (US Black use) the introduction of a white person into a Black person's life with the express intention of profiting financially by catering to their sexual wants *Klein.*

snow job n. an untrue but totally convincing story; a conman's patter *Caron.*

snoz n. see: snozzle *Southern & Hoffenberg.*

snozzle n. the nose (cf: schnozzle) *Runyon:1.*

snuff v. to murder, to kill; abbrev. snuff out *Sanders.*

snuff it v. to die *Humphries.*

snuff movies n. films, usu. pornographic, which climax in the actual death of one of the participants, usu. an actress; snuff movies were allegedly common in California around the time of the psychotic Manson Family, c.1969, though no one seems to have seen or to possess a copy *Sanders.*

snuggies n. (US campus use) female underwear; not particularly winter thickness *Underwood.*

so a. homosexual; 'Is he so?' (cf: that way) *Q. Crisp, 'The Naked Civil Servant', 1975.*

soak n. a drunkard.

soak v. to extort money from *The People's Comic.*

so-and-so **1.** euph. for any derog. name, esp. sonofabitch (qv); **2.** unspecified object, thingamijig *Bruce:1.*

soap opera n. the daily radio and TV dramas – 'The Archers', 'Coronation Street', etc. – which tell the interminable tale of supposedly 'ordinary life'; fr. the original show 'The Goldbergs', used by US sponsor Proctor & Gamble to advertise their soap and similar products (cf: sitcom) *Green:2*.

SOB see: sonofabitch.

sob sister n. see: agony aunt.

sob story n. a pitiful tale, which may reduce the listener to tears, whether or not it has any basis in truth or is designed merely for felonious purposes.

sob stuff n. distressing facts, stories, etc.; often used to obtain sympathy and poss. money too.

sock v. to hit, to punch *Farrell*.

sock it to me! (excl.) amaze me, surprise me, etc.; fr. the catchphrase used in 'Rowan & Martin's Laugh-In', TV 1960s, *Uneeda Comix*.

socko a. wonderful, excellent, esp. in show business use and *Variety* magazine *Thompson*.

sock the clock punch the time clock *Chandler: Notebk*.

sod n. **1.** an unpleasant person; fr. abbrev. sodomite, but sexual reference purely coincident; **2.** (US campus use) a drunkard; pun on sot *Underwood*.

sod about v. to mess around, to waste time, etc.

sodding a. adj. from sod (qv); derog. intensifier *Performance*.

sod widow n. an actual widow, whose husband has died, rather than a grass widow, whose husband is merely away; the corpse is 'under the sod' Runyon.

soft a. fr. soft in the head: stupid, dull, foolish *Breslin*.

soft-cop n. a sucker, esp. some form of community/social worker whose sympathies can be exploited *Robins*.

softie n. a weakling; a man whose external toughness hides a sentimental soul *Heller*.

soft money n. notes, bills, paper money *Klein*.

soft number n. an easy job.

soft-pedal v. to play down, to diminish, to keep a 'low profile'; fr. pedal on a piano.

soft soap n.,v. flattery, thus the act of flattering someone *Hotten*.

soft touch n. one who can easily be touched (qv), ie solicited for money.

soggies n. (UK 'society' use) breakfast cereal; a hangover from nursery talk *Barr*.

SOHF n. (UK 'society' use) (acro.) *S*ense *O*f *H*umour *F*ailure; often discerned in someone who fails to appreciate the throwing of bread rolls, etc. *Barr*.

sold a. successfully persuaded (cf: sell) *Norman:2*.

soldier n. (US Mafia use) a lower echelon member of a Mafia family, the run-of-the-mill gangsters who fight the gangwars.

sold on a. convinced, fascinated by (cf: sell).

solid! excl. of approbation, implying a firm bond, honesty, excellence, etc.

solitary as a bastard on Father's Day (Aus. cp) extremely lonely *Humphries:2*.

so long goodbye, poss. fr. Hebrew *shalom*: the basic word of greeting and farewell, lit. 'peace' *rr*.

sombitch n. see: sonofabitch *Vidal*.

some hope! (negative excl.) no hope whatsoever.

some mothers do have 'em (cp) describing a particularly foolish or absurd person *BBC-TV, situation comedy title, 1970s*.

someone blew out his/her pilot light (US campus use) cp referring to anyone considered somewhat odd, high on drugs, etc. and who thus has 'lost direction' *Bernbach*.

some people! (cp) derisory or critical comment by the speaker on the opinions or more likely the activities of others; the details are unspoken but will be a condemnation of what 'some people; are doing.

something else n. excl. or description of approval, or wonder *Bruce:2*.

something the cat brought in n. a distasteful, prob. dirty/unkempt,

object or person *Wodehouse:MOJ.*
son of a bitch n. derog. general term of abuse *Higgins:1.*
sonofagun (euph.) sonofabitch (qv) *Bruce:2.*
sook n. (Aus. use) coward, crybaby *Humphries:2.*
sooner n. (Aus. use) a lazy person; one who would 'sooner' loaf around than work or, in context, fight *Neaman & Silver.*
SOP (police use) (abbrev.) *S*tandard *O*perating *P*rocedure *Vidal.*
sophisticated lady n. (US Black use) cocaine (cf: girl) *Folb.*
sopor n. (drug use) (abbrev.) soporific, any form of barbiturate drug *Stone.*
soppy a. (juv. use) vapid, naïve, esp. romantic; sometimes intensified as *soppy date*; fr. sopping wet (?).
sore a. angry, irritated *McBain:1.*
sorehead n. a grumpy, irritable person *Dunne.*
sorry and sad n. (rhyming sl.) dad = father *Wright.*
sort n. **1.** (Aus. use) a companion of either sex; **2.** (UK use) a girl *Humphries.*
sort out v. to deal with, esp. violently *Tidy.*
soul n. the essential quality of Black being, unavailable, however much aped and pirated, to anyone who is not Black (and American).
soul a. Black; fr. soul n. (qv); thus *soul food, soul sister etc. Price:2.*
soul child n. (US campus use (Black students)) anyone with conspicuous Black pride and identity *Underwood.*
soul kiss n. a deep kiss, involving putting one's tongue into one's partner's mouth (cf: french kiss) *Jay & Young.*
soul shake n. see: slap five *Folb.*
sound n. (street gang use) conversation; talk *Salisbury.*
sound v. (street gang use) to tease, to joke with *Salisbury.*
sound off v. to boast, brag.
sounds n. music, spec. records.
sounds and tunes n. (US campus use) songs *Underwood.*
soup and fish n. a dinner jacket; fr. the food one eats when wearing it *Wodehouse passim.*
souped-up a. intensified, accelerated; usu. of a car that has been modified by its owner to exceed the basic factory-created performance; fr. soup = engine fuel (?) *Humphries:2.*
souse n. a drunkard (cf: soak).
soused a. drunk; fr. souse (qv) *Schulberg.*
sov n. (abbrev.) sovereign: a pound sterling *Newman:1.*
so what? widely used term of disinterest, a rejoinder to the previous speaker's announcement, revelation, or whatever.
sozzled a. drunk *Wright.*
SP (racing use) (abbrev.) *S*tarting *P*rice, thus: basic information, facts *Griffith.*
space v. (US teen. use) to daydream, to drift off; fr. spaced out (qv) *Pond.*
space cadet n. (drug use) any heavy user of drugs, esp. cannabis or hallucinogens who is, thus, continually 'flying' *Sanders.*
spaced see: spaced out *Goldman.*
spaced out **1.** intoxicated by a drug; esp. the hallucinogens; fr. the image of flying through space; **2.** generally disorientated, with or without drugs *Tuff Shit Comics.*
spacey a. **1.** anything that simulates the intoxication of LSD or other hallucinogens **2.** see: spaced out *McFadden.*
spade n. a Black person, esp. West Indian or African; fr. 'black as the ace of spades' *Price:2.*
spag n. (Aus. use) (abbrev.) spaghetti: derog. term for Italian *Wilkes.*
spag bol n. (UK 'society' use) aka: *spag bog*: spaghetti bolognese (most likely in some adulterated British version); a retained juv. use *Barr.*
spaghetti n. (hi-fi use) the collection of wires usually found behind the linking amplifiers, record decks, etc. *Sony Corp., ad., 1983.*

spaghetti bender n. (derog.) Italian; fr. popular Ital. foodstuff *BvdB.*

spank v. to beat up *Austin.*

spare a. overwrought, distraught *'Minder', Thames TV, 1983.*

spare prick at a wedding absolutely useless; usu. a cp: *as much use as a . . .*

spare tyre n. the roll of flesh that surrounds an overweight stomach (cf: bagel, love handle).

sparkers see: spark out *Powis.*

sparkler n. jewellery, spec. diamonds *Powis.*

spark out v. fall fast asleep *Norman:2.*

sparks n. an electrician, usu. theatrical and film use.

sparrow fart n. dawn *Humphries.*

spas n. (student/school use) useless, clumsy, incompetent and thus socially unacceptable person; abbrev. spastic *Underwood.*

spastic a. **1.** convulsed with laughter and thus incapable of coherent mental or physical activity; **2.** see: spas.

spaz n. a fool, an idiot, an unappealing person; fr. spastic (qv) *Harpers/Queen 1/83.*

speaker n. (US Black use) a gun *Major.*

spear v. **1.** (ice hockey use) to stab at another player with the shaft of one's stick; an illegal foul *D. Atyeo, 'Blood & Guts', 1979*; **2.** (US prison use) to arrest *Chandler: Notebk.*

spearchucker n. a Black; fr. tribal/African origins *Price:1.*

spear the bearded clam v. (Aus. use) to have sexual intercourse *Humphries.*

special n. (pimp use) a client who has any particular tastes: costumes, bondage, foot-fetishes, etc. *OUI 8/75.*

speck n. (US Black use) a Black person *Folb.*

speed n. any amphetamine-based stimulant drug *Price:2.*

speedball n. a mixture of cocaine and heroin, either injected or sniffed by the user *ES 24/3/83.*

speed freak n. **1.** (drug use) a user of amphetamines; **2.** (US Black use) one who enjoys driving or being driven at high speed.

speed limit (bingo use) 30; fr. urban speed limit in UK, 30 mph.

spend a penny v. (euph.) to urinate; fr. the penny (pre-decimalization) charge in public lavatories, now risen with inflation to 10p *James Tucker, 'The Novels of Anthony Powell', 1976.*

spew v. to vomit *Norman:3.*

spew one's guts v. to vomit violently, thus, figuratively, to make a full confession of crimes. (cf: spill one's guts).

spic n. **1.** (derog.) Puerto Rican, Mexican (but cf: wetback); orig. used for Italian, mispron. of 'spaghetti' or 'no speaka da English' *Price:2*; **2.** (US campus use) course in Spanish; fr. **1** *Underwood.*

spick n. see: spic **1** *Jenkins.*

spider n. (US campus use) a hard worker; fr. the industrious arachnid *Bernbach.*

spiel n. patter, speech, line (qv); esp. of salesman or market stallholder.

spiel v. **1.** to gamble; fr. Yiddish: to play; **2.** to patter, to talk glibly, to 'shoot a line'.

spieler n. (illegal) gambling club; fr. Yiddish 'to play' *Norman:2.*

spiff n. a dandy; fr. spiffy (qv) *Dunne.*

spiffed up a. dressed particularly well; fr. spiffy (qv) *Price:3.*

spifflicated a. drunk *Chandler: LG.*

spiffy a. excellent, wonderful, neatly dressed; fr. mid-19th C. *Price:3.*

spike n. **1.** hypodermic syringe *Caron*; **2.** a lodging house, orig. local authority workhouse or lodging house *G. Orwell, 'Down and Out in Paris and London', 1933.*

spill v. **1.** (drug use) to miss the vein when making an injection and thus waste the heroin/water mixture *Goldman*; **2.** see; spill the beans *rr.*

spillin' n. (US Black use) a gunfight in which quantities of bullets are fired and wounds inflicted *Klein.*

spill one's breakfast v. to vomit *Dunne.*

spill one's guts v. (UK cant) to confess one's crimes in full.

spill one's nut v. to confess, to make an admission *Gruber*.

spill the beans v. to confess, to let out a secret, to talk unguardedly *Waterhouse*.

spill the works v. see: spill the beans *rr*.

spin v. (UK police use) to search, usu. in *spin a drum*: to search a house *Powis*.

spin n. (taxi use) an authorized cab rank *LL*.

spin a drum v. (UK police use) to search a suspect's premises *Neaman & Silver*.

spirit n. (US Black use) jazz or blues music *Klein*.

spit-bit n. (US Black use) smooth, persuasive talk *Klein*.

spit out of the window v. (homosexual use) to spit out one's partner's semen after fellatio; on to a towel, a tissue, etc. *Legman*.

spitter n. (baseball use) a spitball, now outlawed as a foul pitch *Sanchez*.

spiv n. obs. and for historical use only: a flashy, sharp individual who exists on the fringes of real criminality, living by his wits rather than a regular job; poss. origins: fr. reverse of *VIPs*; fr. police abbrev. 'suspected persons and itinerant vagrants'; most likely from Romany for 'sparrow', used by gypsies as derog. ref. to those who existed by picking up the leavings of their betters, criminal or legitimate.

spivmobile n. an exceptionally ostentatious and flashy car, such as might be driven by a spiv (qv) or his successors (cf: pimpmobile) *T 5/10/83*.

splang n. (US Black use) sharp words *Klein*.

splash the boots v. to urinate *Humphries*.

splendiferous a. intensifier of 'splendid' *Hotten*.

splib n. (abbrev.) slip-de-wib: a fellow Black person *Milner*.

splice the mainbrace v. to drink; fr. nautical use *Hotten*.

spliff n. a marijuana cigarette; esp. West Indian and Rastafari use *Thelwell*.

splish and splash v. (US Black use) to debate a topic; to ponder without coming to a decision *Klein*.

split v. to leave. fr. the subsequent division in the group that such a departure makes (?); also fr. 18th C. UK use: to move, run, gallop, etc. *Price:2*.

split beaver n. see: wide-open beaver.

splitsville n. the end of a relationship, a divorce, etc.

split the cup v. (US Black use) to deflower a virgin *Klein*.

splosh n. tea *Norman:2*.

splosh it on v. to bet heavily, esp. at racetracks.

splurge v. to spend freely, generously and foolishly.

spoiler n. (journalistic use) a reporter who uses any methods, ethical or otherwise, to steal or otherwise ruin a rival paper's supposed scoop *'World In Action', Granada TV, 1983*.

spondulicks n. money *Waterhouse*.

spook n. **1.** a Black person *Norman:2*; **2.** (US use) an intelligence agent, esp. CIA; derived fr. the Yale University secret society 'Skull & Bones' from amongst whose members were recruited the personnel of the OSS, the Second World War predecessor of the CIA *Esq. 1976*.

spook v. to scare, to unnerve *Grogan*.

spooked a. (gambling use) a crooked, marked deck of cards; under the influence of a malign spirit *Austin*.

spoon n. (drug use) two grams or one sixteenth of an ounce of heroin *Grogan*.

spoon v. (US campus use) to eat together *Underwood*.

sport n. **1.** a playboy, a man about town, with accent on gambling, womanizing and other areas of the fast life *Heller*; **2.** general term of address to a man, esp. Aus. use.

sporting life n. the 'good' life: money, liquor, women, all the desired pleasures of the flesh (cf: sport) *Schulberg*.

spot v. to advance on credit *Tuff Shit*

Comics.

spot on perfect, exactly right, accurate.

spot one out v. (US Black use) to ascertain the characteristics, hidden or otherwise, of a given person (cf: peep one's hole card) *Klein.*

spray one's tonsils v. (homosexual use) to ejaculate in one's fellator's mouth *Legman.*

spread a technicolour rainbow v. (US campus use) to vomit (cf: technicolour yawn) *Neaman & Silver.*

spread eagle n. a position of heterosexual intercourse.

spread the broads v. to play cards, esp. to cheat or to play a swindling game such as 'find the lady' (qv) (cf: broads) *Powis.*

spread the bull v. to talk boastfully, if inaccurately, of one's prowess (cf: bull, bullshit) *Farrell.*

spring v. to get a person out of prison; to have someone released *Humphries.*

spring it v. to reveal (a plan), with some element of surprise *Wodehouse: PGM.*

spritz v. fr. Yiddish: 'spray': in show business use: to perform a stage monologue with much impromptu ad libbing, free-associating, etc. à la Lenny Bruce *Goldman.*

sprog n. a child; orig. milit. use: recruit *Obs. 20/3/83.*

spruik v. (Aus. use) to speak in a way that resembles a spruiker (qv) *Dennis.*

spruiker n. (Aus. use) **1.** a loud and continual talker; **2.** spec. a barker for a fairground/carnival sideshow or a cinema, theatre or similar entertainment, who stands on the street to ballyhoo (qv) the show and attract an audience *Humphries:2.*

spud n. a potato *Wodehouse: COJ.*

spud-bashing n. peeling potatoes; orig. milit. use, when the job was compulsory and part of kitchen fatigues.

spunk n. **1.** semen, thus; **2.** courage, bravery, guts *Schulberg.*

spunko a. (UK teen. 'society' use) an attractive, intelligent and fashionable male.

spunky a. courageous, brave, plucky.

Spurs n. Tottenham Hotspur Football Club.

SQPQ (UK 'society' use) (acro.) *S*uspiciously *Q*uiet, *P*robably *Q*ueer; note appended to the name of a possible male escort by a debutante or her mother *T 18/7/83.*

Squad n. (abbrev.) the Flying Squad (cf: Sweeney) *Newman:1.*

squaddy n. regular private soldier *A. F. N. Clarke, 'Contact', 1983.*

square n. **1.** a traditional, conservative person; fr. jazz use *Grogan*; **2.** (Black pimp use) a naive person, a sucker (qv), anyone who believes in white America's promises; one who has little sexual sophistication *Milner.*

square v. to put right, spec. to deal with problems, often by using influence, bribes, threats, etc. *Wodehouse: PGM.*

square away v. to deal with, to settle; fr. milit. use *Higgins:3.*

squarebrain n. (US Black use) a fool, a dullard, with overtones of conservatism *Folb.*

square broad n. (Black pimp use) any woman not a prostitute *Milner.*

squaredom the world of the unsophisticated, the unwordly, the unhip (qv) *Greenlee.*

square-eyes n. one who watches an excess of TV and thus, supposedly, develops eyes the same shape as the screen.

squarehead n. (derog.) German; fr. the severe 'Prussian' haircuts (?) *BvdB.*

Square John n. a respectable member of society (cf: John Q. Public) *Pearce.*

square one off v. to pay; can be used quite legitimately, but often carries a sense of corruption/bribery etc. *Humphries:2.*

square shake n. a fair deal, honest treatment *Algren.*

square shooter n. honest, trustworthy person *Farrell.*

square to the wood (US Black use) intensifier of square (qv) *Folb.*

square with v. to make amends, to make up for, to even up *rr.*
squashed a. very drunk *Bernbach.*
squat see: diddley-squat (qv) *Higgins:1.*
squatter n. the buttocks *Rawson.*
squawk n. (UK prison use) any form of petition, to the Governor or to the Home Secretary *LL.*
squawk v. to complain; like some raucous bird *Runyon.*
squeaky-clean a. as clean as one could imagine; so shiny and taut that it almost squeaks with its own perfection *Whitcomb.*
squeal n. (US police use) the report of a crime by a member of the public *McBain:1.*
squeal v. (US police use) **1.** to report a crime to the police *McBain:1*; **2.** to inform against one's partners in crime *rr.*
squealer n. an informer *Edgar Wallace, bk. title, 1927.*
squeeze n. **1.** (UK criminal use) silk; fr. the quality of the fabric which will squeeze into a minuscule space *Powis*; **2.** (US Black use) a close friend; fr. physical affection (cf: main squeeze) *Folb.*
squibbed off a. shot, murdered. fr. 19th C. UK cant *squib*: to fire a gun *Chandler: Notebk.*
squid n. (US campus use) a particularly hard worker *Bernbach.*
squiff out v. to collapse through drunkenness; fr. squiffy (qv) *Chandler: LG.*
squiffy a. drunk; fr. skew-whiff (qv) *Dickson.*
squillion a hypothetical and enormous number, a multiple of many millions *Obs. 26/6/83.*
squire general term of address, no particular rank or intimacy indicated *Newman:2.*
squirrel n. (US campus use) **1.** an eccentric person; **2.** the female pubic hair; **3.** a female *Underwood.*
squirrelly a. (US campus use) eccentric, odd *Underwood.*
squirt n. a small, insignificant person, often of a child *Runyon.*
squirt game n. drinking the cheapest forms of alcohol for intoxication's sake alone; fr. squirt: very cheap beer *Norman:2.*
squizz n. a glance, a brief look; fr. quiz, quizzical, etc. *Humphries:2.*
SRO (acro.) *S*tanding *R*oom *O*nly; orig. entertainment use, by extn. anything that sells out, a full house *Green:2.*
SS n. (acro.) *S*uspended *S*entence *Higgins:3.*
stab n. a try, an attempt; thus *make a stab at*: to try; fr. a lunge with a knife.
stable n. (Black pimp use) those women currently working for a given pimp *Milner.*
stache n. (US campus use) (abbrev.) moustache *Underwood.*
stacked a. well-built, of a woman *Algren.*
stack up v. to emerge, to develop; to maintain (or fall beneath: 'don't stack up') a given standard *Thompson: J.*
stag n., a. an unaccompanied man at a dance or similar gathering *Price:1.*
stage-door johnny n. a man, poss. rich, who hangs around theatre stage doors hoping to meet his female idols *NYRB 29/9/83.*
stage fright n. (rhyming sl.) light = light ale *Powis.*
stag film n. a pornographic film; enjoyed by stags (qv) *Bruce:1.*
stag party n. the traditional eve-of-wedding all-male party given for a bridegroom and featuring an excess of drink, probably a stripper and possibly a prostitute.
staked long and deep (US Black use) the investment of large sums of cash *Klein.*
stake-out n. the surveillance of a suspect by police stationed in clandestine hiding places *Fiction Illus. 3.*
stalk n. **1.** cheek (cf: neck) **2.** the (erect) penis *Powis.*
stalking n. (taxi-driver use) London cabbies' illegal practice whereby one keeps the meter on 'hired', although

one has no actual fare, while cruising the streets looking for what may be a very lucrative fare, for whom one *will* stop *Powis.*

stall n. (US cant) a pickpocket's assistant who blocks the passage of the intended victim *Neaman & Silver.*

stall v. to play for time, to make excuses, to delay *Hotten.*

stallion n. **1.** (US Black use) a tall, good looking woman, poss. highly sexed *Milner*; **2.** a man with greater than average sexual powers (cf: steed, stud).

stammer and stutter n. (rhyming sl.) butter *Jones: J.*

stamping ground n. one's home territory, one's area of operations (cf: manor; turf).

stand n. an erection.

stand at ease n. (rhyming sl.) cheese *Jones: J.*

standing on the top step (UK criminal use) of a man on trial who is facing the likely prospect of a maximum sentence *LL.*

stand on me! (excl.) believe me! *Performance.*

stand over v. (Aus. use) to demand (money) with menaces; thus *stand over man*: a thug, a heavy (qv); fr. menacing position the demander adopts *Wilkes.*

stand pat v. to stay as one is; fr. poker use: a player who does not wish to change his hand.

stand point v. (Can. prison use) to be on the alert; fr. milit. point: the lead man of a patrol *Caron.*

stand still for v. tolerate, permit, accept *Stone.*

stand to n. (rhyming sl.) stand to attention = pension *Powis.*

stand up v.t. to fail to arrive for a scheduled meeting, to break a date *Junker.*

stand up v. **1.** to confess (cf: put one's hand up); **2.** to withstand pressure, esp. police questioning *Higgins:1.*

stand up guy n. an honest, dependable person, one who 'stands up to be counted' *Higgins:1.*

stank n. **1.** (US Black use) the anus; fr. possible malodorousness *Klein*; **2.** (US Black use) the vagina (cf: stank = anus) *Folb.*

star n. **1.** (UK prison use) a first offender; abbrev. star prisoner *Cole*; **2.** (US black use) a man's favourite woman; a very attractive woman; fr. show business use *Folb.*

star fucker n. see: celebrity fucker *D. McLintick, 'Indecent Exposure', 1983.*

starkers a. nude; fr. stark naked *Humphries.*

stark, staring bonkers a. absolutely crazy *Denis Healey, 1983 election campaign.*

star of the line n. (US Black use) a pimp's favourite whore within a stable (qv) (cf: star) *Klein.*

stars for studs (US campus use) course in basic astronomy *Birnbach.*

starters n. initial actions, plans, etc. *Powis.*

starve the lizards! (Aus. use) see stiffen the lizards *Wilkes.*

stash v. to hide. fr. 18th C. cant *stash*: put a stop to, or fr. Fr. *cacher*: to hide *Higgins:1.*

stash n. **1.** a hiding place, usu. for drugs *Goldman*; **2.** (US campus use) any drug, esp. cannabis; fr. stash: hiding place for that drug *Underwood.*

stat (medical use) immediately, emergency; used to summon medical staff over the public address system *Breslin.*

static n. difficulties, aggravation; fr. radio use *Higgins:1.*

stay loose the equivalent of 'goodbye' in communities influenced by California's post-hippie era 'new therapies' (cf: hang loose) *Mcfadden.*

stay on one's case v. to attack, to harass continually and consistently *Folb.*

steady n. a regular girl/boy-friend *Howard.*

steady the Buffs! (cp) keep calm, don't lose control, etc.; poss. milit. origin fr. Buffs: the East Kent regiment.

steam n. (drug use) PCP (phencyclidine); (cf: angel dust, hog) *Sanders*.
steam v. to be annoyed, to talk aggressively *Heller*.
steamed up a. **1.** tense, annoyed; **2.** fighting drunk *Wilkinson*.
steamer n. (rhyming sl.) steam tug = mug = fool, sucker (qv) *Powis*.
steam in v. to commit oneself completely, esp. in a fight (cr: wade in).
steaming a. intensifier, euphemistic overtones, since usu. in negative use, ie *steaming great prawn*: absolute, utter fool *Capital Radio 1983*.
steed n. sexual expert although he does the 'riding' (cf: stallion, stud).
steel pot n. (US milit. use) a GI helmet *Del Vecchio*.
steerer n. (gambling use) one who tempts players into a poker game or similar opportunity for them to lose their money *Algren*.
stench trench the vagina *Cole*.
stencil n. (drug use) a long, thin marijuana cigarette *Folb*.
step v. (US Black use) to work as a prostitute; poss. fr. *stepney*: a white-slaver's temporary best girl (?) or more simply fr. her 'street-walking' *Folb*.
step fast v. (US Black use) do whatever is necessary to survive in a harsh world *Folb*.
step on v. to adulterate narcotics for more profitable sales *Goldman*.
step on one's dick v. see: step on one's prick *Bruce:2*.
step on one's prick v. to make a fool of oneself *Thompson*.
step out on the green v. (US Black use) to challenge to a fight; fr. 'going outside' to some supposed turf *Folb*
stepper n. (US Black use) a prostitute *Folb*.
steppin' n. (US Black use) the street-walking that a prostitute must carry out to meet her customers *Klein*.
stew n. (abbrev.) stewardess, air hostess *Higgins:2*.
stewed a. drunk *Runyon:1*.
stewed as a prune a. extremely drunk *Wodehouse: GB*.
stewed to the eyebrows a. very drunk (cf: stewed to the gills) *Wodehouse: MOJ*.
stewed to the gills a. extremely drunk *Algren*.
stick n. **1.** a marijuana cigarette *Selby:1*; **2.** (Black pimp use) a prostitute *Milner*; **3.** the penis (cf: creamstick) *Folb*; **4.** a reprimand, a criticism.
stick v. to stab with a knife *Sillitoe*.
stick around v. to stay close-by *White*.
stick him on! (UK police use) charge him (with a crime)! what he is 'stuck on' is the police station charge sheet *Powis*.
stick in the mud n. an old-fashioned, conservative person.
stick it! (excl.) (abbrev.) stick it up your ass; thus a derog. reply to a given question, ie 'What shall I do with this?' or in response to an opinion with which one disagrees *Uneeda Comix*.
stick it to v. **1.** to copulate; **2.** to tease, to malign, to attack *Price:3*.
stick it up v. to take advantage of, esp. financially *Humphries:2*.
stick it up your jumper! (derog. cp) (usu. children's use) rejecting the previous speaker's idea, opinion, insult, etc. *John Lennon & Paul McCartney, 'I Am The Walrus', 1967*.
stickman n. **1.** the member of a pickpocket gang who is handed the stolen goods by the actual pickpocket who does the physical stealing; the stickman must also try to hinder any attempts to capture his confederate by police or public *Powis*; **2.** a good lover, a potent, experienced male; fr. stick = penis (qv) *Price:2*.
stick one on v. to hit *Keyes*.
stick one's bib in v. (Aus. use) to interfere, to intrude *Wilkes*.
stick one's neck out v. exceed one's brief, to interfere in affairs in which one is not directly concerned and often, having stuck out one's neck, to figuratively have one's head cut off *Schulberg*.

sticks n. **1.** articles of household furniture; fr. their wooden construction *Hotten*; **2.** anywhere other than the big cities; fr. sticks = trees *Newman:2*.

sticksing (West Indian use) picking pockets *Powis*.

stick up n. an armed robbery; thus *to stick up*.

stick-up artist n. armed robber *Grogan*.

sticky a. (Aus. use) (abbrev.) stickybeak (qv): inquisitive, curious *Baker*.

sticky-beak n. (Aus. use) an inquisitive person; one who 'sticks their nose in' *Humphries:2*.

sticky-fingered a. habitually larcenous, one to whose fingers things are always sticking.

stiff n. **1.** a corpse; fr. rigor mortis *Price:2*; **2.** a note; usu. between prisoners in a gaol, or passed illicitly into a gaol by a relation, etc. *Norman:3*; **3.** an average person; often with description: working stiff (qv) etc.; poss. fr. stiff = corpse, ie one so dull as to be 'half-dead' anyway; or as one who can be stiffed (qv) due to their rectitude *Higgins:3*; **4.** (horseracing use) a useless, losing horse and thus an erroneous, losing wager *Bukowski:1*.

stiff v. to cheat, to rob.

stiff a. **1.** very drunk; and passed out cold *Higgins:1*; **2.** depending on context, harsh ('a stiff penalty') or expensive ('a stiff fine') *Wodehouse: PG*.

stiff as a crutch (Aus. cp) completely penniless, totally broke (qv) *Baker*.

stiffen v. to bribe, to corrupt *Runyon*.

stiffen the lizards! (Aus. use) exclamation of surprise, shock, etc. *Humphries*.

stiffie n. an invitation; fr. the card on which it was printed *T 18/7/83*.

stiffin' and jivin' n. (US Black use) unreal, phoney conversation (cf: stiff = cheat, jive) *Klein*.

stiff 'un n. (horseracing use) a horse that appears, for whatever reason, not to have been ridden to its full competitive capacity (cf: stiff = dead).

sting n. a reasonably large sum of money – $500 average – obtained by some form of deception or hustle (qv) *Milner*.

sting v. to steal, both in fact and as merely overcharging *Goldman*.

stinger n. (US Black use) a hotplate which is run from two wires attached to a light socket *Klein*.

stink n. **1.** a fuss, a furore *Farrell*; **2.** (US Black use) the vagina (cf: stank) *Klein*.

stinker n. **1.** a promiscuous woman (cf: scrubber) *Cole*; **2.** anything or person considered particularly unpleasant *Wodehouse: AAG*.

stink finger manual stimulation of the female genitals *Folb*.

stinking a. **1.** aka: *stinko*: very drunk *Junker*; **2.** (abbrev.) stinking rich: very well-off.

stinko a. very drunk *Goulart*.

stinkpot n. (US Black use) the vagina (cf: fish) *Folb*.

stinky finger n. see: stink-finger *Pearce*.

stir n. prison; fr. Romany *sturiben*, to confine, or fr. stir = porridge (qv) *Cole*.

stir v. to gossip maliciously, to cause trouble deliberately by so doing.

stir bugs a. (Can prison use) insane from too long a confinement in gaol (cf: stir crazy) *Caron*.

stir crazy a. deranged from an excess of prison *Caron*.

stirrer n. an unpleasant, malicious gossip.

stir the possum v. (Aus. use) to create a disturbance, to start things moving, to jolt the general apathy; fr. animal's habit of keeping quite still for long periods (cf: play possum) *Wilkes*.

stitch n. (US preppie (qv) use) anything or anyone seen as amusing. Thus intensified as *stitch and a half* fr. physical 'stitch' that can accompany laughter *Bernbach*.

stitch up v. for the police to ensure a conviction by planting evidence, faking confessions, etc.; fr. sewing up a garment neatly and conclusively *Newman: 1.*

stockbroker Tudor n. fake Tudor architecture, with emphasis on exposed beams, to be found in the wealthy commuter villages of the Home Counties wherein live many brokers (cf: pseudie Tudie).

stogie n. **1.** cigar, abbrev. Conestoga *SF Comic*; **2.** (drug use) an over-sized marijuana cigarette, fr. **1** *Folb.*

stoked a. **1.** drunk *Dickson*; **2.** (US teen. use (esp. California) elated, delighted, very pleased, thrilled, etc. *Pond.*

stoked out a. exhausted *Wolfe: 5.*

stomp n. (US Black use) a shoe; fr. its potential use *Klein.*

stomp v. to beat up *Price: 2.*

stompers n. (US campus use) boots, esp. cowboy boots *Underwood.*

stone a. absolutely, purely, completely *Price: 2.*

stoned a. **1.** intoxicated with some form of drug *Caserta*; **2.** drunk.

stoneface n. a totally unemotional person; Buster Keaton (1898–1966) the unsmiling silent era comedian was 'The Great Stone Face' *Dunne.*

stoneginger a. absolutely certain; fr. a phenomenally successful racehorse *Newman: 1.*

stone me! excl. of surprise.

stones n. testicles; thus courage, bravery, etc. (cf: balls) *Price: 2.*

stones and bones (US campus use) course in prehistory *Dickson.*

stone the crows! excl. of surprise, wonder, alarm *Dennis.*

stonewall v. to put up barriers; to obfuscate, to prevaricate *Price: 3.*

stonicky n. (UK criminal use) a cosh; original naval use: a rope's end, used for punishment *Powis.*

stonkered a. drunk; orig. milit. use: out of action *Humphries.*

stony a. (abbrev.) stony broke: absolutely penniless.

stooge n. **1.** (show business use) a comedian's assistant or 'straight man' who feeds lines for his jokes; **2.** any underling (cf: gofer) *Higgins: 1.*

stooge v. to work for as an assistant or underling.

stoolie n. (abbrev.) stool-pigeon (qv) *Vidal.*

stool-pigeon n. an informer, one who makes a confession implicating others.

stoop v. (US Black use) to indulge in sexual intercourse (cf: get down) *Klein.*

stop moing me! (US preppie (qv) use) a demand made of one prep school boy to another who he feels is pushing or jostling him unnecessarily *Bernbach.*

stoppo driver n. a getaway driver. fr. *take stoppo*: to be forced to run away *G. F. Newman, 'Law & Order', BBC-2 TV 1977.*

stop work (bingo use) 65; fr. male retirement age *Wright.*

stork v. (US campus use) to make pregnant; fr. myth of storks bringing babies *Underwood.*

stoush n.,v. (Aus. use) a fight; to have a fight *Lawson.*

stove lid n. (derog.) a Black person; fr. blackening of the utensil *Runyon.*

straight n. **1.** a conventional person; **2.** a cigarette (cf: joint); **3.** in outlaw terminology: someone one can trust, and thus, usually not at all straight **1** *Wolfe: 2*; **4.** (homosexual use) a heterosexual person *Stanley.*

straight a. (drug use) cured of one's sickness (qv) by an injection of heroin *Larner.*

straight arrow n. an honest, clean-living, clean-cut, upright, if naive and unsophisticated person *Junker.*

straighten v. **1.** to bribe successfully *Newman: 1*; **2.** to settle an argument or a grudge by fighting *Cole.*

straightener n. a bribe *Powis.*

straight goods n. the absolute truth *Wodehouse: MJ.*

straight shit **1.** the truth *Higgins: 1*; **2.** utter lies.

straight shooter n. an honest, dependable, trustworthy person *Vidal.*

straight shot n. (US Black use) sexual intercourse without any means of contraception (cf: bareback) *Klein*.

straight up (excl.) honestly, really *Performance*.

strain the potatoes v. aka: *strain the spuds*; to urinate *Humphries*.

strap v. (UK police use) to interrogate intensely but, in theory, without force *Powis*.

strapped for cash a. impoverished, poor *Sanders: 2*.

straps it to his ankle description of a man with a supposedly extra-large penis; often used ironically of a sexual braggart.

Strat n. (abbrev.) Stratocaster guitar *Dury*.

streak n. (US campus use) an exciting time, esp. at a party *Underwood*.

streetified a. (US Black use) well-versed with the ways of the urban lifestyle as seen on the inner-city streets (cf: street smart) *Klein*.

street people n. the derelict remainder of the hippies and similar 'beautiful' people of the 1960s, now reduced to begging, living rough and often addicted to narcotics.

street smart a. able to survive in the inner city or the ghetto streets despite a lack of material, bourgeois advantages (cf: streetified).

street wise a. see: street smart.

strength n. the facts, the details of a situation *Griffiths*.

stretch n. (UK criminal/prison use) 12 months sentence *Norman: 1*.

stretched a. very drunk *Neaman & Silver*.

strewth! (euph.) God's truth *Payne*.

strictly! (US campus use) excl. really, honestly, absolutely, etc. *Underwood*.

strictly from in the style of, derivative of, exactly like fr. beatnik/jazz use, thus *strictly from Dante Burroughs: Jr*.

stride v. (US Black use) to perform with great skill *Folb*.

strides n. (Aus. use) trousers *Humphries*.

strike a light! general excl. of surprise, shock, amazement, etc. (cf: strike me blind, strike me pink).

strike it rich v. to gain sudden wealth *Wright*.

strike me blind! general excl. of surprise, amazement; implies calling on God/the gods to make some concomitant gesture (cf: strike me pink!).

strike me pink! see: strike me blind! *Wodehouse: AAG*.

strike out v. **1.** attempt to make sexual contact and fail through the other party's lack of interest; fr. baseball use *Jay & Young*; **2.** to die; fr. baseball use *Neaman & Silver*.

strike paydirt v. to gain one's objective, often but not invariably financial; for a journalist, for instance, the 'dirt' could be a given revelation; fr. mining use, esp. for gold.

striker n. a match *Norman: 2*.

string n. the penis *Bukowski: 1*.

string along v. to deceive someone over a period of time; fr. the image of dragging a toy along on the end of a string *Farrell*.

string and nuggets n. the penis and testicles *Bukowski: 1*.

string bean n. **1.** a skinny person; **2.** (US Black use) a very thin penis *Folb*.

stringer n. (newspaper use) a local correspondent, often with his own job, who works on a regular but freelance basis for a national newspaper *Sanders: 2*.

stripe n. a scar, usu, the result of being slashed with an open razor *Norman: 2*.

stripe v. to slash with a cut-throat razor *Norman: 2*.

stripped to the buff a. naked, without one's clothes (cf: in the buff) *Hotten*.

stroke v. (US Black use) to have sexual intercourse *Folb*.

stroke book n. pornographic book or magazine; fr. its use in masturbation *Goldman*.

stroked out a. exhausted *Wolfe: 2*.

stroke one's beef v. to masturbate.

stroll n. (US pimp use) those streets or blocks on which prostitutes ply their trade *Shulman*.

stroll on! (excl.) 'you must be joking!' *Newman: 1*.

strong a. (euph.) pornographic; use restricted to advertisements in such magazines.
strong arm v. (criminal use) to rob someone through threats and potential, rather than actual violence.
strong arm man n. a thug, a hoodlum, a gangster (cf: standover man) *Larner*.
stroppy a. bad-tempered, irritable; fr. obstreperous *Keyes*.
strung out a. **1.** spec addicted to narcotics; **2.** unhappy, depressed *SF Comics*.
strunz n. fr. Ital: rubbish, shit *R. Stone, 'A Flag For Sunrise', 1981*.
stub one's toe v. (euph.) to menstruate (cf: sprain one's ankle) *Rawson*.
stuck on a. **1.** obsessed with, devoted to *Seale*; **2.** in love with.
stuck-up a. (school use) arrogant, snobbish, reserved; from the sticking of one's nose in the air.
stud n. **1.** (white use) a sexually active male *Wolfe: 5*; **2.** (Black use) a sophisticated male, but no sexual connotation *Major*.
study v. (homosexual use) to appraise a potential sexual conquest/partner *Stanley*.
stuff n. **1.** (US Black use) things or activities in general, varying as to context; **2.** drugs, spec. heroin *Higgins: 1*.
stuff v. **1.** to defeat, to outwit *Higgins: 5* ; **2.** to copulate.
stuffed a. put down, mocked, denigrated *Higgins: 5*.
stuffed shirt n. pompous, aristocratic but ineffectual person; a bore *Schulberg*..
stuffer n. a drug addict; fr. stuff (qv) *R. Stone, 'Dog Soldiers', 1975*.
stuffing (US Black use) tricking, conning a victim *Klein*.
stuffy a. **1.** wealthy, rich *Powis*; **2.** pompous, snobbish *Wodehouse: GB*.
stumblebum n. shambling, useless, foolish person *X*.
stumer n. a dud cheque or other fraudulent monetary draft *LL*.
stumm and crum a. extremely quiet, 'silent as the grave' (cf: shtum) *Powis*.
stump n. the penis *Klein*.
stump v. (US Black use) to rob or mug a person; fr. stomp (?) *Klein*.
stung a. (Aus. use) drunk *Humphries: 2*.
stunt v. (US pro football use) to produce particularly baffling plays *Jenkins*.
stupe n. (abbrev.) stupid; a fool, an idiot *Heller*.
style v. to show off, to strut around *Milner*.
stymied a. in difficulties; frustrated; fr. golfing use.
sub v. to give an advance on wages, a loan; fr. subsistance (money) *Payne*.
sub up v. to hand over money, whether owing or not; fr. sub (qv).
subway dealer n. (US cant) a crooked card sharp who deals from the bottom of the pack; fr. subway = underground *Neaman & Silver*.
suck v. **1.** (US campus use) cf: suck wind *Underwood*; **2.** to make someone into a victim of one's plans, tricks, etc; (?) back formation fr. sucker (qv) *Klein*; **3.** to be worthless, pointless *Higgins: 1*.
suck-ass a. useless, pointless, unpleasant – all deriving from the need to be obsequious *Price: 3*.
suck ass v. to curry favour; to attempt to win over someone *Klein*.
sucker n. **1.** (euph.) fucker; generally derog. description *Price: 2*; **2.** the victim of any kind of crooked plan; the bettors at casinos *Wodehouse: PGM*.
sucker-bait n. young girls hired by casinos to appear available and thus lure and distract gamblers *Sharpe: 1, 1982*.
sucker-weed n. (drug use) inferior or even bogus marijuana; for the consumption of the gullible only *Folb*.
suck face v. (US campus use) to kiss (cf: chew face) *Bernbach*.
suck hind tit v. to curry favour (cf: suck ass) *Higgins: 4*.
suck it and see! (cp) aimed derisively

at someone who has asked what is considered a stupid or impudent question.

suck off v. to fellate*Bukowski: 7.*

sucks to you! disdainful, dismissive cp; usu. school use *Wodehouse: AAG.*

suck up n. one who curries favour with others; a creep (qv).

suck up to v. to curry favour, to be obsequious, to grovel shamelessly in return for favours, esteem, etc. (cf: bootlick) *Hotten.*

suck wind v. to be on one's last legs, to be struggling; fr. image of gasping for breath *Price: 2.*

suds n. (US teen. use) beer; fr. the product's intense soap-suds-like fizziness and (to UK palates) taste *Underwood.*

Sue City n. (US teen. use) involved in a court case or similar legal situation (cf: — City) *Sculatti.*

suede n. (Black use) a Black person *Milner.*

suedehead n. a form of skinhead (qv) whose hair was grown slightly longer than the usual absolute bald look and thus presents a slight fuzz, slightly reminiscent of suede.

suffering cats! aka:*suffering Christ!*: mild excl.

sugar n. **1.** money; fr. rhyming sl. sugar and honey *Runyon*; **2.** (US Black use) semen; thus Bessie Smith: 'Want Some Sugar in My Bowl' *Neaman & Silver*; **3.** general term of endearment, can be used of and to either sex *L. Reed, 'Take a Walk on the Wild Side', 1972.*

sugar! (euph.) shit! (cf: fudge!) *Rawson.*

sugar daddy n. an older man who is willing to provide the various material wants of his younger mistress *Waits.*

sugar pimp n. a pimp who prefers charm and persuasion to threats and violence when dealing with his girls (cf: sweet mack) *Milner.*

suited down a. (US Black use) well dress *Folb.*

sumbitch n. see: sonofabitch *Jenkins.*

summertime ho n. (pimp use) occasional prostitute who works, not necessarily in summer, but only when she needs the money or the mood takes her; often incl. high school girls who turn to whoring in summer holidays *OUI 1975.*

sunbeam n. (Aus. use) an item of crockery or cutlery laid out on the table but still unused and as such as bright and clean as a sunbeam *Humphries: 2.*

sunk a. hopeless, finished, no chance; fr. nautical use *Big Ass Comics 1.*

Sunday punch n. one's best effort; fr. boxing use *P. Pringle & W. Arkin, 'SIOP', 1983.*

sunny side (abbrev.) sunny side of the street: the good, easy, materially satisfying life.

sunshine n. **1.** a variety of LSD, fr. the orange colour of the pills containing the drug: **2.** generally affectionate term of address *Payne.*

superfly a. (US Black use) excellent, first rate; of people, situations, drugs, etc. *film title 1969.*

supergrass n. (police/criminal use) an informer who betrays a large number of important fellow-criminals, thus helping with the solution of a number of hitherto unresolved crimes (cf: grass) *Mortimer.*

super honkie n. (US Black use) an exceptionally authoritarian white person (cf: honkie) *Klein.*

supersoul n. (US campus use (Black students)) an exceptionally sophisticated, hip (qv) Black (cf: soul) *Underwood.*

sus a. (abbrev.) suspicious; thus the 'sus laws': controversial powers that permitted the police to stop and search persons allegedly suspected of a crime and which were considered as racist by the Black and Asian communities *Norman.*

susfu (milit. use) (acro.) *s*ituation *u*nchanged, *s*till *f*ucked *u*p (cf: snafu) *Byrne.*

suss out v. to understand, to work out, to discover; fr. suspicious *Robins.*

sussy a. (abbrev.) suspicious (cf: sus)

Newman: 1.

Susy n. (rhyming sl.) Susy Anna = tanner (qv) = 6d. (old pence) = 2½p. *Wright.*

swab jockey n. **1.** (USN use) a sailor who mops down the ship's decks; **2.** (USMC use) derog. for sailors in general *Uris.*

swack n. (US Black use) the penis *Klein.*

swacked a. drunk *Dickson.*

swaddy n. a soldier; fr. 18th C. *swad*: soldier *Hotten.*

swag n. **1.** (US Black use) liquor *Folb*; **2.** (cant.) loot; almost obs; a part of traditional villain with mask, striped jersey and bag marked 'swag'.

swag v. to take forcibly, to arrest *Norman: 2.*

swagging (US prison use) stealing, spec. stealing state-owned property *Rawson.*

swags n. (butchers' backsl.) sausages *Cole.*

swailer n. (UK criminal use) a cosh *Powis.*

SWALK (acro.) *S*ealed *W*ith *A* *L*oving *K*iss; usually found on the back of envelopes (cf: NORWICH).

swallow (it) v. to accept, esp. a lying story that one is told; fr. swallowing a bait.

swamp v. (US prison use) to arrest *Chandler: Notebk.*

swan about v. to wander blithely and carelessly without a care in the world; like a swan gliding over water.

swank v. **1.** to boast, to show off; **2.** to pretend *Powis.*

swanky a. smart, sophisticated, chic *Goulart.*

swap cans v. (US prison sl.) to take alternate active/passive roles in anal intercourse fr. can (qv) *Legman.*

swap spit v. (US campus use) to kiss, usu. a French kiss (qv) *Bernbach.*

swartzer n. fr. Yiddish *schwartz*: black, thus any Black person *Newman: 1.*

swear and curse (cuss) v. (rhyming sl.) bus *Wright.*

sweat n. a problem, a worry, a struggle, a challenge; anything that works up real or figurative sweat *Wodehouse: PF.*

sweat v. to worry about, to take trouble over.

sweat hog n. (US campus use) exceptionally unattractive female *Underwood.*

sweat it out v. to endure hardships and difficulties in the hope of achieving solutions/successes in the end.

sweats n. the sweating that is one of a heroin addict's withdrawal symptoms *Price: 2.*

swede n. ignorant country person; fr. urban conception of the country's main product, foodstuff, etc; thus *Swedey*; Metropolitan Police nickname (punning on Sweeney, qv) for Operation Countryman, an investigation into alleged corruption carried out by officers of rural/provincial forces *Norman: 1.*

Swedish n. (sexual use) the use of rubber garments in sex; refers to the sweating one experiences in a Swedish sauna bath *Maledicta.*

Sweeney n. (rhyming sl.) Sweeney Todd = Flying Squad *Ian Kennedy Martin, Euston Films, TV series, 1977.*

sweet n. (US Black use) a male homosexual *Folb.*

sweet a. excellent, perfect, simple (cf: handsome) *Linda Brown.*

sweet as a nut (UK criminal use) easy, simple, no problems, delightful, esp. of a robbery or other 'job' *Powis.*

sweet daddy n. aka: *sweet poppa, sweet sugar*; a male lover *Folb.*

sweet FA (abbrev.) sweet Fanny Adams (qv) = (euph.) sweet fuck all = nothing at all.

sweet Fanny Adams (euph.) sweet fuck all = nothing (cf: sweet FA).

sweetheart contract n. a union-employer contract that favours the company over its employees *Selby: 1.*

sweet kid n. (Can. prison use) a younger prisoner who joins up with an older man (cf: punk) *Caron.*

sweetman n. (UK criminal use) a

ponce who runs only one prostitute and lives off her earnings alone *Powis*.

sweet pea n. girl-friend *Runyon*.

sweet potato pie n. (US Black use) **1.** an attractive girl or boy; **2.** male or female genitals; example of sex = food *Folb*.

sweet talk v. **1.** to persuade, to charm, to lull into (false) confidence; **2.** spec. to seduce *Thompson: J*.

swell a. excellent, wonderful, delightful.

swell n. an aristocrat, a sophisticated, rich person, a toff (qv) *rr*.

swellhead n. (US Black use)**1.** a braggart, a boaster; **2.** one who has passed out through drug use *Klein*.

swift a. smart, clever, cunning; of a policeman: any illegal activities, esp. during an arrest *Underwood*.

swift 'un n. corrupt police procedure when arresting a suspect (cf: stitch up, fit up, bit swift) *Newman: 1*.

swig v. to drink, to gulp down; since 17th C.*Runyon*.

swill v. to drink heavily; in New South Wales fr. 1916–55 pubs took 'last orders' at 6 pm and the resultant rush of the all-male drinkers was termed 'the six o'clock swill'; fr. the desperate, animal-like gulpings of the drink.

swindle sheet n. **1.** (boxing use) the accounts made up by a manager and shown to his fighter; bitter fighters felt that these rarely had much relevance to the actual money involved; **2.** expense accounts in general *Heller*.

swing v. **1.** (homosexual use) to fellate *Legman*; **2.** (US teen. use) to achieve the supreme level of well-being and satisfaction *Sculatti*; **3.** to arrange husband/wife swapping parties; **4.** to carry on an affair with someone; **5.** to enjoy an active and varied sex life *Bruce: 2*.

swing both ways v. to practise bisexuality.

swing daddy n. (US Black use) an attractive, well-dressed male; a male lover *Folb*.

swing either way v. see: swing both ways *McFadden*.

swinger n. **1.** one who leads an active and varied sex-life; **2.** (contact magazine use) one who participates in wife-swapping parties *Stone*.

swing it v. to cope, to deal with a situation *Price: 2*.

swing like sixty v. (US teen. use) to perform at one's peak, to achieve ultimate success/pleasure *Sculatti*.

swing shift n. a work shift that bridges late afternoon and early evening or early morning and early afternoon *Waits*.

swing the lamp v. (UK milit. use) to tell exaggerated stories; fr. the lamp that swung inside a tent as the tales were told *Neaman & Silver*.

swing the lead v. to malinger, to avoid one's duties; orig. milit. use *Wright*.

swing with v. to ally oneself to a group; to agree with a concept *McFadden*.

swing with v. to enjoy, to appreciate *Southern*.

swipe n. (US Black use) the penis; fr. swipe = hit, or kidney-wiper (qv) (?) *Klein*.

swipe v. to steal *Wodehouse: AAG*.

swish n. a homosexual male; fr. his effeminate style *Burroughs: Jr*.

swish v. to accentuate one's homosexuality.

Swish Alps n. (US homosexual use) gay area in the Hollywood Hills (cf: Boystown, swish) *White*.

Swiss a. (US teen. use) neutral, of no specific opinion; fr. trad. role of Swiss in international relations *Sculatti*.

switched on see: turned on *Powis*.

switcheroo n. the opposite, the reverse *Stone*.

switch-hitter n. a bisexual. fr. baseball use: an ambidextrous batter *Jay & Young*.

Swone one (UK 'society' use) Battersea, London SW11 (sw-one-one) *Barr*.

swoop n. (police use) a raid; a sudden

arrest *Folb*.

swordsman n. male sexual athlete *S. Alexander, 'Very Mucha Lady', 1983.*

swuft a. (US campus use) pun on swift (qv) *Underwood*.

syph n. aka: *siff*: (abbrev.) syphilis *Bukowski: 2*.

sypho n. (Aus. use) syphilis.

syphon the python v. to urinate *Humphries*.

syrup n. (rhyming sl.) syrup of figs = wig *Powis*.

tab n. **1.** the bill, account, credit *Price:1*; **2.** (abbrev.) tabloid newspaper *Schulberg*.

tabbed a. (US Black use) well dressed *Folb*.

tack n. **1.** food orig. naut use: ship's biscuit *Farren;* **2.** money *Howard*.

tacky a. unattractive, second-rate, off-putting, poor taste *Variety 19/1/83*.

tackyhead see: BB head *Folb*.

taco bender n. (derog.) Chicano; fr. popular Mexican food (cf: bagel bender) *Folb*.

taco head n. (derog.) Mexican, Chicano (cf: taco bender) *Dunne*.

Tad n. Irish Catholic, fr. Thaddeus, popular Irish name *Higgins:5*.

taff a. (backsl.) fat *Cole*.

Taffy n. Welshman; fr. Dafydd, Welsh version of David *BvdB*.

Taig n. (derog.) Roman Catholic, spec. used by Protestants in N. Ireland.

tail n. **1.** young boys suitable for homosexual relation *Legman*; **2.** a woman, women; **3.** sexual intercourse *Higgins:1*; **4.** the posterior, the buttocks; **5.** the vagina; 'a piece of tail'.

tail v. to follow, to keep under police surveillance *Higgins:2*.

tailgate v. to drive a car closely (too closely) behind the one in front *Higgins:2*.

tailormade n. (UK prison use) a factory-produced cigarette (cf: roll-up) *Cole*.

take n. **1.** bribery, thus *on the take*: receiving regular bribes *Bruce:2*; **2.** (Aus. use) a thief, a villain *Ready*.

take v. to accept bribery *Higgins:2*; **2.** to arrest; abbrev. thief-take *Higgins:2*.

take a back seat v. to accept a secondary role voluntarily (cf: play second fiddle) *Neaman & Silver*.

take a bath v. to lose badly, in business, sport, gambling *Higgins:3*.

take a Brody v. to commit suicide by leaping from a bridge; in fact the original Stephen Brody only promised, amid much publicity to leap from the Brooklyn bridge in New York; his eventual reneging on this promise led to the theatrical use of the phrase to denote a (much touted) flop *Pynchon*.

take a dive v. (boxing use) for a fighter deliberately to lose a fight (cf: go in the tank, etc.) *Bukowski:6*.

take a dump v. to excrete, usu. in sense of incontinence *Price:2*.

take a fall v. to be arrested; to be imprisoned (cf: fall money) *Higgins:2*.

take a flying fuck! derisory, dismissive exclamation *Dunne*.

take a gander v. to look at, to glance at; fr. the bird's long neck *Chandler:LG*.

take a hike v. to leave; esp. as a command to someone the speaker wishes to go away *'Hill Street Blues'*,

Thames TV, 1983.

take a hinge at v. to look at; fr. the turning of one's head *Schulberg.*

take a leak v. urinate *Waits.*

take an application v. (Black pimp use) to interview a woman as a prospective prostitute *Milner.*

take a nose-dive v. to collapse, to fail utterly; fr. flying use *Gruber.*

take a pop (at) v. **1.** to make an attempt; **2.** to hit someone.

take a powder v. to escape, to run away; the 'powder' is supposedly a laxative *Himes:1.*

take a rain check v. to defer until a later, and unspecified, time; fr. sporting use: a check (ticket) issued for future use if a baseball game was cancelled due to rain *Uris.*

take a running-jump! excl. of dismissal or dislike.

take a run-out powder v. see: take a powder *Runyon.*

take a screw at v. to stare at in aggressive manner; thus 'who you screwin'?' as ritual challenge to a fight (cf: screw) *Robins.*

take a shine to v. to find attractive, appealing, of an object or more likely, a person; fr. shiner: sweetheart.

take a shot v. to try, to make an attempt *Higgins:4.*

take a turn on shooter's hill (US Black use) to have sexual intercourse *Klein.*

take away n. a cafe or restaurant that supplies food that can be taken out and eaten elsewhere (cf: take-out).

take care of v. **1.** to kill; **2.** to bribe *Runyon.*

take care of business v. (Black use (though increasingly widespread)) to deal efficiently with matters in hand *Milner.*

take care of number one v. aka: *look after number one*: to put oneself first, no matter what the situation.

take for an airing v. see: take for a ride *Runyon.*

take for a ride v. **1.** (criminal use) to assassinate, usu. by taking the victim out in a car and killing him/her at some stage, then dumping the body far from one's base; **2.** to deceive, to fool, to trick (usu. for financial gain) *Runyon.*

take it! (homosexual use) excl. demanding fellatio *Legman.*

take it any way v. (homosexual use) to enjoy pedication or fellatio *Legman.*

take it on the chin v. to suffer hardship and adversity without complaint; fr. boxing use.

take it on the lam v. to run away, to escape (cf: lam) *Runyon.*

take it up the ass v. to submit to anal intercourse *Legman.*

take no shit v. brook no arguments, accept no diversions, irritations *Higgins:1.*

taken short forced to make an emergency visit to the lavatory *Newman:3.*

take off v. **1.** to leave; also an excl. go away!; **2.** to use heroin; fr. getting high (qv) *Larner.*

take-off artist n. (US criminal use) a successful robber, rapist or killer; anyone who does the job then 'takes off' *Stone.*

take one down a peg v. to reduce a person, usu. in their own excessive esteem *Hotten.*

take one's lumps v. to acccept and deal with one's problems and setbacks *Schulberg.*

take one's meat out of the basket v. (homosexual use) to reveal one's genitals to another man *Legman.*

take one to the cleaners v. to remove all of a victim's assets, either in a wager or by extortion or similar legal or illegal means *Vidal.*

take one's best hold v. to prepare oneself emotionally for dealing with a problem *Klein.*

take one's best shot v. do the best one can; try one's hardest.

take on some backs v. (US Black use) to have anal intercourse *Folb.*

take out v. to kill, to destroy a specific target; fr. its complete removal *Higgins:1.*

take-out n. **1.** food that can be consumed off the premises where it is purchased (cf: take away); **2.** (US conman use) a convenient 'phone message' that arrives for the conman when it appears that his marks (qv) are becoming suspicious and permits him to vanish before problems start cropping up; usu. arranged, for a price, with a friendly barman or similar *Thompson:J.*

take-out guy n. the man in a crooked card game who always wins and as such attracts attention away from the real cheat who is manipulating all winning and losing cards (cf: mechanic) *Breslin.*

take tea with v. (UK criminal use) to outsmart a clever person or to defeat someone in authority *Powis.*

take the air v. to leave, to escape *Runyon.*

take the big jump v. (US western use) to die *Adams.*

take the biscuit v. to beat all rivals, esp. with implication that the person, announcement, even, etc. is even more startling, appalling than might have been expected.

take the bus v. (US teen. use) to go on the cheap, to bargain-hunt; fr. bus, as opposed to airfares *Sculatti.*

take the cake v. to be the best, to carry off a prize; fr. the awarding of a cake as prize, but not always congratulatory.

take the dairy off v. to divert suspicion *Norman:2.*

take the easy way out v. to commit suicide *Neaman & Silver.*

take the fall v. to volunteer oneself as a victim, usu. as the alleged perpetrator of a crime, in the place of the real villain *Dunne.*

take the gas v. to endure punishment, esp. in a boxing ring *Heller.*

take the knock v. **1.** to accept the blame (cf: take the fall); **2.** to suffer an unpleasant surprise *Wodehouse:AAG.*

take the mickey v. to tease *T 12/9/83.*

take the piss v. to tease.

take the rap v. **1.** (criminal use) to take a punishment, often a prison sentence, that is actually due to someone else (cf: take the fall), thus; **2.** to take the blame when one is not the guilty party *Wodehouse:AAG.*

take the scenic route v. (US teen. use) to concentrate on pleasure at the expense of efficiency or speed; fr. touring in car or train *Sculatti.*

take the wind v. to leave *Runyon.*

talent n. attractive young women, esp. those standing around at a party, in a club or dancehall, etc. *Powis.*

talk a blue streak v. to talk both fast and at great length *Runyon.*

talk business v. (US Black use) to seduce; to shoot a line (qv) *Folb.*

talker n. (pimp use) a client who wishes only to talk, either of sex or merely of his (wretched) life *OUI 8/75.*

talk fuck v. to murmur or shout obscenities during sexual intercourse for the gratification of one or both partners *Klein.*

talk game v. (Black pimp use) to chatter about pimping, whoring and those involved *Shulman.*

talking n. (lesbian use) having a relationship with another woman while in prison *Maledicta.*

talking out of the side of one's neck (US Black use) talking surreptitiously to ensure that one's conversation remains unheard by eavesdroppers *Klein.*

talking shit **1.** talking nonsense; **2.** (Black use) any verbal byplay, banter between men, flirtation between man and woman, etc. *Milner.*

talking trash (euph.) talking shit (qv) *Milner.*

talk like a book v. to appear well-educated and literate.

talk out of school v. to tell tales, to talk unguardedly.

talk talk and walk walk v. (US Black use) to do whatever is natural and comfortable *Folb.*

talk that talk v. (US Black use) to chatter inconsequentially *Klein.*

talk the hind leg off a donkey v. to talk continually and obsessively, seemingly with no sign of ever stopping.

talk through one's ass v. to talk nonsense; thus coarse cp: be quiet/ shut your mouth and give your ass a rest *Bleasdale*.

talk through one's hat v. to talk nonsense, talk rubbish *Heller*.

talk through the back of one's neck v. to talk nonsense, rubbish.

talk to the engineer, not the oily rag (cp) deal with the boss, not an assistant *ad for Olympus cameras, 1982*.

talk turkey v. to talk honestly, about the facts; to talk business fr. the bird's central role in traditional Christmas dinner (cf: get down to brass tacks) *PT*.

tall a. (US Black use) a large quantity, esp. of money *Klein*.

tallawah a. (West Indian use) honest, honourable, decent *Powis*.

tall poppies n. (Aus. use) conspicuously high earners or other VIPs *Wilkes*.

T and A (abbrev.) *T*its and *A*ss (qv) *Bruce:1*.

tangle assholes v. see: lock assholes *Higgins:1*.

tank n. (Can/US prison use) a holding cell *Caron*.

tank v. (US campus use) to drink heavily *Underwood*.

tanked (up) a. drunk *Wodehouse passim*.

tanker n. a prizefighter who has agreed to accept cash in return for losing a given fight; ie to 'take a dive' into the tank (swimming pool) *'On The Waterfront', directed E. Kazan, 1954*.

tank fight n. (boxing use) a contest in which one fighter has been bribed to lose; *tanking* has been extended to other sports, ie tennis, as cited in *Obs*. 26/6/83 'the deliberate throwing of a match'.

tank town n. a small, insignificant town; fr. the positioning of water tanks at such railway stops, thus providing the only reason why a train might need to stop there (cf: jerkwater town) *Price:3*.

tanner n. sixpence, thus post-metrication, 2½ pence.

tan one's hide v. aka: *tan one's arse*: to beat severely; of a child, to spank severely; fr. tannery (leather-making) use.

tan-tracker n. (Aus. use) homosexual male (cf: brown, Brown Family, etc.).

tap v. to borrow, or attempt to borrow money; fr. tapping their arm to attract attention (cf: put the arm, bite on).

tap a keg v. (US use) to urinate; fr. brewery use *Neaman & Silver*.

tap city n. the state of being unable to raise a stake for further betting (cf: tap).

taped up a. (US Black use) a girl already with a boy-friend; thus secured from other admirers *Klein*.

tapioca a. (US campus use) absolutely broke (cf: tap city, tapped out) *Bernbach*.

tapped out a. out of money, nothing to use for further betting.

tarfu (milit. use) (acro.) *t*hings *a*re *r*eally *fu*cked-*u*p *Rawson*.

tarnation! euph. excl. that substitutes for damnation! *Rawson*.

tarp n. (abbrev.) tarpaulin *rr*.

tart n. **1.** spec. promiscuous woman, prostitute; **2.** any girl, not esp. derog; girl-friend *Humphries*.

tart about v. for a girl or woman to act like a tart **1** (qv).

tart up v. to decorate, to ornament *Austin*.

tash n. (abbrev.) moustache *Sillitoe*.

taste n. **1.** (criminal use) a share, of a bribe, of the proceeds of a robbery, etc. *Newman:1*; **2.** a sample of drugs *Grogan*.

taste bud n. the clitoris *Klein*.

tasty a. **1.** of a person: smart, sharp, prob. criminal; **2.** of a thing; valuable, worthwhile, usu. some form of criminal plan *Newman:1*.

tat n. (US conman use) con tricks performed with dice; fr. tatts (qv) *Thompson:J*.

ta-ta goodbye! *Performance*.

taters aka: *taties*: fr. rhyming sl. taters in the mould = cold *Norman:2.*
tatts n. dice; orig. *tats*: crooked dice, fr. 16th C. *Powis.*
taxi-cabs n. (rhyming sl.) crabs = body lice *Norman:2.*
TB (UK teen 'society' use) *T*rès *B*rill.: absolutely wonderful (cf: brill) *P. Wickham.*
T-bone (US Black use) common Black nickname *Klein.*
TCB see: take care of business.
tea n. **1.** alcohol *Higgins:3;* **2.** marijuana *Goldman.*
teahouse n. a house or apartment where people gather specifically to buy and enjoy marijuana (cf: tea **2**) *Klein.*
tealeaf n. (rhyming sl.) thief *Norman:1.*
team n. **1.** a posse of police; **2.** a gang of criminals.
team cream n. (homosexual use) an orgy *Stanley.*
team-handed working in a group; thus spec. two-handed, five-handed, etc. *Farren.*
tear ass v. to move extremely quickly, to drive very fast *Price:2.*
tearaway n. a minor gangster, a small-time villain *Norman:2.*
tear into v. see: rip into.
tear-jerker n. (film use) a heavily romantic film, with either a sad or happy conclusion, either of which should guarantee a weeping audience; similarly used to describe mawkish ballads/love-songs *Whitcomb.*
tear loose v. (US Black use) to escape, fr. person or situation *Klein.*
tear off v. to rush away, to leave at speed *Barr.*
tear off a strip v. to criticise severely, to reprimand; orig. milit. use.
tear one a new asshole v. to attack savagely, either physically or verbally.
tear one's ass v. to criticise severely *Himes:1.*
tearoom n. (US homosexual use) a public toilet popular for casual sex and assignations (cf: cottage) *Jay & Young.*
tearoom queen n. a homosexual who hangs around public lavatories for sex *Stanley.*
tear up v. (US Black use) to enjoy oneself; to do something with relish *Folb.*
teaspoon n. (drug use) half a spoon (qv) of narcotic drugs *Klein.*
technicolour yawn n. (orig; Aus. use; now general) the act of vomiting; fr. the multicoloured effluvia so produced *Humphries.*
Teddy Bear n. (Aus. use) a show-off, esp. a cricketer who jokes around on the field and plays to the crowd; fr. rhyming sl. lair (qv) *Wilkes.*
teddybear n. (US Black use) a plump but nonetheless sexy woman *Klein.*
Ted Frazer n. (rhyming sl.) razor, always a cut-throat open model *Powis.*
teed off a. annoyed, irritated, upset *Seale.*
teed up a. drunk *Dickson.*
tee kay n. (butchers' use) (abbrev.) town killed, ie English meat (cf: cold) *Cole.*
teensie-weensie a. (juv. use) very small, minuscule *Thompson:J.*
teenybopper n. young girl, usu. in early teens, with a predeliction for rock music and the boys who play it.
tee-tee a. (US milit. use) in Vietnam, very small *Del Vecchio.*
tekram n. (backsl.) market, spec. Covent Garden *Powis.*
Tel almost invariable nickname for Londoners called Terry *'Minder', Thames TV, passim.*
telephone J/O (homosexual use) telephone jerk off; masturbation while using the telephone, not necessarily while exchanging a specifically erotic conversation *Jay & Young.*
telephone numbers extremely large sums of money; fr. the digits used in big city exchanges.
tell it like it is v. (Black, hippie, now general use) to be absolutely honest; to reject dissembling.
tell it to the marines! (excl.) dismissive statement of disbelief in a previous, far-fetched statement; fr. naut. use: sailors had a low opinion of

Marine intelligence *Price:1.*

tell me another! (cp) indicating disbelief and implying that the previous speaker is telling not facts but a string of jokes.

tells n. (poker use) nervous tics, mannerisms, idiosyncrasies – all of which help to inform rival players of a players state of mind and of cards *Alvarez.*

Ten n. (US criminal use) (abbrev.) the Ten Most Wanted Criminals List, est. 1930s by J. Edgar Hoover, head of the FBI *Dunne.*

ten n. the ideal woman or man; fr. the film *10* directed by Blake Edwards (1979); ten is also used for sexual intercourse in schoolboys/girls petting scale of 1 to 10 *White.*

ten cent bag n. (drug use) $10 bag of marijuana (cf: dime bag) *Folb.*

tender box n. (homosexual use) a young boy with alluring buttocks *Klein.*

ten-four message received and understood; fr. the US police 'ten codes', 10:4, thus *10:15* civil disturbance, *10:31* crime in progress, etc. *Jenkins.*

ten-two traditional payment for sex in US: $10 for the girl, $2 for the room.

texan rude (backsl.) next door *Cole.*

texan rude nam n. (backsl.) lit. next door man, thus neighbour *Cole.*

Texas steel n. (US prison use) a prison *Klein.*

TGIF (acro.) *T*hank *G*od *I*t's *F*riday (cf: poet's day).

TH (backsl.) eight *Cole.*

thanks a bunch thank you very much, poss. ironic use; bunch synonymous with many, thus 'many thanks' *Griffith.*

thanks for nothing (cp) exclamation of annoyance and contempt.

that'll pin your ears back (cp) that will surprise you (and poss. cause you trouble).

that's news to acknowledge one's interest in whatever one has just been told *Klein.*

that's so ill! (Valley Girls (qv) use) all-purpose denunciation of an object or activity; ie I want to be sick! *Pond.*

that's the ball game (cp) that's it; no arguments accepted; forget it; fr. sporting use *'T.J. Hooker', Thames TV, 1983.*

that's the shot! (Aus. use) excl. of general approval *Wilkes.*

that's the ticket just what is wanted, the ideal thing *Hotten.*

that's the way the cookie crumbles one must accept the facts, like it or not *Junker.*

that's torn it that has ruined it, spoiled it *Wodehouse:MOJ.*

that way a. homosexual (cf: so) *Jay & Young.*

THC (abbrev.) *t*etra*h*ydro*c*annabinnol, the active chemical substance in cannabis, which gets users 'high' (cf: tincture).

the gun n. (US milit. use) an M-60 light machine gun, thus termed by troops in Vietnam *Del Vecchio.*

the rabbit died (cp) I am pregnant; fr. the test used to determine pregnancy *Dunne.*

there'll be blue murder if... (cp) warning against performing any action with inevitably disastrous consequences.

there'll be hell to pay see: there'll be blue murder.

there's one born every minute (cp) refers to an event or a person that has exhibited great foolishness; fr. a dictum of master-showman P.T. Barnum (1810–91) to whom 'one' was a sucker (qv).

thespian n. a lesbian, pun on that word, plus alleged prevalence of *male* homosexuals in theatre (?) *Maledicta.*

thick a. **1.** (US campus use) emotionally involved, romantically attached; abbrev. thick with *Underwood*; **2.** (US Black use) something intellectually demanding, a deep topic *Klein*; **3.** stupid, dull, foolish *Barr.*

thickie n. a fool; fr. thick (qv) *Dury.*

thing n. **1.** use. as *one's own thing*: one's lifestyle, one's opinion etc.;

2. (euph) the penis *Dunne.*
thingummibob n. anything, often small, to which one cannot put a name.
thingmummijig n. see: thingummibob (cf: whatchamacallit).
thingummy n. indefinite noun for any nameless object *Wodehouse:PGM.*
thinker n. the mind *R. Chandler, 'The Little Sister', 1949.*
thinks it's just to pee through (cp) denigrating an unsophisticated, inexperienced youth who supposedly has yet to appreciate the alternative function of his penis.
thin on the ground sparse, well spread-out.
third degree n. (police/criminal use) the beating up and similar physical abusing of suspects by policemen in order to extract confessions; allegedly outlawed in last couple of decades, but reality proves otherwise.
third leg n. the penis (cf: short arm) *Neaman & Silver.*
Third World briefcase n. a large, portable stereophonic tape-deck/radio, particularly popular among Black youths in US and UK (cf: ghettoblaster, boofer-box, etc.) *Green:2.*
thirty-eight n. .38 pistol *Higgins:1.*
this is where we came in (cp) we've come full circle, we're back where we started; refers to conversation or discussion rather than physical movement; fr. the cinema's non-stop 'continuous performances'.
thoroughbred n. (pimp use) a prostitute with style, sophistication, knowledge; younger than an old-timer (qv) and generally considered among the elite of her profession; fr. horseracing use *OUI 8/75.*
thoroughbred black(US Black use) the ideal Black girl *Klein.*
thousand eyes n. (US Black use) a particular style of man's shoe with many perforations in the leather *Folb.*
thousand yard stare n. (milit. use) the look in the eyes of a soldier who has been shattered by his experience of combat but who must continue fighting; orig. during the Vietnam War; looking into the middle distance.
thrash v. (Aus. use) to drive at great speeds (usu. teen. use) *Ready.*
threads n. clothes; fr. jazz/beatnik use, 1950s *Price:2.*
three balls n. (US Black use) a Jew; fr. traditional three brass balls that hang outside a pawnshop *Folb.*
three-bullet Joey (US Black use) the police *Folb.*
three-card monte n. the three-card trick (cf: find the lady) *Powis.*
three-dollar bill n. eccentric, odd; no such currency exists (cf: nine-bob note).
three-hour tour n. (US teen. use) anything too tedious to be tolerated *Sculatti.*
three-letter man n. (euph.) homosexual; orig. the letters were f-a-g, now g-a-y *Rawson.*
three-piece set n. aka: *three-piece suit* the male genitals *Neaman & Silver.*
three squares n. (abbrev.) three square meals; regular eating *SF Comic.*
three-sheet v. to advertise, thus to boast, to brag. fr. carnival/theatre use: a three-sheet poster is larger than usual *Green:2.*
three sheets to the wind drunk; also: six sheets, four sheets, etc.
threesome n. group sex involving three people of same or mixed sexes *Jay & Young.*
three tears and a bucket (US Black use) cp. meaning 'I should care less' (qv) *Klein.*
three-time loser (US cant) n. a prisoner who has been convicted of two crimes worthy of prison sentence and faces life sentence or execution if convicted a third time *Fiction Illus.3.*
three-way deal n. sex involving three partners at once; thus *four-way deal*, etc. (cf: threesome) *Price:2.*
three-way girl n. a prostitute who will offer any orifice in her body to clients.
thrill and chill n. (US Black use) a sexual experience so wonderful it

sends chills up one's spine *Klein.*

throat n. (US campus use) anyone who works harder than the average – and enjoys it *Bernbach.*

through and through n. (US Black use) a wholly admirable (Black) person *Klein.*

through the gate (cricket use) for a batsman to be bowled by a ball that slips through the space between his bat and his pads *BBC Radio, 1983.*

through the nose a. very expensive *Sharpe:1.*

throw v. to have sexual intercourse *Folb.*

throw a buttonhole on v. (US Black use) to have anal intercourse *Folb.*

throw a moody v. to become sulky, truculent, ill-tempered *Bleasdale.*

throw a punch v. to defend oneself, verbally as well as physically; fr. boxing use *Klein.*

throw a seven v. (Aus. use) to faint, to collapse; fr. seven as the losing throw in a game of craps dice *Wilkes.*

throw down on v. to blame someone; fr. cant use: hold a gun on *Burroughs:Jr.*

thrower n. (UK criminal use) in three-card monte (qv) gangs, the member who actually deals the three cards and exercises the fraudulent sleight-of-hand *Powis.*

throw hands v. (US Black use) to punch, to hit *Seale.*

throw in v. to add, to include *Capital Radio 1983.*

throw in one's hand v. to give in, to surrender; fr. card use.

throw in the sponge v. **1.** see throw in the towel; **2.** to die; fr. boxing use *Rawson.*

throw in the towel v. to give in, to capitulate; fr. boxing use, whereby the seconds of a losing fighter toss his towel into the ring to save him from any further punishment.

throw iron v. see: pump iron *Seale.*

throw one for a loop v. to disturb; to worry considerably, to put off one's stride *Thompson:J.*

throw one's cookies v. to vomit *Higgins:1.*

throw one's hat in the ring v. to join a contest, to register one's candidacy or opinion *T 16/6/83.*

throw one's voice v. (Aus. use) to vomit *Humphries:2.*

throw one's weight about v. to act in an arrogant, aggressive manner *Thompson:J.*

throw some dirt on v. (US Black use) to malign, to slander *Klein.*

throw the baby out with the bathwater v. to be so keen on eliminating the large-scale errors that one simultaneously tosses out the less visible but highly valuable entities hidden amongst them.

throw the book at v. to discipline heavily, to reprimand severely; the 'book; is the 'book of rules' that one has contravened.

throw up v. to vomit *Price:1.*

thumb n. (US Black use) a fight *Folb.*

thumper n. (US milit use) M-79 grenade launcher *Del Vecchio.*

thunder-box n. **1.** a lavatory *Humphries*; **2.** a portable commode *E. Waugh, 'Officers & Gentlemen', 1955.*

thunder chicken n. (US Black use) an unattractive or unpleasant female *Folb.*

tick n. **1.** unpleasant, insignificant person; fr. the vermin *Wodehouse: VGJ*; (US campus use) **2.** overweight person; **3.** a greedy or selfish person; *Underwood*; **4.** credit; fr. abbrev. ticket, since 17th C. *Hotten.*

ticker n. **1.** a watch; fr. its mechanism *Wright*; **2.** the human heart; fr. the regular beat *Runyon:1*; **3.** accountant; who ticks off sums of money *Payne.*

ticket n. **1.** (UK police use) a warrant to search or to arrest *Powis*; **2.** a person, esp. used by 'mods' of early 1960s *The Who, 'Quadrophenia', 1973.*

ticketty-boo a. fine, wonderful, all in order, etc. fr. that's the ticket (?); orig. naval use.

tickle n. **1.** (UK police use) a piece of information; it 'tickles one's fancy';

2. (UK criminal use) a successful and lucrative crime fr. tickling trout (?) *Powis.*

tickled a. amused, pleased; tickled pink (qv): extremely amused *Runyon:1.*

tickled pink a. extremely pleased or amused *Wodehouse:MOJ.*

tickled to death delighted, very happy, amused *Heller.*

tickle one's pickle v. to masturbate *Maledicta.*

tickler n. a junior official or assistant who is used by his superior(s) to disseminate to still lower ranks such policies that the leaders wish adopted, without making face-to-face contact themselves *PT.*

tickle the ivories n. to play the piano, fr. the ivory keys.

tick one off v. (US campus use) to prompt thoughts in the hearer *Underwood.*

ticky-tacky a. vulgar and banal, tasteless, unsophisticated, corny (cf: tacky) *Whitcomb.*

tiddler's bait (rhyming sl.) late *Cole.*

tiddly a. slightly drunk; fr. rhyming sl. *tiddly wink* = drink *Cole.*

tiddly wink n. (rhyming sl.) Chink = Chinese *Dury.*

tied up a. busy *Higgins:1.*

tie off v. (drug use) to tie up a vein and isolate it prior to injecting narcotic drugs *Caserta.*

tie one on v. **1.** (UK and US use) to be drunk *Schulberg*; **2.** (Aus. use) to provoke a fight *Baker.*

tie-up n. (drug use) the rubber tube, handkerchief, string or other object used for tying off a vein prior to injecting narcotics *Burroughs:1.*

tiger for n. (Aus. use) an enthusiast for a given task: fr. the aggression of the animal *Wilkes.*

tight a. **1.** mean, avaricious, ungenerous; fr. tight-fisted and tightwad (qv) *Higgins:2*; **2.** very close, friendly, intimate *Dunne*; **3.** reasonably, but not excessively drunk *Bernbach.*

tight-assed a. repressed, self-denying, puritan *Higgins:5.*

tightbuck n. (homosexual use) the foetal position, popular for tying up participants in sado-masochistic sex *Jay & Young.*

tighten up one's game v. (US Black use) to take control of one's life, of a given situation in which one is interested *Folb.*

tightwad n. an ungenerous, mean person *BvdB.*

tight-weak a. (poker use) a weakness in one's play that develops when a player is too frightened about losing his money *Alvarez.*

tight with a. very friendly with someone; fr. physical/mental intimacy.

Tijuana bible small, illustrated pornographic book; named for the era when US citizens saw Tijuana, Mexico, as the Port Said of Central America (cf: eight-pager).

tile loose a. eccentric, foolish, 'not all there'.

till hell freezes over see: till the cows come home.

till the cows come home for an indefinite time; for ever.

Tilly n. (homosexual use) the police *Stanley.*

time and a half n. payment of the basic wage plus 50% extra – for overtime or similar bonus payment; thus, *double time*: double the basic rate, *two and a half-time*, etc.

tin n. (US police use) the official police badge (cf: potsy) *Neaman & Silver.*

tin-arsed a. (Aus. use) thick-skinned, impervious to pain, lucky *Wilkes.*

tin can n. (USN use) destroyer *Pynchon.*

tincture n. (drug use) tincture of cannabis (cf: THC) *Green:1.*

tincture n. a drink; fr. 'Dear Bill' column, lampooning Denis Thatcher, husband of Prime Minister Margaret, in *Private Eye* passim.

tinhorn a. second rate, inferior, superficially flashy *rr.*

tinkle v. to urinate; often children's use *Vidal.*

tinkle n. a ring on the telephone; usu: give one a tinkle *Performance.*

tinnie n. (Aus. use) a can of beer; now general, orig. surfer use *Humphries: 2.*

Tinsel Town n. Hollywood, Calif. fr. its glittering, fantasy image *CB.*

tin soldier n. (prostitute use) a man who wishes no actual sex but only to act as a servant or 'slave' to the prostitute; usu. fr. middle or upper-class background *Paul Bailey, 'An English Madam', 1982.*

tin-tack n. (rhyming sl.) the sack = dismissal from a job *Franklyn.*

tip n. (abbrev.) tip off, but used as any reason for an arrest, not simply information given to the police *Seale.*

tip v. (US Black use) **1.** to cheat on one's lover or mate; **2.** to perform an illicit act; **3.** to be in a place where one should not be *Folb*; **4.** (US campus use) to drink heavily; fr. tipple *Underwood.*

tip in v.t. to inform against *Higgins: 1.*

tip off v. to warn.

tip out v. (US Black use) to have sex with anyone other than one's spouse or regular lover (cf: tip, v. **1**) *Major.*

tippin' a. (US Black use) in full control; on top of one's game; fr. 'tip-top' *Klein.*

tipsy a. slightly drunk *Bruce: 1.*

tip the wink v. to warn, to signal, usu. with an actual wink, but also figuratively *Hotten.*

tired a. (homosexual use) to describe an exceptionally dull and boring person *Stanley.*

tired and emotional (euph.) extremely drunk; coined in *Private Eye* fr. the popular euph. to mask the activities of the famous.

tired people n. (US Black use) weak or displeasing people *Klein.*

tired woman n. (US Black use) a female who lacks sophistication, who is not streetwise (qv) *Klein.*

tit n. **1.** something extremely simple and usu. rewarding, esp. a criminal scheme. fr. the simplicity of a child's finding its mother's breast; **2.** a breast *Price:1* thus; **3.** anything considered to resemble a breast, or, more often, the nipple; a button or small switch, etc. *Price: 1.*

tit for n. (pron. titfer) rhyming sl. tit for tat = hat *Powis.*

tit man a man who finds a woman's breasts her most attractive feature (cf: ass man, leg man).

tit mag a magazine, à la *Playboy*, *Penthouse*, *Hustler*, etc. which features scantily clad girls, interspersed with varying amounts of prose, reviews, etc. but in effect, for all other pretensions, an aid to masturbation.

tits and ass burlesque show; cheap sex-orientated entertainment which features strippers, etc. (cf: T&A) *White.*

tits on a bull a. (cp) utterly useless; usu. 'no more use than tits on a bull'.

tits-up a. (Can. prison use) dead; thus laid out on one's back *Caron.*

titty n. the female breast (cf: tit); orig. the nipple, as diminutive of tit *Vidal.*

tizzy n. a panic, a 'state', of flap.

TJ (abbrev.) *T*i*j*uana, Mexico.

TKO v. (boxing use) (acro.) to achieve *T*echnical *K*nock-*O*ut *Higgins: 1.*

TLC (abbrev.) *T*ender *L*oving *C*are.

TNT **1.** (abbrev.) *T*wo *N*ifty *T*its: the female breasts *Rawson*; **2.** (US Black use) a popular name for dynamite, thus describing anyone or anything that is metaphorically 'dynamite', wonderful, exceptional, etc. *Klein.*

toast n. (US criminal use) a long and epic poem, often trad. in prisons *Goldman.*

toast v. (West Indian use) for a disk jockey to perform his own lyrics to the background of a reggae song, usu. in a dub (no lyrics, only bass and rhythm lines) version.

toasted a. (drug use) very high (qv) *Folb.*

toby n. (UK police use) an area, a police division fr. 19th C. *toby*: highway, the road; thus those roads the division supervises (cf: manor) *Powis.*

toch eno! (backsl.) hot one!, ie look

out, take care, etc. *Cole*.

toches n. fr. Yiddish: posterior, buttocks *Rosten*.

toddle off v. to leave *Wodehouse passim*.

to die a. (US campus use) excellent, wonderful, perfect, ie that boy is to die pretty, etc. *Bernbach*.

to-do n. an argument, a set-to, a lively situation *Parade 7/83*.

Tod Sloan (rhyming sl.) alone; thus on one's Tod (qv) *Cole*.

toe popper n. (US milit. use) in Vietnam, the M-14 anti-personnel mine which maims the foot *O'Brien*.

toe queen n. foot fetishist (cf: queen) *Stanley*.

toe-rag n. orig. a tramp (from the foot-bindings they wear); currently any unappetizing (old) person; UK prison use: any highly unpopular person, young or old *Dury*.

toes lively a. very fast *Cole*.

toey a. (Aus. use) nervous, touchy *Wilkes*.

toff n. aristocrat; anyone considered either to be or to be posing as a superior person; also *you're a toff*: you're very kind/generous; thank you very much *Dury, 'Laughter', 1981*.

toffee n. nonsense; flattery; fr. the 'sweetness' of its content (?) *Powis*.

toffee-nosed a. snobbish, arrogant; fr. toff (qv) *Keyes*.

together a. aware, in control, united, happy, *au fait*, sophisticated.

togged to the bricks a. (US Black use) dressed in absolute chic and style *Major*.

togs n. clothes *Vidal*.

toilet n. anywhere considered disgusting, esp. show business use for a third-rate venue *Goldman*.

toilet talk n. obscenities, coarse language *Humphries*.

toke n. (US Black campus use) a marijuana cigarette; fr. toke, v. (qv) *Folb*.

toke v. to puff on a marijuana cigarette (cf: toke, n.) *Wolfe: 2*.

Tom (abbrev.) Uncle Tom (qv) *Greenlee*.

tom n. **1.** a prostitute working in Mayfair (cf: Edie) *Austin*; **2.** (rhyming sl.) tomfoolery = jewellery *Norman: 2*; both meanings date prior to 1959 Street Offences Act, but with new upsurge of street prostitution during the current economic depression they may revive; **3.** (abbrev.) Tommy, a British soldier *A. F. N. Clarke, 'Contact', 1983*.

tom v. for a Black person to act in an inferior and obsequious manner to whites; to act as a Black stereotype; fr. Uncle Tom (qv).

Tom and Dick v. (rhyming sl.) to be sick *Dury*.

tomato n. girl, woman; fr. the luscious ripeness of the fruit *Runyon*.

tom-cat v. to strut around looking for sexual conquests; fr. the animal.

Tom, Dick & Harry n. any men, young or old, irrespective of given names.

tomfoolery n. (rhyming sl.) jewellery *Cole*.

Tom Mix n. (rhyming sl.) fix = problem, predicament; fr. film cowboy (1880–1940) *Powis*.

tommy rollocks n. (rhyming sl.) bollocks = testicles.

tommy tucker n. (rhyming sl.) supper *Jones: J*.

tom out v. (US Black use) for one Black to inform against another; fr. Uncle Tom (qv) *Folb*.

Tom Pepper n. a liar; fr. nautical use: TP was a mythical sailor who was ejected fr. Hell for lying *Newman: 3*.

toms n. (Aus. use; rhyming sl.) tomtits = shits = diarrhoea, food poisoning *Humphries: 2*.

Tom Slick (US Black use) a Black police informer (cf: Uncle Tom) *Folb*.

tom thumb n. (rhyming sl.) rum *Jones: J*.

tomtit n. (rhyming sl.) shit = excretion *Powis*.

ton n. one hindred, esp. of money; orig. gambling use, but spread elsewhere, esp. to sport.

tongue v. **1.** (homosexual use) to perform cunnilingus *Legman*; **2.** to kiss with each partner's tongue in the other's mouth *Price: 2*.

tongue bath n. see: around the world *Legman*.

tongue lash v. to perform fellatio or anilingus *Klein*.

tongue sushi n. (US preppie (qv) use) French kissing (qv); fr. sushi: Japanese raw fish, a popular dish (cf: swap spit) *Bernbach*.

tonight's the night! (cp) underlining the speaker's expectation of something exciting/important, esp. of a possible seduction.

tonk n. (Aus. use) a male homosexual, or an effeminate, if heterosexual male *Wilkes*.

tons a. (US campus use) very, extremely, really, etc. *Underwood*.

ton-up boy n. aka: *Rocker*: member of a motorcycle gang; fr. ton: 100 mph *Mandelkau*.

tony a. classy, sophisticated, chic; fr. Fr. *ton*: tone *Higgins: 3*.

too Irish stew! (rhyming sl.) too true! *Cole*.

tool n. **1.** (US campus derog. use) a very hard worker *Bernbach*; **2.** penis *Vidal*; **3.** weapon, usu. gun or knife *Norman: 2*; **4.** burglar's implement, spec. jemmy (qv) *Powis*; **5.** (US campus use) a stupid, useless person *Underwood*.

tool around v. (US campus use) to drive around at random in a car *Underwood*.

toolbox n. the vagina; fr. tool 2 *Maledicta*.

tooled up a. carrying a weapon (cf: tool **3**) *Mandelkau*.

toolhead n. (US campus use) a fool, an idiot; fr. tool = penis (cf: prick, etc.) *Underwood*.

tool in v. (US campus use) to arrive, usu. at speed *Underwood*.

too much! excl. of surprise, shock *Stanley*.

too right! excl. of agreement *Ready*.

tooshie n. buttocks, fr. Yiddish *tuchus Goldman*.

toot n. (drug use) **1.** cocaine *Price: 3*; **2.** a device for inhaling cocaine; **3.** a measure of cocaine, usu. one line (qv).

toot v. to inhale cocaine.

toothpick n. (US Black use) **1.** a thin marijuana cigarette; **2.** a pocket knife *Folb*.

tooti-frooti n. (US Black use) (derog.) homosexual male.

tootle v. to ring cheerily, of a telephone or horn *Wodehouse: MOJ*.

toot one's horn v. to experience the immediate post-inhalation high from cocaine; the top of one's head is 'lifted' like that of a boat whistle (cf: toot) *Safire*.

toots n. **1.** a girl; **2.** general form of address, usu, to a female.

tootsie n. see: toots (**1**, **2**) *Bruce: 2*.

tootsie roll n. (US Black use) an attractive female; fr. US sweet of that name; plus ref. to jellyroll (qv) (?) *Klein*.

top v. **1.** to surpass *Higgins: 3*; **2.** to kill, esp. to execute by hanging; thus *top oneself*: to commit suicide *Caron*.

top bollocks n. female breasts.

top cat n. (US Black use) the leader of a group, esp. of a clique of down-and-outs *Klein*.

top dog n. the boss, the senior member of an organization, a leader.

top drawer a. socially elite, aristocratic, upper class *Chandler: LG*.

top hole! excellent, wonderful, perfect, etc.

topkick n. (US Army) first sergeant *Grogan*.

top man n. the dominant partner in a homosexual sado-masochist couple (cf: bottom man) *Jay & Young*.

top notch a. excellent, first class *Payne*.

top-off n.,v. (Aus. use) informer, to inform; to 'finish' a person off *Wilkes*.

top of the house (bingo use) **1.** 99; **2.** 100.

topped up a. drunk *Powis*.

tops n. **1.** (gambling use) doctored dice used for cheating purposes *Runyon*; **2.** the best, the winner *Vidal*; **3.** at the most, at the top estimate *Dunne*.

top sergeant n. (homosexual use) a

masculine lesbian; fr. milit. use *Legman.*

top shelf a. (US Black use) excellent, first class, the best *Klein.*

top up v. to end up, to conclude *Newman.*

torch v. to commit arson; fr. tool employed *Breslin.*

torch for v. see: carry a torch.

torch song n. a love song that takes as a theme unrequited love or a dead affair (cf: carry a torch) *Runyon.*

torn down (US Black use) most distressed, miserable; (cf: bring down) *Major.*

torpedo n. a thug, a hoodlum; the 'weapon' used by a gang boss and sent out to destroy enemies *Fiction Illus. 3.*

TOS n. (US pimp use) (abbrev.) *T*ricks *O*ff the *S*treet; usu. used by hotel clerks in those hotels which let out rooms to working prostitutes: men picked up in the street (cf: trick) *Shulman.*

tosh n. **1.** nonsense, rubbish *H. L. Mencken, 'A Carnival of Buncombe', 1947*; **2.** form of address (cf: mush, moosh); poss. fr. Scot. dial *tosh*: smart, neat, thus a smart, neat person *LL.*

tosheroon n. half a crown (obs.) *Norman: 3.*

toss in the bucket v. to imprison (cf: can) *Algren.*

toss off v. to masturbate.

toss one's cookies v. (US campus use) to vomit *Bernbach.*

toss one's tacos v. (US campus use) to vomit; spec. when eating Mexican food (?) *Bernbach.*

toss the squares v. (US Black use) to pass a pack of cigarettes; fr. the packet's shape *Klein.*

total v. **1.** to crash one's car so badly as to render it beyond repair – a total disaster; **2.** to destroy or maim anything or any one.

total blowchoice (Valley Girls (qv) use) 'well, kinda cool (qv), but really, who cares?'; appealing but irrelevant *Pond.*

totally a. (Valley Girls (qv) use) intensifier to mean utterly, absolutely, completely, etc. *Harpers/Queen 1983.*

total wreck n. (rhyming sl.) a cheque *Wright.*

to the bad in debt, 'in the red'.

totty n. young girl, usu, sexually available; fr. 19th C.a high-class prostitute *Keyes.*

touch v. to borrow money from (cf: tap) *Wodehouse: GB.*

touch base v. to communicate with, to check in; fr. baseball use.

touch of the seconds second thoughts, last minute hesitation *Powis.*

touch of the tar brush n. derog. phr. implying, often erroneously, that someone has a degree of non-white blood *Sharpe, 'Indecent Exposure', 1973.*

touch-on n. an erection *Newman: 2.*

touch up v. to molest sexually *Tidy.*

tough a. (US campus use) admirable; on bad = good analogy *Underwood.*

tough shit! (excl.) so what! see if I care! response indicating little or no sympathy with the speaker *Jay & Young.*

tough stuff (US Black use) (on good/bad reversal) anything appealing, pleasing in the realms of sex or drugs *Klein.*

tough titties bad luck *Price: 2.*

touristas n. any form of stomach upset contracted on a foreign holiday; fr. Sp. (cf: Montezuma's revenge, etc.) *Neaman & Silver.*

tout n. (IRA use) informer *'Harry's Game', LWT, 1983.*

town bicycle n. highly promiscuous girl or woman, who is constantly 'ridden' (cf: town pump).

town pump n. highly promiscuous girl or woman (cf: town bicycle).

town punch n. see: town pump, town bicycle *Underwood.*

toys n. appliances designed to increase sexual pleasure or fantasies: dildoes, vibrators, whips, chains, etc. *Jay & Young.*

toy-boy n. a young attractive boy popular among older, richer women.

track n. (Black use) the world of pimping, hustling, confidence tricks, etc., the Eastern cities are the *fast track*, California and the West are the *slow track*, *soft track Milner*.
track v. to maintain emotional/verbal stability, to keep on the right track *McFadden*.
tracks n.punctures and scar tissue that accumulate on the veins of a regular drug addict who injects himself with a given drug *Burroughs: 1*.
trade n. (homosexual use) a man with whom one has (commercial) sex *Jay & Young*.
tram line n. a scar (cf: stripe) *Norman: 1*.
tramp n. a promiscuous woman *Price: 2*.
tramps's lagging n. (UK prison use) a sentence of 90 days in jail; commonly that meted out for vagrancy *LL*.
tranks n. (abbrev.) tranquillizers: barbiturates, Librium, Valium, etc.
trap n. **1.** mouth (cf: keep one's trap shut) *Higgins: 3*; **2.** a place, spec. a nightclub; fr. the extortionate prices charged those lured within (?) *Runyon*; **3.** (US prostitute use) the number of customers a ho (qv) is assigned as a daily tally by her pimp to reach a given financial target *Shulman*.
trapeze artist n. a woman who enjoys cunnilingus, esp. as part of sex exhibitions *Legman*.
traps n. drums *Algren*.
trash n. (abbrev.) white trash: poor (Southern US) whites *Wolfe: 2*.
trash . **1.** to break windows, destroy appliances, etc. as part of a demonstration; coined by the radical Weathermen movement, c.1969. fr. trash: rubbish, garbage *White*; **2.** to malign someone else (cf: rubbish, v.).
trash around v. to slum; acting poorer than one is *White*.
trashed a. very drunk *Bernbach*.
trashmouth n. (US campus use) anyone who regularly uses profanity or obscenity *Underwood*.
tremblers n. female breasts, usu. large, thus able to tremble *Whitcomb*.
triangle n. an three-way relationship: two men, one woman, or two women, one man both heterosexual and male and female homosexual *Legman*.
trick n. **1.** the client of a prostitute, whether hetero- or homosexual; the implication is of conning any such client into parting with money *Higgins: 1*; **2.** (homosexual use) any casual sex partner *White*: **3.** a period of work, usu. physically demanding or unpleasant; fr. nautical use *trick*: turn at the wheel *Powis*.
trick v. (homosexual use) to pick up a partner for casual, unpaid sex *Jay & Young*.
trick baby n. (US Black use) the illegitimate child born to a prostitute; given no positive evidence to the contrary, she assumed the father to have been one of the paying customers *Iceberg Slim, book title*.
trick bag n. (US Black use) an unpleasant and disadvantaged position *Klein*.
trick cyclist n. pun on psychiatrist (cf: shrink).
trick flick n. (homosexual use) a pornographic film (cf: stag film) *Stanley*.
trick towel n. (homosexual use) a towel for wiping oneself after intercourse *Stanley*.
Trick Willy n. (US Black use) a gullible Black man *Klein*.
triff a. (abbrev.) terrific, wonderful *Capital Radio 1984*.
triflin' (US Black use) acting irresponsibly; as a parasite fr. SE trifling *Klein*.
trigger (man) n. a gunman working for organized crime (cf: soldier).
trim n. (US Black use) the female genitalia *Folb*.
trimmer n. (Aus. use) anything excellent, wonderful, approved of; fr. 19th C. *trimming*: excellent, first-rate, etc.
trip n. **1.** spec. the experience that follows the taking of LSD; **2.** any form of experience, event *Hoffman: a*.

triple clutcher n. (euph.) motherfucker; coined by Black truck-drivers in US Army fighting in Korean War *Rawson*.
triple hip a. (US Black use) extra-smart, very wise *Major*.
trip out v. to lose control, to leave normality; fr. the LSD trip (qv) *Price: 2*.
tripper n. (drug use) one who takes LSD or similar hallucinogens.
-tripping general suffix denoting a style of action or opinion: *power-tripping*: asserting oneself over others; *head-tripping*: thinking, etc. *McFadden*.
trippy a. **1.** bizarre, strange, disturbing; fr. LSD trips (qv) *ES 23/9/83*; **2.** (Valley Girls (qv) use) excellent, first-rate, etc. *Pond*.
trip to the moon n. (homosexual use) anal intercourse (cf: moon) *Legman*.
trolling see: cruising; fr. SE: saunter along *Junker*.
tromp v. to tramp around *Higgins: 4*.
trophy n. (US campus (spec. U. of Arkansas) half a gallon of alcohol *Underwood*.
troppo a. (Aus. use) mad, insane, fr. effects of the tropical heat (cf:Doolally) *Humphries*.
Trot n. (abbrev.) Trotskyite; used indiscriminately for any hard-left group in the UK; thus media use of *trot-slot*: a programme that concerns itself with or apparently propagandizes for such groups.
trots n. diarrhoea (cf: runs) *Higgins: 4*.
trotter n. (UK criminal use) a deserter from the British armed forces; one who is 'on the trot', running *Powis*.
trotters n. **1.** feet *Wright*; **2.** racehorses.
trouble and strife n. (rhyming sl.) the wife *Cole*.
trout n. (US Black use) **1.** the vagina; **2.** a female *Folb*.
truck v. to move, to travel; esp. in hippy rallying cry of 1960s: 'Keep on trucking!' *Underwood*.
truck driver n. (US Black use) an ostentatiously 'masculine' homosexual, poss. dressed in trucker, or similar macho clothes (cf: butch, rough trade) *Major*.
trucking moving, struggling along; esp. as *keep on trucking*: exhortation to continue with one's life *Trashman, Berkeley, Calif. 1969*.
trumpet n. the telephone *Powis*.
try it on. v. to attempt to get away with anything, usu. that which one is not entitled to have.
try-on n. an attempt to try it on (qv).
ts (abbrev.) *t*ough *s*hit, often used ironically or mockingly as well as sympathetically *Uris*.
TS n. (abbrev.) *T*rans-*S*exual (cf: TV) *Maledicta*.
TTFN (cp) (abbrev.) *T*a-*T*a *F*or *N*ow = goodbye; orig. created and popularised on comedian Tommy Handley's BBC Radio show 'ITMA' (It's That Man Again); Dorothy Summers, as 'Mrs Mopp' (the comic charlady) actually used the cp; currently featured by BBC Radio-2 disc jockey Jimmy Young *Whitcomb*.
tub n. a boat, spec. the tubs (qv) *Runyon*.
tube n. **1.** (UK prison use) a prison officer who makes a habit of listening for information from prison informers (cf: bubble) *LL*; **2.** television, fr. cathode ray tube, a basic component of the TV; **3.** (Aus. use) a can of beer *Humphries*.
tube v. (US campus use) to do badly at work; fr. 'go down the tubes' *Underwood*.
tubed a. very drunk; thus vanishing 'down the tubes' *Dickson*.
tube it v. to watch television *Underwood*.
tubesteak n. (US Black use) the penis *Folb*.
tubs n. **1.** (obs.) transatlantic liners; **2.** drums *Algren*.
tub thumper n. a vehement preacher, either clerical or secular *Hotten*.
tubular a. (Valley Girls (qv) use) even better than awesome or massive (qqv), prob. fr. surfers' use of *tube*: the inside

curve of a good wave *Harpers/ Queen 1983*.

tuches n. see: toches.

tucker n. (Aus. use) food; devel fr. use at 19th C. gold diggings: rations *Humphries: 2*.

tuckered out a. exhausted, worn out *Runyon: 1*.

tuck up v. to defraud, to steal from *Newman: 1*.

tucked up a. (UK police use) captured without any chance of escape fr. 17th C. cant *tuck (up)* : to hang.

tug n. an arrest (cf: pull) *'The Sweeney', Thames TV, passim*.

tumble v. **1.** to seduce, to have intercourse *Thompson: J*; **2.** to realize, to notice *Newman: 1*.

tummler n. **1.** fr. Yiddish: noise, disorder; 'the life and soul of the party'; a person who talks a great deal but accomplishes little; **2.** (show business use) the MC of a (Jewish) hotel in Catskill Mts, NY (cf: Borscht belt) *Rosten*.

tump over v. (US campus use) to knock over; fr. SE tumble *Underwood*.

tuna n. **1.** (US campus use) a girl-friend, a female *Bernbach*; **2.** (US Black use) a female and by extension, the vagina (cf: fish) *Folb*.

tuned in a. aware of what is going on, at one with the nuances and niceties of a situation or conversation; fr. radio use (cf: hip).

tune off v. to calm someone down; esp. when this will stop them from 'broadcasting' facts detrimental to one's own interest; fr. radio use *PT*.

turd n. **1.** piece of excrement; since 11th C. *Price: 1* thus; **2.** an unappealing person.

turd-burglar n. (Aus. use) homosexual male; fr. anal intercourse.

turd-packer n. homosexual *Legman*.

turf n. **1.** spec. the area controlled by a given US urban street gang; **2.** the area with which one is familiar and which in turn recognizes one as a regular figure *Greenlee*.

turf out v. to eject, to throw out; supposedly on to some grass.

Turk n. (homosexual use) one who enjoys anal intercourse; fr. racial cliché *Legman*.

turkey n. **1.** a failure, an incompetent *Price: 1*; **2.** a dull, incompetent, unappealing person *Junker*; **3.** an appalling, unquestionable disaster; esp. in show business.

turkey-neck n. the penis; fr. supposed resemblance *Bukowski: 6*.

turkey on a string n. (US Black use) one who is infatuated and thus easily led and controlled *Folb*.

turkey shoot n. (milit. use) a combat in which one's own side wins without any difficulty, killing and destroying on a large scale *Esq. 6/83*.

turking n. sexual intercourse *Powis*.

turn n. (Aus. use) a party (usu. teen. use) *Ready*.

turn around v. (police use) to persuade a criminal to turn informer *Higgins: 2*.

turned on a. aware, sophisticated, up to the minute; fr. image of the awareness gained through drug use *SF Comics*.

turnip greens n. (US Black use) marijuana; fr. popular 'soul food' *Folb*.

turn it up! stop doing that; since 17th C.*Dury, 'Do It Yourself'*.

turnkey job n. a commission in which one major contractor delivers the finished product to the client and deals with all sub-contractors and affiliates himself; thus on completion all the client need do is 'turn a key' and his machine, factory, new house, etc. is all ready to start operations *Thompson: J*.

turn off v. repel sexually *Jay & Young*.

turn on n. a thrill, sexual or otherwise *McFadden*.

turn on v. **1.** to take drugs; as in Dr Timothy Leary's exhortation: 'turn on, tune in and drop out' *Goldman*; **2.** to stimulate sexually, to appeal to someone *Jay & Young*.

turn one's crank v. to give pleasure *Underwood*.

turn one's face to the wall v. to die *Algren: 2.*

turn on the waterworks v. to start crying *Neaman & Silver.*

turn out v. **1.** (pimp use) to run a prostitute on the streets *OUI 8/75*; **2.** (Hells Angel use) to use a woman for multiple sex *Mandelkau.*

turn over v. **1.** (police/criminal use) to search a house or apartment, usu. with the maximum of damage, mess, etc. *'Minder', Thames TV, 1983*; **2.** (homosexual use) to allow anal intercourse; fr. the physical act that may precede it *Legman.*

turn the set out v. (US Black use) to disrupt (permanently) a given situation or occasion *Folb.*

turn the tables v. (homosexual use) for a male homosexual prostitute to blackmail a client *Legman.*

turn tricks v. to engage in prostitution (cf: trick) *Price: 2.*

turn up n. surprise *Lynda La Plante, 'Widows', Thames TV, 1983.*

turn up one's toes v. to die *Barr.*

turps n. (Aus. use) any form of alcohol; thus *on the turps*: drinking (heavily) (cf: metho) *Ready.*

turtles n. (rhyming sl.) turtle doves = gloves, spec. those worn by housebreakers to hide fingerprints *Powis.*

tushie n. fr. Yiddish: *tuchus* = buttocks *Price: 1.*

tushroon n. (US Black use) money (cf: tosheroon) *Major.*

tuskie n. (US Black use) a large marijuana cigarette; resembling an elephant's tusk (?) *Folb.*

TV n. (acro.) *Trans Vestite* (cf: TS) *Jay & Young.*

twang v. to engage in spontaneous sexual intercourse; since 17th C. *Klein.*

twang one's wire v. to masturbate *Humphries.*

twank n. (prostitute use) an older man who enjoys watching girls at work but has no personal interest in sex.

twat n. vagina; thus a term of abuse; since 17th C. *Powis.*

tweedler n. (UK police/criminal use) a stolen vehicle which is passed off as perfectly legitimate for sale to a sucker (qv). *Powis.*

tweedling (UK police/criminal use) selling stolen property or even non-existent property to innocent purchasers who assume the goods are legitimate *Powis.*

tweeked a. (Valley Girls (qv) use) very drunk or drugged *Pond.*

twenties n. (US conman use) one asks the store clerk for change for $20 rather than give the right, small amount of money; then, after pocketing that, you find the right money, say 20 cents, and offer that, simultaneously asking for or just snatching back the $20 bill *Thompson: J.*

twenty-nine and wake-up (US prison use) the period between receiving a notice of parole and one's actual release, ie a month (cf: wake-up) *Klein.*

twerp n. idiot, nincompoop *Waterhouse.*

twig v. to understand *Payne.*

twirl n. **1.** (UK prison use) a prison officer – from the keys he carries and twirls *Norman: 1*; **2.** (UK criminal use) a key, spec. a skeleton or duplicate key *Powis.*

twist n. **1.** a girl, woman; fr. rhyming sl. twist and twirl = girl; **2.** the passive member of a lesbian relationship *Stanley.*

twisted a. **1.** extremely intoxicated by a specific drugs, esp. the hallucinogens or cannabis; **2.** annoyed, out of emotional control *Stone*; **3.** very drunk *Bernbach.*

twister n. **1.** (US Black use) a front-door key *Major*; **2.**an untrustworthy person, a crook *Wodehouse: PGM.*

twit n. fool, idiot; fr. twerp + twat (qqv) (?) *L. Deighton, 'Close-Up', 1974.*

two n. (criminal use) a two-year sentence *Mortimer.*

two and eight n. (rhyming sl.) a state, a panic *Norman: 2.*

two-bit second-rate; inferior; lit. worth 25 cents *R. Newman, 'Almost Made It To The Top', 1979.*
two-bob a. (Aus. use) inferior, useless, second-rate; lit. worth 2s. (10p) (cf: two-bit) *Wilkes.*
two bricks short of the load someone who is 'not all there', a dunce *Obs. 6/2/83.*
two cents worth n. one's personal opinion, a remark about a given topic *Larner.*
two-dollar words n. any language considered 'difficult' or 'intellectual' by its user, most likely a speaker who claims to despise/avoid such locutions; usu. derog. *Dickson.*
two ducks (bingo use) 22 (from the shape) *Wright.*
twoed-up (UK prison use) two men in the same cell; thus **threed-up**, etc. *Cole.*
twoer n. £200 *Newman: 1.*
two fat ladies (bingo use) 88; fr. the shape *Dury, 'Laughter', 1979.*
two little crutches (bingo use) 77, fr. alleged shape *Wright.*
two pence short of a bob eccentric, slightly crazy; fr. *bob = 1s. Humphries: 2.*
two shakes of a lamb's tail immediately, at once; usu. *In . . .*
twot n. see: twat *Griffith.*
two-time v. to cheat, esp. to double-cross.
two-timer n. a cheat, a double-crosser *rr.*
two-timing a. duplicitous *Himes: 1.*
two-way man n. a male prostitute who is willing to act as passive or active partner in pedication or fellatio *Legman.*
typer n. typewriter *Bukowski: 2.*
T-zone a. (US teen. use) lost in one's own world, spaced out (qv), in a state of transcendental bliss *Sculatti.*
tzuris n. bad luck, endless problems; fr. Yiddish: troubles *Rosten.*

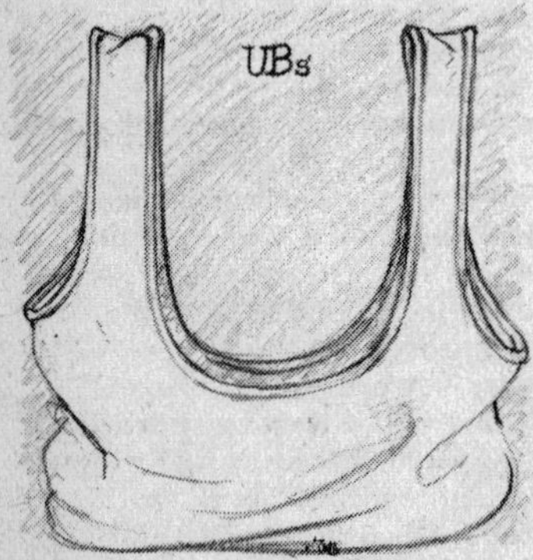

UBs n. (US campus use) (abbrev.) underbodies = underwear, usu. female use *Underwood*.

Ugandan discussions n. (euph.) sexual intercourse; popularly thought to have derived from the alleged discovery, *in flagrante delicto* of Uganda's Minister of Foreign Affairs (female) in an airport lavatory, and so underwritten by *Private Eye*, which magazine coined the phrase, aka *talking about Uganda*; latterly repudiated by Corinna Adam, whose letter to *The Times* (Sept 1983) claims that in 1971 a passionate literary critic was the first to offer this excuse.

U-ie aka: *U-ey*, *youee* a U-turn.

umbrella n. (boxing use) an incompetent boxer who 'folds up' when hit by his opponent *Runyon:1*.

umbrella brigade n. (UK police use) the Special Branch; who may dress in the Whitehall uniform of bowler hat and rolled umbrella *Powis*.

umpteen unspecified large number or amount; orig. milit. use, deliberately replacing a specific number with a noncommittal 'um' for communications secrecy.

unbuttoned a. unprepared, caught by surprise, taken unawares (cf: naked, a.).

uncle n. a pawnbroker.

Uncle n. (abbrev.) Uncle Sam (qv) = the USA, spec. the US military forces or other authorities (FBI, CIA, etc.) *Higgins:1*.

Uncle Bert n. (rhyming sl.) shirt *Jones: J*.

Uncle Dick see: Tom and Dick *Powis*.

Uncle Fred n. (rhyming sl.) bread (food) *Jones: j*.

uncle nabs n. (US Black use) the police; fr. nab, v. (qv) *Folb*.

Uncle Ned n. (rhyming sl.) bed *Wright*.

Uncle Sam the USA, esp. the armed forces of the USA; Uncle Sam (the equivalent of the UK's Britannia or John Bull) is always pictured as a bewhiskered, high-hatted old gentleman, garbed in red, white and blue.

Uncle Tom n. a subservient Black person, fitting willingly into the stereotyped and inferior image refined by generations of white supremacy *Seale*.

Uncle Tom v. (US Black use) to act in a subservient, obsequious manner to whites (cf: tom v.) *X*.

uncool a. unpleasant, square (qv), emotional, rude; various negative meanings as to given context (cf: cool) *Wolfe:2*.

under glass a. imprisoned, arrested; as in a museum *Chandler: Notebk*.

under house a. (US teen. use) in an uncontrollable state, emotionally unstable, furious; fr. under house arrest *Sculatti*.

underlay n. (horseracing use) a horse

that starts a race at odds lower than those listed in the 'morning line' that preceeds each day's racing *Bukowski:1*.

under one's own steam alone and unaided; fr. railway use.

undertaker job n. **1.** a hopeless proposition, thus 'dead'; **2.** (gambling use) a horse or greyhound which is deliberately – for the odds sake – not meant to win, whatever legitimate bettors may presume *Runyon:1*.

under the cosh see: under the gun.

under the gun under great pressure, stress *Price:3*.

under the influence a. drunk; 'of alcohol' is assumed *Neaman & Silver*.

under the odds a. easy, better than expected; fr. betting use *Mortimer*.

under the table a. **1.** clandestine, secret, corrupt *Larner*; **2.** drunk; one has fallen there

under the weather a. **1.** drunk; **2.** not feeling perfectly well, miserable *Rawson*.

underwear n. (pimp use) a client who enjoys buying or otherwise employing the prostitute's used underwear *OUI 8/75*.

under wraps a. secret, hidden away; as in a new design, esp. milit.

unglued a. unstable, emotional, lacking control *McFadden*.

uni n. (abbrev.) university *Humphries:2*.

uniform n. (homosexual use) any member of the armed forces: less freq. policemen, firemen, etc. (cf: rough trade) *Legman*.

union card n. (US campus use) a university degree certificate *Underwood*.

union wage n. (US Black use) the police; the sole motivation for their activities (?) *Folb*.

university of life n. that college attended by those who claim personal experience as infinitely superior to academic knowledge (cf: school of hard knocks) *Whitcomb*.

unkjay n. (Pig Latin) junkie (qv) *Algren*.

unload v. to get rid of; spec. to break off an affair *Dury*.

unlucky for some (bingo use) 13; the number most prone to superstitious interpretation *Wright*.

unreal a. **1.** (Aus. surfer use) unbelievable, unacceptable, unpleasant; an all-purpose negative that depends for precise meaning on context; **2.** (Aus. use) term of all-encompassing approbation as used by upper-middle class Aus. teenage girls *Humphries*; **3.** (US campus use) as **2.**

unsus a. (abbrev.) unsuspicious: plausible. (cf: sus, sussy) *Norman:2*.

untogether a. anyone not in full possession of their faculties; a situation that is less than satisfactorily under control (cf: uncool).

up against the wall a. (US campus use) dumb, foolish, stupid; fr. 1960's radical slogan: 'Up against the wall, motherfucker', and its root, the putting of prisoners against a wall to face a firing squad *Underwood*.

up a gumtree a. (orig. Aus. use, now general) in trouble, facing a problem; fr. the chasing of an animal into such a tree.

up-and-downer n. a fight, a tussle *Mortimer, 'Rumpole and the Golden Thread', 1983*.

up and dust v. (US Black use) to leave in a hurry; to run away *Klein*.

up and up a. fair, honest, straightforward *Schulberg*.

up a tree a. (US campus use) annoyed, emotionally unstable; fr. out of one's tree (qv); or fr. a cat perched, spitting down at an adversary, high in a tree *Underwood*.

upchuck v. to vomit (cf: throw up) *Farina*.

up for grabs a. **1.** available, on the market; **2.** vulnerable *Bruce:2*.

upfront a. open, honest, outspoken, outgoing *McFadden*.

up her like a rat up a drain (cp) the assumption that a given woman will be freely, easily and speedily sexually available to the speaker.

up in the paints a. depending on

context: old, high, superior; all meanings infer something more extreme; fr. gambling use: *paints* = high (royal) cards *Runyon:1*.

upper crust a. conceited, snobbish; fr. the 'crust' that sits on the great 'pie' of society *Underwood*.

uppers n. amphetamines (cf: speed).

uppity a. cheeky, arrogant, one who refuses to 'know their place' (cf: hincty) often as *uppity nigger*: a Black person who refuses to fall into a second-class line *Neaman & Silver*.

ups see: uppers.

upsadaisy! soothing excl. offered a fallen child as one picks it up again.

up shit creek without a paddle a. in deep trouble *Humphries*.

upside a. (US Black use) next to, up against *Folb*.

upstairs n. (US Black use) the mind *Klein*.

upstate n. (New York criminal use) prison; the main New York state prisons being in upstate New York *Selby:1*.

upta a. (Aus. use) aka: *upter* useless, no use whatsoever; fr. *up to shit* *Lambert*.

up the chute anal intercourse (cf: poopchute) *Price:2*.

up the creek a. **1.** (Aus. use) pregnant (cf: up the flue, etc.); **2.** in trouble, facing problems (cf: up shit creek) *Ready*.

up the duff a. pregnant (cf: up the spout).

up the flue a. (Aus. use) pregnant (cf: up the spout, duff, etc.) *Ready*.

up the gazoo **2.** up the anus; **2.** to excess *Higgins:5*.

up there Cazaly! (Aus. use) cry of encouragement; fr. Australian Rules player Roy Cazaly (1893–1963), star of the South Melbourne team, and especially noted for his athletic leaps into the air for a 'mark' *Ready*.

up the river a. in gaol, fr. the penitentiary at Ossining ('Sing-Sing') which is sited up the river from New York City.

up the spout a. **1.** pregnant (cf: up the duff, knocked up); **2.** in the pawnshop *Baker*.

up the stairs on trial; fr. the steps that lead from the cells beneath the Old Bailey up into the dock.

up the steps see: up the stairs *Powis*.

uptight a. **1.** tense, annoyed; **2.** close, friendly; **3.** OK, satisfactory, good *SF Comics*.

up to here a. bored, disgusted, utterly intolerant of an event, someone's statements, actions, etc.

up to snuff a. efficient, capable, aware *D. McLintick, 'Indecent Exposure', 1983*.

uptown a. sophisticated, worldly, rich; fr. that area of US cities considered residential, rather than *downtown*, where business is carried on *Capital Radio 1983*.

upways n. (US Black use) a snobbish, stand-offish person *Klein*.

up West the West End of London, as seen either from the East End or from the Western or suburban areas *Dury*.

up your ass! to hell with you! 'stick it . . .' is taken as read.

up your jacksie! alternative version of up your ass! (qv).

up yours! excl. of contempt; abbrev. of up your ass! (qv).

use v. to be taking or addicted to narcotics *Higgins:1*.

use one's loaf v. to think, to work things out; fr. rhyming sl. loaf of bread = head (qv).

user n. a drug addict.

use the English v. (rare) to wriggle one's buttocks while being penetrated anally; fr. snooker use *Legman*.

ute n. (Aus. use) (abbrev.) utility vehicle, small truck *Ready*.

UVs n. (US teen. use) (abbrev.) ultraviolet rays, thus sunshine; *soak up UVs*: to get a tan *Pond*.

v a. (UK 'society' use) (abbrev.) very *Barr*.

vag n. (US police use) a charge of vagrancy.

Valley Girls n. teenage Californian girls, spec. the daughters of the affluent middle-classes in the Los Angeles area; the description, and the core vocabulary was coined by Moon Unit, daughter of rock star Frank Zappa, c.1980; slang etymologists will note that the bulk of the vocabulary descends directly from surfing, US college, drug user, and general US teen. terminology.

Vallie n. (drug use) (abbrev.) Valium *Humphries:2*.

vamoose! go away! fr. Sp. *vamos*! *Schulberg*.

vamp on v. (US Black (radical) use) to make an unjust attack; to arrest; also used, when aimed at the oppressor to correct, to upbraid, to force him to mend his ways *Seale*.

Vaseline Heights n. (US homosexual use) gay centre of Portland, Ore. fr. the lubricant uses of Vaseline *White*.

veg n. (abbrev.) vegetable = moron, madman.

vegetable a. (US campus use) very drunk *Underwood*.

vegetarian n. (US cant) prostitute who refuses to offer fellatio to her clients, who 'won't eat meat' *Neaman & Silver*.

veg out v. (US campus use) to let oneself slip into a totally apathetic and passive state; to vegetate *Neaman & Silver*.

Vera Lynn n. (rhyming sl.) gin; fr. the 'forces' sweetheart' of the Second World War *Wright*.

Vera Vice n. (homosexual use) the police vice squad *Stanley*.

verbal v. (UK criminal/police use) for the police to fake a confession by claiming that one's statement under interrogation – the verbal – admitted to all the crimes for which in court one is pleading not guilty *Powis*.

verbals n. (UK police/criminal use) a statement to the police either voluntarily or during and after interrogation *Powis*.

verboten a. fr. Ger.: forbidden *Price:2*.

very swift (UK criminal use) the taking of grossly unfair advantage by the police *Powis*.

vet prostitute n. a senior member of the stable, responsible for teaching and disciplining her younger sisters; fr. abbrev. veteran *Klein*.

Vette n. (abbrev.) Corvette *Higgins:5*.

vg (UK 'society' use) (abbrev.) *v*ery *g*ood *Barr*.

vibes n. (abbrev.) vibrations: atmosphere, feelings; thus *good vibes* or *bad vibes*; fr. 1960s hippie use *Uneeda Comix*.

vicious a. (Valley Girls (qv) use) wonderful, excellent, etc. (on bad =

good premise) *Pond*.

vig n. (abbrev.) vigorish (qv) *Higgins:3*.

vigorish n. (US bookmaker use) interest on a loan, or debt; fr. SE vigorous (?), since it 'intensifies' the payments, by increasing them.

-ville general suffix, fr. abbrev. for 'village', and esp. popular in jazz and beatnik eras.

Ville n. HMP Pentonville (cf: the Scrubs).

vine n. **1.** (US Black and teen. use) a suit *Goldman*; **2.** (UK criminal use) (abbrev.) the grapevine, the unofficial underground network of information *LL*.

vineyard n. (US Black use) ironic ref. to anywhere that alcoholics congregate (cf: shooting gallery) *Klein*.

vino n. wine *SF Comics*.

virgin n. a criminal with no convictions *Higgins:2*.

vitamins n. (drug use) any drugs available in pill or capsule form *Folb*.

W n. (UK police use) a warrant – arrest, search, etc. *Norman:2.*

wack n. aka: *wacker*: Merseyside term of address to a male *Payne.*

wacky a. amusing, jolly, funny; one of the many words popularized during the Beatlemania craze of the mid-1960s.

wade in v. to commit oneself wholeheartedly, esp. to a fight.

waffle n. (US criminal use) a male homosexual *Legman.*

waffle stompers n. (US campus use) heavy boots with thick cleated soles that resemble a waffle iron *Underwood.*

wag n. (US police use) a vagrant *Chandler: LG.*

wag v. (US Black use) to procrastinate, to find it hard to make any decisions; fr. wag = vagrant (qv) *Klein.*

wail v. to abandon one's inhibitions, to lose oneself in a given activity; esp. used of musicians during an improvised solo, or of sexual pleasure *Bruce:2.*

wake it up! (Aus. use) hurry up, get on with it *Ready.*

wake up v. see: wise up.

wake-up n. (drug use) **1.** a heroin user's first injection of the day *Grogan*; **2.** any form of stimulant and amphetamine *Folb*; **3.** (US milit. use) in Vietnam, the last day of a tour in Vietnam; thus days left calculated as 'X and a wake-up'; similarly used in US prisons; one 'wakes up' in an institution, but goes to bed in freedom *Del Vecchio.*

walkabout n. the public mingling with attendant crowds of any celebrity, esp. a member of the UK Royal Family.

walk-about money n. daily expenses, petty cash rather than a large amount that needs investing or depositing somewhere *Runyon.*

walker n. a man, often rich, invariably personable and socially acceptable, who accompanies the wives of very prominent men – Presidents, chairmen, etc. – to parties, on shopping expeditions, to the theatre, etc. *Green:2.*

walking papers n. (US prison use) official notice to inform a prisoner that he/she has finished a given sentence *Klein.*

walk on! (US campus use) term of dismissal, disbelief, contempt (cf: stroll on!) *Bernbach.*

walk on one's cap-badge to be very drunk; orig. milit. use *Dickson.*

walk on rocky socks v. (US use) to walk unsteadily owing to an excess of drink *Neaman & Silver.*

walk the bricks v. (US police use) to patrol a foot beat rather than work from a patrol car *Dunne.*

walk the check v. (US campus use) to walk deliberately out of a restaurant without paying the check (bill)

Underwood.

wallah n. a person, a man; fr. Anglo-Indian (milit.) use, thus through to UK general use *Dury.*

wallflower n. (UK prison use) a prisoner obsessed with the possibility of escape; fr. dance/party use: one who doesn't want to join in *LL.*

wallflower week those days during which a woman is menstruating and thus, traditionally, sexually inactive *Rawson.*

wallop n. beer, alcohol in general; Second World War milit. use for beer only *A. Green 1983.*

walloper n. (Aus. use) a policeman; fr. his activities *Baker.*

wallopies n. (US campus use) female breasts, esp. large ones *Underwood.*

Wall Street didn't jump (US teen. use, cp) anything that fails to produce the anticipated/desired excitement from bystanders; let alone produce an effect on the US economy *Sculatti.*

wall-to-wall a. everywhere, all over; like carpet *Higgins:1.*

wally n. **1.** an unfashionable, unintelligent, 'suburban' person, lacking in taste and sophistication; **2.** a trainee policeman *Newman passim*; **3.** a pickled cucumber.

waltz v. to achieve something easily, esp. in sporting use *'Minder', Thames TV, 1983.*

wampum n. money; fr. American Indian word for money *Vidal.*

'wana n. (abbrev. and corruption) marijuana *Folb.*

wang n. penis *Bruce:1.*

wangle v. to obtain what one wants, often through a degree of manipulation or cunning.

wang-tang n. (US Black use) anything, esp. on a sexual level, that is especially desirable *Klein.*

wank v. to masturbate. this sp. has generally superseded *whank.*

wanker n. **1.** spec. a masturbator; **2.** derog. general description: lazy, incompetent person *Farren.*

wanna be n. (US Black use) a fantasist, one always says 'I wanna be . . .' *Folb.*

wanna do a thing? (US Black use) cp asking a passing woman if she fancies intercourse *Klein.*

wanna go out? (prostitute use) ritual come-on from a prostitute to a passing male *Rawson.*

want to make something of it? (cp) ritual request that may well herald a fight, but still gives the other person the chance to back down.

warm a. (US teen. use) a very attractive, sexy girl; deliberate understatement of hot (qv) *Pond.*

wash n. (West Indian use) the mash of cheap grain and sugar that is distilled to produce the home-made spirit that are sold in shebeens (qv) *Powis.*

wash v. see: launder *PT.*

washed up a. useless, exhausted, a failure *Heller.*

wash-out n. a failure *Jay & Young.*

wash out v. to remove, to cancel, to dismiss *Jay & Young.*

WASP n. (acro.) White Anglo-Saxon Protestant, the predominant racial group in the USA.

was she worth it? (bingo use) 76; fr. former price of UK marriage licence, 7/6d *Wright.*

waste v. to kill, esp. milit. use *O'Brien.*

wasted a. **1.** utterly overcome by a given drug *Price:2*; **2.** killed, esp. in a battle *O'Brien*; **3.** very drunk *Bernbach.*

watch one's ass v. to take care, to take note, to be warned *Bruce:2.*

watch one's lip v. to mind one's manners, to talk politely *Chandler: LG.*

watch queen n. a male homosexual voyeur fr. queen (qv) *Stanley.*

watch the ant races v. to be excessively drunk, probably face down on the bar or the floor *Neaman & Silver.*

watch the dickey-bird! (cp) photographers' (both professional and amateur) exhortation to their subjects to ensure smiling and alert faces for the picture; smiles are also encouraged by *say cheese.*

watch the submarines v. (US use) to indulge in sexual by-play *Neaman & Silver.*

Water n. the River Thames; thus *over the Water*: South of the Thames. *Newman:1.*

waterboy n. (boxing use) a useless boxer who accepts money to lose fights (cf: tanker, take a dive, etc.) *Runyon.*

watermelon man n. (US Black use) a drug seller *Klein.*

water of life n. (US Black use) semen.

water sports urinating on a partner for sexual stimulation (cf: golden shower) *Jay & Young.*

wax v. see: wax one's tail *Underwood.*

waxed a. (US Black use) of anyone whose personality and characteristics are known well (cf: peep one's hole card) *Klein.*

wax one's tail v. to beat up; also used by milit. fliers for taking the advantage in an aerial dog-fight, getting on the enemy's tail *Wolfe:6.*

wax up v. (US Black use) **1.** to propitiate someone whom one has insulted or annoyed (cf: apple-polish); **2.** to hide evidence *Klein.*

way a. (Valley Girls (qv) use) very, extremely, etc.; fr. way-out (qv) (cf: total) *Pond.*

way out a. bizarre, fantastic, exceptional; fr. hippie use in 1960s *Thompson.*

ways n. the style and standards of the US Mafia *Higgins:3.*

way to go! excl. of approval, ie. 'that's the right way to go . . .'.

wazz n. urination.

wazzocked a. drunk *Obs. 13/3/83.*

weak a. poor, disappointing *Salisbury.*

weakheart n. (West Indian use) policeman *Powis.*

wear a cut glass veil v. to attempt unsuccessfully to hide one's homosexual preferences *Legman.*

wear a mourning veil v. attempt to hide one's homosexual proclivities *Legman.*

wearing the ring a. (US Black use) infatuated with someone, thus sexually exclusive as if, in theory, married *Folb.*

wear it v. (US cant/police use) to take the blame for a crime even when not actually guilty *'The Stone Killer', film 1973.*

wear one's badge v. to wear an outward sign of being a homosexual; formerly this was a red tie, now obs. *Legman.*

wear the dog v. (US Black use) to go around looking deeply depressed (but, cf: put on (the) dog) *Klein.*

wear the trousers v. to dominate; usu. implying that the female half of a relationship is the one who dictates the rules (formerly 'wear the breeches' *Hotten*).

weasel n. (rhyming sl.) weasel and stoat = overcoat *Powis.*

wedge n. a thick, chunky roll of banknotes, usu. folded in half *Powis.*

wedgeass n. general derog. term of abuse *Uris.*

weed n. **1.** (commercial use) the practice of pocketing a certain amount of the cash that should be placed untouched into one's employer's tills *Green:2*; **2.** marijuana *White*; **3.** a cigarette, spec. the tobacco it contains *Uris.*

weedhead n. (drug use) marijuana smoker *De Lannoy & Masterson.*

weedy a. weak, cowardly, spineless; either juv. or upper-class UK use; fr. gardening use *Barr.*

Wee Georgie Wood a. (rhyming sl.) good; fr. music hall star *Wright.*

weekend n. (UK prison use) a very short period of imprisonment *LL.*

weekend ho n. (pimp use) part-time prostitute, often without a pimp but poss. helping out her boyfriend with cash *OUI 8/75.*

weekend man n. (US Black use) a family man who can only manage the street life at weekends *Klein.*

weekend warriors n. part-time prostitutes, amateurs who work weekends only *Neaman & Silver.*

weenie n. the penis, usu. children's use; fr. supposed resemblance to a wiener or other sausage *Vidal.*

weepie n. (film use) a film whose main effect is to reduce its audience to tears, usu. consciously romantic; thus – on model of *three alarm fire*, etc. – *three-handkerchief weepie*: a very emotional film (cf: tearjerker).

weeping willow n. (rhyming sl.) pillow *Jones: J.*

weigh in v. to join in, esp. in an argument; fr. racing use.

weigh into v. to attack verbally, to criticize *Capital Radio 1983.*

weigh off v. (UK criminal/police use) to sentence a convicted prisoner *Norman:1.*

weight n. **1.** one pound of marijuana, cannabis; **2.** one ounce of heroin *Larner.*

weirdo n. an eccentric, a peculiar person *Bruce:2.*

weird out v. to horrify, to play mental games *Price:3.*

welch v. aka: *Welsh*: to refuse to pay a gambling debt or other bill; fr. the ethnic slur.

welcher n. aka *Welsher*: anyone who refuses to pay their debts, gambling or otherwise *Performance.*

welfare mother n. (US Black use) any woman, irrespective of status *vis-à-vis* welfare, who is poorly dressed and unkempt *Folb.*

well a. very; thus *well tasty*, *well sus* (qqv) etc. *Newman:1.*

well away a. **1.** drunk; **2.** making headway in a given seduction.

well heeled a. rich; fr. quality of shoes, *inter alia.*

well hung a. a well-endowed male.

wellies n. (abbrev.) wellington boots *May.*

Wellies n. (Exeter University (UK) use) the public-school educated, upper-middle and upper-class students who are seen as playing, rather than working their way through college; fr. wealthy, and fr. green wellingtons such students wear for various rural pleasures *T 3/10/83.*

well in a. **1.** (UK use) popular, secure, entrenched; **2.** (Aus. use) wealthy, affluent *Wilkes.*

wellington n. (Aus. rhyming sl.) wellington boot = root = sexual intercourse *Humphries.*

well-lined a. rich, prosperous; fr. 'lining one's pockets' *Humphries:2.*

well-oiled a. very drunk (cf: neck oil).

Welsh v. see: welch.

wen n. (backsl.) new, thus: *teg a wen eno* get a new one *Cole.*

went down like a pork chop at a Jewish wedding (cp) extremely unpopular; fr. the Jewish religious prohibition of pork *A. F. N. Clarke, 'Contact', 1983.*

were you born in a barn? (cp) aimed at anyone who has failed to shut a door.

were you born in a tent? (Aus. use) see: were you born in a barn? *Wilkes.*

West Hams n. (rhyming sl.) West Ham reserves = nerves *Powis.*

wet a. (US Black use) suspicious (cf: fishy) *Klein*; **2.** weak, spineless, usu. an upper-class word, spec. of members of Tory party who do not back Mrs Thatcher's hard line monetarist economics.

wet n. a drink *Hotten.*

wetback n. **1.** an illegal Mexican immigrant to the USA; fr. the condition of the immigrants who traditionally swim the Rio Grande as the best means of beating border checks, thus; **2.** (derog.) Mexicans in general *Vidal.*

wet behind the ears a. naïve, inexperienced, gauche *Gruber.*

wet blanket n. a dreary person, a spoilsport; fr. a wet blanket being used to quench fires.

wet foot n. a naïve, inexperienced, innocent person *Powis.*

wethead n. (US Black use) a simpleton, an innocent, a novice (cf: wet behind the ears) *Folb.*

wet one's pants v. to panic, to lose control. fr. the involuntary urination that may follow great fear *Thompson: J.*

wet one's whistle v. to take a drink; fr. *whistle* throat; dates fr. 14th C.

Neaman & Silver.
wet the baby's head v. to drink in celebration of a baby's birth.
whack n. share, usu. of money *Griffith.*
whack v. **1.** to charge money, usu. *whack for . . . Higgins:1*; **2.** to hit.
whack-a-doo n. lunatic, eccentric *Price:3.*
whacked out a. **1.** crazy, insane, eccentric *Price:3*; **2.** under the influence of a given drug or of alcohol *Goldman.*
whacking a. general intensifier usu. in *whacking big*, *whacking horrible*, etc. *Wodehouse: PGM.*
whacko a. crazy, insane, eccentric.
whacko n. an unstable or mentally ill person *Price:2.*
whack off v. to masturbate *Price:1.*
whacko the diddle-oh (Aus. use) a remark offered on seeing an attractive girl *Humphries.*
whack out v. to kill, to murder; fr. whack 2 *Bruce:2.*
whacky a. see: whacked out.
whale the piss out of v. see: whale the shit out of *Higgins:3.*
whale the shit out of v. to beat viciously *Higgins:1.*
wham n. (US Black use) a large, aggressive man who finds few rivals on the street *Klein.*
wham bam thank you ma'am (cp) epitomizing brief sexual intercourse intended on the whole for male satisfaction only (cf: bip bam . . .).
whammy n. a punchline; anything devastating and beyond a similarly powerful response.
whang n. the penis (cf: wang) *Vidal.*
whangee n. a cane *Wodehouse: JO.*
whap v. to hit; fr. onomatopoeia (?) *Higgins:2.*
whap that thing! (US Black use) congratulatory remark to a passing woman, implying her supreme sexiness *Klein.*
wharfie n. (Aus. use) docker; fr. wharf *Bickerton.*
what are you pushing? (US Black use) what sort of car do you drive? *Klein.*
what a turn-up! what a surprise; fr. turn up for the book, racing use *'Widows', Thames TV, 1983.*
what can I do you for? (cp) facetious reversal of usual 'what can I do for you?' *BBC-1 TV 1983.*
whatchamacallit n. anything to which one cannot give a name when required (cf: thingummibob).
what-d'you-call-it n. see: whatchamacallit *Wodehouse: MOJ.*
what else is new? deprecating comment on anything the previous speaker has said, esp. if that speaker had intended to make a big impression *Price:3.*
what gives? fr. Yiddish: *vi geht's*: how goes it? what's happening (qv), what's new, etc. *Rosten.*
what in blue blazes? excl. of extreme surprise, absolute confusion, etc.
what's biting you? what's the matter? what's the problem? *Manser.*
what's cooking? what's going on? (qv) *Hoffman.*
what's going on? common greeting (cf: what's happening?).
what's happening? a greeting: hello and how are you; what are you/have you been doing? (cf: what's shaking?) *Seale.*
whatshisface n. a reference to anyone whose name one has (temporarily) forgotten *Dickson.*
what's in it for me? (cp) an honest statement of selfishness.
what's it in aid of? what exactly is the reason for all this?
what's it to you? aggressive reply to a questioner implying that whatever it may be, it is none of his/her business.
what's new? see: what's happening?
what's shaking? a greeting: hello and how are you (cf: what's happening?) *Price:2.*
what's that when it's at home? (cp) deliberate misunderstanding of a word or statement which the speaker is implying to be too 'clever' for his/her understanding.
what's the big idea? (excl.) more a

threat than a question; usu. asked when someone is doing or saying something of which the speaker disapproves *Manser*.

what's the percentage? what's the point? what's the intention? fr. gambling use *McFadden*.

what's your poison? aka: *name your poison*: jocular invitation to a fellow drinker to make a choice of drink at a party or in a bar.

what the dickens? (excl.) euph: what the devil? *Hotten*.

what the hell! general excl. of surprise, shock, alarm, etc. *Wodehouse: MOJ*.

whazood a. (US campus use) drunk (cf: wazzocked) *Underwood*.

wheel n. (abbrev.) big wheel (qv) *Selby:1*.

wheeler-dealer n. entrepreneur, operator (qv) *Higgins:4*.

wheelie n. trick riding on the back wheel only of a motorcycle *Higgins:1*.

wheelman n. expert car driver, either for police or for criminals *Powis*.

wheels n. a car *Shulman*.

when the chips are down (cp) in the final event, at the denouement, when one has no option; fr. poker use.

when the crow shits (Aus. use) aka: *when the eagle shits*: payday *Wilkes*.

when the morning comes (US Black use) when hard times finally disappear *Klein*.

where it's at the right place, the ideal situation, opinion, experience; an expression of approval/affirmation *Bruce:2*.

where one is coming from see: where you're at *McFadden*.

where's the fire? (cp) where are you running to? what's the hurry? *Farrell*.

where you're at what your stance is on a particular topic, your attitude and opinion, the way you live: esp. popular in the new therapies of California (cf: where you're coming from) *McFadden*.

where you're coming from how you are feeling, what your opinions are; esp. used in new therapies of California *Price:2*.

whiff n. an odour, a smell.

whiff v. to smell *Wilkinson*.

whip around n. a collection, usu. of money – for a round of drinks, a present to a third party, etc.

whip it on me **1.** to explain and inform one of facts and events; **2.** (drug use) to inject one with narcotics *L. Reed, 'Sister Ray', 1967*.

whip off v. (US campus use) masturbate *Underwood*.

whip one's ass v. to beat completely and comprehensively, whether or not with violence *Price:1*.

whip one's wire v. (US campus use) to masturbate *Underwood*.

whipped a. (US campus use) dominated, subservient, meek *Underwood*.

whipped cream n. (US Black use) semen *Folb*.

whips n. (US Black use) **1.** the white establishment; **2.** the police *Folb*.

whip shack n. (US Black use) anywhere one can have sexual intercourse (cf: killing floor) *Folb*.

whip up v. to create or make something quickly, at short notice *Dunne*.

whisper n. a rumour, usu. of impending crimes *Newman:2*.

whistle n. (rhyming sl.) whistle and flute = suit *Dury*.

whistle and toot n. (rhyming sl.) loot = money *Cole*.

whistle-blower n. a scandalmonger, an investigator who reveals facts that disturb an hitherto satisfactory – if corrupt – status quo. *Newman:2*.

whistle Dixie v. to boast, to brag without substance *Dave Anderson, 'Count-Down to Superbowl', 1969*.

whistle in the dark v. to hazard a guess, to speculate wildly.

whistle up v. to send for; fr. naut. 'whistling up the wind'.

white a. honest, upright, fair-dealing; fr. the characteristics the white (Anglo-Saxon) races like to assume they have, as opposed to 'lesser' (coloured) breeds; usu. as 'you're a white man . . .', 'that's white of you' *Wodehouse: MOJ.*

white bread (US preppie (qv) use) anything pertaining to WASP (qv) styles; bland, unexciting (cf: yankee white) *Bernbach.*

whitecoat n. (taxi-driver use) the senior examiner at the Police Public Carriage Office, in charge of the testing of London taxi drivers *Powis.*

white cross n. (drug use) amphetamine pills with a white cross cut into one surface *Underwood.*

white-haired boy n. especial favourite, one who can, in the right eyes, do no wrong.

white hat n. (USN use) an officer; fr. his uniform cap *Pynchon.*

white lady n. (Aus. use) methylated spirits *Wilkes.*

white lightning n. illicit homebrewed whisky or poteen *Wolfe:1.*

white line fever n. **1.** the obsessive use of cocaine; fr. the lines of the powdered drug that are snorted (qv) by users; **2.** an obsessive driver; fr. white lines that divide traffic lanes.

white liver n. a homosexual who has no interest whatsoever in women *Legman.*

white meat n. (Black use) a white girl, regarded in a sexual context punning on the genteel euph. for the 'breast' of a chicken (cf: dark meat).

whites n. (drug use) amphetamines (cf: reds) *Green:1.*

white shirt n. (UK prison use) a senior prison officer, who wears a white rather than blue (for junior ranks) shirt *Cole.*

white shit n. heroin *Higgins:1.*

whitewash n. **1.** in sport, the complete defeat of one team by another; **2.** (political use) a cover-up, the official denial or burying of facts detrimental to their own power, no matter how important such facts are to the public *PT.*

Whitey n. (Black use) the white race in general *Greenlee.*

whiz n. **1.** a pickpocket *Powis*; **2.** amphetamine (cf: speed) *Cole.*

whiz-pop n. (US campus use) a stupid person *Underwood.*

whizz off v. to leave quickly, to go somewhere fast *Barr.*

who cut the cheese? popular cp (usu. college, school use): who farted? (qv).

whodunnit n. (UK prison use) meat pie; the 'murder victim' is the prison cat *LL.*

whole bag of tricks n. everything necessary to deal with a given situation.

whole ball of wax n. see: whole kit and caboodle *'T. J. Hooker', Thames TV, 1983.*

whole bang shoot n. everything relevant and involved.

whole boiling lot absolutely everything.

whole kit and caboodle n. the lot; everything there is *Runyon.*

whole shebang n. absolutely everything; orig. US milit. use *shebang*: a soldier's tent, where his possessions were kept.

whoop it up v. to have a noisy, ostentatious good time *NYRB 29/9/83.*

whopper n. a particularly gross lie; fr. whopper = a big one *Hotten.*

whopping a. enormous, very large; usu. school use only *Hotten.*

whore n. **1.** a promiscuous woman, but not necessarily (not even usually) an actual prostitute *Underwood*; **2.** (poker use) the queen *Uris.*

whore scars n. (US Black use) the scars left from continuous injections of narcotics (cf: tracks) *Major.*

who you screwin'? aggressive question aimed at someone who is staring, or perhaps is not, but with whom the speaker wishes to start a ritual that might lead to a fight *Robins.*

whup v. (US Black use) to attack, to beat up; fr. whip *Folb.*

whup the game v. (US Black use) to succeed in life (cf: have it knocked) *Folb.*

why keep a dog and bark yourself? (cp) urging one to use all available facilities if one is fortunate enough to have access to them.

wicked a. (US Black use) excellent, wonderful (cf: bad).
wicked lady n. (UK prison use) cat o' nine tails *EN 12/11/57.*
wicked thing n. (US Black use) an extraordinary event or situation *Klein.*
widdle v. to urinate *Dury, 'Spasticus Autisticus', 1981.*
wide a. (police use) corrupt; since 16th C. *Newman:2.*
wide boy n. a minor villain dabbling in various schemes to get rich quick (cf: spiv) *LL.*
wide-open a. vulnerable, undefended; fr. boxing use *Schulberg:2.*
wide-open beaver n. a photograph or film shot of the inner labia (cf: split beaver).
widgie n. (Aus. use) the female counterpart of a bodgie (qv) *Ready.*
Widow n. nickname for Veuve Cliquot champagne; fr. Fr. *veuve* = widow.
widow n. (drug use) black widow (qv) *Underwood.*
-widow n. suffix to denote a woman who is left behind while her husband devotes himself to a given obsession, usu. sport or a hobby; thus *golf-widow*, *bicycle-widow*, etc. *McFadden.*
widow maker n. (US milit. use) see MA *Del Vecchio.*
wienie n. **1.** the penis; **2.** a fool, an incompetent (both fr. wienie, lit. wienerwurst or frankfurter) *Underwood.*
wife n. the supposedly subservient, 'female' partner in a homosexual couple *Legman.*
wig n. the head, the brain or its functions.
wig bust (US Black use) the altering of a natural crinkly Black head of hair into a straight 'process' (qv) style *Klein.*
Wig City a. (US teen. use) eccentric, unbalanced, nearly insane (cf: wiggy) *Sculatti.*
wigged out see: wiggy.
wigging n. a reprimand, a telling off; fr. ear-wigging *Hotten.*
wiggy a. odd. bizarre, unpleasant, disturbing; fr. wig = head (qv) *Wolfe:1.*
wig out v. **1.** to lose control, to have a breakdown; fr. wig (qv) *Price:2*; **2.** enjoy oneself, lose one's inhibitions *Seale*; both fr. wig = head (qv).
wild a. eccentric, bizarre, weird, odd *Bruce:2.*
wild about very keen on, excited by; often in negative 'I'm not exactly wild about . . .' *T 12/9/83.*
wild-ass a. crazy, insane, unbalanced *Higgins:1.*
wildcat n. (US Black use) someone who participates intensely and also to his own advantage in the street life *Klein.*
wild prints n. (police use) fingerprints that as yet have not been identified *McBain:1.*
Wilkie Bard n. (rhyming sl.) **1.** (theatre use) a professional card, used to get free admission to the theatre by an actor; **2.** (plural): playing cards; fr. the comedian *Wright.*
willie peter n. (US milit. use) white phosphorus, usu. in form of incendiary artillery round or grenade *Del Vecchio.*
willies n. nerves, worries, tension *Bruce:2.*
willy n. the penis, usu. children's use only.
wimmin n. women, preferred sp. among some radical gay women who thus censor even the written 'men' *Jay & Young.*
wimp n. weakling *Payne.*
windbag n. a boastful, loud-mouthed (qv) person.
wind jammer n. (Aus. use) homosexual male.
window dressing n. any form of illusion, cosmetic adornment, etc. which is used to hide the facts of an unpleasant and thus publicly or personally unpalatable reality.
wind up v. **1.** to bring to a conclusion, to end up, to find oneself somewhere,

to result *Larner*; **2.** to tease, usu. maliciously; fr. winding up clockwork to 'make it go' *Payne*.

wind up merchant n. someone who specializes in teasing, possibly to the point of at least verbal retaliation *Robins*.

Windy City n. Chicago; fr. its weather *title of musical, 1983*.

wing-ding n. a boisterous, noisy party *Major*.

wing it v. to improvise, to ad lib, to play a situation by ear without practice or rehearsal; fr. a bird's flying *Price:3*.

winker-stinker n. (US prison use) the anus (cf: roundeye) *Klein*.

winkle n. penis *Dury, 'Do It Yourself', 1979*.

winkle-pickers n. highly pointed boots or shoes, orig. favoured by Teddy Boys in 1950s but latterly absorbed into the wide variety of 1980s teen. fashions. (cf: roach-killers).

winks n. (US campus use) sleep; fr. *forty winks* = a nap *Underwood*.

wino n. an alcoholic, usu. living in poverty; fr. the cheap wine that he/she drinks *Gothic Blimp Works No.4*.

wipe v. (Aus. use) to forget, to dismiss from one's mind *Wilkes*.

wiped out a. exhausted *Price:1*.

wipe out n. **1.** a failure; **2.** (ski/surf use) a spectacular fall from skis or surfboard.

wipe out v. to beat up *Larner*.

wire n. the pickpocket who actively steals from his victim, rather than the various accomplices on his team (cf: hook) *Chandler: Notebk*.

wired **1.** spec. using some form of amphetamines; **2.** tense, nervous, irritable; full of 'electricity' *Higgins:2*.

wired up a. see: wired *Wilkinson*.

wire up v. (US Black use) to explain the current situation, to tell what has been/is happening; fr. electrical use *Klein*.

wise a. **1.** stupid, foolish; in ironic use (cf: wise guy) *Thompson*; **2.** homosexually experienced *Legman*.

wise-ass a. see: *smart ass* (qv) *Motor City Comics*.

wise guy n. anyone who thinks they are particularly knowing or clever; thus a person too clever for their own good *Price:2*.

wise guys n. the Mafia; both positive and negative meanings of the phrase *Higgins:2*.

wisenheimer n. a know-it-all, a self-appointed smart fellow.

wise up v. to act sensibly, to cease from being stupid.

wish (up)on v. to foist something – an article, a task, etc. – on someone who in no way had requested the burden.

with it a. sophisticated, chic, aware of current fashions, styles, language, etc., fr. 1960s 'Swinging London' era.

with knobs on! the same to you, and more so! usu. children's use.

wizard a. (UK 'society' use) excellent, wonderful; general term of approval used only by prep school boys when both young and adult *Barr*.

wodge n. thick, chunky, dense lump.

wog n. (derog.) any non-white, esp. Indian; poss. from *golliwog* or acro. *W*esternized *O*riental *G*entleman *Farina*.

wog-box n. a large, portable stereo tape-recorder-cum-radio, particularly beloved of ghetto youths (cf: ghettoblaster, Third World briefcase) *Cole*.

Woler n. (UK 'society' use) Rolls Royce motor car (cf: Roller) *Barr*.

wolf n. **1.** predatory male pursuing women for sex; **2.** (homosexual use) the active partner in anal intercourse *Legman*.

wolfing it v. (US Black use) to talk big but fail to back up such boasts with actual performance *Klein*.

wolf-pussy n. (US Black use) unpleasant vaginal odours *Klein*.

wollied a. drunk.

wolly n. **1.** a uniformed (junior) policeman; criminal and detective branch use *Newman:1*; **2.** a fool, a stupid, boring person poss. fr. *wall-eyed*: squinting, short-sighted *Obs. 13/3/83*.

wollyhumper n. (rock music use) a bouncer (qv) employed by a rock band to make sure no fans manage to climb on stage while they play or, if they have climbed up, to throw them down again; fr. wolly = tedious person *P. Marchbank.*

womon n. woman, preferred sp. by some radical gay women (cf: wimmin) *Jay & Young.*

wonelly a. (Valley Girls (qv) use) admirable, very good, etc; fr. *one hell of a . . . Pond.*

wonga n. money *Cole.*

wonk n. (US campus use) anyone who works harder than the rest of the students see fit *Bernbach.*

wonky a. unsteady, unstable, out of kilter.

wooden v. (Aus. use) to knock down, knock out; fr. the use of a blunt instrument (?) *Wilkes.*

woodener n. (UK prison use (rare)) a one-month sentence; fr. the wooden spoon once issued and rhyming sl. wooden spoon = moon = month = short sentence *LL.*

wooden kimono n. see: wooden overcoat *Rawson.*

wooden overcoat n. a coffin, often used in fictional versions of organized crime *Rawson.*

wooden spoon n. (UK sports use) a metaphorical prize for the competitor or team who comes last in a sporting contest (cf: leather medal) *ST 6/3/83.*

woodie n. (surfer use) a wood-panelled station wagon, beloved of surfers in US and Australia *Beach Boys, passim.*

woof v. **1.** (US Black use) to speak continually and forcefully, often requiring no replies, only an audience; fr. canine barking (cf: yap) *Klein*; **2.** (US Campus use) to vomit; fr. 'barking' noise that accompanies intense vomiting *Bernbach.*

wool n. **1.** spec. female pubic hair, thus; **2.** a girl or woman *Jenkins.*

Woolies n. nickname for Woolworth department stores (cf:M&S).

Wooloomooloo Yank (Aus. use) a relatively unsophisticated person who attempts to ape the supposedly hip style of an American.

wooly-back n. an unsophisticated, country person; who thus resembles his sheep *Bleasdale.*

Woop Woop n. (Aus. use) an imaginary place which is a byword for backwardness and remoteness; its inhabitants are *woops* Wilkes.

woozy a. **1.** vague *J. Tucker, 'The Novels of A. Powell', 1976*; **2.** under the influence of drugs or drink, poss. of a blow on the head.

wop n. Italian (derog.); fr. Sp. *guapo*:a dandy, which was taken up in Sicily during an occupation and thus taken to US by 19th C. immigrants *Price: 2.*

word! (US teen. use) excl. of approval, admiration, agreement, etc. fr. my word! *E. Beyer.*

word freak n. (pimp use) a client who wishes the prostitute to speak in obscenities for his sexual gratification *OUI 8/75.*

word up! see: word!

work n. (US cant/police use) the written records held by illegal bookmakers *Neaman & Silver.*

work a crowd v. to ply one's trade to an audience – begging, preaching, etc.

work a ginger v. (Aus. use) for a prostitute and her accomplice to rob her customer (cf: murphy game) *Baker.*

working from a book (Black pimp use) a pimp who conducts his business through his book of addresses and telephone numbers for his girls' clients; this method of work cuts down on many of the problems – esp. the police – that are met in street prostitution *Milner.*

working girl n. a prostitute *Farren: passim.*

working stiff n. an average, unexceptional working man *Whitcomb.*

workoholic n. anyone who is obsessed by working and thus very rarely stops (cf: -oholic).

work one's ass off v. to work extremely hard.
work one's butt off v. see: work one's ass off *Higgins: 5*.
work one's ticket v. to malinger, to escape onerous duties by shamming illness or similar unsuitability; fr. Br. Army use, obtaining a discharge through faking illness.
work out v. to exercise *Higgins: 1*.
work over v. to beat up (qv); to hurt to any extent short of murder *Higgins: 1*.
works n. the equipment used by a heroin addict for injecting him/herself (cf: outfit) *Grogan*.
work the hole v. (US cant) to rob drunks who have passed out in the subway *Burroughs: 1*.
work the room v. to chatter to people at a party or meeting; fr. show business use in which a entertainer will move through the audience at a nightclub, chatting to people and using them in his/her act *D. McLintick, 'Indecent Exposure', 1983*.
work the well v. (US cant) for a pickpocket to use the crush getting on and off buses for stealing from travellers *Neaman & Silver*.
World n. (US milit. use) in Vietnam, the USA *Del Vecchio*.
worm farm n. an eccentric, one whose mind is 'full of worms' *McFadden*.
worse things happen at sea (cp) somewhat empty words of consolation when nothing deeper seems available to the speaker.
wotcher Cockney greeting, fr, 'ehat cheer', which dates back at least to 16th C.
would I shit you . . . you're my favourite turd (US cp) in answer to the previous speaker's 'Don't (bull)shit me . . .' *Price: 1*.
wouldn't tell one the time of day (cp) said by one who ignores a given person completely, spurning any and all advances *McFadden*.
wouldn't touch it with a ten foot barge pole see: don't fancy yours!
wouldn't touch it with yours (cp) popular phrase betw. two men observing a woman when the speaker finds her unattractive; 'yours' is the penis.
wow v. to delight, to enthrall, to please very much; esp. show business use. fr. excl. of approval and acclaim.
wowser n. (Aus. NZ use) a puritan, a self-appointed censor, a 'Mrs Grundy' (or Mrs Whitehouse).
WPLJ (abbrev.) *W*hite *P*ort and *L*emon *J*uice.
wrap n. end, conclusion; fr. film use: a wrap: the end of a day's shooting *Jenkins*.
wrapped (Aus. use) see rapt *Wilkes*.
wrapped tight (US teen. use) feeling fine, happy *Safire*.
wrapping n. (US teen. use) clothes, esp. female *Sculatti*.
wrap up v. to stop talking, esp. as a command: *wrap up!*
wreck v. (homosexual use) **1.** to degrade a fellow homosexual when he is not expecting it; **2.** see: ruin *Stanley*.
wrecked a. **1.** heavily affected by a given drug; **2.** very drunk *Bernbach*.
wrinklies n. the old; mainly UK upper/upper-middle class youth use (cf: crumblies, dusties) *ES 11/5/83*.
write off n. anything that is completely destroyed, beyond all hope of repair and thus, in orig, service use, must be written off the inventory.
write scrip(t) v. to give out prescriptions for narcotics *Grogan*.
writing doctor n. (drug use) a doctor who will write prescriptions for narcotics and ask no questions about the user (cf: write scrip(t), hungry croaker) *Stone*.
wrong guy n. an incompetent, an untrustworthy person; spec. an informer *Higgins: 1*.
wrong side of the tracks the poor, undesirable area of a town; fr. the building of many US towns athwart the railway tracks.
wrong 'un n. **1.** (cricket use) a googly; **2.** an untrustworthy, incompetent person.

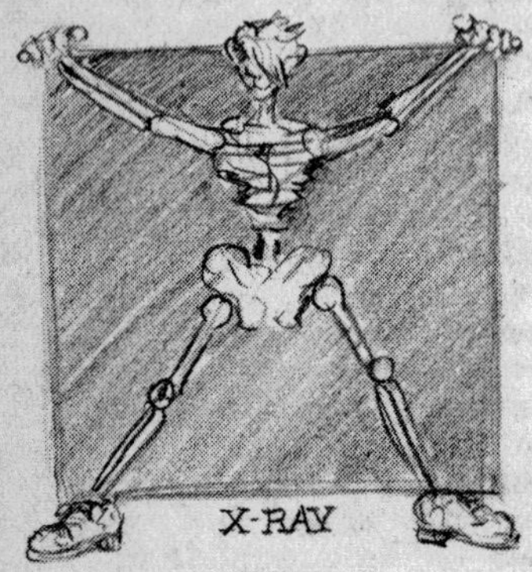

xed out (US Black use) tricked, fooled *Klein*.

X ray n. (film use) a still photo *Chandler: Notebk*.

Y n. (abbrev.) Young Men's Christian Association (YMCA).

yacoo n. (US Black use) **1.** a white person; **2.** a racist; both fr. *Yacub*: the devil-figure white man in Black Muslim mythology *Folb.*

yak v. to talk, usu. garrulously; like a raucous bird *Price:1.*

yakka n. (Aus. use) work; fr. Aborigine *Humphries.*

yakkety-yak n. meaningless, if enthusiastic and earnest, chatter *Sanders:2.*

yank v. to drag, to pull *Selby:1.*

yap n. the mouth; usu. in derog. sense: 'shut your yap!' etc. *Price:2.*

yap v. to talk, esp. to shout at, like a dog *Higgins:1.*

yard n. one hundred, usu. money.

yardbird n. **1.** (US milit. use) a recruit, a rookie (qv) *Uris*; **2.** civilian dock workers in US naval dockyards *Pynchon*; **3.** (US Black use) anyone confined to a restricted area – home, a prison, etc. – by the authority of an unassailable superior *Klein.*

yard Negro n. see: house nigger *X.*

yarra a. (Aus. use) insane; fr. mental hospital at Yarra Bend, Victoria *Wilkes.*

yawp v. to talk loudly, foolishly; to nag (cf: yap) *Algren.*

yea a. use. as *yea big, yea high*: this big, this high.

year dot n. a very long time ago; usu. *from the year dot*: for ever.

yeasting (US Black use) exaggerating, boasting; fr. the way in which yeast makes otherwise flat dough rise up *Major.*

ye gods! mild. oath; abbrev. ye gods and little fishes! *Wodehouse:AAG.*

yellib n. (butchers' backsl.) belly; both human and as a cut of meat *Cole.*

yellow a. cowardly *Selby:1.*

yellow ass n. a light-coloured Black girl *Jones.*

yellow-bellied a. cowardly *Gruber.*

yellow girl n. a Mulatto *Himes:1.*

yellowjackets n. barbiturates; fr. colour of pills *Higgins:1.*

yellow peril n. (derog.) any oriental person, the Communist Chinese *BvdB.*

yellows n. pills, usu. tranquillizers *Dury.*

yellow sheet n. (US police use) a criminal's record of arrests (cf: rap sheet, form) *Neaman & Silver.*

yenep n. (butchers' backsl.) penny *Cole.*

yennom n. (butchers' backsl.) money *Cole.*

yenta n. a nagging, whining person, usu. of a woman; fr. the character Yenta Telebende, created at the Lennox Theatre in Harlem, 1920s, and Yiddish: 'shrew, gossip (cf: kvetch) *Neaman & Silver.*

yes-man n. an obsequious, subservient person, esp. in business, who always says 'yes' to his superiors, in the belief that is what they like to hear.

yid a Jew; both derog. and general use, depending on context *Big Ass Comics 1.*

Yiddle n. a Jew (cf: yid) *Schulberg.*

Yidney n. (UK 'society' use (derog)) Sidney, Australia; fr. Jewish population of the city (cf: Jew York).

yikes n. **1.** worries, nervousness; **2.** excl. of surprise, shock *Higgins:1.*

yob n. **1.** (backsl.) boy, no spec. pejorative connotations *Cole*; **2.** an uncouth, vulgar youth, prob. fr. backsl. boy *Powis.*

yobbo n. extension of yob (qv) and as such poss. even more pejorative.

yodel v. aka: *yodel in the canyon of love*: to perform cunnilingus *Legman.*

yodel in the canyon v. aka: *dive/grin/sneeze. . .*: perform cunnilingus *Folb.*

yodel up the valley v. to perform cunnilingus *Humphries.*

yok n. **1.** (theatrical use) a belly laugh *Rosten*; **2.** (Jewish use) a Gentile (cf: goy).

yoo-hoo boy n. an effeminate homosexual; allegedly given to shouting 'yoo-hoo!' at all and sundry *Legman.*

you ain't just whistling 'Dixie' (US cp) you really mean what you're saying, you're not just being flippant.

you and me (bingo rhyming sl.) 3 *Wright.*

you and me n. (rhyming sl.) tea *Powis.*

you and who's army? (children's (usu.) cp) addressed to anyone who is threatening violence *Manser.*

you bet! excl. of absolute aggrement, confidence.

you can say that again! (cp) underlining the speaker's agreement with the previous statement.

you can't take it with you (cp) urging someone to spend their money, enjoy their possessions, etc.; the un-named journey is beyond the grave.

you can't win 'em all (cp) self-explanatory; offering some slight comfort.

you could have knocked me down with a feather (cp) indicating maximum surprise and shock.

you don't know the half of it! (cp) self-explanatory, with the assumption that the speaker *does G. Vidal, 'Myron', 1974.*

you don't look at the mantelpiece when you're poking the fire (cp) a woman's looks are irrelevant if she's sexually available.

you got it! (excl.) general affirmative reply, usu. to a yes/no question and often Black use *Underwood.*

you know the great interjection of the illiterate; it means nothing more than its parallel: *er.*

you know it is! (US Black/teen. use) yes indeed, you're right, etc.; any form of emphatic agreement *Malcolm McLaren, LP, 1983.*

youknow what n. sexual intercourse *Rawson.*

you know where n. (euph.) depending on context: if sexual: the vagina or penis; if hostile, the anus.

you'll be a long time dead (cp) addressed to anyone the speaker feels is wasting time, not putting his life to its best advantage, etc.

you'll be sorry! semi-jocular cry of warning fr. those who have experienced a situation to those who are about to encounter it; orig. use amongst Second World War troops.

young blood n. junior members of an organization, firm, team, etc., recruited in the hope of their providing a degree of vital rejuvenation.

young blood n. (US Black use) the up and coming youth who are learning the mores of the street life *Folb.*

young in the head (US Black use) childish, immature *Folb.*

you pays your money and you takes your choice (cp) self-explanatory.

your (yer) actual an emphatic intensifier of a person or object: 'your actual Rolls Royce', etc.; supposedly coined by Peter Cook for sketches in *BBC-TV's 'Not Only . . . But Also',*

1960s.

you reckon? semi-rhetorical response: is what what you really believe?

you're darn tootin' you're absolutely right *Whitcomb.*

you're singing my song! you and I agree in every way; you're my kind of person *Thompson:J.*

your guess is as good as mine (cp) don't ask me, I don't know either.

your mother n. (homosexual use) oneself, thus 'your mother needs a drink', etc. *Maledicta.*

your mother! (US teen. use) rejoinder to an insult, implying that whatever that insult is, it applies most to the speaker's own mother (cf: dozens).

yours truly jocular reference by a speaker to him/herself *Wolfe:5.*

you scratch my back and I'll scratch yours (cp) promising mutual aid in a given situation; 'one good turn deserves another'.

youthquake n. the upsurge of (radical) youth in 1960s, early 1970s; not only potentially revolutionary, this essentially disaffected young bourgeoisie also offered a huge purchasing base to those who wished to exploit it *Hoffman:a.*

you've got a nerve! (cp) how dare you!

you wouldn't read about it! (cp) describing anything amazing, unbelievable, and proving that nature is infinitely more bizarre than mere art.

you wrote the book! (cp) used when offering what is appreciated as gratuitous advice to one whose ideas are the same as, if not an improved version of, one's own *Humphries:2.*

yo-yo n. a fool, an unpredictable person whose moods and actions go up and down *Price:2.*

yuck! all-purpose juv. excl. of distaste.

yucky a. unpleasant, disgusting; with overtones of stickiness or smelliness; usu. juv. use.

Yug n. (abbrev.) Yugoslav.

yuks n. see: yoks *Bruce:2.*

yummy n. attractive teenage girl, 'good enough to eat' *Farren.*

yummy a. tasty, delicious, flavoursome *Vidal.*

yum-yums n. (drug use) any drugs in pill or capsule form *Folb.*

yuppie n. (US use) young, upwardly mobile professional (cf: preppie) *ST 29/4/84.*

yutz n. penis; fr. Yiddish *Price:3.*

Z v. (US teen. use) to sleep; fr. the noise of one's breathing; sleep is often indicated in cartoons by 'Z-z-z-z-' issuing fr. sleeper's mouth *Pond.*

za n. (US campus use) (abbrev.) pizza *Bernbach.*

zaftig a. fr. Yiddish: juicy: a plump. buxom woman *Rosten.*

zap n. energy, enthusiasm *Bukowski:1.*

zap v. **1.** to shock, to alarm *Jay & Young*; **2.** to kill, esp. milit. use *A.F.N. Clarke, 'Contact', 1983.*

zazzle n. (US Black use) sexual desire or sensuality *Major.*

Z-bird n. (US teen. use) a failure, a loser; fr. position of Z at end of alphabet *Sculatti.*

Z'd out (US teen. use) unable to wake up properly, still sleepy (cf: Z) *Pond.*

zeek out v. (Valley Girls (qv) use) to act outrageously, to lose control, esp. through drugs/drink *Pond.*

zero n. a nobody, a totally useless and insignificant person *R. Crumb, 'Shuman the Human', c.1967.*

zero in v. to concentrate on, to focus on *Wolfe:2.*

zero minus (US campus use) utterly, completely impossible, unacceptable; less than nothing *Underwood.*

zilch zero, nothing *Underwood.*

zing n. energy, enthusiasm *Runyon.*

zinger n. a witty line, a one-line joke or repartee *Goldman.*

zip zero, nothing.

zip n. **1.** a speedy, energetic, mobile person *Price:1*; **2.** speed, enthusiasm, fervour, energy.

zip v. to run around energetically, to be highly energetic *Price:3.*

zipalid n. a complete moron; fr. *zipperlid*: one whose head has been 'unzipped' and the brain removed *E. Barker.*

zip-five (US prison use) a maximum of five years sentence *Larner.*

zip-gun n. homemade gun, favoured by US street gangs.

zip it up! be quiet, shut up! (cf: zip one's lip) *Klein.*

zip one's lip v. to stop talking *Klein.*

zippy a. fast, speedy.

zits n. acne spots *Junker.*

zizz n. a nap, a snooze, a brief sleep (cf: Z) *Dickson.*

zod n. (Valley Girls (qv) use) an eccentric, a strange person; fr. 'he's odd' *Pond.*

zombie n. **1.** (US Black use) a very African looking person short of stature, with a dark complexion and broad features *Klein*; **2.** (UK prison use) any prison officer who looks permanently miserable and humourless *LL.*

zoned a. (US preppie (qv) use) utterly exhausted, burned out; in the twilight zone (?) *Bernbach.*

zonked a. see: stoned *Wolfe:2.*

zonker n. anyone who takes drugs to excess *Wolfe:2.*

zonko n. (US campus use) boring, dull person and thus socially unacceptable *Underwood.*

zoom off v. to exit at speed, to leave quickly.

zoom one out v. to amaze, to fascinate, to surprise (cf: blow one's mind).

zoon out v. (Valley Girls (qv) use) see: *zeek out Pond.*

zot (US campus use) zero (in an examination) *AS 50 (1965).*

zowie n. keenness, enthusiasm, energy.

Zs n. sleep; (pron. with US Z = zee, not zed) *O'Brien.*

zubber n. (film use) a man dressed in top hat, white tie, tails, spats and a cane *Chandler: Notebk.*

Bibliography

NB: All editions cited were published in London unless otherwise specified.

Adams Ramon F. Adams, *Western Words*, 2nd revised edn, U. of Oklahoma Press, Norman, Okla., 1968.
Algren Nelson Algren, *The Man with the Golden Arm*, Doubleday, NY, 1949.
Algren:2 Nelson Algren, *A Walk on the Wild Side*, Corgi Books, 1964.
Alvarez A. Alvarez, *The Biggest Game in Town*, André Deutsch, 1983.
AS *American Speech* magazine, U. of Alabama Press, 1925–.
Austin Max Austin, *Out*, Arthur Barker, 1978.
Baker Sidney J. Baker, *The Australian Language*, 2nd edn, Currawong Publishing, Sydney, 1966.
Baker:2 Mark Baker, *Nam*, Sphere Books, 1982.
Barr Ann Barr & Peter York, *The Official Sloane Ranger Handbook*, Ebury Press, 1982.
Bernbach Lisa Bernbach, *The Official Preppy Handbook*, Eyre Methuen, 1981.
Bickerton Anthea Bickerton, *Australian/English*, *English/Australian*, Abson Books, Bristol, 1976.
Big Ass Comics *Big Ass Comics 1*, Rip Off Press, San Francisco, 1969.
Bleasdale Alan Bleasdale, *Boys from the Blackstuff: Five Plays for Television*, Granada Publishing, 1983.
Breslin Jimmy Breslin, *The World of Jimmy Breslin*, Hutchinson, 1968.
Bruce:1 Lenny Bruce, *How to Talk Dirty and Influence People*, Peter Owen, 1966.
Bruce:2 *The Essential Lenny Bruce*, ed. John Cohen, Ballantine Books, NY, 1967.
Bukowski:1 Charles Bukowski, *Erections, Ejaculations, Exhibitions and General Tales of Ordinary Madness*, City Lights Books, San Francisco, 1972.
Bukowski:2 Charles Bukowski, *Notes of a Dirty Old Man*, City Lights Books, San Francisco, 1973.
Bukowski:3 Charles Bukowski, *Post Office*, Black Sparrow Press, Santa Barbara, 1971.
Bukowski:4 Charles Bukowski, *Factotum*, Black Sparrow Press, Santa Barbara, 1975.
Bukowski:5 Charles Bukowski, *Women*, Black Sparrow Press, Santa Barbara, 1978.
Bukowski:6 Charles Bukowski, *South of No North*, Black Sparrow Press, Santa Barbara, 1973.
Bukowski:7 Charles Bukowski, *Ham on Rye*, Black Sparrow Press, Santa Barbara, 1982.
Burroughs:1 William Burroughs ('William Lee'), *Junkie*, Ace Books, NY, 1953.
Burroughs: Jr. William Burroughs Jr, *Kentucky Ham*, Pan Books, 1975.
BvdB Lester V. Berrey & Melvin Van Den Bark, *The American Thesaurus of Slang*, 2nd edn, George G. Harrap, 1954.

Byrne Josefa Heifetz Byrne, *Mrs Byrne's Dictionary of Unusual, Obscure & Preposterous Words*, Granada Publishing, 1979.
Caron Roger Caron, *Go-Boy!*, Hamlyn Paperbacks, 1979.
Carson Tom Carson, *Twisted Kicks*, Arrow Books, 1983.
Caserta Peggy Caserta, *Going Down With Janis*, Futura, 1975.
CB *The Complete CB Slang Dictionary*, Merit Publications, N. Miami, 1980.
Chandler:FML Raymond Chandler, *Farewell, My Lovely*, Hamish Hamilton, 1940.
Chandler:LG Raymond Chandler, *The Long Good-bye*, Hamish Hamilton, 1953.
Chandler: Notebk *The Notebooks of Raymond Chandler*, ed. Frank MacShane, Weidenfeld & Nicolson, 1977.
Cole Nicholas Cole, private lists 1982/1983.
De Lannoy & Masterson William C. De Lannoy & Elizabeth Masterson, 'Teenage Hophead Jargon', American Speech xxvii:1, 1954.
Del Vecchio John M. Del Vecchio, *The Thirteenth Valley*, Sphere Books, 1983.
Dennis C. J. Dennis, *The Sentimental Bloke*, Angus & Robertson, Sydney, 1957.
Dickson Paul Dickson, *Words*, Arena Books, 1983.
dl *Dreams of Love*, comics, IW Enterprises, NY, n.d.
Dunne John Gregory Dunne, *True Confessions*, Circus Books, 1979.
Dury Ian Dury, *The Ian Dury Songbook*, Blackhill Music, 1979.
Farina Richard Farina, *Been Down So Long It Seems Like Up To Me*, NEL, 1968.
Farrell James T. Farrell, *Studs Lonigan*, Constable, 1936.
Farren Mick Farren, *The Tale of Willy's Rats*, Granada Publishing, 1974.
Fiction Illus. *Fiction Illustrated*, vols. 1 & 3, Pyramid Publications, NY, 1976.
Folb Edith A. Folb, *Runnin' Down Some Lines*, Harvard University Press, 1980.
Franklyn Julian Franklyn, *A Dictionary of Rhyming Slang*, 2nd edn, Routledge & Kegan Paul, 1981.
Goldman Albert Goldman (from the journalism of Lawrence Schiller), *Ladies and Gentlemen, Lenny Bruce!*, W. H. Allen, 1975.
Goulart Ron Goulart, *The Hard-Boiled Dicks*, T. V. Boardman, 1967.
Greaser *Greaser Comics*, Rip Off Press, San Francisco, 1972.
Green:1 Jonathon Green, *The Book of Drugs*, unpub. ms., 1974.
Green:2 Jonathon Green, *Newspeak: A Dictionary of Jargon*, Routledge & Kegan Paul, 1983.
Greenlee Sam Greenlee, *The Spook Who Sat by the Door*, Allison & Busby, 1969.
Griffiths Leon Griffiths, The Bengal Tiger, TV script, Euston Films, 1979.
Grogan Emmett Grogan, *Ringolevio*, Little, Brown, Boston, 1972.
Gruber Frank Gruber, *The Last Doorbell*, Sydney Pemberton, Manchester, 1951.
Heller Peter Heller, *In This Corner*, Dell Publishing, NY, 1973.
Higgins:1 George V. Higgins, *Cogan's Trade*, Secker & Warburg, 1981.
Higgins:2 George V. Higgins, *The Friends of Eddie Coyle*, Secker & Warburg, 1972.
Higgins:3 George V. Higgins, *The Digger's Game*, Secker & Warburg/Ballantine Books, NY, 1973.
Higgins:4 George V. Higgins, *The Rat on Fire*, Secker & Warburg, 1981.
Higgins:5 George V. Higgins, *A City on a Hill*, Secker & Warburg, 1975.
Himes:1 Chester Himes, *Cotton Comes to Harlem*, Frederick Muller, 1966.
Himes:2 Chester Himes, *The Big Gold Dream*, Panther Books, 1968.
Hoffman Alice Hoffman, *Property Of*, Hutchinson, 1978.
Hoffman:a Abbie Hoffman, *Woodstock Nation*, Vintage Books, NY, 1969.

Hotten John Camden Hotten, *A Dictionary of Modern Slang, Cant, and Vulgar Words . . . by a London Antiquary*, 2nd edn, Hotten, 1860.
Howard Kent Howard, *Small Time Crooks*, Cooperbooks, n.d.
Humphries Barry Humphries, *Barry McKenzie*, strip cartoon, *Private Eye* passim.
Humphries:2 Barry Humphries, *A Nice Night's Entertainment: Sketches & Monologues 1956–1981*, Granada Publishing, 1981.
Jay & Young Karla Jay & Allen Young (eds.), *The Gay Report*, Summit Books, NY, 1979.
Jenkins Dan Jenkins, *Semi-Tough*, Star Books, 1978.
Jones LeRoi Jones (Imamu Amiri Baraka), *Tales*, McGibbon & Kee, 1969.
Jones:J Jack Jones, *Rhyming Cockney Slang*, Abson Books, Bristol, 1971.
Junker Howard Junker, *The Fifties*, *Esquire* magazine, 1969.
Keyes Thom Keyes, *All Night Stand*, W. H. Allen, 1966.
Kidder Tracy Kidder, *The Soul of a New Machine*, Allen Lane, 1982.
King Stephen King, *The Raft*, *Twilite Zone* magazine, June, 1983.
Klein Ronald Klein, PhD, *Jailhouse Jargon & Street Slang*, unpub. ms., 1983.
Lambert Eric Lambert, *Twenty Thousand Thieves*, Corgi Books, 1955.
Landy Eugene S. Landy, *The Underground Dictionary*, Simon & Schuster, NY, 1967.
Larner Jeremy Larner & Ralph Tefferteller, *The Addict in the Street*, Grove Press, NY, 1964.
Laugh in the Dark *Laugh in the Dark*, comics, Last Gasp Eco-Funnies, Berkeley, 1971.
Laurie Peter Laurie, *Scotland Yard*, The Bodley Head, 1970.
Lawson Henry Lawson, *Complete Prose Works*, Angus & Robertson, Sydney, 1948.
le Carré John le Carré, *The Little Drummer Girl*, Hodder & Stoughton, 1983.
Legman G. Legman, 'The Language of Homosexuality: A Glossary'; as Appendix VII in Henry, G. W. *Sex Variants: A Study of Homosexual Patterns*, NY, 1941.
LL Paul Tempest, *The Lag's Lexicon*, Routledge & Kegan Paul, 1950.
McBain Ed McBain, *Shotgun*, Hamish Hamilton, 1969.
McFadden Cyra McFadden, *The Serial: A Year in the Life of Marin County*, Picador, 1978.
MacInnes:1 Colin MacInnes, *Absolute Beginners*, MacGibbon & Kee, 1959.
MacInnes:2 Colin MacInnes, *City of Spades*, MacGibbon & Kee, 1957.
MacInnes:3 Colin MacInnes, *Mr Love & Justice*, MacGibbon & Kee, 1960.
Major Clarence Major, *Black Slang*, Routledge & Kegan Paul, 1971.
Maledicta *Maledicta: The International Journal of Verbal Aggression*, VI: 1–2, 1982.
Mandelkau Jamie Mandelkau, *Buttons: The Making of a President*, Open Gate, 1971.
Manser Martin H. Manser, *A Dictionary of Contemporary Idioms*, Pan Books, 1983.
Maurer David W. Maurer, *Language of the Underworld*, U. of Kentucky Press, Lexington, Ky, 1981.
May Jonathan May, *Confessions of a Gas-Man*, Sphere Books, 1977.
Michaels Leonard Michaels & Christopher Ricks (eds.), *The State of the Language*, U. of California Press, Berkeley/Los Angeles, 1980.
Milner Christine & Richard Milner, *Black Players: The World of Black Pimps*, Michael Joseph, 1972.

Moore Charles Moore, *CB Language in Great Britain*, Star Books, 1981.
Mortimer John Mortimer, *Rumpole & the Golden Thread*, Penguin Books, Harmondsworth, 1983.
Motor City *Motor City Comics*, Rip-Off Press, San Francisco, 1969.
Neaman & Silver Judith S. Neaman & Carole G. Silver, *A Dictionary of Euphemisms*, Hamish Hamilton, 1983.
Newman:1 G. F. Newman, *A Villain's Tale*, Sphere Books, 1977.
Newman:2 G. F. Newman, *A Detective's Tale*, Sphere Books, 1977.
Newman:3 G. F. Newman, *A Prisoner's Tale*, Sphere Books, 1977.
Newspapers: *The Times* (T), *Guardian* (G), *Daily Telegraph* (DT), *Financial Times* (FT), *Daily Mail* (DMa), *Daily Express* (DE), *Daily Mirror* (DM), *Sun* (Su), *Daily Star* (DS), *(Evening) Standard* (ES), *Sunday Times* (ST), *Observer* (Obs), *Mail on Sunday* (MoS), *Sunday Telegraph* (STe), *Sunday Express* (SE), *News of the World* (NoW), *Sunday Mirror* (SMi), *Sunday People* (SP).
Norman:1 Frank Norman, *Bang To Rights*, Secker & Warburg, 1958.
Norman:2 Frank Norman, *Stand On Me*, Secker & Warburg, 1960.
Norman:3 Frank Norman, *The Guntz*, Secker & Warburg, 1962.
Norman:4 Frank Norman, *Banana Boy*, Secker & Warburg, 1969.
O'Brien Tim O'Brien, *If I Die in a Combat Zone*, Calder & Boyars, 1973.
OED *The Oxford English Dictionary*, 12 vols. plus Supplement, Oxford University Press, 1933; Supplements A–G (1972), H–N (1976), O–Scz (1982), OUP.
Partridge:1 Eric Partridge, *Slang Yesterday and Today*, 4th edn, Routledge & Kegan Paul, 1970.
Partridge:2 Eric Partridge, *Dictionary of Slang & Unconventional English*, 2 vols, 7th edn, Routledge & Kegan Paul, 1970.
Partridge:3 Eric Partridge, *A Dictionary of the Underworld*, 3rd edn, Routledge & Kegan Paul, 1968.
Partridge:4 Eric Partridge, *A Dictionary of Catch Phrases*, Routledge & Kegan Paul, 1977.
Payne Andrew Payne, *You Need Hands*, TV script, Euston Films, 1981.
Payne:2 Andrew Payne, *Dream House*, TV script, Euston Films, 1981.
Pearce Donn Pearce, *Cool Hand Luke*, Secker & Warburg, 1966.
People's Comic *The People's Comic*, Golden Gate Publishing, San Francisco, 1972.
Performance Film, directed Nicholas Roeg, produced Donald Cammell, 1970.
Pond Mimi Pond, *The Valley Girl's Guide to Life*, Dell Publishing, NY, 1982.
Poston Lawrence Poston III & Francis J. Stillman, 'Notes on Campus Vocabulary', *American Speech* magazine xlix, 1964.
Powis David Powis, *The Signs of Crime*, McGraw Hill (UK), 1977.
PT *The Presidential Transcipts: The Complete Transcripts of the Nixon Tapes*, Dell Publishing, NY, 1974.
Price:1 Richard Price, *The Wanderers*, Chatto & Windus, 1975.
Price:2 Richard Price. *Bloodbrothers*, Houghton, Mifflin, Boston, 1976.
Price:3 Richard Price, *The Breaks*, Simon & Schuster, NY, 1983.
Pynchon Thomas Pynchon, *V*, Jonathan Cape, 1963.
Rawson Hugh Rawson, *A Dictionary of Euphemisms and Other Doubletalk*, Macdonald, 1983.
Ready Susan Ready, private lists, 1983.
Rechy:1 John Rechy, *City of Night*, McGibbon & Kee, 1964.
Rechy:2 John Rechy, *The Sexual Outlaw*, W. H. Allen, 1978.
rr *Realistic Romances*, I. W. Enterprises, NY, n.d.

Robins David Robins & Philip Cohen, *Knuckle Sandwich*, Penguin Books, Harmondsworth, 1978.

Rodgers Bruce Rodgers, *The Queens' Vernacular*, Straight Arrow, San Francisco, 1972.

Rosten Leo Rosten, *Hooray for Yiddish!*, Elm Tree Books, 1983.

Runyon Damon Runyon, *Runyon On Broadway*, Constable, 1950.

Safire William Safire, *On Language*, Avon Books, NY, 1980.

Sanchez Thomas Sanchez, *Hollywoodland*, Magnum Books, 1981.

Sanders Ed Sanders, *The Family: The Story of Charles Manson's Dune Buggy Attack Battalion*, Avon Books, NY, 1972.

Sanders:2 Ed Sanders, *Tales of Beatnik Glory*, Stonehill Publishing, NY, 1975.

SF Comics *San Francisco Comic Book 2 & 3*, Rip Off Press, San Francisco, 1970.

Salisbury Harrison E. Salisbury, *The Shook-Up Generation*, Ace Books, NY, 1961.

Schulberg Budd Schulberg, *On The Waterfront*, The Bodley Head, 1956.

Schulberg:2 Budd Schulberg, *What Makes Sammy Run?*, The Bodley Head, 1941.

Sculatti Gene Sculatti, *Cool: A Hipster's Dictionary*, Vermilion, 1983.

Seale Bobby Seale, *Seize the Time*, Arrow Books, 1970.

Selby Hubert Selby, Jr, *Last Exit to Brooklyn*, Calder & Boyars, 1966.

Sharpe:1 Tom Sharpe, *Vintage Stuff*, Secker & Warburg, 1982.

Sharpe:2 Tom Sharpe, *Wilt*, Secker & Warburg, 1976.

Shulman Alix Kates Shulman, *On The Stroll*, Virago Press, 1983.

Sillitoe Alan Sillitoe, *The Loneliness of the Long-Distance Runner*, W. H. Allen, 1959.

Simmons Donald C. Simmons, 'Some Special Terms Used in a U. of Connecticut Men's Dormitory', *American Speech* magazine xlix, 1969.

Skeat W. W. Skeat, *Etymological Dictionary of the English Language*, Oxford University Press, 1879–82.

Southern Terry Southern, *Red Dirt Marijuana & Other Tastes*, Jonathan Cape, 1971.

Southern & Hoffenberg Terry Southern & Mason Hoffenberg, *Candy*, New English Library, 1968.

Stanley Julia P. Stanley, 'Homosexual Slang', *American Speech* magazine xlv, 1970.

Stone Robert Stone, *Dog Soldiers*, Secker & Warburg, 1975.

Teresa Vincent Teresa, 'A Mafioso Cases the Mafia Craze', in *The Crime Society*, ed. Francis Ianni & Elizabeth Rheuss-Ianni, NAL, NY, 1976.

Thelwell Michael Thelwell, *The Harder They Come*, Pluto Press, 1980.

Thompson Hunter S. Thompson, *Hells Angels*, Penguin, 1966.

Thompson:J Jim Thompson, *Four Novels*, Zomba Books, 1983.

Tidy Bill Tidy, *The Cloggies*, cartoon strip, *Private Eye* passim.

Tuff Shit *Tuff Shit Comics*, Print Mint, Berkeley, 1972.

TZ *Twilite Zone* magazine, Twilite Zone Publications, NY, 1980.

Underwood Gary Underwood, 'Razorback Slang', *American Speech* magazine li, 1976.

Uneeda *Uneeda Comix*, Print Mint, San Francisco, 1969.

Uris Leon Uris, *Battle Cry*, Alan Wingate, 1953.

Usborne Richard Usborne, *Wodehouse at Work to the End*, Barrie & Jenkins, 1977.

Vidal Gore Vidal, *Duluth*, Heinemann, 1983.

Vizinczey Stephen Vizinczey, *An Innocent Millionaire*, Hamish Hamilton, 1983.

Waits Tom Waits, *Small Change*, Warner Bros. Records, 1976.
Waterhouse Keith Waterhouse, *In the Mood*, Michael Joseph, 1983.
Webb James Webb, *Fields of Fire*, Granada Publishing, 1981.
Webster *Webster's Third New International Dictionary*, G & C Merriam, NY, 1966.
Wentworth Harold Wentworth & Stuart Berg Flexner, *Dictionary of American Slang*, 2nd Supplemented edn, Thomas Crowell, NY, 1975.
Whitcomb Ian Whitcomb, *Rock Odyssey: A Musician's Chronicle of the Sixties*, Doubleday, NY, 1983.
White Edmund White, *States of Desire*, André Deutsch, 1980.
Wilkes G. A. Wilkes, *A Dictionary of Australian Colloquialisms*, Routledge & Kegan Paul, 1978.
Wilkinson Tony Wilkinson, *Down & Out*, Quartet Books, 1981.
Wodehouse:P P. G. Wodehouse, *The Pothunters*, A & C Black, 1902.
Wodehouse:MJ P. G. Wodehouse, *My Man Jeeves*, Newnes, 1919.
Wodehouse:IJ P. G. Wodehouse, *The Inimitable Jeeves*, Herbert Jenkins, 1923.
Wodehouse:COJ P. G. Wodehouse, *Carry On, Jeeves*, Herbert Jenkins, 1925.
Wodehouse:VGJ P. G. Wodehouse, *Very Good, Jeeves*, Herbert Jenkins, 1930.
Wodehouse:TJ P. G. Wodehouse, *Thank You, Jeeves*, Herbert Jenkins, 1934.
Wodehouse:RHJ P. G. Wodehouse, *Right Ho, Jeeves*, Herbert Jenkins, 1934.
Wodehouse:YMS P. G. Wodehouse, *Young Men in Spats*, Herbert Jenkins, 1936.
Wodehouse:CW P. G. Wodehouse, *The Code of the Woosters*, Herbert Jenkins, 1938.
Wodehouse:EBC P. G. Wodehouse, *Eggs, Beans & Crumpets*, Herbert Jenkins, 1940.
Wodehouse:JM P. G. Wodehouse, *Joy in the Morning*, Herbert Jenkins, 1947.
Wodehouse:MS P. G. Wodehouse, *The Mating Season*, Herbert Jenkins, 1949.
Wodehouse:JO P. G. Wodehouse, *Jeeves in the Offing*, Herbert Jenkins, 1960.
Wodehouse:PF P. G. Wodehouse, *Performing Flea*, Herbert Jenkins, 1961.
Wodehouse:PB P. G. Wodehouse, *A Pelican at Blandings*, Herbert Jenkins, 1969.
Wodehouse:GB P. G. Wodehouse, *The Girl in Blue*, Barrie & Jenkins, 1970.
Wodehouse:MOJ P. G. Wodehouse, *Much Obliged, Jeeves,* Barrie & Jenkins, 1971.
Wodehouse:PGM P. G. Wodehouse, *Pearls, Girls & Monty Bodkin,* Barrie & Jenkins, 1972.
Wodehouse:AAG P. G. Wodehouse, *Aunts Aren't Gentlemen*, Barrie & Jenkins, 1974.
Wolfe:1 Tom Wolfe, *The Kandy-Kolored Tangerine Flake Streamline Baby*, Jonathan Cape, 1966.
Wolfe:2 Tom Wolfe, *The Electric Kool-Aid Acid Test*, Weidenfeld & Nicolson, 1969.
Wolfe:3 Tom Wolfe, *The Pump House Gang*, Weidenfeld & Nicolson, 1969.
Wolfe:4 Tom Wolfe, *Radical Chic & Mau-Mauing the Flak-Catchers*, Farrar, Straus & Giroux, NY, 1970.
Wolfe:5 Tom Wolfe, *Mauve Gloves & Madmen, Clutter & Vine*, Farrar, Straus & Giroux, NY, 1976.
Wolfe:6 Tom Wolfe, *The Right Stuff*, Farrar, Straus & Giroux, NY, 1979.
Wolfe:7 Tom Wolfe, *From Bauhaus to Our House*, Jonathan Cape, 1982.
Wolfe:8 Tom Wolfe, *In Our Time*, Pan Books, 1980.
Wright Peter Wright, *Cockney Dialect & Slang*, Batsford, 1981.
X *The Autobiography of Malcolm X*, with the assistance of Alex Haley, Hutchinson, 1966.